FIFTH EDITION

Teaching Young Children

AN INTRODUCTION

Michael L. Henniger

WESTERN WASHINGTON UNIVERSITY

PEARSON

Boston Columbus Indianapolis New York San Francisco Upper Saddle River
Amsterdam Cape Town Dubai London Madrid Milan Munich Paris Montreal Toronto
Delhi Mexico City São Paulo Sydney Hong Kong Seoul Singapore Taipei Tokyo

Vice President and Editorial Director:
  Jeffery W. Johnston
Senior Acquisitions Editor: Julie Peters
Development Editor: Bryce Bell
Editorial Assistant: Andrea Hall
Vice President, Director of Marketing:
  Margaret Waples
Senior Marketing Manager: Christopher D. Barry
Senior Managing Editor: Pamela D. Bennett
Senior Project Manager: Linda Hillis Bayma
Senior Operations Supervisor: Matthew Ottenweller

Senior Art Director: Diane C. Lorenzo
Text and Cover Designer: Candace Rowley
Cover Image: Fotosearch
Photo Researcher: Lori Whitley
Media Project Manager: Rebecca Norsic
Full-Service Project Management: Mary Tindle,
  S4Carlisle Publishing Services
Composition: S4Carlisle Publishing Services
Printer/Binder: R.R. Donnelley & Sons Company
Cover Printer: Lehigh Phoenix/Hagerstown
Text Font: ITC New Baskerville Std

Credit and acknowledgments for materials borrowed from other sources and reproduced, with permission, in this textbook appear on appropriate page within text, or below.

Illustration appearing on page 306 courtesy of Laura Prieto-Velasco, artist and metalsmith based in Chicago, IL.

Every effort has been made to provide accurate and current Internet information in this book. However, the Internet and information posted on it are constantly changing, so it is inevitable that some of the Internet addresses listed in this textbook will change.

Photo Credits: Scott Cunningham/Merrill, pp. 2, 11, 18, 60, 71, 114, 292, 236, 292, 335, 357; Katelyn Metzger/Merrill, p. 15, 390; © BananaStock Ltd., 27, 148, 154, 166; © thislife pictures/Alamy, p. 34; Courtesy of the Library of Congress, p. 37, 46; Courtesy of the Centenary of the Montessori Movement, pp. 41, 86, 142; Bill Anderson/Photo Researchers, Inc., p. 45; © Monkey Business Images, p. 63; Anthony Magnacca/Merrill, p. 65, 170, 354; © Kati Molin/Shutterstock, p. 106; © Janine Wiedel Photolibrary/Alamy, p. 109; © Richard Hutchings/PhotoEdit, p. 113, 250; Silver Burdett Ginn, p. 120, 432; © Myrleen Ferguson Cate/PhotoEdit, p. 127; © Michelle D. Bridwell/PhotoEdit, p. 132; Comstock/Thinkstock, p. 137; PhotoDisc/Getty Images, p. 174; © Catchlight Visual Services/Alamy, p. 179; © Monkey Business/Fotolia, p. 193; Laima Druskis/Merrill, p. 202; Pearson Learning Photo Studio, p. 206; © Michael Newman/PhotoEdit, p. 210; © Tom McCarthy/PhotoEdit, p. 211; Scott Cunningham/Merrill: The Kids on the Block is an educational company that uses puppets to teach children about disabilites, differences, and social concerns. Created in 1977, the educational puppet curriculums are in use worldwide by more than 1,700 community-based troupes. For information, call 1-800-368-KIDS or visit www.kotb.com., p. 221; © Robin Nelson/Photo Edit, p. 226; Antropov, p. 232; © Unlisted Images, Inc. All Rights Reserved, p. 247; © Golden Pixels LLC/Shutterstock, p. 262; © Tom Prettyman/PhotoEdit, p. 274, 412; John Bulmer© Dorling Kindersley, p. 278; Getty Images – Stockbyte, p. 279; John Paul Endress/Modern Curriculum Press/Pearson Learning, p. 285; © nyul/Fotolia, p. 299; David Mager/Pearson Learning Photo Studio, p. 304, 378; Corbis RF, p. 308; © Fancy/Alamy, p. 310; ©3445128471/Shutterstock, p. 324; Doug Menuez/Getty Images, Inc. – Photodisc, p. 329; © Will Hart/PhotoEdit, p. 336; Diego Cervo/Shutterstock, p. 369; © Andia/Alamy, p. 373; Jacky Chapman/Alamy, p. 393; Ray Ellis/Photo Researchers, Inc., p. 400; © pressmaster/Fotolia, p. 403, 425; Annie Fuller/Pearson, p. 406, 455; © Paul Conklin/PhotoEdit, p. 418, 444; © Onoky/SuperStock, p. 430; Krista Greco/Merrill, p. 437; © ene/Shutterstock, p. 460; © Stephen Coburn/Shutterstock, p. 466; Superstock Royalty Free, p. 471; Lori Whitley/Merrill, p. 473; © Huntstock.com/Shutterstock, p. 476

Library of Congress Cataloging-in-Publication Data
Henniger, Michael L.
Teaching young children : an introduction / Michael L. Henniger. — 5th ed.
  p. cm.
Includes bibliographical references.
ISBN-13: 978-0-13-265710-5
ISBN-10: 0-13-265710-4
  1. Early childhood education. I. Title.
LB1139.23.H45 2013
372.21—dc23

2011030724

10 9 8 7 6 5 4 3 2

www.pearsonhighered.com

ISBN-13: 978-0-13-265710-5
ISBN-10: 0-13-265710-4

preface

Young children are exciting to be around and enjoyable to work with, but teaching them is far from easy. Students new to the field of early childhood education need to develop an awareness of both the challenges and the joys involved in working with young children. This book presents both perspectives, providing a comprehensive, balanced overview of early childhood education.

This text is designed to be reader-friendly and uses a clear, informative, and personal writing style. Throughout the text, the reader encounters concise, research-based overviews of important topics. Vignettes concerning children and early childhood professionals, as well as questions presented throughout the chapters, help readers to understand young children and encourage readers to reflect on teaching and learning, and to discuss the topics presented with others.

Unique Features

Teaching Young Children: An Introduction is unique in several ways. It focuses on:

- **Five essential elements of early education.** Understanding child development, play, guidance, working with families and communities, and diversity—all are frequently explored in the prose and through boxed features in every chapter, and one chapter near the beginning of the book is devoted to each essential element.
- **Curriculum and play.** The book emphasizes appropriate curriculum for young children in six content-area and domain-related chapters, environments in two chapters, and play in another chapter.
- **Concrete applications.** Helpful program strategies are a focus of this text and specifically address infants and toddlers, preschoolers, and children in the primary grades.

Multimedia Feature

- **Integrated videos, articles, and artifacts. MyEducationLab™** for Introduction to ECE, a Pearson website containing resources for readers of this text, includes classroom videos, student and teacher artifacts, resources for professionalism, and more.

New to This Edition

As with every revision of this text, the content and references from the previous edition were carefully edited and updated. Beyond that, however, this fifth edition has gone through even more extensive revisions that include language changes to make the text more inclusive, stronger organization, revised features, and more extensive additions of content.

- **Inclusive Language.** Because of the thoughtful reviews that came in from colleagues around the country in preparation for this edition and the insights gained from reading Janet Gonzalez-Mena's wonderful book titled *50 Strategies for Communicating and Working with Diverse Families* (Gonzalez-Mena, 2010), this edition now uses more inclusive language to represent the diversity of early childhood education settings and the children and families that are found there. The changes include consistently using the following terms:

  - **Families** rather than *parents*, to emphasize the diversity of family situations
  - **Children** rather than *students*, except in reference to primary classrooms
  - **Early childhood professional** or **caregiver** and **teacher** rather than *teacher*, except when talking about primary classrooms
  - **Program** or **setting** rather than *classroom*, except when describing primary education

- **Stronger Chapter Organization.** Each chapter of the text was carefully analyzed so that content would be organized logically and efficiently to improve readability. Chapter opening objectives were aligned with major headings and concluding summaries. Content for virtually every chapter was significantly reorganized to enable the reader to better understand the material presented. In most chapters, this simplified the organizational structure, making the content easier to follow.

- **Revised Features.** In addition to updating and improving the content of the features found in this text, three significant revisions were made to specific features:

  - **Developmentally Appropriate Practice.** The National Association for the Education of Young Children has identified developmentally appropriate practice (DAP) as the foundation for all teaching and learning in early childhood settings (Copple & Bredekamp, 2009). From its beginnings, this text has emphasized this approach. To further highlight developmentally appropriate practice, the feature formerly called *Into Practice* underwent significant revision and now focuses on presenting the reader with practical examples of DAP related to the chapter content.

  - **Observing Development.** Reviewer feedback made it clear that the *Observing Development* feature found in earlier editions, while valuable, needed to be more focused and easier to use by beginning students. These changes were implemented, and the revised feature has been placed in the body of the text to emphasize its importance and the connections of the observation to chapter content.

  - **Technology Explorations and Activities.** Formerly titled *Multimedia Explorations and Activities*, the revised title reflects the new focus of the feature on technology options being used in early childhood settings. By broadening the focus beyond computers to include such options as digital cameras and a variety of Internet tools, this revised feature will help prospective early childhood professionals envision the technology options available to them. Rather than being found at the end of each chapter, this feature is now located in the body of the text.

- **End-of-Chapter Discussion and Reflection.** A new section at the end of each chapter, *For Reflection and Discussion,* encourages thoughtful reflection and provides questions to inspire class discussion.

- **Content Additions.** While content additions and deletions were made throughout the text, several key changes were made for this fifth edition:
  - **Recent American Contributors.** David Weikart, Lilian Katz, Joe Frost, and Louise Derman-Sparks were added to Chapter 2 as important contributors to the field of early childhood education.
  - **Waldorf Education.** This was added as an important model early childhood program in Chapter 3.
  - **Early Brain Development.** The writings of Shonkoff and Phillips (2000) and Galinksy (2010) on early brain development are discussed in Chapters 4 and 6.
  - **Diversity.** To further enhance the diversity emphasis of the text, new information on family diversity (linguistic diversity and foster children) was added to Chapter 7 and religious diversity content was added to Chapter 8.
  - **Health and Wellness.** The content in Chapter 12 was broadened beyond physical development and now includes added content on health (medical and dental health, childhood illnesses, and healthy adults) and safety (environmental risks, accident prevention, and abuse and neglect).
  - **Curriculum Implementation Cycle.** To assist students in understanding the process of creating and implementing curricula in early childhood settings, a curriculum implementation model was added to the content of Chapter 11. Based on developmentally appropriate practice, the model includes three repeating steps: identifying children's needs and interests, planning the curriculum, and engaging in assessment.
  - **Theatre and Dance.** New content related to theatre and dance was added to Chapter 16.
  - **Bullying.** New bullying content was added to Chapter 13.

Five Foundational Themes

This textbook provides a framework for understanding how to teach children from birth through age 8 by clearly identifying and discussing five essential elements of early childhood education. Each of these five essential elements is discussed in an individual chapter dedicated to the topic (see Part II). Each element is a critical component of quality programs for young children and is woven throughout the text. Each element is highlighted and explored in every chapter by special feature boxes:

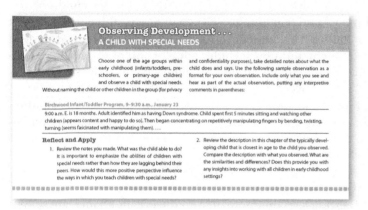

Observing Development

UNDERSTANDING CHILDREN AND THEIR DEVELOPMENT. This is a key aspect of working with young children. Caregivers and teachers know that before planning learning activities for early childhood settings, they need to have a firm grasp of each child's interests and developmental abilities. Observation is a proven technique used regularly by early educators for this purpose. The *Observing Development* feature integrated into each chapter lists traits and behaviors to observe, factors to consider and reflect upon, and specific applications and strategies to use to support and enhance development.

Celebrating Play

OPPORTUNITIES TO PLAY. Young children need times during their day to engage in quality play experiences, both indoors and outdoors. Play is one of the most important ways for young children to learn about the world around them. *Celebrating Play* features appear in each chapter to illustrate how play can be used to promote development in all domains.

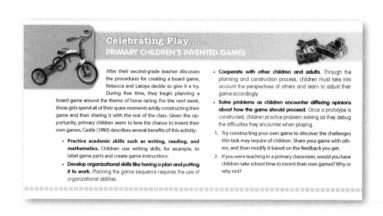

Developmentally Appropriate Practice . . .
PLANNING GUIDANCE STRATEGIES

Much of the guidance in the early childhood settings consists of preventing problems from occurring in the first place. This can be accomplished by planning ahead and defining potential problems. For example, a cooking activity can get out of hand quickly if you leave part way through the process to gather some forgotten ingredients or needed utensils. Sharp knives or tempting taste treats may be too much for children while you are away. So, as you plan for activities, take time to think about what you can do to prevent problems from occurring as children proceed through them. Consider the following:

- **Gather all needed materials.** As in the previous cooking example, having all the materials needed for planned activities together and ready to go can prevent many problems from occurring in the first place.
- **Consider space needs.** Some activities have specific space needs for safety and freedom of expression. For example, woodworking activities often involve hammers and saws, and cramped spaces can lead to inadvertent accidents when children move with these relatively dangerous tools. Another enjoyable activity for young children is movement to music with colorful scarves. To move freely and creatively, however, requires considerable space for each child.
- **Provide several popular toys.** When setting up a creative play center, include more than one of the same popular toy

so there are fewer problems with sharing. For example, having two or three popular trucks in the block center makes it possible for several children to engage in similar play themes.

- **Think about potential conflicts.** Part of your planning should include thoughts about potential conflicts that might occur between children and ways in which these conflicts can be resolved. In the computer area, for example, several children might want to use a new software program at the same time. You could set a time limit and have a buzzer go off when time is up or set up two or three chairs at the computer so that several children can work together using the same software.
- **Plan for clean-up time.** Although many activities are exciting for young children, cleaning up the messes made can be less attractive. Cleaning up a creative fingerpaint activity, for example, could be facilitated by assigning different roles to children. Some could be responsible for hanging up wet paintings, others could put away paints, and a third group could be responsible for wiping the table clean.
- **Schedule time for transitions.** It takes time for children at all levels within the early childhood range to transition from one scheduled activity to the next. Children may need directions on where to go or what they need to take with them, or information about the things they will see or do. It will also take time to physically move from one activity to the next. Planning for these transition times helps make them smoother and less traumatic for children and adults.

Developmentally Appropriate Practice

EXAMPLES OF EFFECTIVE PRACTICE. The National Association for the Education of Young Children (NAEYC), has identified characteristics of quality learning activities and teaching practices found in infant/toddler, preschool, and primary settings (Copple & Bredekamp, 2009). These characteristics help early childhood professionals engage in developmentally appropriate practice. The *Developmentally Appropriate Practice* features provide specific examples of activities and practices that are age-appropriate, individually appropriate, and consider social and cultural contexts.

Family Partnerships

WORKING WITH FAMILIES. The development of mutually supportive relationships with families is another essential element of teaching and learning in early childhood settings. Strong relationships and effective involvement help ensure maximum opportunities for growth and development in young children. The *Family Partnerships* feature in each chapter presents ways in which early childhood professionals can partner with family members to positively influence the lives of young children.

Family Partnerships . . .
WORKING WITH DIFFICULT FAMILY MEMBERS

While it would be ideal if every family were pleasant, positive, and easy to work with, the reality is that some will find fault with nearly everything you do. There are many possible explanations for these challenging families. Some may have had poor school experiences themselves and come to your early childhood program with many negative associations. Keyser (2006) identifies four other categories of family–teacher conflicts: (a) conflicting family and program needs; (b) differing views of teaching and child development; (c) inadequate communication; and (d) cultural differences.

Regardless of the reason, you will need to develop strategies to help you improve your interactions with these difficult families. The following options should be considered:

- **Increase communications.** While the human tendency is to step back from difficult interactions, it is important to increase them. For example, make it a point to regularly send a positive note or e-mail message telling difficult families about something good that has happened with their child.
- **Listen calmly and carefully.** Difficult families may say things that are hurtful and make you defensive. By being a calm and

careful listener, you are more likely to be able to identify the problem the family member is having and begin to work toward a solution.

- **Build on family strengths.** Just as it is important to look for the positive characteristics of every child and to build on them in your early childhood program, it is equally important to identify the positive attributes of difficult families so that you can use these qualities for the betterment of the children (Souto-Manning, 2010). For example, a difficult father who experienced failures as a student himself may be an excellent carpenter who could help you design and build a flowerbox planter for your program. Allowing the parent to contribute in a positive way to the program has the potential to strengthen his relationship with you.

1. Given the information in this chapter on the benefits of family involvement, how important is it to work effectively with all families, including difficult ones? What will you do to increase your success in working with difficult families?
2. How do you typically deal with confrontations? Do you welcome the challenges or try to avoid them? What does this tell you about your future interactions with difficult families?

Celebrating Diversity . . .
HOLIDAYS

The holidays we celebrate have their roots in family and culture. Some, such as Christmas and Hanukkah, are directly linked to religious beliefs. Others, like Halloween and Groundhog Day, have become traditional celebrations over time. In either case, the appropriateness of celebrating these holidays needs to be carefully determined. Kostelnik, Soderman, and Whiren (2011) identify several potential problems with these celebrations. Because children often have many opportunities to celebrate these events outside the program setting, blocks of children's lives tend to be dominated by holidays, leaving less time for other important learning options. In addition, the authors emphasize that caregivers and teachers who choose to celebrate holidays in early childhood settings run the risk of adding to cultural or religious stereotypes. The decision about whether or not to celebrate specific holidays is best made collaboratively among early childhood professionals, families, and children (National Association for the Education of Young Children, 2007).

The traditions surrounding holidays that are valued by different people can provide important opportunities for children to learn about diversity. When holidays are chosen carefully, and activities are planned that respect the cultures and religious perspectives represented by each of the children in your group, they can be a positive element of the curriculum. The National Association

for the Education of Young Children (2007) provides the following suggestions for making decisions about holidays:

- Families and early childhood professionals need to ask why children should learn about this holiday and whether it is developmentally appropriate.
- Celebrations should be connected to specific children and families within the group.
- Children should be encouraged to share their feelings and information about the celebrations they have.
- Every group (but not every holiday) represented within the early childhood setting should be honored through celebration of a holiday.
- Activities should demonstrate respect for the customs of different cultures.
- Families and early childhood professionals should work together in planning these special events.

1. Do you think that holidays that come from different cultures and religious groups constitute meaningful diversity experiences as described in this chapter? Why or why not?
2. How do you feel about celebrating holidays that conflict with your religious/cultural heritage? Discuss these feelings with others.

Celebrating Diversity

DIVERSITY AND YOUNG CHILDREN. An understanding of, and respect for, diversity is the final essential element of early education. Differences due to culture, gender, religion, income level, and physical and/or mental capabilities influence each of the other four essential elements and must be studied, understood, and discussed in early childhood settings. The *Celebrating Diversity* feature in each chapter presents issues that caregivers and teachers need to understand and apply.

An Emphasis on Curriculum, Environments, and Play

The six chapters that emphasize curriculum discuss the content areas and domains that readers will need to understand and integrate when creating enjoyable, playful, educational experiences for young learners. The chapter on play and the two separate chapters on planning indoor and outdoor environments are unique.

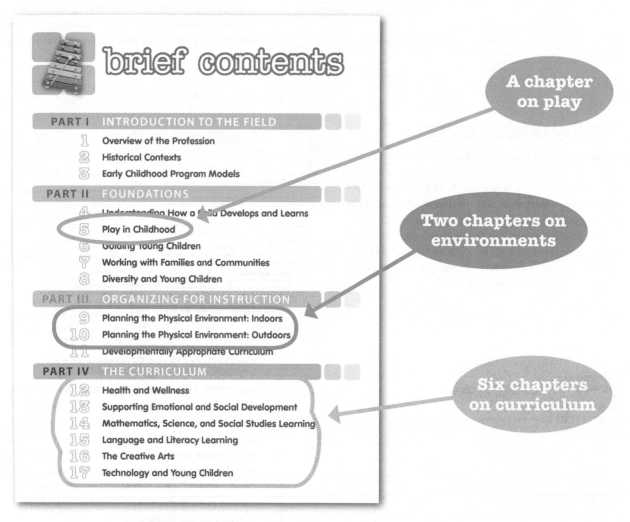

A chapter on play

Two chapters on environments

Six chapters on curriculum

- **Three chapters on play and environments.** Although other texts present information on planning outdoor play environments, this text provides complete chapters identifying the outdoor and indoor play areas as significant components of early education. A chapter on play (Chapter 5) offers a strong rationale for including play in the classroom.

- **Six chapters on curriculum.** In addition to chapters on physical development, emotional and social learning, the cognitive curriculum, literacy learning, and the arts curriculum, the concluding curriculum chapter on technology is unique in its description of play-oriented, developmentally appropriate technology experiences.

Concrete Applications

To help students bridge the gap between theory and practice, **concrete strategies** are listed in many of the five boxed features. These strategies give students a real-world flavor for what teaching in early education settings requires. Applications are culturally and developmentally appropriate, research-based, and classroom-tested.

Developmentally Appropriate Practice . . .
GUIDING VIOLENT PLAY

One thing you have undoubtedly discovered by now is that young children love to imitate significant others. Unfortunately, many of the role models for young children come from the television programs and movies they watch. Many of these programs include violent characters such as those in the classic cartoon about Wile E. Coyote, the movie *The Secret of NIMH,* and adult action heroes like Jet Li. It should come as no surprise, then, that we sometimes find even very young children engaged in play of a violent nature. Although children typically do not intend to hurt one another, the end result of violent play is often just that. In addition, it is important for young children to learn better strategies than violence for dealing with disagreements. Consider the following strategies for guiding children away from violence in their play:

- **Avoid pretend weapons.** Make sure no toys resembling weapons are brought from home. Suggest nonviolent uses for sticks and other neutral objects that children pretend are weapons.

- **Redirect play themes.** If children are playing out a cartoon theme such as "Dragon Ball Z" and becoming violent, try to redirect the play without entirely changing the theme. Having some knowledge of the characters being imitated helps with this task.

- **Rehearse verbal responses.** Be prepared with simple, direct responses to violent play. "I won't let you play in that way. Someone might get hurt." "You need to find another way to play Teen Titans so that no one gets hurt."

- **Remain calm, but firm.** Your responses to violent play will impact how children accept your intervention. Make sure to use a calm but firm voice.

- **Model appropriate behavior.** In some situations, it may be effective to actually join in the play and through your actions show children more appropriate ways to interact.

- **Seek family support.** Make sure to share with family members both the importance of intervening in violent play and the strategies you are using in school, so that they can support you at home.

Family Partnerships . . .
INVOLVING FAMILIES IN READING

One of the most important things you can do as an early childhood professional is to develop ways to successfully involve families in reading aloud to their children at home. The research indicates that this is the single most important activity needed for success in reading (International Reading Association, 1998). While this may seem to be a simple task, it actually requires careful planning and constant effort. Families lead busy lives and often forget (or do not realize) that this effort is critical to success in reading.

While the following list of suggestions is not complete, it should get you thinking about what you can do to increase the likelihood of families and children sitting down together to read.

- **Provide a rationale for reading.** Because of their busy lives, families need to be highly motivated to spend some of their precious time reading to children. Collect research and writing that supports this position and send home regular reminders in newsletters or other written communications summarizing the views expressed.

- **Suggest good children's literature.** There are literally thousands of books available to children of all ages and reading abilities. Families need guidance about what books might be appropriate for their children and where they might be found. Send home lists periodically (you may wish to tie them

to the concepts you are emphasizing in class) so that families will consistently know about quality literature they can read.

- **Prepare reading backpacks.** Prepare one or more backpacks, each equipped with a good children's book, a note to the family explaining what they should do and why, and some suggestions for extending the reading task into other activities. At the end of each day, send a backpack home with one of the children to use overnight. Make sure every child regularly has the opportunity to take home the backpack.

- **Conduct family meetings.** It may be useful to have families come together for an evening meeting in which you explain the importance of reading aloud to children and provide some examples of quality children's literature and where it can be found. Discussing this topic with others may also encourage "reluctant family readers" to get involved in this important task.

1. Talk to an early childhood caregiver or teacher about the challenges of involving families in reading to their children. From your discussion, do you think most families believe that reading to their own children as infants, toddlers, and preschoolers is an important task? Why or why not?

2. Do you enjoy reading for pleasure? How will you work to instill this attitude in the children you teach?

MyEducationLab

The power of classroom practice.

MyEducationLab™ "Teacher educators who are developing pedagogies for the analysis of teaching and learning contend that analyzing teaching artifacts has three advantages: it enables new teachers time for reflection while still using the real materials of practice; it provides new teachers with experience thinking about and approaching the complexity of the classroom; and in some cases, it can help new teachers and teacher educators develop a shared understanding and common language about teaching. . . ."[1]

As Linda Darling-Hammond and her colleagues point out, grounding teacher education in real classrooms—among real teachers and students and among actual examples of students' and teachers' work—is an important and perhaps even an essential, part of training teachers for the complexities of teaching in today's classrooms. For this reason, we have created a **MyEducationLab™**—an online learning environment that provides the context of real classrooms and artifacts that research on teacher education tells us is so important. The authentic in-class video footage, interactive skill-building exercises, and other resources available on MyEducationLab offer pre-service teachers a unique and valuable education tool. This exciting new learning and teaching tool is designed to help learners and future teachers develop the essential skills needed to succeed in the classroom, while helping instructors save time in teaching courses.

To enhance the coverage of the core concepts discussed in the book, MyEducationLab is organized topically. This organization allows flexibility, focusing on core concepts within a course rather than on individual chapters. This way, regardless of how a course is organized—by following the text's chapter sequence or an adapted sequence—the assignable activities and learning units are easy to find and incorporate into any unit of study. Whenever the MyEducationLab logo appears in the text, follow the simple instructions to access the interactive assignments, activities, and learning units on MyEducationLab. Additionally, a full listing of assignments, activities, and other resources (identified by topic area) is available on the site for ease of use. For each topic covered in the course you will find most or all of the following resources:

Connection to National Standards

Now it is easier than ever to see how coursework is connected to national standards. Each topic on MyEducationLab lists intended learning outcomes connected to the appropriate national standards. All of the Assignments and Activities and all of the Building Teaching Skills and Dispositions in MyEducationLab are mapped to the appropriate national standards and learning outcomes as well.

---

[1]Darling-Hammond, l., & Bransford, J., Eds.(2005). *Preparing Teachers for a Changing World*. San Francisco: John Wiley & Sons.

Assignments and Activities

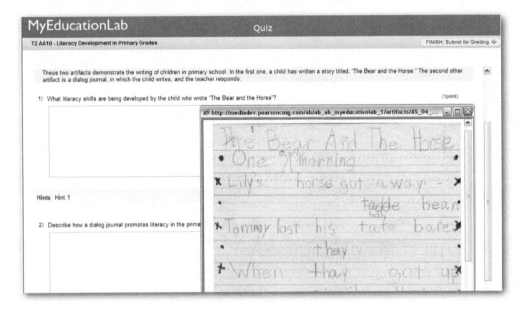

Designed to enhance student understanding of concepts covered in class and save instructors preparation and grading time, these assignable exercises show concepts in action (through video, cases, and/or student and teacher artifacts). They help students deepen content knowledge and synthesize and apply concepts and strategies they read about in the book. (Correct answers for these assignments are available to the instructor only under the Instructor Resource tab.)

Building Teaching Skills and Dispositions

These learning units help students practice and strengthen skills that are essential to quality teaching. After presenting the steps involved in a core teaching process, students are given an opportunity to practice applying this skill via videos, student and teacher artifacts, and/or case studies of authentic classrooms. By providing multiple opportunities to practice a single teaching concept, each activity encourages a deeper application of text content, as well as the use of critical thinking skills.

IRIS Center Resources

The IRIS Center at Vanderbilt University (http://iris.peabody.vanderbilt.edu)—funded by the U.S. Department of Education's Office of Special Education Programs (OSEP)—develops training enhancement materials for pre-service and in-service teachers. The Center works with experts from across the country to create challenge-based interactive modules, case study units, and podcasts that provide research-validated information about working with students in inclusive settings. In your MyEducationLab course we have integrated this content where appropriate.

Teacher Talk

This feature emphasizes the power of teaching through videos of master teachers telling their own compelling stories of why they teach. These videos help teacher candidates see the bigger picture and consider why the things they are learning are important to their career as a teacher. Each of these featured teachers has been awarded the Council of Chief State School Officers' Teachers of the Year award, the oldest and most prestigious award for teachers.

Course Resources

The Course Resources section on MyEducationLab is designed to help students put together an effective lesson plan, prepare for and begin their career, navigate their first year of teaching, and understand key educational standards, policies, and laws.

The Course Resources Tab includes the following:

- The **Lesson Plan Builder** is an effective and easy-to-use tool that students can use to create, update, and share lesson plans.
- The **Preparing a Portfolio** module provides guidelines for creating a teaching portfolio that will allow students to practice effective lesson planning and prepare a high-quality portfolio.
- **Beginning Your Career** offers tips, advice, and other valuable information on the following:
  - **Resume Writing and Interviewing.** Includes expert advice on how to write impressive resumes and prepare for job interviews.
  - **Your First Year of Teaching.** Provides practical tips to set up a first classroom, manage student behavior, and more easily organize for instruction and assessment.
  - **Law and Public Policies.** Details specific directives and requirements teachers need to understand under the No Child Left Behind Act and the Individuals with Disabilities Education Improvement Act of 2004.

Certification and Licensure

This section is designed to help students pass their licensure exam by giving them access to state test requirements and sample test items complete with correct answers.

The Certification and Licensure tab includes the following:

- **State Certification Test Requirements:** Here students can click on a state and be taken to a list of state certification examinations and state departments of education.
- **Licensure Exams** provides guidelines for passing the Praxis exam, including:
  - A **Practice Test** Exam with practice test questions
  - **Case Histories** with practice test questions
  - **Video Case Studies** with practice test questions
- **State and National Standards:** This section provides links to state and national standards where available.
- **National Evaluation Series™ by Pearson:** Here students can see the tests NES has available in addition to having access to sample test items with descriptions and rationale for correct answers.
- **ETS Online Praxis Tutorials:** Here students can complete practice test items and receive descriptions and rationale for correct answers in preparation for the Praxis tests that individual states require.

Book Resources

Study Plan

A MyEducationLab Study Plan is a multiple choice assessment tied to chapter objectives, supported by study material. It offers multiple opportunities to master required course content as identified by the objectives in each chapter:

- **Chapter Objectives** identify the learning outcomes for the chapter and give students targets to shoot for as they read and study.
- **Multiple Choice Assessments** evaluate mastery of the content. These assessments are mapped to chapter objectives, and students can take the multiple choice quiz as many times as they want. Not only do these quizzes provide overall scores for each objective, but they also explain why responses to particular items are correct or incorrect.
- **Study Material: Review, Practice and Enrichment** give students a deeper understanding of what they do and do not know related to chapter content. This material includes text excerpts, activities that include hints and feedback, and interactive multi-media exercises built around videos, simulations, cases, or classroom artifacts.

Visit www.myeducationlab.com for a demonstration of this exciting new online teaching resource.

New! CourseSmart eTextbook Available

CourseSmart is an exciting new choice for students who want to save money. As an alternative to purchasing the printed textbook, students can purchase an electronic version of the same content. With a CourseSmart eTextbook, students can search the text, make notes online, print out reading assignments that incorporate lecture notes, and bookmark important passages for later review. For more information, or to purchase access to the CourseSmart eTextbook, visit www.coursemart.com.

Ancillaries

Online Instructor's Manual

This updated manual includes suggestions for teaching and additional instructional resources such as handouts. "For Discussion and Action" offers prompts for in-class activities. "Building Your Personal Library" provides key reference books related to chapter content.

Electronic Test Banks

Test items in multiple-choice, true/false, and essay format are available to instructors in the Online Test Bank in MS Word and in various LMS formats.

Pearson MyTest

This powerful assessment generation program helps instructors easily create and print quizzes and exams. Questions and tests are authored online, allowing ultimate flexibility and the ability to efficiently create and print assessments anytime, anywhere. Instructors can access Pearson MyTest and their test bank files by going to www.pearsonmytest.com to log in, register, or request access. Features of Pearson MyTest include the following:

Premium assessment content

- Draw from a rich library of assessments that complement your Pearson textbook and your course's learning objectives.
- Edit questions or tests to fit your specific teaching needs.

Instructor-friendly resources

- Easily create and store your own questions, including images, diagrams, and charts, using simple drag-and-drop and Word-like controls.
- Use additional information provided by Pearson, such as the question's difficulty level or learning objective, to help you quickly build your test.

Time-saving enhancements

- Add headers or footers and easily scramble questions and answer choices—all from one simple toolbar.
- Quickly create multiple versions of your test or answer key, and when ready, simply save to MS-Word or PDF format and print.
- Export your exams for import to Blackboard 6.0, CE (WebCT), or Vista (WebCT).

Online PowerPoint Slides

PowerPoints of key concepts from the text are available to instructors on the Instructor's Resource Center at www.pearsonhighered.com. Easily accessed and organized by chapter, they are colorful, simple, and straightforward, and may be customized to fit instructors' needs.

Acknowledgments

No book of this complexity can be completed without the assistance of a great many competent and supportive people. Grateful thanks are given to Mary Tindle, project editor at S4Carlisle Publishing Services, and to the following staff at Pearson: Julie Peters, senior acquisitions editor; Linda Bayma, senior project manager; and Lori Whitley, photo researcher. Their support and assistance throughout this process have been invaluable.

I also thank the reviewers for their thoughtful commentary and helpful suggestions: Heather Batchelder, University of Central Florida; Priscilla Garcia, Laredo Community College; Kimberly Hale, East Tennessee State University; Kristen Stephens, Duke University; Kathy Wolf, Guildford Technical Community College; and Clover Wright, California University of Pennsylvania.

On a personal note, I want to say a special word of thanks to my wife, Lisa, for all her support throughout this and prior editions of this text. Between us, we have six wonderful children, all of whom need some form of parenting every day. Because of my work responsibilities as a university administrator and my time spent in revising this text, my parenting role has sometimes been more limited than I would like. Lisa has always been there to make up the difference. She works tirelessly to make sure that each of our children knows they are deeply loved. Her ready smile, encouraging words, and uncomplaining attitude have helped me through many difficult days. Thank you, Lisa, for all that you do to support me in my work. It won't be long now, and I'll be retired and able to join you as a full partner in the parenting process!

Michael Henniger

brief contents

contents

 # special features

Developmentally Appropriate Practice

Technology Explorations and Activities

Teaching Young Children

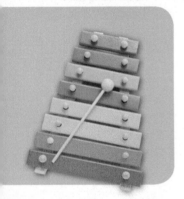

Overview of the Profession

IN THIS CHAPTER YOU WILL

- Develop an understanding of the essentials of early care and education.

- Learn about the many different types of programs for young children.

- Identify the sources of funding for early childhood programs.

- Determine the roles, responsibilities, and skills needed for teachers of young children.

- Investigate the current training typical of teachers in early care and education.

- Become familiar with the resources for professional development available to early childhood educators.

Adrienne has just been offered the job she interviewed for last week. After spending several years at home caring for her children, she decided to reenter the workforce.

One of the first challenges she faces, however, is finding quality child care for her daughter and son: 4-year-old Alyssa and 2-year-old Mark. During the past few months, Adrienne and her husband have been exploring the many different early childhood programs available in their community.

Adrienne knows how important it is to her children's growth and development that they continue to be stimulated and well cared for when she is not with them. Therefore, she and her husband have been visiting preschool and child-care centers in her area, meeting with teachers, talking with other parents, touring classrooms, and observing the children enrolled in these different programs. They have also been collecting information on teacher-to-student ratios, staff qualifications and turnover rates, and the approach to early care and education in each program.

Finding affordable, high-quality programs where Alyssa and Mark will have plenty of personal attention and many opportunities to learn and play will take careful planning, but with so many possibilities, the right option is sure to present itself.

Perhaps, like Adrienne, you have had some exposure in one form or another to early care and education. Alternatively, this may be your first introduction to working with children from birth to age 8. In either case, this book will help you begin to explore a most interesting and challenging profession. Because this is an introductory text, however, a great many issues are only briefly described. You will need much more study and practice before you have the knowledge and skills necessary to teach at this level. As you read through the chapters of this book, discuss what you are learning with others, and observe children and teachers in the classroom, you will develop a deeper understanding of the field of early care and education.

This first chapter introduces you to the many different types of programs associated with early care and education and describes the professional aspects of becoming an early childhood educator. Before discussing these issues, however, the chapter begins with an overview of the five essential elements of early care and education.

 # Essentials of Early Care and Education

MyEducationLab

Visit the MyEducationLab for *Teaching Young Children* to enhance your understanding of chapter concepts with a personalized Study Plan. You'll also have the opportunity to hone your teaching skills through video- and case-based Assignments and Activities as well as Building Teaching Skills and Disposition lessons.

Early care and education is a unique field of study and practice organized around five key elements (summarized in Figure 1–1). Understanding these foundational components and their interrelationships will help you develop a clear understanding of what is needed to work with young children. Early childhood teachers and caregivers must understand all of these elements and deal with their implications in their classrooms.

Understand Children and Their Development

The first of these essential elements is an understanding of child development and learning. Early childhood educators believe that educational experiences are based first on children's needs and interests. To know these needs and interests, adults must understand children, both individually and collectively. By studying child development, teachers of young children know the normal patterns of behavior for children at specific ages. They also realize that individual differences exist between children, and they can identify those variations. This knowledge helps early

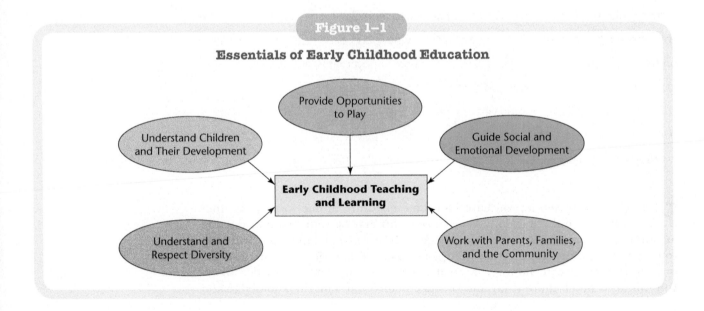

Figure 1–1

Essentials of Early Childhood Education

Observing Development . . .
GENERAL DEVELOPMENTAL ABILITIES

Choose one of the age groups within early childhood (infants/toddlers, preschoolers, or primary-age children) and observe **general developmental abilities**. Without naming the children observed (for privacy and confidentiality), take detailed notes about what children do and say. Use the following sample observation of preschool children as a format for your own observation. Include only what you see and hear, saving your interpretations for the reflections that follow the sample observation:

Playful Beginnings Preschool, October 23, 9:30–10:00 a.m.

Language/communication strategies (actual words, gestures)	Physical activities observed	Social interactions with peers and adults
1. "Teacher Kelly, come look at my picture."	1. C., age 3, stacked four blocks and then immediately knocked them down.	1. E., M., and D. are finger painting, occasionally looking to see what others are doing.
2. . . .	2. . . .	2. . . .

Reflect and Apply

1. Was there anything surprising or interesting that you heard or saw children doing?

2. Based on this one observation, what did you learn about general developmental abilities at this age level?

3. Were there more similarities or differences among the children you observed? What does this observation tell you about teaching and learning in early childhood settings?

---

childhood caregivers and teachers to select materials and activities that will create optimal learning opportunities in the classroom. The *Observing Development* feature found in each chapter of this text will help you to understand children and how they develop. The feature in this section prompts you to look at aspects of general developmental abilities of children, reflect on what you observe, and consider how you might apply your understanding to children of various ages to maximize their development.

The following vignette illustrates how one effective teacher applies her understanding of child development with her students:

Lavelle Peters is preparing for the coming week in her kindergarten classroom. She remembers overhearing Noell and Jaleen talking excitedly about the recent class field trip to the zoo. The Primate House was particularly interesting to several members of the class. Planning some activities centering on this interest seems appropriate and fun. Lavelle uses her general knowledge of child development and individual differences to select books, computer software, and discussion topics about monkeys, baboons, and gorillas for the coming week.

The approach described in this vignette is very different from the typical procedures used to develop the curriculum in many primary classrooms. Textbooks used by teachers carefully organize and structure the content taught in elementary schools and present it in a specific sequence. In science, for example, the textbook may call for the study of insects first, followed by birds, and, later still, the investigation of primates. Rather than considering children and their developmental needs and interests first, teachers who use this curriculum-centered approach with students allow the teaching materials to dictate the sequence and appropriateness of learning activities.

Provide Opportunities to Play

A second essential ingredient found in early childhood programs is the provision of times during the school day in which children can engage in play. Play is one of the major ways in which young children learn about the world around them. Rather than having adults *tell* children what they need to know (an efficient strategy for many adult situations), children need the chance to manipulate real-world objects, interact with others, and learn for themselves important information about their environment. When children have large blocks of time to choose their own materials and playmates, the learning that takes place can be quite amazing.

Lattice and Malcolm are in the block area in their preschool classroom. They are working together building a road, a schoolhouse, and a parking garage. Lattice is struggling to find just the right block for her portion of the roadway. Malcolm suggests she try the "long, long one like mine," and Lattice discovers that his idea solves her problem nicely. As these children continue their play together, they solve additional problems, practice the important skill of cooperation, and indirectly learn about the mathematical properties of their play materials.

While most parents and teachers recognize play as an enjoyable experience for children, many fail to see the learning potential of this important activity. Consequently, play is often viewed as frivolous and is excluded from what is seen as more meaningful work experiences in the classroom. Early childhood educators, however, believe that play is a crucial way in which children learn about language, develop intellectual concepts, build social relationships and understandings, strengthen physical skills, and deal with stress. In short, play enhances every aspect of child development and is an essential ingredient in early care and education.

The *Celebrating Play* feature found in each chapter of this text will provide additional information about the importance of play and examples of classrooms effectively using play. *Celebrating Play . . . In the Primary Grades* (found in this section) provides an excellent example of how a primary teacher used this important activity for meaningful science learning.

Guide Social and Emotional Development

The third key element of early care and education emphasizes the importance of guiding the young child's social and emotional development. Although educating the mind is critical during the early years, caregivers and teachers of young children find it equally important to help children develop a strong sense of self, learn to relate in positive ways with adults and peers, and work through the many positive

Celebrating Play . . .
IN THE PRIMARY GRADES

While most preschool teachers include many opportunities for children to play, most primary classrooms are organized around tasks that exclude play as an option for learning (Koralek, 2005; Stone, 1995). With the heavy emphasis on teacher-directed learning found at this level, little time is left for this valuable activity. Yet play can provide many opportunities for primary children to create, problem solve, and learn about the world around them.

Wassermann (2000) has clearly identified ways in which children in the primary grades use play to enhance language development, learn concepts, and build social relationships. She is considered one of the leading advocates for play at this level. She gives the following example of a second-grade classroom in which play is effectively used:

As I walk through the door, the sight dazzles me. Five groups of children are working in investigative play groups with dry cells, buzzers, low-wattage light bulbs, and switches. They are carrying out inquiries with these materials. Bob (the teacher) has used the following activity card to guide them.

Use the materials in this center to find out what you can about electricity and how it works.

- What can you observe about the dry cells? The buzzers? The light bulb?
- Talk together about your observations and make some notes about what you did. (p. 21)

Wassermann describes the intensity and enthusiasm of the children involved in this playful activity. Everyone is busy exploring the materials provided. Many choose to continue the science activity rather than go outside for recess. No discipline problems arise. This playful task has created an ideal situation for creatively learning about science.

1. Based on Wassermann's description, what are three or four benefits of play in the primary classroom?
2. From what you know of play so far, do you think it should be included in the primary classroom? If you were a primary teacher, would you encourage your children to play? Why or why not?

and negative emotions they experience. Guiding young children in these areas requires a solid background in child development and a sensitive, insightful adult.

Carly is a quiet but capable 4-year-old in Ingrid Siegelman's prekindergarten classroom. Lately, however, her behavior has been less than desirable. Carly seems distracted and simply stares into space much of the day. She clings to her mom when brought to school and doesn't want to stay in the classroom. Ingrid decides to contact Carly's mom and telephones her at home that evening. Through the course of the conversation, Ingrid finds out that Carly's grandmother died suddenly and the whole family is grieving her loss. Knowing this, Ingrid plans to choose some books for the literacy center next week that might be helpful and will make an effort to take some extra time to work with Carly one-on-one to see if she can draw her into a conversation about her grandmother. With follow-up, Ingrid feels certain that she will be able to make progress in helping Carly.

Some adults, particularly at the primary level, may downplay this activity as tangential to the main mission of education, yet Ingrid and other early childhood teachers recognize it as a critical component of their teaching role. The development of effective social skills and the promotion of emotional health are essential elements of the early childhood curriculum. While this makes the teacher's role more complex, the overall benefits to children are immense.

Work with Families and the Community

The fourth essential element of early care and education is the development of mutually supportive relationships with families and the community. Although this concept has more recently gained support among educators in general, early childhood professionals have had a long tradition of working closely with families and community members. Effective two-way communication, a climate of caring, and the involvement of families in the educational process all provide early childhood caregivers and teachers, and families and their children with many benefits.

 Larry Marshall is in his second year of teaching third-grade children. He tried to communicate with families and get them involved last year, and he has worked even harder this term to build stronger relationships. The results have been truly surprising. Larry expected to see greater student progress and satisfaction and is pleased to find these results. An unanticipated result, however, is the value that families have found in the informal conversations and observations they have during their time in the classroom. One parent confided that she was learning some very helpful discipline tips from watching Larry in action. She was using similar techniques at home with good success and feeling much better about this aspect of her parenting. Larry also finds that he is personally benefiting from his work with families. When they share their special talents in the classroom, for example, Larry is challenged and invigorated by the experiences along with the children.

The *Family Partnerships* feature found in each chapter of this text will highlight key issues that will help you develop and maintain these essential relationships. The *Family Partnerships* feature in this section describes the importance of effective communication strategies and identifies key options that you will want to use regularly. Read about them now and respond to the questions posed at the end of the feature.

Understand and Respect Diversity

The final essential element of early education is an understanding of, and respect for, the many elements of diversity that have an impact on the lives of young children. Cultural backgrounds, religion, income level, family circumstances, variances due to gender, and physical/mental differences among children all influence development and learning. Furthermore, each of the other four previously mentioned essentials of early childhood is impacted by diversity. The following examples help highlight the importance of diversity and its interrelatedness with the other essential areas:

- **Development and diversity.** Two-year-old Sabrina has a hearing loss. After being fitted for a hearing aid next month, she will start attending an early learning program designed to help her catch up with her peers in oral language development.
- **Guidance and diversity.** At group time, you are introducing Corinne, a new Asian-American student in your preschool classroom. Four-year-old Andy says, "Mrs. Amada, why does her skin look different?"

Family Partnerships . . .
COMMUNICATION IS THE KEY

As with all healthy relationships, the key to effective partnerships with families is to engage in effective communication. You will need to know about and use several key elements of good communication, including the following:

- **Use of voice.** The loudness, pitch, speed of delivery, and tone of one's voice all help determine the message received by someone else. A calm, moderately pitched voice makes it more likely that families and others will be able to hear and respond to the messages you send.

- **Body language.** Body posture, hand gestures, and facial expressions all send important messages to others. For example, leaning forward while communicating with families indicates interest and a desire to engage in effective communication. You will want to be sure to send this kind of positive nonverbal message as you interact with families.

- **Word choice.** Because words individually and collectively convey so much meaning, it is important to think carefully about the words you use when communicating with families. While it is important to be honest with them, saying that their child is outspoken rather than belligerent may lead to a more productive conversation.

- **Situational variables.** Such things as the clothes you wear, the choice of chairs for seating, and the location in which you communicate all influence the interactions you have with families. For example, when choosing the clothes to wear for family–teacher conferences, make sure to select items that are professional without appearing too elitist.

- **Listening skills.** Because good communication requires both speaking and listening, it is important for you to truly listen when families are speaking so that you accurately hear their messages. It takes concentration and practice to be a good listener, but making the effort will pay big dividends in relationships with families.

1. Based on your life experiences to date, how important are good communication skills in human relationships? In what ways would good communication skills positively influence relationships with families?

2. Do a self-assessment of your communication skills at this time. What do you see as your personal strengths and weaknesses as a communicator and listener?

- **Play and diversity.** After school, 7-year-old Audrey likes to get out her paint set and create imaginative pictures using a variety of vibrant colors. Her twin brother, Darian, prefers racing around the cul-de-sac on his bicycle, weaving around a self-constructed obstacle course.

- **Families and diversity.** At the open house, 5-year-old Franklin has just introduced you to Denise and Angela, his parents. They mention their interest in occasionally helping out in the classroom.

The *Celebrating Diversity* feature found in each chapter of this text introduces additional key understanding regarding this important topic. The *Celebrating Diversity* feature found on page 10 describes the growing religious diversity in America and the implications of this change. Read the feature now and respond to the questions before continuing on.

The Scope of Early Care and Education

Although quality early childhood programs will have each of the five key elements previously described, they also exhibit many differences because of the children these programs are designed to serve. A program for infants and toddlers, for

Celebrating Diversity . . .
AMERICA'S GROWING RELIGIOUS DIVERSITY

While American religious beliefs are still primarily Christian, there are many diverse traditions and practices within the subgroups that consider themselves Christian. For example, the beliefs of Mormons, Seventh-Day Adventists, and Jehovah's Witnesses differ significantly from Protestant groups such as Lutherans and Presbyterians.

In addition, there are growing numbers of other faiths present in most schools and communities across the nation. As greater numbers of immigrants from non-European countries have found their way to America (Hoefer, Rytina, & Baker, 2010), they have brought with them a growing diversity of religious beliefs. In the United States, the Jewish, Buddhist, Muslim, and Hindu religions are the largest non-Christian groups (Pew Forum on Religion and Public Life, 2008). Diana Eck (2001) makes a startling pronouncement about religious diversity in America today when she says, "The United States has become the most religiously diverse nation on earth" (p. 4).

With this growing religious diversity come many opportunities for teachers of young children to help themselves and their children to understand and respect the various belief systems that exist within their classrooms. Teachers need to become aware of the religious diversity within their schools and classrooms, understand the differences in traditions and practices that exist between religions, and make sure to plan activities and discussions that respect this diversity of beliefs.

1. Will your religious beliefs influence your ability to accept the diverse beliefs that will be held by the children and families you will be working with? Give a rationale for your response.

2. At this point, can you identify ways in which religious diversity will change the ways in which you will work with young children and their families? For example, how would you celebrate holidays such as Ramadan and Hanukkah in your classroom if you have children for which they are important?

example, is going to look quite different from one designed to meet the needs of primary-age children. In this section, infant/toddler, preschool, child-care, children with special needs, and primary education programs will be described to provide you with a beginning understanding of the similarities and differences that exist between them.

Infant/Toddler Programs

The fastest growing segment of early childhood programming is the infant/toddler component (birth to 2 years of age). Until fairly recently, most very young children were cared for by family members in the home. Over the last few years, however, research has found that 38% of children from birth to age 2 spend more than 35 hours each week in child care out of the home and another 17.3% spend between 15 and 34 hours per week in such care (Capizzano & Main, 2005). As these numbers continue to grow, the impact on low-income families is particularly strong. The need for quality infant/toddler care is especially important for this group of children and their families (Children's Defense Fund, 2010). Although most current infant/toddler programs operate in home environments with small groups of children, the number of center-based options where larger groups of very young children receive care is increasing. In either homes or centers, the major challenge for a teacher is to form a close relationship with each child in his or her care. Consistently and lovingly

A major challenge for infant and toddler caregivers is to consistently meet children's physical and emotional needs.

meeting the needs of very young children is an extremely important and challenging task (Petersen & Wittmer, 2008).

Each of the chapters in this text includes several features titled *Developmentally Appropriate Practice*, which are designed to provide you with practical ideas that are consistent with national standards for early childhood programs (Copple & Bredekamp, 2009). They provide insights into what you will be doing in the classroom as an early care and learning professional. The feature found in this section provides you with an example of the daily routine for an adult working with toddlers. Take a look at this schedule to get a beginning idea of what it would be like to work in this setting.

Preschool Programs

Traditionally, preschool programs were designed for children between the ages of 3 and 5 as a way to enhance social and emotional development. These nursery school options became popular in the 1920s and continue to be highly valued by many middle-class families. More recently, prekindergarten programs have been promoted as a way to help children identified as being at risk of failing in the K–12 system develop the skills they will need to be successful in later years. Many preschool programs today have also expanded their age range downward to include 2-year-olds.

Rather than being full-day programs, most preschool classrooms operate halftime or less. A common model is to enroll children for three to five half-day sessions per week. With the increasing numbers of single parents and dual-career families, however, these partial-day sessions are often combined with the chance for children to participate in full-day child care as well. Preschool students may be in the same classrooms and working with the same adults as children in child-care options, thus making it difficult to separate the two programs.

Child-Care Programs

Child-care programs are designed to provide children with quality care and education for full days. With more parents working full-time, the need for childcare options for young children continues to grow. Typically, child-care programs provide education and care for children from the beginning to the end of the parents' workday. It is not uncommon for some children to be in a child-care setting from 6:00 a.m. until 6:00 p.m. As indicated earlier, other children may attend part days for a preschool experience.

A variety of child-care options are available. The most common type is called the **family home child care**. These programs operate out of the caretaker's home and enroll only a small number of children. **Child-care centers** are programs located in buildings either designed for, or remodeled to be used with, young children. More children are typically enrolled in these programs, with several teachers hired

Developmentally Appropriate Practice . . .
A CENTER-BASED PROGRAM FOR TODDLERS

A typical center-based toddler classroom can have as many as six or seven children under the care of one adult. While additional assistance may be available during portions of the day, much of the care is provided by this one person. Caregivers working with toddlers spend considerable time assisting with activities such as eating, sleeping, and toileting. They work to make these interactions enjoyable parts of the day as they playfully and lovingly meet the needs of young children. The schedule of events for toddlers should be in a predictable sequence, provide for active and quiet times, and encourage quality adult–child and child–child interactions. The following schedule is typical of what you would find in a center-based program for toddlers. Try to imagine yourself spending extended time in this setting, engaged in the tasks described here.

6:00 a.m.   **Arrival, quiet activities.** Caregiver greets individual children as they arrive. Parents sign in and share any last minute instructions. Some children may simply need to be held and cuddled, while others are ready for quiet play in one of the classroom centers.

7:30 a.m.   **Prepare for breakfast.** Caregiver checks diapers and washes hands in preparation for breakfast.

7:45 a.m.   **Breakfast and free play.** Children and caregiver share breakfast together. As children finish their meal, they are transitioned to free play in art, water play, and sensory activities.

9:00 a.m.   **Diaper changing/potty training.** The caregiver works with any children who haven't recently had a diaper change or spent time in the bathroom.

9:15 a.m.   **Music, stories, finger plays.** Children are encouraged to participate in a group experience with singing, storybooks, and movement activities.

10:15 a.m. **Outdoor play.** Weather permitting, children are taken outside to the playground to use the materials and equipment found there. In unpleasant weather, children engage in indoor large muscle activities on simple climbing equipment.

10:45 a.m. **Quiet activities, puzzles, art, play dough.** In preparation for lunch, children engage in quiet activities while the caregiver takes care of toileting needs and washing hands.

11:00 a.m. **Lunch.** Lunch provides another opportunity for the caregiver and children to sit down together and enjoy food and relaxed discussion/conversation time.

11:30 a.m. **Rest time.** While some children do not sleep, all of the children are encouraged to lie down and rest for an extended period following lunch.

1:00 p.m.   **Quiet activities.** Since some children may sleep for extended periods, those who are awake are engaged in more quiet activities with puzzles, art, and play dough.

2:45 p.m.   **Diaper changing/potty training.**

3:00 p.m.   **Snack time.** Nutritious snacks are set up at a table and children can individually come and eat.

3:15 p.m.   **Outdoor play.**

4:00 p.m.   **Indoor free play.**

5:00 p.m.   **Story time and parent pick-up.** Parents are expected to pick up their children by 6 p.m. Story time gives a quiet end to a busy day.

to work with different groups of children. **School-based child care** is becoming a more popular option in many locations. Public and private schools are setting aside space in their elementary school buildings for child-care programs under their direction. **Corporate child care** is also growing in popularity. An increasing number of businesses are offering on-site child care as a convenience and service to their employees because the benefits far exceed the costs (Bright Horizons Family Solutions, 2010). **Before- and after-school care** is a final option available in many

Technology Explorations and Activities . . .
CHILD CARE EXCHANGE

There are a great many Internet resources available to assist you in learning more about young children, their development, and strategies for effectively working with them. One important option is the Child Care Exchange. This organization has been in operation for more than 30 years, providing information to educators in early childhood programs through its *Exchange* magazine, books, seminars, and conferences. Their website has an assortment of free articles and information for early educators. Take some time now to review their Internet site to learn more about this resource.

Research, Reflect, and Respond

1. Do an Internet search for Child Care Exchange and research the options available at the site. What did you find that was of interest to you?

2. After reviewing the website, reflect on the information presented there. Talk with others about the benefits of the materials located on this site.

3. You may wish to sign up for the free ExchangeEveryDay electronic newsletter. It is available five days a week and provides very good information to adults working with young children.

---

settings. These programs may be provided at the elementary school, or children may travel to other sites to receive this care.

A feature found in each chapter of this text is called *Technology Explorations and Activities*. It uses Internet resources to expand your knowledge and understanding of key issues. Above you will find information on the Child Care Information Exchange website. This is a good option for free daily information about early care and education. After reading this feature now, you will want to review the site carefully to see what information it contains that would be useful to you as a future early childhood professional.

Programs for Children with Special Needs

Early childhood programs designed for children with special needs are also available in most communities. Federal legislation over the past three decades has mandated these important options. **Public Law (PL) 94–142**, enacted in the mid-1970s, requires that, beginning at age 3, all children with special needs be provided a free and appropriate public education. Later revisions of this act extended the availability of these programs downward to include birth to age 3. In 1990, after several more revisions, the act was renamed the **Individuals with Disabilities Education Act**. It was last amended in 2004. This law is intended to educate children with special needs in classrooms with their normally developing peers. This effort has led to early childhood special education programs that are blended with other options for young children. The *Developmentally Appropriate Practice* feature in this section provides additional information on a special needs preschool.

While many educational efforts for children with special needs are integrated with other early childhood programs, **early intervention programs** for children with special needs are also available (U.S. Department of Education, 2009). These programs are designed to help identify children's disabilities and assist them in growth and development. Options for infants and toddlers are most common and often combine limited small-group experiences with home visits where the family and home visitor work together to support the young child's development.

Developmentally Appropriate Practice . . .
A SPECIAL NEEDS PRESCHOOL

With the school year about to begin, Monica, the head teacher for the special needs preschool, is getting ready for her new group of students. She is reviewing the written information she has on each of the children with special needs in the class. There will be nine students: seven children with special needs and two "typical" children to serve as peer models. While Patti and Kara, her two classroom aides, are busy setting up centers and the speech therapist and occupational therapist are down the hall reviewing last year's Individualized Education Plans (IEPs) for returning students, Monica considers the challenges she will face in meeting the needs of such a diverse group of students: Evan is a quiet 4-year-old boy with Down syndrome who has delays in his language, physical, and intellectual development. Stephanie is a 3-year-old who was recently diagnosed with autism. She has difficulty understanding how to engage in conversations with others and taking part in group interactions. Angie has mild cerebral palsy and slower speech and motor development. Brian is in his second year in the preschool and has significant problems in his social interactions with adults and other children. Mark is a 4-year-old with speech delays of unknown origins. Esther has a birth defect known as spina bifida and spends her time at the preschool in a special wheelchair/bed. Sam has significant vision problems and is considered legally blind. In addition, he has sensory integration difficulties.

Each of the children just described will eventually spend most of his or her time in "regular education" classrooms. As it is likely that you will have children with special needs in your future classrooms, it is important for you to begin thinking about the following:

- **Emphasize commonalities first.** Every child with special needs shares much in common with other children in your classroom (likes, dislikes, positive/negative personality characteristics, strengths/weaknesses, etc.). Make sure to find those similarities and build on them in your teaching. Mark, for example, despite his speech delays, loves to construct with blocks; he can build complex structures and engages in creative play in that center.

- **Define what the child can do.** Rather than focusing on what the child cannot do, work on identifying and building on the child's capabilities. Esther, despite spending her time in a wheelchair, has a great love of books and is beginning to read some simple beginning children's books on her own.

- **Include the child in classroom life.** Make a special effort to find ways in which a child with special needs can be included in all aspects of the activities planned each day. One of the characteristics of children with Down syndrome, like Evan, is that they tend to stand back and watch rather than actively participate in many activities. But when Monica works to include him at group time, he interacts well with her and other students.

Kindergartens

It may surprise you to know that publicly funded programs for 5-year-old children are a relatively new option in many states. Many public schools either did not provide kindergarten or offered it only for families who were able to pay for the service. Today, however, publicly funded kindergarten is available to virtually all children in the United States at age 5 (Cascio, 2010).

Traditional kindergartens in the United States were half-day programs designed to help children develop social, emotional, and cognitive skills through a play-oriented experience. Despite the many benefits of this focus, many programs today are more academic and present a curriculum that looks much like that of the first-grade classroom. One reason for this more academic focus is the increased pressure from state and federal agencies to improve the literacy, science, and mathematical understandings of young children. Federal legislation, such as the

Primary children learn many valuable concepts using manipulative materials.

No Child Left Behind Act of 2001, provide financial incentives to schools that make good academic progress as measured on standardized tests and penalize those that demonstrate poor performance. Consequently, kindergarten teachers spend more of their classroom time engaged in these more academic subjects and have fewer opportunities for other very valuable experiences. In part to accommodate this more academic focus, many kindergarten classrooms are now full-day programs that meet 3 to 5 days a week.

Primary Education

Grades 1 through 3 in elementary schools are referred to as primary education and have been a part of American schooling from colonial times. For most of this period, the methods and materials for teaching at this level have mirrored those used with older elementary students. Instruction was teacher-directed and included mostly small- and large-group teaching combined with independent work for students.

Beginning in the 1960s and 1970s, the popularity of theorists such as Piaget (Flavell, 1963), Bruner (1966), and Dewey (1929) led to new teaching strategies for primary education. Educators began to view young elementary students as more like preschool and kindergarten children in their thinking rather than older elementary students. More opportunities to learn through hands-on manipulation of objects and interaction with peers were implemented. Although instruction at the primary level remains teacher-directed in a majority of classrooms, more primary teachers are starting to engage in a variety of interesting teaching and learning strategies. The **multiage classroom**, in which two or three grades are grouped together for instruction, is one option being tried. For example, rather than having separate groups of 5-, 6-, and 7-year-old children, students are mixed together in the same room. Multiage classrooms can be traced back to the one-room schoolhouses that existed in America until the early part of the twentieth century. A renewed interest in this option began in the 1980s. In these classrooms, younger children learn from their interactions with older classmates, and older students reinforce their own understandings as they work with younger students. Because early childhood professionals have many of the same students for more than 1 year, there tend to be stronger adult–student relationships in multiage settings. Both research and practice suggest that these classrooms enhance child development (Carter, 2005; Kinsey, 2001). Multiage classrooms produce students who have more positive attitudes toward schooling, demonstrate stronger leadership skills, have greater self-esteem, and engage in fewer aggressive behaviors.

Another creative option being used with primary children is called **looping** where the teacher remains with the same group of students for several years. For example, a first-grade teacher could work with the same students from first through third grades before "looping" back to a new group of first-grade students at the end of the 3-year period. An **integrated curriculum**, in which mathematics, reading, science, and social studies are all learned simultaneously through the teaching of specific themes, is another creative option being used in the primary grades. An example of a theme that might be of interest to a group of second-grade students is hurricanes. As children read about them, write their own stories, learn about the impact of hurricanes on people around the nation, and create graphs of hurricane activity, they are engaged in meaningful integrated learning. Creating **classroom centers** where children can independently explore materials and activities of their own choosing in playful ways is yet another strategy used in many primary classrooms.

Funding: Who Pays for Early Education?

Another way to conceptualize programs for young children is to look at who pays for the services. In general, it is either the public (through local, state, or federal funds), the families who have children involved in the early childhood program, or some combination of these two. In this section, we will look at these options in more detail.

For-Profit Programs

Most child-care programs are run as businesses to generate profits for their owners. Some of the largest of these include Knowledge Learning Corporation, Le Petite Academy, Learning Care Group, and Bright Horizons (Neugebauer, 2006). The Knowledge Learning Corporation is the parent company for the well-known KinderCare child-care program. KinderCare has approximately 1,700 franchised centers nationwide in 38 states (KinderCare, 2010).

The revenue generated from parent fees is the major source of income for virtually every for-profit program. The money received is used to pay for teacher salaries, space/housing costs, and toys and equipment used in the program. In addition to the large national child-care options, there are many locally owned for-profit centers as well as child-care programs in family homes. These community entrepreneurs may or may not have expertise in early education. Because of this variance in knowledge and training, some programs offer excellent education and care while others leave much to be desired.

The costs for quality child care can be high, with those for infant/toddler care reaching as much as $14,000 annually (Matthews, 2009). The greatest single expense for any child-care program is the salaries paid to care providers. Because adult–child ratios for infant/toddler programs must, of necessity, be the lowest (Copple & Bredekamp, 2009), these options are the most expensive for families. Generally speaking, as children get older, the costs for quality care tend to decrease. Nonetheless, low-income families typically find it difficult to pay the high rates being charged for quality care. Without the availability of state and federal funding, these options would be out of reach for many families.

Cooperative Programs

Another early education option for families is often referred to as the **parent cooperative**. Although typically not traditional for-profit programs, parents are usually responsible for paying their children's educational costs. These expenses are kept low by involving parents as assistant teachers in the classroom. Each family unit is expected to spend a specified number of hours each month helping out in the classroom. This allows the program to operate with fewer paid adults and makes the overall costs to parents lower. Many community colleges and universities operate cooperative programs for their students. High school child-care programs for teen parents may also follow this cooperative model and require family participation to reduce overall program costs. In addition to keeping the educational expenses low, early childhood cooperatives are excellent parent–education experiences. By participating in a school environment with specially trained adults, parents have many opportunities to learn about children and gain experience in positively interacting with them. Discussing common problems with others whose struggles are similar is also helpful to many families.

Federally Funded Programs

The federal government spends a relatively small amount of its budget on programs for children in their early years. However, the support it does provide meets some important needs. The most well-known early childhood program funded by federal money is the **Head Start** program. Begun in 1964 as an attempt to help low-income 4-year-olds catch up academically with their more advantaged peers, Head Start has withstood the test of time as an important program for young children. Typically educating children who are 3 to 5 years old, the Head Start program is considered comprehensive because of its emphasis on all aspects of the child's development. In addition to focusing on social, emotional, intellectual, language, and physical development, Head Start programs emphasize good health and provide resources and assistance with medical, dental, nutritional, and mental health needs. Although not all children who are eligible are served because of underfunding, approximately 904,000 participate nationwide. Head Start has four major components (Administration for Children and Families, 2010a):

- **Education.** In addition to providing learning experiences to stimulate intellectual development, the Head Start program emphasizes social and emotional growth as well. Children participate in indoor and outdoor play experiences and engage in more structured learning.
- **Health.** Head Start places a strong emphasis on early identification of health problems, because many children served have never seen a doctor or dentist. This comprehensive health care includes medical, dental, mental health, and nutritional services.
- **Parents are viewed as the single most important influence on the child's development.** It is therefore essential for parents to be involved in parent education, in the classroom, in program planning, and in operating activities.
- **Social services.** This component of Head Start is an organized method of assisting families in assessing their needs and then guiding them to resources to help meet those needs.

The **Early Head Start** program, which focuses on families with children younger than 3 and pregnant women is a more recent option that has become available because of the successes experienced in Head Start and due to the growing awareness that working with even younger children pays big dividends in the long run. There are approximately 650 Early Head Start programs nationwide, serving more than 66,000 children and their families. Because research results indicate that this early intervention option is effective, it is likely that the Early Head Start program will continue to grow (U.S. Department of Health and Human Services, 2010).

Federal funds help support programs for children with special needs.

Another group of programs receiving federal money is designed for **children with special needs**. Options that include children with special needs in regular classrooms and those providing separate services are funded in part by national government dollars. Generally, the level of federal support is less than what it actually costs to educate children with special needs. State or local assistance is used to make up the difference.

Elementary schools benefit from additional federal support authorized by 2001's No Child Left Behind Act. As mentioned earlier, this act provides substantial amounts of money to help schools improve the academic achievement of students who are disadvantaged and those identified as at risk for future failure in school (U.S. Department of Education, 2010). While these funds are not adequate, they do provide considerable incentive for schools to engage in more intensive academic programs. As more educators recognize the importance of the early years in overall academic performance, increasing numbers of elementary schools are spending these federal dollars on literacy, mathematics, science, and social studies programs for kindergarten and primary-age children.

Military child care is another type of early childhood program funded by the federal government as a benefit to those engaged in military service around the world. Beginning with the *Military Child Care Act of 1989*, the U.S. military has become one of the largest employer-sponsored child-care programs in the country and is recognized as a model for others seeking to provide quality care (Zellman & Gates, 2010).

State and Locally Funded Programs

In recent years, despite funding some important educational options, the federal government has cut back other types of assistance to children and families. As a result, state and local governments have had to either increase their financial support or cut programs. In addition to providing public K–12 education for all, state and local agencies help fund a variety of other options for children and families. Some states, for example, supplement the federal money designated for Head Start so that more children from low-income families can be served. Washington State's Early Childhood Education and Assistance Program (ECEAP) is one such example (Washington State Department of Early Learning, 2010). State and local support for the inclusion of children with special needs is also common. Local governments and philanthropic organizations, such as United Way, also give money to nonprofit programs for children and families.

Corporate Child Care

Many corporations today recognize the importance of assisting employees in the challenges of work and family life. A significant part of this effort to be more responsive to family needs is the provision of corporate child care. A small but growing number of businesses are providing on-site child care for their employees' children. These programs are usually jointly funded, with corporations partially subsidizing the costs and parents paying the balance. Businesses that have implemented child-care programs cite many important benefits (Bramble, 2010):

- Lower employee absences, tardiness, and turnover
- Improved productivity, morale, and health
- Enhanced community and public relations

Eli Lilly and Company, a major manufacturer of pharmaceuticals, is an example of a family-friendly corporation. Lilly recognizes that when it supports the health and well-being of its employees, it creates a win-win situation that leads to greater productivity and employee loyalty. They list several benefits that the company offers to help employees meet the many challenges of parenting and family life (Eli Lilly and Company, 2010):

- **Resource and referral service for child care and elder care.** Employees with children or aging parents can use this service to find options for after-school programs, summer camps, emergency back-up care, sick child care, and elder care options.
- **On-site child development centers.** Employees may choose to have their infants through kindergarten-age children cared for at a center located right at the work site. These centers also provide back-up care when regular arrangements are not available.
- **Maternity and parenting leaves.** The first few months of parenting are particularly stressful. Lilly recognizes this and provides parents with opportunities to take time off to make this important adjustment.
- **Nursing mother stations.** Access to quality electric breast pumps and children on-site allows nursing mothers to easily continue to breast-feed their young children.

You can make your future classroom more family friendly by having the following:

- **Resources for children and families.** Arrange to have pamphlets available providing information on such things as public library times, community agencies that provide services to families (counseling, housing, low-cost medical care, etc.), and local options for after-school and back-up child care.
- **An open-door policy.** Make sure families know that they are always welcome in your classroom by regularly inviting them to participate. Welcoming family involvement as you communicate with them via letters, newsletters, telephone calls, and e-mail messages helps ensure that they will become more involved in the life of your classroom.
- **Parent-to-parent interactions.** Provide a directory that includes parent/guardian and child names and contact information, plan an evening parent meeting to address a topic of interest to families, or host a lunch or dinner potluck social activity to bring families together.

Although corporate child care has powerful benefits for employees, many corporations still find it difficult to provide this option, especially in tight financial times (Van der Pool, 2009). The investment of time, energy, and resources is difficult for even large corporations to manage. Rather than taking full responsibility for a child-care program, many businesses are contracting with private child-care corporations to provide on-site care. For example, Bright Horizons (2010) promotes itself as the world's largest provider of corporate child care, with more than 600 centers worldwide. Despite many challenges, on-site corporate child care should continue to grow in the years ahead.

College- and University-Supported Programs

Many colleges and universities have child-care programs for students and employees of the institution that provide similar benefits to those stated previously for corporations. Generally, the expenses for these child-care options are shared. Some support is provided by the college or university, with families who use the service paying the balance.

In addition to the obvious child-care benefits, college and university programs are often designed to serve as research and training sites. Faculty who want to study child development or examine the effectiveness of a specific teaching strategy often can use the child-care facility for this purpose. In addition, programs that prepare students to work with young children may use campus child-care programs as sites for their students who need direct experience working with young children. For example, students in the Human Development and Family Sciences program at the University of Texas at Austin may take a 10-hour-per-week practicum experience in the Priscilla P. Flawn UT Child and Family Laboratory as part of their preparation to work with young children (University of Texas, 2010).

 # Teaching Young Children

Now that you have had some initial exposure to the field of early care and education, take a more personal look at what teaching young children is like. This will help you to understand the preparation and skills needed to work in the field. Look at your own personal characteristics and compare them with those needed to be successful in the programs described here. Is there a good match? If so, your interest in early care and education could lead to a productive career choice. If not, you may need to think carefully about what you would need to do and learn in order to prepare yourself to be successful in this profession. In some instances, you may find that other careers are better suited to your personality and skills.

The Power of Teaching

Most of us can remember one or more teachers who have had a powerful impact on our lives. Perhaps it was an act of kindness, a belief in you as a person, or the excitement this person brought to the classroom. Unfortunately, others may remember teachers who callously or carelessly hurt the students around them through their words or actions. Teachers have great power to do either much good or considerable harm.

Haim Ginott (1972), a famous child psychologist, had the following to say on this important topic:

> I have come to a frightening conclusion. It is my personal approach that creates the climate. It is my daily mood that makes the weather. As a teacher, I possess tremendous power to make a child's life miserable or joyous. I can be a tool of torture or an instrument of inspiration. I can humiliate or humor,

hurt or heal. In all situations it is my response that decides whether a crisis will be escalated or de-escalated, a child humanized or de-humanized. (p. 13)

The power of teaching is real at all levels, but perhaps even more so when adults work with young children. You will have the power to build fragile egos, develop positive social skills, and lay the foundation for later academic learning. Or, conversely, you have the power to break down, destroy, or significantly damage all aspects of the young child's growth and development. How do you see yourself using this power? Would you use it to positively assist child growth and development? If so, this is a positive sign that you should continue to consider teaching as a potential career choice.

Roles of the Early Childhood Educator

Teachers and caregivers working with young children serve in many roles as they assist students in their development. Figure 1–2 provides a visual summary of the many important responsibilities assumed by those working with young children. The most obvious role is that of *facilitator of learning*. Helping children know more about the world around them has been a time-honored expectation. Because young children are naturally curious about nearly everything, it is also an exciting role. Teachers and caregivers also serve as *counselor* to the children in their care. Obviously, early childhood personnel do not have specific training as counselors, but they use many of the same skills as they guide children in their social and emotional development. For example, helping Alanna recognize that she is mad at Derrick for taking her toy truck and helping her to learn ways to manage her anger are important forms of early counseling.

More routine tasks also are expected of teachers and caregivers, especially those who work at the prekindergarten level. The role of *janitor*, for example, may be shared among preschool teachers. While larger programs may hire a specialist, many caregivers and educators also serve as a *cook* for their children as they prepare

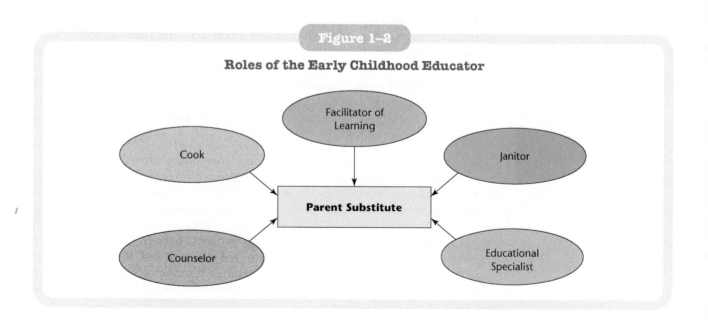

Figure 1–2

Roles of the Early Childhood Educator

Facilitator of Learning

Cook

Janitor

Parent Substitute

Counselor

Educational Specialist

nutritious snacks and possibly meals. Although it is very important to get children involved in the basic chores of the program, it is often necessary for the adult to go beyond the basics in providing these services.

Early childhood personnel also serve as *educational specialists*. Because of the integrated nature of the early childhood curriculum, it is necessary for teachers and caregivers to be comfortable with and to lead children in music, art, and physical education experiences. While these specialists may be available at the elementary level, the best early childhood educators add to the limited opportunities provided by others.

In summarizing many of these roles, teachers of young children may also become a *parent substitute* for their students. Most parents fulfill their responsibilities well while children are in the home. However, young children continue to need parenting in the school environment even when their own families are not around. Love, guidance, encouragement, assistance, and modeling are all needed by young children and are essential components of the early childhood educator's role.

Responsibilities of the Early Childhood Educator

In addition to their specific roles, early childhood teachers and caregivers also assume important responsibilities as they work with young children. Overall, the early childhood professional's foremost responsibility is to be an advocate for children and their families (Russell, 2009). **Advocacy** simply means promoting the causes of children and families. Taking leadership in helping meet the needs of children and families is an important responsibility that early childhood educators must assume. While the challenges are numerous, every individual interested in the well-being of children and families must get involved. Following are several important reasons why early childhood educators should make advocacy for children and families a high priority:

- **Importance of the early years.** It is critical that young children and their families receive the best possible education and care because the early years are such a critical period in overall child development. Decision makers at all levels need to repeatedly hear this message.
- **Powerless children and families.** It is virtually impossible for children to speak for themselves about their educational, emotional, and physical needs. Many families also need the support of articulate, dedicated professionals advocating on their behalf.
- **Low priority of early education and care.** The lack of program support for young children and families at the state and federal levels is painfully obvious. Early educators and others must work hard to raise the priority of young children and families in the eyes of others.

While it may sound challenging and time consuming to engage in advocacy, it is actually something you can do now as a natural part of your interactions with others. For example, as you communicate with others not engaged in early learning, you can emphasize the importance of this time period for overall development. What you are learning right now from your college course work can be shared with others. Take the time to communicate with neighbors, friends, family, and others about the critical importance of supporting young children and their families. This kind of advocacy effort may eventually lead you to additional advocacy efforts such as writing letters to politicians or attending community meetings to speak out on behalf of children and families.

An additional responsibility of early childhood educators is continuing education. Research by scholars in the discipline as well as innovations by educators in the classroom contribute to our understandings of how best to educate young children. To keep up with this growing body of knowledge, teachers of young children should continue to take classes, attend workshops, and read the professional literature available to them. The closing sections of this chapter focus on opportunities for continuing education and professional development.

A final responsibility of early childhood professionals is that they must know and follow a shared code of ethical conduct, based on a set of core values with deep historical roots in the field of early care and education. The code of ethical behavior developed by the **National Association for the Education of Young Children (NAEYC)** provides guidelines for responsible behavior in relation to students, families, colleagues, and society. Figure 1–3 summarizes the major components of this code. Members of NAEYC agree to engage in conduct that demonstrates high standards, and they commit to monitoring the behavior of others in the profession. This Code of Ethical Conduct was first adopted by the organization in 1989 and was revised most recently in 2005. It was reaffirmed and updated in May 2011. By continually refining and strengthening this document, NAEYC is demonstrating its strong commitment to professionally responsible behavior on the part of all early childhood educators.

Figure 1–3

Summary of the NAEYC Code of Ethics

Section I: *Ethical Responsibilities to Children.*

Childhood is a unique and valuable stage in the human life cycle. Our paramount responsibility is to provide care and education in settings that are safe, healthy, nurturing, and responsive for each child. We are committed to supporting children's development and learning; respecting individual differences; and helping children learn to live, play, and work cooperatively. We are also committed to promoting children's self-awareness, competence, self-worth, resiliency, and physical well-being.

Section II: *Ethical Responsibilities to Families.*

Families are of primary importance in children's development. Because the family and the early childhood practitioner have a common interest in the child's well-being, we acknowledge a primary responsibility to bring about communication, cooperation, and collaboration between the home and early childhood program in ways that enhance the child's development.

Section III: *Ethical Responsibilities to Colleagues.*

In a caring, cooperative workplace, human dignity is respected, professional satisfaction is promoted, and positive relationships are developed and sustained. Based upon our core values, our primary responsibility to colleagues is to establish and maintain settings and relationships that support productive work and meet professional needs. The same ideals that apply to children also apply as we interact with adults in the workplace.

Section IV: *Ethical Responsibilities to Community and Society.*

Early childhood programs operate within the context of their immediate community made up of families and other institutions concerned with children's welfare. Our responsibilities to the community are to provide programs that meet the diverse needs of families, to cooperate with agencies and professions that share the responsibility for children, to assist families in gaining access to those agencies and allied professionals, and to assist in the development of community programs that are needed but not currently available.

Source: Reprinted from the *NAEYC Code of Ethical Conduct and Statement of Commitment,* revised April 2005, reaffirmed and updated May 2011. Copyright © 2011 by the National Association for the Education of Young Children. The full text of all current NAEYC position statements is available at www.naeyc.org/positionstatements

Skills Needed to Teach Young Children

The responsibilities and challenges of working with young children make it one of the most difficult occupations. The best teachers and caregivers are successful in taking advantage of their personal strengths and in building their teaching ability through many interactions with children and others. Good educational practice requires skills in three main areas: interacting with children, preparing the environment, and working with other adults.

Interacting with children. The early childhood educator spends much of her day engaged in informal interactions with children. "Kelly, please put the puzzle back on the shelf before you get out another toy. . . . Adrian, that must have really hurt. Tell Mark how that makes you feel. . . . I'm not sure what ants eat, Ariel, but we can probably find some information on the computer." Times like these provide many opportunities to assist child growth and development. Sensitive teachers and caregivers learn when to step in and communicate with individual children and when it is best to simply stop and observe what is taking place.

Caregiving and teaching also requires skills in working with both small and large groups of children. Getting their attention, maintaining students' interests in a project or topic, making smooth transitions from one activity to the next, and presenting information in an exciting way are just some of the skills a teacher must use to be successful in working with a group of young children. Often, educators must use several skills almost simultaneously to make sure everything moves along smoothly.

Preparing the environment. Early educational experiences are best when children actively manipulate materials. This process of learning by doing allows the young child to build stronger understandings of the world around her. This requires that the adult carefully plan and prepare the materials in the learning environment. Knowing about student interests and needs, the early childhood educator must organize and plan for materials that can stimulate the young child's understanding. By regularly rotating new materials in and out of the classroom and playground, teachers and caregivers can continually challenge children to learn from their surroundings.

Ramona has just finished her week with 18 four-year-olds. Before heading home, however, she plans on spending the next few hours getting the classroom ready for next week. Ramona will spend much of her time setting up a new dramatic play center with a post office theme. In addition, there are new books to be added to the reading corner, art materials to organize, manipulative toys to exchange for new items, some interesting rocks to put out at the science table, and new props to add to the block center. The time Ramona spends in preparing the classroom today will help make next week another great learning experience for her students.

Working with other adults. Most people come to an early childhood setting to work with children, but they often find themselves interacting with other adults. Communicating and working effectively with other caregivers, teachers, aides, and administrators will make the many tasks associated with teaching and learning more manageable. In addition, strong relationships with families and community members are essential in an early childhood classroom. Many teachers and caregivers are surprised to learn about the importance of these adult relationships. Furthermore, making interactions with other adults' work is not an easy task. They require the use of different strategies and a new mind-set to be successful.

Should I Enter the Profession?

Take a careful look at the roles, responsibilities, and skills described in this chapter. Can you envision yourself as an educator of young children? The challenges of care-giving and teaching are very real. The rewards are also clearly identified. Only one question remains: Is working in the early childhood classroom a career you should pursue? While *you* must make this decision, others can assist in this process. The *Into Practice* feature in this section gives ideas for personal reflection on teaching as a career. In addition, you can consider doing any or all of the following as you reflect on teaching as a possible career:

- **Observe early childhood teachers at work.** If possible, observe several teachers so that you see a variety of teaching styles. Try to critically analyze all that the teachers are doing while interacting with children. Can you see yourself doing the same sorts of things?

- **Spend time working with children.** The more time you can spend interacting with children, the better your chances of determining if there is a good match. Try seeing yourself as a teacher and putting on all of the roles (facilitator of learning, counselor, etc.) discussed earlier.

- **Ask for feedback from others.** Teachers who can observe you working with young children are probably the best source of information about your teaching ability. Ask them to be honest with you. Everybody has both strengths and weaknesses. Find out about both.

- **Analyze your potential.** Although self-analysis may be a struggle, it is often helpful to critique your own skills. Identify your personal strengths and weaknesses. How do they match the roles and skills of teachers?

While self-reflection is only one of many ways to develop a better understanding of your capabilities and motivation to teach, it is often a good starting point for exploring the issue. Prior experiences as well as personal strengths and weaknesses all influence our ability to become an effective teacher. With this in mind, for each of the roles and responsibilities of the early childhood educator defined in this chapter, spend some time thinking about personal experiences, strengths, and weaknesses that will influence your potential as an early childhood teacher. The organizing questions that follow are designed to help you get started with this process of reflection. It may be beneficial for you to do this exercise more than once. Try it out now as you begin to read and study about early care and education and then reflect again on these same issues as you complete the text.

- **Past experiences.** What experiences with people or children have you had that would influence your ability to manage the roles and responsibilities of an early childhood educator?

- **Personal strengths.** What personal strengths do you think would help you effectively engage in the roles and responsibilities of an early childhood educator?

- **Potential weaknesses.** What personal traits do you have that you think may decrease your effectiveness in carrying out the roles and responsibilities of an early childhood educator?

As you investigate early care and education as a career option, you will realize that you are stronger in some roles and more skilled in certain areas than in others. Which aspects of the job might be more difficult for you? What could you do to make the difficult roles more workable for you? Fortunately, quality educational programs can help guide and train you in these areas.

Making the decision to become an educator is often a difficult one that requires careful reflection and considerable time. It is important to begin this process now as you initiate your study of early care and education. As you read each succeeding chapter and discuss with classmates issues related to its content, continue to reflect on how well you fit into the role as an adult working with young children. It may even be useful to stop at the end of your introductory course in early care and education and take another look at the ideas presented in this chapter. After several opportunities to evaluate these issues, you will be much better prepared to make a realistic appraisal of your potential as an early childhood educator.

Another, more practical, consideration that you will want to explore as you think about a career in early learning is the availability of jobs in prekindergarten and primary settings. There are a number of signs indicating that opportunities to work with young children will continue to grow. One sign is the very strong data identifying the economic benefits of early learning. A longitudinal study of low-income preschool students from the mid-1960s indicates that quality early learning leads to fewer students needing special education services as well as lower crime rates (Holzman, 2005). When special education services and prison time are avoided, taxpayers save many times the costs of the preschool experience. This message is being heard and understood by those in business and industry, who are applying pressure to increase opportunities for children to participate in early learning experiences (Clothier & Poppe, 2010). In addition, increased numbers of job opportunities exist today for those interested in prekindergarten education due to the growing numbers of elementary schools around the nation that now include these learning options in public school settings (Bureau of Labor Statistics, 2009). Finally, jobs in primary settings continue to be available due to teacher retirements and those who are choosing to leave the profession. This trend is expected to continue at least into the next decade (Bureau of Labor Statistics, 2009).

Professional Preparation of Early Childhood Professionals

Teacher education programs are clearly defined for those preparing for K–3 classrooms. Adults seeking to work in prekindergarten settings often find a variety of paths to their goal. In many cases, a high school diploma is the only requirement for beginning work with children younger than age 5 despite the many complex roles and responsibilities that these skilled adults must assume. Increasingly, however, a 2-year college preparation program or a 4-year degree is required for those working in prekindergarten settings.

Adults working in early childhood classrooms have a variety of roles. Classroom assistants, caregivers, teachers, educational specialists, and supervisors all play important roles. Because these different roles exist within the early childhood classroom, the training required to prepare for them varies. Most adults working with young children follow one of three main routes for their initial training: the

Child Development Associate (CDA) credential, a 2-year teacher preparation program at a community college, or a 4-year-degree program at a college or university. Master's and doctoral programs are also available for those interested in continuing to increase their knowledge of early education and those preparing to teach adults in community college and university settings.

The CDA Credential

The CDA credential, a national program designed to improve the qualifications of those who teach in prekindergarten classrooms, is a non-degree option that is based on demonstrated competencies in six areas: (a) maintaining a safe and healthy learning environment, (b) advancing physical and intellectual competence, (c) supporting social and emotional development, (d) establishing positive relationships with families, (e) ensuring a well-run program meeting individual needs, and (f) maintaining a commitment to professionalism. The CDA program is operated by the Council for Professional Recognition, a nonprofit organization located in Washington, DC. The main goal of the council is to improve the professional status of those working in early childhood settings (Council for Professional Recognition, 2010).

Practical experiences with young children are an important component of both 2-year and 4-year programs.

Two-Year, or Associate Degree, Programs

Many community colleges offer 2-year programs that prepare interested students to teach in prekindergarten programs and serve as administrators at this level. NAEYC (2011) has developed professional preparation standards for associate degree programs. Providing a combination of child development course work, early childhood instructional methods, and practical experiences with young children, these programs generally provide excellent preparation for teaching in infant/toddler and preschool classrooms. The following content summary is an example of a 2-year program in early care and education (semester system):

Introduction to early care and education	3 credits
Practicum experiences	10 credits
Curriculum development	3 credits
Creativity and play	3 credits
Working with families	3 credits
Children with special needs	3 credits
Child development	5 credits
Language and literacy	3 credits
Cognitive development	3 credits
Social and emotional development	3 credits
Infant and toddler care	3 credits

Some community colleges have designed an **Associate of Arts in Teaching** degree option that is intended to better prepare students who are planning to complete a 2-year degree and then transfer to a 4-year college or university to pursue state teacher certification (Dallas County Community College District, 2010). In some instances, students interested in early care and education complete the 2-year program and then take a position working with young children that doesn't require state teacher certification.

Four-Year Programs

Numerous programs exist at 4-year colleges and universities to prepare students to work with young children. NAEYC (2009) has developed professional preparation standards for these degrees. Typically, options at colleges and universities are of three main types:

- **Child development/family studies programs.** Located in colleges other than education, these programs typically prepare students to work in prekindergarten settings for children birth to age 5.
- **Early care and education programs.** These options most often prepare students to teach children who are 0–5 or 0–8 years, depending on state certification requirements, and are typically housed in a unit within the department or college of education.
- **Primary education programs.** Some colleges and universities offer programs that prepare students to work in K–3 classrooms with state teacher certification at that level. These options are typically housed within an elementary education department or program.

Coordinating Efforts

Unfortunately, for many years little effort was made to have 2-year colleges and 4-year institutions work together to articulate student course work and to help students move to the next step in the educational sequence. Students seeking training in early care and education have often been blocked from making smooth transitions by colleges and universities who battle over issues of quality and comparability of course work.

These roadblocks are slowly beginning to erode, and national professional organizations are working to ensure that students can move through a continuum of educational experiences leading to increasingly advanced early childhood training (NAEYC, 2009). Furthermore, in order to improve the academic performance of young children, the No Child Left Behind Act of 2001 (NCLB) has provided additional incentives to have highly qualified teachers in every early childhood classroom. (Schools that don't meet the NCLB standards for highly qualified teachers may lose important financial support provided by this act.) It is essential that prospective educators be provided clear and easily negotiated paths to working in early childhood classrooms.

Advanced Degrees

Master's degree programs that are appropriate for those working with young children are found at many 4-year colleges and universities across the nation. Some offer advanced preparation for teaching in the early childhood classroom at the prekindergarten, the primary, or the entire early childhood range from birth through age 8. In addition to programs for teachers, other master's degree options lead to advanced preparation in areas such as child development, parent education, early childhood program administration, child psychology, English language learning, and special education. A master's degree is the minimum educational level needed for teaching college students at most 2- and 4-year colleges and universities.

If you are interested in eventually teaching full-time at the college level, you should plan on completing a doctoral degree program in early care and education, child and family studies, or a related field. These doctoral degree options, while available in every state, are more limited in number than programs at the master's degree level. Normally, one or two public universities and a similar number of private institutions in each state offer course work and degree programs at the doctoral level that would prepare you to teach other adults interested in working with young children.

 # Resources for Professional Development

Although professional development begins with initial training, this process will continue throughout your career as an early childhood professional. Your growth as an educator continues as you gain experience in the classroom, make careful observations of children, have conversations with other educators, and attend professional conferences. By actively participating in professional organizations, subscribing to professional journals, and being aware of other sources of information on early care and education, you can continue to grow in your ability to meet the needs of children and families.

Professional Organizations

Two major professional organizations emphasize early care and education. By far the largest and most influential is NAEYC. With a membership of approximately 100,000, NAEYC promotes quality education and care for children from birth to age 8 and their families. Members receive the journal *Young Children*, which provides teachers and others with many practical ideas for the early childhood classroom. More recently, NAEYC began publishing the *Early Childhood Research Quarterly* for those interested in studies of children, families, and curriculum. In addition, the organization publishes an important list of books for early educators and holds an annual conference that attracts approximately 25,000 national and international participants. State and local affiliates of NAEYC provide additional opportunities for workshops and professional growth for early childhood educators.

The second major professional organization for early educators is the **Association for Childhood Education International (ACEI)**. Although the focus of this organization is broader, with an emphasis on children from birth through adolescence, the early years have been a major interest of many members. Smaller in size than NAEYC, ACEI has nonetheless had a significant influence on the directions of early care and education. Members receive the journal *Childhood Education* and have the opportunity to participate in national and regional conferences. Books and other publications are also available through the national headquarters. Finally, ACEI offers a research publication titled the *Journal of Research in Childhood Education*.

Other professional organizations that have special interest groups or that focus on aspects of early care and education are also available. Some examples of these groups include the following:

- American Montessori Society
- Council for Exceptional Children
- Association for Supervision and Curriculum Development
- International Reading Association
- National Council of Teachers of Mathematics
- Society for Research in Child Development

Journals

In addition to the previously mentioned journals from NAEYC and ACEI, many other professional publications are available to help those involved in early care and education. These can be divided into two broad groups: (a) research publications emphasizing child development and family issues and (b) journals that focus primarily on ideas useful to the practitioner. Following are some examples of research journals dealing with child development and family issues:

Child Development

Developmental Psychology

Early Child Development and Care

Merrill Palmer Quarterly

Monographs of the Society for Research in Child Development

Journals published for practitioners include the following:

The Arithmetic Teacher

Child Care Information Exchange

Day Care and Early Education

Dimensions of Early Childhood

Early Childhood Education Today

The Reading Teacher

Reference Materials

One set of tools that early educators use as they work to increase their knowledge of children and learning is a rich collection of reference materials. In addition to journals, many books provide insights on issues relating to early care and education. For example, numerous texts are available that describe in more detail the importance of play in child development. These resources provide a more in-depth understanding of issues of interest to caregivers and teachers.

The **Educational Resources Information Center (ERIC)** is an important reference system that can provide quick and detailed assistance in locating information on children and families. This computer-based information retrieval system is free of charge to users. Funded by the Institute of Education Sciences, U.S. Department of Education, ERIC can help educators locate articles, books, and microfiche on topics of interest. The ERIC system provides an abundance of information and resources relating to young children and families.

Another reference option that is growing rapidly with the expansion of materials on the Internet is websites with information on children and families. Most colleges and universities, professional organizations, and government agencies now have websites with links to other useful Internet sites. Keep in mind, however, that not every website has accurate information based on current research and best practices. The following are examples of some of the many quality websites that are available:

- National Association for the Education of Young Children: www.naeyc.org
- The Annie E. Casey Foundation: www.aecf.org
- Children's Defense Fund: www.childrensdefense.org
- National Board of Professional Teaching Standards: www.nbpts.org
- National Center for Education Statistics: nces.ed.gov

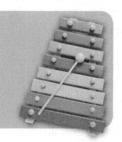

summary

Essentials of Early Care and Education

This chapter has provided you with a broad introduction to the field of early care and education. The five essential elements include understanding child development, providing quality play experiences, guiding children's social and emotional development, working with parents and families, and understanding the importance of diversity in child growth and development.

Programs for Young Children

The different types of early care and education programs include infant/toddler programs, preschool education, child care, programs for children with special needs, kindergarten, and primary education.

Sources of Funding for Early Care and Education

The issue of who should pay for early care and education is significant; the various options include programs for profit, federally funded programs, state and locally funded programs, corporate child care, and college/university-supported programs.

Working with Young Children

This chapter also addressed the important work of teaching and caregiving in the early years. An understanding of the adult's roles and responsibilities and of the skills needed will help you to decide if this is a good career choice for you.

Professional Preparation of Early Childhood Caregivers and Teachers

Different educational paths are available to those wanting to enter the field, including the CDA credential, an associate of arts degree in early care and education from a community college, and a 4-year bachelor's degree. In addition, options are available that allow teachers and caregivers of young children to participate in continued professional development.

Resources for Professional Development

Early childhood educators have numerous professional organizations, journals, and reference materials available to assist them in professional development.

for reflection and discussion

1. Are the five essential elements of early care and education described in this chapter unique to the field or are they common to all levels of education?
2. Which of the early childhood programs described in this chapter is of most interest to you personally? Is this an area you may want to pursue as a career?
3. Should prekindergarten programs be funded by either state or federal dollars? Write 2 to 4 paragraphs giving a rationale for the stance you take.
4. Share with a small group of peers what you see as your personal strengths and weaknesses and how they will impact your ability to work with young children.
5. If you choose to pursue a career in early care and education, what do you see as the long-term educational experiences you will need? Create a potential plan for your own professional development by listing these educational experiences. Share your plan with others and collaborate on strengthening your plan.

MyEducationLab

Go to Topic 12: Professionalism/Ethics in the MyEducationLab (www.myeducationlab.com) for *Teaching Young Children* where you can:

- Find learning outcomes for Professionalism/Ethics along with the national standards that connect to these outcomes.
- Complete Assignments and Activities that can help you more deeply understand the chapter content.
- Apply and practice your understanding of the core teaching skills identified in the chapter with the Building Teaching Skills and Dispositions learning units.
- Access video clips of CCSSO National Teachers of the Year award winners responding to the question, "Why Do I Teach?" in the Teacher Talk section.
- Listen to experts from the field in Professional Perspectives.
- Check your comprehension on the content covered in the chapter with the Study Plan. Here you will be able to take a chapter quiz, receive feedback on your answers, and then access Review, Practice, and Enrichment activities to enhance your understanding of chapter content.

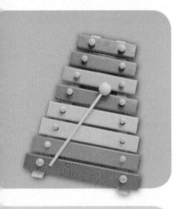

Historical Contexts

IN THIS CHAPTER YOU WILL

- Learn about the European and Early American influences on early care and education.

- Read about more recent Americans who have made significant contributions to the field.

- Review historical events that have influenced directions in early education.

It is a beautiful spring day, and Ms. Gregory's kindergarten class is excitedly exploring the outdoors. Marta and Gina are digging contentedly in the garden in preparation for some later planting. Erik and Daniel have discovered an anthill and are down on their hands and knees carefully observing the scurrying workers. Nateesha and Elizabeth have taken two tires and are building their own pretend bird's nest by collecting twigs and grass for the base of the nest. Several children are playing a loosely organized game of tag and are running gleefully around on the grassy field. Still others are playing on the climbing structure in the middle of the playground, while three children swing and chat on the swing set nearby.

While everyone is so actively engaged, Ms. Gregory has taken the opportunity to carefully observe her children's actions. She is particularly interested in their social interactions and is focusing on the friendship patterns and general communication strategies children use as they interact with their peers. Ms. Gregory is pleased with the skills she is seeing her students use.

Although the preceding scene is typical of many early childhood classrooms, it may surprise you to know that these options have not always been available to children. For most of recorded history, for example, boys were the only ones to receive formal education. Playing outdoors and learning from nature were not promoted until the eighteenth century. Toys and equipment designed specifically for young children appeared around the middle of the nineteenth century, and formal playground equipment became available near the beginning of the twentieth century. Careful observations of children's actions were first promoted in the late nineteenth century and weren't commonly used by early childhood educators until the early twentieth century.

This chapter examines the historical roots of current practice in early care and education. By examining the people and events from the past that have shaped early care and education, you can develop a deeper understanding of this exciting field.

Historical Figures Influencing Early Care and Education

Key people from the past who have had a major impact on directions in early care and education will be identified and discussed here. Understanding the contributions of these individuals provides insight into the theory and practice of programs for young children. Some of the people discussed in the following paragraphs are **theorists**. Although they identified and discussed important issues related to children and teaching, they did not actually put these ideas into practice working with children. Others were **practitioners** who, in addition to presenting new and interesting ideas about child development and learning, actually worked in early childhood settings with young children.

European Contributors

For the past several centuries, European countries have been the leaders in promoting innovative educational theory and practice. Many of the key methods and materials used in early childhood settings today can be traced to European theorists and practitioners. Figure 2–1 provides a visual timeline of these key contributors.

Martin Luther (1483–1546). While Martin Luther is best known for his impact on Christian religious reformation, he also had a significant impact on educational thinking and practice. Because of his conviction that the Bible was the key to Christian reform, Luther began to promote improved education, particularly the ability to read, as an essential element in German society. According to Luther, in order to establish a personal relationship with God, everyone needed to be able to read the Bible.

As an early educational theorist, Martin Luther suggested many revolutionary ideas for his time (Braun & Edwards, 1972):

- **All towns and villages should have schools.** This was not common in Luther's time, but leaders of the day began to take the idea seriously.
- **Both girls and boys should be educated.** Up until this time, education was almost exclusively for boys. Luther's emphasis on everyone reading the Bible, however, required that all children be taught basic academic skills.
- **Schools should foster intellectual, religious, physical, emotional, and social development.** This concept of educating the whole child is an essential element of early care and education today.

John Amos Comenius (1592–1670). Comenius was another early educational theorist who presented many new and important ideas about children and learning. Although his interests were broader than early care and education, one of his books in particular addressed issues that dealt with teaching young children. Titled *School of Infancy* (Comenius, 1896), this text describes many ideas that are very much a part of early education today. He suggested, for example, that the first years of life are crucial to overall development and that adults must take advantage of this time to assist the child's growth. Comenius also believed that movement and activity were sure signs of healthy learning experiences. Young children, he stated, learn best from natural, real-world experiences.

In other writings, Comenius also made clear his views on the teacher's role in learning, and identified who he felt should be educated. His goal for education was, "To seek and find a method by which the teachers teach less and the learners learn more, by which the schools have less noise, obstinacy, and frustrated endeavor, but

MyEducationLab

Visit the MyEducationLab for *Teaching Young Children* to enhance your understanding of chapter concepts with a personalized Study Plan. You'll also have the opportunity to hone your teaching skills through video- and case-based Assignments and Activities as well as Building Teaching Skills and Disposition lessons.

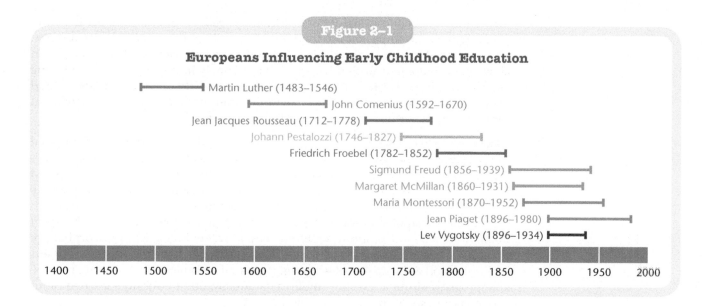

Figure 2–1

Europeans Influencing Early Childhood Education

Martin Luther (1483–1546)

John Comenius (1592–1670)

Jean Jacques Rousseau (1712–1778)

Johann Pestalozzi (1746–1827)

Friedrich Froebel (1782–1852)

Sigmund Freud (1856–1939)

Margaret McMillan (1860–1931)

Maria Montessori (1870–1952)

Jean Piaget (1896–1980)

Lev Vygotsky (1896–1934)

1400   1450   1500   1550   1600   1650   1700   1750   1800   1850   1900   1950   2000

more leisure, pleasantness" (Braun & Edwards, 1972, p. 31). Comenius advocated for enjoyable educational experiences and for students who could take charge of their own learning. He, too, promoted the idea that all children should be educated. Rather than teaching just the sons from wealthy families, Comenius wanted all boys and girls, bright and dull, rich and poor, to receive an education.

Jean Jacques Rousseau (1712–1778). Although Rousseau lived a tumultuous and undisciplined life, which included the abandonment of all five of his children, his

Jean Jacques Rousseau

educational writings have had a significant influence on the direction of early childhood theory and practice. Rousseau's best-known book, titled *Emile*, describes the ideal early education of an imaginary child (Rousseau, 1762/1979). From his writings, it is clear that Rousseau was advocating educational experiences that were very different from what children of his day were receiving. He proposed the following:

- **Negative education.** By this, Rousseau meant that formal educational experiences should be postponed until children are 12 years old.

- **Learning from nature.** Young children could learn all they needed to know from the natural world around them. Books should be forbidden during this period.

- **Education should focus on sensory experiences.** Touching, tasting, and experiencing new sights and sounds were Rousseau's building blocks for early learning.

- **Children need to choose their learning experiences.** Rousseau believed that when left to their own devices children would select the best tasks for developmental progress.

- **Childhood is a stage in development.** One of the first to make this claim, Rousseau recognized that children can be distinguished from adults in more ways than just size. They think differently, reason differently, and require different ways of learning.

Rousseau's educational theory, although idealistic and naive as presented in *Emile*, significantly impacted the thinking of many later theorists and practitioners. Often referred to as a *naturalist*, his belief in the innate goodness of children and in allowing development to simply happen has strongly influenced current thinking and practice in early care and education. Much like a flower grows with water and good soil, young children often do well when adults prepare a quality environment for learning, then step back and watch for the results.

Johann Pestalozzi (1746–1827). Pestalozzi, an early childhood practitioner, was inspired by the writings of Rousseau and was determined to apply Rousseau's principles in raising his own children. While he quickly learned that the unlimited freedom proposed by Rousseau needed to be tempered with adult guidance and limits, Pestalozzi continued to believe in Rousseau's basic ideas and worked to refine their implementation.

In 1799, Napoleon invaded Switzerland and left the town of Stanz with a great many homeless and destitute children. Pestalozzi took charge of an orphanage there, and his educational career took root. Working with children whom others had written off as incapable of learning, Pestalozzi was able to demonstrate remarkable progress within a few short months. Gradually, other educators learned of his programs and spent time studying his methods.

Pestalozzi's most well-known publications were actually novels written for the general public of his day. Although the characters in these books portrayed many of his educational thoughts through their actions, most of what we know about Pestalozzi's methods and theories comes from the writings of others (e.g., Guimps, 1890). Pestalozzi has been described as a great teacher who made every effort to love and care for his students in addition to educating them. He modeled much of what we currently do in early care and education, including the following:

- **Careful observation of children.** Pestalozzi was a perceptive observer of children and used what he saw to plan learning experiences for them.
- **Recognizing the potential in each child.** He saw every child as having the ability to learn, given the right circumstances. He believed in their potential, when others had given up on them.
- **Importance of teacher–student relationships.** Pestalozzi believed that before children could learn they needed a strong relationship with their teacher. Once the confidence and affection of each child had been won, learning was a much simpler process. The *Developmentally Appropriate Practice* feature found in this section describes strategies for building these strong relationships.
- **Strengthening peer relations.** Pestalozzi encouraged older children to tutor younger students and, in general, promoted good relations among his students.
- **Sensory learning.** Pestalozzi recognized the importance of learning experiences that took advantage of young children's natural interest in using their senses.

Friedrich Froebel (1782–1852). After discovering he had the interest and abilities to be a good teacher, Froebel spent time studying the techniques of Pestalozzi. Although he liked much of what he saw, Froebel eventually developed his own approach to teaching. His educational interests were broad: Froebel wanted to remake all of education. Needing to begin somewhere, however, he focused initially on working with 5-year-old children. Froebel named the program he developed for this age group the *kindergarten* (meaning "children's garden" in German). His techniques and materials gradually became popular throughout Germany and later were adopted by educators in the United States.

Developmentally Appropriate Practice . . .
GUIDING CHILDREN BEGINS WITH STRONG RELATIONSHIPS

Pestalozzi was one of the first early childhood practitioners to emphasize the importance of strong adult–child relationships. Since that time, many others have reinforced this concept and see these relationships as key to the guidance process. Here are some suggestions for building relationships with young children:

- **Be a good role model.** Make sure that you are engaging in the same behaviors you want for your children. For example, if you want them to sit in chairs, rather than on the tables, be sure you do the same thing yourself. "Please" and "thank you" should be your verbal responses if you want those replies from students.

- **Make time for positive interactions.** When you have a high number of positive interactions with students, it makes it easier to work through the more difficult times together. Be sure to make a conscious effort to take the time needed to have quality interactions with your students by doing such things as spending time talking with them, sharing snacks or lunch together, and periodically playing games with them.

- **Demonstrate high expectations for children.** When children know that you think positively enough of them to have high expectations, they know that you believe in them and want the best for their lives. Continually reinforce your high expectations with both words and actions.

- **Show children you care.** A hug when a child is feeling sad, a pat on the back for a job well done, and positive words of encouragement are all examples of ways in which children come to know that you care about them as individuals.

Froebel is often referred to as the father of the modern kindergarten. His methods and materials gained popularity in two main ways. First, during his lifetime, many European and American women went to Germany to study his techniques before returning to implement them in their own classrooms. Second, Froebel wrote two popular books that outline his approach to teaching young children. In *Education of Man* (Froebel, 1886), he describes his teaching materials and techniques. *Mother-Play and Nursery Songs* (Froebel, 1906) emphasizes the role of mothers in the young child's development.

Froebel's contributions to early care and education were many. One important concept was his emphasis on the benefits of childhood play. Froebel extolled the virtues of play throughout his writings:

> It gives, therefore, joy, freedom, contentment, inner and outer rest, peace with the world. It holds the sources of all that is good. A child that plays thoroughly, with self-active determination, perseveringly until physical fatigue forbids, will surely be a thorough, determined man, capable of self-sacrifice for the promotion of the welfare of himself and others. (Braun & Edwards, 1972, p. 67)

The *Observing Development* feature in this section provides you with an opportunity to study firsthand the many virtues of play. As you observe and reflect on the many benefits of play, consider again the high praise that Froebel had for this important aspect of child development.

How important were the social interactions to the actual play activities observed? Could the play have continued without the social interactions or were they an essential component?

Observing Development...
CHILDHOOD PLAY

Choose one of the age groups within early childhood (infants/toddlers, preschoolers, or primary-age children) and *observe* **childhood play** either indoors or outdoors. Take detailed notes of what children do and say. Use the following sample observation as a format for your own observation. Include only what you see and hear, saving your interpretations for the reflections that follow the sample observation:

Custer Elementary Playground, 10:30–11 a.m., October 23

Objects used in play	Play activities	Social interactions
1. Four children are bouncing a ball between them.	1. Two children are swinging on the swings and talking animatedly about the upcoming school carnival.	1. One child is playing away from the other children, using a stick to dig in the dirt.
2. ...	2. ...	2. ...

Reflect and Apply

1. How did children use toys and equipment in their play? What toys were they playing with?

2. What could children potentially be learning (language, concepts, social skills, emotional understandings) from the activities you observed?

Froebel also emphasized the value of singing at home and in school as a pleasant and effective way to learn. He encouraged mothers to spend time singing with their children and also incorporated songs and musical experiences into his kindergarten classroom. Froebel believed that music helped build teacher–student and parent–child relationships, was an excellent tool for teaching young children concepts, and was also fun for both children and adults. The *Developmentally Appropriate Practice* feature found in this section describes four important values of singing in the early childhood classroom.

Another important classroom management technique found in settings for young children had its origins in Froebel's kindergarten. During observations of young children engaged in play, Froebel was intrigued by the number of times they joined hands and made a circle. He incorporated this natural tendency into his teaching, and what we now call **circle time** was born. Froebel recognized that seating children in a circle for group experiences brought them together in a setting that was easy to manage while creating a more personal atmosphere that helped improve interactions and instruction.

Maria Montessori (1870–1952). The courage and determination of Maria Montessori are exemplified by her initial choice of careers. Near the end of the nineteenth century, despite numerous challenges, she became the first female physician in Italy. She then focused the many analytical and observational skills developed in her medical training to what became her true passion—working with children.

Montessori's first educational interest was in mental retardation. She felt that institutionalized children were eager for learning experiences and could, if given appropriate instruction, grow more normally. Like Pestalozzi before her, Montessori

Developmentally Appropriate Practice . . .
SINGING IN THE KINDERGARTEN

Froebel, the father of the modern kindergarten, was an early proponent of singing in the classroom (Moore & Campos, 2010). For example, Froebel created songs that helped young children understand the properties of each of the new play materials he introduced during circle time. The songs also helped children to understand how to use these materials in appropriate ways.

If you have ever spent time observing or participating in a kindergarten classroom, you know that most teachers use singing for a variety of purposes. Following are four of the most important of these:

- **Singing for the pleasure of the activity itself.** Songs such as "The Wheels on the Bus" for young children are engaging and fun. When done right, singing is an activity that most children find highly pleasurable.

- **Breaking up work periods.** In addition to simply singing for fun, many kindergarten teachers find that a lively song with accompanying movements is a good way to break up a more academic work period. It provides a pleasurable break in the routine while allowing students to move, stretch, and momentarily change their focus.

- **Using songs to enliven routines.** Another common strategy is to use a good song to help make daily routines more enjoyable. For example, while cleaning up is a chore that most children recognize as important, it is not a very exciting task. Many teachers sing a simple repetitive clean-up song during the actual clean-up time to alert children to this part of the daily schedule and help make the activity a more playful part of the school day.

- **Teaching concepts.** Many wonderful CDs are available that contain a variety of songs that teachers can use to teach concepts to young children. Ella Jenkins and Hap Palmer are classic examples of performers who have long been involved in producing such CDs. Songs can teach such things as mathematical concepts ("Five Little Speckled Frogs"), principles of language ("ABC Song"), understanding feelings ("It's All Right to Cry"), and body parts ("Head, Shoulders, Knees and Toes"). Many children can learn better and more quickly with the assistance of a good song.

Maria Montessori

took up the cause of young children whom the rest of society had rejected. After careful observations of children classified as retarded and the study of earlier educators such as Itard (1801/1962), Seguin (1907), and Froebel (1886), Montessori was ready to begin her educational career.

In 1898, Montessori assumed the directorship of a school for "defective" children. Her reputation as an educator began to grow when she prepared these "idiot" children to successfully pass examinations for primary certificates. At the time, these examinations were typically the highest educational accomplishment of most Italians.

Montessori's most well-known educational program opened in 1907 and was called the **Casa dei Bambini** (Children's House). Located in the slums of Rome, Casa dei Bambini was the setting in which Montessori further developed her theories about children and refined her teaching techniques. Montessori detailed her fascinating ideas in several books (e.g., Montessori, 1949/1967), and other writers also have summarized her work (e.g., Lillard, 1972, 1996).

Developmentally Appropriate Practice . . .
INEXPENSIVE OUTDOOR PLAY

When Margaret McMillan allowed her children to play outdoors, she discovered that students tended to gravitate to several inexpensive materials that they found there:

More than any other place our children love the great heap of stones and builders' rubbish that the masons have left behind them after building our extension. To put up some kind of house, to fix some kind of tent, and to sit inside—that is the aim and desire of all the children of five and over. And the making of this house is a more popular occupation than any other, except of course the making of mud hills and trenches and the filling of dams and rivers. (McMillan, 1919, p. 106)

Children today can enjoy the same experiences that McMillan described:

- **Loose parts.** Teachers can collect an assortment of boards, bricks, tires, and donated building materials so that children can construct their own play spaces for hours of inexpensive fun.

- **Natural materials.** The availability of water, dirt, sand, and pea gravel can provide many hours of creative play for young children. While these materials are messy and may present storage problems, they are a low-cost and attractive alternative to the expensive playground equipment typically found on playgrounds.

- **Garden area.** A small area for digging and planting can provide many opportunities for creative play experiences outdoors. A few shovels, trowels, hoes, and buckets are all that are needed once the garden space has been initially prepared for use.

- **Shrubs and plants.** With some planning and preparation, a few carefully placed shrubs and plants can be used to form natural play spaces and quiet areas for children. These plantings can also be used for engaging science experiences as children observe flowers, fruits, seeds, and new growth.

Margaret McMillan (1860–1931). Margaret McMillan and her sister Rachel had a significant impact on early education in England at about the same time Montessori was gaining popularity in Italy. The McMillan sisters were early activists concerned about the health problems of children growing up in low-income areas in London. To help correct the health issues they identified, the McMillans founded the **Open-Air Nursery**. After Rachel's untimely death, Margaret continued to refine their program for young children.

The Open-Air Nursery was designed for children from 1 to 6 years of age and, as the name implies, emphasized outdoor play. The McMillans felt that the health benefits of outdoor activities were just what their children needed. They provided children with opportunities for gardening, playing in a sandbox, and building with scraps of materials in the "rubbish heap." The *Developmentally Appropriate Practice* feature found in this section provides additional information on engaging young children in quality outdoor play experiences like those emphasized in the Open-Air Nursery.

In addition to this emphasis on outdoor play, the Open-Air Nursery provided baths, clean clothes, healthy meals, medical and dental care, and opportunities for learning experiences. Because they focused on the health and well-being of the whole child, the Open-Air Nursery was an early model for the current Head Start program.

Margaret McMillan emphasized several important concepts in her program that are considered important in early education today:

- **Facilitating emotional development.** McMillan recognized that young children need more than physical health and intellectual stimulation to develop normally. Emotional well-being was equally important and needed to be addressed by teachers.
- **Parent involvement.** Monthly parent meetings, home visits, strong parent–teacher relations, and support for families during crises were all emphasized in the Open-Air Nursery.
- **Children's art.** McMillan considered children's spontaneous drawings and artwork important to their overall development and made sure they were encouraged.

Lev Vygotsky (1896–1934). Vygotsky was a Russian scholar who began his study of developmental psychology and education in the 1920s. Unfortunately, his death from tuberculosis at age 37 prematurely ended a brilliant career. Nonetheless, Vygotsky's contributions have been substantial. Three important concepts from Vygotsky's work have significantly influenced early care and education. First is the **zone of proximal development**, the most well-known of his ideas (Vygotsky, 1978). The zone of proximal development is the gap between the child's independent performance of a task and that which he can perform with the help of a more skilled peer or adult. Children who are functioning in their zone are being challenged and growing with the assistance of others at a maximum rate. Second, Vygotsky's thinking about the relationships between language and thought in childhood have also influenced teaching and language learning in the early years. Third is the value of play in the development of symbolic thinking and the overall growth of children. The *Celebrating Play* feature found in this section discusses in more detail Vygotsky's thoughts on childhood play.

Sigmund Freud (1856–1939). Near the start of the twentieth century, Freud began his study of human personality and emotional development. He created a complex theory that is often referred to as *psychoanalysis*. In relation to early care and education, perhaps the most important aspect of Freud's theory is his psychosexual stages of development. Freud believed that personality was strongly influenced by the ways in which children learned to expend what he called sexual energy from one stage to the next (Thomas, 1985). He defined five major stages that children pass through as they develop their personalities:

- **Oral stage (0–1).** The mouth is the location of satisfying or frustrating experiences. Exploring objects by sucking on them and nursing at the mother's breast are examples of a positive release of what Freud called sexual energy.
- **Anal stage (1–3).** The child is developing sphincter and bladder control, which allows parents to begin work on toilet training. While the child receives pleasure from eliminating the bowels and bladder as needed, parents want the child to delay until a toilet is available.
- **Phallic stage (3–5).** The child's genitals become important objects of pleasure during this period. Children want to touch themselves while parents often try to discourage this behavior.

Celebrating Play . . .
VYGOTSKY'S THOUGHTS ON PLAY

Although Vygotsky's ideas on play do not really qualify as a theory, his writings about play have become very influential in our thinking about its importance (Berk, 1994). In particular, he believed that make-believe (dramatic) play was a major contributor to the child's social, language, and cognitive development. Vygotsky's high regard for play can be seen in the following quote:

Play creates a zone of proximal development in the child. In play, the child always behaves beyond his average age, above his daily behavior; in play it is as though he were a head taller than himself. As in the focus of a magnifying glass, play contains all developmental tendencies in a condensed form and is itself a major source of development. (Vygotsky, 1978, p. 102)

Kara is a fearless 5-year-old who loves to climb to the top of the jungle gym on the playground. Her close friend Aleesha, however, is more timid. As the two climb, Kara tells Aleesha where to place her hands and feet and constantly reinforces her efforts. With this help, Aleesha climbs nearly to the top of the play structure. She is playing in her zone of proximal development.

Vygotsky felt that imaginary play has two critical features that help make it so influential in the child's development:

- Play creates an imaginary situation that allows the child to work through desires that are unrealizable.

Andrew is learning as a 3-year-old that he must wait for his turn many times in the preschool situation. He does not want to do this, and his imaginary play allows Andrew to work through these feelings.

- Play contains rules for behavior. If children are to successfully complete a play scene, they must follow the accepted rules for social behavior in the situation they are enacting.

Kathryn wants to be the mommy and must conform to the rules of maternal behavior for the play sequence to work.

1. Earlier in this chapter Froebel was quoted as saying that play gave children joy, freedom, and contentment. Are Vygotsky's ideas on play compatible with those of Froebel? Why or why not? What do you see as the similarities and differences between the two perspectives?

2. Choose an age/grade that currently appeals to you as a future teacher. For that level, identify two or three specific examples of ways in which play according to Vygotsky could be beneficial for children at that age.

- **Latency stage (5–11).** The genitals remain the focus of sexual energy, but children work to suppress their wants. They tend to work and play with others of the same sex partly to control their sexual energies.

- **Genital stage (11+).** At puberty, the child enters this final stage. While the focus of sexual energy remains on the genitals, the means of satisfaction now becomes sexual orgasm. Young people become very interested in others of the opposite sex.

While many today disagree with Freud's heavy emphasis on sexual energy and its gratification in childhood, his theory had a major influence on child-rearing practices during the twentieth century. Rather than rigidly excluding what Freud termed pleasurable sexual activity at each stage, parents and child-care providers were encouraged to relax a little and allow children to experience gratifying experiences (Thomas, 1985).

Jean Piaget (1896–1980). Piaget is another theorist who has had a major impact on early education. A true scientist from an early age, Piaget published his first research investigation at the age of 10. He began his lifelong investigation of humankind's acquisition of knowledge shortly after completing his doctoral studies.

Preschool children construct their knowledge of the written word through early scribbles.

Piaget took a job analyzing responses to standardized intelligence tests and was intrigued by children's incorrect answers. After carefully questioning and observing many different children (including his own), Piaget published his theories concerning intellectual development. These theories have given rise to what is often called **constructivist learning** (Kamii & Ewing, 1996), because they suggest that individuals actively construct knowledge on an ongoing basis. In other words, Piaget theorized that we are all constantly receiving new information and engaging in experiences that lead us to revise our understanding of the world.

In a constructivist learning environment, the child creates rather than receives knowledge, and the teacher guides or facilitates this process of discovery. Unlike a traditional classroom where the teacher might lecture or perform demonstrations in front of a group of passive students, children in a constructivist environment actively learn by doing. For early childhood educators, this approach makes good sense. After all, children learn a great deal without being formally taught. They are able to understand, communicate, move, and function in the world around them long before they encounter schoolteachers, handouts, tests, homework, and report cards. They learn all these things by simply interacting with their environment.

Some characteristics of a constructivist learning environment include the following:

- Learning is a social and collaborative endeavor rather than a solitary activity.
- Activities are learner-centered rather than teacher-centered.
- Activities are often cross-disciplinary, encouraging students to make connections and integrate information, rather than compartmentalize it.

Jean Piaget

- Topics for inquiry are driven by students' interests rather than strict adherence to a fixed curriculum.
- Emphasis is on understanding and application rather than rote memorization or copying.
- Assessment is through authentic measures rather than traditional or standardized testing.

Piaget's studies of children continue to influence contemporary educators in many ways. The best-known component of his research was a definition of stages of intellectual development (Piaget, 1950). Less well-known is Piaget's research on moral development in children (Piaget, 1965). Piaget also studied play in childhood (Piaget, 1962) and found that child development was enhanced through these experiences. His work is discussed in more detail in Chapter 4.

American Influences

The twentieth century ushered in a period of rapid growth and improvement in American education. Several theorists and practitioners from the 1900s have had a significant impact on the direction of early care and education today. They relied heavily upon the European leaders described previously while striking out in new directions to influence young children and their development. The American theorists will be described first, followed by key early childhood practitioners. Figure 2–2 gives a visual timeline of these key theorists and practitioners.

John Dewey

John Dewey (1859–1952). Dewey's career began as a teacher of philosophy at the university level. After spending time at several institutions, he settled at the University of Chicago in 1894. It was here that Dewey began to apply his philosophical ideas to the study of education. As his concepts took shape, Dewey's fame spread, and the **Progressive Movement** in American education was born.

The last half of the nineteenth century was a period of rapid growth in the availability of education in America. Although this was a major step forward, at the start of the twentieth century many were questioning the generally accepted methods and content of schooling. Dewey's ideas were a catalyst for the reform efforts of progressive education in the 1920s and 1930s. Braun and Edwards (1972) summarize the major ideas associated with Dewey as follows:

- **Education should be integrated with life.** To make education meaningful, it must be associated with real-life events.
- **Education should preserve social values.** The common values of the culture need to be taught and supported by the schools.
- **True education occurs in social situations.** Dewey felt very strongly that learning was strengthened through social interactions with peers and adults.

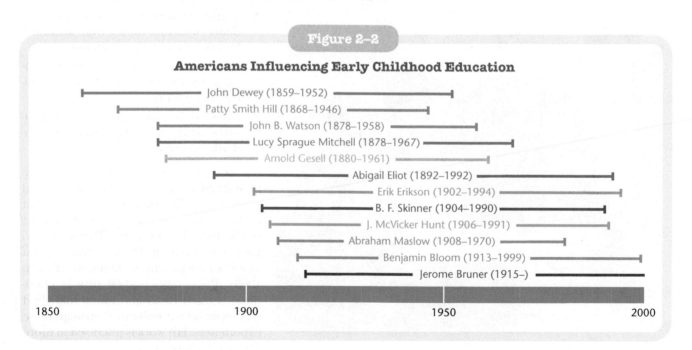

Figure 2-2

Americans Influencing Early Childhood Education

John Dewey (1859–1952)
Patty Smith Hill (1868–1946)
John B. Watson (1878–1958)
Lucy Sprague Mitchell (1878–1967)
Arnold Gesell (1880–1961)
Abigail Eliot (1892–1992)
Erik Erikson (1902–1994)
B. F. Skinner (1904–1990)
J. McVicker Hunt (1906–1991)
Abraham Maslow (1908–1970)
Benjamin Bloom (1913–1999)
Jerome Bruner (1915–)

1850   1900   1950   2000

- **Children's instincts and powers create starting points for education.** An understanding of child development and individual needs and interests is necessary for teachers who are planning learning experiences for children.
- **Active learning is essential.** Children must be intellectually and physically involved in their classrooms to truly learn from their experiences.

Erik Erikson (1902–1994). Erikson was a German-born psychoanalyst who came to the United States after having internalized much of the Freudian theory described previously. While accepting much of what Freud developed, he worked to extend and refine the psychoanalytic theory of personality development. Thomas (1985) proposes three main additions that Erikson made to Freud's earlier work:

- **Emphasis on the healthy personality.** While Freud was often perceived as having studied neurotic personalities, Erikson's theory helps us understand how healthy personalities develop.
- **The epigenetic principle.** Erikson proposed that growth in personality, like other aspects of development, follows a clearly defined plan that is primarily determined by genetics. It develops according to steps "predetermined in the human organism's readiness to be driven toward, to be aware of, and to interact with a widening radius of significant individuals and institutions" (Erikson, 1968, p. 92).
- **Psychosocial stages of development.** Erikson defined eight stages in the development of the personality. These stages begin at birth and end in old age.

Abraham Maslow (1908–1970). Maslow is considered a key advocate of what is called *humanistic psychology*. Humanists propose an optimistic picture of children that emphasizes these traits:

- **The basic "goodness" of the child.** Human needs, emotions, and capacities are seen as basically positive. Life experiences are what lead to such things as cruelty and destructiveness.
- **Human needs.** Behavior is seen as motivated primarily by the person's efforts to fulfill a series of needs. Successfully meeting needs leads to healthy development; conversely, those who have unmet needs will face difficulties.
- **The importance of self.** Although humanists differ in their interpretation of self, it is seen as the integrator of human experiences and the "central core" of an individual that grows and changes over time (Maslow, 1968).

Maslow's major contribution to humanistic theory was the development of a **hierarchy of needs**. He proposed that basic needs such as food, shelter, and clothing must be satisfied before higher-level needs such as belongingness and affection can be met.

Benjamin Bloom (1913–1999). Bloom's writings led to an increased interest in early care and education. He did much to popularize the importance of development during the early years of life. Bloom also promoted the idea that human intelligence was strongly influenced by environmental factors. In his book, *Stability and Change in Human Characteristics* (Bloom, 1964), he stated:

> . . . the data suggest that in terms of intelligence measured at age seventeen, about 50 percent of the development takes place between conception and age four, about 30 percent between ages four and eight, and about 20 percent between ages eight and eighteen. . . . The evidence from studies of identical twins reared separately and reared together as well as from longitudinal

studies in which the characteristics of the environments are studied in relation to changes in intelligence test scores indicate that the level of measured general intelligence is partially determined by the nature of the environment. (p. 88)

Jerome Bruner (1915–). At the same time that Bloom was identifying the early years as critical to intellectual development, Bruner published his influential book, *The Process of Education* (1960). In it, he challenged educators at all levels by stating that the "foundations of any subject may be taught to anybody at any age in some form" (p. 12). In other words, he believed that young children can and should be taught the basic concepts and the methods of studying such subjects as mathematics, science, and social studies. These early experiences could then be built upon in later years to enhance intellectual understandings even further. Bruner also promoted what he called *discovery* (or *inquiry*) *learning*, in which students are encouraged to discover for themselves the important elements of a given discipline. In this approach to learning, teachers guide their students as they discover meaningful understandings of the world around them.

Arnold Gesell (1880–1961). With medical training and a doctorate in psychology, Arnold Gesell had unique qualifications for his work in early care and education. Gesell used his education to research the developmental patterns of childhood. Interested in studying children's maturational characteristics, he spent 30 years as director of the Yale Clinic of Child Development. In this position, he created a comprehensive collection of data describing normal child development. For children from birth through adolescence, Gesell identified observable changes in growth and behavior that he categorized into 10 major areas. Gesell authored or coauthored several books (see, for example, Gesell & Ilg, 1949) that summarized for readers the typical or normative behaviors of children. This information became very popular with both parents and teachers who needed clear descriptions of normal child behaviors. Gesell's descriptions continue to be used and are discussed further in Chapter 4.

Patty Smith Hill (1868–1946). Hill, an important early childhood practitioner, was trained in Froebel's methods of kindergarten education. In addition, she was strongly influenced by the work of John Dewey. By blending the thinking of these two different but compatible theorists, she was able to create a strong curriculum for young children. Hill's educational efforts became the foundations of kindergarten practice in the United States.

Hill is credited with two important innovations. First, she helped found the laboratory nursery school at Columbia University Teachers College in 1921. This model program helped train many fine teachers of young children while providing a research site for faculty at the college. Her second contribution was to help organize the National Association for Nursery Education. This group was later renamed the National Association for the Education of Young Children (NAEYC), which is currently the largest and most influential organization of early childhood educators.

Lucy Sprague Mitchell (1878–1967). While Patty Smith Hill worked at Columbia University Teachers College, Lucy Sprague Mitchell labored under similar circumstances, also in New York. Mitchell is credited with helping start the laboratory nursery school at the Bureau of Educational Experiments in 1919. She initiated an excellent model program for young children where researchers could study children and their development. She also trained prospective teachers who left to start their own nursery

Family Partnerships . . .
LETTERS HOME

Just as Abigail Eliot was a strong proponent of effective relationships with families, you will need to plan for a variety of positive interactions with them as well. An effective and commonly used strategy is to regularly send home letters. They are generally one or two pages in length and describe happenings in the classroom. Although the content of these letters varies among classrooms, some typical components would be information about projects being worked on in class, notice of upcoming field trips and special productions that would be of interest to parents and guardians, and ideas about what families can do at home to support the activities in class.

If you choose to do a letter to families, consider the following in developing them:

- **Use your best writing skills.** Families expect the teachers of their children to be good written communicators. If you send home a letter with even a few spelling, grammar, or punctuation errors, parents and guardians may well think less of your teaching abilities. Make sure to write, edit, and rewrite whatever you send home.

- **Consider the first languages of parents and guardians.** In many homes today, the language spoken and read by parents and guardians is not English. If you find this to be the case in your classroom, you may need to get a translator to rewrite your letter in the appropriate language/languages so that these families can also have the benefit of your communications.

- **Develop a strategy for making sure the letters get home.** After spending time writing a great letter, you want to make sure that it reaches parents and guardians. Some teachers create a folder for family communications and make sure that these folders go home on the same day each week so that parents and guardians can be expecting them. Another option that also saves paper (and the environment) is to send letters home electronically.

1. What do you see as the advantages and disadvantages of letters as a form of communicating with families?

2. Can you see yourself regularly using letters to communicate with parents and guardians? Why or why not?

---

school programs in other locations. The Bureau of Educational Experiments was later renamed the Bank Street College of Education. This program has been influential over the years in defining important directions for early care and education.

Abigail Eliot (1892–1992). Abigail Eliot made important contributions to early care and education through her work with nursery school children from low-income families. After working with the McMillan sisters in their Open-Air Nursery in London, Eliot served as director of the Ruggles Street Nursery in Boston beginning in 1922. Like the Open-Air Nursery, Eliot's school became an early model for the current Head Start program.

The Ruggles Street Nursery had the following characteristics:

- Child-sized equipment
- Comprehensive program (including health care, to meet the needs of the whole child)
- Variety of materials (Froebelian, Montessori, and McMillan materials)
- Full-day program (including nap)
- Work with parents (the *Family Partnerships* feature found in this section suggests strategies for written communications that will help improve your ability to work with parents and guardians)

Recent American Contributors

Although there are many recent American early educators who have contributed significantly to the directions of early care and education, four will be discussed here. These four, along with their most significant contribution, are David Weikart and the High/Scope program, Lilian Katz and the project approach to learning, Joe Frost and the importance of outdoor play, and Louise Derman-Sparks and the anti-bias curriculum.

David P. Weikart (1938–2003). David Weikart began work with the Ypsilanti Public Schools, in Ypsilanti, Michigan in 1957 as a school psychologist. After working in the district for 5 years, he began the Perry Preschool Project in 1962, which was so named because it was housed in the Perry Elementary School in Ypsilanti (Schweinhart, 2004). This program developed out of Weikart's interest in helping African-American children do better in school. At a time when IQ was considered fixed and children were believed to have simply been born with whatever innate abilities they had, Weikart believed that he could help these young African-American children improve their IQs and enter public school with more chance of success (Hanford, 2009).

The experimental program was a huge success, with IQ scores going up an average of 15 points for children who had been in the program for 2 years. Over time, however, Weikart and his researchers found that these initial gains "washed out" and IQ scores of children in the program fell (Hanford, 2009). Undaunted, Weikart still believed that children were making significant gains from being a part of his program and he decided to quit his job with the Ypsilanti schools so that he could devote his full attention to perfecting the curriculum and studying the results of his work with young African-American children.

Along with several colleagues, he then set up the High Scope Educational Research Foundation to carry on his work (High Scope Educational Research Foundation, 2010). Since that time, long-term research findings have been conducted when students were 14–15, 19, 27, and 40. Results have been very positive and conclusive. Quality early education does make a difference for children from low-income families. At age 14, students were performing significantly better than expected on IQ tests (compared with a control group of their peers), had higher grades, and were more positive about being in school (Hanford, 2009). By the age of 40, these same Perry Preschool children were doing much better in life than peers from similar backgrounds. They were more likely to be employed, made more money, were less likely to use social services, and were more likely to say that they had positive relations with their families (Schweinhart et al., 2005). Weikart's pioneering work has had a powerful effect on teaching and learning in early childhood settings.

Lilian Katz. Lilian Katz is a modern leader in early education and care who spent more than three decades as a professor of early childhood education at the University of Illinois, Urbana–Champaign. She is the author of more than 150 publications, including articles, chapters, and several books on early childhood education. In addition, Dr. Katz founded two journals: *Early Childhood Research Quarterly* and *Early Childhood Research and Practice*.

One of her most important contributions has been to popularize the **project approach** to learning in the classroom. Her book, written with Sylvia Chard and titled *Engaging Children's Minds: The Project Approach* (Katz & Chard, 2000), is considered a key reference on the subject. Projects can be defined as in-depth studies of topics of interest to a class, a group of children, or an individual.

Each issue of the online journal *Early Childhood Research and Practice,* founded by Dr. Katz, provides an example of a project created by a classroom teacher. For example, the spring 2007 issue describes a hospital project undertaken by 3-, 4-, and 5-year-old children (Sanchez, 2007). Following an initial classroom discussion about health and taking care of your body, children began playing doctor in the dramatic play area. Children then got interested in visiting a health care facility where they could learn more about doctors and health care. Activities leading up to and following the field trip provided students with an in-depth and meaningful study of health care. By observing, listening, and talking to children about their interests, teachers were able to plan an extensive hospital study that became a valuable learning experience for all involved.

Joe L. Frost. Born during the 1930s depression in rural Arkansas, Frost lived a childhood like many others, filled with considerable time spent outdoors playing with whatever was lying around. There were no playgrounds or fancy toys, so he made do with natural objects that were found in the outdoors. These early experiences were to later greatly influence the course of his career (University of the Incarnate Word, 2010).

After earning a doctorate from the University of Arkansas, Dr. Frost took his first university job at Iowa State University. During the next 10 years, Frost published 10 books on children and poverty, including *The Disadvantaged Child* with Glenn Hawkes (Frost & Hawkes, 1970) and *Early Childhood Education Rediscovered* (Frost, 1968). Both texts were highly acclaimed and helped lead policy makers and students alike to a greater interest in the field of early childhood education.

In 1966, Dr. Frost left Iowa State University to take a position at the University of Texas in Austin where he taught for the remainder of his career. It was here that he reconnected with his childhood play experiences and became a leading proponent of play, particularly in outdoor settings. He also has been a tireless advocate for play in outdoor settings and has written extensively on the subject (see, for example, Frost & Henniger, 1979; Frost & Sweeney, 1996; Frost & Wortham, 1988). His most recent book, *Play and Child Development,* is in its fourth edition (Frost, Wortham, & Reifel, 2012).

Within the last two decades, early childhood professionals have been suggesting that another option for play is through the use of electronic media. The *Technology Explorations and Activities* feature in this section, is designed to help you reflect on the importance of this option. Read the information now and compare technology use with the information presented in this chapter on childhood play.

Louise Derman-Sparks. Louise Derman-Sparks started her career as a teacher in the Perry Preschool Project (see entry on David Weikart). Working with low-income children from diverse backgrounds was a passion that began for her in the early 1960s and stayed for the remainder of her career. While serving as a teacher in the

Technology Explorations and Activities . . .
PLAYFUL ELECTRONIC GAMES FOR YOUNG CHILDREN

There are many different kinds of free electronic games on the Internet for young children to enjoy using a desktop computer or tablet. These games can provide many hours of fun and learning. One key to your success in using these activities in your classroom is to have reviewed them carefully so that you understand both the limitations and values for children. One example of an Internet game of this type is the Boohbah Zone. It is based on the television series Ragdoll's Boohbah Show and is designed for preschool-aged children. Another example is PBS Kids, which uses games and activities that are based on popular PBS television shows. Choose one of these options, do an Internet search, and then review its contents based on the questions and activities described here.

Research, Reflect, and Respond

1. Spend some time playing on the website you have chosen. Try to imagine how a young child would respond to the activities presented. What ages of children do you think would be attracted to this site? Do you think they would enjoy the activities presented over an extended period of time? Why or why not?

2. Review the quote on play by Froebel earlier in this chapter. Do you think Froebel would have considered this activity a playful one? Why or why not?

3. Would you consider using this website with young children in an early education setting? Why or why not? Do you think families should be made aware of the site as being useful in the home? Give a rationale for the response you give.

Perry Preschool Project, she helped develop the curriculum of what came to be known as the High/Scope program (Hanford, 2009).

In 1989, Derman-Sparks published a book through the National Association for the Education of Young Children titled *Anti-Biased Curriculum: Tools for Empowering Young Children.* She published this work as the culminating experience of the Anti-Bias Curriculum Task Force, a group in which she played a leading role. In the *Anti-Biased Curriculum,* she presents ground-breaking ideas about how young children, with the assistance of their caregivers and teachers, can learn to overcome the biases they will face in their homes, extended families, and communities. She provides numerous ideas that caregivers and teachers can use to assist children in this process. This text has a very strong influence on the directions of diversity education in early childhood settings today. In 2010, the NAEYC updated and republished this important book under the title *Anti-Bias Education for Young Children and Ourselves* (Derman-Sparks & Edwards, 2010).

Two other books of note that were co-authored by Derman-Sparks are *Teaching/ Learning Anti-Racism: A Developmental Approach* (Derman-Sparks & Phillips, 1997) and *What If All the Kids Are White?* (Derman-Sparks & Ramsey, 2006). In both of these books, Derman-Sparks expands upon the diversity themes she presented in her earlier work.

Louise Derman-Sparks was a human development faculty member at Pacific Oaks college in California for 33 years (1974–2007). She is now retired but continues to write and speak about issues of diversity and young children.

Historical Events Influencing Early Care and Education

The insights of many early educators have enriched the teaching and learning of young children over the past several centuries. However, historical and recent events as well as people have influenced the directions of early care and education. During the last hundred years in America, several key occurrences have significantly shaped the ways in which we teach and care for young children.

Child Study Movement

The end of the nineteenth century and beginning of the twentieth century brought a rapidly growing interest in studying children and their development (Weber, 1984). This period is known as the Child Study movement. It may surprise you to know that the main reason for this newfound urge to understand children was the realization that children are qualitatively different from adults. Although we accept this today as common knowledge, for much of the history of humankind, children were viewed simply as miniature adults (Aries, 1962). As people began to recognize that differences existed between children and adults, they were forced to investigate these variations. The Child Study movement was born.

This research effort was important to early care and education for two main reasons. First, the interest in studying children generated a great deal of very useful child development information. People like Arnold Gesell were observing children and carefully documenting typical child development and the variations between children. This information is still very much in use as an initial planning guide for teachers of young children.

The Child Study movement was also an important catalyst in the growth of laboratory nursery schools. To better understand young children, colleges and universities throughout the nation created nursery schools as research sites for faculty (Braun & Edwards, 1972). Some key programs were established during this period:

- **Bureau of Educational Experiments.** Lucy Sprague Mitchell was the guiding force behind this program, which began in 1919. Eventually, this became the Bank Street College of Education in New York.
- **Columbia University Teachers College.** This program, under the direction of Patty Smith Hill, began in 1921.
- **Merrill–Palmer Institute.** Edna Noble White was this program's first director, beginning in 1922.
- **Yale Guidance Nursery.** Arnold Gesell was instrumental in this nursery program, started in 1926.

In addition to providing research sites for the Child Study movement, the laboratory nursery schools were models of excellence in early education and also stirred interest in prekindergarten programs. As adults learned of these opportunities and recognized the benefits for the development of children, more options became available across the country. Preschool programs for children with disadvantages and cooperative nursery schools are two examples of this increased interest.

The Great Depression

Surprisingly, the U.S. Great Depression of the 1930s had an important impact on early care and education. Major federal efforts to put people back to work ended up promoting the cause of prekindergarten education. The Works Progress Administration (WPA) took unemployed schoolteachers, custodians, cooks, and nurses and gave them jobs in government-sponsored preschool programs (Steiner, 1976). The main benefit of these efforts was that nursery education became more widely recognized, which led to acceptance by the American public. Early efforts at parent education were another important spin-off of the WPA programs. Unfortunately, significant problems also surfaced as a result of the WPA nursery schools. The unemployed educators put to work teaching in the nursery programs were given little or no training for their new roles. The assumption (a false one) was that because they knew how to teach older students, they could easily manage younger children. Teachers were also paid very low wages for their services. The WPA was able to pay teachers only a fraction of their prior salaries. The perception that began to develop during this period was that teachers of young children did not need much training or salary for the work they were doing.

World War II

As America reluctantly became involved in World War II, those left at home were called upon to keep the economy running. The government gave special priority to war-related industries to make sure the equipment needed for the war effort was produced on time. Both government and industry encouraged many women with young children to work in these industries, creating a temporary need for child care. Federal money was made available to provide for this care.

The most well-known child-care program from this period was located at the Kaiser Shipyards in Portland, Oregon (Hymes, 1978). Under the guidance of James Hymes, this program implemented many innovations:

- **Specially designed building.** While most child-care facilities today are remodeled business sites or portions of church facilities, the Kaiser program had a carefully designed building with many innovative design features.
- **Located at the work site.** Because the building was at the work site, there were opportunities for mothers to nurse during break times, have lunch with their children, and participate in center activities.
- **Open 24 hours a day.** To accommodate workers around the clock, the center was open 24 hours a day.
- **Special attendance times.** Parents could occasionally leave their children for an extra session so that they could have some time to enjoy a special event or recreational activity.
- **Infirmary for sick children.** A special room was available for children who were sick. Parents could be assured that their child was receiving good care even during times of illness.
- **Family consultant.** An adult was available to assist parents in finding needed community resources.
- **Home food service.** Parents could use the child-care food service to order a hot meal to take home with them.

At the war's end, programs such as the one at the Kaiser Shipyards were simply closed as women returned to their traditional roles as homemakers. Quality options for child care virtually disappeared for several decades and are just now beginning to reemerge. The innovations in child care implemented during World War II continue to be a model for present-day child-care programs.

The Launching of *Sputnik*

In 1957, the launching of Russia's first Earth-orbiting satellite created a great uproar in America. Called *Sputnik I*, this satellite launch represented to many our decline as a society. We were behind the Russians in the race to conquer this new frontier. Something must be done, people said, to reverse this truly alarming situation. The consensus among many people was that we needed to do a better job of educating children so that American scientists could eventually catch up with their Russian counterparts (Braun & Edwards, 1972).

This attitude led to both positive and negative results. One clear benefit was a renewed interest in preschool education. The general thinking seemed to be that if we started earlier, we could better educate our children. The early years began to be recognized as an important developmental period that needed to be taken advantage of and carefully studied. Another positive result was the increased public support for early education. People were more willing to provide financial assistance for programs that showed promise. More federal money, in particular, was available during the 1960s and 1970s to demonstrate new models of early education and for research on teaching and learning at this level.

Unfortunately, there were also negative outcomes in education stemming from the launching of *Sputnik*. One of the most problematic was an overemphasis on intellectual performance. The concern over lagging abilities in mathematics and science in particular led many early educators and the general public to place too much importance on the intellectual activities of young children. While the traditional preschool emphasized all aspects of the child's development, the growing expectation was for programs that could demonstrate improved intellectual performance. A second problem associated with *Sputnik's* launch was the demand for quick and lasting results. The American public, while providing support for new educational efforts, anticipated speedy solutions that would rapidly help us catch up with the Russians—a wholly unrealistic expectation.

The War on Poverty

The presidencies of John F. Kennedy and Lyndon B. Johnson saw a marked increase in the federal government's efforts to help low-income families break free from the grip of poverty. The cornerstone of this "War on Poverty" was the provision of national monies to fund early childhood programs designed for young children from disadvantaged backgrounds (Hymes, 1978). The thinking of policy makers was that the cycle of poverty could be broken only by providing quality educational experiences for children from low-income families. These children would then end up in better-paying jobs, and all of society would benefit. Beginning in 1964, the federal government provided money to local sites for preschool-age children from low-income families.

The most well-known program to come out of this period was the Head Start program. The early research conducted on the effectiveness of Head Start was disappointing (Coleman, 1966). It showed minimal initial success in improving children's intelligence scores, and the gains that were made eventually washed out by the time children reached the third grade. Other federally funded programs begun during the War on Poverty had similar disappointing results (Bronfenbrenner, 1974).

The inability of Head Start and other compensatory education programs to produce long-term IQ score gains in their students led many to believe that a more concentrated effort over a longer period of time was needed. **Project Follow Through**, begun in 1969, was funded by the federal government as a way to continue this assistance to children from low-income families in the primary grades. A variety of model programs were funded at sites across the country, and others conducted research to determine their effectiveness. Although the research results continued to be disappointing, Project Follow Through had a significant impact on early education. Most importantly, these programs created a stronger link between preschool and primary education. Most of the Project Follow Through models used many of the same techniques that had been successful at the preschool level to assist primary-age children in their development. Early childhood educators began to view children from birth through age 8 as similar in many ways and started planning educational experiences that reflected this perspective.

No Child Left Behind Act

One of the most significant recent events to impact the lives of children and their families is 2001's No Child Left Behind Act, designed to provide schools and teachers with the support needed to allow all children to have a quality education. The act states: "The purpose of this title (act) is to ensure that all children have a fair, equal, and significant opportunity to obtain a high-quality education and reach, at a minimum, proficiency on challenging state academic achievement standards and state academic assessments" (U.S. Department of Education, 2010).

Three provisions of this act have particular relevance to early care and education. The first of these provisions is that renewed efforts are being made to ensure that all children can read. One of the positive outcomes of this emphasis is that the federal government tripled its funding of reading instruction in support of this goal. And in elementary schools across the nation, K–3 teachers are putting even more effort into helping all children learn to read.

Second, the No Child Left Behind Act is intended to strengthen teacher quality by requiring states to put a highly qualified teacher in every classroom. Early childhood programs that are funded with either state or federal dollars (such as Head Start) are increasingly requiring all teachers to have completed bachelor's degrees in early care and education. Increasing the qualifications of early childhood teachers is a positive outcome that will have a positive impact on student learning. At the same time, however, in order to attract and retain highly

Celebrating Diversity . . .
LEAVING NO CHILD BEHIND

The No Child Left Behind Act, signed into federal law by President George W. Bush on January 8, 2002, has a noble purpose: to make sure that all children have the opportunity to obtain a high-quality education so that they can be successful in life (U.S. Department of Education, 2010). All children, regardless of socioeconomic status, disability, race, or gender, should have access to quality education. While this is an admirable sentiment, there are many who say that this act cannot attain its goal without addressing several other important factors (Children's Defense Fund, 2010). They include the following:

- **Health insurance coverage.** More than 9 million children in America lack adequate health coverage. Children in poor health find it more difficult to learn.

- **Parent education.** Because parents are the most influential people in children's lives, they need to receive training and assistance to do their jobs well.

- **Greater access to quality preschool education.** While the No Child Left Behind Act recognizes the importance of having children come to school ready to learn, no provisions are made to increase the opportunities for preschool learning for those children who need it most.

- **Addressing the conditions of poverty.** Poverty can lead to homelessness, poor nutrition, and environments that are unsafe for children. Abuse, neglect, and violence are frequently associated with poverty. Children in these circumstances have much greater difficulty being successful in school.

1. How do the risk factors described here influence success in early childhood settings? Are some of these factors more problematic than others? Why or why not?

2. What can and should you do as a future teacher to help children and families who face the kinds of problems discussed here?

---

qualified teachers it is also necessary to have correspondingly higher salaries for these teachers, which is currently not the case.

Finally, this act strongly promotes English competence for limited-English-proficient (LEP) students. The federal agencies responsible for assisting non-English-speaking students have been consolidated, and federal money is available to help LEP children to quickly and effectively learn English. While there is considerable argument over what kinds of programs and teaching strategies are best for helping LEP students develop English proficiency, the commitment and financial support of the federal government will help keep this important issue at the forefront of school and public agendas.

The *Celebrating Diversity* feature found in this section provides another perspective on leaving no child behind. Unlike the federal legislation, which focuses on student academic success, many educators and others suggest that school performance is closely linked with non-academic factors that have a strong influence on child health and well-being. Until these issues are addressed, they contend, there will be only limited success in improving academic performance. Read the feature now to learn more about this perspective.

summary

Historical Figures Influencing Early Care and Education

This chapter introduced key historical figures who have had a significant impact on early care and education. Major figures from Europe include Martin Luther, John Amos Comenius, Jean Jacques Rousseau, Johann Pestalozzi, Friedrich Froebel, Maria Montessori, Margaret McMillan, Lev Vygotsky, Sigmund Freud, and Jean Piaget. In the United States, John Dewey, Erik Erikson, Abraham Maslow, Benjamin Bloom, Jerome Bruner, Arnold Gesell, Patty Smith Hill, Lucy Sprague Mitchell, and Abigail Eliot have had a significant impact on early education.

More Recent American Contributors

Four important, more recent American contributors were discussed for their roles in shaping early care and education: David Weikart for his role in creating the High/Scope program, Lilian Katz and her leadership in the project approach to learning, Joe Frost for emphasizing the importance of outdoor play, and Louise Derman-Sparks for the development of the Anti-Bias Curriculum.

Historical Events Influencing Early Care and Education

The Child Study movement, America's major economic depression of the 1930s, World War II, the launching of *Sputnik*, the 1960s War on Poverty, and the No Child Left Behind Act are all important events influencing early education.

for reflection and discussion

1. Which of the key historical figures presented in this chapter is of most interest to you and why? Spend some time reading more on this individual and discuss your findings with others.

2. Louise Derman-Sparks has had a strong influence on early childhood education through the development of what she terms the anti-bias curriculum. Discuss with others the negative influences that bias towards children and families can have on teaching and learning.

3. Do some research on the No Child Left Behind Act. You may want to talk to a child care provider or teacher to get their perspectives. What are the potential positive aspects of this important piece of legislation? Can you see problems that could come from the act?

MyEducationLab

Go to Topic 2: History in the MyEducationLab (www.myeducationlab.com) for *Teaching Young Children* where you can:

- Find learning outcomes for History along with the national standards that connect to these outcomes.
- Complete Assignments and Activities that can help you more deeply understand the chapter content.
- Apply and practice your understanding of the core teaching skills identified in the chapter with the Building Teaching Skills and Dispositions learning units.
- Check your comprehension on the content covered in the chapter with the Study Plan. Here you will be able to take a chapter quiz, receive feedback on your answers, and then access Review, Practice, and Enrichment activities to enhance your understanding of chapter content.

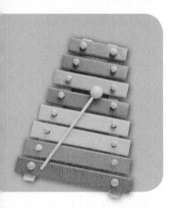

 3

Early Childhood Program Models

IN THIS CHAPTER YOU WILL

- Study the Montessori program and its implications for teaching young children.
- Investigate the High/Scope curriculum for infant/toddler, preschool, and primary classrooms.
- Review Waldorf education and its application to young children.
- Consider the Bank Street model for early education.
- Identify the elements of the Reggio Emilia program and its applications in the United States.

Amanda is taking her first course in early care and education and is trying to make sense of all that she is learning. The issue she is currently struggling with concerns early childhood program models. Amanda has learned about Montessori education, the High/Scope model, the Bank Street program, and the Reggio Emilia approach. Is one better than the others for young children?

The programs that she has studied share many similarities, which makes it more difficult to sort out her thoughts. Amanda's thinking is further complicated by the fact that she likes different elements of each model. Additional information would be helpful to her as she evaluates the options. It would be nice, for example, to see each of the programs in action, but the local early childhood centers do not clearly identify themselves with the specific models Amanda has studied.

The issues you face as you read this chapter will probably mirror those that Amanda identified in the preceding scenario. Several clearly defined models for early care and education are currently in practice; making conclusive judgments about them without in-depth study, however, is difficult. Also, pure models of the different approaches are hard to find, making it unlikely that you can observe each of the models in action. While it is difficult to find examples of the models described here, you need to be aware of the different program options used to educate young children and understand their similarities and differences. Also, take time to think about which models appeal to you personally, and plan to learn more about them later. Remember, this is just the beginning point for your understanding of early care and education.

This chapter presents an overview of five major program models for early care and education and discusses the key elements of each. These options significantly influence the philosophy and approach to learning that occurs in early childhood programs across the country. Figure 3–1 summarizes the key features of each approach.

CHAPTER 3

Figure 3–1

Key Features of Five Early Childhood Programs

Program	Key Features
Montessori education	Work experiences rather than play. Special materials for specific learning tasks. Carefully prepared classroom environment.
High/Scope program	Based on the theory of Jean Piaget. Use of a plan-do-review sequence. Classroom organized into centers. Emphasis on cognitive development.
Waldorf education	Began with the work of Rudolf Steiner. Believe in the unity between the spirit, body, and mind. Uncluttered, warm, homelike, and aesthetically pleasing spaces.
Bank Street model	All aspects of child development are addressed in the curriculum. Freud, Erikson, Piaget, and Dewey all influence the model. Commercial equipment supplemented with teacher-made and child-made materials. Emphasis is on an integrated curriculum.
Reggio Emilia approach	Emphasis on in-depth projects to facilitate learning. A workshop area is used to record in visual form what is learned. Families are expected to share responsibilities in educating children. Strong collaboration exists among staff members.

 ## The Montessori Program

MyEducationLab

Visit the MyEducationLab for *Teaching Young Children* to enhance your understanding of chapter concepts with a personalized Study Plan. You'll also have the opportunity to hone your teaching skills through video- and case-based Assignments and Activities as well as Building Teaching Skills and Disposition lessons.

The teaching and writing of Maria Montessori led to a unique model for early learning that has had a significant influence on the methods and materials used by early childhood professionals today. As with each of the models described in this chapter, the Montessori approach has both strong supporters and vocal critics (Roopnarine & Johnson, 2009).

Montessori education began as a program for children from 4 to 7 years of age in low-income families. Today, the principles of this approach are being used with infant/toddler through high-school-age students. Although most of these options are private schools for predominantly middle-class students, approximately 200 public school programs nationwide are using the Montessori method (North American Montessori Teachers Association, 2010).

Montessori programs in the United States are generally associated with one of two major organizations. The American Montessori Society is a group of educators in the United States dedicated to implementing the ideas of Montessori in this country. This association has taken Montessori's methods and materials and modified them where needed for use in American schools in an attempt to make the approach more widely accepted here (American Montessori Society, 2010). The more traditional methods and materials that Montessori developed are promoted through the Association Montessori Internationale. Montessori programs throughout Europe, India, and the rest of the world generally associate themselves

This Montessori teacher shows students how to complete their work tasks.

with this organization. Some American programs also affiliate with the international association (Association Montessori Internationale, 2010).

Montessori's Work Experiences

One major difference between Montessori education and many other early childhood programs in the United States is the emphasis on **work tasks** rather than play times (Montessori, 1965). Although these concepts share similarities, the differences are significant.

While children are free to choose the materials they want to spend time with during work times, these items are used in very specific ways. Before the child is allowed to spend time independently on a task, the adult demonstrates how the materials are to be used. Precise steps are clearly presented, and any deviations from these procedures result in a new demonstration of the task by the early childhood professional or redirection into a different work activity. When children are developmentally ready to use the task in the prescribed way, they are then free to use the materials during choice times.

An example of a work task used in Montessori classrooms is the spooning of dried peas. On a child-sized tray, the Montessori professional organizes two bowls (one filled with dried peas) and a spoon. When a child shows interest in these materials, the adult carefully demonstrates how the child should place the bowls, hold the spoon, and move the peas from one bowl to the next without spilling. Once the child has demonstrated appropriate spooning techniques, he is then free to engage in this work task as often as he wants.

Very different from Montessori's work tasks are the **play experiences** found in most preschool programs. Play tends to be much more open-ended than the learning opportunities designed by Montessori. Children have many choices of interesting materials and use those toys and equipment in their own unique ways. Play materials usually do not require demonstration by the adult. Children understand their use and simply take them from their storage location and engage in play. A set of wooden blocks, for example, is an excellent play material that leads to building castles, roads, towers, or anything else that comes to mind. The *Celebrating Play* feature found in this section compares the thinking used in creative play with thought processes in Montessori's work tasks. Read the feature now and respond to the questions posed as you continue to learn about Montessori methods and materials.

Montessori Materials

Montessori's ideas of work and play and her views of child growth and development provide a clear rationale for the materials in Montessori settings. Because of her work with poor children in the slums of Rome, Montessori felt very strongly that the materials used in her programs should be beautiful (Lillard, 1996). They

Celebrating Play . . .
ENCOURAGING DIVERGENT THINKING

While the work tasks described in this section by Montessori can definitely benefit children and their development, many early childhood educators emphasize the values of play experiences for young children. For example, Doris Fromberg (2002), in her book *Play and Meaning in Early Childhood Education*, describes astrophysicist Michio Kaku's projections for the kinds of thinking needed by adults in the twenty-first century. Adults need to do three important things:

1. envision more than one answer to a question;
2. take imaginary leaps and act on them;
3. adapt to rapid change.

The world will need people who can think flexibly, collaborate with others, and feel comfortable with the predictably unpredictable. (Fromberg, 2002, p. 3)

Fromberg goes on to say that play is the vehicle that young children use to develop these skills. When children play, rather than engaging in the convergent thinking associated with Montessori tasks, they are engaged in a process of divergent thinking that allows them to resolve the dilemmas they face in daily life. Take, for example, Irina, a 4-year-old preschool child playing in the art center. She has been working on her painting for the past 20 minutes and is carefully painting with red, blue, and yellow colors to fill her easel paper. Irina accidentally mixes colors and finds that when she does it leads to new and interesting options. As she gets excited about her discovery, she experiments with new combinations to find out the colors that result. Through her play, Irina is developing the skills she will need to be a creative, problem-solving adult.

1. Reread the sections in this chapter describing Montessori's work tasks and the section on play experiences. Compare and contrast work tasks and play. What are the similarities and differences?
2. As a future early childhood professional, are you more likely to promote work tasks as defined by Montessori or more open-ended play experiences? Give a rationale for your preference. Is there room for both play and work tasks in early childhood settings? Why or why not?

---

were constructed with care from only the finest woods and other materials and carefully finished to look and feel good to children. For many of her children, this equipment was one of very few contacts with truly beautiful materials. Montessori designed her equipment with other specific characteristics in mind as well (Standing, 1962):

- **Careful attention to concept development.** Each piece of equipment was designed to teach specific concepts to children as they used them.
- **Graduated difficulty/complexity.** As children develop, they need increasingly challenging materials to stimulate their continued growth.
- **Self-correction.** Whenever possible, Montessori-designed materials are self-correcting, eliminating the need to consult an adult.
- **Sensory orientation.** Montessori considered all the senses to be important, and she designed her materials to stimulate their use as part of the learning process.

One popular Montessori work task is the cylinder block. Several different types are used, some varying only in the depth of the cylinder, others only in the diameter (see Figure 3–2a). The more difficult ones require the child to differentiate both depth and diameter. Children take the cylinders out and place them carefully on the table and then replace them in the appropriate holes.

Figure 3–2

(a) Montessori Cylinder Blocks (b) Button Frame

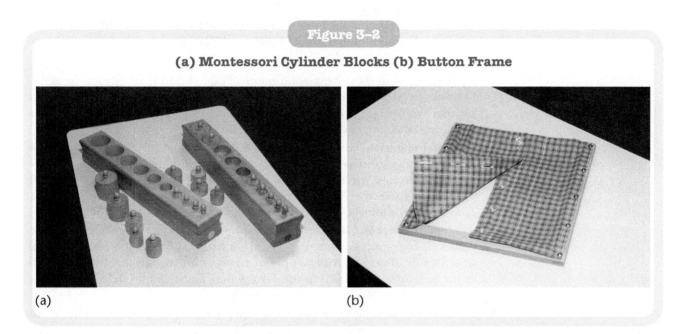

(a)   (b)

Another common material found in Montessori programs is the buttoning frame (Figure 3–2b). There are several variations of these wooden frames, all of which have two half-sheets of fabric attached. Some have buttons, and others have tying materials that children use to connect and disconnect the two pieces of fabric. This task develops fine motor skills and prepares children to dress themselves.

Classroom Organization

Montessori carefully organized the materials and equipment in her classroom so that children could easily and effectively use them (Lillard, 1996). One characteristic of this organization was the child-sized equipment she used. Montessori designed tables and chairs with young children's bodies in mind. She also constructed storage shelves, sinks, drinking fountains, toilets, and other equipment at the appropriate height for young children. Montessori wanted children to independently and easily use the available equipment.

Precise organization is another characteristic of the work spaces in a Montessori program. The early childhood professional stores each activity in a specific place and carefully organizes the materials for easy use by children. The adult organizes many of the work tasks on trays so that children can take them to their own work space, use the materials, and return them to their proper storage spot. The washing-up tray, for example, is stored on a shelf in the home living center and typically contains a child-sized pitcher, bowl, washcloth, soap, soap dish, and apron, all neatly organized for children's use.

A third characteristic of organization is the use of individual work spaces for each child. Typically, a small rug or mat defines the personal space children need for their work tasks. During work time, children bring out their rug, place it on the floor or at a table, and then select the task they want to use. These mats encourage children to focus their energies on the work before them rather than being distracted by the activities of others.

Montessori programs are loosely organized into centers that differ somewhat from other early childhood settings. Lillard (1972) identifies four categories of materials that are used in each of these centers:

- **Daily living materials.** This equipment allows children to engage in activities associated with their own physical well-being or provides opportunities for them to manage the indoor environment. Materials for washing up and a child-sized dustpan and broom are examples of these options.

- **Sensorial materials.** Montessori saw the development of all the senses as an important way to help young children learn. These materials help enhance sensory awareness while assisting in intellectual development. One example is Montessori's sound cylinders, which the adult uses to help children discriminate between sounds of different objects placed in wooden cylinders.

- **Academic materials.** Children use this equipment to learn language arts, mathematics, geography, and science. There is a natural progression from sensorial to academic materials. An example of an academic material is the collection of metal shapes that children use for tracing. These shapes help develop the physical skills children need for later writing tasks.

- **Cultural and artistic materials.** This equipment helps prepare children for later artistic expression. For example, Montessori professionals believe that children need practice in walking a line on the floor as they prepare for future music and dance expression. As children develop their sense of balance and gain better control over their hands and feet, they develop the skills needed for rhythm and dance experiences.

Role of the Early Childhood Professional

The formal training of Montessori professionals is extensive. Prospective candidates must thoroughly study child development, understand the educational values of all the materials used in the program, become sensitive to the appropriate times to present work tasks to children, and gain experience in interacting with children.

Adults in a Montessori classroom operate on three basic principles (Montessori, 1965):

- **A carefully prepared environment.** The first and most important task of a Montessori professional is to thoroughly prepare the indoor environment. When children can work with materials that meet their developmental needs, they spend many productive hours engaged in work tasks that enhance learning and development.

- **An attitude of humility.** Montessori professionals recognize that children's inner needs are very difficult to understand, and adult attempts to assist in meeting these needs are often misguided. Therefore, truly effective early childhood professionals must approach their roles humbly, while constantly evaluating their own motives and the needs of children.

- **Respect for the child's individuality.** A thorough understanding of child development and individual differences is essential for the Montessori professional. Knowing and respecting these differences within and between children helps the adult focus on the positive characteristics each child possesses.

Montessori's ideas, materials, and teaching strategies have a relatively small but loyal group of supporters both in the United States and around the world. The strong emphasis on highly structured work tasks, however, is generally in conflict with the play orientation of most American early childhood programs. In America, Montessori's approach is most popular with families who seek a more structured learning environment in which to stimulate child development.

Children Served

Montessori's original work with children focused on ages 4–7. As interest in her methods and materials grew, she began to expand the ages served. While the focal point for this model remains on preschool and kindergarten children, Montessori programs can be found that serve the needs of infant/toddlers, elementary school children, and students in their middle and high school years. A review of American Montessori Society (2010) programs in California, for example, found the following early childhood options:

- **Infant/toddler programs.** Several programs provide Montessori education for children beginning at 18 months, with a few admitting infants from 2 months of age.
- **Programs for ages 3–6.** Nearly all of the Montessori schools in California included this age range as an option for families.
- **Programs for ages 6–9.** Montessori educators believe that children of this age have very similar needs, interests, and abilities. Montessori programs often group these children together in the same setting. Several California programs provided this option.
- **Programs for children 9–15.** Some of the Montessori programs listed also offer educational options for students in late elementary through the middle school years and into early high school.

Montessori educators also believe that children with special needs and those who are gifted and talented can benefit from their methods and materials. Because of the individual treatment each child receives, many families with gifted children in particular seek out Montessori programs for their children (Hoagie's Gifted Education, 2010). The *Celebrating Diversity* feature found in this section describes some common educational options for gifted students.

 # The High/Scope Curriculum Model

The High/Scope curriculum model has had a major influence on early care and education for the past 50 years (Hanford, 2009). David Weikart and others created the Perry Preschool Program in the 1960s as a model approach designed to help disadvantaged preschool children develop the skills needed to succeed in either public or private K–12 school systems. The program emphasizes the importance of teaching the cognitive understandings needed for academic success in reading and mathematics (DeVries & Kohlberg, 1987).

After initially receiving federal support in the 1960s, a private organization called the High/Scope Foundation took over responsibility for continuing to promote the model. David Weikart, who was the leading visionary and driving force behind the High/Scope program from its beginning, served as president of this foundation until 2000, when he retired (High/Scope Foundation, 2010). This curricular approach, although originally designed for preschool-age children, has been successfully used with infant/toddlers and primary-age children in more recent years (Bredekamp, 1996; Post & Hohmann, 2000).

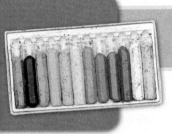

Celebrating Diversity . . .
PROGRAMS FOR CHILDREN WHO ARE GIFTED AND TALENTED

Although none of the program models described in this chapter are designed exclusively for children who are gifted and talented, each can accommodate these students and provide quality educational experiences for them. Most programs for gifted and talented children begin in the primary grades. Three approaches to gifted education are commonly found in the United States (Davis, Rimm, & Siegle, 2011):

- **Separate education.** In this option, children who are identified as gifted and talented are isolated from others and taught in a separate program within the school. While providing potential benefits, this option runs counter to the current emphasis on integrating children with special needs into the regular program setting.
- **Accelerated education.** In accelerated programs, children who are gifted and talented skip grades in the school system, work with older children and their teacher to learn more advanced topics, or use accelerated materials more independently in their regular programs. Although it moves gifted and talented children more rapidly through required

subjects, this approach may fail to stimulate and challenge these students.

- **Enrichment education.** Children in this program type remain in their regular program setting and receive experiences that extend and expand learning through special projects and activities. This option allows children who are gifted and talented to socialize and interact more normally with their peers while still receiving the stimulation they need for exciting learning experiences. Enrichment programs support the effort to integrate all children with special needs in the regular classroom.

1. During your own schooling, did you know someone you would consider gifted or talented? What options did the school provide to support this student? Did this person develop to his or her potential? Why or why not?

2. Identify the potential strengths and weaknesses of each of the approaches to gifted education described here for primary-age children.

3. Do you think primary-age children can and should be identified as gifted or talented? What are the benefits and potential problems?

Theoretical Basis

The High/Scope curriculum is grounded in the theoretical perspectives of Jean Piaget, who believed that children learn best when they build understanding through direct experiences with people and objects in the world around them. Applying Piaget's theories in classrooms has led to the development of several programs that are collectively called *constructivist* in their approach. The High/Scope curriculum is the best-known example of this type. DeVries and Kohlberg (1987) and Kamii and DeVries (1978) have described their thoughts on constructivist education in separate books. Studying the perspectives presented in these resources will add further insights into the High/Scope model.

While emphasizing the development of the whole child, High/Scope focuses on strengthening cognitive skills through active, hands-on learning experiences. This cognitively oriented curriculum is founded on the belief that children cannot understand themselves without first being able to place themselves in time and space and to classify and order objects and events (Weikart, Rogers, Adcock, & McClellan, 1971).

The High/Scope program is designed to help children develop logicomathematical and spatiotemporal understandings of the world around them (Hohmann & Weikart, 1995). **Logicomathematical relationships** include organizing objects into groups according to common characteristics and ordering items from smallest to largest. These tasks are based on Piaget's studies of logic and number. **Spatiotemporal relationships** focus on helping children understand relational concepts such as up/down, over/under, and inside/outside. Event sequences and cause-and-effect relationships are also emphasized.

The Plan-Do-Review Sequence

To help children develop stronger conceptual understandings, the High/Scope curriculum uses a procedure called the **plan-do-review sequence** (Hohmann & Weikart, 1995). The teacher encourages children to plan the tasks they want to accomplish during free-choice time, engage in those activities, and then spend time later in the day reflecting on what they learned.

Children typically engage in planning time in small groups of four or five, while working with an early childhood professional. Children identify activities they would like to try during work time, and the adult helps them refine their thinking to produce a clear, structured plan for the work period ahead. The High/Scope professional uses a variety of motivational strategies to assist children in making decisions about their school day. For example, a set of pretend walkie-talkies could be used to help children communicate their plans to others. The *Developmentally Appropriate Practice* feature found in this section provides additional ideas about planning with children.

Developmentally Appropriate Practice . . .
PLANNING WITH CHILDREN

The planning component of the plan-do-review sequence in the High/Scope program is considered essential for both children and adults. It helps children make good decisions about the activities they choose during playtimes. The following hypothetical dialogue between an early childhood professional working with one of her 4-year-old children highlights the planning process taking place in a typical small-group session:

Adult: Miranda, here is Muppet the Puppet. Can you tell her what you plan on doing today during work time?

Miranda: **(puts puppet on her hand and speaks to it):** Muppet, I think I'll go to art today.

Adult: Tell Muppet what you plan to do when you get there, please.

Miranda: Well, probably paint at the easel.

Adult: That's a good choice, Miranda. You haven't painted at the easel for several days. Anything else you want to tell Muppet?

Miranda: . . . Nope.

Adult: Remember at group time I mentioned that there were both wide and narrow brushes to use at the easel? Do you want to use one or the other, or both?

Miranda: I think I will try the wide one first and then maybe the narrow one.

Some other options you could consider using to help young children plan include the following:

- **Audio recorder.** Have children speak into a microphone attached to an audio recorder, explaining their choices of activities for the play period. Play back what the child has said to reinforce the choice(s) made.

- **Spyglass.** Use the cardboard cylinder from an empty paper towel roll as a "spyglass." Ask each child to look through the spyglass and find a center in the indoor environment that he or she would like to visit during playtime and describe the activities to engage in.

- **Camera.** If you have a digital camera, you could ask the children to take a picture of the center they want to visit and then describe the activities they want to engage in there. Or, you could simply ask children to look through the camera viewfinder and identify the center they are interested in visiting.

Adults often refer to the "do" time in the High/Scope curriculum as *work time;* it directly follows the planning period. In this model, early childhood professionals organize program space into areas where children spend their work time with blocks, art projects, quiet activities, and dramatic play. High/Scope professionals provide children with a large block of time (usually 40 to 60 minutes) to carry out their planned activities.

Review time is the last of the three components of the plan-do-review sequence and typically follows the work period. Adults can conduct this recall time either in small groups or as a whole class. Again, the early childhood professional assists children in reviewing their work experiences in a variety of developmentally appropriate ways. Drawing a picture of the block structure built, discussing whom children spent time with, and reviewing the plans made earlier in the day are examples of the techniques used during this period.

The Curriculum

Early childhood professionals in the High/Scope program emphasize eight **key experiences** as they plan for their time with children (Weikart et al., 1971):

1. **Active learning.** Adults expect children to initiate and carry out their own tasks in the early childhood setting. They encourage manipulation of materials for all aspects of the High/Scope curriculum.

2. **Using language.** Early childhood professionals emphasize oral and written language. They encourage children to talk with others about their experiences and feelings as they go through the program day.

3. **Experiencing and representing.** Children need many opportunities to experience through their senses and to represent those activities through music, movement, art, and role-playing.

4. **Classification.** The ability to notice similarities and differences among objects grows during the early childhood years. Adults provide many opportunities for children to grow in their understanding of classification because of its importance in later mathematical learning.

5. **Seriation.** Another important foundation for mathematics is the ability to order objects from smallest to largest on the basis of some criteria such as length, weight, or width.

6. **Number concepts.** Understanding, for example, what *fiveness* means is another mathematical concept that High/Scope professionals promote.

7. **Spatial relationships.** Children gain understandings of concepts such as under/over, up/down, and in/out as they interact with materials in their environment.

8. **Time.** Although an understanding of time develops slowly, children gradually learn concepts about seasons, past and future events, and the order of activities as they work with tasks and communicate their results to adults and others.

Structure of the Class Day

The High/Scope model emphasizes that the best learning experiences occur when children have a consistent classroom routine. Adults carefully plan special events such as field trips and discuss them with children ahead of time. This adherence to a planned sequence of events helps give children the control they need to learn successfully from the people and materials in their environment (Hohmann & Weikart, 1995).

Quality materials lead to active engagement and learning.

A typical half-day classroom schedule in the High/Scope program includes the following elements:

- **Planning time.** The day begins with time in small groups where children plan their work experiences with the assistance of an adult. Children have consistent opportunities to share their ideas and plans with High/Scope professionals and then learn to act on their choices.

- **Work time.** This period is generally the longest time children spend in any one activity during the day. Children select their activities for this time based on the planning conducted earlier and engage in the tasks at their own pace. During this time, High/Scope professionals observe and assist where needed.

- **Clean-up time.** This period offers an opportunity to restore order to the environment following work experiences. It also becomes additional learning time as children sort and return materials to their proper storage locations.

- **Recall time.** Children have the opportunity each day to summarize what they have learned during the work period. This recall period helps bring closure to the earlier planning and work times and assists children in building stronger conceptual understandings.

- **Small-group time.** Adults carefully plan structured activities and conduct them with four or five children in a small-group setting. They encourage children to participate in activities that build upon their backgrounds and experiences and add new cognitive understandings.

- **Large-group circle time.** This component of the class day consists of 10 to 15 minutes of games, songs, finger plays, sharing, and a short story. Circle time helps children develop group social skills as they engage in a variety of motivating experiences.

A full-day High/Scope program includes several additional elements (Hohmann, 1996). One of these is outside time. Being outdoors provides children with additional opportunities for play and work experiences in that setting. Full-day programs also include mealtimes where further occasions for learning are presented. Most full-day programs provide both breakfast and lunch for children. Finally, a nap/quiet time gives children the chance to rest and prepare for further learning later in the day.

The High/Scope Professional's Role

Early childhood professionals in a High/Scope program work with children to strengthen their overall development, while specifically emphasizing cognitive skills. There are four key components to these interactions with young children:

- **Adults as active learners.** High/Scope educators are active learners themselves as they work with children. By modeling excitement and interest in learning, they encourage children to do the same. This attitude also helps them prepare more interesting activities and materials for use in the program.

- **Careful observers.** Early childhood professionals need to make thorough, detailed observations of children to understand their developmental abilities and plan motivating activities for them. The High/Scope program has developed an observation guide called the Child Observation Record (COR) to assist teachers in this effort (Schweinhart, 1993).
- **Environmental planning and organization.** A key role for High/Scope professionals is preparing the environment for students' work and play activities. Although adults maintain overall consistency in the environment, children need new materials to stimulate their growth and development. Minor modifications each week help keep children involved in their school day.
- **Positive interactions with children.** High/Scope professionals work hard to communicate effectively with children. These positive interactions include being a good listener, asking challenging open-ended questions, and motivating children to reach higher levels of understanding.

Research on the High/Scope Model

From its beginnings as the Perry Preschool Project, the High/Scope program has conducted research on program effectiveness. Because of the diligence of the program founders, some of the best long-term research on the effectiveness of early childhood programs for children from low-income families comes from High/Scope. Having kept track of former students for almost 50 years, the program research provides convincing evidence of the values of early education. Schweinhart et al. (2005) summarize these findings from interviews with former students who are now adults:

- A higher percentage of High/Scope participants had completed high school than non-program students.
- Fewer students had been arrested.
- More adults from High/Scope had a job at age 40 than those not attending the program.
- Program graduates had median annual earnings that were $5,000 higher as adults.
- Nearly three times as many former students owned their own homes.
- Fewer female students had treatment for mental impairment or had to repeat a grade.

These results translate into considerable savings to the public. Lower costs for special education, jails, and police interventions; higher income levels; and less reliance on welfare services all mean that early intervention programs can be highly cost-effective. Schweinhart (2003) estimates a savings of approximately $7 for every dollar invested in early intervention programs.

Children Served

In 1962, David Weikart's original intervention program was designed to serve young children in what was originally called the Perry Preschool Project. Over time, however, the children being served spanned all ages within the early education range. In addition to preschool children, the High/Scope model has been successfully used in these settings:

- **Infant/toddler programs.** High/Scope has developed and published teaching strategies, key experiences, and assessment tools that are used in infant/toddler settings that parallel those originally designed for preschool children (Post & Hohmann, 2000).
- **Primary education settings.** The High/Scope model has proven effective in both public and private primary school settings. Active learning and a balance of teacher-planned and child-planned activities are hallmarks of the primary model.

 # Waldorf Education

The first Waldorf school began in 1919 at the Waldorf-Astoria cigarette factory in Stuttgart, Germany, as a school for employees' children. Waldorf education was the brainchild of Rudolf Steiner (1861–1925), who had a strong interest in the spiritual dimensions of education (Ullrich, 1994). This first school defied the educational conventions of the time by educating boys and girls together, being open to all children regardless of educational background, and including preschool through high school-aged children (Edwards, 2002).

Steiner founded a new spiritual movement he termed Anthroposophy, which is a unique blend of science and mysticism. His spiritual beliefs had a strong impact on the educational program he developed. This mystical quality can be seen in the following quote about Waldorf early childhood education: "The first seven years of life are a time of tremendous growth and transformation. Having left the spiritual worlds, the child begins the journey of incarnation, and the soul and spirit have to struggle to adapt to the vessel of the body" (Waldorf Early Childhood Education Association of North America, 2010).

Although Waldorf education is still a relatively small program in the United States, with 147 schools nationwide (Association of Waldorf Schools of North America, 2010), Waldorf education has some famous parents, including Paul Newman, Joe Namath, John Delorean, and Mikhail Baryshnikov. Waldorf schools numbered more than 900 worldwide in 2010 (Waldorf Schools, 2010).

Theoretical Perspectives

Steiner believed that there was a unity among the spirit, body, and mind and that good education was a tool for keeping these three elements in balance (Edwards, 2002). His educational philosophy is based on the notion that children pass through three 7-year periods of growth, each of which has its own special needs for learning. According to Steiner, a child's growth spirals ever upward from birth through age 21 (Ullrich, 1994). The three periods he defined are these:

- **Birth to age 7.** Children learn through imitation and doing. Imaginary play is seen as the most significant way in which young children develop intellectually, physically, and emotionally. Oral language (not written), storytelling, and songs are at the heart of the educational curriculum for this age (Schwartz, 2008).
- **Ages 7 to 14.** Children learn best when they stay together as a group for this entire period and work with the same Waldorf professional. This leads to a very close-knit classroom unit that grows together intellectually and socially

through an adult-directed curriculum that operates without the use of any standard textbooks. Adults are expected to develop an integrated, multisensory curriculum that relies more on oral listening and memory than is typical for other programs for this age (Edwards, 2002).

- **Ages 14 to 21.** For the high school years and beyond, Steiner believed that young people were ready to use rational and abstract thinking as they focused on ethics, social responsibility, and the content of rigorous academic subjects.

Role of the Waldorf Professional

The adult's role in Waldorf education changes with the ages of the children. Those working with younger children are more nurturing and supportive, while Waldorf educators working with older children encourage more independence on the part of their students. Adults at the preschool and primary levels are responsible for carefully preparing the environment, with a particular emphasis on color, natural materials, and props that have minimal details for imaginative play (Schwartz, 2008). The environment at this age should be a space that is uncluttered, warm and homelike, and aesthetically pleasing.

In Waldorf education, particularly at the primary level, the teacher is a performer as s/he leads or models whole-group activities that integrate academics, the arts, and a sense of spirituality (Edwards, 2002). The teacher is also the spiritual/ moral leader of the class and is expected to create a sense of community and model caring and concern (Ullrich, 1994). Teachers encourage childhood wonder, curiosity, belief in goodness, and a love of beauty (Edwards, 2002). Those interested in becoming a Waldorf teacher attend Rudolf Steiner College in California for training (Rudolf Steiner College, 2010).

Sample Teaching Strategies

While some of the language used by Rudolf Steiner and other Waldorf educators appears mystical and is at times difficult to understand, a number of techniques used in Waldorf classrooms are easily applied to all early childhood settings (Costello-Dougherty, 2009). These include the following:

1. **Greet students with a handshake.** Look each child directly in the eye and welcome them as they enter the program at the beginning of the day. This helps children understand that adults care deeply about them and want children to develop to their full potential.

2. **Create a buddy system.** Have older children pair up with younger students to develop strong peer relationships. This helps them develop strong self-esteem and assists in social and emotional development.

3. **Integrate art into the curriculum.** Art presents a wonderful opportunity for children to clarify their understandings in all curriculum areas. It provides young children with creative experiences that enhance their sense of wonder and their appreciation of beauty in the world.

4. **Plan for gardening and outdoor nature activities.** Outdoor activities such as gardening and nature walks are great ways for valuable science learning to take place. They provide sensory experiences that cannot be duplicated in any other setting.

5. **Incorporate music and rhythm activities.** These are additional strategies for integrating the curriculum through the arts. Both rhythmic movement to music and music making integrate mind, body, and spirit in Waldorf programs.

6. **Promote active movement for quality learning.** Adults in Waldorf education work hard to get children physically moving as they learn. For example, a Waldorf educator might encourage counting out numbers by tapping feet as children begin learning about multiplication in a primary setting.

7. **Use storytelling for developing basic conceptual understandings.** For example, the adult might introduce an arithmetic operation through an oral storytelling experience in which the numbers are characters in the story (Edwards, 2002).

 # The Bank Street Model

A fourth important model for early care and education called the **Bank Street approach** was developed at the Bank Street College in New York. Initially designed in the 1930s at what was then called the Bureau of Educational Experiments, this model continues to have a strong influence on theory and practice in the field.

Although this program also promotes a constructivist approach similar to that of the High/Scope curriculum, Bank Street is best described as a **developmental interactionalist model** (Weber, 1984). The Bank Street curriculum addresses all aspects of child development in a setting that encourages both interpersonal interactions and learning experiences that integrate intellectual, social, and emotional understandings.

Theoretical Underpinnings

The Bank Street approach identifies three major theoretical perspectives that form the foundation for the model (Mitchell & David, 1992):

- **The psychoanalytic perspective.** The writings of Freud and others, particularly Erik Erikson, clearly describe children's psychological, social, and emotional development. This information guides the Bank Street professional's planning for these aspects of development.

- **Piaget's cognitive developmental theory.** Piaget's ideas on how human intelligence changes during the early childhood years are the basis for this component of the Bank Street curriculum.

- **John Dewey and progressive education.** Dewey emphasized the importance of social learning experiences and the value of active involvement of children in the educational process. Both of these ideas strongly influence the Bank Street model.

Program Goals

The Bank Street program has four broad goals (DeVries & Kohlberg, 1987). The first of these is to *enhance competence*. This goal includes building not only children's knowledge and skills but also the more subjective elements of competence, such as self-esteem, resourcefulness, and resilience.

A second broad goal of the program is to *develop individuality*, or identity. Adults encourage children to develop qualities of selfhood. Bank Street professionals assist children in the process of learning what makes them unique and help them to build on their individual strengths. The program fosters an attitude of independence by allowing children to make choices, develop preferences, and learn from their mistakes.

A third goal is to *positively influence socialization.* Young children need considerable practice and assistance as they work through the complex process of becoming social beings. Learning to recognize and respond appropriately to the points of view of others is one major challenge they face. The ability to use a variety of communication strategies to interact positively with adults and other children in work and play situations requires much additional practice.

The final goal of the Bank Street model is an *integration of functions.* Children are guided in understanding the interrelatedness of things and people in the world around them. For example, rather than compartmentalizing the teaching of mathematics or science, the Bank Street program integrates these subjects into the study of topics such as recycling or aging. In an influential new book called *Mind in the Making,* Galinsky (2010) suggests that one of the seven essential life skills that all children need is the ability to make connections. Bank Street educators who are helping children understand the interrelatedness of things and people in their world are building this essential life skill.

Governing Principles

Understanding child development and then using that information in the planning of activities for young children is essential in the Bank Street model. Mitchell and David (1992) identify six general developmental principles that guide the program:

- **Child development is a complex process.** Some general concepts are helpful in describing this process, such as stages of development and moving from simple to more complex behaviors. It is important to realize, however, that each child differs from the average and that development varies among children.

- **Behavior varies and is often unpredictable.** Although it would be nice to have a checklist that allows us to predict what children will do next, many factors may cause children to engage in more mature behavior today and in less-advanced interactions tomorrow.

- **Developmental progress includes both stability and instability.** Periods of stability allow children the opportunity to consolidate their understandings and refine concepts. As children approach developmental milestones and are challenged to develop new understandings, they face times of uncertainty and instability in their knowledge. Both are necessary for healthy development.

- **Motivation to learn about the world lies within each child.** Given an exciting environment that can be freely explored, children will actively engage in learning about the world around them.

- **Developing a sense of self is essential.** Critical to overall development is the process of learning about capabilities and understanding one's uniqueness. Children who develop a positive self-concept become active, independent learners.

- **Conflict is necessary for development.** As children mature, their ideas and wants come into conflict with others. Children need strategies for dealing with these natural conflicts in positive ways.

Curriculum and Materials

The activities and materials found in a Bank Street program reflect the goals and principles previously described. One essential characteristic is a learning environment that allows children to choose their preferred activities and materials (DeVries & Kohlberg, 1987). Areas for building with blocks, dress-up, sand and water play, books, and art are typical in this model. During much of the class day, children are allowed to choose the activities and materials that they want to use for play and work experiences.

Although commercial toys and equipment are common in Bank Street programs, classrooms also use adult-made and child-made materials (Mitchell & David, 1992). Some simple rhythm instruments made by the Bank Street professional, for example, could be selected by children during choice time for exploration and use. In addition, adults in the Bank Street program encourage children to make their own books, read them to others, and then place them in the book area for others to enjoy.

Another important characteristic of the Bank Street model is its emphasis on an integrated curriculum (Weber, 1984). Rather than attempting to separate mathematics, science, and literacy topics, for example, Bank Street professionals work hard to integrate these content areas into experiences that focus on thematic studies that are of interest to children. A field trip to a local park for a group of second-grade children might lead to a discussion of the problems associated with litter and the broader topic of what happens to our garbage. The teacher in this primary setting could develop this theme into several activities that combine mathematical, science, and literacy skills. The *Developmentally Appropriate Practice* feature in this section describes another example of integrating the curriculum through a woodworking project.

Strong two-way communication with families is yet another valued component of the Bank Street program (Mitchell & David, 1992). Families are important allies in the educational process. They provide adults with much useful information about attitudes, feelings, and stressors while assisting in essential ways with developmental progress. Effective communication between home and school is the foundation needed for taking full advantage of all that families have to offer.

Children Served

Like most of the other models described in this chapter, the Bank Street program began as an option for prekindergarten children. Over time, it has expanded its focus (Bank Street College, 2010) to include the following:

- **Infancy Institute.** Each year, the Bank Street College offers a 3-day conference that addresses issues related to infants and toddlers, and their families. It is designed to help those who work with this age group to implement Bank Street principles in their work.

- **Center for Emotionally Responsive Practice.** Focusing primarily on school-age children, the center helps schools address the social and emotional development of children and the relationships of these aspects of development with the child's learning potential.

- **Professional Development for After-School Program.** This Bank Street program provides professional development opportunities for after-school educators. The focus is on providing curriculum and instruction strategies in the arts and literacy.

- **Learning in the Natural World.** Bank Street now offers the Tiorati Workshop for Environmental Learning. It emphasizes integrating environmental science methods and concepts across the curriculum.

Developmentally Appropriate Practice . . .
INTEGRATING THE CURRICULUM THROUGH WOODWORKING

Adults implementing the Bank Street approach to teaching and learning might well include woodworking in the program as a means of encouraging learning in several subject-matter areas. The following example highlights how woodworking could be used to promote an integrated curriculum in a second-grade classroom:

It is springtime and Mr. Hanson's second-grade class has just returned from a nature hike around the school neighborhood. As students reflect on what they observed at group time, many mention the birds they saw and heard. They ask questions about what birds eat and where they live. It is evident that this is a good topic for future study. After further discussion, children begin to show an increased interest in birdhouses. Several were seen on the walk through the neighborhood.

Mr. Hanson agrees to set up an area in the classroom next week where children can build their own birdhouses from scraps of wood. In preparation for this opportunity, interested children are to collect information about local birds and their natural habitat. Others will research the design features of different birdhouses and the construction challenges of each. During independent work time over the next several days, children excitedly locate information on the Internet, check books out of the school library to read, interview family members and neighbors who have birdhouses, sketch their plans, and complete step-by-step directions for constructing their birdhouses.

At a later class meeting, the children decide that once the construction process is complete, they will work on donating the birdhouses to interested groups around the community. The local senior citizens center, community churches, and the city parks department are mentioned as possibilities. These organizations will need to be contacted once the birdhouses are finished.

As students prepare for and complete their woodworking activities, they are engaging in an integrated curriculum. With the assistance of Mr. Hanson and other students in the class, children are reading, writing, learning about their local community, engaging in scientific inquiry, and using a variety of mathematics skills. These learning opportunities flow naturally from the tasks of preparing for and building the birdhouses.

Following are some other possible integrated learning experiences using woodworking that could be included in a primary classroom:

- **Putting on a class play.** In addition to constructing the props needed for the play, students can practice reading and writing and engage in dramatic activities.

- **Building a scale model of a local building or landmark.** Students can research local architecture/history, practice measuring and computational skills, learn about proportion, and better understand building principles as they construct their model.

- **Constructing classroom gardening boxes.** If students are interested in gardening activities, constructing gardening boxes that can be filled with soil and kept in the classroom will allow opportunities to engage in scientific inquiry as they observe, record, and make hypotheses about the growth of plants over time.

The Reggio Emilia Program

In recent years, the preschool programs of Reggio Emilia, Italy, have captured the imaginations of early childhood educators in the United States. These programs got their start shortly after World War II, under the leadership of Loris Malaguzzi. He was generally credited with being the founder and leading proponent of the Reggio Emilia approach prior to his death in 1994. Using what is referred to as a **project approach** because of the emphasis on in-depth investigations of topics of interest to children and teachers, the educational experiences these preschools provide are truly remarkable (Hendrick, 2004). With adult help, children in Reggio Emilia schools document their learning through insightful and detailed conversations, photographs, and artwork. The *Technology Explorations and Activities* feature in this section describes in more detail the use of digital cameras as one method for documenting children's learning.

Technology Explorations and Activities . . .
USING A DIGITAL CAMERA TO DOCUMENT CHILD LEARNING

Digital cameras are a way of life today for most people. They are easy to use, inexpensive (once the camera is purchased), and compatible with a variety of other electronic media. Young children can quickly learn to use them, and since a poor quality picture is easily deleted and replaced by a better one, adults find it much easier to just hand over the camera for children to use.

Digital cameras are being used regularly in early childhood classrooms for everything from identifying classroom procedures (Wacona Elementary School, 2010) to teaching science lessons (Neumann-Hinds, 2007). The Reggio Emilia program model discussed in this chapter would also suggest that using the digital camera to document student learning would be a productive use of that technology. Digital photographs of projects that show the starting points, processes used, and end results of efforts are an excellent way for children to show others their thinking and learning.

Research, Reflect, and Respond

1. Spend some time searching the Internet for information about using digital cameras with young children. Describe the different ideas you found useful.

2. Find and read about the project on dinosaurs presented later in this section on Reggio Emilia. Think about how you could use a digital camera as one of several tools to document learning for this project. Discuss your thinking with others and then compile a comprehensive list of ideas for documenting learning with the digital camera.

An exhibit that includes photographs and projects completed by children in the Reggio Emilia schools and titled "The Hundred Languages of Children" has been touring the United States for the past several years and provides many examples of experiences in the Reggio Emilia classroom. After 25 years touring as "The Hundred Languages of Children," the exhibit now is titled "The Wonder of Learning" (Reggio Children, 2010).

> Few walk away unmoved by its visual impact. They remember the carefully selected photographs, most often grouped in sequences, that serve as vibrant records of children's experiences and explorations as they investigate various aspects of a particular theme. Even more beguiling are the extraordinary pictures and objects made by the children themselves. (Hendrick, 1997, p. 28)

What makes the Reggio Emilia model so remarkable? According to program founders, it is a combination of fundamental ideas that must all be present for the model to be successful (Gandini, 1993). Many of these components are present in other programs for young children. The difference may be in the intensity with which they are applied in Reggio schools (Bredekamp, 1993). The following sections describe the key elements of this unique program.

The Environment

The physical space in a Reggio Emilia program is designed to foster communication and relationships. Children are encouraged to learn from each other, the adults, and families in a setting that is discovery-oriented and attractive to them. The basic message that Reggio Emilia professionals attempt to convey as they set up the environment is that learning is a pleasurable, social activity (Hendrick, 2004).

Reggio Emilia programs are full of children's own work. Although this is true of many early childhood settings in the United States, the differences are in the breadth and depth of these representations by children of what they have learned.

Paintings, collages, sculptures, drawings, mobiles, and photographs are present in every nook and cranny of the environment. They are displayed so that families, educators, and other children can better understand the process of children's thinking.

One special space found in the Reggio model is called the **atelier**. The program sets aside this special workshop area for recording in visual form what students learn as they engage in projects of their own choosing (Edwards, Gandini, & Forman, 1998). The atelier contains a wealth of tools and resource materials that children can use for their documentations. Under the direction of a trained specialist, children work cooperatively to construct summaries of their learning experiences.

Children, Families, and Reggio Emilia Professionals

Reggio Emilia professionals view children as active, curious, and eager learners. When interesting materials and activities are present and when adults give children thoughtful guidance, children can engage in quality educational experiences.

Families are considered essential in the Reggio Emilia approach and are expected to share responsibilities in educating children (Hendrick, 2004). Some families participate regularly in the program, while others are involved in special events or engage in educational activities planned specifically for them. The *Family Partnerships* feature in this section describes some simple strategies for providing families with the understandings they need to support child growth and development. Strong family support and communication will help you better meet the needs and interests of the young children you teach.

Reggio Emilia professionals are partners with children and families in the educational process. Careful observation and strong communication skills allow them to develop plans for assisting the learning experiences for each child in the program. In addition, adults see themselves as learners and continue to grow in understanding along with children.

Cooperation, Collaboration, and Organization

Additional key elements of the Reggio Emilia model are the cooperation and collaboration among staff members in each program and throughout the system (Gandini, 1993). Reggio Emilia professionals work in pairs in early childhood settings and view themselves as equal partners in gathering information about children and making plans to enhance children's growth and development. Through active cooperation, adults and program administrators make it possible for children to achieve the lofty goals of the program.

Cooperation and collaboration are more effective in a system that is highly organized. Reggio Emilia professionals work within a structured system that is designed to make planning and discussions about children more effective. The program sets aside a minimum of 6 hours each week for meetings of professional staff members, preparing the environment for children, meetings with families, and in-service training (Hendrick, 1997).

The Atelierista

A specialist trained in the visual arts and referred to as the **atelierista** is hired for each Reggio Emilia program. This atelierista works with the other school professionals and children to develop projects summarizing learning experiences (Edwards et al., 1998). The atelier (workshop/studio area), with its tools and art materials, is the focal point for the atelierista's efforts. By guiding other adults and children as they

Family Partnerships . . .
THE IMPORTANCE OF FAMILY EDUCATION

For much of American history, new families could rely on their own parents and/or extended family members to help them learn the many complex tasks associated with raising children. Families lived close to one another, and it was relatively easy to get advice and support.

As families have become more mobile, however, this support system is available less often. Assume, for example, that it is midnight and your infant daughter is coughing and crying from what is apparently a new cold. You would like some ideas about medicines that would be safe for her to take or things you could do to make your daughter more comfortable. Although you might call your family or a favorite aunt for advice if they were living in the same community, it is less likely that you would do so if they are living in a different part of the country and in a different time zone. The advice and support you need and want is just not as readily available.

Parenting is a very difficult job that can be made easier with the assistance of others who have experienced or are experiencing similar challenges. Because extended families are not as able to manage this task, you should consider taking time as an early childhood professional to create opportunities for family education. There are a variety of ways in which this could happen:

- **Informal sharing opportunities.** Family education can be as simple as having family members come together for a potluck dinner and then gather in groups of four or five to take some time to get to know one another, share their parenting concerns, and receive advice from others.

- **Parenting network.** You could also help set up a telephone/e-mail exchange network so that interested families could seek advice from others when needed.

- **Community parenting expert.** Every community has professionals whose job includes helping families be more effective in their many roles. You could invite an expert to come and share with your families.

- **Parenting resources.** Have a variety of parenting books and resources available for families to check out for further study at home. This would give families the opportunity to grow in their understanding of appropriate responses to childhood issues without bringing them together as a group.

1. What are your attitudes about helping future families deal with their parenting concerns? Do you think this is something you will enjoy or find a burden? Why do you feel this way?

2. Do you think early childhood professionals and programs should be involved in family education activities? What makes you think this way?

---

proceed through several refinements of their projects, the atelierista contributes significantly to the work efforts in Reggio Emilia programs.

The Importance of Documentation

A critical part of the Reggio Emilia model is the process of **documenting learning experiences** (Hendrick, 2003). Children are expected to describe for others the work they have accomplished and the processes they have used in discovering new knowledge. This documentation can take a variety of forms, including the following:

- **Transcriptions** of children's remarks and discussions.
- **Photographs** of activities in and around the classroom.
- **Art media representations** of experiences (group murals, sculptures, paintings, drawings, etc.).

Documentation serves several important functions (Hendrick, 2003). First, it helps families become more aware of children's learning and development. In addition, Reggio Emilia professionals use these representations of learning to better understand children and to assess their own teaching strategies. Reviewing documentation with others also encourages a sharing of ideas among adults and promotes professional growth. Children benefit as well, seeing that their efforts are valued by adults and consolidating their understandings by being able to communicate them to others.

Projects

A project can be defined as the extended study of a topic that is of interest to a group of children. It is an in-depth investigation of aspects of the topic that often takes place over a period of several weeks or months (Katz & Chard, 2000). Adults assist in the process by focusing the attention of children on those elements that are important for deeper understandings.

Although the Reggio Emilia program is a recent example of the project approach in early education, the methods have been a part of educational experiences since at least the 1920s and the work of John Dewey. The "open education" movement in the United States in the 1960s and 1970s relied on project work. Also, the writings and work of Lilian Katz (Katz & Chard, 2000) and others (see the online journal *Early Childhood Research and Practice* for examples) have also focused on project learning in the United States.

Four key steps are involved in implementing project work:

- **Selecting a topic.** This is a very important step that generally requires considerable guidance from the early childhood professional. The topic possibilities are limited only by the imaginations of children and adults but should be based on children's own firsthand experiences. They should also be topics that children can investigate in the school setting.

- **Beginning the project.** Adults encourage children to share their own understanding of the topic through drawings, writings, or dramatic play. This helps everyone involved start with a common understanding of the issue being studied.

- **Doing the project.** Children and early childhood professionals engage in gathering new information on the topic primarily through real-world experiences. Taking field trips, carefully observing and manipulating objects, and talking directly with people who have additional information on the topic can all be productive ways of collecting new knowledge. In-depth projects often last several weeks and captivate the interests of both children and adults. Ideas for these projects come from the experiences of both children and adults and lead children to an advanced understanding of the world around them.

- **Ending the project.** Children need procedures for consolidating the new information they have gathered. They can summarize what they have learned through artwork, photographs, displays, or a discussion with others not involved in the project. The *Developmentally Appropriate Practice* feature in this section describes in more detail the procedures children use to document their accomplishments.

Hendrick (1997) describes how children and adults in a Reggio Emilia program developed a project related to birds on the playground. The Reggio Emilia professionals remembered how children during the previous school year were very interested in promoting birds visiting the playground and had built a small lake and birdhouses as projects. The adults then prepared questions and possibilities to present to children to see if they were interested in following up on these earlier efforts.

> Then they had the first meeting with the children. The children's conversation was full of ideas and surprises as, in the course of it, they became more and more involved. First, they explored the idea of repairing what had been constructed the previous year, and then they thought of improving the

Developmentally Appropriate Practice . . .
DOCUMENTING PROJECT WORK

A well-known project from the Reggio Emilia program dealt with the topic of dinosaurs (Rankin, 1993). After adults realized that their children had an interest in dinosaurs and suggested taking it up as a project, several children chose to participate in an investigation that lasted for 44 separate sessions over a 4-month period. The Reggio Emilia professionals and the atelierista first determined children's beginning level of knowledge about dinosaurs, then helped them find more information to broaden their understanding. After investigating the topic for several sessions, children were ready to begin some initial documentation of their learning. By vote, children selected the Tyrannosaurus Rex as the dinosaur they wanted to create using materials available to them in the atelier. A group of four girls handled this step in the following manner:

> The girls chose styrofoam as their medium. This material turned out to be rather easy to work with as it was easy to handle and the shape and size of the styrofoam pieces often suggested to them different parts of the dinosaur. They had to ask for Roberta's (the Atelierista's) help only at specific times; she did some things they were unable to do, such as attaching pieces of foam in a stable way with a piece of wire. A satisfying, three-dimensional, approximately four-foot high, highly decorated Tyrannosaurus Rex resulted, along with a stronger friendship among these particular girls. (Rankin, 1993, p. 198)

Some other possible ways of documenting learning in this dinosaur project might include these:

- **Drawings.** Children could draw their understanding of the Tyrannosaurus Rex, giving dimensions, naming parts, providing skeletal diagrams, and depicting such things as sleeping and eating habits.
- **Slide show.** Children could download clip art from the Internet and combine them into a slide show to share with others.
- **Videotape.** Children could create a script (much like a play) in which they described what they had learned about the Tyrannosaurus Rex. By videotaping their efforts, they could document their learning and share it with others.

---

area by adding several amenities for the birds to make them feel welcome in their playground. Finally, they became very enthusiastic about the idea expressed by one child of constructing an amusement park for the birds on the school's playground. (Hendrick, 1997, p. 23)

This discussion led to several children drawing what they thought should be included in the amusement park for birds. The adults discussed the idea further and presented more questions and suggestions to the children, and gradually the idea began to take shape. A project was born and eventually implemented by children and adults in the Reggio Emilia program.

Children Served

Loris Malaguzzi, the founder of the Reggio approach, first implemented the program with children ages 3 to 6. Today, the program includes the following groups:

- **Prekindergarten education.** In the United States, this remains the predominant age group served using the Reggio approach. In particular, projects and documenting children's learning are components that are becoming increasingly evident in these settings.
- **Infant/toddler programs.** In Italy, Malaguzzi and other early educators introduced programs in 1970 for infants and toddlers beginning at 3 months of age (Hendrick, 2004). These programs are beginning to have an influence on the curriculum and teaching that occurs in infant/toddler settings in the United States.

Observing Development...
PROGRAM CHARACTERISTICS

Choose one of the age groups within early childhood (infants/toddlers, preschoolers, or primary-age children) and *observe* program characteristics. Use the following sample observation as a format for your own observation. Include only what you see and hear, saving your interpretations for the reflections that follow the sample observation:

Sunny Day Preschool, April 23, 11–11:30 a.m.

Classroom materials	Classroom organization	Adult/child interactions
1. Dramatic play center with dress-up clothes, hats, scarves, belts, and shoes. 2. . . .	1. Centers: art, music, dress-up, blocks, group area, manipulatives, science. 2. Space for adults/families.	1. "J., you need to put the blocks back on the shelf and join us for group time." 2. A. is using the teacher-made game in the science area with adult assistance.

Reflect and Apply

1. Based on your observations, do the toys and materials used by children resemble any that were described in this chapter for different model programs? What were the similarities and differences you noticed between the toys and materials in the model programs discussed and the ones you observed?

2. Did you observe adult behaviors that were similar to the ones described in the model programs presented in this chapter? Discuss what you found with classmates.

3. Would you consider the program you observed to be closer in format to one of the model programs described in this chapter than to others? What made you think this?

Having read about different models of early learning, take a few minutes now to read the *Observing Development* feature that follows. Consider going into an early childhood setting and observing for characteristics of the models presented.

summary

The Montessori Program

In Montessori education, children engage in self-selected work experiences in an environment that is carefully prepared by the early childhood professional. Montessori materials are designed to be used by children in specific ways that are first demonstrated by the educator.

The High/Scope Curriculum

The High/Scope program is based on Piaget's theory and emphasizes the importance of learning through direct experiences with people and objects. High/Scope professionals help children develop deeper cognitive understandings through the plan-do-review sequence.

Waldorf Education

Waldorf education began with the work of Rudolf Steiner and emphasizes t. blending of science and mysticism. Professionals using the Waldorf approach in early childhood settings work to create a space that is uncluttered, warm and home-like, and aesthetically pleasing.

The Bank Street Model

The Bank Street approach stresses the interrelatedness of all aspects of the child's development and the importance of enhancing the development of the whole child. This approach emphasizes the use of an integrated curriculum that is created by the Bank Street professional based on the needs and interests of individual children.

The Reggio Emilia Program

In the Reggio Emilia program, children engage in extensive project work that allows them to study topics of interest in great depth. Children document the results of their studies through detailed artwork or another form of media to summarize what was learned so that they can share this knowledge with others.

for reflection and discussion

1. Choose one of the early childhood program models described in this chapter and research it more carefully. Share what you found with others.
2. Compare and contrast two of the models in this chapter. What are the similarities and differences between the two? Which of the two models best fits your current thinking about how you want to interact with children and why?
3. Which program model did you like the least and why?
4. Make a list of ideas presented in the various program models that were new to you. Choose three that you would like to try with children. Discuss these ideas with others.

MyEducationLab

Go to Topic 5: Program Models in the MyEducationLab (www.myeducationlab.com) for *Teaching Young Children* where you can:

- Find learning outcomes for Program Models along with the national standards that connect to these outcomes.
- Complete Assignments and Activities that can help you more deeply understand the chapter content.
- Apply and practice your understanding of the core teaching skills identified in the chapter with the Building Teaching Skills and Dispositions learning units.
- Check your comprehension on the content covered in the chapter with the Study Plan. Here you will be able to take a chapter quiz, receive feedback on your answers, and then access Review, Practice, and Enrichment activities to enhance your understanding of chapter content.

4

Understanding How a Child Develops and Learns

IN THIS CHAPTER YOU WILL

- Learn about developmentally appropriate practice.
- Gain insight into the relationships among child development, learning, and teaching.
- Study differing perspectives on development.
- Review characteristics of children at different ages and stages of development.
- Identify strategies for learning about children and their development.

It is time for another school year to begin, and you sit down to study the class list for your second-grade students. Patrick's name is familiar to you. Other teachers have warned that he is a handful and that you should be prepared for a very busy, bright, sensitive, easily excitable child. Patrick has been tested and qualifies for the school's gifted program, yet often is off-task and gets into trouble. But Patrick's name is not the only one you recognize. Of the remaining 25 names on the list, three are on medication for attention-deficit/hyperactivity disorder, two are receiving special education assistance, and four more come to you with very low reading scores. Interestingly enough, this is considered a typical classroom. As their teacher, what can you do to prepare for this diverse mix of children? How will you meet Patrick's need for challenging experiences while working effectively with the children in your class who have special needs? The remaining students on the roster also have diverse abilities that require your teaching expertise. This is shaping up to be another challenging and exciting year.

As difficult and challenging as the preceding scenario appears, this classroom experience is manageable. Early childhood educators across the country face these dilemmas each year and consistently find creative ways to deal with them. One essential ingredient for success in this process is an understanding of the overall patterns of child development and learning. The more you know about normal child development and variations from these typical patterns, the better able you will be to plan appropriate learning experiences for your early learning setting. In the same way, an understanding of different theoretical perspectives on how children learn and develop allows you to see children through new eyes and create lessons and activities that meet the needs of all your children. The *Technology Explorations and Activities* feature that follows provides ideas on how to access child development information on the Internet.

Technology Explorations and Activities . . .
INTERNET RESOURCES ON CHILD DEVELOPMENT

In this chapter, you will learn about developmentally appropriate practice, important child development theories, and the similarities and differences in development between children. Take a moment and choose one of the topics in the chapter that is of particular interest to you. Do an Internet search on that topic to gather more information. Be sure to think carefully about the sites you review. Some will have more credibility than others, and you will want to use sources that can provide the best, most accurate information.

Research, Reflect, and Respond

1. First, critique the Internet sites that were available on the topic you chose. How would you assess the quality of the sites you reviewed? What criteria did you use to determine the quality of the site?

2. What did you learn about the topic that you chose? Share your findings with classmates.

3. Based on this exercise, how helpful do you think the Internet will be to you as a future early childhood professional? Why do you think this?

The Developmentally Appropriate Classroom

Basing the curriculum on an in-depth understanding of child development and learning is often referred to as **developmentally appropriate practice**. Rather than focusing first on what is to be learned, the early childhood professional in a developmentally appropriate classroom begins by working hard to understand the developmental abilities of children and then makes decisions about what should be taught. This philosophical approach to teaching and learning is at the heart of high-quality early childhood programs. The National Association for the Education of Young Children (NAEYC) has been the leader in promoting developmentally appropriate practice through its position statements and books on the subject. To date, NAEYC has published three editions of a book outlining the characteristics of developmentally appropriate practice (Bredekamp, 1987; Bredekamp & Copple, 1997; Copple & Bredekamp, 2009) for children birth through age 8.

One of the features found in each chapter of this text is titled *Developmentally Appropriate Practice.* It presents real-world examples of what developmentally appropriate practice looks like in early childhood settings. NAEYC's latest book on the subject (Copple & Bredekamp, 2009) highlights many more examples of developmentally appropriate practice for infants and toddlers (0–3), preschool children (3–5), kindergarten children (5–6), and children in the primary grades (6–8).

Developmentally appropriate practice has three dimensions (Copple & Bredekamp, 2009). The first is referred to as *age appropriateness,* or what is suitable for the age of the child based on developmental averages (called *norms*) for that age. When a kindergarten teacher selects a game that requires the child to count to 10, she is using knowledge of age appropriateness to choose an activity within the developmental abilities of the typical 5-year-old. The second dimension to developmentally appropriate practice is called *individual appropriateness.* This takes into account what is appropriate for each child based on his unique personality and experiences. When David's mom shares with you her son's interest in collecting rocks, and you decide to have some books in your third-grade classroom about different kinds of rocks, you are using individual appropriateness as you plan your curriculum. The final dimension is the *social and cultural context.* Early childhood professionals are

MyEducationLab

Visit the MyEducationLab for *Teaching Young Children* to enhance your understanding of chapter concepts with a personalized Study Plan. You'll also have the opportunity to hone your teaching skills through video- and case-based Assignments and Activities and Building Teaching Skills and Disposition lessons.

knowledgeable of the home lives and community experiences of children and families and build on these contexts as they plan activities in their programs. Knowing about student connections with homeless families, reading a book on the topic, and discussing its implications is an example of using this social and cultural context to plan a part of the program day.

Developmentally appropriate programs share four important characteristics that are summarized in Figure 4–1. The first essential element is that *learning is viewed as an active process*. Children in a developmentally appropriate program are busy exploring their indoor and outdoor environments and interacting with other children and adults. Play is a vital element of this active learning. Bredekamp (1987) states it this way: "child-initiated, child-directed, teacher-supported play is an essential component of developmentally appropriate practice" (Bredekamp, 1987, p. 3).

Another important characteristic of developmentally appropriate practice is that it *considers all aspects of the child's development*. The child's physical, emotional, and social development are valued just as highly as intellectual development. All areas of development are integrated into the activities planned for the early childhood program (Epstein, 2009). Similarly, understanding and preparing for children of all ability levels is critical in a developmentally appropriate classroom. The needs of children who are gifted as well as those with disabilities must be considered and met for a person to be an effective caregiver or teacher in early childhood settings.

Active family involvement in the educational process is also considered critical to developmentally appropriate practice. Families can contribute time and talents both at home and in the classroom to assist you in the learning process. Their knowledge of the child's developmental history provides you with invaluable information to assist in planning individually appropriate activities (Copple & Bredekamp, 2009).

Finally, early childhood professionals engaged in developmentally appropriate practice provide children with *multicultural, nonsexist materials and experiences* in their programs. The early childhood years are generally seen as critical to the development of multicultural and nonsexist attitudes (Maschinot, 2008). Derman-Sparks and Edwards (2010), in their book on anti-bias education, emphasize the importance of preparing the environment and providing experiences for young children so that they learn to be comfortable with themselves and the diverse people around them.

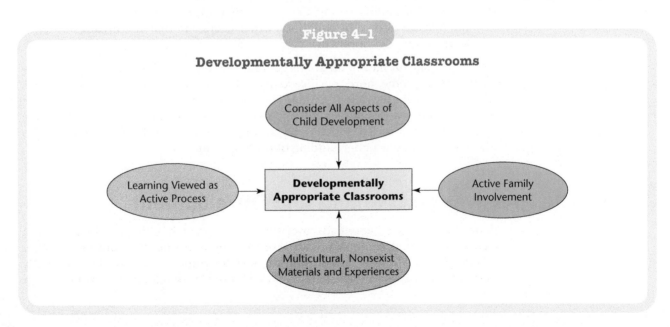

Figure 4–1

Developmentally Appropriate Classrooms

NAEYC (Copple & Bredekamp, 2009) has identified 12 key principles of child development that help early childhood professionals make good decisions about what constitutes developmentally appropriate practice:

1. All areas of development (physical, social, emotional, and cognitive) are closely related and influence one another.

2. Child development is a relatively orderly process, with new skills and abilities building on those previously learned.

3. Development proceeds at different rates for individual children and varies for different aspects of development within the same child.

4. The combination of biological maturation and childhood experiences leads to developmental growth and learning in young children.

5. The experiences of young children have a profound cumulative effect on their growth and development both during their early years and in later life. There are also critical periods during which certain kinds of development and learning are more readily accomplished.

6. Child development moves toward increasing complexity, greater self-regulation by the child, and higher levels of symbolic and representational thinking.

7. The combination of secure and consistent relationships with adults and positive peer relations leads to the highest levels of child development and learning.

8. The social and cultural settings in which children live and learn have a powerful impact on their development.

9. Children use a variety of active mental strategies to learn about the world around them. Consequently, adults need to use a wide range of strategies and interactions to support these differing ways of learning.

10. Play is an essential way in which young children develop self-regulation. It also is an important strategy for promoting language, intellectual, social, and emotional development.

11. Children develop and learn best when they are encouraged to work at a level just beyond their current abilities. They also need many opportunities to practice the skills they have just learned.

12. Persistence, initiative, and flexibility are attitudes and approaches to learning that are formed by childhood experiences and that also greatly influence learning and development.

Now that you have read about general principles of developmentally appropriate practice, some more specific examples may help you further understand this important concept for early learning. The *Developmentally Appropriate Practice* feature in this section gives examples for infants/toddlers, preschoolers, and school-age children engaged in developmentally appropriate practice. Read these examples now to enhance your understanding of this important concept.

Key Perspectives on Learning and Development

Many attempts have been made over the years to explain child development and learning. It should come as no surprise that there are no easy answers to these complex issues. However, armed with the insights from a variety of theorists, early educators can have a much better understanding of developmental processes in

Developmentally Appropriate Practice...
EXAMPLES OF DEVELOPMENTALLY APPROPRIATE PRACTICE

When caregivers and teachers of young children plan programs that are developmentally appropriate, they use an understanding of child growth and development to plan activities that take advantage of children's abilities and interests. Developmentally appropriate practice, in addition to being used to plan appropriate activities, also influences the materials used, the organization of the early childhood setting, guidance strategies, and the daily schedule. The following examples are intended to highlight the many different facets of developmentally appropriate practice in programs for infants/toddlers, preschool children, and those in the primary grades:

Infants/Toddlers

- Routines in the day, such as diaper changes, are made as enjoyable as possible by adults when they play simple games like "Peek-a-Boo," smile and talk to children, and have a positive attitude about these parts of the child's day.
- Pictures of infants and their families are hung on the walls so that children can see them. Adults take the time needed to talk to children and show them the pictures on a regular basis.
- Rattles, balls, squeeze toys, stuffed animals, and chewing toys are all available for children to grasp, drop, shake, chew, and manipulate.

Children Who Are 3-, 4-, and 5-Year-Olds

- Each week, early childhood professionals take materials out of each center and replace them with other interesting and developmentally challenging options. For example, in the manipulative center, five new puzzles of differing complexity are added to replace the ones that have been out for the past week. LEGO bricks are removed and Lincoln Logs are added in their place. Play dough is added as a new option for children to explore.
- During the past week, two children who are normally friendly to each other engaged in name-calling. Knowing this, the adult talks to both families to find out if they are aware of any problems or issues. The adult then reads a story at group time that brings up the topic of name-calling and discusses the issue with the class.
- The schedule each morning has been constructed to allow children 45 minutes in the morning for center time. During this period, children can choose the center they wish to attend and the activities that they want to engage in.

Children Who Are 6-, 7-, and 8-Year-Olds

- Knowing that most young children have difficulty sitting still for any length of time, teachers organize the schedule so that children have short breaks during academic periods to sing a song or get up and "get the wiggles out" by doing some simple stretching exercises.
- Children have the opportunity to work in groups several times each day so that they can learn from each other in a social context. In some instances, the teacher identifies the small groups, while in others the children themselves decide on groupings.
- Children are encouraged to engage in long-term projects that interest them. For example, three second-grade students who have a fascination with spiders are encouraged to develop a science report on this topic that they can share with the rest of the class.

---

childhood. Several key theorists stand out as providing perspectives that are essential for those who work in the field of early care and education. The works of Bowlby, Maslow, Gardner, Montessori, Vygotsky, Erikson, Piaget, and Bronfenbrenner provide a wealth of insights into child development and learning.

John Bowlby (1907–1990)

Early in his work in child guidance, British researcher John Bowlby became concerned about the ability of children raised in institutions to form lasting relationships with others. He developed an explanation for these behaviors that is referred to as an *ethological theory* (Thomas, 1985), because he studied relationship building within an evolutionary context. Bowlby proposed that children who grew up in orphanages were unable to love because they had not had the opportunity to form a solid attachment to a mother-figure early in life (Bowlby, 1969). This **attachment** is an emotional bond that occurs between two people and is essential to healthy relationships. Bowlby's work led him to suggest that this bonding process begins at birth and is well under way by about 6 months of age. During this time, infants typically attach themselves to their primary caregiver. From about 6 to 18 months, a young child separated from an attachment figure (often the mother) will be quite upset and engage in frequent crying. Fear of strangers is another common behavior during this period.

Damon (1983) identifies four stages in the attachment process:

- **Preattachment (Phase I)** lasts from birth to approximately 12 weeks of age. During this time, children make little distinction among people in their vicinity. They turn toward them, follow them with their eyes, and are generally more content when others are around.

- **Attachment-in-the-making (Phase II)** is the period from about 12 weeks to 6 months of age. At this point, children continue to be interested in people around them. They do not express concern when strangers are introduced during this period. The main change at this phase is that infants become more enthusiastic in their responses to their primary caregivers. They begin to clearly prefer that key person who is providing for their basic needs.

- **Clear-cut attachment (Phase III)** begins around 6 months of age and continues to about 2 years. Now, the young child clearly discriminates between people who provide primary care and others. As children begin to explore the world around them, they use the attached person as a secure base from which they move out to interact with people and things. The bonds between primary caregivers and the child are strong, and it is hard for the child to be separated from these attachment figures. Strangers produce more anxiety and concern for children during this phase as well.

- **Goal-corrected partnership (Phase IV)** finds the 2-year-old beginning to develop relationships with attached persons that are more complex and that start to recognize the goals and plans of the attached adults. Up to this point, the child has focused on having needs met, and the attachment bond is a rather one-sided relationship. Slowly, these partnerships mature, and the increased opportunities for reciprocal interactions benefit both the child and the adult.

Although infants typically develop a primary attachment to one caregiver, other attachment bonds can also be significant. Fathers, siblings, relatives, and other important caregivers can be attachment figures to the young child. Mary Ainsworth, a key American researcher to study attachment, describes these as *secondary attachments* (Ainsworth, 1973) and discusses the importance of these bonds in her work.

Bowlby (1969) also describes the more positive aspects of this attachment relationship. As the infant/toddler becomes more confident in his caregiver bonding, he becomes more able to use the attached person as a base from which to explore. If, for example, a mother and her 1-year-old son go to the park for the afternoon, the strongly attached child will typically remain close for a short time and then move off to briefly explore his new surroundings. This sense of confidence and competence allows young children to learn more about the world around them and continue to grow stronger both emotionally and intellectually.

Clearly, the attachment relationship has important implications for early childhood programs. Caregivers working with infants and toddlers need to be aware of the importance of attachment and be prepared to deal with the separation problems that many children will face when attached caregivers leave. Another issue is the effect of high turnover rates in child-care centers on secondary attachments. Raikes (1993) found that children who spent at least 9 months with a high-quality caregiver were more likely to develop a secure relationship and that attachment security was enhanced.

Abraham Maslow (1908–1970)

Maslow's ideas about human development are often referred to as *humanistic theory* (Schunk, 2008) because of the emphasis on the development of self. He proposes that people have needs that must be met in order to become and stay healthy. Maslow's **hierarchy of human needs** is summarized in Figure 4–2. The most basic needs are at the bottom and strongly impact each person's ability to meet higher-level needs. The first level of needs is often referred to as **deficiency needs** (Maslow, 1968) because their absence causes physical and/or emotional illness. The top two levels of needs are called **growth needs** and are the individual's attempts at becoming a more satisfied and healthy person. These needs can be described as follows:

- **Physiological needs.** The need for food, clothing, and water are considered the most basic. Life itself is not possible without having these needs met. Even when they are not met for short periods of time, the consequences can be

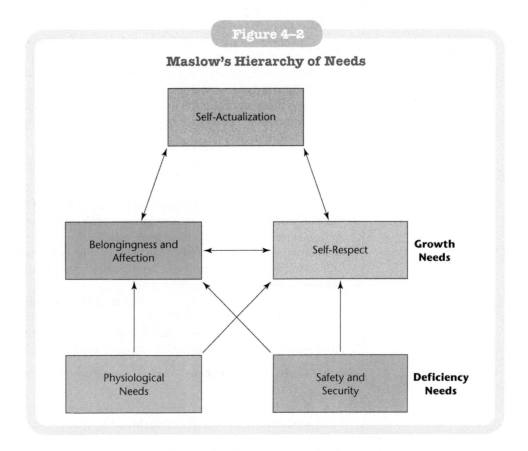

Figure 4–2

Maslow's Hierarchy of Needs

significant. For example, coming to an early learning program without break-fast is going to make it difficult for the young child to learn.

- **Safety and security needs.** All human beings also need to live in a safe and nonthreatening environment. Not having these needs met can cause serious physical or emotional health problems.
- **Belongingness and affection.** The need to be part of a group and feel loved is another important aspect of healthy living. When these needs are met, the individual is more able to reach out to support and encourage others.
- **Self-respect.** At a slightly higher level than belongingness and affection, every person needs to be valued by others and to have high self-esteem. Quality schooling experiences, when combined with the meeting of lower level needs, helps strengthen the young child's developing sense of self.
- **Self-actualization.** Maslow suggests that the highest point of every person's development occurs when he or she engages in self-actualization. For brief periods, individuals at this level perform at their maximum potential.

Maslow's theory, in addition to providing insights about the importance of human needs, provides hope for those who work with children from difficult circumstances. He suggests that when previously unmet basic needs are provided for, the child can move ahead and develop more normally. For example, the child who lives in a physically abusive home is under incredible stress and is likely to experience many difficulties in early childhood settings. Yet, if this child is removed from the abusive environment or if the abuse is eliminated, healthy growth is again possible. This encouraging perspective has support in the research literature (Skeels, 1966) and should help you be more optimistic toward even the most difficult circumstances.

Maslow's hierarchy of needs makes it clear that early learning is much more complicated than many people believe. Rather than focusing solely on academics, you must also be concerned with children's needs and must do your best to make sure these needs are consistently being met. Although it is not possible for any one person to meet all of the needs of each child, it is necessary to work to meet as many needs as possible. This must begin with an awareness of any needs of children that are not being met.

Howard Gardner (1943–)

As a faculty member at Harvard University, Howard Gardner has promoted a new view of intelligence in his many writings. Rather than seeing intelligence as a single, general capacity that each of us possesses, he suggests that people have at least eight distinct types of intelligence. This **theory of multiple intelligences** (Gardner, 1993) has prompted many to rethink the ways in which learning takes place and the techniques used to measure intelligence.

Gardner identifies eight intelligences that people possess to greater or lesser degrees (Gardner, 1983, 1999). In addition, he is currently researching the possibility of a ninth intelligence that is tentatively being called existential intelligence. Following are the eight identified intelligences:

- **Linguistic intelligence** is seen in people who speak or write creatively and with relative ease.
- **Logical-mathematical intelligence** can be seen in people who reason effectively and engage in high-level mathematical and scientific inquiry.

- **Spatial intelligence** allows people like engineers and sculptors to form refined mental models of the spatial world around them.
- **Musical intelligence** is found in people who are especially talented in singing or playing a musical instrument.
- **Bodily kinesthetic intelligence** helps people solve problems and fashion products using their body or body parts. Athletes and dancers have high bodily kinesthetic intelligence.

Two additional intelligences are referred to as the personal intelligences:

- **Interpersonal intelligence**, the first personal intelligence, is the ability to understand and interact with other people at a high level.
- **Intrapersonal intelligence**, the second personal intelligence, is the ability to have a deep understanding of self.
- **Naturalistic intelligence** was recently added to the original seven categories (Gardner, 1999). The person strong in this intelligence has special abilities in recognizing differences in the natural world.

Gardner's notion of multiple intelligences reminds us that children come to the early childhood setting with many different talents and skills that we as educators need to recognize and respect. Too often, schools prize linguistic and logical-mathematical intelligences and overlook the rest (Gardner, 1999). When we are sensitive to the other intelligences, children see themselves as more successful and competent. Recognizing a variety of intelligences also means that early childhood professionals must plan their curriculum differently.

Maria Montessori (1870–1952)

Maria Montessori developed what is referred to as a maturational theory of child development. Through her work with young children in Italy, she developed an intriguing theory and many practical strategies that have significantly influenced early care and education. Based on her readings and observations of children, Montessori believed that children pass through numerous sensitive periods during their progress to adulthood (Montessori, 1949/1967). She viewed these periods as genetically programmed blocks of time when young children are especially eager and able to master certain tasks. For example, Montessori suggested that there is a sensitive period for walking when the infant/toddler spends considerable time and effort in learning to walk. As most families can attest, it becomes almost an obsession for children as they struggle to master this important task.

Another important idea that Montessori promoted was the concept of the **unity of the mental and physical** (Lillard, 1996). Until Montessori, Western educational thought had been influenced by Descartes, who viewed people as divided into two parts: the intellectual and the physical. Her readings and work with children led Montessori to the opposite conclusion. That is, full development of the intellect is not possible without physical activity. Learning through doing is a cornerstone of Montessori's educational approach.

Montessori also believed that during the first 3 years of life children have **absorbent minds** (Montessori, 1967). Because children's minds are not fully formed during these years, she reasoned that they must learn in ways different from adults. Montessori believed that children unconsciously absorb information from the environment around them and, like a sponge, simply soak up information into their developing minds. This information also forms their minds in preparation for later, more advanced thought.

Montessori also believed that children pass through stages in their growth and development. She described five specific periods of growth:

- **Birth to age 3.** During this period, children unconsciously absorb information from the world around them.
- **Age 3 to 6.** Gradually, children bring the knowledge of the unconscious to a conscious level.
- **Age 6 to 9.** Children build the academic and artistic skills necessary for success in life.
- **Age 9 to 12.** A knowledge of the universe gradually opens up to children during this period.
- **Age 12 to 18.** Children explore areas of special interest in more depth (Lillard, 1972).

Lev Vygotsky (1896–1934)

Although he lived a short life, Vygotsky's theory of development has had a significant impact in his homeland of Russia and more recently in the United States. Often referred to as a *sociocultural theorist* (Schunk, 2008), Vygotsky's theory states that development is primarily influenced by the social and cultural events of each individual's life. Interactions with other children and adults are the primary vehicles children have for learning about the world around them. Language becomes a crucial tool for learning because it is the primary way we communicate and interact with others. It allows us to talk about our social interactions and is essential in the thinking process.

A major focus of Vygotsky's research was the relationship between language and thought. After considerable study, he concluded that this relationship changes over time. Initially, there is little connection between the two. Over time, however, language and thought partially overlap to form what Vygotsky called **verbal thought**. The child now learns concepts that also have word labels (Thomas, 1985). Language and thought never totally merge; however, both children and adults continue to use nonverbal thought and non-conceptual speech. Figure 4–3 provides a pictorial representation of these relationships.

Vygotsky (1962) is perhaps best known for a concept referred to as the **zone of proximal development**. This is the developmental area between the child's independent performance of a task and those tasks he can perform with a more skilled peer or adult's help. The child builds knowledge of the world when he is in this zone of proximal development and receives guidance from a more skilled peer or adult. Vygotsky believed that educational tasks should be planned to challenge each child at the top of his zone of proximal development.

Like those of the other theorists discussed, Vygotsky's ideas have many practical implications for early childhood professionals, including the following:

- If the child's *social and cultural experiences* play such a major role in development, it is critical to understand and build on the experiences children bring to early childhood settings.
- Because *relationships with peers and adults* are so critical to development, the early childhood professional must work hard to foster strong adult–child and peer relations.

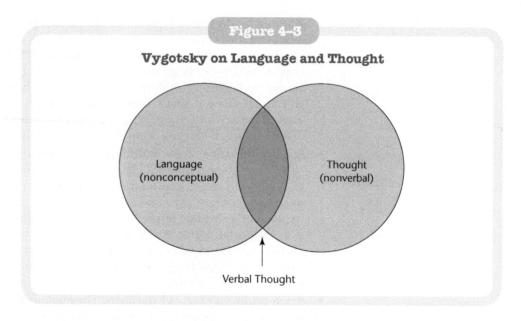

Figure 4–3

Vygotsky on Language and Thought

Language (nonconceptual)

Thought (nonverbal)

Verbal Thought

- Understanding and supporting *child language development* is essential and is a critical aspect of learning and development in early childhood settings.
- Teaching strategies such as *project learning* in which small groups of peers work together to attain a common goal are important options for young children.

Erik Erikson (1902–1994)

Erikson's theory of human development is one of only a few that describe human behavior from birth through old age. It is often called a *psychosocial theory* because of its emphasis on psychological development through the person's interactions within her social environment (Trawick-Smith, 2010). Erikson proposes that humans pass through a series of eight stages from birth to old age. Each stage has a major issue that must be addressed, which Erikson refers to as a *psychosocial crisis* for that time of life (Erikson, 1963). Successful resolution of the psychosocial crisis of the current stage provides a stronger foundation for approaching the next crisis.

The first four of Erikson's stages are important for early care and education and are briefly discussed next. The title for each stage identifies the psychosocial crisis for that stage, with the first descriptor representing the positive resolution of the crisis:

- **Stage 1: Trust versus Mistrust.** For the first year of life, children are dealing with the trustworthiness of their primary caregivers. If family members and others provide consistent care and meet the child's physical and emotional needs, a sense of trust begins to develop and the young child can start to trust others. One way in which early care settings can support the development of trust is to have the same adult provide primary care for individual infants and toddlers whenever possible. Consistent and competent care for daily routines such as changing diapers, providing meals, and engaging in play help very young children develop a greater sense of security and trust in the adults in their lives.
- **Stage 2: Autonomy versus Shame and Doubt.** From approximately 1 to 3 years of age, young children make initial attempts at doing some things for themselves.

Wanting to dress and feed themselves helps give young children a sense of independence. When not allowed to engage in these activities, they may develop a sense that they are not capable and experience what Erikson calls shame and doubt. Beginning independence is promoted when children are allowed to make appropriate choices for themselves. Choosing between grapes and apple slices at snack time, making choices about the play centers they want to participate in, and selecting a book for adult reading are all examples of ways in which caregivers and teachers can help promote child autonomy.

- **Stage 3: Initiative versus Guilt.** During the preschool and kindergarten years, children are developing a sense of initiative by making plans, setting goals, and working hard to accomplish tasks. Families and early childhood professionals need to encourage the child's natural curiosity to allow this growing initiative to blossom. Providing larger blocks of time for projects of interest to children is an important strategy for developing initiative. Caregivers and teachers know that it often takes 30 minutes or more for preschool and kindergarten children to begin a task, explore and create, and then prepare to move on to the next part of the day.

- **Stage 4: Industry versus Inferiority.** The elementary school years (ages 6 to 12) are spent in Erikson's fourth stage of psychosocial development. A child develops a sense of industry through learning the skills necessary to be successful in society. Children begin comparing themselves with others and identifying their own particular strengths and weaknesses. During the primary school years, it is important for teachers to give children accurate feedback about their developing skills, which helps in the development of a sense of industry. Feedback should be given privately and with sensitivity. "Miguel, you read that passage more smoothly today. You are recognizing many more words now, and it is making a real difference. Keep up the good work!"

Both the adults in early care settings and the families of the children who go there play key roles in assisting children with successful resolution of each of these psychosocial crises. They must be constantly aware of the impact of their words and actions on young children. Demonstrating trustworthiness, allowing some independence, encouraging planning and exploration, and praising children's accomplishments help ensure positive resolutions to each of these stages of psychosocial development.

Jean Piaget (1896–1980)

Piaget's long and productive career is difficult to summarize, because of the breadth of his writing and research. In general, Piaget was interested in studying how knowledge develops in human beings. Through careful observations and ingenious experiments with children, he created an influential theory of development. A basic element of this theory is the notion that regardless of age, people form mental concepts about the world that he refers to as schemas. These schemas are general ways of thinking about or interacting with things in our environment. As we take in new information from the world around us, we can *assimilate* that information into already existing schemas to strengthen our understanding of that mental concept. A 3-year-old, for example, may already have a schema for *dog* that includes experiences with short-haired dogs such as dalmations, Labradors, and boxers. Upon meeting a new breed of short-haired dog such as the dachshund, the child can assimilate that new information into his schema for dog. When new information does not fit already existing schema, however, the schema must then be modified to *accommodate* this new knowledge. The same 3-year-old, upon meeting a curly-haired poodle, must change or modify his schema for dog to accommodate this new piece of information.

The best-known and most influential aspect of Piaget's work is his four stages of intellectual development (Flavell, 1963). Piaget states that everyone passes through each of these stages at approximately the same ages and that ways of knowing about the world vary significantly from one stage to the next:

- **Sensorimotor intelligence.** From birth to about age 2, children are in Piaget's stage of sensorimotor intelligence. During this time, children learn about the world through sensory experiences and motoric activity. The infant's sucking and shaking of various objects are examples of early ways of learning about things in his environment through physical manipulation and sensory exploration.

- **Preoperational intelligence.** Children from approximately 2 to 7 years of age (most of the early childhood years) engage in preoperational thinking. During this stage, children begin to use symbolic thinking rather than exclusively learning through sensory and motor interactions with the world. Preoperational children make initial attempts to be logical but are unsuccessful by adult standards. Since they are **egocentric** in their thinking, children have a difficult time seeing things from any perspective other than their own. Taking things literally is another characteristic of this stage.

- **Concrete operations.** From 7 to 12 years, children engage in concrete operational thinking. The child becomes more successful in thinking logically and systematically, especially when dealing with concrete objects. At this stage, the child understands conservation, recognizing that matter does not change in quantity or mass when moved or manipulated. Children are less egocentric and more able to see the perspectives of others.

- **Formal operations.** Piaget suggests that from adolescence on we enter the stage of formal operations. At this point, the abstract and logical thinking necessary for scientific investigation are possible.

Piaget was also an early proponent of the **constructivist approach** to learning and development. He believed that children create knowledge of the world for themselves as they interact with the people and things in their environment. This approach has had a significant impact on education in general and on early care and education specifically. Although he spent little time defining the educational implications of his theory, others have suggested many connections. Piaget's theory implies active learning during the early childhood years. Hands-on manipulation of materials and objects in the world provides the child with much information to assimilate and accommodate. His theory also suggests that understanding how children gain knowledge about their world is essential to planning for future learning (Kamii & Ewing, 1996). A third basic implication of Piagetian theory is that the learning environment must allow for manipulation of objects and interactions with other children and adults.

Urie Bronfenbrenner (1917–2005)

Bronfenbrenner (1979) created an influential theory of human development called the **ecological model** to describe the many different social systems that contribute to the overall development of the child. He proposes four major systems that influence children's growth. These systems are described in the following list and are represented pictorially in Figure 4–4:

- **Microsystem.** This includes close relationships within the home, school, neighborhood, and church. These are the earliest and some of the strongest influences on the young child's development.

- **Mesosystem.** These factors include the interactions and relationships among home, school, neighborhood, and church. For example, the communications and interactions between families and early childhood professionals have an impact on the child's development. The *Family Partnerships* feature in this section provides more insights into the benefits of family and community relationships.

- **Exosystem.** The exosystem consists of local governmental agencies, the family members' workplace, mass media, and local industry. Although the influences of these elements are less direct, it should be clear that they all impact the overall development of children.

- **Macrosystem.** The macrosystem includes the dominant beliefs and ideologies of the culture. Because the child is immersed in cultural experiences, these cultural beliefs also strongly influence the child's development.

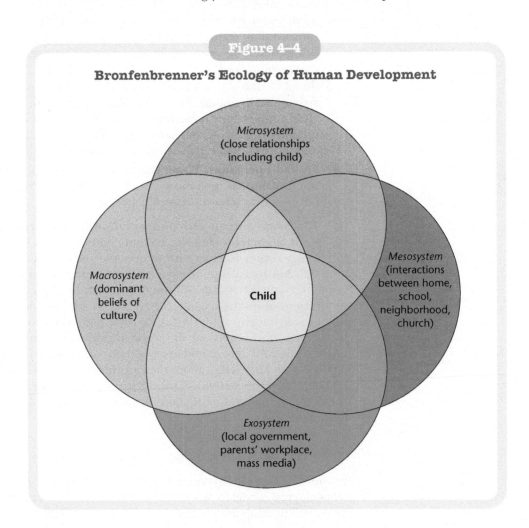

Figure 4–4

Bronfenbrenner's Ecology of Human Development

Family Partnerships...
BENEFITS OF FAMILY AND COMMUNITY RELATIONSHIPS

The mesosystem described by Bronfenbrenner includes the family and community as significant influences on the lives of young children. But how would it benefit you as an individual early childhood professional to establish strong relationships with families and community members? Because it takes considerable effort to have positive home/school/community interactions, there must be obvious benefits to you and your children for this to become a priority activity. Several important benefits can be identified:

- **Enhancing student learning.** Family and community members can strengthen student learning when they volunteer in the early childhood setting. For example, retired members of the community have a wealth of experiences and talents that they may enjoy sharing with children. Conversely, taking young children out into the community for field trips (for example, visiting the fire department) also provides many valuable opportunities for learning.
- **Celebrating accomplishments.** Family and community members can provide significant financial and emotional support for the work that caregivers and teachers do in early childhood settings. For example, when they are invited to watch the class play that was developed by children, family and community members have a clearer understanding of the learning that is taking place and are more supportive of the teacher's efforts.
- **Support change.** With the involvement of family and community members, positive changes are more likely to occur. For example, a group of interested families and community members could work with school personnel to plan, raise money for, and help install a creative playground for young children.

1. Do you think the benefits listed for strong family and community relationships make it worth the effort it will take to develop them? Why or why not?

2. How do you think you will feel about working to have strong family and community relations? Describe your feelings.

3. What personality characteristics do you have that will either make it easier or harder for you to work with families?

Jack Shonkoff and Deborah Phillips

Two current researchers at Harvard University are often credited with much of today's strong public and research interest in early childhood development. Jack Shonkoff is a physician and professor at Harvard University, as well as the founder and director of the Center on the Developing Child there. Deborah Phillips is professor of psychology at Georgetown University. Their popular book *From Neurons to Neighborhoods* (Shonkoff & Phillips, 2000) highlights several key points about development during the early years. This edited book summarizes the work of the Committee on Integrating the Science of Early Childhood Development, under the direction of the National Research Council and the Institute of Medicine. The charge of the committee was to review and critique a growing body of research on early childhood development.

The findings from their extensive review emphasize the critical importance of the early years for later development. From birth to age 5, a child's brain growth and overall development proceed at rates far greater than at any other time in life. They found that this early development provides an essential foundation for later development if the child's environment and experiences are quality ones. Conversely, when children grow up with poverty, fear, and limited stimulating life experiences, early development is hindered. These early hardships are difficult to overcome in later life. The reviewed research indicated that significant differences in what children know and are able to do are clearly evident by age 5.

A more specific contribution from the research review conducted by Shonkoff and Phillips has been a more extensive understanding of early brain development. Prior to their efforts, many believed that brain development during the early years was predominantly a function of what children inherited genetically from their parents. Shonkoff and Phillips (2000) demonstrate that early brain development, while significantly influenced by genetic inheritance, is also strongly influenced by the young child's environment and early experiences. When children receive good nutrition, have many opportunities for quality early experiences, and have positive nurturing relationships with adults, brain growth is maximized. Conversely, when children experience high levels of stress in their environment from chronic fear and anxiety, receive poor nutrition, have fewer stimulating experiences, and are given an inconsistent and/or low level of care from their families and other adults, brain development can be far less than optimal.

At a recent symposium on early brain development (Haskins, 2010), Jack Shonkoff highlighted four core concepts regarding early brain development:

1. Early experience literally shapes the structure of young brains. Positive experiences lead to rapid brain growth and integrated brain functions, while less positive ones produce less effective growth and integration.

2. The young brain builds basic neuron connections first and then develops more complex connections. Through early experiences, these neuron connections assist the child in all aspects of development, including conceptual, emotional, social, and language development. For example, as adults respond to infant sound-making with facial expressions, gestures, and repeating the sounds of the child, infant brains process these interchanges and create brain connections that lead to early language learning.

3. Cognitive, social, and emotional functioning are all interrelated and linked to the growing connections being made in the brain. Each of the areas influences development in the others, making it difficult to understand and study functioning in one area without knowledge of the others. So, for example, a child learning to read has a much harder time being successful when she is preoccupied by a home environment that fills her with fears and anxieties.

4. The ability of the brain to change decreases over time. Brain flexibility changes dramatically over just a few short years. It's harder for the brain to adapt and change as the child gets older. Consequently, society is best served by helping young children develop to their highest potential rather than trying to assist them later in life.

A second outcome of Shonkoff and Phillip's book has been the growing emphasis on self-regulation as an important issue in early childhood development (Galinsky, 2010). From infancy onward, young children are slowly moving from a state of near-total dependence on others to doing more and more on their own. This process of self-regulation occurs in fits and starts, but in healthy children it moves ever onward toward greater self-control. It begins in infancy with tasks such as learning to regulate sleep and wakefulness to conform to the typical night/day cycle of the adult world. Later self-regulatory tasks in early childhood include learning to manage emotions constructively and learning to maintain attention or focus on specific tasks. These developmental tasks are both personal and social as children learn to regulate themselves and their interactions with others. A fundamental responsibility of families, caregivers, and early childhood professionals is to provide opportunities for guiding the young child's movement from dependence to more productive self-regulation.

The emphasis on brain research led by Shonkoff and Phillips has helped energize interest among early childhood professionals about the significance of brain development during the early years. An important new book by Ellen Galinsky (2010) titled *Mind in the Making* helps synthesize both the research and practical implications of this brain work. In her book, Galinsky proposes that every young child needs to develop seven essential skills to be successful in life. Together, these seven essential skills are referred to as executive functions of the brain. They make it possible for us to manage our behaviors as we strive to reach established goals. All of these seven skills are considered critical for successfully navigating life in the twenty-first century and must be promoted during the early childhood years.

- **Focus and self-control.** In our fast-paced world, children are bombarded by a wealth of information that must be either addressed or discarded. Young children need to develop skills that allow them to focus on what is important. They also must learn to give up immediate rewards (develop self-control) so that they can reach more important goals later.

- **Perspective taking.** Children need to develop the ability to consider the perspectives of others by looking at the actions or words of peers and adults in new ways and thinking carefully about these different perspectives. Although this is a very difficult task, even for many adults, early childhood professionals can assist in the development of this important skill.

- **Communicating.** Effective oral and written communications are at the heart of all positive interactions and lead to deeper understandings between people. Families and early childhood professionals need to spend considerable time and effort working with children to help them clearly understand what is being communicated by others, reflect on this message, and respond appropriately.

- **Making connections.** Children also need to develop the ability to make connections between understandings. For example, an infant who has been fed using a child-sized spoon may be gradually introduced to a fork and come to the eventual understanding that both can be used for eating.

- **Critical thinking.** Children need to learn how to sort through all of the information that comes their way and discriminate between what is reliable and useful and what should be discarded. Critical thinking requires children to develop the ability to reason like a scientist as they make sense of the information that surrounds them.

- **Taking on challenges.** Life today is filled with many challenges that must be faced almost daily by children and adults. Whether these challenges are positive or negative, they often lead to stress. Although many children try to avoid stressful situations, early childhood professionals need to assist children by providing them with strategies that they can use in facing challenges directly and positively.

- **Self-directed, engaged learning.** Early childhood professionals also need to create an environment in which children, families, and educators are all learning and growing together. In this learning community, children are able to develop skills that help them become self-directed, engaged learners.

Children: Developmental Similarities and Differences

Imagine for a moment the process a creative chef uses for cooking a culinary delight. Although the process may not be conscious, the knowledgeable cook understands the characteristics of each of the foods used in a recipe. The length of time needed to cook, the food's properties when mixed with other ingredients, and its consistency, color, and aroma are just some of the bits of information the creative chef relies on before beginning the process of cooking. In much the same way, a creative early childhood caregiver or teacher must know a great deal about children and their typical developmental patterns before beginning their work. These understandings become the basis for the planning and teaching that will follow. Unfortunately, there are few recipes to follow to ensure success in early childhood settings.

From study and experience in working with children, the best caregivers and teachers know what is normal for a group of young children.

- A *kindergarten teacher*, for example, knows that a typical 5-year-old child should be able to string a set of 10 beads and that he has the fine motor skills to begin to enjoy the writing process (Charlesworth, 2011).
- *Preschool teachers* have learned that many young children have difficulty separating from their parents when they arrive at school. The tears and clinging are normal reactions to the stress of leaving loving parents.
- *Third-grade teachers* understand the importance of peer relationships and work hard to encourage positive interactions among students. In these and many other similar ways, teachers use their knowledge of child development to begin the process of planning and teaching.

Knowledge of what is typical for a given group of children must be supplemented with an understanding of the variations that exist among children of the same age. Children develop at different rates. The reasons for these deviations are complex but are some combination of genetic factors and environmental influences. Finding and using this information about individual differences among children is very useful to the early childhood professional in planning the curriculum. Talking to a 3-year-old child's family, for example, could help you understand that this child's delay in climbing may be partially due to a broken leg at age 2. Observing kindergarten children at play, you may discover that a child needs help in making friends. Or the second-grade teacher who analyzes a fairy tale that one of her students has written may learn of the child's special writing talents. The longer you work with children, the more sensitive you become to the general patterns of development and the subtle variations between children. These building blocks of knowledge and understanding form the foundations for good teaching and learning.

Infants and Toddlers

The first 3 years of life are characterized by rapid growth in all areas of development. The young child moves from being someone who is totally dependent on others to someone who is able to walk and talk and begin to interact with peers and adults. This period is also a critical foundation for all of the development that is to follow. Families and caregivers need to understand the developmental patterns of this period. Figure 4–5 provides a summary of some typical behaviors of infants and toddlers.

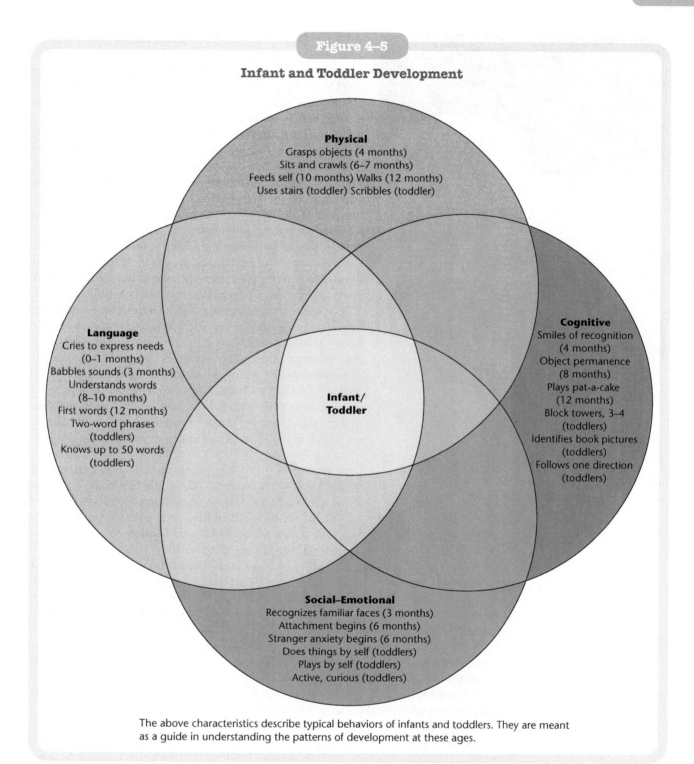

Figure 4–5

Infant and Toddler Development

Physical
Grasps objects (4 months)
Sits and crawls (6–7 months)
Feeds self (10 months) Walks (12 months)
Uses stairs (toddler) Scribbles (toddler)

Language
Cries to express needs
(0–1 months)
Babbles sounds (3 months)
Understands words
(8–10 months)
First words (12 months)
Two-word phrases
(toddlers)
Knows up to 50 words
(toddlers)

**Infant/
Toddler**

Cognitive
Smiles of recognition
(4 months)
Object permanence
(8 months)
Plays pat-a-cake
(12 months)
Block towers, 3–4
(toddlers)
Identifies book pictures
(toddlers)
Follows one direction
(toddlers)

Social–Emotional
Recognizes familiar faces (3 months)
Attachment begins (6 months)
Stranger anxiety begins (6 months)
Does things by self (toddlers)
Plays by self (toddlers)
Active, curious (toddlers)

The above characteristics describe typical behaviors of infants and toddlers. They are meant as a guide in understanding the patterns of development at these ages.

Infants explore their world by touching, tasting, and shaking objects within their reach.

Infant development. Newborn Jenny has just arrived home and is already causing quite a stir in the household. She seems so helpless and unaware of her surroundings. Yet, Jenny is quickly learning about her family members and the world around her. Although her first movements are reflexive, she quickly begins to develop more purposeful activities. Nursing is quickly mastered, and Jenny's cries take on a variety of meanings from "I'm wet" to "feed me!" She is learning about her world through her senses and motor activities. Dropping, squeezing, sucking, seeing, and hearing are some of the many ways in which Jenny is making sense of her world during her first year of life. By the middle of her first year, Jenny is sitting up when propped, grasping objects, and rolling over. Her understanding of language is growing rapidly, and she is babbling the sounds used to make up words. At this point, Jenny has also begun the attachment process to her significant caregivers and becomes upset when they are not with her.

As Jenny's first birthday approaches, she is taking her first steps and speaking her first words. These are major milestones that dramatically change her interactions with others. No longer dependent on others to get from one place to another, Jenny is free to explore her environment more independently. Words open up a new and more precise way of communicating with others, and Jenny is using this tool to her full advantage. Jenny's total dependence on caregivers has changed significantly over the past 12 months.

One-year-olds. Matt has just turned 1 and is already off exploring his environment. From his first shaky steps just a few weeks ago, he is now becoming more confident and stable in his gait. By the end of his second year of life, he is able to run and effectively navigate up and down stairs. This newfound mobility allows Matt to expand his horizons and learn even more about his growing world.

Matt's language is also growing by leaps and bounds. Beginning the year with just a few words that were understandable mostly to family members, Matt's vocabulary will expand to approximately 300 words by year's end. He is also now able to put together words and form simple two-word sentences. Matt understands much more of the verbal communications from others than he is able to repeat himself.

Toward the end of this year, Matt will be able to mentally represent objects and events as symbols. Although he still learns much from his senses and motor activity, he can now engage in symbolic thought. Matt can now imitate the actions of others and get involved in simple make-believe play. The *Celebrating Play* feature in this section provides additional information on infant/toddler play.

Matt's push toward more independence can be difficult for his family members and caregivers. Although he wants to do as much as he can by himself, he still needs and wants closeness and assistance. Finding that delicate balance between independence and assistance is often difficult for both Matt and his family. Patience and calmness are virtues for adults at this point.

Two-year-olds. As a 2-year-old, Serena is making the transition from babyhood to childhood. She continues to gain body control, with improved walking and running

Celebrating Play . . .
INFANT AND TODDLER PLAY

When most people think about children playing, the image that comes to mind is probably one of preschool or elementary children engaged in playful interactions. Those writing about children's play, however, also make it clear that even the very youngest of children engage in play. Doris Fromberg (2002), for example, provides the following examples of infant/toddler play:

> The 6-month-old lay on a carpet under a table. A mirror was attached to the underside of the table. The teacher had attached a knitted ribbon loop to the infant's ankle. When he moved his leg down, the ribbon pulled down a soft, red stuffed toy. His entire body shook with excitement as his legs and arms waved in the direction of the toy. When he raised his leg, the toy moved higher. With repeated play, he began to pull his toes closer to his mouth. (p. 16)

As individual toddlers finished their meal, they began to pull playthings from a low shelf. Several children walked around the open, low-pile carpeted space with pull toys. Several children sat with a teacher in a construction activity with miniature animals. The children piled animals into a central "zoo" and alternately walked toward the shelf of pull toys. Four other children stood at a table on which the teacher had taped paper. The teacher commented, "Jenny's using a red crayon; Hal is writing with a brown crayon. . . ." (pp. 16–17)

1. Compare and contrast the play of preschool children presented earlier in this chapter with those noted for infants/toddlers. What are the similarities and differences?

2. Do you think that play for infants and toddlers is as important for growth and development as play for older children? Why or why not?

and small muscle development. Serena spends considerable energy in refining her skills by repeating over and over again the things she is learning. For example, she will put together a simple puzzle many times before she is ready to move on to the next activity.

Serena's language continues to grow exponentially. Her vocabulary will triple by year's end to approximately 1,000 words. Serena's sentences have grown as well, with many including three or more words. Conversations with others become more interactive, with Serena able to listen and talk in appropriate contexts.

Along with her growing language abilities, Serena is developing deeper conceptual understandings of her world. She remains curious and excited about exploring the natural world around her. Serena has a lively imagination and enjoys using it in her play with others.

Although Serena's social skills are growing, she is still likely to play alongside, rather than with, other children. And rather than ask for a toy, Serena might just take it. Her newly acquired ability to communicate more effectively is often not enough to avoid conflict in many situations, and Serena reverts to throwing a temper tantrum.

Children Age 3 through 5: The Preschool Years

The years from 3 through 5 are often referred to as the *preschool years*. Many young children are entering a school-like setting for the first time. Although growth has slowed somewhat from the frantic pace of the earlier years, development is still rapid during this period. A 3-year-old is very different developmentally from his 5-year-old friend, and each year brings new milestones. Figure 4–6 identifies some of these developmental highlights.

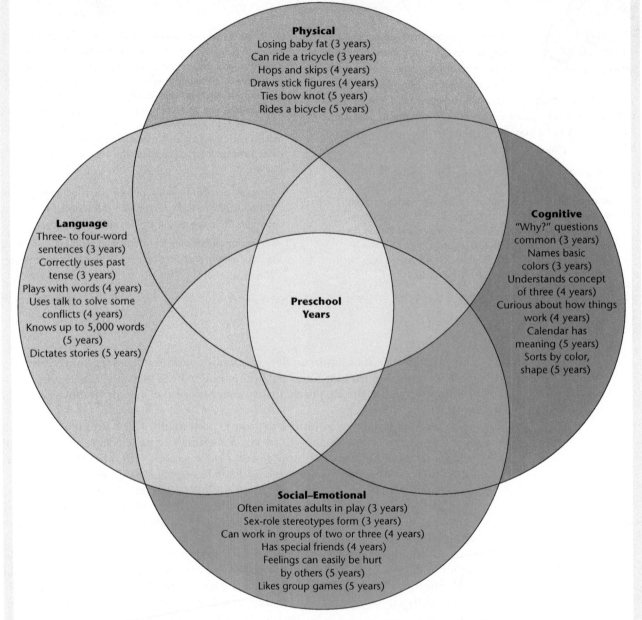

Figure 4–6

Development of Children Age 3 through 5: The Preschool Years

Physical
Losing baby fat (3 years)
Can ride a tricycle (3 years)
Hops and skips (4 years)
Draws stick figures (4 years)
Ties bow knot (5 years)
Rides a bicycle (5 years)

Language
Three- to four-word
sentences (3 years)
Correctly uses past
tense (3 years)
Plays with words (4 years)
Uses talk to solve some
conflicts (4 years)
Knows up to 5,000 words
(5 years)
Dictates stories (5 years)

Preschool Years

Cognitive
"Why?" questions
common (3 years)
Names basic
colors (3 years)
Understands concept
of three (4 years)
Curious about how things
work (4 years)
Calendar has
meaning (5 years)
Sorts by color,
shape (5 years)

Social–Emotional
Often imitates adults in play (3 years)
Sex-role stereotypes form (3 years)
Can work in groups of two or three (4 years)
Has special friends (4 years)
Feelings can easily be hurt
by others (5 years)
Likes group games (5 years)

The above characteristics describe typical behaviors of children 3 through 5. They are meant as a guide in understanding the patterns of developement at these ages.

Three-year-olds. Mario is very much a child and no longer a baby. He has lost most of the baby fat that gave him that chubby look of younger children. Mario's physical skills have grown, and he is able to balance on one foot, unbutton and button clothing, and ride a tricycle. He has achieved bowel and bladder control and can use the toilet with limited supervision.

Mario's language continues to develop as his vocabulary increases and his sentence structure improves. He is better able to engage in a real conversation with others, talking *with* rather than just *to* others. Mario is full of questions about his world and constantly asks for information about the people and things around him.

During this year, Mario is developing conceptual understanding through playing with people and things. His pretend play has become more complex, and Mario can now include two or three other children in the scenarios he creates. Although his attention span is still relatively short, Mario can use his lively imagination to play out complex themes, especially those in which he imitates adult roles. In the block corner, Mario often constructs and then names what he has made.

Socially and emotionally, Mario continues to make significant progress. He can now establish and maintain short-term friendships with others and begins to enjoy playing *with* rather than *near* his buddies. Mario is learning to use social skills such as taking turns, but he finds it difficult to use these emerging skills consistently. His imaginary friend, Buffy, is often included in play themes around home and in school. Mario is often frightened by large dogs and horses and needs comforting when he encounters these animals. The *Developmentally Appropriate Practice* feature in this section talks about strategies you can use to assist children with the difficult-to-master social skill of sharing. Like Mario, many young children are only beginning to use this important social skill.

Four-year-olds. Mary is an active and confident 4-year-old. Having mastered the basics of movement, she is constantly testing her physical limits to improve her skills. Mary climbs higher, runs faster, and pumps vigorously on the swing to challenge her motor skills.

Mary's language has now matured to the point that she can communicate with others using fairly sophisticated words and sentences. Language becomes a plaything for Mary, and she loves rhyming and nonsense words. Bathroom talk, tall tales, and swearing are also parts of her experimentation with language.

Highly interested in how things work, Mary is constantly asking questions that challenge the adults who work with her. Her interest in the concepts of life and death lead her to explore the world of insects and small animals. Mary will often name her artwork and begins to draw and paint objects that represent things and people in the world. Number concepts are beginning to develop, and Mary enjoys games and songs that incorporate them. Mary understands time as a sequence of events and appreciates a consistent routine to her day.

Most 4-year-old boys and girls enjoy playing with dolls.

Developmentally Appropriate Practice...
GUIDING CHILDREN WHO HAVE DIFFICULTY SHARING

Although young children are capable of many things at an early age, it is also important to keep in mind what they are unable to do . . . yet. As with the example of 3-year-old Mario in this section, many young children have difficulty sharing toys and equipment in the classroom. Adults working with preschool children need to be prepared to deal with the problems that this may bring. The following strategies are commonly used to help children who are struggling with sharing:

- **Have two or more of the most popular toys.** When possible, have two or more toy trucks, popular dolls, magnifying glasses, floor pillows, or shovels to use for gardening and make sure they are available to the children. This will not eliminate problems, but it might make it easier to share a popular item among several children.

- **Set time limits with toys and equipment.** If, for example, three children want to use the two toy trucks available in the block center, give each child a time limit (perhaps 10 minutes) for playing with the toy. Set a timer so that you do not forget, and then try to get the child who doesn't have the desired toy involved in another activity for the next few minutes.

- **Identify ways in which children can use the equipment together.** For example, if three children want to play the same game on the computer, see if you can set them up so that all three can be seated around the screen with specified roles. The additional benefits of playing together may well outweigh the challenges of getting them involved in a cooperative activity.

- **Give children words to use in sharing situations.** Because of their more limited language skills, preschool children often use physical actions in their place. If a young child wants a stapler but one is not available, a common response is simply to take it away from someone else. You can help them with the language they will need to use in sharing. "Rather than taking the stapler away from Lise, ask her if you can use it to staple your pages together. Tell her you will return it when you are done."

- **Ask older children to identify and discuss possible solutions.** As children mature, they are more able to work toward their own solutions to sharing. You will need to facilitate their problem solving by encouraging them to identify solutions, suggesting modifications to potential solutions, and making sure that children agree to a common solution.

Mary's friendships are becoming stronger, and she has clear preferences for playmates. These special friends change regularly, however. Play has now become a truly social activity during most times with others. Occasionally, however, Mary still likes to go off by herself for some quiet time. Turn taking and sharing are becoming easier for Mary because she is beginning to recognize the value of cooperation. However, her growing skills and confidence often lead Mary into confrontations with others. She wants to be the leader and is bossy and assertive in her relationships with peers.

Five-year-olds. Abdul has calmed down a bit from a few short months ago. He is now much more interested in fine motor activities and spends considerable time building with Legos, cutting paper, making artwork, and engaging in beginning writing activities. Abdul's interest in swinging, climbing, and running is still strong, and he engages in these activities in a fluid, coordinated, confident manner. He also has fun throwing and catching from short distances.

Abdul's language use is now fully developed, with a vocabulary of several thousand words. He can construct complex sentences and accurately use grammatical forms in communicating. He eagerly learns new words that give him labels for the ever-expanding world he is exploring. Socially, Abdul has solidified his friendships at school and in the neighborhood. Although he will play with others, his strong preference is to be with his special friends. Cooperative play themes, in which children take on roles, is a common component of Abdul's activity. He is aware of rules and begins to enjoy simple games.

Abdul's conceptual knowledge is expanding rapidly. His understanding of numbers has improved, and he can now accurately count 10 objects and count by rote to 20. He can sort objects by either color or shape. He knows the purpose of a calendar and can tell time by the hour. Abdul also understands the concepts of *tomorrow* and *yesterday*.

Children Age 6 through 8: The Primary School Years

Although the life of a primary-age child has changed dramatically with the introduction of formal schooling, developmental characteristics through this period closely resemble those of earlier years. Children are still working hard to understand and construct social relationships, deal with their emotions, and learn about their world through hands-on manipulation of objects and interactions with peers and adults. Figure 4–7 summarizes some important developmental milestones during the primary school years.

Six-year-olds. Christy is a normal, busy 6-year-old who enjoys practicing newly acquired skills. Although her physical growth has slowed, she likes to test the limits of her body with challenging activities such as acrobatics and jump rope. Christy just got a new bicycle and is working hard to master two-wheeling. Other activities that require good balance such as skating and skiing are also fun for her.

Christy has many friends, most of whom are other girls. Her playmates change regularly, however, with new friends being added and old ones set aside. Christy is making comparisons between herself and her peers, which is leading her to recognize personal strengths and weaknesses.

Although Christy still has some minor articulation errors, she is eager to talk with adults and others. It is hard to get her to be quiet long enough to enter the conversation. She is making significant progress in putting her thoughts into writing and enjoys practicing this newfound skill.

Christy's school days are filled with learning to read and developing early math skills. She is making steady progress with these very complex tasks.

Christy collects rocks and enjoys sorting and classifying them. Although she enjoys simple games in school and at home, winning and losing are very difficult for Christy, and she is happier when they are de-emphasized.

Seven-year-olds. At 7, Gordon values his and others' physical competence. Sports figures like LeBron James and Alex Rodriguez, are important to him. Gordon is a typical boisterous 7-year-old and enjoys rough-and-tumble play with his friends. He needs daily opportunities to engage in active play. Sitting still does not seem to be a part of his makeup.

Gordon's rate of vocabulary development has slowed, but language learning remains significant. He is learning Spanish in an after-school enrichment program and is finding this to be a fun activity. His ability to communicate in writing is improving steadily, and Gordon enjoys writing long, fantasy-oriented stories to share with his friends and family. Although he likes to work alone, his overriding desire is to be part of the group. Peer pressure to conform to the in-group's expectations

Figure 4–7

Development of Children Age 6 through 8: The Primary School Years

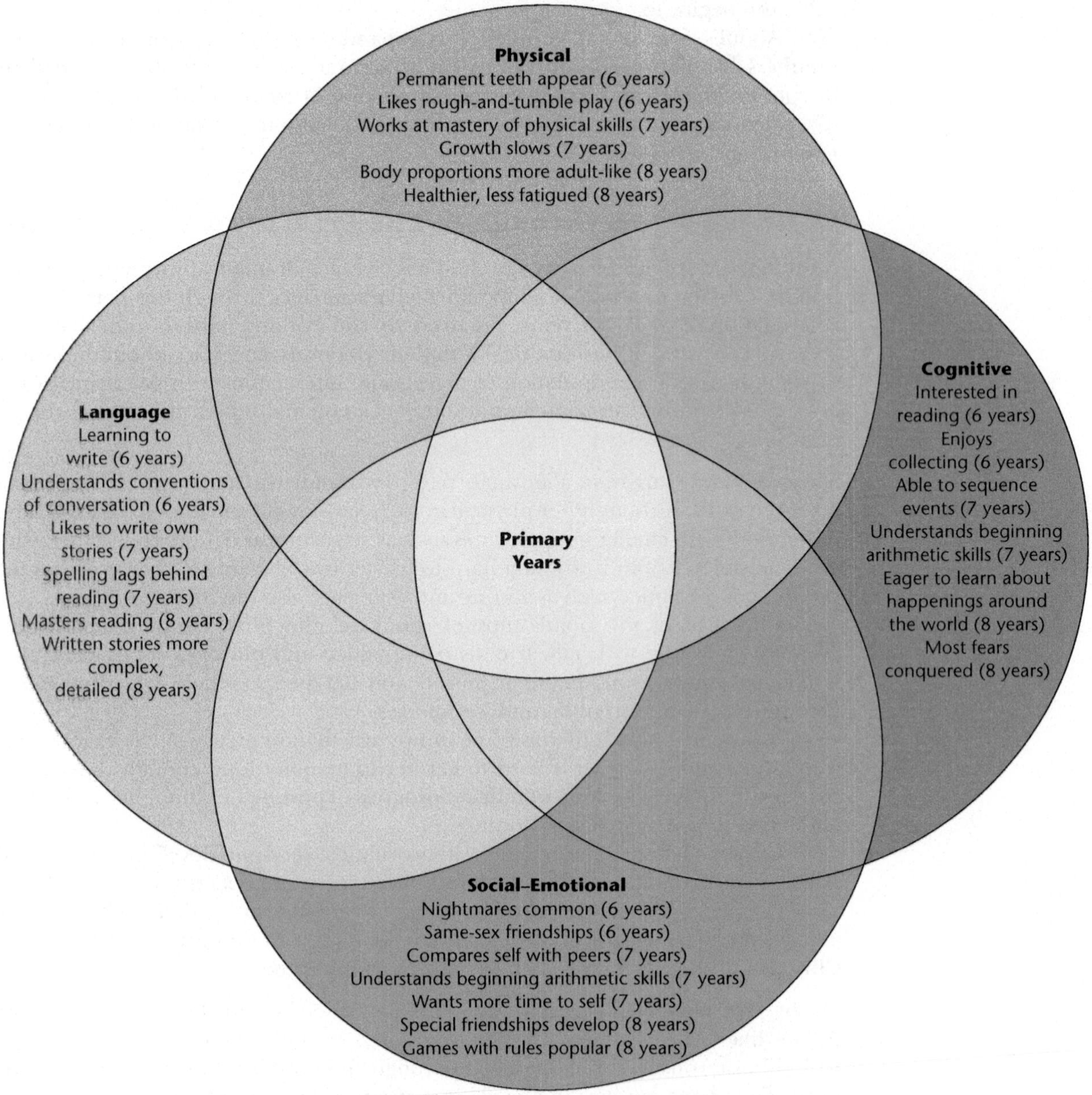

Physical
Permanent teeth appear (6 years)
Likes rough-and-tumble play (6 years)
Works at mastery of physical skills (7 years)
Growth slows (7 years)
Body proportions more adult-like (8 years)
Healthier, less fatigued (8 years)

Language
Learning to
write (6 years)
Understands conventions
of conversation (6 years)
Likes to write own
stories (7 years)
Spelling lags behind
reading (7 years)
Masters reading (8 years)
Written stories more
complex,
detailed (8 years)

**Primary
Years**

Cognitive
Interested in
reading (6 years)
Enjoys
collecting (6 years)
Able to sequence
events (7 years)
Understands beginning
arithmetic skills (7 years)
Eager to learn about
happenings around
the world (8 years)
Most fears
conquered (8 years)

Social–Emotional
Nightmares common (6 years)
Same-sex friendships (6 years)
Compares self with peers (7 years)
Understands beginning arithmetic skills (7 years)
Wants more time to self (7 years)
Special friendships develop (8 years)
Games with rules popular (8 years)

The above characteristics describe typical behaviors of children 6 through 8. They are meant as a guide in understanding the patterns of developement at these ages.

Participating in peer group activities is very important to most 7-year-olds.

is growing. Mood swings are common for Gordon, as well as complaints of not being liked and concerns over competence when he compares himself with peers. Gordon's thirst for knowledge about the world around him appears boundless. He wants to know how the real things he encounters work, and he spends considerable energy on tasks that interest him. Gordon has mastered the basics of reading and has learned the arithmetic operations of addition, subtraction, and multiplication.

Eight-year-olds. Marissa is beginning to look more adult-like in her physical appearance. Her body proportions are subtly changing in preparation for the more dramatic changes of puberty just ahead. Marissa's movements are now quite fluid and graceful, and she uses good posture when seated. She is, in general, healthier and less easily fatigued than she was as a 7-year-old.

Marissa is very aware of the differences between herself and the boys in her class, and she works hard to separate herself from "those geeks." Her friends are all girls, and she likes it that way. Her group of friends is becoming more exclusive, and it is difficult for them to add new members. Although closeness with her family is still important to her, Marissa is beginning to separate herself from her teacher and finds this relationship less important than it was a year ago.

Marissa's hungry mind is eager to know more about her expanding world. In addition to her desire to know more about people and relationships in her family and neighborhood, Marissa can conceptualize nations around the world and is curious about life there. She has an Internet pen pal in Australia and enjoys learning about school and family life there. Marissa is beginning to show an interest in historical events and can conceptualize and discuss future events.

Children with Special Needs

Every early childhood setting is filled with a wonderful diversity of children. One of the major reasons for this diversity is the growing trend to place children with special needs in the regular program. It is important to understand both the strengths they bring to the early childhood setting and their unique needs. Although every child has distinctive attributes, children with special needs are often categorized as disabled, at-risk, or gifted.

Children with disabilities. A child who is **disabled** is unable to do something or has difficulty with a specific task. Seven-year-old Angela, for example, uses a wheelchair and is unable to walk. She is a child with a physical disability. All other aspects of Angela's development are normal, however. Other children with disabilities may have several areas of development that are affected. Brian, for example, has a significant hearing loss and is delayed in his oral language development. Because he has difficulty hearing others and communicating with them, Brian also struggles with social relationships. The types and severities of childhood disabilities are many and varied.

Some children have mild disabilities, while others are faced with moderate to severe ones. For example, at age 7, Aretha has trouble distinguishing between letters such as *b* and *d* as she reads. She has been diagnosed as having a mild learning disability. Jason has Down syndrome, congenital heart defects, and severe mental retardation. His disabilities are much more problematic to his overall development. Hallahan, Kauffman, and Pullen (2009) have suggested the following as categories of disabilities that are often encountered by early childhood professionals:

- **Intellectual and developmental.** This disability is characterized by significant limitations in brain functioning that affects conceptual, social, and adaptive skills.

- **Learning disabilities.** Children with learning disabilities have problems understanding or using spoken or written language and this affects their ability to learn in the early childhood setting.

- **Attention deficit/hyperactivity disorder (ADHD).** This is a chronic condition that includes inattentive, hyperactive, and impulsive behaviors that frequently get in the way of learning and social development. The *Celebrating Diversity* feature in this section provides additional information on ADHD.

- **Emotional or behavioral disorders.** These are identified as chronic and extreme behaviors that are unacceptable because of social or cultural expectations.

- **Communication disorders.** Children with communications disorders have difficulties in either producing or understanding verbal communications and face challenges in learning and interacting with others.

- **Deafness and hard of hearing.** This disability includes both children who cannot hear, even with assistive devices, and those who use hearing aids.

- **Blindness or low vision.** Children who lack the ability to see and those who have impaired vision have special needs in the early childhood classroom.

- **Autism spectrum disorders.** The three most common autistic disorders include the relatively mild Asperger's syndrome, a mid-range disability called pervasive developmental disorder not otherwise specified, and the more severe autism. All three types of autism affect the child's social interactions, communication abilities (nonverbal and/or verbal), and repetitive behaviors and interests. Willis (2009) shares a number of strategies that are effective in working with young children with autism spectrum disorder.

- **Low-incidence, multiple, and severe disabilities.** These disabilities occur infrequently, typically involve more than one area of development, and require intense, ongoing support from others.

- **Physical and other health impairments.** Children who have physical limitations or health problems that interfere with school attendance or development to the extent that special services, equipment, or facilities are needed.

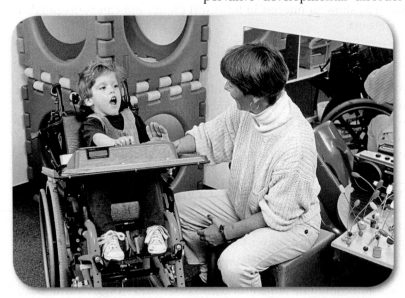

Children with special needs are valued in early childhood settings.

Celebrating Diversity...
ATTENTION-DEFICIT/HYPERACTIVITY DISORDER

Children who used to be classified as hyperactive are now described as having attention-deficit/hyperactivity disorder (ADHD). Statistics indicate that 4.5 million children in the United States have been diagnosed as having this disorder (Centers for Disease Control and Prevention, 2010). Boys tend to be diagnosed more often than girls as having ADHD. For those diagnosed with this disorder, stimulant medications are frequently prescribed by physicians to counteract this behavior pattern (National Institutes of Health, 2009). Unfortunately, significant side effects are associated with continued use of stimulants, and its overuse is questioned by many. Appetite and sleep disturbances, increased heart rate and blood pressure, and addiction have all been associated with stimulant medications.

Early childhood professionals who recognize and understand the implications of ADHD are better able to meet their needs:

Characteristics of Children with ADHD

- Impulsive (acting without thinking of the consequences)
- Short attention spans (difficulty concentrating on a task or activity)
- Difficulty in organizing thoughts and work
- Easily distracted from the task at hand
- In constant motion (find it hard to sit still and to refrain from fidgeting)

Guidance Considerations

- Provide consistent routines in school day.
- Keep children away from distracting noises and active areas.
- Make eye contact while giving clear directions.
- Create a signal that reminds children to get back on task.

1. Have you known someone who has been diagnosed with ADHD? What were some characteristics of this person's behavior? How did ADHD influence this person's school performance?

2. Can you see any problems associated with classifying children with ADHD? What are your concerns? What are the benefits?

At-risk children. Children who are **at risk** may experience developmental delays due to negative genetic or environmental factors such as poverty, low birth weight, or maternal diabetes. At-risk children have not been identified as having disabilities, but may have difficulty in early childhood settings without adequate intervention. For example, Joy, who is only a few days old, is experiencing neonatal abstinence syndrome because of her addiction to cocaine. She became addicted during the prenatal period and is at risk in her future development. Joy needs to receive special assistance to help her through this difficult beginning.

Early care and education has long been involved in helping at-risk children prepare for success in the formal schooling process. Head Start and other similar programs, for example, were created to meet the needs of young, low-income children who can benefit from additional support in their learning and development.

Particularly during the prekindergarten years, educators are reluctant to classify children as having particular disabilities. Developmental patterns at these early ages vary greatly. Yet, children who have experienced early risk factors often need assistance to develop more normally and avoid later intervention. Either biological or environmental factors can lead to the child being identified as at-risk. Biological risk factors may occur either during pregnancy or after birth. Premature birth, low birth weight, maternal diabetes, and severe illnesses are all biological factors that may place children at risk in their development.

At age 2, Monica got into the cleaning agents under her mom's sink and swallowed samples of several types. After an emergency visit to the hospital for a stomach pump, she has been recovering nicely. Her child-care center has been asked to carefully watch for signs of longer-term problems associated with this traumatic event. Monica is considered at risk for at least the short term.

Environmental factors play a major role in creating at-risk conditions for children. Poverty, homelessness, child abuse, and poor parenting are all key factors that can cause children to be at risk in their development.

Andrew is 3 years old and has just begun to attend the local Head Start program. His mother is 18, a single parent on welfare who is struggling to get her life together. Andrew's overall development is lagging behind his peers, and he is considered at risk.

Five-year-old Bonnie has just been placed in temporary foster care. Her parents are suspected of neglect. Bonnie frequently comes to school dirty, unkempt, hungry, and tired. The school staff has been notified, and she is being watched for signs of problems in her overall development.

Having read about children with special needs, take some time now to observe them in an early childhood setting. The *Observing Development* feature that follows will provide you with some guidelines for making this observation.

Gifted children. Children who are **gifted** demonstrate excellence in an area of development that is well beyond that of most children of the same age. For example, Armon taught himself to read at age 4. At age 6, he is reading long chapter books that are challenging to many 10- to 12-year-olds. He is enrolled in a gifted program at his elementary school.

Traditionally, IQ tests have been used to identify giftedness, and very high intellectual functioning is seen by many as the true mark of a gifted person. More recently, people such as Howard Gardner (Gardner, 1999) have suggested that intelligence comes in many forms, and high levels of expertise in music, art, sports, and relationships are also evidence of giftedness. For example, Taylor began piano instruction at age 3, and now at age 5 is reading and playing classical music for pleasure. Her musical giftedness is obvious to all who listen to her play.

Giftedness is a complex concept that is difficult to define. One popular description follows:

Children and youth with outstanding talent who perform or show the potential for performing at remarkably high levels of accomplishment when compared with others of their age, experience, or environment (National Society for the Gifted and Talented, 2010).

Observing Development . . .
A CHILD WITH SPECIAL NEEDS

Choose one of the age groups within early childhood (infants/toddlers, preschoolers, or primary-age children) and observe a child with special needs. Without naming the child or other children in the group (for privacy and confidentiality purposes), take detailed notes about what the child does and says. Use the following sample observation as a format for your own observation. Include only what you see and hear as part of the actual observation, putting any interpretive comments in parentheses:

Birchwood Infant/Toddler Program, 9–9:30 a.m., January 23

9:00 a.m. E. is 18 months. Adult identified him as having Down syndrome. Child spent first 5 minutes sitting and watching other children (appears content and happy to do so). Then began concentrating on repetitively manipulating fingers by bending, twisting, turning (seems fascinated with manipulating them). . . .

Reflect and Apply

1. Review the notes you made. What was the child able to do? It is important to emphasize the *abilities* of children with special needs rather than how they are lagging behind their peers. How would this more positive perspective influence the ways in which you teach children with special needs?

2. Review the description in this chapter of the typically developing child that is closest in age to the child you observed. Compare the description with what you observed. What are the similarities and differences? Does this provide you with any insights into working with all children in early childhood settings?

No one list of characteristics describes children who are gifted. Certain traits and abilities, however, do seem to be common to many. Unusually strong language skills may indicate giftedness. These children frequently have a large and complex vocabulary and are able to use their words to create elaborate oral stories, songs, and rhymes. Early reading and writing are often demonstrated as well.

Strong skills of observation enable gifted children to pay attention to details that allow them to master concepts more quickly. Four-year-old Amy, for example, notices many differences in the colors and body parts of the ladybug caught on the playground this morning. She asks the adults around her many questions and is eager to look through the book in the library center that describes bugs.

Gifted children are often more willing to take risks and problem solve as they learn about their world. Curiosity and a willingness to explore possibilities make them eager to grow in their understanding of people and things. Eight-year-old Jerrod, for example, is constructing a castle out of blocks after reading a story about medieval times. He is having difficulty constructing a roof that meets his expectations and tries several possibilities before getting it the way he wants it.

summary

The Developmentally Appropriate Classroom

The characteristics of developmentally appropriate practice are a cornerstone of early care and education. Early educators must understand its dimensions, characteristics, and principles. This approach to teaching and learning is essential in high-quality early care and education.

Key Perspectives on Learning and Development

Caregivers and teachers need to understand the theories and concepts of John Bowlby (attachment), Abraham Maslow (hierarchy of needs), Howard Gardner (multiple intelligences), Maria Montessori (maturational theory), Lev Vygotsky (sociocultural theory), Erik Erikson (psychosocial theory), Jean Piaget (stages of intellectual development), Urie Bronfenbrenner (ecological theory), and Jack Shonkoff and Deborah Phillips (early brain development and self-regulation).

Children: Developmental Similarities and Differences

An understanding of the developmental characteristics of children from infancy through 8 years of age allows teachers to successfully prepare materials and activities for young children. Children with special needs (disabled, at-risk, and gifted) are an important part of early education; teachers need to understand and prepare for educating all children.

for reflection and discussion

1. Write a description of what you see as the key characteristics of developmentally appropriate practice.
2. Describe attachment and its influence on social and emotional development of young children.
3. Discuss with others how Maslow's description of a hierarchy of needs would influence teaching and learning in an early childhood setting.
4. Based on the readings you have done in this chapter, what similarities exist across children in the early childhood years? List these similarities, then compare your list with those of your classmates.

MyEducationLab

Go to Topic 2: Child Development/Theories in the MyEducationLab (www.myeducationlab.com) for *Teaching Young Children*, where you can:

- Find learning outcomes for Child Development/Theories along with the national standards that connect to these outcomes.
- Complete Assignments and Activities that can help you more deeply understand the chapter content.
- Apply and practice your understanding of the core teaching skills identified in the chapter with the Building Teaching Skills and Dispositions learning units.
- Check your comprehension on the content covered in the chapter with the Study Plan. Here you will be able to take a chapter quiz, receive feedback on your answers, and then access Review, Practice, and Enrichment activities to enhance your understanding of chapter content.

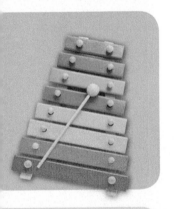

5

Play in Childhood

Your kindergarten children have just been dismissed for their morning recess. However, rather than heading down to the teacher's lounge today, you spend a few minutes watching your students engage in play just outside your classroom windows. It is amazing how busy they have become. Two minutes ago, they were listening quietly to the story you had chosen, but now the playground supervisor has her hands full. Phillip and John are already rolling around on the grass, enjoying the spring weather and the chance to engage in rough-and-tumble play. Maria and Chelsea are laughing and talking as they swing back and forth with their friends. Charlie and Andy are playing cops and robbers and chasing several girls excitedly around the playground. Joe is new to your class and is currently just observing the actions of others. The sandbox has attracted Albert and Amy, who are planning the castle they intend to build. Eric and Austin are climbing and swinging from the monkey bars, trying to outdo one another. The excitement and enthusiasm are evident. What is less obvious is all the learning that is taking place through the varied play experiences. If only others knew how valuable play can be during childhood, it would be much easier to include it as part of your school day. Just yesterday, a family member was quizzing you about the importance of play in the classroom, and once again you were explaining the many benefits of this natural part of childhood.

Unfortunately, the most common perception of play is that it is a fun but frivolous activity. Many families, the general public, and some early childhood professionals and administrators view play as a nice treat for children who have spent time engaged in more serious learning tasks. They question, however, its role in the early childhood curriculum. Despite its benefits, many find it difficult to rationalize play as a major learning tool. In this era of student assessment and educator accountability, more formal mathematics, science, social studies, and literacy learning tend to take precedence over all other activities.

This chapter begins by defining what constitutes childhood play and then identifies its many benefits. As you learn more about play by reading this chapter and discussing its contents with others, you will be better able to develop a strong rationale for including it in the early childhood curriculum. You will also find this information helpful in clarifying others' misconceptions about this important activity. Hopefully, as research continues to identify the many benefits of play (Fromberg & Bergen, 2006; Ginsburg, 2007; Wright & Neuman, 2009), it will find even greater acceptance among educators and others for its important role in development and learning.

Defining Play

It may be surprising to realize that childhood play is actually a difficult term to define. Garvey (1990) helps us understand the challenges of defining play through the following imaginary dialogue between a mother and her son:

> "Tom, I want to clean this room. Go out and play."
>
> "What do you mean, 'go out and play'?"
>
> "You know what I mean."
>
> "No, I don't."
>
> "Well, just go out and do whatever you do when you're having too much fun to come in to dinner."
>
> "You mean toss the tennis ball against the garage? Finish painting my bike? Practice standing on my head? Tease Andy's sister? Check out the robin eggs?" (p. 2)

The broad category of activities called play also includes a great variety of other behaviors, such as swinging, sliding, running, digging in the dirt, building with blocks, dancing to music, making up nonsense rhyming words, dressing up, and pretending. Because of this variety, no one definition of play can adequately describe its many facets. Understanding and using several different definitions helps you to better understand the complexities of play.

Characteristics of Play

One approach frequently used to define play is to list common characteristics of these experiences. Early researchers such as Huizinga (1955), Mitchell and Mason (1948), and Dearden (1968) all created lists of common characteristics of play. From these lists, four attributes stand out as essential to our understanding of the term. These characteristics are summarized in Figure 5–1. When all four characteristics are present, the activity is clearly play. However, when none of the characteristics are evident, the activity does not fit any of the commonly held definitions of play.

- **Activity level.** Play is *active*. When children play, movement often involves both large and small muscles. Children are using their bodies and manipulating the natural and human-made materials that they find in their play environments. Rather than passively taking in information, children involved in play are engaged in learning about the world by constructing knowledge through active interaction with people and things (Wright & Neuman, 2009).

MyEducationLab

Visit the MyEducationLab for *Teaching Young Children* to enhance your understanding of chapter concepts with a personalized Study Plan. You'll also have the opportunity to hone your teaching skills through video- and case-based Assignments and Activities as well as Building Teaching Skills and Disposition lessons.

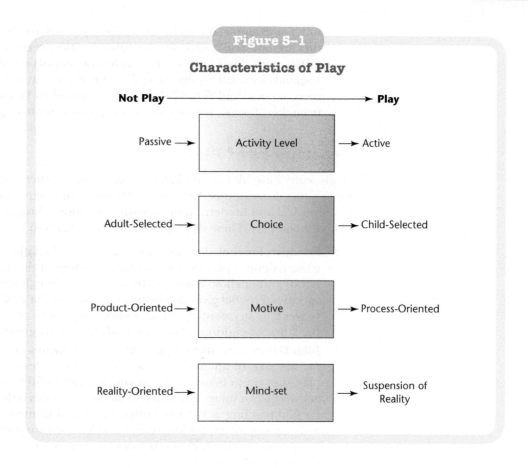

Figure 5–1

Characteristics of Play

Not Play ⟶ Play

Passive ⟶ | Activity Level | ⟶ Active

Adult-Selected ⟶ | Choice | ⟶ Child-Selected

Product-Oriented ⟶ | Motive | ⟶ Process-Oriented

Reality-Oriented ⟶ | Mind-set | ⟶ Suspension of Reality

- **Choice.** Play is child selected (Copple & Bredekamp, 2009). Quality play experiences are those in which the child chooses to participate. Consider, for example, a family member who tells her 6-year-old child to clean her room. For most children, the request to clean something would be met with groans and protests, and it would not be thought of as a playful event. This child, however, could choose to clean her bike in preparation for an upcoming ride and find the task enjoyable and generally playful. When the child chooses the task, it becomes fun and rewarding and is more likely to fit a broad definition of play.

- **Motive.** Children are motivated to play because of the pleasure of the activity. It is process-oriented rather than product-oriented (Bruner, 1972). Four-year-old Michael is constructing a road out of blocks. He makes it wide enough for the truck he is using and includes several intersections and curves. Once the road is built and he has used it for his truck play themes, Michael will be ready to dismantle it and move on to other projects. This process-orientation gives children in play the freedom to explore and experiment without fear of failure. There is no right or wrong way to play, so children can try a variety of play options, knowing that it is the road traveled rather than the destination that is the most important aspect of this activity.

- **Mind-set.** Play usually requires a suspension of reality. When children play, they set aside the realities of their world and enjoy activities that are often silly but fun. For example, the child who makes up nonsense rhyming words knows that they are not "real" words, but he still enjoys the process of creating them. Piaget (1962) calls this a *ludic set*. This ludic (or playful) mind-set allows children to suspend their knowledge of reality and engage in activities that are creative, spontaneous, and fun. Children who pretend to be astronauts or characters from their favorite movies are creating a ludic set to engage in this play.

Descriptors of Play

While some have identified characteristics of play, other writers' have defined play using short descriptions that identify its essential components. Descriptions from key historical and modern figures provide additional insights into the complexities of childhood play. These descriptors are summarized in Figure 5–2.

- **Friedrich Froebel,** described in Chapter 2 as the father of the modern kindergarten, defines play as "the natural unfolding of the germinal leaves of childhood" (Mitchell & Mason, 1948, p. 103). Although this description gives few specifics, Froebel gives us a beautiful metaphor for childhood play. He characterizes it as an essential and necessary component of childhood. Play is part of the fabric of children's lives and leads to healthy growth and development.

- **John Dewey** suggests that play consists of activities not consciously performed for the sake of any result beyond themselves (Dewey, 1929). When children play, they do so because the process is meaningful to them. The doing of the activity gives it value. The end product, if any, holds little meaning for the child. A child painting at the easel often has a goal in mind as she covers the page with vibrant colors, but the real joy of the activity is just engaging in the painting process itself. Once the painting is completed, she is ready to move on to the next challenge.

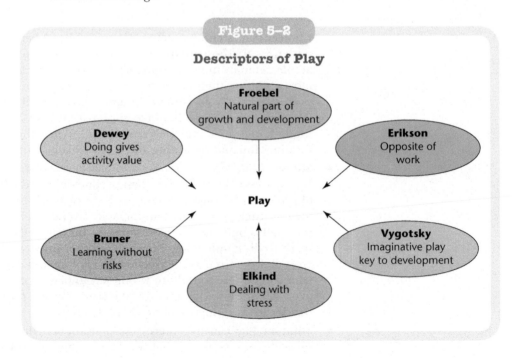

Figure 5–2

Descriptors of Play

- **Erik Erikson** defined play by contrasting it with work:

  When man plays he must intermingle with things and people in a similarly uninvolved and light fashion. He must do something which he has chosen to do without being compelled by urgent interests or impelled by strong passion. He must feel entertained and free of any fear or hope of serious consequences. He is on vacation from social and economic reality—or as is most commonly emphasized: he *does not work.* (Erikson, 1963, p. 212)

- **Jerome Bruner** writes about low-risk learning opportunities:

  Play appears to serve several centrally important functions. First, it is a means of minimizing the consequences of one's actions and of learning, therefore, in a less risky situation. . . . Second, play provides an excellent opportunity to try combinations of behavior that would, under functional pressure, never be tried. (Bruner, 1972, p. 693)

  Play, according to Bruner, can be seen as a prime opportunity for children to take risks without fear of failure. Bruner's definition also suggests that childhood play and creative activity are closely linked. When fear of failure is low and children can explore and experiment in their play, the possibilities for creative outcomes are greatly enhanced. For example, a young girl building with Legos can creatively explore and experiment without fear of failure. There is no right or wrong way to build with these materials.

- **Lev Vygotsky** views imaginative play as a key to the overall development of the child (Berk, 1994) by challenging the child to increasingly higher levels of functioning:

  Play creates a zone of proximal development in the child. In play, the child always behaves beyond his average age, above his daily behavior; in play it is as though he were a head taller than himself. As in the focus of a magnifying glass, play contains all developmental tendencies in a condensed form and is itself a major source of development. (Vygotsky, 1978, p. 102)

- **David Elkind** identifies the importance of play in dealing with stress. He states, "Basically, play is nature's way of dealing with stress for children as well as adults" (Elkind, 2001, p. 198). This perspective may be initially surprising, in part because it does not describe all play behaviors. But for a significant portion of children's activities, stress reduction is an important part of the play experience.

 Four-year-old Robert's mother is pregnant. Getting ready for a new brother or sister is stressful for him. Mom and dad are busy making preparations, there is less time and energy for the other children, and just making sense of the upcoming changes takes considerable time and energy. Robert's play in the dress-up corner at preschool reflects his attempts to make sense of these changes and work through the stresses of this coming event.

It is important to emphasize again that none of the characteristics or descriptions presented here is sufficient, in and of itself, to fully explain this complex phenomenon we call play. However, each provides additional insight to help us in our understanding of this important component of early care and learning. Collectively, they paint a clearer picture of this important concept.

Developmentally Appropriate Practice . . .
A PRETEND GROCERY STORE IN PREKINDERGARTEN

When given the time and appropriate materials, prekindergarten children can have great fun pretending as they play out a theme you have prepared as the early childhood professional. One example of this type of activity is to set up a grocery store in the dramatic play center. This theme can also be successfully used as a transitional activity during the early part of the kindergarten year.

Materials Needed

Grocery bags

Empty food containers such as soup and vegetable cans and cereal boxes (use your imagination)

Pictures or posters of food items

Telephone

Assorted baskets

Plastic foods

Play money (coins and paper)

Notepads for making out grocery lists

Sticky notes for pricing groceries

Writing utensils

Cash register

Adding machine

Shelves for storing foods

Checkout table

Mathematics and Literacy Learning

Children who are provided with these kinds of materials can take on the roles of shoppers, grocery checkers, and clerks. Some can price the groceries, others can shop for bargains on a budget, while a third group can be checkers. As they engage in these roles and have fun, young children are also learning a great deal. For example, they may be developing early mathematical skills by counting, comparing sizes, weighing, learning about money, and estimating. Children strengthen communication skills as they talk and listen in the roles they assume in the grocery store. Some may even make pretend "grocery lists" and practice some prewriting skills as they shop.

Why Children Play: Theories

Just as there are a variety of definitions of play, many different theories have been proposed to explain why children engage in this activity. Although no one theory is fully satisfying, together they add much to our understanding of a child's motivation to play. Ellis (1973) organizes theories of play into two categories: classical and contemporary. The classical theories are older and generally less complex in their explanations of why children play. Contemporary theories are more recent and provide a more detailed rationale for this childhood activity.

Classical Theories

Three classical theories add insights into why children play:

- **Surplus energy theory** suggests that each of us generates a finite level of energy that must be expended. Our first priority is to use that energy on survival. What is left over accumulates until it reaches a point where it must be used up. Play becomes the vehicle for expending that extra energy. This theory suggests that children play more than adults because they are not burdened with survival tasks. This theory has considerable appeal. Many times, children seem to need to use up their surplus energy. Yet, there are other times when children clearly are operating on energy reserves but still very much want to continue in their play.

- **Relaxation theory** is the opposite of the surplus energy theory and suggests that people play because of a deficit of energy. When we engage in tasks that are relatively new to us or that are demanding in some way, fatigue sets in and relaxation is needed to replenish our energy. Because children encounter more new tasks and challenges than adults do, they need to spend more time relaxing in play. This theory clearly has application for children in the primary school years. With the many new academic tasks they face, play becomes an important opportunity for rest and recuperation. Recess and indoor play breaks give children much-needed opportunities to get away from work-like experiences to reenergize.

- **Pre-exercise theory** views play as an opportunity to practice the skills necessary for adult life. When puppies engage in play fighting, for example, they are practicing survival skills they need in adult life. A young boy who pretends to be a daddy is also developing abilities for his future role as a parent. This theory proposes that through their play children practice dealing with such things as fear, anger, curiosity, assertion, and submission.

Children of all ages engage in meaningful play.

Contemporary Theories

While the classical theories previously described add some insights into why children play, they tend to be more limited in their scope. Three newer theories describe in more detail the rationale for childhood play. The psychoanalytic theory, play as arousal seeking, and the cognitive structures theory are all described in the paragraphs that follow and are summarized in Figure 5–3.

A more recent description of why children play is the **psychoanalytic theory**. Many have contributed to this perspective, but it is based primarily on the work of Sigmund Freud. He suggests that play is motivated by what he calls the *pleasure principle* (Freud, 1938). Pleasure is achieved, according to Freud, through wish fulfillment in play. When 7-year-old Maya pretends to be an astronaut, she is gaining pleasure by becoming that important person for a short period of time. Play provides an opportunity for children to bend reality and gain gratification.

This theory also suggests that play has significant therapeutic value. When children encounter unpleasant situations or stressful circumstances, play becomes the child's vehicle for mastering them. By playing out mom and dad fighting, 5-year-old Jemal can begin to make sense of this unpleasant event and eventually set it aside and move on to other play themes. A specific branch of therapy for children who have experienced severe stress is based on this premise. It is called *play therapy* (see, for example, Axline, 1947). Trained therapists use this approach to help victims of

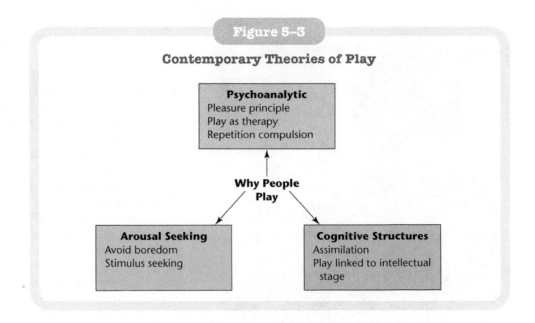

Figure 5-3

Contemporary Theories of Play

child abuse and those who have experienced other traumatic events come to grips with difficult and complex experiences.

Other theorists have expanded upon Freud's ideas concerning childhood play. One such person is Waelder (1933), who added the concept of the *repetition compulsion*. He identified the almost compulsive way in which many children will repeat an unpleasant experience in their play over and over again. Waelder states that children may find some events too difficult to assimilate all at once. They often need to play them out over and over again, until finally diminishing their intensity. For example, Brown, Curry, and Tittnich (1971) describe an event in which several kindergarten children observed a man who was critically injured on the street adjacent to their playground. In observations of later play experiences, it was clear to the writers that these children needed to repeat this very unpleasant and difficult event over and over in order to make better sense of it. Throughout the school year, this accident-related play theme reappeared regularly as children worked through their feelings.

Another more recent theory that has been proposed to explain why children play is called **play as arousal seeking**. Ellis (1973) developed this theory from a number of research studies that make a case for a new drive—the drive for optimal arousal. In an attempt to avoid boredom on the one hand and overstimulation on the other, people strive to reach just the right level of excitement. Each of us is engaged in behavior that can be called *stimulus seeking*. Play is a major opportunity for most of us to be stimulated. Not all stimulus seeking, however, is play. When 5-year-old Angie challenges herself to climb one level higher on the climber or 4-year-old Micah jumps off a 3-foot-high box, each is doing a bit of thrill seeking. These behaviors are somewhat risky and therefore more exciting for the children engaged in them. Although this theory again does not explain all types of children's play, it applies readily to many childhood activities.

A final theory about childhood play comes from the work of Piaget (1962). He explains this activity in terms of children's **cognitive structures**. As children learn about the world, they are adding to their *schema* or conceptual understandings.

These schema are strengthened through the dual processes of assimilation (taking in information from the environment and fitting it into an already existing schema) and accommodation (adjusting schema to take into account new input from the environment that does not fit existing structures). Piaget suggests that when children play they are engaging primarily in the process of assimilation. As children take in information during play, they are unconsciously growing in their understanding of the world.

Piaget also proposes that the play children engage in is strongly influenced by their intellectual stage of development. For example, he suggests that during the sensorimotor stage of intellectual development (approximately birth to age 2), children engage primarily in functional play. These simple, repetitive muscle movements match the cognitive functioning of the child during the sensorimotor period. Piaget's play stages have been expanded upon by Smilansky (1968) and are described in more detail in the next section of this chapter.

Cognitive and Social Play

People who have studied childhood play often categorize it according to either its cognitive or its social elements. **Cognitive play** categories identify the intellectual functioning of children during play. **Social play** categories describe how children gradually become more able to relate effectively with others as they play.

Cognitive Play

As suggested earlier, Piaget (1962) developed cognitive play categories that match each of his first three intellectual stages of development. Smilansky (1968) modified this approach slightly by defining a fourth cognitive play category. Her cognitive play stages have been widely accepted as an effective way to understand and study childhood play.

- **Functional play.** From birth to about age 2, children play by engaging in simple, repetitive muscle movements. Functional play develops physical skills and is done because the activity is pleasurable. The toddler who is learning to walk spends considerable time practicing the muscle movements necessary to get from one spot to the next. An infant shaking a rattle is also engaging in functional play. This play type is the predominant one during the first 2 years, but it does not end at that time. Primary children swinging on swings or running happily across the playfield are participating in functional play.

- **Construction play.** Children from about 2 to 3 years of age are involved primarily in actually making something out of the materials available to them. For example, when using a set of blocks, Alyssa can begin to create simple structures such as towers. The intellectual skills needed for building are a step above those required for functional play. Older children also engage in construction play, but it is the 2-year-old's primary cognitive play type.

- **Dramatic play.** From about age 3 to 7, children pretend that one object is something else, or they take on a role other than that of a child. For example, 4-year-old Lisa pretends to be a teacher and imitates what she has seen her preschool teacher do by encouraging her playmates to try new pretend

Developmentally Appropriate Practice . . .
GAMES FROM OTHER CULTURES

Orlick (1978) suggests that one good way to better understand different cultures is to play childhood games from around the world. Games provide young children with enjoyable ways to indirectly learn about the attitudes, values, and interests of different cultures. The following examples are just two of the many possibilities that early childhood professionals can consider using in their programs.

Pin

This game of cooperation is played by Native American children in Guatemala. A wooden pin is set up at a moderate distance from a throwing line. (The group can decide the length.) The object is for the team to work together to get the first ball that is rolled (lead ball) to touch the pin without knocking the pin over. The first player rolls her ball, and the subsequent team members try to roll their balls so that they nudge the lead ball closer to the pin. The game is won when the lead ball is touching the pin. If the pin is knocked over, the player who knocked it over starts a new game by rolling the first ball (Orlick, 1978, p. 76).

Muk (Silence)

This game comes from the Inuit people in Alaska and centers around laughter. Players begin by sitting in a circle. One player moves into the middle of the circle. He then chooses another player, who must say "Muk" and then remain silent and straight-faced. The person in the middle uses comical expressions and gestures to try to "break the muk." The player who breaks the muk is dubbed with a comical name and replaces the person in the middle (Orlick, 1978, p. 81).

Because of the current interest in multicultural education, there are many publications that present options for games from other cultures. Some are excellent activities, while others should not be used with young children. Choose games from other cultures that

- **De-emphasize competition.** While it is often difficult to eliminate competition entirely, it is important for young children to have games that involve minimal competition. The game *Pin*, described previously, has a competitive element but places more emphasis on the need to cooperate for a common goal.

- **Are developmentally appropriate.** Do not use games that are too advanced for a child's physical or mental development. For example, *Mancala* is an excellent African board game for older primary children, but it requires cognitive skills that most preschool children do not possess, and it should not be used at this age level (Orlick, 1978, p. 78).

- **Are enjoyable.** Clearly, there is little benefit to having children play a game they will not enjoy. It is important for them to laugh, have fun, and be successful with the activities you choose. The game *Muk*, described previously, should meet these criteria for primary children.

foods in the housekeeping center. She must use considerable intellectual skill to imagine the sequence she plays out with her peers. Research indicates that dramatic play is crucial as a foundation for later academic learning (Smilansky & Shefatya, 1990) and should be encouraged both at the preschool and early elementary levels.

- **Games with rules.** At approximately 7 years of age, children enter Piaget's stage of concrete operations and begin to engage in games with rules. These activities require children to agree to a set of rules before beginning play and to accept the defined penalties for breaking the rules (Piaget, 1965). The *Developmentally Appropriate Practice* feature in this section describes some examples of games from other cultures that can be introduced to primary-age children as an engaging way to help them learn about different cultures.

Observing Development . . .
SOCIAL PLAY

Choose one of the age groups within early childhood (infants/toddlers, preschoolers, or primary-age children) and *observe* social play. Focus all of the children in the group and take careful note of the social play you observe. Use the following sample observation as a format for your own observation. Place an x or check on the right-hand side each time you observe a new occurrence of social play.

Lakeway Elementary Playground, 2–2:30 p.m., March 23

Solitary Play (child plays alone)	X X
Parallel Play (playing beside, not with, others)	
Associative Play (similar play behaviors, borrowing/sharing play materials)	X X X
Cooperative Play (work to attain common goal)	X X
Cooperative-Competitive Play (activities leading to team victory)	X

Reflect and Apply

1. How did the social play you observed compare with the social play types identified in this chapter? How many children played together? What play materials were used? What were the activities the children engaged in?

2. Did the children you observed engage in more than one type of social play? From your perspective, why or why not?

3. What did you learn about how children play socially and about what you can do as an adult to facilitate this important aspect of play? Share your insights with others.

Social Play

A number of researchers and writers have suggested different categories to describe children's social play. The work of Mildred Parten (1933), however, has stood the test of time as one of the best and most descriptive summaries of the three social play stages of prekindergarten children. Seagoe (1970) identifies one additional social play type for primary children. After you read about these social play types, take the time to observe children engaged in social play. The *Observing Development* feature above will give you that opportunity.

Following are the four social play types:

- **Solitary play.** Until about 2½ years of age, children play alone, with toys that are different from those of children playing nearby. They make no attempt to get close to or interact with others. Clearly, the level of social interaction at this point is very low. Despite its lack of social interaction, however, solitary play should be encouraged as part of the young child's activities. Much of a primary child's day, for example, is spent in independent seat work. Children who have learned to be comfortable in solitary play are more likely to succeed in working independently.

- **Parallel play.** From about 2½ to 3½ years, children continue to play independently, but now they do so among their peers and they use toys that

In parallel play, children play beside, but not with, others.

are similar to those of the children around them. Just as parallel lines run side by side, children in this play stage play beside, but not with, others. There is an awareness of the children nearby but little interaction. Andre and Kelly are playing with play dough at the art center in their preschool program. They occasionally glance at each other's efforts but spend most of their time just molding their chunks of dough. They are engaging in parallel play.

- **Associative play.** At about 3½ years of age, children begin to truly play with others. Children borrow and loan play materials, and the group members engage in similar activities. Parten (1933) suggests that, at this point, the associations are more important than the play activity itself. Children begin to form small play groups and spend considerable time moving from one activity to the next, with playmates remaining together. Watch children of this age swinging on swings, for example. They enjoy the swinging but spend more of their efforts talking and laughing with their friends. When a group leader decides it is time to move on, others make the move as well. Being with the other children has become more important than the activity itself.

- **Cooperative play.** Beginning at about 4½ years of age, children continue to play in groups, as they did in associative play, but now they demonstrate division of labor, working on a group project or cooperating to attain a common goal. When four kindergarten children decide to build a town with blocks, and each takes a specific part of the town to build, play has become cooperative. It is important to note that, although cooperative play requires practicing important social skills, it is not always a desired play type. Think about three preschool children who decide to torment a fellow classmate. Although each takes on a separate role and the children are working toward a common goal, the play is unpleasant for the targeted child.

- **Cooperative-competitive play.** Seagoe (1970) identified a social play type for older children, beginning at about age 7 or 8, that she called cooperative-competitive play. It involves activities that are formally patterned toward team victory. Organized team sports such as soccer and baseball are examples of this play type. The social understanding needed for cooperative-competitive play is more advanced than that required for the cooperative play described by Parten. The *Celebrating Play* feature in this section talks about the benefits of having primary children invent games that they can then play with classmates. Once they are ready for cooperative-competitive play, this can be a very motivating learning experience.

Celebrating Play . . .
PRIMARY CHILDREN'S INVENTED GAMES

After their second-grade teacher discusses the procedures for creating a board game, Rebecca and Latoya decide to give it a try. During free time, they begin planning a board game around the theme of horse racing. For the next week, these girls spend all of their spare moments avidly constructing their game and then sharing it with the rest of the class. Given the opportunity, primary children seem to love the chance to invent their own games. Castle (1990) describes several benefits of this activity:

- **Practice academic skills such as writing, reading, and mathematics.** Children use writing skills, for example, to label game parts and create game instructions.

- **Develop organizational skills like having a plan and putting it to work.** Planning the game sequence requires the use of organizational abilities.

- **Cooperate with other children and adults.** Through the planning and construction process, children must take into account the perspectives of others and learn to adjust their game accordingly.

- **Solve problems as children encounter differing opinions about how the game should proceed.** Once a prototype is constructed, children practice problem solving as they debug the difficulties they encounter when playing.

1. Try constructing your own game to discover the challenges this task may require of children. Share your game with others, and then modify it based on the feedback you get.

2. If you were teaching in a primary classroom, would you have children take school time to invent their own games? Why or why not?

Benefits of Play

Jay and Aaron are excitedly rummaging through the junk pile used for outdoor play at their preschool. This collection of bricks, boards, old tires, and assorted building materials has them thinking of the many different structures they might construct. There is no thought in their minds of the learning potential of these tasks. These two young boys are merely playing. Yet, mathematics, language usage, social skills, basic physics principles, and more may all be enhanced as they play out their fantasies.

Growing numbers of professionals outside the field of early childhood education, and families of young children are recognizing the benefits of play. For example, the American Academy of Pediatrics (2006) recently published a clinical report affirming the social, emotional, and cognitive benefits of play. In addition, groups such as the International Play Association (IPA, 2010), the Association for Childhood Education International (Isenberg & Quisenberry, 2010), the Alliance for Play (Miller & Almon, 2009), and the National Association for the Education of Young Children (Copple & Bredekamp, 2009) have been promoting the importance of childhood play for several decades. Unfortunately, there are still large numbers of adults who fail to understand its importance (Elkind, 2006). For that reason, it is critical that the many benefits of play be shared with families, other early childhood

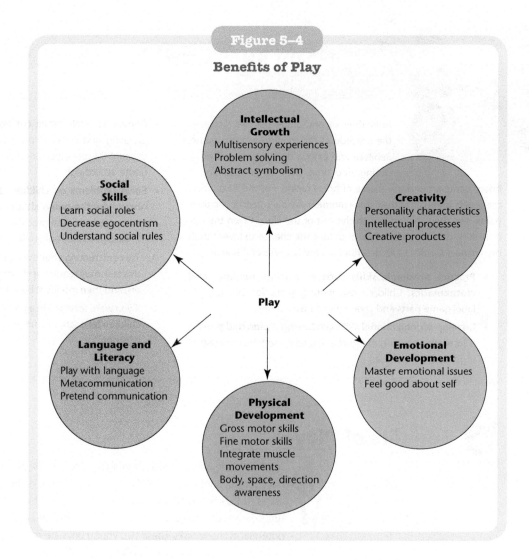

Figure 5–4

Benefits of Play

professionals, administrators, and the general public. Every aspect of the child's development is enhanced through play. It is just not obvious to many people at first glance. Figure 5–4 summarizes the benefits of play.

Intellectual Growth through Play

Because many people assume that the primary goal of schooling is to feed the intellect, this discussion on the benefits of play begins with information on how play enhances cognitive development. Using Piaget's terminology, *cognitive development* is the process of building more elaborate schema or concepts about the workings of the world. Play builds schema in three important ways:

1. **Multisensory experiences** with things and people in the child's environment lead to enhanced conceptual development (Bruner, 1966; Piaget & Inhelder, 1969). Play provides the most natural and enjoyable opportunities for these

experiences and, therefore, is a major tool that children use to understand their world. When 7-year-olds David and Jessica construct cardboard castles during free choice time, they are internalizing the information they read in their social studies text. Their play has expanded and solidified several existing schema.

2. **Effective problem solving** is another major asset in intellectual development. Children who can make sense of the problems they face and work through them are adding greatly to their understanding of the world and their ability to work through future problems. Evidence points to a clear link between play and problem solving. Children who engage in creative play experiences are better at convergent (Vandenberg, 1980) and divergent (Pepler & Ross, 1981) problem solving. Play frees up children to explore and experiment in ways that lead to important intellectual understanding.

> When 4-year-olds Kelly and Sarah play in the dramatic play area, they discover that they do not have the props they need to become pilots. After yesterday's field trip to the airport, they are very excited about this play theme. Kelly discovers a headset from the listening center and decides it can be used "for one of those things pilots listen and talk through." sarah arranges several child-sized chairs into rows for the passengers. After several minutes of preparation, they have created the basic props they need for their play, and they begin the process of acting out their respective roles.

During play, children encounter and master new problems as well. Play provides many chances for practicing problem solving.

3. **Mastering abstract symbolism** is a third major way in which play assists in intellectual development by helping children master abstract symbolism. This is especially true when children engage in dramatic play. As they pretend, children arbitrarily assign meaning to objects they are using in their play. A block is temporarily viewed as a door to the castle, child-sized chairs in rows become passengers seating on an airplane, or a magnifying glass becomes "that thing doctors use." Objects become arbitrary, abstract symbols for real items needed for dramatic play. Nourot and Van Hoorn (1991) state this same concept as follows: "In its complex forms play is characterized by the use of symbols to represent objects, ideas, and situations not present in the immediate time and place" (p. 41).

Children who are able to manipulate abstract symbols in their play are more likely to succeed in managing symbols in school. Both reading and mathematics are fundamental components of formal education that require frequent manipulation of arbitrary and abstract symbol systems. Smilansky and Shefatya (1990) emphasize that children who are good at dramatic play are going to be more successful with these and other academic tasks. Art experiences provide children with additional opportunities to manipulate symbols and should be readily available in early childhood settings. The *Technology Explorations and Activities* feature in this section asks you to consider the merits of electronic art for young children.

Technology Explorations and Activities . . .
PLAYFUL ELECTRONIC ART

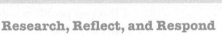

This chapter has emphasized the many important benefits of play in the lives of young children. Typically, this means that children use blocks, paper, dolls, puppets, and other real world toys and materials to engage in quality play experiences. But another option being promoted by some is the use of computer games and activities as tools for creative play. One such option is Bomomo, an interactive art-like activity available free on the Internet. Children can use a desktop computer or a tablet to playfully engage in art-like activities. Do an Internet search for this website and spend some time exploring the activities presented there.

Research, Reflect, and Respond

1. After spending time exploring the options on the Bomomo website, reflect on your reactions to the activities. Did you find it enjoyable? Do you think young children would find it a fun site to explore? What ages of children do you think would find it interesting?

2. Compare and contrast Bomomo art with the paper, crayons, and paints more typically found in early childhood settings. Do you think one is more valuable than the other? Why or why not?

3. Look back over the characteristics of play identified in this chapter. Using those characteristics as a guide, do you think Bomomo is a playful activity? Why or why not?

Building Social Skills

In addition to its role in cognitive development, play is an important tool for strengthening social skills in three main ways:

1. **Learning about social roles.** As they play, children have many opportunities to learn about the social world in which they live. The give and take that occurs as children interact helps them learn about social roles. Following a trip to the fire station, for example, a group of first graders try out this role in their play outdoors. They are consolidating and integrating their understandings of this important work situation.

2. **Decreasing egocentrism.** Piaget describes children in the preoperational stage of intellectual development (approximately 2 through 7 years of age) as egocentric. He means that it is difficult for children at this age to see things from another person's perspective. Play provides them with many opportunities to decrease egocentrism (Piaget, 1962). To maintain a play sequence, children are forced to acknowledge other viewpoints and modify or adapt the activity accordingly. For example, Ariel and Reetha are playing train conductors. Ariel is upset because "only boys should wear the conductor's hat." Reetha, however, feels that girls can, too. These two will need to recognize their differing perspectives and work out a solution to continue the play sequence.

3. **Understanding the rules of social interaction.** Play also allows children to learn and practice the principles that underlie all social exchanges (Nucci & Killen, 1991). Such tasks as listening, speaking, taking turns, leading, and following are all guided by commonly understood rules. For example, we all understand that if several people in a group have something to contribute to the conversation, only one can speak at a time. To do otherwise would lead

Play provides many opportunities for literacy learning.

to mass confusion. Children learn this and other similar rules for social interactions as they become involved in their many play experiences.

Chantel and Marta both want to be teacher as they play during free time in kindergarten. As they realize that it works best to have only one teacher at a time, the girls practice the art of negotiation and compromise so that the play may continue. They learn social rules in a safe and enjoyable way as they proceed.

Language and Literacy Development

Through play, children also enhance oral and written language skills. Garvey (1990) suggests that every aspect of language can be better understood through play. Phonology (sounds of language), grammar, and meaning are all playfully explored as children engage in their free-choice activities. Garvey proposes four different types of play with language:

1. **Play with sounds and noises.** Children explore the sounds used to form words and experiment with putting them together in creative and fun ways.
2. **Play with the linguistic system.** In their play, children begin to understand how sounds combine to form words, and recognize the structure and ordering of words in sentences.
3. **Spontaneous rhyming and word play.** Through simple rhyming games, children learn about the structure of words and their meanings.
4. **Play with the conventions of speech.** By using and breaking the rules for conversation, children learn how to effectively communicate.

In addition to playing with language, children use language in and around their play experiences. **Metacommunication statements** are used to structure and organize play. "Let's pretend this rope is a snake." "First we'll go to the market, then the toy store." **Pretend communication statements** are appropriate to the roles children have adopted. "Hush, baby! Mom is on the telephone!"

During the preschool and primary school years, children learn about the written language around them as well. Play can provide many opportunities to facilitate literacy development.

Cindy and Erik, both age 4, are playing in the restaurant set-up in the dramatic play area at their child-care center. Erik takes orders by scribbling on a notepad and passing the orders on to Cindy, who cooks up some imaginary foods. Anook has built a town out of blocks modeled after the story he has just read in his second-grade classroom. Once the town is completed, he writes an imaginary tale describing life in his town.

Developmentally Appropriate Practice . . .
TOYS FOR LANGUAGE LEARNING

During the preschool and primary years, young children are growing daily in their understanding of language. One thing that caregivers and teachers can do to help stimulate language learning is to provide a variety of toys for children to use in their play. While virtually every piece of play equipment has the potential to stimulate language learning, some seem to be used most productively by young children. Following are four examples of this type:

- **Puppets.** Handheld puppets are fascinating to many children. As soon as they pick them up, they begin a running dialogue with others as they speak through the puppet. Even many shy children find this an easy way to engage in social communications with others.

- **Telephones and cell phones.** By their very nature, telephones and cell phones encourage young children to pretend they are calling and talking to someone else. These conversations with peers and adults give children many opportunities to speak, listen, and learn more about the rules that govern social interactions. In the home, cell phones also provide excellent opportunities to engage in meaningful written communications through the use of text messages.

- **Audio recorders.** Children are often amazed to hear themselves on an audio recording. Once instructed on the proper use of an audio recorder, they can enjoy making endless recordings of communications with others.

- **Electronic toys.** Many of the "talking" electronic toys (such as those from the LeapPad® company) provide numerous opportunities for young children to hear sounds and words spoken and then practice repeating them in a game-like format.

When appropriate props are available, play becomes a rich resource for literacy learning (Owocki, 1999; Riley & Jones, 2010). The *Developmentally Appropriate Practice* feature in this section provides ideas for toys that can be effectively used with preschool and primary children for language and literacy learning.

Physical Development and Health

For many, play is epitomized by children running, climbing, jumping, and moving. The pure joy of these simple physical activities is warmly remembered. Children using their large muscles in these activities are strengthening their **gross motor development**. Beginning in infancy, children improve neuromuscular coordination through repeated use of their large muscles. Batting at a mobile as an infant, walking during early toddlerhood, running and climbing at the preschool level, and swinging and skipping in the primary years are all examples of how play enhances gross motor development (Pica, 2004).

Play activities also include use of smaller muscles for a variety of tasks. **Fine-motor development** is refined through cutting, lacing, buttoning, painting, and writing experiences in play. Building with Legos®, putting together puzzles, sand and water play, woodworking projects, play dough, and dressing dolls are additional examples of play activities that promote fine-motor development.

As children mature, they use their muscles in continually more complex ways, integrating large and fine muscle movements with visual perception. Play allows frequent practice of these complicated actions. Hitting and catching a ball, jumping rope, playing hopscotch, and using the monkey bars are all examples of these

Developmentally Appropriate Practice . . .
INFANT/TODDLER EXPLORATION AND MOVEMENT

Because very young children learn a great deal from their physical interactions with the environment, it is essential to provide materials and activities that stimulate exploration and movement. The High/Scope program, a nationally validated model of early learning, identifies exploration and movement as two of the ten key experiences for infants and toddlers (Post & Hohmann, 2000). The following information provides a more detailed description of these two key experiences along with some suggested materials and activities that support them:

Exploring objects. Infants and toddlers need numerous daily opportunities to explore with their hands and feet, and with each of their senses. Examples include the following:

- Safe and nontoxic infant/toddler toys that can be shaken, dropped, mouthed, carried, and used as tools to complete a task.
- Interesting patterns and bright/colorful objects for visual exploration.

- Sound-making toys like rattles and noisemakers; music and nature tapes or CDs for listening.

Movement. As very young children slowly develop greater mastery of physical movement and learn intellectually about the things in their environment through exploration, they also develop greater social and emotional maturity. Examples include the following:

- Crawling and walking lead the infant/toddler to greater levels of independence and more motivation to further explore the environment.
- Climbing an incline or stacking objects gives a heightened sense of self and leads to an attitude of "I can do it!"
- Greater physical mobility puts infants and toddlers in closer proximity to other children and adults. Social exchanges that begin with looks, touches, and vocalizations slowly grow into early attempts at interactions with others.

more difficult coordinated movements. In addition, play allows children to develop a better awareness of body, space, and direction. As they move their bodies, children learn about up, down, in, out, over, under, left, right, and more as they climb, swing, crawl, and run. Playing in the gym or outdoors is particularly good for body awareness learning. The *Developmentally Appropriate Practice* feature in this section provides additional thoughts on physical development during the infant/ toddler years.

While play is important for physical development, activities that promote *healthy young bodies* are also critical in early childhood settings. Today, as many as one fourth of all children between the ages of 2 and 5 are overweight (Huber, 2009). Other statistics indicate that obesity affects fully one-third of all children (Crosnoe, 2010). Regardless of the exact numbers, it is clear that young children need to be given many opportunities to engage in vigorous physical activities in indoor and outdoor settings. Caregivers and teachers need to plan for extended periods of time for young children of all ages to engage in these important tasks.

Despite the strong need, there are indications that nearly half of all young children do not receive the amount of physical activity recommended by the National Association for Sport and Physical Education (Tucker, 2008). Part of the reason for this is that in many elementary schools across the nation, traditional recess time is either being reduced or lost, despite the many benefits that are associated with it

(Jarrett & Waite-Stupiansky, 2009). Caregivers and teachers of young children need to work hard to counteract these troublesome trends by planning activities that encourage more physical activities:

- **Infants and toddlers** need to develop fundamental motor skills and find pleasure in being physically active. This foundation of physical activity can then be built upon in later years (Deiner & Qui, 2007).
- **Preschool children** are ready for more vigorous physical activities and should be encouraged to run, jump, and be active, particularly in outdoor settings.
- **Primary children** can be encouraged to engage in active games that stimulate large muscle use over more extended periods of time (Jarrett & Waite-Stupiansky, 2009).

Emotional Development

Play is an excellent vehicle for helping children with their emotional (also called *affective*) development (Ginsburg, 2007; Miller & Almon, 2009). In their play, children can master emotional issues such as anxiety, frustration, normal developmental conflicts, traumatic situations, unfamiliar concepts, and overwhelming experiences.

Four-year-old Raul just had a very exciting trip to the museum, although his initial experience was a bit overwhelming. Just inside the door to the museum was a huge skeleton of a Tyrannosaurus rex. When his father told Raul that this was once a living animal, he was shocked. How could anything that big ever have lived? During the days and weeks that follow in preschool, Raul played out his wonderment by making dinosaurs with play dough, drawing dinosaurs, building dinosaur cages with the blocks, and fighting dinosaurs on the playground. It will take him many weeks to play through this interest, but when it is completed, Raul will have mastered a complex emotional issue.

Another major emotional benefit of play is that it gives children numerous opportunities to feel good about themselves. Because there is no right or wrong way to play, children have successful experiences that positively influence their self-concept.

Annette, age 18 months, is playing with a set of nesting blocks in her toddler class, experimenting with building a tower. Although this was not the intended use for this toy, Annette has managed a stack of three blocks—her tallest yet. Her success is evident in the huge smile that seems to fill her whole face. She is feeling good about herself right now.

Play and Creativity

Sometimes, thoughts of the creative process bring to mind those rare individuals who invent marvelous new products or play a musical instrument better than anyone else. These truly gifted individuals certainly add richness to the lives of those around them. Yet, each of us has creative potential that can be expressed in different and enjoyable ways. Early childhood professionals need to look for and nurture this aspect of each child's personality.

Creativity, like play, is not an easy concept to define. Hughes (1999) identifies three important elements of creativity: (a) personality characteristics; (b) intellectual processes; and (c) creative products. These are described in the following text. Comments follow about how play provides numerous opportunities to strengthen each of these elements:

- **Personality characteristics.** Creative people have specific personality characteristics that lend themselves to engaging in creative activity. They tend to be mentally flexible, spontaneous, curious, and persistent. Particularly in young children, these characteristics are still forming. Play provides many daily opportunities to stimulate these attributes. Wassermann (1992) states it this way: "The creation of new ideas does not come from minds trained to follow doggedly what is already known. Creation comes from tinkering and playing around, from which new forms emerge" (p. 134).

- **Intellectual processes.** Creativity can also be viewed as a way of thinking. Individuals who are creative approach situations or problems with an open mind and an ability to look at them in unusual ways. Play again presents young children with a variety of settings in which they can practice this open-minded exploration and problem solving. Goertzel and Goertzel (1962) studied the early years of 400 famous adults and discovered that a common thread for these creative individuals was the opportunity to explore their areas of interest and play with things and ideas. For example, Frank Lloyd Wright was encouraged by his mother from an early age to play with colored papers and cubes of wood. She felt that these play experiences would stimulate his intellectual development.

- **Creative products.** Adult creativity sometimes results in an original product or contribution that benefits humanity. Young children rarely engage in this kind of creative activity. However, a child who uses paints to create a new and unusual product for that child is engaging in work that could be the precursor to adult creative products. By encouraging these early creative efforts, adults working with young children help build attitudes and experiences that may lead to more creative products during adulthood. Clearly, play will not make a creative genius out of every child. However, it does help stimulate each person's creative talents.

Gared is having fun painting in his second-grade classroom. As he deftly strokes paint on the paper, he gains a sense of control over the elements he is working with. Gared feels good about himself and his artwork. When he gets positive feedback from his classmates and adults, his pleasure increases even further. Gared's continued success in art will bolster his attitude about school and increase his willingness to try out his creative skills in other areas of school life.

 ## Facilitating Childhood Play

Play seems to be such a natural part of childhood that it is difficult to imagine children needing help with this part of their lives. However, the many hours spent in front of the television and other electronic media, the overscheduling of children's lives, and a reluctance of many families to let their children go outside and play for safety reasons have all taken their toll on children's play abilities. In addition, many adults fail to recognize the importance of play in children's lives. Children today often need the help and support of caring adults to engage in quality play experiences.

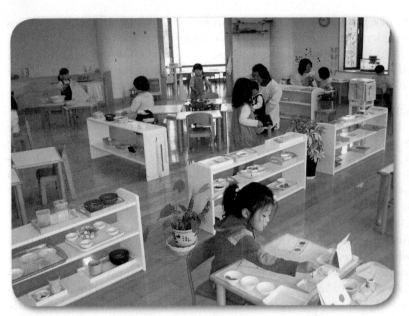

Early childhood professionals need to carefully prepare children's play environments.

Preparing the Play Environments

One important role adults have in facilitating play is to prepare the places where children play. Caregivers and teachers need to provide materials and create spaces for play both indoors and outdoors if quality experiences are to take place there (Copple & Bredekamp, 2009; Curtis & Carter, 2003; Mashburn, 2008). Time and energy must be spent in carefully planning these environments. Materials should change regularly, so that children have opportunities to play with new toys and equipment often. A variety of challenges should be available for the diverse abilities that children bring with them to their play. As a general rule of thumb, there should be at least one-and-a-half play options per child, both indoors and outside. For a class of 25 kindergarten children, this means that between 40 and 50 play options should be available so that each child has a variety of choices.

Part of preparing the play environments includes making every effort to plan settings so that all children can engage in creative play experiences. Children at all levels of social, emotional, physical, and intellectual ability need to be considered while planning the indoor and outdoor environment. The *Celebrating Diversity* feature in this section provides more information and suggestions on how this planning should take place.

Creating a Climate for Play

The early childhood professional must create an atmosphere that lets children know that play is valued. One way to do this is to allow plenty of time for play (Elkind, 2006; Ward, 1996). Quality play experiences can seldom be completed in 10 or 15 minutes. A minimum of 30 minutes (more is better) is needed for creative indoor and outdoor play.

 As Meesha begins her second-grade art project, she needs a few minutes to see what is available today in the way of materials, then time to settle on an idea, and finally additional opportunity to do her art activity. Once her project is complete, Meesha needs time to share ideas with others in the art center and to clean up before moving on to the next activity.

An adult's response to children as they play also strongly influences the climate for play. Making encouraging statements to children when they share, commenting on the positive uses of play materials, and just being nearby to assist as needed all help children know that play is valued. "Philip, thank you for sharing the blocks with Cheri! The two of you are creating some amazing structures!" "Cassandra, I like the

Celebrating Play...
ENGAGING ALL CHILDREN IN PLAY

Play can be considered the "universal language" of childhood. All children, regardless of their cultural heritage, gender, ability, and socioeconomic status, engage in play. It is important for you to realize that the similarities in play experiences between diverse groups of children are much greater than the differences. Having said that, here are some important thoughts about the play you will observe among the diverse children you will have in your future early childhood settings:

- **Culture and play.** There are many games that are very similar across cultures. For example, variants of "hide and seek" games are found in nearly every cultural tradition (Kirchner, 2000). It is important for early childhood professionals to emphasize these similarities as they engage children in play activities.

- **Gender and play.** Boys and girls, while engaging in many similar activities, tend to play somewhat differently. Boys are more often engaged in active/aggressive play, while girls tend to spend more time in play that develops language and relationships (Fromberg, 2002). Both sexes need to be encouraged to participate in activities that are outside their normal preferences.

- **Disabilities and play.** Children with special needs enjoy play experiences as much as any other child. While disabilities may delay the typical developmental patterns of play, when appropriate activities and materials are provided, quality play experiences result (Casey, 2008).

- **Socioeconomic status and play.** Children from low-income families tend to have fewer opportunities for play than their more advantaged peers. Consequently, their play skills are often less well developed (Smilansky & Shefatya, 1990). However, because of the importance of play in children's development, children from low-income families need even more opportunities for creative play.

1. Given the importance of childhood play (see following section), should every single child in your future early childhood program be encouraged to engage in play? Why or why not?

2. Based on what you now know about childhood play, what can you do to encourage all children to participate in meaningful play experiences? Identify two or three specific ideas that you could implement.

way you combined the blue and yellow paints in this part of your picture. It makes an interesting contrast to the rest of your work." An adult's comments and actions are essential in promoting quality play experiences.

Promoting the Importance of Play

Families and other adults are often unaware of the tremendous potential for learning through play. Particularly in the primary classroom, these skeptics must be helped to understand the rationale for including this activity. When families and others come to value play, children will have more and better opportunities to spend time playing. The *Family Partnerships* feature in this section describes some ways in which you can encourage play at home.

In addition, you may need to educate other early childhood professionals and administrators about the values of play (Riley & Jones, 2010). Wasserman (2000) has written an excellent book that emphasizes the importance of play in the primary grades. She describes clearly how children who engage in creative play experiences build cognitive and linguistic skills that are invaluable in the schooling process. They also gain confidence in their abilities to be creative problem solvers.

The primary grades are particularly difficult years for teachers who want to encourage play in the classroom. The strong push from most administrators and families is to spend instructional times engaged in more academic pursuits. Yet, the

Family Partnerships...
ENCOURAGING PLAY AT HOME

Because of the importance of childhood play, one of your roles as a future caregiver or teacher of young children is to make sure that, in addition to including play in the early childhood setting, play is encouraged as an option in the home environment as well. Unfortunately, many families are either unaware of play's importance or simply do not provide children with the encouragement they need to get involved in creative play experiences. With the incredibly fast pace of family life today, many children are not engaging in much creative play at home. There are several steps you can take to help encourage play at home:

- **Share the values of play.** Your first task will be to make sure that families know how valuable play is in the overall development of children. You will need to share this message repeatedly and in as many different ways as possible so that there is no mistake about its importance. E-mail messages, newsletters (both electronic and paper), and personal communications are all options that you can use to share with families the importance of play.

- **Encourage families to turn off the television and other electronic media.** In many homes, most of a child's free time is spent watching television and using a variety of electronic media such as computers, video games, and cell phones. While these activities have their place, when they take away opportunities for creative childhood play they are being misused (Elkind, 2006).

- **Provide time to play.** The busy nature of family life makes it difficult for children to engage in play. If valuable structured activities such as swim lessons, dance classes, and music lessons take up most of a child's free time, there will be few opportunities for creative play experiences. Encourage families to make time for creative play. Children need to have a balance of structured and unstructured times.

- **Find play partners.** Many of the richest play experiences are ones that occur in small groups. However, children today typically do not simply wander outside or next door for some quality play experiences. For a variety of reasons, families must now spend time and effort to bring children together for play. While this is an extra commitment for adults, it pays rich dividends in the quality of play experiences for children.

- **Supply play materials.** While they need not cost a lot, families should make sure that creative play materials are available for young children to use at home. For example, collecting some old adult clothes, shoes, jewelry, and hats for dress-up play is a relatively simple and inexpensive option for creative play at home.

1. Think back to your own childhood and the play experiences you had at home. What things do you remember? Can you see yourself encouraging families to provide similar opportunities for their children? Why or why not?

2. Do you think children engage in fewer play experiences at home than they did 20 or 30 years ago? Do you think it is important to encourage more play at home? Why or why not?

benefits of play for children 5 through 8 are still very strong (Riley & Jones, 2010). Stone (1995) provides several concrete suggestions for becoming an advocate for childhood play in the primary grades. Some of these are as follows:

- **Understanding the values of play.** This is an important first step for early childhood professionals. They need to be clear about the many benefits of play before promoting it with others.

- **Posting the values of play prominently in the early childhood setting.** Both children and families can be visually reminded of the importance of play.

- **Providing evidence of how learning is enhanced through play.** By displaying examples of things children have invented or problems they have solved through play, others can see concrete evidence of the value of play.

- **Sharing good articles on play with others.** Provide articles from experts on the benefits of play to families on a regular basis. The Companion Website for this chapter lists some good examples of this type of article.

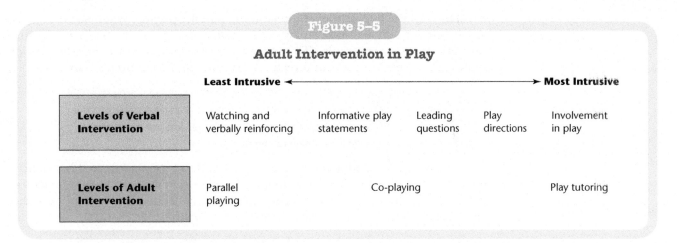

Figure 5–5

Adult Intervention in Play

Least Intrusive ◄————————————————————► Most Intrusive

Levels of Verbal Intervention	Watching and verbally reinforcing	Informative play statements	Leading questions	Play directions	Involvement in play

Levels of Adult Intervention	Parallel playing	Co-playing	Play tutoring

Adult Involvement in Play

As much as possible, children should be allowed to engage in play with little or no adult involvement. When given these opportunities, most children will play meaningfully and well. Because of the nature of children and the play experience, however, there are times when adults need to become more directly involved in play so that they can enrich the experience or move it in a different direction. This is not something the caregiver or teacher should take on lightly, because an adult's participation can actually undermine the child's creativity, spontaneity, and choices for play. After carefully assessing the need for involvement in play, the adult should participate at the lowest level possible. Figure 5–5 summarizes two different descriptions that writers have presented for adult intervention in children's play.

Heidemann and Hewitt (1992) suggest a model for adult intervention that primarily emphasizes verbal involvement, beginning first with the least-intrusive verbal intervention strategies and working toward more active involvement as needed.

- **Watching and verbally reinforcing** is the least-intrusive intervention. Adults who simply observe children at play or who verbally reinforce positive play behaviors are intervening at a low level to extend and strengthen play.
- **Informative play statements** give children ideas for strengthening their play without directly asking them to do so. (Example: "Doctors usually work with one patient at a time so they can help each one with their problems.")
- **Leading questions** are somewhat more intrusive since they often require a verbal or physical response by the child. Their intent is to give children ideas for extending and enriching the play sequence. (Example: "Where will you go when you have finished your grocery shopping?")
- **Play directions** inform children of actions they should take to strengthen their play. (Example: "Phillip, while you are waiting for a turn on a trike, you can be the police officer and tell the cars which way to go.")
- **Involvement in play** is the most intrusive, but may be needed to get children who are struggling with a theme to engage in quality play behaviors. It is important to emphasize once again that, ideally, play should be child-initiated and child-directed. Only when the play is faltering should adults intervene and then at the least intrusive level possible.

Johnson, Christie, and Yawkey (1987) describe a second model of adult intervention in play, which includes three levels of adult involvement in children's play. They call the lowest level of intervention **parallel playing**. When an adult plays beside, but not with, children and uses the same materials as the other participants, she is engaging in parallel play. This play type allows children to see the adult model positive play behaviors without directly intervening in the children's activities.

 Hermione notices that several toddlers in her program are having difficulty finding productive ways to use the play dough in the art center. She sits down at the table, tears off a piece of dough, and begins to roll it out into long snakes while quietly humming to herself.

The next level of adult involvement is referred to as **co-playing**. In this instance, the adult actually enters the children's play but allows them to control the activities. By taking on a needed role and, again, modeling appropriate play responses, the adult can subtly influence the direction and complexity of the play.

 As Antoine watches the play in the dress-up corner of his kindergarten classroom, he notices that children are struggling with the role of patient at the doctor's office. Walking into the center, he volunteers to be the next patient and helps children see how this person should interact with the doctors and nurses by playing out the role.

The highest level of involvement in play by early childhood professionals is called **play tutoring**. Taken from the work of Sara Smilansky (1968), this form of participation requires the adult to take at least partial control of the play situation. The adult now gives children directions or suggestions that lead the play into new areas. It is possible to engage in play tutoring while participating in the children's play or to guide them from outside the play sequence. In either instance, the adult must intervene in such a way that children can learn from the suggestions being made and can reinitiate their own leadership of the play events as quickly as possible. As with the verbal interventions described earlier, it is important to remember that adult participation should be limited in duration and done at the least-intrusive level possible.

 As Ellen passes by the block center in her third-grade classroom, she notices that Awesta and Carrie are struggling with the castle they are trying to build. She states: "Before you two go any further in your building, perhaps you should review the book you have and then sketch the castle you would like to construct. That may give you the ideas you need to continue your project."

 summary

Defining Play

Childhood play is far more complicated and diverse than most people realize. Understanding the characteristics and definitions of childhood play help clarify the meaning and value of this important childhood activity.

Why Children Play: Theories

An understanding of theories, both classical and contemporary, adds further insights into why children play. Because of its complexities, no one theory can adequately explain why children play. Theories are generally classified as either classical (surplus energy, relaxation, pre-exercise) or contemporary (psychoanalytic, play as arousal seeking, cognitive structures).

Cognitive and Social Play

Researchers and writers have categorized play according to either its cognitive or its social elements. The four cognitive play stages of Smilansky describe increasingly complex intellectual activities that occur during play. Mildred Parten identifies four levels of social interactions in childhood play.

Benefits of Play

Play provides opportunities to enhance all aspects of child development. The intellectual, social, linguistic, physical, and emotional benefits of play define a strong rationale for including play in the early childhood setting.

Facilitating Childhood Play

The adult's role in facilitating play includes preparing both the indoor and outdoor environments, creating a climate for quality play, and using techniques for constructive adult intervention/involvement.

for reflection and discussion

1. Write a description of what you see as the key characteristics of childhood play.
2. Discuss with others the theories presented in this chapter of why children play. Which do you think best describes why children engage in play, and what are your reasons?
3. Write 2 to 3 paragraphs explaining whether or not you believe play is valuable in primary settings. Share your viewpoint with your classmates.
4. What role to support and promote childhood play will you feel comfortable in assuming as an early childhood professional?

MyEducationLab

Go to Topic 2: Child Development/Theories in the MyEducationLab (www.myeducationlab.com) for *Teaching Young Children*, where you can:

- Find learning outcomes for Child Development/Theories along with the national standards that connect to these outcomes.
- Complete Assignments and Activities that can help you more deeply understand the chapter content.
- Apply and practice your understanding of the core teaching skills identified in the chapter with the Building Teaching Skills and Dispositions learning units.
- Check your comprehension on the content covered in the chapter with the Study Plan. Here you will be able to take a chapter quiz, receive feedback on your answers, and then access Review, Practice, and Enrichment activities to enhance your understanding of chapter content.

Guiding
Young Children

IN THIS CHAPTER YOU WILL
- Define guidance in early childhood settings.
- Understand the key components of guidance.
- Learn to apply guidance in a variety of contexts within early childhood settings.

Free choice time has just begun in your preschool program. Nineteen 4-year-olds are busily engaged in play in the different centers, and things are moving along nicely. Suddenly, you hear Tasha and Ariel arguing over an accessory in the block center. Going over to investigate, you discover that they both want to use the same toy elephant in their separate block-building activities. Just as you finish helping them work through this dilemma, you notice Hector standing near the edge of the manipulative center watching the other children playing there. After bending down and resting a hand on his shoulder, you suggest some play options that you think might help him get involved in the available activities. Moments later, Christa is screaming and pounding the floor in the art center. She has accidentally mixed the blue and yellow tempera paints on her easel paper and she is very upset. Christa is so angry that your only option is a brief time-out so that she can calm herself down and get ready to re-engage in center activities. Although you know that time-outs get overused in many settings, in this instance it makes good sense. Group time is next on your schedule, and everything is going well until you mention your new pet cat. Now everyone wants to talk at once, and it takes several minutes to get the discussion back on track. This is proving to be another typical day, with many opportunities to practice your guidance skills.

Although the preceding scenario might sound unusual, it is really a pretty average day in the life of an adult in an early childhood setting. Young children are learning a great deal more than just conceptual knowledge as they grow and develop. They are also learning about their feelings, how to interact with their classmates, and being part of a group. This means that you will need a variety of guidance techniques to assist them in their development. These skills do not come naturally to most people and require both understanding and practice. This chapter is designed to help start you on the road to understanding and using effective guidance techniques.

What Is Guidance?

Sometimes the words you use make a big difference in the message others hear. Think about the words *guidance* and *discipline*, for example. When you hear the word *discipline*, what comes to mind? For most people, it brings thoughts of what you do when children have done something wrong. Guidance, however, often conjures up images of helping and assisting children in their growth and development. Although the two words have much in common and can be used interchangeably in many contexts, **guidance** is generally considered a broader concept, incorporating all the adult does or says to influence the behavior of the child. **Discipline** is an important component of the guidance process in which the adult is dealing with children who misbehave.

Building Self-Esteem

Guidance consists of several interrelated elements. One important element is the process of helping young children strengthen their feelings of self-esteem or self-worth. **Self-esteem** is a psychological concept that refers to the subjective assessment of one's abilities and skills. Kostelnik, Whiren, Soderman, and Gregory (2009) identify three dimensions to self-esteem: competence, worth, and control. They define **competence** as the belief in one's ability to accomplish tasks and achieve goals. **Worth** can be viewed as the extent to which people like and value themselves. **Control** is the degree to which people believe they can influence the events around them. Although the development of self-esteem is, in many ways, a lifelong venture, early childhood professionals play a critical role in the child's early efforts in esteem-building.

Aretha is new to your preschool program and hesitates when it is her turn to pour juice for snack time. When you encourage her to do so, she can serve herself without spilling. Aretha has added a bit to her sense of competence and will likely continue to expand her horizons as she becomes more involved in preschool activities.

Although Mica struggles with mathematics in your third-grade classroom, you know that he does excellent artwork. You have just complimented him for the clay pot he has made. The ready smile and obvious pleasure he displays help you know that Mica's sense of competence has been enhanced.

Supporting Emotional and Social Development

A second element of guidance emphasizes the adult's role in assisting young children to understand and address social/emotional issues. Emotionally, children are just beginning to make sense of the many different feelings they experience. During the early childhood years, they need help from adults to identify their feelings and then learn appropriate ways in which they can deal with them (Katz, 1984).

Two-year-old Randall has just fallen off the climber on the playground, scraped his elbow, and is crying. The early childhood professional sits down, holds Randall, and says, "That must have hurt and scared you when you fell off the climber. It's okay to cry. I'm just going to hold you for a minute before we go in for a bandage."

MyEducationLab

Visit the MyEducationLab for *Teaching Young Children* to enhance your understanding of chapter concepts with a personalized Study Plan. You'll also have the opportunity to hone your teaching skills through video- and case-based Assignments and Activities as well as Building Teaching Skills and Disposition lessons.

Learning to relate socially to other people is a difficult and complex task. Children in the early childhood years are constantly struggling with appropriate ways to interact with others. Caregivers and teachers must regularly take time to assist children in this important process.

As Darla enters the block center in her kindergarten classroom, Mark blurts out, "Go away, Darla! We don't want any girls in the block area!" Clearly, the classroom teacher will need to help Mark develop better ways to communicate with Darla.

Adults provide critical guidance when they give children labels for the feelings they see them express and then suggest effective ways for children to manage their emotions.

Growing toward Self-Regulation

A third important element of the guidance process is the work that early childhood professionals engage in to help children as they grow in their abilities to self-regulate (Shonkoff & Phillips, 2000). From infancy onward, young children are slowly moving from dependence on others to doing more and more on their own. This healthy growth toward greater independence requires considerable assistance from adults in early childhood settings. Good guidance during the early childhood years should eventually create within children the ability to guide themselves. Independence and self-control develop slowly and painfully in most people over a long period of time. Yet, these elements are important to becoming healthy, fully functioning adults. For example, the influence of peers becomes strong during the middle-school years. It is essential that we help young children become more able to self-regulate, so they can resist the negative push to experiment with drugs and other potentially harmful activities that present themselves during these years. We also need children to be able to demonstrate self-control as they manage their anger and frustrations in positive ways, rather than resorting to the increasingly common aggression and violence that many are using to deal with feelings (Piotrowski & Hoot, 2008).

Caregivers and teachers of young children need to create an atmosphere that encourages self-regulation. Sometimes that means stepping back and letting children work things out themselves. It may take longer and be a more difficult task, but when children learn that they can do it on their own, they gain independence (Shonkoff & Phillips, 2000).

Armondo and Dee are two members of a cooperative learning group in your second-grade classroom that is working on gathering information on sea life. They have just asked you for assistance in learning about whales, a special interest of yours. It would be easier (and probably more fun) to spend some time helping them with this task, but since you know that they can find this information in the resources you have provided, you direct them to the books and computer software you have in the science center.

Another important way in which early childhood professionals can help children develop self-regulation is by demonstrating their own methods for managing difficult situations (Committee for Children, 2010). When an adult remains calm and shows children constructive ways to deal with and express feelings, she is inviting children to engage in similar activities. Gradually, with continued verbal guidance and appropriate modeling, children begin to learn appropriate options for self-regulation.

Two 4-year-olds in the block area need your assistance. Briana just hit Rory with a block. After placing Briana in time-out and comforting Rory, you return and say, "Briana, I am angry with you right now. You hit Rory with that block and it really hurt him! I'm too angry to discuss it right now, so we will talk about this when the others leave for lunch in five minutes."

 ## Components of Guidance

Before becoming more specific about several distinct components of guidance, some reminders about children and early childhood professionals are needed. First, it is essential to remember that *each child is unique.* Just look around any early childhood setting, and you can see many of the more obvious differences among children. What may not be quite so clear are the varying responses they have to guidance techniques.

Two-year-old Marissa is quite happy to have you take her by the hand and gently lead her to the next play event when she struggles to get involved. Four-year-old Greg, however, is more likely to respond positively when given two options from which he can choose.

Adding to the complexity of guidance decisions is that *every situation is unique.* Caregivers and teachers must have a variety of guidance options available so that they can meet the needs of each child and the unique situations they create in their day-to-day interactions.

Today, Talia and Pam are fighting over the paints available at the easel. Because of their relative maturity levels, you decide to remind them that they need to share and ask them to try to work it out themselves. Yesterday, when Craig and Ilyia were having trouble using one of the manipulative toys together, you stepped in and helped them work through their conflict. You decided that they needed your help to work through the issues involved.

Not only are guidance techniques different because children and situations vary, but it is also important to remember that *every early childhood professional is unique.* There is no one right way to guide young children and no one ideal caregiver or teacher. Excellent early childhood professionals come with all sorts of different personalities and techniques that work for them.

Raelean is a new second-grade teacher who spends many extra hours organizing her class day. By carefully planning her activities, Raelean finds that she is more confident and her students are actively engaged in learning. Mary, however, is more spontaneous and gets really excited about her teaching. She is always coming up with crazy (but fun) ways to get her third-grade students involved in the learning process. Both are highly capable teachers with very different strengths that they bring to their classrooms. It should not be surprising to find that these two teachers tend to use a different mix of guidance strategies as they teach children.

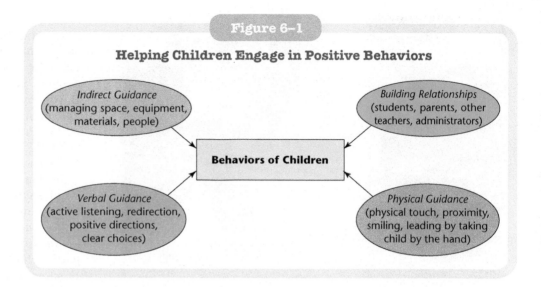

Figure 6–1

Helping Children Engage in Positive Behaviors

Indirect Guidance
(managing space, equipment, materials, people)

Building Relationships
(students, parents, other teachers, administrators)

Behaviors of Children

Verbal Guidance
(active listening, redirection, positive directions, clear choices)

Physical Guidance
(physical touch, proximity, smiling, leading by taking child by the hand)

As described in this text, there are five main components to guidance. The first four are attempts on the part of the early childhood professional to help children engage in positive behaviors. These include indirect guidance, building relationships, physical guidance, and verbal guidance. They are summarized in Figure 6–1. Despite the adult's best efforts, however, there are times when none of these will be successful and problem behaviors will occur. It then becomes necessary to use discipline, the fifth component of guidance. Each of these elements will be discussed in the sections that follow.

Indirect Guidance

Much of what a caregiver or teacher does to influence children's behaviors is indirect. This behind-the-scenes work and planning help prevent problems from occurring in the first place. By managing the space, equipment, materials, and people in the child's environment, adults can eliminate many potential conflicts. Hearron and Hildebrand (2009) identify three components of indirect guidance:

- **Forming appropriate expectations based on an understanding of children.** Clearly, taking courses about child development and reading what others have identified as typical of children at different ages is one way to form appropriate expectations for children. Another option is to observe them carefully. This will allow you to see the specific skills and understandings of individual children and to prepare for them in your program. A third way of understanding children is to talk to their families. For example, when Dimitri's dad tells you of his son's passion for collecting sea shells, you can plan a display in the science center for the following week.

- **Managing space and time to create an environment that supports positive behavior.** There are many important ways to indirectly manage the environment. One strategy is to arrange activities in interesting ways that invite children to participate. For example, you could begin a sand structure in the sandbox outdoors so that preschool children are encouraged to add on their own ideas. Another strategy is to prepare materials so that children can use them safely

The caregiver placed this water activity where the contents would not splash other children or surrounding materials and left space around the table for children to freely move.

and with a minimum of adult help. Arranging the art supplies neatly on shelves next to the art table so that children can readily get them for projects is one example of this. A third strategy is, when rotating toys and equipment in and out of centers so that they remain new and interesting, to store the materials you do not want children to use out of sight. Finally, your indirect management should include planning the lengths of time set aside for different activities. For example, because of the attention spans of prekindergarten children, group times should be short, with singing and movement activities interspersed between listening and responding times.

- **Planning an indoor and outdoor curriculum that engages the whole child.** It may surprise you to realize that the activities you prepare for young children can have a direct impact on their positive and negative behaviors in your early childhood program. When activities are of high interest, children are much more likely to spend their time actively engaged with the materials presented and positively interacting with their peers. The converse, however, is also true. When activities are poorly chosen or planned, children are much quicker to engage in problem behaviors. For example, planning an integrated math/science/literacy activity for second-grade students based on observed interests in which they are actively observing, discussing, and recording plant growth prior to writing a report on their findings can be a motivating time for children and lead to more positive engagement in the activity.

Time spent in indirect guidance helps create a smooth-running and pleasant program. By reducing the number of misbehaviors, it frees up the adult for more positive interactions with children. Indirect guidance is well worth the effort you will invest. Sometimes, good indirect guidance means that early childhood professionals need to give up some preconceived notions about what should be happening in their early childhood settings. The *Celebrating Play* feature in this section provides an example of this type. When children engage in creative play experiences, they tend to be noisy and messy. Part of indirect guidance during play, then, is to allow this noise and messiness to occur (within limits, of course!). Read the feature now for more information on this aspect of indirect guidance.

Building Relationships

A second important key to effective guidance is the relationships you establish with children, families, and other colleagues and administrators throughout the early childhood setting (Heimes, 2009). Effective interactions among all those who work with young children will greatly influence healthy growth and learning. The most critical relationships are those you establish with children. These can be built in

Celebrating Play . . .
NOISE AND MESSINESS: PART OF THE PLAY?

It is choice time in your second-grade classroom, and Mrs. Hanson, your elementary school principal, has just walked in the door. Children are actively engaged in creative play in the three centers you have set up, but the noise level is rather high. Matt, Carolee, and Arlene are busy talking and constructing a southern plantation based on their social studies unit. Norm, Sandy, Molly, and Kareena are animatedly discussing their play options in the art center. Several others are engaged in productive but noisy tasks throughout the room. You can tell that Mrs. Hanson is distracted by the sounds of busy players. She is probably wondering, "Is all this noise really necessary?"

Hakeem and Albert have just asked your permission to get a bucket of water and make mud pies in the sandbox. It is a beautiful spring day and you have just consented. But now you are beginning to wonder about your decision. Both children are having a great time but are covered from head to foot with wet sand. You hope that no family members drop by before you can get the boys cleaned up. It always seems to be a challenge to keep children from getting too messy when they are involved in creative play experiences.

These are not isolated incidents but are fairly typical of many play situations. Noise and mess do seem to be a normal part of children's play. That does not mean, however, that there are no limits. Noise levels can become too high, and children may need to be reminded of appropriate voices for play indoors and out. A certain amount of messiness is also typical of most play. Creative art projects, block structures in progress, and manipulatives being used all create a cluttered environment. Children learn rather quickly, however, that at the end of a play sequence, things can and should be picked up before they begin the next activity. The mess from play should be temporary and manageable. By allowing appropriate levels of noise and messiness, you are indirectly guiding students in their efforts to engage in creative play.

1. What could you say to Mrs. Hanson to help her understand the need for some noise as children play?

2. What are your personal attitudes about noise and messiness in an early childhood setting? Do you think these attitudes might influence children's play activities when you teach?

---

part, through the positive interactions you have throughout the day. A pat on the back for a job well done, an engaging smile when greeting each child in the morning, and words of encouragement are all examples of relationship-building interactions. Sometimes, however, it is important to plan contrived situations to get better acquainted with students. Name-game activities at the start of the school year to get better acquainted with students are examples of this type of interaction.

Establishing quality relationships with families is also important to good guidance in early childhood programs. The *Family Partnerships* feature in this section provides an example of a specific strategy that is effective in strengthening these relationships. When strong family-program relationships are encouraged through activities like potluck socials, families are much more likely to support what takes place in the program. This helps make guidance easier to implement. Good communication is the key to strong home–school relationships and is important to master in your work with families.

Physically Guiding Children

Physical touch, body language, and proximity are additional components of effective guidance for young children. Perhaps the most important and controversial component of physical guidance is touch. Despite the fact that it is such a natural way of relating to young children, adults are becoming much more cautious about touch. Many are avoiding physical contact entirely, even at the preschool

Family Partnerships...
BUILDING RELATIONSHIPS BY CREATING A WELCOMING EARLY CHILDHOOD SETTING

If you want to have strong relationships with families, an excellent starting point is to create a program where they feel welcome and comfortable (Souto-Manning, 2010). This means that you will need to find ways to create a space that looks and feels right for families. There are several ways to create this welcoming space:

- **Make your room visually appealing to families.** Your first responsibility in organizing your room is to have a space that is appealing to children. At the same time, however, there are ways to make the room visually interesting to families as well. Having a colorful space that is clean and well cared for can make a big difference in its appeal to others. You can also display children's work around the room so that families know you value their work. Welcome signs in the languages spoken in the home will also help families feel at ease there.

- **Be personally welcoming to families.** It is often the little things you do or say that help families feel at home in your room. A friendly smile is one example. Finding the time to greet each family member when he or she comes to the room is another. Being courteous and respectful of all families is another way in which you can be personally welcoming.

- **Create a space for families.** Space will always be in short supply in your room. There never seems to be enough to use for all the ideas you will have for children, let alone creating a space for families. But think about creating a multi-use area that can be a spot for families to use when they visit but also a space for children the rest of the time. For example, you could bring in a comfortable stuffed chair for visiting adults that can be used as a quiet reading area during other parts of the day. Or simply having a bulletin board with a welcoming sign and interesting items for families to read while they are waiting can create a sense of space for them.

1. Do you remember being in an educational setting that you felt was welcoming to families? What characteristics of the space made it feel that way?

2. Is it important to make families feel welcome in your future early childhood setting? Why or why not? Can you think of additional ways in which your space could be welcoming?

---

level (Carlson, 2006). From one perspective, it is understandable why early childhood professionals are taking this stance; they are scared. The threats of lawsuits and possible job loss from inappropriate touch are strong deterrents. Despite these complications, however, and in spite of all that has been written recently about the inappropriate ways in which adults touch young children, it is important to use good touch as a guidance strategy. What better way is there to let young children know that we care about them and want to help them deal with the many problems they face? Carlson (2006) writes:

> Young children need positive human touch, and lots of it, in all its forms—carrying, swinging, rolling, holding, a backrub, a hug, a pat, a high-five, rough-and-tumble play, even massage. Nurturing touch from their caregivers is essential for children to feel loved and secure. . . . Moreover, teachers must understand that withholding touch can be just as physically and emotionally harmful to a child as sexual abuse or physical abuse such as hitting, grabbing, spanking, and shaking. (pp. 2–3)

Adults and children vary in their comfort levels with physical touch. Some adults are not comfortable holding children close in an embrace or encouraging children to sit on their lap. However, a gentle pat on the shoulder, high fives, and handshakes all communicate to children that we care. Children also differ in their need for touch. Caregivers and teachers must be sensitive to these variances and respond accordingly.

Physically guiding young children involves more than the all-important use of touch. It also includes such things as proximity, gestures, and body language. For example, the child who is struggling to stay on task may well benefit from being close to an adult. This physical proximity of the adult often calms and redirects children to more positive behaviors. In addition, gesturing and body language are other aspects of physical guidance that are effective in early childhood settings. We send children many messages about what we expect when we smile, raise an eyebrow, or point with a finger. Taking them by the hand and leading them to a more positive activity is another effective physical guidance strategy for many children. Physically turning children gently at the shoulders and redirecting them toward a desired activity also works well for many children.

Verbal Guidance

Communication is another important element of child guidance. The words we use as adults strongly influence the behaviors of young children. An excellent beginning for effective verbal communication is the ability of the adult to be a good listener. **Active listening** is a technique that helps early childhood professionals be more effective in the communication process (Gordon, 1974). The adult begins by being open and approachable and listens carefully to what the child is saying and doing. Then, in her own words, the caregiver or teacher repeats back what she has heard the child say. "Damion, it sounds like you are mad at Ian because he took the truck you wanted to use." When adults use active listening, they let children know they are trying hard to help them identify feelings and respond to those emotions in appropriate ways.

Another form of verbal guidance is called **redirection**. Two-year-old Andrew is fascinated by climbing and is preparing to move from his chair to the nearby table. His caregiver, knowing Andrew's love of books, takes him by the hand and says, "Andrew, let's go find a book to read." For the youngest children, redirection becomes a way to divert or distract the child from an undesirable behavior into a more appropriate activity. For older children, adults can verbalize a substitute for the problem behavior: "Rachelle, you will need to get your own blocks from the shelf. Martin is using those."

When early childhood professionals initiate verbal messages, they should use positive directions, telling the child what to do, rather than what *not* to do. When an adult says, "Don't jump off the table!" it is almost as if the child does not hear the "don't" and is further encouraged to engage in the inappropriate behavior. In addition, *don't* statements fail to tell the child what it is you would rather have her *do*. The statement "Climb down off the table, please" clearly identifies what you expect and makes it easier for most children to comply.

You can also strengthen verbal communication by making it clear when children have choices. Many times, choices are appropriate and useful to children in developing independence and decision-making skills. "Gary, would you like to use the computer now that Carla has finished, or are you interested in continuing with your math project?" Other times, however, adults inadvertently give children choices when they really do not mean to do so. Young children think more literally than adults do, so when they hear phrases like, "Would you like to sit down now for group time?" they may well assume that you have given them a choice. Another common problem many adults have is ending their statements with "okay?" "Philip, it's clean-up time now, *okay?*" Without meaning to do so, adults have given children an implied choice by the words they have used. Hearron and Hildebrand (2009) give additional suggestions for making verbal guidance more effective with young children:

- Get down on the child's level and speak quietly and directly as you make eye contact.
- Place the action part of your guidance statement at the beginning ("Hold tight, or you might fall out of the swing").
- Give directions at the time and place you want behavior to occur.
- Give logical and accurate reasons for your requests.
- Keep competition to a minimum in your verbal guidance.

As you begin using verbal guidance strategies, remember that young children will come to the early childhood setting with varying English language abilities. When you work with limited-English-speaking and non-English-speaking students, you will need to adjust your verbal guidance to meet the language abilities you encounter. The *Celebrating Diversity* feature in this section provides more information on the increasing numbers of non-English-speaking children and families in this country. Read the information now and reflect on its implications for the ways in which you will use verbal guidance strategies.

Celebrating Diversity . . .
ENGLISH-SPEAKING CHILDREN AND THEIR FAMILIES

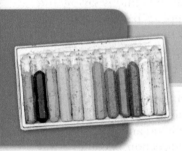

The United States is currently experiencing the largest influx of immigrants since the early 1900s (U.S. Department of Education, 2010a). With this increase comes a growing diversity in the languages spoken by children and their families. Spanish, Chinese, Tagalog (Filipino), Korean, Vietnamese, Arabic, Hindi, and Russian are among the most common non-English languages being spoken. Data indicate that 21% of families speak a language other than English in the home and that most of the children in these settings have limited English proficiency (U.S. Department of Education, 2010b). This means that as a future caregiver or teacher of young children it is highly likely that you will be working with children and families who speak languages other than English at home.

While working with non-English-speaking children and their families will have its challenges, it is also a rich learning opportunity for all. For example, non-English-speaking children bring a wealth of cultural traditions that provide exciting learning experiences. The similarities and differences in foods, holidays, and clothing across cultures are better understood by children when they can talk to families that have lived in other countries. In addition, learning some simple words and phrases in the native languages of students in the class can create opportunities for meaningful learning experiences.

Not only do children learn and grow from having non-English-speaking classmates, but you as the early childhood professional can also benefit. As you interact with children and their families, you will learn about the diverse life experiences these families have had and will increase your understanding of different cultures. For example, hearing about the general level of poverty in India from an immigrant family would broaden your comprehension of worldwide hunger and bring to life the challenges of trying to address this issue. The potential for personal growth as an early childhood professional is greatly enhanced by working with non-English-speaking immigrant families.

1. In the community or region in which you are currently living, are there large populations of non-English-speaking families? What do you know about the culture and language of these families? How can you learn more?

2. In what ways will working with limited-English-speaking and non-English-speaking children and families influence the guidance strategies you use?

Discipline Strategies

Despite the best intentions of the early childhood professional to prevent problems from occurring, children will still engage in behaviors that require some form of discipline. Discipline, however, does not need to be heavy-handed, punitive, or mean. The emphasis of good discipline is on changing student behaviors from less desirable to more desirable. Early childhood professionals can use a variety of discipline strategies to deal with issues as they arise. The appropriate option depends not only on the situation and the children involved but also on the adult's personality. Knowing about, and being able to effectively use, several discipline options allows the creative professional to make good choices in many different situations. These discipline options are summarized in Figure 6–2.

One strategy recommended by Thomas Gordon (1974) is to use what he calls an **I-message**. This communication statement includes the personal pronoun *I*, the feelings experienced by the adult, and the actions that caused those feelings. The *I-message* itself is frequently followed by a brief explanation from the adult to help explain why the feelings are important.

 Kelsey has just come in late from recess for the second time this week, and you decide to use an I-message. "Kelsey, I get frustrated when you come in late from recess. You distract the rest of the class and miss many of my directions for the next lesson."

Rather than criticizing a child for an undesirable behavior, an I-message identifies the feelings of the adult and helps the child see how his behavior influences others. If the relationship between the early childhood professional and the student is strong, often the child will voluntarily change his or her behavior and act more responsibly.

Dreikurs, Grunwald, and Pepper (1982) propose the use of **natural and logical consequences** as effective discipline strategies. Both options make a clear link between the child's inappropriate behavior and the consequence for that activity.

Figure 6–2

Discipline Options

I-message	I, followed by feelings experienced by the adult, ending with what behavior caused the feelings
Natural consequences	A naturally occurring result of the child's behavior
Logical consequences	The teacher establishes a consequence that has a logical link to the child's behavior
Positive reinforcement	Anything that follows a behavior and increases the likelihood it will occur again
Punishment	Anything that follows a behavior and decreases the likelihood it will occur again
Ignoring	Avoiding verbal and nonverbal responses to attention-seeking behavior
Problem solving	Using techniques of counseling, the teacher and student work together to resolve difficulties

With natural consequences, the adult simply lets the inherent outcomes for certain actions take place.

On a cool, fall day, you remind your kindergarten children to put on their coats before heading out to the playground for recess. Larissa hears your reminder but decides to ignore it. After discussing the situation with her individually, you allow her to experience the natural consequence of going outdoors for a few minutes without her coat: she is cold.

A major drawback to natural consequences is that many times they either do not occur or are potentially dangerous to the child. In those instances, a logical consequence is needed. The adult establishes the consequence and makes a logical link between the child's behavior and the resulting discipline strategy. For example, if Karma runs down the hallway as students go to music class, a logical consequence would be to have her start over and walk down the hall at your side. If possible, it is best to discuss these consequences before they are implemented with a child. Furthermore, stating logical consequences in a choice format helps students make stronger connections between their behavior and its results. In discussing Karma's behavior with her before the next music class, the adult could say, "Karma, you need to walk down the hallway to music or you can walk next to me. You choose."

Many educators use a group of discipline strategies that are collectively referred to as **behavior modification**. Based on the theoretical perspectives of behaviorists such as B. F. Skinner (1974), three basic techniques are associated with this approach. They are positive reinforcement, punishment, and ignoring. While these techniques are used extensively in K–12 classrooms, they should be applied thoughtfully and less often in early childhood settings (Shiller & O'Flynn, 2008). The following paragraphs identify some of the more appropriate uses of behavior modification for young children and make clear which strategies should never be used in the early childhood setting.

Positive reinforcement is anything that follows a behavior and increases the likelihood that it will occur more often in the future. Smiles, high fives, and positive comments are all considered positive reinforcers for children when they increase behaviors that precede them. Sometimes, things that adults would normally consider negative interactions may actually be reinforcing to some children. A stern verbal response by the early childhood professional may be reinforcing to certain children who really need to get any kind of attention from adults. Conversely, a typically reinforcing action like a pat on the back may not be viewed as such by some children. Carefully watching the child's reactions to the interactions will help determine whether or not they are reinforcing. While candy and other physical rewards are considered positive reinforcements by behavior modification proponents, they should not be used in early childhood settings.

Punishment is another strategy associated with behavior modification and is defined as any event or action that follows a behavior and decreases the likelihood that the behavior will occur again. A common punishment used by many early educators is **restitution** (Dreikurs, Grunwald, & Pepper, 1982). When a child engages in an inappropriate behavior, the caregiver or teacher insists that the child engage in activities that correct or "make up for" the problem.

Angie is an active first-grade student who tends to doodle on her desk instead of doing her project work during small group time. As her teacher, you notice that Angie is daydreaming and scribbling on her desk while others in the group are working to complete their portions of a long-term project. You take Angie aside and tell her that she needs to go into the bathroom, get some paper towels and soap, and clean her desk. She is making restitution for her problem behavior.

Some forms of punishment are widely viewed by early childhood experts as inappropriate in working with young children. Corporal punishment (spanking), for example, should not be used because it is harmful to adult–student relationships and creates an atmosphere of fear and anxiety (Paintal, 1999). Although spanking is a traditional discipline approach used in many homes, early childhood educators should never resort to corporal punishment in disciplining children. Humiliation and intimidation are two other punishments that are extremely harmful to relationships and self-esteem. They, too, have no place in early childhood settings.

The third strategy typically associated with behavior modification is **ignoring**. Often when children misbehave, they are seeking attention from adults. The class clown is typically engaging in attention-seeking behavior. Ignoring can be a powerful strategy for attention-seeking children if the adult can refrain from giving any verbal or nonverbal feedback for the inappropriate behavior. When both adults and other children consistently ignore attention-getting behaviors that are not too disruptive to the rest of the class, attention-seeking children quickly learn that these inappropriate strategies are no longer effective.

Another set of discipline options available to early childhood professionals is often referred to as **problem-solving strategies**. These are very different from the behavior modification techniques just described. Rather than being initiated and directed by the adult, the problem-solving approach is a cooperative effort that engages both the student and the early childhood professional in working through the issues of concern together. Similar problem-solving approaches were developed by both Glasser (1969) and Gordon (1974) and have been successfully applied to working with children of all ages. The basic approach used in problem solving is to work with children much as a counselor interacts with his clients. Built on a strong foundation of good communication and positive relationships, the adult and child

- Work together to identify the problem behavior
- Discuss the implications of the behavior
- Brainstorm possible solutions
- Agree on a plan
- Check periodically to make sure the plan is working

The process is relatively time-consuming and requires a private space and time to work through the issues, so you should reserve this technique for more problematic behaviors that cannot be resolved in other ways. The *Developmentally Appropriate Practice* feature in this section provides an example of an adult using problem solving as a guidance option with a young child.

Problem-solving strategies can also be used effectively in group settings. Implementing the same basic techniques described previously, early childhood professionals can conduct class meetings in which group problems are identified and resolved. Gartrell (2006) describes a second-grade teacher who had several children engaging in problem behaviors during bathroom breaks. She called a classroom meeting where everyone was given a chance to speak and each student was treated with respect. The class was able to work through the problem and identify a solution that was agreeable to all. With the teacher's assistance, the class began by clarifying their problem behaviors, then discussed the implications of their actions, brainstormed possible solutions, and agreed on a plan of action that was agreeable to all. With adult assistance, preschool children can also benefit from this group problem-solving strategy.

Developmentally Appropriate Practice . . .
AN EXAMPLE OF PROBLEM SOLVING

The following example of an individual problem-solving meeting should help you understand both the challenges and benefits of this discipline technique:

Habib, one of Chelsea Evan's second-grade students, is what many people would call a "class clown." He regularly engages in silly actions to bring attention to himself. Yesterday, he "accidentally" tipped over his chair and fell noisily to the floor. Today, during quiet reading time, he burped loudly and then laughed self-consciously, causing several other children to giggle and disrupting the concentration of others. Having tried several other simpler strategies, Chelsea decides to hold a problem-solving meeting with Habib. After asking the class to return to their reading, she walks over and quietly asks Habib to stay in from recess for a few minutes so that they can discuss his behavior. The following dialogue highlights the key points of this meeting:

Teacher: Habib, I want you to know that I really enjoy having you in my class. You are smart, contribute to class discussions, and are fun to be around. But there are times when the things you do disrupt the class. Can you tell me what you did earlier today that was disruptive?

Habib: Yeah, I burped and then laughed.

Teacher: Right, and do you know why that was a problem?

Habib: I guess it made it hard for the rest of the class to keep on reading.

Teacher: Yes, that's it. I've been thinking about why you do things like tip over your chair and burp during quiet time, and I think you're trying to do things so that others will notice you and like you. And even though everyone wants to be noticed and liked, it should not get in the way of others learning. We need to think of some better ways for you to get some attention from the class. One thing I thought of was for you to spend a few minutes during group time sharing something you like to do. Is that something you would like to try?

Habib: Well . . . I guess so. But what would I share?

Teacher: I heard you talking recently about your baseball card collection. Would you be interested in telling us about it?

Habib: That would be awesome! I have a collection that my brother gave me and I've added to it. That would be fun.

Teacher: Okay, let's plan to have you share at group time on Thursday. We'll start with that and then talk again next week to see if there are other things we should do.

Guidance Applications

The components of guidance presented here are all important to an overall plan for positively managing child behaviors in early childhood settings. Having learned about them, you can now look more carefully at how guidance can be applied to different areas of working with young children. Following are strategies for using guidance to help children deal with feelings and emotions, manage routines, engage in positive social interactions, and participate in group settings.

Feelings and Emotions

Throughout the early childhood years, children are beginning the lifelong process of recognizing and appropriately responding to their feelings. This difficult, yet extremely important, task requires insightful interventions by the adult. By helping children recognize and deal with their feelings, the caregiver is laying the groundwork for mature coping mechanisms in adulthood. Opportunities to deal with feelings come up regularly, as Furman (1995) indicates in the following example: Two policemen arrive at the door of a preschool lunchroom with a 4- or 5-year-old boy in tow. The officers had found the child wandering around near the school and had assumed he belonged there. After being told that he did not, the policemen went on their way, leaving behind many young children who had mixed emotions about this event. Rather than ignore this experience, adults spent time with the students discussing their concerns, making the visit a learning opportunity for them.

The *Developmentally Appropriate Practice* feature in this section talks about the feelings and emotions children experience when faced with traumatic events. As much as we would like to shield young children from personal, community, and societal disasters, many children end up confused and traumatized by them. Read the feature now for more information on this difficult topic.

Accept feelings as valid. An important starting point in guiding children through the emotions they experience is to help them realize that feelings themselves are valid responses to life situations. A preschool child who is saddened by his father's departure at the beginning of the school day is not going to be helped by an adult attempting to talk him out of those feelings. Feelings are just that—feelings. They are not right or wrong, good or bad. Feelings simply exist. Helping children recognize this important concept makes it easier for them to respond more effectively to their feelings.

Seven-year-old Ingrid has just described to you, through her tears, the anger and frustration she feels because of an incident on the playground. Two of her friends have decided to exclude her from their play activities because of a perceived slight. Ingrid is angry and hurt. Your response as her classroom teacher could begin with some variation of the following: "Ingrid, I can understand your feelings of anger right now. It hurts when others treat you that way."

Be calm and direct. In many circumstances, emotions lead to turmoil. In childhood, that may mean such responses as tears, hitting, or screaming. Whether they are directed toward the adult or other children, or are merely expressed, it is helpful for the early childhood professional to remain calm and deal with these emotional responses as directly and simply as possible. When the adult is calm, the child is more likely to regain control and begin to work through her emotions. Body language, words spoken, and tone of voice all contribute to an appropriate adult response to children's emotional outbursts. Even when the child does not initially express a problem behavior, a calm demeanor will help ensure a better resolution to the feelings being experienced.

Help the child verbalize emotions. Although children experience emotions from a very early age, it takes considerable practice for them to identify and label these elusive feelings (Furman, 1995). For younger children, the basic feelings of sadness, fear, anger, excitement, and happiness need to be given names by caring adults.

Four-year-old Latoya is smiling broadly as you discuss the upcoming field trip at group time. "Latoya, your face is telling me that you are excited about going on the field trip to the farm this afternoon!" By giving her feeling a name and describing what you are observing, you are helping Latoya to gain experience in identifying her feelings.

Older children continue to benefit from this assistance, when adults verbalize the emotions children experience. Children who have succeeded in identifying the more basic feelings can be assisted in identifying more subtle emotions such as

Developmentally Appropriate Practice...
HELPING CHILDREN DEAL WITH TRAUMA

Although it is often difficult for adults to admit, many children experience periods of significant trauma. It may be a world event such as the terrorist attacks on New York's World Trade Center on September 11, 2001. The drawing included here shows airplanes crashing into a tall building. This may be one way in which young children may respond to such an event. While they may have great difficulty understanding such events, children can see and feel the hurt and anguish of family members and others and will need considerable help in responding to the traumatic events they encounter. The adult may say to the child who made this drawing: "Tell me about what you have drawn." Or "Did you see planes crashing into a building on TV? What happened when your family saw this on TV?"

Young children may also experience trauma associated with the community in which they live. Natural disasters like floods and tornadoes, drive-by shootings, and auto accidents are all events that may directly impact children and their families. Finally, situations within the family itself can produce trauma for children. Severe financial difficulties, child or spousal abuse, the death or disability of a family member, and divorce are some of the more common traumatic events children experience. Reports indicate that 71% of children have been exposed to at least one traumatic event in the course of a year (Berson & Baggerly, 2009). Caregivers and teachers of young children must be prepared to provide children with support and guidance as they work to cope with traumatic events. Following are some strategies for assisting children and their families:

- **Be a good listener or observer.** Some children may be able to verbalize to you or other children the challenging situations they face. If so, take the time needed to listen carefully and draw out what they know and believe. Most young children, however, will not be able to talk about traumatic events, because they have neither the language nor the cognitive understanding to do so. In these situations, the early childhood professional needs to carefully watch for telltale changes in child behaviors and/or the introduction of new play themes that may signal the occurrence of traumatic events.

- **Provide support to children and families.** The support provided by early childhood professionals is very individualized, depending on both the traumatic event itself and the time and energy commitment possible on the part of the adult. It might include a special family conference to brainstorm strategies that could be used both at home and at school to support the child. It might also mean spending extra time with a troubled child to show him or her you care. Support could also take the form of volunteering for periodic after-hours care so that other family members can have more time to work through the issues they face.

- **Seek professional advice and assistance.** Many traumatic events experienced by children and families require the help of trained professionals with expertise that goes well beyond the natural abilities of most adults. These professionals should be called on early and often to provide the strategies needed to be of significant assistance to families.

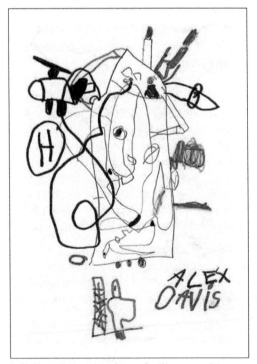

Collaborative artwork can facilitate positive social interactions.

loneliness, annoyance, and worry. This verbalization process is an important beginning point for eventual mastery and control of feelings.

Suggest alternatives. Inappropriate responses to negative emotions are common in childhood. It is easier and perhaps more natural to strike out either physically or verbally than to work through these feelings in a more mature way. Children need considerable help and practice in dealing with their emotions. In addition to serving as models for appropriate responses, you need to give children concrete suggestions for dealing with feelings.

> Two-year-old Meesha has just taken a toy truck away from Ben and caused him to cry. You suggest, "Meesha, I know you wanted that truck, but Ben was playing with it. When you want something Ben is using, you need to ask him for it." Most children will need many reminders from caring adults before they begin to understand that there are better ways to get what they want.

As children get older, early childhood professionals may try to get students more involved in this process of selecting appropriate alternatives for dealing with feelings. Rather than making a direct suggestion, the adult may ask the student for his or her ideas (Gordon, 1974).

> Eduardo has just called his third-grade friend Allen a "geek" for not wanting to work together on a writing project. Allen's feelings are hurt, and Eduardo is mad at him. You respond to Eduardo, "Allen was hurt when you called him a 'geek.' Can you think of a better way to tell him that you are mad because he did not want to work on the writing project with you?"

Of course, it may still be necessary to help children at this age select appropriate strategies for dealing with their feelings.

Routines

During the early childhood years, children's routines are an important part of their daily experiences. As they move through the school day, they encounter a variety of regularized events that often require adult assistance to successfully manage. When these components of the day are consistently managed and children know what to expect, they are more comfortable and relaxed in school (Koralek, 2008).

Arrival and departure. The beginning and end of the day are important times for children. Early childhood professionals need to plan for these times carefully to reduce problems during these transitions. For many children in the infant/toddler and preschool years, leaving the security of their families for the school setting can be a frightening experience. Greeting children at the door and guiding the less secure ones through a consistent routine help make the arrival time more positive. Even with older children, a consistent beginning to the school day helps ensure a productive start for both adults and children (Koralek, 2008). Similarly, at the end of the day, it is important to routinely take time to summarize what has taken place that day and bring closure to the many things the children have accomplished in a predictable and recognizable way. Helping children leave with a good feeling about the day also increases the chances for beginning the next class session on a positive note.

Transitions. At first glance, the times between the activities of the school day may seem unimportant. Often, however, they can be a prime time for problem behaviors if you fail to plan for them (Evans, 2007; Hemmeter et al., 2008). Children need clear directions and procedures for transitioning from one event to the next. Think about a group of kindergarten children getting ready to move from group time to recess. If the classroom teacher were to say, "Okay, children, recess is next. Go get ready," children would likely respond in a variety of ways, many of which could be problematic. Several might head to the bathroom at the same time, making for crowded conditions there. Others could line up for a drink, while yet another group could head to their tables to finish up an art project before moving to the coat area. If expectations are not clearly explained, these transition times can be very confusing and frustrating to both children and adults. Good caregivers and teachers know what they want children to do at transition times and clearly describe their expectations.

Snack/meal time. Another important routine that requires clear adult guidance is snack/meal time. For the infant/toddler, eating is a frequent and essential part of the day. Caregivers must work carefully with families to understand each child's eating schedule, food preferences, and routines. In addition to regular meal times, preschool and primary children need a nutritious snack both mid-morning and mid-afternoon to ensure high energy levels and involvement in program activities. Whether these snacks are prepared by staff or brought from home, children need clear expectations for how snack time is to proceed. Should children sit together in small groups and visit with peers and an adult? Or do students pick up a snack, return to their desks, and continue working? What are the expectations for children serving themselves and cleaning up afterward? The early childhood professional must address, and the children must understand, all these issues (and more) to have a consistently pleasant snack time. Snack time should foster independent student behavior and create a relaxed atmosphere for eating and visiting with others.

Caregivers must make sure children understand what behavior is expected of them at snack time.

Toileting. For the youngest children, toileting in early childhood settings means diaper changing. Until approximately 2 years of age, most children have not developed the bladder and bowel control to use a toilet. Adult caregivers at the infant/toddler level must simply accept this aspect of young children as normal and natural and work to make these times as pleasant as possible (Petersen & Wittmer, 2008). Talking, singing, and playing games as diapers get changed help make this time more interesting and enjoyable for all. As children begin the toilet-training process, caregivers must work carefully with families to consistently use similar toileting procedures and communicate about issues and problems as they arise. Well after toilet training has ended, some children will occasionally have accidents. How the early childhood professional reacts to these situations will make a big difference in how the child feels about himself. A casual, calm approach will help minimize the embarrassment the child will likely feel.

Rest times. The younger the child, the more significant the rest-time routine is in the child's life. Infants and toddlers take frequent naps throughout the day and need consistent, caring adult interactions before and after these times (Petersen & Wittmer, 2008). Each child will be different, with routines learned at home and differing sleep needs. Consistent communication with families helps make these routines more successful for the youngest children. During the preschool years, rest/nap times are usually found only in full-day programs and typically occur in the early afternoon. Generally, it is best to have all children spend some quiet time on a mat or cot. During this time, some will actually nap while others rest. Caregivers must work hard to create an atmosphere in which sleep is possible for those who need it and rest time is pleasant for others. Back rubs, soft singing, reading a book, and quiet conversations may help children during this time.

Social Interactions

Throughout the early childhood years, children are learning to relate socially to one another and to adults. This process of becoming social beings is a complex one that requires considerable adult guidance and has a significant impact on overall development (Bowman & Moore, 2006). In addition to helping young children engage in positive social interactions, adults also need to help them identify, avoid, and respond to an array of less positive behaviors such as teasing and bullying (Gartrell & Gartrell, 2008). The *Developmentally Appropriate Practice* feature found in this section provides strategies that adults can use to help children deal with these difficult social interactions. Read this information now and reflect on the challenges presented when children tease and bully one another.

Developmentally Appropriate Practice . . .
DEALING WITH TEASING AND BULLYING

Early childhood professionals are increasingly aware that they must address the issues of teasing and bullying, especially in the primary grades (Gartrell & Gartrell, 2008; Piotrowski & Hoot, 2008). Children are seeing family members, neighbors, and television actors engaging in teasing and bullying behaviors and are trying out similar tactics in their interactions with peers. And while boys tend to initiate the majority of these incidents, both boys and girls are recipients of these negative behaviors (Gropper & Froschl, 1999).

Froschl and Sprung (1999) provide several suggestions for adults in dealing with teasing and bullying behaviors:

- **Address the teasing and bullying early and often.** Many adults tend to ignore a large percentage of these problem behaviors. While it is important to let children work things out on their own when possible, teasing and bullying are not a natural or necessary part of childhood. When intervention takes place regularly, children learn that adults expect more positive interactions between children.

- **Talk about teasing and bullying.** Children need the chance to talk about what makes them uncomfortable indoors and on the playground. Several good books such as Tomie dePaola's *Oliver Button Is a Sissy* are available to use as discussion starters (Gartrell & Gartrell, 2008).

- **Develop program rules that discourage teasing and bullying.** Children can participate in rule-making activities that help them learn what teasing and bullying behaviors look and sound like and what consequences will be implemented when they occur.

- **Promote noncompetitive games.** Games that promote cooperation and friendship can be used both indoors and outdoors to help children develop more positive ways of interacting with each other.

- **Involve families in the process.** Families need to be active participants in understanding the problems with teasing and bullying, and in discouraging them both in the early childhood setting and at home. Early childhood professionals who work to communicate with families on this topic will gain valuable assistance in dealing with the problems.

Goals for positive social interactions include the following:

- Showing sympathy and kindness
- Demonstrating helping
- Accepting food or toys
- Engaging in sharing
- Showing positive verbal and physical interactions
- Comforting others in distress
- Exhibiting concern
- Taking the perspective of others
- Demonstrating affection (Wittmer & Honig, 1994)

Caregivers and teachers can use many strategies to help facilitate these goals (Jones, 2008). While it takes time and energy to promote positive social interactions, adults can expect significant progress on the part of children, resulting in environments in which conflict and frustrations are kept to a minimum.

Be a careful observer. An excellent starting point for dealing with many issues is to make thorough and regular observations of children. The more you know about children and their typical patterns of interaction, the better able you will be to help them in their social development. When direct observations are supplemented with information provided by other adults and families, the chances for success in guiding social interactions dramatically increase.

Many times, these observations can be informal and require little preparation. As preschool children play during center time, for example, the adult can focus attention on small groups of children and make brief notes about the ways in which they interact socially. With older children, teachers may not have as many opportunities to stop and observe, but when important behaviors occur, they can make mental notes and then record short written statements at a later, more convenient time.

 Juan's interruption during reading group today is something you want to remember, but you do not have time to stop during the lesson. Later, after announcing snack break, you take a minute to jot down a note about his behavior for future reference.

On other occasions, more formal observations may be necessary to clarify the behaviors about which you are concerned. By choosing the appropriate observation method and creating an accurate picture of the child's activities, you have taken the first step to help children improve their social interactions.

Can children solve their own problems? A major reason many people choose early education and care is that they like children and want to assist them in their growth and development. That desire to help is strong among caring adults and in most instances is a real asset. At times, however, this helping attitude actually can be harmful to children. It is useful to remember that even at very young ages, a major goal of guidance is to help children grow toward independence. This may mean stepping back a bit and allowing children to at least try to work through issues by themselves. Gordon (1974) suggests that adults should mind their own business more often and see what children can do to resolve their own problems. Perhaps just hesitating briefly before stepping in will allow children the time they need to successfully work through their social conflicts. It is sometimes difficult to do, but pausing before you intervene could pay big dividends in terms of encouraging more independent behavior among young children.

Define the limits of acceptable behavior. Clearly, children do need help in many social interactions. Hurting others either physically or emotionally, for example, cannot be allowed. When you recognize the need for intervention, step in and provide it. Frequently, problems with social interactions create strong emotions. You can begin by following the strategies outlined in the previous section for helping children deal with their feelings. In addition, however, it is often useful to clearly define for children the limits of acceptable behavior.

One way to do this is by setting and consistently applying program rules. As surprising as it may first seem, children actually are far more comfortable in an environment where rules are clearly understood and consistently enforced. Their need to test the limits decreases, and they are then free to explore and experiment within the known boundaries. With a few well-chosen and easy-to-understand rules, the early childhood professional can create a consistent and fair program climate. More effective social interactions are one positive result of these clearly defined rules.

Another aspect of defining limits is to help children understand through examples which social behaviors are acceptable and which are not. They know that hitting, biting, kicking, and swearing are unacceptable. Unfortunately, many interactions are not so easily categorized as right or wrong. Take, for example, talking back. Although it is certainly acceptable for children to ask for clarification on an assignment or task, many other responses the child might make would be considered talking back.

 Yolanda's second-grade teacher has just told her to clean up her desk and get ready for recess. If she responds by saying: "No, I'm not ready yet!" that would be talking back to her teacher. However, if she said: "Can I finish my story first?" that would be acceptable. The gray areas need to be carefully defined for students so that they clearly know what is acceptable and what is not.

Help children become more prosocial. Honig and Wittmer (1996) have reviewed extensive research that suggests that child-sensitive, high-quality care will promote more positive social interactions in early childhood settings. Specifically, early childhood professionals who engage in the following activities will help children become more prosocial:

- Emphasize cooperation rather than competition.
- Teach cooperative and conflict-resolution games and sports.
- Set up materials and spaces that facilitate cooperative play.
- Use children's literature that promotes prosocial behaviors.
- Lead discussions that deal with positive social interactions.
- Include class projects that provide opportunities for children to help others.
- Invite adults who have helped others in the community to talk about their experiences with your children.

The *Technology Explorations and Activities* feature in this section describes a program that many early childhood professionals are using to help children become more prosocial. In particular, the program is designed to address violence, bullying, and teasing.

Technology Explorations and Activities . . .
THE SECOND STEP PROGRAM

Professionals in early care and education have taken the principles of guidance described in this chapter and developed specific guidance programs to help children become more prosocial and address the problem behaviors of young children. The Second Step program (Committee for Children, 2010) is a well-known example of this type. It is a planned program designed to develop prosocial behaviors in children and help them avoid violence, bullying, and child abuse. Do an Internet search for Second Step and spend some time reviewing the components described for early childhood settings.

Research, Reflect, and Respond

1. After reviewing the Second Step program, what did you like about the options presented for violence prevention among young children? Were there things that you didn't like?

2. How do you think young children would react to the activities presented on the website? Do they appear to be developmentally appropriate?

3. Compare the strategies used in the Second Step program with those described in this chapter. What are the similarities and differences?

Group Guidance

When you gather young children together in groups, new guidance strategies need to be considered to ensure that these experiences are positive. Children must learn many new behaviors for small- and large-group times to go well. Taking turns speaking, listening while others are talking, and sitting without disturbing neighbors are all important social skills that require considerable practice and discussion before children can successfully manage them. With careful planning and preparation, you can successfully manage these group experiences.

Consider the physical setting. The physical space used for group times is important. If children are too crowded or uncomfortable, they will be less likely to cooperate and enjoy the experience. Normally, a carpeted area with children seated on the floor is the best arrangement for a large-group meeting. Placing them in a circle also allows for better eye contact and a more intimate setting for communication. Some caregivers and teachers find that, for younger children, taping a circle on the rug is helpful to remind them visually of the approximate size of the group circle. Removing unnecessary distractions also increases the likelihood that children will be able to focus their attention on the adult's agenda.

Small-group experiences are often held at tables seating four to six students. In some instances, however, the purpose for the small group may make it more appropriate for children to sit on the

Placing children in a circle creates a more intimate setting with better eye contact and results in more cooperation.

floor in a carpeted area. You should position yourself so that you can periodically scan the activities occurring in other areas. While your primary responsibilities are to the small group, taking the time to look up briefly to see what is happening in the rest of the room will help improve your understanding of total program functioning.

Careful planning and organization. The group experience requires thorough preparation and thought (Jones, 2008). The group time should include active and quiet components, times for children to participate, times for them to listen, and a fairly consistent routine to add stability. The length of time should be tailored to the age of the children, with 10 to 15 minutes being an adequate group time for 3-year-olds and 20 or 25 minutes more workable for second graders. The actual activities will vary according to the purposes of the group time.

An opening group time for a first-grade classroom might look like this:

8:30	Greetings and opening song
8:35	Lunch count, weather, calendar
8:40	Action songs/story
8:45	Dismissal to desks for daily oral language

Although this seems to be a rather simple group experience, each individual component needs careful planning for productive use of the time.

Mixing active and quiet times. The activity level of young children is definitely high, making it difficult for them to sit still and listen to an adult for any length of time. Moving, touching, and talking to others are natural ways for children to learn about the world around them. Although it is important for children to learn to manage their wiggles and to listen to you for short periods, these are not easy things for most children to do. You can help this process along by actively involving children in group experiences. Having children share their thoughts during group time is one involvement technique. By asking appropriate questions and allowing time for children to respond, adults engage students' minds in the issues being discussed. Singing active songs is another favorite of many early childhood professionals.

Movement and music mesh very well in early childhood settings and allow children to participate physically during group time. Simple games and exercises also add movement and interest to group times. The traditional Simon Says is a time-honored favorite that can be added to a group experience to break up longer stretches of quiet sitting times. The best early childhood professionals have a long list of these fun activities to use as needed to add spice to group times throughout the day. Some examples include

- **Songs.** The Eensy Weensy Spider; Head, Shoulders, Knees, and Toes; The Hokey Pokey; The Wheels on the Bus
- **Activities.** Follow the Leader, stretching, clapping to music, marching in place to music, rolling a ball inside the circle of children
- **Games.** Duck, Duck, Goose; Be My Mirror; Simon Says; Heads-Up, Seven-Up

Now that you have read about guidance in early childhood settings, take some time to observe how early childhood professionals put these concepts into practice. Use the *Observing Development* feature that follows to make your observation.

Observing Development . . .
GUIDANCE TECHNIQUES

Choose one of the age groups within early childhood (infants/toddlers, preschoolers, or primary-age children) and *observe* **guidance techniques**. Use the following sample observation as a format for your own observations of guidance strategies:

Glenhaven Head Start Program, 10–10:30 a.m., November 3

Guidance technique	Strategy observed
Indirect Guidance (managing space, equipment, materials, people)	1. Rug in block area (keeps noise down while children use blocks). 2. . . .
Building Relationships (words and actions)	1. Adult gives C. a hug after a fall.
Physical Guidance (physical touch, proximity, smiling)	1. Adult approaches child who says "Don't do that anymore!" 2. . . .
Verbal Guidance (active listening, redirection, positive directions, clear choices)	1. "H., please use your indoor voice."
Discipline strategies (I-message, natural/logical consequences, positive reinforcement, punishment, ignoring, problem-solving)	1. "P., I really like the way you cleaned up the art area before heading outside."

Reflect and Apply

1. Did you find adults consistently using the guidance techniques described in this chapter? Were other strategies used that you thought were more or less effective than the ones in this chapter?

2. After observing in an early childhood setting, which of the components of guidance do you think are the most important and why?

3. What discipline strategies did you observe and how effective were they in changing child behaviors?

summary

What Is Guidance?

Child guidance includes nurturing each child's self-esteem, helping children develop skills in dealing with social-emotional issues, and allowing children to grow toward increasing levels of self-regulation.

Components of Guidance

Guidance includes indirect guidance, building relationships, physical guidance, and verbal guidance. When these attempts at encouraging positive behaviors in children are unsuccessful, caregivers and teachers need to use the fifth component of guidance: discipline.

Guidance Applications

Guidance is used by early childhood professionals to assist children in dealing effectively with feelings and emotions, the routines of the day, social interactions, and group learning experiences. Examples of applications for each of these categories are presented.

for reflection and discussion

1. How is guidance different from the more traditional discipline that was so much a part of our own schooling experiences? Discuss your response with others.

2. List four or five indirect guidance strategies that you could use in your future early childhood setting.

3. Discuss with others the discipline strategies described in this chapter. Which ones do you like and why?

4. List three or four routines that are important in early childhood settings and describe how you can manage these times in your future program. Discuss your thoughts with others.

MyEducationLab

Go to Topic 9: Guiding Children in the MyEducationLab (www.myeducationlab.com) for *Teaching Young Children*, where you can:

- Find learning outcomes for Guiding Children along with the national standards that connect to these outcomes.

- Complete Assignments and Activities that can help you more deeply understand the chapter content.

- Apply and practice your understanding of the core teaching skills identified in the chapter with the Building Teaching Skills and Dispositions learning units.

- Check your comprehension on the content covered in the chapter with the Study Plan. Here you will be able to take a chapter quiz, receive feedback on your answers, and then access Review, Practice, and Enrichment activities to enhance your understanding of chapter content.

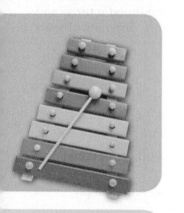

 7

Working with Families and Communities

IN THIS CHAPTER YOU WILL

- Learn about the diversity of family situations.
- Develop insights regarding the benefits and potential conflicts of involvement.
- Identify tools for building strong relationships.
- Learn about strategies for involving families.
- Clarify the role of community members in early education.

Your third year of teaching first grade has just begun. The content and materials for teaching are well organized. You are feeling comfortable with your guidance and discipline strategies. Perhaps this is the year to begin involving families more consistently in their children's learning. You are already sending home a weekly letter, making telephone calls with positive comments, and holding family–teacher conferences in the fall and spring, but you know that much more could be done. Having family members volunteer in the classroom is rather scary, but it is clear from what you have read and heard from others that this type of involvement has many benefits. Providing ways for families who cannot come in during the school day to participate at home would also be of significant value to you and your students. If they are interested, you could plan to have a social event such as a potluck to get families better acquainted. And you have been thinking about collecting and organizing information about community resources to assist families with their many needs. It looks like this will be another busy and productive year.

Early childhood professionals recognize that although they have a major influence on children's lives, their impact pales in comparison with the significance of family interactions. For one thing, they have spent, and will continue to spend, far more time with their children than early childhood professionals ever can. In addition, the bonds created between families and children are hard to match in the program setting. Early childhood professionals need to recognize this fact and work with families to make sure that children have the best opportunities for growth and development. When caregivers and teachers (like the one in the opening scenario) understand family situations and plan strategies for working with them, everyone benefits. The *Observing Development* feature in this section will allow you to observe this family–child dynamic and reflect on its importance.

Observing Development . . .
FAMILY–CHILD INTERACTIONS

Go to a park or playground and observe family–child interactions for one of the age groups within early childhood (infants/toddlers, preschoolers, or primary-age children). It is best to seek permission to observe (giving your reasons for doing so) before you begin. Pay particular attention to the ways family members and children communicate and interact with one another. Use the following sample observation as the format for collecting information on family–child interactions:

Arroyo Park, 2:30–3 p.m., October 2

Family-Child Interaction	Observation
Words Spoken, Tone of Voice	1. "A., be careful not to get your dress dirty!"
	2. . . .
Nonverbal Messages	1. Adult gives C. a swat on the bottom for pushing another child at the climber.
	2. . . .
Involvement of Family in Play	1. Adults spend time on bench observing play (unless they need to get up and intervene).
	2. Older siblings play alongside younger children.

Reflect and Apply

1. Which of the verbal messages shared between adults and children are ones you would consider relationship-building? Could you use any similar messages in your future work with children?

2. Which of the nonverbal strategies you observed could help promote adult–child relationships? Would they be effective in your future early childhood setting?

3. What did this observation tell you about the strength of the adult–child relationship you observed? If you were that child's caregiver or teacher, how would your understanding of this relationship influence the ways in which you interacted with this child?

MyEducationLab

Visit the MyEducationLab for *Teaching Young Children* to enhance your understanding of chapter concepts with a personalized Study Plan. You'll also have the opportunity to hone your teaching skills through video- and case-based Assignments and Activities as well as Building Teaching Skills and Disposition lessons.

It is essential to involve family members who might be the child's primary caregivers in the educational process. Community members provide further resources and support for teaching and learning in early childhood settings. Neglecting these important connections will definitely influence the quality of programs for young children. Families and community members have much to offer early childhood programs in terms of support, insights, and skills. The effort expended in establishing strong working relationships with these individuals will pay big dividends.

The importance of family and community relationships is emphasized in the accreditation standards of the National Association for the Education of Young Children (2009). In addition to being an integral component of every standard, two of the standards address families and community specifically:

- **Standard 2—Building family and community relationships.** Students prepared in early childhood degree programs understand that successful early childhood education depends upon partnerships with children's families and communities.

- **Standard 4—Using developmentally effective approaches to connect with children and families.** They (students) understand and use positive relationships and supportive interactions as the foundation for their work with young children and families.

 ## Family Life Today

 Margaret Smith's third-grade classroom has a mix of families. Some of her parents had children as young teens and others waited until much later in life. One of Margaret's families is homeless, several qualify for food stamps, and a few are upper middle class. Several single-parent families, remarriages, and a gay couple add further diversity to her family configurations. Ethnic and religious differences create an even more varied mix of values, attitudes, and traditions among her families.

It does not take much insight to realize that families today look much different from the way they did just a generation or two ago. The idyllic picture of mom, dad, and two or three children living happily down the street in the house with the white picket fence is just not as likely today. Family situations vary widely, and educators not only must know what those possibilities look like but must be ready to work effectively with diverse families. In the following paragraphs, a number of important family constellations are described to help you better understand the diverse mix you will encounter in future early childhood settings. For each of the family types identified, some general attributes are presented. Be aware that although these may be typical, each family situation is unique. For example, although many single parents may find it difficult to commit the time and energy needed to be involved in early learning, some single parents you work with may not fit this pattern.

The Extended Family

Not too many years ago, it was fairly common to find families and their relatives living in the same community or general area. Aunts, uncles, and grandparents were available to help with child care and give advice on how to parent. This support system was often helpful, especially to first-time parents as they struggled with the many challenges of raising children. Although some of these extended families still exist, they are now the exception rather than the rule. Despite the fact that many still need and want the support that the extended family provided, few have found an adequate replacement. Early childhood professionals can assist in this process by helping families create networks with others in similar situations to provide one another with support.

Divorced and Single-Parent Families

One of the most common family situations that you will encounter is the single-parent family. National statistics indicate that 26% of children under age 18 are living in families with only one parent (Forum on Child and Family Statistics, 2010). In most cases, the missing parent is the father. Single-parent families headed by mothers are far more likely to be living at or below the poverty level than two-parent families. It is estimated that approximately 40% of all single-parent families headed by women are poor, compared with only about 8% of two-parent families (Annie E. Casey Foundation, 2010). In addition to having low incomes, single parents as a group tend to be busy with work commitments and child-rearing responsibilities, which may leave less time for things like family–teacher conferences and helping out in early childhood settings. You will need to be sensitive to these time constraints and find creative ways to work with single parents and their children. It is also important to communicate with and involve non-custodial parents (typically fathers) when legally possible. For example, it may be necessary to schedule separate family–teacher conferences for non-custodial parents so that they can be included in their child's learning and development.

Blended Families

 Ramon is a new 4-year-old in your early childhood program. His mother and stepfather have recently married and created a blended family with four children, two each from their previous marriages. The family has been working hard to redefine roles and responsibilities. Although many positive attributes can be found in this blended family, everyone is struggling to adjust.

Divorce, as previously described, impacts a great many families. It leaves young children without one of their parents and creates many stresses for all involved. In many circumstances, family dynamics are further complicated by the eventual remarriages that frequently occur. As in the previous example of Ramon, these blended families create challenges for both adults and children as new relationships are established. Approximately 54% of women remarry within five years, creating situations in which the children are raised by a stepparent (Bramlett & Mosher, 2002). While adults are learning to mesh parenting styles and are combining efforts to manage complex households, children are adjusting to a variety of new relationships. Children in newly blended families may respond by withdrawing socially or acting out. Careful observation and sensitive interactions may be required of you in order to assist children and families with these complex changes.

Two-Career Families

Today's economic realities find a great many intact families in which both adults work outside the home so that the family can maintain a desired lifestyle. In other two-parent families, both adults have career aspirations and are employed full-time outside the home. Because of these two sets of circumstances, children in two-career families today tend to have less time to spend with their families. In addition, when both adults work outside the home, they may have fewer opportunities to be actively involved in early childhood settings. While there are numerous exceptions to this generalization, early childhood professionals must understand the complexities of this family type and adjust their involvement strategies to ensure that busy lifestyles and limited flexible time can be managed.

Older and Younger Parents

Another change in family composition that impacts working with young children is the age of parents themselves. People are having children at both older and younger ages. Teen pregnancies and birth rates among unmarried women remain high in the United States as compared with other industrialized nations, despite many efforts to make young people aware of the major challenges facing teen parents (Annie E. Casey Foundation, 2010).

Becky is a young single mother of 6-year-old Brian. She got pregnant at 15 and has worked hard to complete high school, keep a part-time job, and be a good mother to Brian. Becky has lived at home to make ends meet and is just now beginning to get herself together both financially and emotionally. Becky is nearly 10 years younger than the typical family members in your program.

At the same time, many couples are choosing to wait until later in life to begin families. This older group of adults tends to be well educated and brings a diversity of life and work experiences to their interactions with early childhood programs. Statistics on older parents are sketchy, but it appears that the numbers are growing (Martin, Kochanek, Strobino, Guyer, & MacDorman, 2005).

Jay and Deedee postponed children for several years while getting established in their careers. Both returned to graduate school to strengthen their career mobility. At age 38, they decided to have their first child. Now in their mid-forties, they have two children, busy professional lives, and a secure financial outlook. Jay and Deedee are nearly 15 years older than the typical family members in your program.

Early childhood professionals can expect to work with parents of all ages and cultural backgrounds.

With young parents, older parents, and every possible age combination in between, early childhood professionals find less common ground on which to base their interactions and communications. Working with families becomes a more individualized event, with more emphasis on the needs, interests, and abilities of the diverse families found in each early childhood setting. Despite the challenges, involving older and younger families should be an essential part of your efforts as a future early educator.

Family Mobility

Another characteristic of families today that significantly impacts early childhood professionals is the relocation of families in new communities. One recent study indicates that approximately half of all households had moved within the past three years (Coulton, Theodos, & Turner, 2009). In some cases, this movement is brought about when one or both adults are promoted to a higher position in a corporation or relocate to find a better job in a new community. Members of the American military community also move frequently. For other families, regular moves are a necessary condition for employment. Hispanic migrant workers, for example, move around the country taking seasonal agricultural jobs. In many parts of the country, the children of these workers move in and out of early childhood settings on a regular and predictable basis. Regardless of the reason, family mobility frequently leads to stress and can impact the family's willingness to be involved. In a military family, for example, the husband may be deployed overseas, while mom and the children remain on a military base. In addition to the same stresses faced by a single parent, this mom may have high anxiety over her husband's safety and have little extra energy and time for involvement.

Homeless Families

Each year in the United States, approximately 1.5 million children are homeless (National Center for Family Homelessness, 2010). They may spend the night in a shelter, an abandoned building, or the family car. While statistics on homelessness are sketchy, it appears that homeless families with children account for a large proportion of those seeking shelter in missions and that these families make up nearly 34% of the homeless (National Center for Family Homelessness, 2010). Clearly, the stress level of homeless families is high, and involvement in early childhood programs tends to be a low priority. In many instances, homeless children either do not attend a program at all or participate only sporadically. You should make a special effort to assist these families by directing them to community agencies that can provide them with services. And, despite the challenges, it is also critical that homeless families remain connected to local early childhood programs. These settings may provide one of the few areas of relative stability for these children.

Gay and Lesbian Families

A small but growing number of children in America have either two moms or two dads. In some cases, these children were born into a heterosexual family that later dissolved when one of the partners discovered his or her sexual orientation. Others were either adopted by their gay or lesbian parents or were conceived through artificial insemination (American Psychological Association, 2010). Although gay and lesbian families currently make up only a small percentage of family totals, there is every indication that early childhood professionals will see increasing numbers in the future. U.S. Census data indicate that 96% of all U.S. counties have at least one same-sex couple with children under age 18 (Gates, 2003). As state and federal laws continue to become more supportive of gay and lesbian couples, and society in general grows more accepting of this family configuration, it becomes increasingly likely that you will be working with gay and lesbian families in your future career.

The *Celebrating Diversity* feature in this section provides additional information about working with gay and lesbian families. A real-life family shares their thoughts on the challenges and joys they face. Read this information now and think carefully about your ability to work with families like this in your future early childhood setting.

Families That Have Children with Special Needs

Families that have children with special needs are much the same as every other family you will work with. They love their children and want the best for them educationally and socially. Families are concerned about parenting strategies that work, want their children to learn and grow in healthy and safe environments, are thrilled when a new developmental milestone is reached, and worry about what is best for their children.

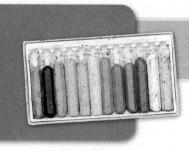

Celebrating Diversity . . .
GAY AND LESBIAN FAMILIES

Ruth Kadish (2006) is lesbian and also a parent of three young children. She and her partner experience many of the same joys and problems faced by all families. They worry about how well their children will do in school, and work to provide them with the support and encouragement they will need for success. Ruth and her partner also encounter many unique challenges because of their sexual preference. They find that some people don't approve of them having children to raise. Others don't consider them a family at all. Ruth describes their efforts to prepare their children both emotionally and practically for the reception they will receive in school: "We can talk to our children about the ways in which all families are different, and give them language to help them talk about their family. . . . We can also work proactively to make our schools welcoming and safe environments for all families" (p. 2).

As you begin to think about working with gay and lesbian families, it is important to realize that they are just like all the other families you will work with. They have the same hopes and aspirations for their children, experience the same feelings of frustration and anxiety toward parenting, and want to support their children in whatever ways they can so that they will be successful. Having said this, however, the presence of gay and lesbian families in your program may well mean further modifications in the ways in which you interact with families and children. For example, you will need to think about how you will respond to the inevitable curiosity of children: "Teacher, why does Marcus have two moms?" It may also mean that you will need to modify slightly the way in which you prepare for celebrations like Mother's Day and Father's Day. It will be important for you to be sensitive to the needs and interests of both adults and children.

1. In what other ways may you need to adapt communications and interactions as you work with gay and lesbian families?

2. How do you think you will feel about working with gay and lesbian families? Do you think that your religious beliefs or family values will make it more difficult to work with gay and lesbian parents? Why or why not?

At the same time, families of children with special needs often face additional burdens and responsibilities that make life a real struggle. Shepherd and Shepherd (1984) describe the range of emotions that many families of children with special needs experience. The following is a sampling of these possible feelings:

- It is a little like everything that everyone else has experienced; it is a lot like nothing anyone else has ever experienced.

- It is feeling like you want to kick in the TV screen every time you see the "Take care of your baby before it is born" public service commercial. I took care of myself when I was pregnant, and our child is handicapped.

- It is being afraid to ask for help because you are fearful that you cannot personally cope with any more blame or guilt.

- It is "dying" from the silence and stares of other people when they meet our son. It is wanting to announce to the whole world that you have a handicapped child and also simultaneously wanting to disappear from the face of the earth for a few moments.

- It is being afraid to even think, much less plan, concerning the future.

- It is dying a little when your son does something inappropriate and others laugh and say, "You are so funny!"

- It is having three specialists all ask you during the same day if anyone in your family has ever been diagnosed as schizophrenic. (Shepherd & Shepherd, 1984, pp. 88–89)

Early childhood professionals working with these families must make every effort to be sensitive to their special needs and feelings. Extra care must be taken to listen carefully, to communicate positively, and to develop good working relationships with them. Remembering that each family unit is unique, you must work to understand the challenges they face and stand ready to assist in whatever ways possible. In addition, families of children with special needs want to feel needed and accepted as part of the early childhood program. Make sure that they, like all families, are welcomed with open arms.

Families with Foster Children

Currently, approximately 800,000 children are in foster care in the United States (Casey Family Foundation, 2008). Children in foster care face many challenges, including living in foster families where there are larger ratios of children to adults, lower household incomes, a higher percentage of adults who haven't finished high school, and greater numbers of adults with disabilities (Casey Family Foundation, 2008). Many children in foster care must change schools one or more times after their placement, leading to additional stress. Children in foster care end up graduating from high school at lower rates than the general population, are expelled from schools more frequently, and are placed in special education at approximately double the rate of the general population (Casey Family Foundation, 2008).

 Jarred and Marissa have just accepted responsibility for another foster child. They have been caring for two other foster children and have two children of their own. Devon is eighteen months and arrived a week ago for what is hoped will be a short foster care stay. There are a total of four children in Devon's family and each has been placed in a separate foster home. Devon's parents are struggling right now. His dad has left the area and appears uninterested in continuing a relationship with any of the children. Devon's mother has been homeless for the last several months and just went into treatment for drug abuse. She hopes to retain custody of the children but is currently unable to care for them.

As an early childhood professional, you will need to work hard to develop strong relationships with foster care families, biological parents, and children like Devon to help them counterbalance the less favorable aspects of family life and foster care. In addition to special efforts at relationship building, you will want to be aware of, and ready to provide, information on resources that may be useful to families and children.

Linguistic Diversity

The United States continues to have growing numbers of families who speak languages other than English in the home. Immigrant families, most of whom speak another language, have grown from 13% of the total U.S. population in 1990 to 22% in 2007 (Mather, 2009). About 40% of this total is from Mexico, while another 20% is from Asia.

In addition to helping children learn English, you will need to use additional strategies for communicating with the families of these children. Parents and older family members who come to this country without English skills have fewer options for learning the language and will need your support to understand and contribute to your early childhood program.

Baahir and Haima moved to the United States 2 years ago from India. They are living in a small Midwestern town with their 3 children enrolled in schools there. Nabha is 3 and enrolled in a Head Start program. She is quickly learning English and fitting in well after being in the program for several months. Gagan is 5 and a typical kindergarten child, full of energy and eager to learn. Taj is the oldest and just started second grade. She, too, is making a good adjustment to life in the United States.

Baahir and Haima, however, are struggling a bit more to adjust. They are slower to learn English, primarily because they have fewer opportunities for instruction. Baahir works as a janitor, and Haima is cleaning houses for a local company. Neither has the time or energy following work to take a class or practice their English skills. Although they would like to be more aware and supportive of their children's schooling, it is difficult because of the language barriers.

Ethnic/Cultural Diversity

Another fact of life today in the United States is that families continue to grow more diverse in terms of ethnic/cultural background. It is estimated, for example, that the non-Hispanic white population in this country will decrease from nearly 75% in 1980 to approximately 47% by the year 2020 (Forum on Child and Family Statistics, 2010). With relatively stable birth rates for whites and considerably higher birth rates for the Hispanic population, in particular, family diversity continues to grow. Other growth factors include the number of immigrants from Asia and other parts of the world (Mather, 2009) and the increase in multiracial families (U.S. Census Bureau, 2000).

Increasing cultural and racial diversity will require changes in what is taught in early childhood settings and will also influence the kinds of interactions that caregivers and teachers have with families. For example, Asian-American families tend to have high academic expectations for their children but also feel that the early childhood program should have considerable autonomy in dealing with academic and guidance-related issues (Olsen & Fuller, 2008). Consequently, they may be less likely to get involved in some aspects of the early childhood program. Adults working with young children and their families must be aware of these cultural/ethnic differences and adjust to them as plans are made to involve families in the educational process (Bang, 2009).

 ## Benefits and Potential Conflicts

Given the family situations described here and the complications they present, you may be wondering whether or not this whole task of involving families is worth the effort it clearly will take. Despite the added time commitments, early childhood professionals who take the time to work with families find the experience richly rewarding for all involved (Souto-Manning, 2010). The insight and support that families can provide to early childhood programs simply have no substitute. Conversely, families often find that they desperately need the support and assistance you can offer. Parenting is an extremely difficult and complex task requiring much guidance and assistance. Children, too, benefit when families and early childhood professionals work together. These relationships become win–win situations where all participants benefit. In the paragraphs that follow, the benefits of involvement for early childhood professionals, families, and children are identified and discussed. These will then be followed by information on potential conflicts you may face.

Benefits to Early Childhood Professionals

 Mrs. Andreson teaches second grade at Northwest Academy. She has worked hard to involve families in the educational process. Although it means some extra effort on her part, she clearly sees many advantages. Involved families are important aides in the classroom and helpmates for field trips. In addition, those who participate in their child's education extend learning into the home and are generally more supportive of the schools.

When caregivers and teachers make the effort necessary to involve families and community members, they benefit in many important ways:

- The involved adults have a greater appreciation of the challenges of working with young children in group settings.
- Families and community members come to value and respect your efforts and are more likely to speak positively with others about early education.
- With added assistance, early childhood professionals can do a better job in their early childhood program (Souto-Manning, 2010). While a family or community member is busy with a small-group art project, for example, the professional is freed up to work with other children.
- Bringing in other adults with unique talents and abilities adds to the excitement of the program and often leaves you feeling more satisfied with your work.
- As early childhood professionals work to involve families and community members, their relationships with children also tend to improve. With more time for each child, increased understanding, and a more exciting program, children will respond more positively to you.

Benefits to Families

The difficult task of parenting is often a struggle for many adults. When families are involved in early childhood programs, they find opportunities for support that make the task a little more manageable (Powell, 1998). Just knowing that other families are struggling with the same issues is reassuring to many. Talking through parenting challenges with others gives family members new ideas and renewed motivation to manage their own concerns.

Conversations with caregivers and teachers combined with opportunities to see them deal with similar issues in early childhood settings provides families with good options to try with their children at home. Families who get involved also gain new insights into their own children's lives in a different setting. All of this tends to strengthen their self-esteem and hone their parenting skills. The Head

Start program has many examples of families who have gotten involved in program activities and gone on to improve their lives in a variety of ways (Administration for Children and Families, 2010b).

Benefits to Children

Kendra has been struggling with reading in her first-grade classroom. After conducting a family–teacher conference, Kendra's teacher has asked two classroom volunteers to each spend time each week listening to her read. At home, Kendra's parents have set aside 20 minutes every evening for family reading time. This combined effort is beginning to pay dividends, and Kendra's reading skills are slowly improving.

When families, community members, and early childhood professionals work together, children's lives are improved. Children who see a variety of concerned adults working to help them improve their school performance respond positively, leading to increased achievement (Fields-Smith & Neuharth-Pritchett, 2009). This involvement makes it clear to children that learning is important; as a result, their motivation to succeed is strengthened. Just as with families, children tend to have improved self-concepts when family members, community members, and early childhood professionals combine efforts on their behalf. It feels good to know so many important people care. Participation also benefits children by providing an enriched school environment. When family members get involved in your setting, more hands-on activities, which simply could not be managed without additional help, become possible. A trip to a local grocery store, for example, to learn about an important community business would not be possible without family members and others to assist along the way.

Potential Conflicts

While most interactions with families are positive, the attitudes and experiences of both families and early childhood professionals can lead to problems in these relationships. Gestwicki (2010) suggests that the barriers to effective family–teacher relationships can be categorized into three areas:

- **Barriers caused by human nature.** Fear of criticism, fear hidden behind a "professional" mask, fear of failure, and fear of differences all can cause problems in family–teacher relationships.
- **Barriers caused by the communication process.** Negative reactions to either the parenting or the teaching role, letting emotions influence communications, and introverted personalities lead to less than positive communications between families and early childhood professionals.
- **Barriers caused by external factors.** Time constraints, appearing too busy to interact, failure to adjust to changing family structures, administrative policies that discourage involvement, and personal problems can cause additional conflicts between family members and early childhood professionals.

Souto-Manning (2010) adds one other significant challenge to family involvement: cultural mismatch. Early childhood professionals and families often have differing cultural expectations about children's development and schooling. These differences need to be understood and addressed if relationships are to be strong.

Family Partnerships . . .
WORKING WITH DIFFICULT FAMILY MEMBERS

While it would be ideal if every family were pleasant, positive, and easy to work with, the reality is that some will find fault with nearly everything you do. There are many possible explanations for these challenging families. Some may have had poor school experiences themselves and come to your early childhood program with many negative associations. Keyser (2006) identifies four other categories of family–teacher conflicts: (a) conflicting family and program needs; (b) differing views of teaching and child development; (c) inadequate communication; and (d) cultural differences.

Regardless of the reason, you will need to develop strategies to help you improve your interactions with these difficult families. The following options should be considered:

- **Increase communications.** While the human tendency is to step back from difficult interactions, it is important to increase them. For example, make it a point to regularly send a positive note or e-mail message telling difficult families about something good that has happened with their child.
- **Listen calmly and carefully.** Difficult families may say things that are hurtful and make you defensive. By being a calm and careful listener, you are more likely to be able to identify the problem the family member is having and begin to work toward a solution.
- **Build on family strengths.** Just as it is important to look for the positive characteristics of every child and to build on them in your early childhood program, it is equally important to identify the positive attributes of difficult families so that you can use these qualities for the betterment of the children (Souto-Manning, 2010). For example, a difficult father who experienced failures as a student himself may be an excellent carpenter who could help you design and build a flowerbox planter for your program. Allowing the parent to contribute in a positive way to the program has the potential to strengthen his relationship with you.

1. Given the information in this chapter on the benefits of family involvement, how important is it to work effectively with all families, including difficult ones? What will you do to increase your success in working with difficult families?

2. How do you typically deal with confrontations? Do you welcome the challenges or try to avoid them? What does this tell you about your future interactions with difficult families?

While it may be impossible to avoid all of these barriers, knowing they exist and thinking through potential ways of dealing with them can help reduce the conflicts that may arise. For example, knowing that talking to a family member about her child's low score on a standardized reading test might cause her to get emotional, you could first highlight the strengths you have seen the child demonstrate in your program and then talk about the test score. Remaining calm, even if a family member criticizes you in some way, may be another necessary response.

No one likes dealing with conflicts that occur in relationships. If you plan to involve families and community members, however, these conflicts will undoubtedly occur. The *Family Partnerships* feature in this section provides strategies for resolving these inevitable challenges.

Building Strong Two-Way Relationships

Healthy human relationships of all sorts have strong communication as a foundation. Friendships, marriages, and family–child relationships all require regular and effective interactions to remain strong. This same basic premise is true for family–teacher relationships as well. When caregivers and families engage in frequent verbal and/or written interactions, their relationships can grow and prosper (Gennarelli, 2004).

Providing Mutual Support

When you think about the friendships you have with other adults, do you recognize the mutual give and take that is necessary to make these relationships work? Strong friendships require mutual support if they are to remain healthy. When the support becomes one-sided, the relationship typically dies. This same idea applies to family–caregiver relationships. If we are to work with families as partners in the educational process, we need to see our interactions as providing support for one another (Daniel, 2009). When family members spend time in early childhood programs, they are providing us with support in the educational process. Other families support you when they assist children with program-related projects at home. The options for family support are many. Creative early childhood professionals will find a number of ways to find and use this support. It is important, however, for you to support the families as well. When we share parenting information with a concerned family member, listen to the struggles families face, or help locate a community resource to meet a family need (Kersey & Masterson, 2009), you are providing valued assistance that will strengthen your relationships with families. This does not mean that you can meet all or even most of the needs of families. Many times, your role is to simply know of resources available within the community and refer families to them when needed. The *Developmentally Appropriate Practice* feature in this section describes some potential ways in which you can support families with infants and toddlers.

Communication: The Key

Without question, the key element needed for effective family–teacher partnerships is strong communication. It is the beginning point and a continuing need in these relationships (Kersey & Masterson, 2009). Calling Mrs. Jackson to mention the extra effort Zachary put into his mathematics today, a brief note to Jennifer's father to thank him for coming on the recent field trip, and just taking the time to say hello to Shaquille's mom when she drops him off for class are all simple, but important, relationship-building communications. Effective understanding and positive interactions result from spending time getting to know one another via thoughtful, quality communications.

Epstein (1995, 2006) suggests that the best early childhood programs work to create partnerships among early childhood professionals, families, and communities. When members of these partnerships work together, children have the greatest opportunities for learning and development. These partnerships lead to six different types of involvement:

- **Parenting.** Establish home environments that support childhood learning. For example, in a weekly letter home to families, you could suggest two to four good books that are available in the school and/or public library for families to read to their children at home.
- **Communicating.** Design effective strategies that encourage two-way communications between home and the early childhood program. Many early childhood professionals use home visits as one of their communication strategies. These visits are highly effective in building relationships and communicating with families about important topics. Home visits are described in more detail in the next major section of this chapter.

Developmentally Appropriate Practice . . .
SUPPORTING FAMILIES WITH INFANTS AND TODDLERS

Families with infants and toddlers lead busy lives. Little things, like the routines of eating, sleeping, and diaper changing, take up considerable amounts of time. Holding, talking, reading, singing, and playing with infants and toddlers are other important parts of parenting very young children. When work responsibilities and/or caring for older children are added to this mix, many families find that they have little time for anything else. When caregivers work to support families with infants and toddlers, even in small ways, the efforts are greatly appreciated. The following list provides some relatively easy ways to assist families with very young children:

- In your weekly newsletter, summarize an effective parenting strategy that families can implement at home.
- Create a list of community resources that support families with infants and toddlers and share it as needed.
- Collect articles on parenting young children and have them available for checkout.
- Identify emergency child-care providers to assist families who need temporary care for their infants and toddlers.
- Set up a parenting group that brings families together on a regular basis to discuss the challenges and joys of parenting infants and toddlers.
- Create a telephone tree for families with infants and toddlers so that they can call each other for advice and support.
- Find doctors and dentists in your community who can offer quality care to new families entering your community.
- Locate businesses and industries in your community with flexible work policies that support families with young children and share as needed.
- Speak up on behalf of families with infants and toddlers in community settings to help improve services and provide support for their many needs.

- **Volunteering.** Recruit and organize family and community volunteers. For example, you may want to recruit families and community members to help tutor the English language learning children in your program.
- **Learning at home.** Provide parents with ideas that they can use to help their children at home. Some early childhood professionals encourage families to check out program materials that come with instructions so that playful learning can occur in the home. The *Celebrating Play* feature in this section provides more details on how you can set up a toy lending library.
- **Decision making.** Give families and community members opportunities to participate in decisions about the early childhood program (Fields-Smith & Neuharth-Pritchett, 2009). For example, early childhood professionals should encourage families that participate in the local parent–teacher organization (PTO) to not only help raise money for program needs, but to also be involved in decisions about how that money is spent.
- **Collaborating with community.** Identify and use community resources to strengthen early childhood programs. For example, you can use business and industry connections in your community to locate and use recycled materials for play and learning in your program (Reusable Resources Association, 2010).

Although only one of the six categories of involvement identified by Epstein specifically addresses communication and its importance in home, school, and community relations, it is not difficult to see that each type requires strong communication

Celebrating Play . . .
A TOY LENDING LIBRARY

Some early childhood professionals are providing families with a valuable service by loaning toys and play equipment from the program to use at home. Because you will put only a small proportion of your total toys and equipment out for play at any one time, a great many others are not in use much of the time. You will rotate toys and equipment through the centers so that there are always new and exciting options for children to play with. The materials that are left in storage can then be loaned to families who would benefit greatly from having quality play materials available in the home.

If at some point in your career you want to consider lending toys to families, you may want to start on a small scale by loaning only one or two toys. Because a large amount of planning and organization is required for a more complete library, starting with one or two toys at a time allows you to implement this strategy with minimal effort. Rather than having a complete lending library, you could then have a "toy of the week" that could be shared with interested families. If you wanted to create a more elaborate toy lending library, it would probably be most successful if you were to seek the support and assistance of others in your early childhood program. By sharing the workload, this project can be made more manageable. Rettig (1998) provides more specific guidelines that will be useful if you decide to set up a toy lending library in your future early childhood setting.

Regardless of the size of your toy lending system, you will need to consider several key steps.

- Develop an easy but effective *checkout system*.
- Find a simple *method of transporting toys* to and from school.
- Have a *list of guidelines* for toy use that can be sent home with the play materials. One simple method for lending a single toy would be to use an old backpack that children could wear home at the end of the day with the play materials inside in a plastic container. Taping guidelines for toy use to the inside of the container lid would be an effective way to make sure they were readily available.

1. Knowing the importance of play, and despite the added work of creating a toy lending system, do you think it would be worth the effort? Why or why not?
2. In what ways would a toy lending system help you educate families about the values of childhood play?

to be effective. The partnerships we seek with families and community members are just not possible without good communication.

Effective Communication Strategies

Given the importance of quality interactions between families and early childhood professionals, it is critical for you to be aware of a variety of communication techniques and the potential strengths and weaknesses of each. No one technique will meet all of your needs for communicating with families. Several methods, each used appropriately, will be necessary to build and maintain partnerships between families and early childhood programs. Figure 7–1 identifies seven essential communication methods, each of which is described in more detail in the following paragraphs.

Telephone calls. One simple but effective technology tool that you can put to good use is the telephone. It is a quick and easy way to communicate simple, positive messages to families (Kersey & Masterson, 2009). A 2-minute call to share with a family member something positive her child did that day will pay big dividends in terms of relationship building. Every family wants to hear these positive messages, so if you decide to use this communication strategy, make sure you contact all families with positive messages about their children.

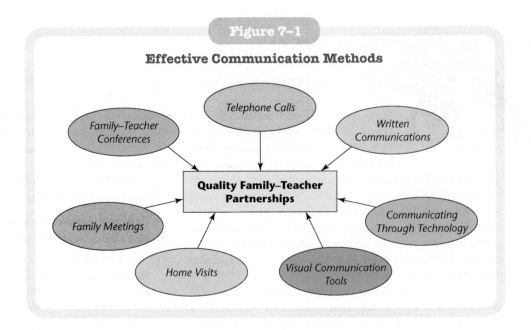

Figure 7–1

Effective Communication Methods

Using the telephone in communicating with families has several other important benefits. In general, it is inexpensive and provides for two-way communications. Most family members are also more comfortable communicating with you from the comfort and convenience of their own homes. You can fit in short telephone calls around an already busy schedule, making it more likely that it is something you will accomplish.

Despite the many benefits, telephone use has some potential drawbacks. Because a phone call does not have nonverbal cues, the phone is not appropriate for more difficult messages that may need to be shared with families. Remember, also, that you do not know what you might be interrupting when you call. It is always best to ask if you are calling at a convenient time. You may need to give the family member the option of talking with you at a later time. Calling a family member on a cell phone has the additional problem of being less private. Either you or the family member could be in a very public place at the time of the call, so sensitive topics need to be avoided.

One final issue should be mentioned regarding telephone use. Consider whether or not you will want to give out your home telephone or cell phone number so that families can contact you outside program hours. Some caregivers and teachers feel very strongly that their life away from their early childhood setting should not be interrupted by work-related business. Others, however, want families to know that they have the opportunity to call when they have a need. If you choose to give out your phone number(s), you may want to let families know the appropriate times to call.

Written communications. A common strategy that early childhood professionals use to exchange information with families is written communications. A wide variety of options are appropriate (Barbour, Barbour, & Scully, 2011):

- **Handwritten notes.** Simple and quick, these notes are sent home as needed regarding individual children. Much like the telephone calls mentioned earlier, these brief notes are simply a little pat on the back for the family and child through sharing a positive event from the program day.

- **Notices to all families.** Caregivers and teachers also find many opportunities to send home written notices to all families about an upcoming event such as a field trip to the zoo.

- **Letters.** One- or two-page letters to families are another possible written communication tool. The *Developmentally Appropriate Practice* feature in this section provides an example of an introductory letter to families that could be sent home prior to the beginning of the school year.

- **Newsletters.** A newsletter is a longer, more complicated written document that usually goes home less regularly. It may contain several pages of information for families, including such things as a calendar of events, articles of interest, samples of children's work, ideas for families to use at home, and a wish list of materials that families could collect for your program. Reichel (2006) provides many practical tips for writing quality newsletters to families.

- **Prepublished materials.** A final category of written materials are those that have been published through other sources. Many public agencies prepare brochures or other written materials that might be useful to you in working with families. Articles in newspapers and magazines (remember to comply with copyright laws if you make multiple copies) are also helpful in communicating important information to families.

As you think about using written communications, consider the following issues. One of the difficulties many caregivers and teachers face with any written material intended for families is how to make sure it gets home. Children of all ages need assistance in getting these messages to their families. In addition, although they provide family members with good information, they seldom encourage a response from the home. When this can be built in, the connection between home and school is stronger.

Perhaps the most important consideration when developing written communications is to make sure that your writing is of the very best quality. What kind of response would families have to a letter from you that had several spelling and grammatical errors? Often, the reaction is surprise, followed by frustration. Early childhood professionals are expected to be good models. Punctuation, grammar, and spelling errors send a negative message home that may be stronger than the more positive intent of the written communication. If writing is something you have to work hard to do well, plan on spending the necessary time to ensure a well-written message.

Communicating through technology. As more homes and early childhood programs invest in computer technology, electronic communications are becoming a more common communication strategy. Keep in mind that families who don't have ready access to technology will need to get the same information in another format. Mitchell, Foulger, and Wetzel (2009) suggest several ways to communicate through technology:

- **Create a program website.** You can either add to your school or program website or create your own. Software such as Google Sites makes this a relatively painless process, even for those with average computer skills.

- **Send individual e-mail messages.** Use e-mail to send positive information about an individual child's activities or accomplishments.

Developmentally Appropriate Practice . . .
A LETTER OF INTRODUCTION

One form of written communication that you may want to use is a letter home to families at the beginning of the year. This letter can be used to tell them something about you as a person, begin the process of building good relationships, and welcome their participation in the life of your program. Following is an example of an introductory letter for a second-grade classroom:

Dear Families:

It is hard to believe that the summer is nearly over and school will begin again in just two short weeks! I have enjoyed a marvelous vacation in which I tended my garden, took short trips for hikes and bicycle rides, and played with my two daughters. This was the first time I have been able to take significant time off over the summer to relax with my family. What a pleasure!

Despite this nearly perfect summer, I am truly excited about the coming school year. Teaching second grade has been a great source of pleasure to me, and I expect this coming year to provide a similar experience. It will be a privilege to get to know you and your child in the coming weeks. To begin this process, I would like to invite you to our school Open House on Friday, September 28, from 6–8 p.m. Bring your family for any part of that time so that you can browse through my classroom and get acquainted with me and Angie Hanson, my Educational Assistant.

Families are always welcome in my classroom. I hope you will be able to find the time to participate in some way. If you cannot assist during the school day, there are other ways for you to get involved. Just let me know of your interest and I will make sure your talents are put to good use. Your participation will be much appreciated.

Again, I look forward to meeting you and your child in the near future.

- **Post or send photos.** With digital cameras, it becomes easy to post photos on your website or even send photos as an attachment to an e-mail message. Families greatly appreciate this view of life in the early childhood program.
- **Post or send at-home activities.** You can either post activities on your website that are designed to extend program learning in the home or send more specific tasks to individual children and families. Either option engages families in extended learning opportunities.
- **Create a family response link or form.** Giving families a way to provide you with feedback about program activities or their child's progress is an invaluable way to help you evaluate the success of your program.
- **Establish a family support discussion forum.** While it may not be possible to get families together physically on a regular basis, they appreciate the chance to voice their questions and comments and receive feedback from you or other families.
- **Communicate logistical information through group e-mails.** This strategy can be effective for quickly sending out information about events that are designed for all families, such as upcoming field trips or conferences.

Visual communication tools. Although written communications are an important part of interactions with families, other options are available. One additional category of communication tools could be called visual displays. Videotapes, DVDs, You Tube videos, and bulletin boards are all important types of visual displays. Many families would like to know what is happening in their children's programs but do not have the chance to drop in on a regular basis. Consider making regular videotapes or DVDs of the activities and then loaning them to families who want to catch a glimpse of their children's daily activities. Similarly, if you have a program website, it is an easy process to create a link to a video on You Tube for families to view online.

Bulletin boards are another form of visual communication that can be used productively in working with families. A wide assortment of information can be shared. Upcoming events, program activities, samples of children's work, articles on parenting or child development issues, and a wish list of materials that families could collect at home are a sampling of items that could be included. A well thought out bulletin board will be read and appreciated by the families who enter your program and have a few minutes to browse. Although bulletin boards have many positive uses, they also have their limitations. Perhaps the most obvious is that families who do not come into your early childhood setting will not see them. Another potential drawback is that bulletin boards do not give families much opportunity to communicate with you. One-way communications definitely have inherent limitations. Finally, be aware that bulletin boards are time-consuming to create and require periodic updating to make sure the information remains current.

Home visits. One of the best ways to get acquainted with families is to take time to go out and meet with them in their homes (Gorter-Reu & Anderson, 1998; Halgunseth, 2009). The early childhood professional sets up an appointment, plans an agenda, and travels to the family's home to meet and talk with them. Home visits have been shown to be highly effective both in teaching families skills that they can use in working with their children (Bronfenbrenner, 1974) and for conducting family–teacher conferences. Perhaps the best way, however, for you to get the most from home visits is to use them to get better acquainted with children and their families.

Many preschool educators have home visits with all of their families before the school year actually begins. These *getting-acquainted visits* typically last 30 to 45 minutes and may include a variety of activities. Some early childhood professionals take a book or a simple activity with them to break the ice with the children who are new to their programs. Young children frequently want to lead a tour around the house and show off their bedrooms and favorite playthings. Home visits are an ideal time to casually share with families a little bit about yourself as a person and what you hope to accomplish during the year. Sharing in this way often encourages families to open up about their lives as well. Refreshments, casual conversation, and an opportunity to get a feel for home life are other common elements of a getting-acquainted home visit.

Home visits are ideal times to casually share with families information about yourself and what you hope to accomplish working with their children.

If you choose to make home visits, consider the following suggestions (Gorter-Reu & Anderson, 1998):

- It is essential that you *make an appointment* with families ahead of time and explain to them the purposes of the visit.
- *Establish a time frame* for the visit (typically 30 to 45 minutes) so that families know what to expect.
- *Think carefully about what you will wear* on the home visit. Remember that first impressions are important and that you want to appear professional but still approachable by families.
- *Avoid note taking* during the home visit itself. Family members generally feel anxious when you do. Drive a few blocks away after the home visit, and then stop to make any needed notes about things you want to remember.

Family meetings. Getting together with families in group settings is another possible communication strategy to be considered. They occur regularly in many early childhood settings. In Head Start programs, for example, family meetings are the second most frequent involvement strategy used (Castro, Bryant, Peisner-Feinberg, & Skinner, 2004). Foster (1994) provides examples of different types of family meetings and describes strategies for making them a success.

- **Social events.** Some family meetings could simply be social times, when you have a chance to get to know families and help them meet others in the program. The traditional school/family potluck and a family fun night are examples of this meeting type.
- **Educational meetings.** Many family meetings are designed to be educational and focus on a topic of interest and importance to a large number of families. "Promoting Childhood Health through Nutrition and Exercise" is one topic that might interest a variety of families.
- **Organizational meetings.** Some meetings are needed to organize a specific task or to deal with the management of the early childhood program. For example, families who are interested in helping to fund playground equipment for your program would need to meet with administrators to help plan the steps they will take.
- **Child performances.** Finally, some meetings provide an opportunity for child performances. While not appropriate for the preschool and toddler years, a musical program or play can be a very enjoyable experience for primary children and their families.

If you plan on incorporating family meetings into your collection of communication tools, be sure to plan them carefully. Families who give up precious evening time to come into your early childhood program will want to get a good return on their investment. Begin by making sure the meeting topics are of interest. A simple questionnaire can be used to determine what families want and need for their group gatherings. Plan a variety of interesting activities that actively involve family members in discussion and learning. Have a carefully planned agenda to keep events moving along smoothly. This planning will pay big dividends in terms of family interest and involvement in your meetings.

Family–teacher conferences. One of the most common communication tools used in early childhood programs is the family–teacher conference. Most programs expect early childhood professionals to conference with families at least once each academic year and more commonly twice. A typical pattern is to have conferences fairly early in the fall and again in the spring. In many early childhood settings, programs will set aside one or two days and additional evening times for conferencing.

Family–teacher conferences have many strengths as a communication tool:

- **They bring families into the program.** Since conferences are typically held in the early childhood setting, families can see firsthand the materials you use and hear personally about your approach to teaching and learning. For some, this may be the only time they enter your physical space.

- **They build rapport with families.** When done well, conferences build positive rapport with families as the early childhood professional and family members discuss the children's strengths, progress, and possible areas for improvement. Face-to-face interactions provide the best opportunities for developing more personal and in-depth relationships.

- **They provide more information.** Conferences allow the sharing of considerable information about the child's progress. As the conversation unfolds, you have many opportunities to tell families about friendships, interactions with other adults, interests, and motivations.

- **They show children's work.** When conferences are held in the early childhood setting, families can actually see projects their children have completed and get a better sense of the learning experiences occurring there. Samples of art work, writing/prewriting activities, books of interest, and mathematics/science projects are examples of the child's activities that can be shared.

Although most family–teacher conferences are pleasant and enjoyable for both family members and early childhood professionals, issues occasionally come up that require you to demonstrate quick thinking and tact to avoid possible problems (Koch & McDonough, 1999). The following purely hypothetical excerpt from a conference situation highlights this issue:

 Margaret is the mother of 5-year-old Louise. During the family–teacher conference, Margaret announces, "You know, I am suspicious of anything Louise does. She has fooled me too many times. Oh, I have read all the books on child psychology, but it has not helped me much. I really do not know what to do with Louise. There are so many things wrong with her!"

As Louise's teacher, you want to understand Margaret's concerns and work effectively with her while helping the parent see the good things Louise does in your program—which is not an easy task. Think about how you might respond to this parent.

The following checklist will help you plan for, and conduct positive conferences with all families:

- **Make an appointment ahead of time and set a time limit for each visit.** You do not want to be rigid, but a schedule is needed to manage all the families who will want to talk to you.

- **Be prepared.** Study all available information on all children, and gather samples of their work. You may want to plan an expected agenda for each conference, while realizing that family comments or concerns may lead you in different directions.

- **Prepare a comfortable place to hold conferences.** It should have adult-sized chairs arranged in such a way that you let families know you see them as partners in the educational process. Make sure the place you choose is private as well, because the information that both of you share is often sensitive.

- **Adjust your pace to that of the family members.** Some of their concerns may be different from yours, but equally important. Be a good listener. Let families do a significant portion of the talking.
- **Make the conference professional.** That means sharing clear, specific information about each child and her strengths and areas for improvement. It also means respecting family information as confidential.
- **Be positive.** It is important to begin and end each conference on a positive note. You cannot ignore the problems, but make sure families know that you notice the strengths their children have demonstrated as well.

Another way to strengthen family–teacher conferences is to include the child. Often referred to as a **three-way conference**, a variety of creative options can be used, such as having the child lead the discussion through the use of a PowerPoint presentation (Young & Behounek, 2006). This conference format has both strengths and possible problems (Taylor, 1999). When children are involved, their anxiety over what is being discussed is eliminated. They can also share their perspectives on conference issues and, along with family members and early childhood professionals, can commit to any plans for improvement. Many times, seeing the interactions between family members and the child in the three-way conference provides insights and important information about family life.

However, the three-way conference has potential problems. For example, the family members may be less comfortable when the child is present. The adults might wish to share information about family life or program interactions that is just not appropriate or helpful for children to hear. In other instances, the adults may downplay the child's problems when he is present. Adults can also make the child feel that he is an unimportant part of the conference process by talking over and around the child. In addition, some argue that younger children may not understand or be ready to participate in the conference.

You may also find that electronic conferences will be an effective strategy to use with some families. The *Technology Explorations and Activities* feature in this section explores this option.

Understanding Beliefs and Attitudes

Good communication skills can help you build strong family and community relationships by providing you with tools to understand the beliefs and attitudes of others and engage in positive dialogue when they differ from your own. Every adult has developed a complex array of beliefs and attitudes that influence virtually every interaction they have with others. As a future early childhood professional, this will be true in your relationships with families and community members.

Martha teaches second grade. One of her personal beliefs is that smoking in its many forms is very unhealthy and that people who do smoke are foolish. This year, she has two families that she knows of who are smokers. With family–teacher conferences coming up in a week, Martha will need to be sure she reminds herself that this attitude toward smoking may influence her interactions with these adults. Martha needs to treat all families with dignity and respect for the sake of the children she teaches.

Technology Explorations and Activities . . .
ELECTRONIC FAMILY–TEACHER CONFERENCES

Although most families want to be involved in their child's early learning, some may not have the option of doing so. But there are newer technologies that can help families participate when it is difficult for them to come into your program to meet face-to-face. One option is to use Skype and the Internet. Skype is a free program that allows anyone with a web camera and microphone to communicate real-time video and sound over the Internet. A teacher in Lacey, Washington, used Skype to conduct a family–teacher conference with a father deployed to Afghanistan. Read about this option at www.king5.com/news/education/Teacher-uses-Skype-for-parent-teacher-conference-89307262.html and reflect on its potential for use in your own early childhood setting. If this link is no longer active, do an Internet search for "Skype and parent teacher conferences" and find other examples to read about.

Research, Reflect, and Respond

1. Have you used Skype to communicate with someone over the Internet? If not, talk to someone who has and get their reactions to this option. If you have used Skype, reflect on the strengths and limitations of this type of electronic media.

2. After reading the Internet article referenced here and thinking through the strengths and limitations of this option, how effective do you think it would be to use Skype to conduct a family–teacher conference? List the potential strengths and limitations from your perspective.

3. Would you use Skype to conduct a family–teacher conference in your future work? Why or why not? Are there other messages/types of communication for which you would consider using Skype?

As indicated in this example, your beliefs and attitudes may be different from those held by families and community members. In some instances, it should be relatively easy for you to set aside your differences and engage in quality interactions that build relationships. In other cases, however, deeply held beliefs and attitudes can cause significant challenges in your relationships with others. It is important for you to be aware of these feelings and how they may impact your work with families and community members. When they are in direct conflict with those of families and community members, it may be difficult to work effectively with these individuals. The following are some examples of beliefs and attitudes that may cause stress in your interactions with others:

- **Religious beliefs.** If you, or the adults you work with, have strong religious beliefs, challenging interactions with families may be the result. For example, a family member may comment: "The Bible says if you spare the rod you will spoil the child. I believe in spanking my children." If your religious beliefs or attitudes about spanking are different from those of this adult, how will you respond? How would this affect your relationship with this family member?

- **People with different ethnic or racial backgrounds.** In Hispanic cultures, early childhood professionals are typically given considerable freedom to guide teaching and learning in the early childhood setting. Many Hispanic families may want to simply turn over these roles to you as the early childhood professional. How will you react to this attitude as you work hard to get all families involved in the learning and development of their children?

- **Single-parent families.** What attitudes do you hold regarding single parents? Some people, for example, feel that they can't be good parents because of the stress from their difficult life circumstances. Single parents, they argue, don't have the time and energy they need to effectively parent their children. Will you be able to set aside this and other generalizations and work to establish good relationships with single parents?

- **Political beliefs.** A community member recently shared in the local newspaper his belief that homeless families are simply not working hard enough to find employment and housing for their loved ones. You are on a community board with this person. Will his attitude toward the homeless influence your ability to work with him?

- **Healthy lifestyles.** You recognize the importance of exercise and healthy eating for young children. One of your families has three members who are obese, including their 5-year-old daughter who is in your class. How will your attitudes influence interactions with this family?

Family-Friendly Schools

Building strong relationships with families also means creating early childhood settings where families are welcomed. Family-friendly settings do the following:

- **Welcome families visually and emotionally.** Banners, bulletin boards, and display cases are developed to help families feel wanted and needed. Reaching out to families as they arrive also helps them feel emotionally welcomed.

- **Accommodate diverse families.** Scheduling conferences at convenient times, communicating with custodial and non-custodial family members, being aware and supportive of family living situations, and adjusting involvement strategies to meet the needs of different families are all examples of this effort to accommodate diverse families. In addition, you should work to accommodate families that are diverse due to cultural background, sexual orientation, or special needs. For example, if your program has African-American children, plan to provide books, dolls, musical experiences, and role models that reflect their cultural heritage. You can also encourage families to bring materials from home to make the early childhood setting more relevant to the diverse families you will serve.

- **Make it easy to get involved.** Rather than creating obstacles that make it more difficult to get involved, family-friendly settings do things to make it easier for families to participate, like providing child care during family–teacher conferences.

- **Demonstrate that family opinions and involvement are important.** Family-friendly settings make sure that family members get involved in meaningful ways and that their opinions are viewed as important in the decision-making process. For example, a family member who serves on a hiring committee for a new staff person should have all the privileges and responsibilities of the other members.

- **Provide assistance and resources.** One almost universal need of families during the early childhood years is assistance with parenting. You can serve as a resource by providing articles and pamphlets on parenting or by developing classes on topics of interest to the group. You should also be ready to provide families with information about community resources that can assist them with a variety of personal needs.

 # Involving Families

Traditional family involvement has focused on developing strategies for bringing family members into the early childhood setting to engage in tasks that support the learning and development of children. While that remains an important component of involvement, many family members find it difficult to actually come into the early childhood setting on a regular basis. For that reason, it is also important to plan ways for family members to get involved in supporting childhood learning and development in the home. The following sections describe several options for involvement in both settings.

In Early Childhood Settings

When you think about involving families in your early childhood setting, you should make sure that the strategies you choose are meaningful to the family members who walk in your door. Some will want to be actively engaged in working with children. Others may be happy doing more clerical tasks such as cutting paper for art projects. Still others find it enjoyable to assist with decision-making tasks such as toy and equipment purchases, food choices for snacks and lunches, and even the hiring of new staff. These needs and interests of families must then be matched with the needs you have for assistance in your program.

Another thing to remember about involving families, is that the options you plan for them must be realistic in terms of your ability to implement them successfully. For example, if you want to have family members come into your preschool and work with children, you will need to think through this seemingly simple task and prepare specific ideas for what you want them to do. Do you want them to read stories to children? If so, you will need to locate books that are both developmentally appropriate and of interest to individual children. Are these books available in your preschool center or will you need to check them out of the local library? What are your goals and expectations for this activity and how will you share this information with the families you involve?

Given the planning and preparation that is needed for even fairly simple tasks, it is important for you to start small with your involvement strategies and gradually add to them as you get more comfortable. This will help ensure that the experiences are good ones for both families and children.

Keeping the above information in mind, here are some initial suggestions for ways in which families can effectively contribute to your program. For more excellent ideas on communicating and working with diverse families, read the book *50 Strategies for Communicating and Working with Diverse Families* (Gonzalez-Mena, 2010).

- Read books to children who are learning English as a second language and spend time talking about the content once the book is completed.
- Engage individual children in activities using a math manipulative to help them develop deeper understandings of numbers.
- Prepare the table, trays, paints, and paper needed for an upcoming finger painting activity.
- Share a talent or interest with the class. An example might be a cooking activity.

- Write down stories told by children that are then illustrated and made into books.
- Assist with a small group of children on a field trip to a dairy farm in the community.
- Spend time with children on the playground as they engage in activities in that setting.
- Talk with children about their work in the community. For example, a firefighter could bring in some of the specialized equipment needed to fight a fire and show how it is used.
- Help children engage in an interesting science activity, such as planting seeds. Begin by reading an appropriate book and then follow with all the steps needed to plant several varieties.
- Tutor an individual child who needs assistance in learning his addition number facts.
- Plan and implement a big buddy program in which older children in the school spend time working with younger ones to build meaningful relationships and develop literacy skills.

At Home

While involving family members in the activities of your early childhood program is important, many find it difficult to find the time needed to do so. In addition, involving families at home may well have even greater potential for positively influencing child growth and development than similar activities in the early childhood program. For example, encouraging a family member to help you prepare and serve nutritious and healthy snacks is a good way to help that person see and discuss the importance of nutrition and diet in child growth and development. On the other hand, having that same family member work with the child at home to create a list of snacks eaten during the past week, and then to create a menu of better (or different) food choices for the coming week may have even more potential for long-term nutritional benefits in the family.

As with planning involvement activities for the early childhood setting, it is important to start with just a few strategies and gradually add other at-home options. Because they typically require more careful written directions than face-to-face interactions do, home involvement activities are even more time consuming to prepare than are similar options in the early childhood setting.

The following list of possible home involvement activities is meant to get you started thinking about the many possibilities that exist. You should consider creating your own list of involvement options.

- Read good books to children regularly so that children recognize the importance of, and pleasures associated with, a good book. Families should be good role models by taking time when children are present to read the newspaper, a magazine, or a book.
- Talk with children about the positive and negative influences of television while viewing it with them. Plan alternative options, such as active outdoor play, that have more value to overall child development.
- Recycle cans, bottles, plastic, and paper so that children see a real-world example of others caring for the environment. Save some of the recycled materials so that they can be used in the early childhood setting for art and construction projects.

- Create a space at home for children to do projects related to the early childhood setting, and then work with them to make sure they get tasks completed.
- With information provided by you, plan, write, and organize the program newsletter for distribution to other families.
- Based on directions provided by you, have the family member prepare a game or activity for use in the early childhood setting.
- Call other families to remind them of the upcoming field trip, and find volunteers to help with transportation and participation.
- Family members can let children know that they think early learning is important. They can discuss ways in which children can be active, positive participants.
- Based on information provided by you, family members can encourage children to eat nutritious foods and exercise regularly to combat obesity.

Connecting with the Community

This chapter has focused primarily on involving families in the educational process. Although families are critical to the success of early education, community members can also provide many important benefits. A great many resources can be productively used to benefit young children. In terms of human resources, the local firefighter, police officer, or retired volunteer can share much with your class. Material resources also abound in most communities. Scrap paper, wood, and other recyclable materials can be located and used effectively (Reusable Resources Association, 2010). Community businesses are often generous in their donations of money and materials in support of local early care and education. When community members are involved, they are also more likely to understand and support your program when talking to others. It makes good sense to work toward involving community members along with families.

Involving the Community in the Early Childhood Setting

The community can be active in early childhood settings in many good ways. One possibility is to allow the early care setting to be used for appropriate community activities. Groups wanting to offer classes in jewelry making or woodworking, recreational activities such as ballroom dancing, or noncredit classes on such topics as health or psychology always need a place to conduct these activities. Community organizations may also need a meeting room and could benefit from a local school's willingness to provide space.

Another important way to involve community members in early childhood programs is to seek out and use resource people to strengthen the curriculum. Community helpers such as doctors and dentists can come into your program and share information with children about good health and dental care. Workers from a variety of occupations can begin the process of career awareness with young children by demonstrating their expertise. Other community members may well be interested in simply volunteering their time and talents to help out in your program.

Finally, community members should be involved in early childhood settings as part of the decision-making process. What is taught, who should serve as caregivers and teachers, and what equipment and supplies should be purchased are all potential issues in which community members should be involved. The Head Start program requires that every local center have representation from families and the community on its policy councils and committees (U.S. Department of Health and Human Services, 2010). These boards make all the major decisions about Head Start activities. Local public schools also are managed by school boards made up of elected community members who agree to oversee the activities of the schools under their control.

Involving the Early Childhood Program in the Community

Early childhood educators and children can also benefit from getting out into the local community. By doing so, programs avoid the tendency to isolate themselves from the rest of life. Perhaps the most common way in which early childhood programs get involved in the community is through the traditional field trip. A well-planned visit to the local bakery could be a wonderful way to help children understand food production and distribution, for example.

Taking children to a fire station can enrich your fire safety curriculum.

With family support, the community can also become a site for observation and for learning separate from program events. In some instances, early childhood professionals can provide families with specific assignments to go out into the community and gain insights into business and community services. For example, a second-grade teacher could encourage families to interview a local businessperson in preparation for an upcoming social studies unit. In other circumstances, providing families with information about upcoming community events and services could lead to important opportunities to learn outside the traditional program setting and day.

Another option for involving early childhood programs in the community is to consider ways in which families and program personnel can give back to the community. Getting involved in a community service project such as planting seedling trees during an Arbor Day celebration could be one way to do this. Another possibility is to adopt a community park and spend time there on a regular basis cleaning and maintaining the grounds. Donating clothing and food to the local women's care facility could be yet another opportunity to help children and families feel that they are contributing to the community in positive ways.

Advocacy and Public Policy

Another very important reason to connect with the community is to make your voice heard in support of children and families. The National Association for the Education of Young Children (NAEYC) published a code of ethical conduct

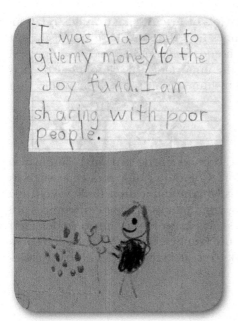

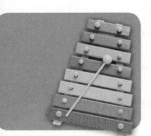

Young children can give back to their community in meaningful ways.

(National Association for the Education of Young Children, 2011). In this document, they make the case that caregivers and teachers must work collaboratively with families, the community, and public agencies to provide the best possible learning and development options for young children. NAEYC states:

> Because of our specialized expertise in early childhood development and education and because the larger society shares responsibility for the welfare and protection of young children, we acknowledge a collective obligation to advocate for the best interests of children within early childhood programs and in the larger community and to serve as a voice for young children everywhere. (p. 6)

There are a variety of ways in which you can serve as an advocate for children and families:

- **Contact elected officials.** When critical issues at the local, state, and national level influence the lives of children and families, consider sending elected officials a quick e-mail message indicating your support or opposition to the action.
- **Educate yourself about critical issues and share your insights with others.** As your knowledge of children, development, and learning continues to grow, your opinions on these matters will count in your interactions with others. Make sure that you are up-to-date on important topics and then share your insights as you communicate with leaders in your community, region, and state.
- **Work to elect officials who support children and families.** Your support in electing key officials who serve in decision-making roles can be invaluable. Start by making sure you are registered to vote. Then, find out which candidates support children and families and work to get them elected.
- **Share your opinions in the media.** It is important that as many people as possible stand up for children and their families. Advocate on their behalf by sharing your opinions in ways such as writing a letter to the editor of your local newspaper. Your voice is needed.

summary

Family Life Today

Decreasing numbers of extended families living in close proximity, divorced and single-parent families, blended families, two-career families, family members at older and younger ages, family mobility, homelessness, gay and lesbian families, families that have children with special needs, families with foster children, linguistic diversity, and ethnic/cultural diversity are all examples of the diverse families present in America today.

Benefits and Potential Conflicts

Early childhood professionals find that involving families and community members helps these adults have a greater appreciation for the challenges of teaching, allows early childhood professionals to do a better job of teaching, and builds relationships with children and their families. Families find that they have more support and ideas for working with their children at home. Children benefit with improved school performance, which helps them see the importance of schooling. Conflicts with families can stem from barriers caused by human nature, the communication process, or external forces.

Building Strong Two-Way Relationships

The key to working with family members is to build strong two-way relationships through mutual support and communication. Communication strategies such as telephone calls, written communications, visual communication tools, electronic communications, home visits, family meetings, and family–teacher conferences are essential to the relationship-building process. It is also important to understand your own beliefs and attitudes and those of the families. Be aware that differences might influence relationships, and then work to create a family-friendly early childhood setting.

Involving Families

When early childhood professionals begin to involve families, they should start with a few options that are carefully planned to help ensure their success. It is important to implement strategies for involving families in the early childhood setting and in the home.

Connecting with the Community

Caregivers and teachers need planned strategies for involving the community in the school and the school in the community. In addition, they serve as advocates for children and families, influencing public policy on a variety of levels.

for reflection and discussion

1. Are there any family circumstances described in this chapter that you will have difficulty dealing with as an early childhood professional? Why do you feel this way?

2. What will you do to reduce conflicts that may occur as you work with families? Discuss your thinking with others.

3. List strategies for creating a family-friendly early childhood setting.

4. Summarize two or three strategies described in this chapter for involving families that you liked and will want to implement in your own program some day, giving a rationale for why you think they are effective. Share these strategies with your classmates and incorporate their feedback.

5. What do you see as the advantages of involving the community in your early childhood setting? Will you also want to involve your program in community activities? Research local organizations and resources in your community that could be beneficial to your program, and vice versa.

MyEducationLab

Go to Topic 3: Family/Community in the MyEducationLab
(www.myeducationlab.com) for *Teaching Young Children*, where you can:

- Find learning outcomes for Family/Community along with the national standards that connect to these outcomes.
- Complete Assignments and Activities that can help you more deeply understand the chapter content.
- Apply and practice your understanding of the core teaching skills identified in the chapter with the Building Teaching Skills and Dispositions learning units.
- Check your comprehension on the content covered in the chapter with the Study Plan. Here you will be able to take a chapter quiz, receive feedback on your answers, and then access Review, Practice, and Enrichment activities to enhance your understanding of chapter content.

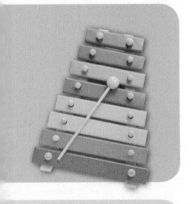

 8

Diversity and Young Children

IN THIS CHAPTER YOU WILL

- Study how people develop attitudes toward diversity.
- Identify ways to encourage acceptance of diverse people.
- Discover inappropriate responses to diversity.
- Learn to integrate diversity throughout the curriculum.

"What an interesting class I have!" you think, as you prepare for next week's activities. "These children are unique in so many ways. In my class of 27 third-grade children, I've got quite a mix. There is Dimitri, who comes to us from Russia. His English has improved by leaps and bounds over the last several months. Carlos and Marianna are Hispanic and benefit so much from the warmth and support of their extended families. Shantel is African American, and Quen has Asian heritage. Each brings a unique personality to the classroom. Then there is Alex. Despite using a wheelchair from a very early age, he is one of the most active and positive children in the group. To make things even more interesting, the class has a higher than normal percentage of boys. It will be even more important than usual to make sure the girls have access to some of the traditionally boy-dominated equipment in the classroom."

Although the preceding scenario may sound rather unusual, in reality, this level of diversity is the norm in many early childhood settings today. Adults working with children need to be prepared for this wonderful mix of children and families. It is important to assist all involved in understanding and appropriately responding to the diversity they will experience.

Diversity is considered an essential element of early care and education in this text because understanding and responding appropriately to diverse children and families is central to the principle that "every child deserves to develop to his or her fullest potential" (Derman-Sparks & Edwards, 2010, p. 2). It is only when we are able to accept and respond to children and families as unique and valued that all children can have the same opportunities for optimal growth and development.

Diversity also directly influences the other essential elements of early care and education. Child development, play, guidance, and working with families are all influenced by diversity. Some examples should help highlight this point:

- **Child development and diversity.** Children with physical disabilities (such as problems with hearing and eyesight) acquire oral and written language differently; boys and girls have variations in their gross and fine motor development (Bee & Boyd, 2010). As programs grow increasingly diverse, the range of developmental abilities you will see as an early childhood professional will continue to expand.

- **Play and diversity.** Children who live in cultures that value competition spend more time playing competitive games (Sutton-Smith & Roberts, 1981); children with autism seldom engage in symbolic play (Atlas & Lapidus, 1987); boys and girls have different toy preferences (Nash & Fraleigh, 1993). Diverse early childhood settings mean you will see, and need to prepare for, wider variations in play behaviors.

- **Diversity and guidance.** Children with attention deficits often need special guidance regarding instructions (Landau & McAninch, 1993); eye contact is considered impolite in some cultures, thus changing the way in which you guide some children. Caregivers and teachers in diverse early childhood settings will need to develop and use guidance strategies that meet the needs of all children.

- **Working with diverse families.** In African-American families, it is common for aunts, uncles, grandparents, and other extended family members to informally adopt children, thus creating unique family constellations for you to work with; the involvement of men in child care and education has increased and changes the mix of families that caregivers and teachers will be working with (National Center for Education Statistics, 2010). The communication and involvement strategies you use will need to take into consideration the diverse families you will be working with. The *Family Partnerships* feature found in this section provides additional information on diverse families; in particular, the issues you will face in working with teen parents.

As American society becomes increasingly more diverse, the importance of this topic will continue to grow. The National Association for the Education of Young Children (2009), in its book titled *NAEYC Standards for Early Childhood Professional Preparation Programs*, emphasizes the importance of diversity by embedding it into each of its six standards. In addition, the document describes four unifying themes, including one titled *"shared professional values"* that includes "a commitment to diversity and inclusion; respect for family, community, and cultural contexts" (p. 3). When early childhood programs are reviewed for accreditation, these elements are carefully studied.

 ## Attitudes toward Diversity

An important starting point in the study of diversity is to address the attitudes of children (and adults) toward people who are different from themselves. Without question, children notice the many distinctions that exist. For example, infants as young as 6 months old notice differences in skin color (Ramsey, 2004). By the age of 2, children not only notice similarities and differences but also ask questions about their observations. Clearly, children find diversity topics interesting and want to talk about and understand them.

Racial/Cultural Attitudes

To understand children's attitudes about racial and cultural differences, it is necessary to begin with those held by the adults around them. Children are strongly influenced by the comments and actions of the significant adults in their lives.

Family Partnerships . . .
WORKING WITH TEEN PARENTS

It may surprise you to learn that the number of teen parents in this country is high. While there was an overall decline in teen parents during the last decade of the twentieth century, America today still has one of the highest teen pregnancy rates among developed countries. Approximately four of every 10 young women in this country become pregnant at least once before their 20th birthday (Annie E. Casey Foundation, 2010). These statistics make it clear that, as an early childhood professional working with young children, your partnerships with families will probably include communicating with and involving teen parents.

Because of these probable connections, it is important for you to be aware of the many challenges faced by very young families and to be prepared to assist them when possible. Teen mothers tend to drop out of school and live in poverty more often than their peers. In addition, they have children with increased health problems, more frequent developmental delays, and a greater likelihood for future difficulties in school (Shore, 2003). As society struggles to reduce the incidence of teen pregnancy, your job will be to work cooperatively and effectively with these very young families in whatever ways you can.

In addition to interacting with teen parents in your early childhood setting, you will want to be aware of other resources within the local community. Teen parents may receive services in several important ways:

- **On-site child care.** Many high schools now provide on-site child care so that teen parents can continue their own schooling while their young children receive quality care. These programs are often cooperative schools, and teen parents are expected to spend time as aides in the early childhood setting, where they learn parenting skills as they interact with other trained early educators.

- **Parenting education.** Teen parents typically have limited knowledge of what it takes to be a parent and few resources for parenting advice. They need assistance from others about expectations for child development, strategies for parenting, and help in managing complex lives under difficult circumstances. Early childhood professionals and community agencies are stepping in to assist teen parents in these important areas.

- **Alternative schooling.** Because of their life situations, teen parents may find it difficult to be successful in a regular middle school or high school program. Many school districts provide alternative schooling options for teen parents and others that offer learning experiences to better meet their needs.

- **Counseling and career education.** School districts and community agencies also provide teen parents with counseling and career education opportunities to help them cope with challenging life circumstances and to take advantage of local resources.

- **Health care.** Because teen parents are often in low-income family situations, they frequently qualify for free or low-cost medical care. Taking advantage of these services can have a major positive impact on the health and well-being of children.

1. What challenges do you think that teen parents face as they continue to mature while raising one or more young children at the same time? What can you do to support teen parents?

2. How do you think you will feel about working with teen parents? How will your attitudes and beliefs influence your interactions?

With the passage of the *Civil Rights Act* in 1964, many people assumed that racial discrimination would end relatively quickly and that attitudes about racial and cultural differences would improve greatly. This has not, however, been the case. Although many people accept and value the racial and cultural diversity of American life, others do not. Unfortunately, some adults continue to pass on to children their misconceptions and negative attitudes about people who are racially or culturally different from themselves.

Children who are exposed to these misconceptions and negative attitudes from the adults around them begin to absorb these same attitudes as early as 2½ years

Diversity is a positive aspect of working with young children and their families.

of age (Ramsey, 2004). Through repeated exposure to family members, neighbors, and others who regularly reinforce this disapproval of people who are different from themselves, children start to internalize these values. These attitudes are often reinforced further when young children watch television, play video games, and listen to music that emphasizes this same negativity (Cortes, 2000). Because both positive and negative attitudes begin to develop early in the young child's life, it is essential for early educators and caregivers to help guide children in the process of valuing racial/cultural diversity.

Attitudes about Gender

Efforts to provide women with equitable opportunities in all aspects of American life have been only slightly more successful than the results for racial/cultural minorities. Take, for example, gender equity in National Collegiate Athletic Association (NCAA) sports. A study by the NCAA indicates that even though equitable funding has been mandated for many years, it will probably be several more years before parity is reached (National Collegiate Athletic Association, 2003).

For more than a decade, the American Association of University Women (AAUW) has studied gender equity issues for girls in the K–12 educational system. Beginning in 1992 with its landmark publication, *How Schools Shortchange Girls*, through its most recent publication on the topic titled *Where the Girls Are: The Facts about Gender Equity in Education* (Corbett, Hill, & Rose, 2008), the AAUW has had a consistent message: Girls don't have the same educational opportunities as boys. While there has been considerable progress over the last several years, girls still take fewer advanced classes in mathematics and the sciences than boys. In addition, girls make up only a small percentage of the students in computer science and computer design courses. Together, these differences in educational preparation mean that women are often not as well prepared for the more science, math, and technology-oriented jobs available in the workplace.

Although most people talk about the importance of gender equity, the subtle (and some not-so-subtle) behaviors of many adults indicate that women are often given lower status in American society and around the world (Frawley, 2005). Think, for example, of the traditional terms we use such as *homemaker* and *housewife* to describe a woman who chooses to stay at home engaged in the critical roles of spouse and mother. Compare those with the terms we use when a woman chooses a career. In addition to the language we use, children are exposed to many adults and media events that promote gender inequities. The family who consistently dresses their young daughter in nice dresses and insists that these dresses stay clean is subtly influencing this young girl's play and interactions with others. These kinds of attitudes on the part of families and others can lead to childhood behaviors and budding perspectives that are less than desirable.

Playing house is important for boys as well as girls.

 Mandy, Ariel, and DeForrest are playing in the dress-up area of their preschool program. Clothes and equipment are available for playing doctors and nurses. Mandy wants to dress up as a doctor and begins to gear up for her role. "Hey!" calls DeForrest. "You can't be the doctor! Girls have to be the nurses!"

Preschool children's attitudes about gender roles (like the one just expressed) are often overgeneralizations made from their observations of, and interactions with, other adults. These early stereotypic responses can be modified by adults who provide children with more diverse examples of women's roles in society. Young children need early and frequent exposure to pictures, stories, and adult models that demonstrate more equitable opportunities for women in America.

Sexual Orientation

The small, but growing number of gay and lesbian families (American Psychological Association, 2010) in the United States means that you are increasingly likely to have children in your early childhood program who have two same-sex parents. Because of strong moral and/or religious beliefs, there are many people who feel that gay and lesbian families should not be recognized as legitimate family units. Attitudes coming from the home will have a strong influence on the thoughts and comments of even the youngest children in your care.

So, in addition to thoughtfully planning ways in which you can support the child and family, you will need to think through, and be ready to address, comments and questions that come up from other children and families. Children will naturally notice and want to have clear information from you about the differences and similarities they see. A typical question you might expect from a young child would be "Why does James have two dads?" You will need to be ready with a simple and honest response. How will you feel about addressing this issue with children?

Children with Special Needs

With the passage of Public Law (PL) 94–142 (the *Education for All Handicapped Children Act*) in 1975, children with special needs began to be included in American public school classrooms. Children without disabilities began to work and play with those who do have special needs. Before this time, they rarely interacted. In 1986, PL 99–457 mandated the inclusion of children from ages 3 to 5 in preschool and kindergarten settings, further encouraging contact between children with special needs and the general population. In 1990, PL 101–336 (known as the Americans with Disabilities Act) was enacted. Viewed as a major piece of civil rights legislation, this law requires equal access to public and private services for individuals with special needs (Heward, 2009). These services include the opportunity to participate in early childhood programs. PL 101–476, known as the Individuals with Disabilities Education Act (IDEA), was also put into law in 1990. This law provided services to individuals aged 18 to 21 with special needs and modified the categories of disability to include such things as autism and attention deficit disorder (ADD). IDEA was amended and reauthorized in 2004.

The opportunity for early and regular interactions between children with and without special needs has led to many benefits for all. Wolery and Wilbers (1994) list the following potential advantages:

Children with special needs

- Are spared the negative effects of separate, segregated education.
- Receive realistic life experiences that prepare them to live in the community.
- Have opportunities to develop friendships with typically developing peers.

Children without special needs

- Can develop more accurate views about individuals with special needs.
- Have opportunities to develop positive attitudes about people who are different from themselves.
- Are provided with models of children who succeed despite many challenges.

 Evan is a fun and lively 5-year-old with Down syndrome. One characteristic of his special need is lower-than-normal muscle tone. This means that Evan's speech is harder to understand and large and small muscle control is delayed. In addition, Evan is slower to develop conceptual understandings and finds it harder than most children to learn new ideas. Despite these challenges, he is actively engaged in learning both at home and in his kindergarten classroom. Evan is one of the most well-liked children in the group.

One result of the current emphasis on meeting the needs of all children with special needs is the implementation of individualized plans designed by early childhood professionals, educational specialists, and families. For infants and toddlers, these plans are called **Individualized Family Service Plans** (IFSP).

Celebrating Play . . .
CHILDREN WITH SPECIAL NEEDS AND PLAY

In your future role as an early childhood professional, you will almost certainly be working with children with special needs. As you begin to think about working with these children, remember that they are people first and only secondarily require special services. Children with special needs are more like their peers than they are different from them. Their needs, interests, and learning styles are often much like every other child in the program. These similarities suggest that play should be considered an important vehicle for learning and development in their lives. As is the case for all children, play provides opportunities for children with special needs to develop social, emotional, physical, language, and intellectual understandings in unique ways.

In a position paper on childhood play published by the Association for Childhood Education International (ACEI), Isenberg and Quisenberry (2010) make a compelling argument for **all** children to have the opportunity for quality play experiences:

> Theorists, regardless of their orientation, concur that play occupies a central role in children's lives. They also suggest that the *absence of play* is an obstacle to the development of healthy and creative individuals. *Psychoanalysts* believe that play is necessary for mastering emotional traumas or disturbances; *psychosocialists* believe it is necessary for ego mastery and learning to live with everyday experiences; *constructivists* believe it is necessary for cognitive growth; *maturationalists* believe it is necessary for competence building and for socializing functions in all cultures of the world; and *neuroscientists* believe it is necessary for emotional and physical health, motivation, and love of learning. (p. 1)

Given this strong statement, it may surprise you to learn that opportunities for play are not always readily available for children with special needs. Because the traditional focus of most programs has been on more direct instruction for children with special needs, caregivers and teachers provide numerous structured learning experiences that help them develop academic and social/emotional skills. One of the consequences of this focus, however, is that there is frequently less time for play. Another problem faced by many young children with special needs is that the materials used in quality play experiences are not easily adaptable for use by them. It is impossible, for example, for a child who uses a wheelchair to take advantage of a creative playground structure if it is not equipped with a ramp for wheelchair use.

1. Go to the ACEI website (http://acei.org/wp-content/uploads/PlayEssential.pdf) and read the position statement in its entirety. Based on the arguments presented, do you agree that play is essential for *all* children? Why or why not?
2. Despite the additional costs, why should children with special needs be provided with the toys and equipment they need to engage in quality play experiences?

From the preschool years and beyond they are called **Individual Education Programs** (IEP). Early childhood professionals participate in the development of these educational plans and then work to implement them in their programs. These important documents are reviewed regularly with families. They require all involved to work cooperatively to meet the needs of children with special needs.

Because of the federal legislation mentioned earlier, an important system is now in place that can help young children develop positive attitudes about people with special needs. Early childhood professionals need to take advantage of these naturally occurring interactions to help children grow in their understanding and acceptance of individuals with special needs. By modeling appropriate interactions and encouraging children to do the same, adults can help ensure the development of healthy attitudes. The *Celebrating Play* feature found in this section describes ways in which you can facilitate these interactions by providing quality play experiences for children with special needs.

English Language Learners

Another form of diversity you will find in early childhood settings is the growing number of children and families whose first language in the home is something other than English. The immigrant population in this country has nearly doubled in the last 10 years, leading to a wide diversity of families who speak languages other than English (Mather, 2009). This will impact you in many different ways. It will change how you plan for, and interact with, both children and families in your program. In some instances, you will have aides and other professionals to help you plan ways to work with English language learners. In other situations, you will need to do the best you can to make adjustments to the teaching and learning options you provide. Having a positive attitude toward children and families who are English language learners is essential.

Jesus and Deangelo are brothers who are new to your Head Start program. Both arrived with their family from Mexico just a month ago. While the boys are quiet and respectful, neither knows much English and they are struggling to adjust. The Head Start adults know some Spanish and are trying to use it where they can to help Jesus and Deangelo feel comfortable in the program. In addition, the bilingual aide has been working with both boys to assist them in adjusting to speaking English. Attempts are also being made to contact and work with the boys' family members. Since both parents are working and speak no English, it has been a challenge for the home visitor to talk with them about the Head Start program.

Take some time now to observe an English language learner in an early childhood setting. The *Observing Development* feature in this section will provide guidelines for making this observation.

Religious Diversity

You may be surprised to learn that the United States is the most religiously diverse country in the world (Eck, 2001). While Christianity is the predominant religion, Judaism, Islam, Buddhism, Hinduism, and other religious beliefs continue to grow in number. Because religion has such a strong impact on beliefs and actions, those in the religious minority are often discriminated against by those in the majority (Derman-Sparks & Edwards, 2010).

As an early childhood professional, you will need to work hard to make every child in your program feel accepted, even when their religious beliefs differ from yours. In its broadest sense, your attitudes are helping children develop their spirituality. Baumgartner and Buchanan (2010) suggest three components of spirituality that are important to include in early childhood settings: (1) *belonging*—all children should feel that they are an integral part of the program experience. When they do, this enhances their feelings of being a part of something larger than themselves. (2) *respect for self and others*—caregivers and teachers who encourage children to respect themselves and others are addressing another important aspect of spirituality. (3) *awareness and appreciation of the unknown*—by helping children be more aware of and appreciate the unknown, you are helping them develop a sense of inquiry, which is at the heart of spirituality. Mardell and Abo-Zena (2010) provide specific examples of how you can explore spirituality in early childhood settings.

Observing Development...
AN ENGLISH LANGUAGE LEARNER

Choose to spend time with either pre-school or primary children and observe an English language learner. Record what you see and hear, putting any interpretations in parentheses. Use the sample observation below as a guide for your own observation:

Cornwall Elementary, Second Grade, 1–1:30 p.m., December 1

1:00 M. works by herself on the mathematics homework. Spends part of the first few minutes staring off into the distance (seems bored or uninterested).

1:05 M. raises hand for assistance from the teacher, who comes to her desk. "What is this word (subtraction)?" Teacher explains term and gets out the button basket to demonstrate 5–3. M. works independently on the next problem.

1:08 . . .

Reflect and Apply

1. Analyze the English language usage of the child. Was it about what you would expect from a child at this age? If not, what were the areas in which the child might need additional assistance?

2. How would you characterize this child's interactions with others? Was she/he able to communicate effectively or was there hesitancy and lower than expected levels of interaction? Do you think this will influence the child's time in the early childhood setting?

3. In what ways did the English skills of the child influence his or her ability to learn? Are there additional strategies that could be used to enhance the child's learning opportunities?

Encouraging an Acceptance of Diversity

It should be clear that early childhood professionals must actively help children develop appropriate attitudes about diversity. The negative opinions children encounter through many hours of media use and interactions with prejudiced adults require careful and frequent effort to overcome. This process should begin with the youngest children and continue throughout the early childhood years. Research indicates that many attitudes are firmly entrenched by 9 years of age and may be difficult to change after that time (Aboud, 1988).

Begin with Self-Analysis

An excellent place to begin this active process of influencing children's attitudes about diversity is with self-analysis. Because you will be one of the most influential adults in the lives of the children you serve, an understanding of your personal attitudes and behaviors is important (Howard, 2006). Although most of us would like to think that we are not prejudiced against those different from ourselves, careful reflection often uncovers many areas that could be improved. One method for developing more accurate self-awareness is through individual reflection and journal writing. The support and assistance of a small group is another strategy that is highly effective. A sampling of activities that could be useful in this process of self-analysis follows (Derman-Sparks, 1989; Derman-Sparks & Edwards, 2010; Derman-Sparks & Phillips, 1997):

- Think about how you would describe or define your racial/ethnic identity. Write about or discuss with others what you find important/not important about this aspect of yourself. Describe how you feel about your racial/ethnic identity.

- Repeat the preceding activity three more times, focusing on your identities in the areas of gender, religion, and ability/disability.

- Either in writing or with a small group, think about and share your views on race, ethnicity, gender, religion, and ableness compared with those of your family.

- Write down lists of acceptable and unacceptable behaviors for boys and girls, and men and women. Discuss these lists with others.

Again, these self-awareness activities are most effective when used with a group of supportive adults who can help one another discuss and deal with the issues uncovered in this analysis. Often, the feelings encountered are painful and difficult to deal with. Help from others may be needed to work successfully through these concerns. Refer to Derman-Sparks (1989), Derman-Sparks and Phillips (1997), and Derman-Sparks and Edwards (2010) for other ideas to assist you in these self-awareness activities.

Talk about Differences

Good early childhood educators have always been effective in recognizing and building on children's natural interests. As captivating topics are identified by children, the creative adult takes the opportunity to discuss them in detail. Through spontaneous dialogue and additional planned activities, children build important understandings of these issues.

As mentioned earlier, young children recognize and want to know more about the differences that exist between people. Whether during a trip through the grocery store, a church activity, community events, or an experience in your early childhood program, children are aware of racial, gender, religious, and ableness issues to which they are exposed. Again, the insightful early childhood professional recognizes these experiences as opportunities for natural and effective discussion times regarding diversity. For example, a young child in your group might remark: "Why does Sarah have two moms?" In addition to providing a calm and factual response to the child, you should take the opportunity this question presents to build deeper understandings of this family structure by providing books like *Anna Day and the O-Ring* (Wickens, 1994) and other materials (such as pictures of diverse families for program walls) that encourage discussions and deeper understandings of these differences.

Talk about Similarities

In all likelihood, young children will recognize and talk about the differences they notice in others. The similarities between diverse peoples, however, may be less obvious to them. You should make an effort to point out to children the similarities that exist among all people. Individually and with groups of children, early childhood professionals should discuss physical similarities, common interests, daily activities that are similar (like playing and school), similarities in games, and toys that are similar across cultures. Following are two tools that may be helpful in dealing with these issues:

- **Books.** Many good books exist to help children explore both the similarities and differences between diverse groups of people (Marshall, 1998; Quintero, 2005). While most were written to highlight the differences, the alert adult can also build in a discussion of similarities.
- **Persona dolls.** Another equally effective technique is the persona doll (Derman-Sparks & Edwards, 2010). Using dolls that are diverse in appearance for storytelling activities allows you to build pretend personalities and lives that are both similar to and different from those of the children in your program.

Expose Children to Diversity

Engaging children in discussions about diversity is too important to be left to chance. Early childhood professionals must plan for a variety of experiences with diversity that are a natural part of the daily activities. Many toys, materials, pictures, books, and experiences can be woven into the curriculum to challenge children to question, compare, and contrast people and experiences that are different from their own. An awareness of the need to plan for these options makes it much more likely that children will develop healthy understandings of diversity.

 Inappropriate Responses to Diversity

Before discussing positive ways of addressing diversity in early childhood settings, it is important to identify two ineffective strategies that are commonly seen. Ignoring diversity and the tourist approach are strategies currently being used by some adults working with young children. Each of these strategies leads to an avoidance of meaningful discussions of human differences in early childhood settings.

Ignore Diversity

One clearly inappropriate response to diversity is to deny that it exists. A typical comment from a adult ignoring diversity would be: "This diversity education business doesn't make sense for my program. My class is all white, and anyway, kids do not notice differences at this age." Hopefully, it is clear to you that ignoring diversity is a misguided approach. Children do recognize and talk about the differences they see. And while limited numbers of early childhood settings today are indeed all white, it is much more likely that you will encounter considerable diversity in your future program. Furthermore, even if it is not diverse, your role is to prepare children for lives in the world, where they will be faced with increasingly greater levels of diversity (Derman-Sparks & Ramsey, 2006). Caregivers and teachers need to weave diversity topics into the curriculum during the early years.

The Tourist Approach

Another ineffective strategy employed in some early childhood programs is to engage in what has been called a *tourist-multicultural curriculum* (Derman-Sparks, 1994). Those who use this approach are typically well-meaning adults who engage in a simplistic, often stereotypic look at different cultures. They take quick little "curriculum visits" to other parts of the world before returning to the more important European-American focus for the majority of the time. Boutte and McCormick (1992) describe the tourist approach as follows: "cooking ethnic foods, examining Native American artifacts at Thanksgiving or discussing African American achievements during Black History month. Certainly, these lessons have merit; however, since they are often isolated and discontinuous, they are actually 'pseudomulticultural' activities" (p. 140).

Although the tourist approach introduces children to aspects of different cultures, it does so in ways that lead children to believe that the European-American perspective is the most important and that other cultures are only tangentially significant. Often, these brief visits lead to stereotypic perceptions of other cultures and therefore sabotage the true goals of studying diversity (Irvine, 2003).

The tourist approach to multicultural education tends to disconnect content learned from the main curriculum. The unintended outcome is to trivialize the contributions of different cultural groups. The unconscious thinking of children could be described as follows: "How can this content we are studying be important? It is only a small add-on to the main topics we are discussing. Studying differences cannot be that important if that is all we are going to do to address it." Clearly, this is not the message we want children to receive through the study of multicultural issues.

Obviously, the tourist approach can also be used by well-meaning adults to address gender, sexual orientation, religious, and ableness issues. When any of these topics is treated as tangential to the main curriculum, children get the message that they are less important concerns. If diversity in general is to be a meaningful component of early childhood programs, this quick-fix strategy must be avoided.

Integrating Diversity throughout the Curriculum

To make sure that diversity topics are viewed by children and families as important elements of the curriculum, a more complex and thoughtful strategy than the tourist approach must be implemented. Issues relating to cultural differences, gender, sexual orientation, religion, and ableness must be made an integral part of the daily activities in the early childhood program (Derman-Sparks, 1999). Rather than brief diversions into interesting but less important areas, the curriculum must be infused with materials, activities, and people that provide regular opportunities for young children to come in contact with meaningful diversity issues (Daniel & Koralek, 2005). There are a number of excellent Internet resources that you can use to integrate diversity throughout the curriculum. The *Technology Explorations and Activities* feature in this section describes one such option.

Art can provide opportunities to discuss meaningful diversity issues.

The Antibias Curriculum

Louise Derman-Sparks (1989) suggests an appropriate title for what is taught in a program that integrates diversity throughout the curriculum: the **antibias curriculum**. She states that, although specific techniques are associated with this approach, each early childhood professional must take the general principles presented and create an appropriate program for his or her specific group of children and their families. The philosophy undergirding the antibias curriculum is value-based: "Differences are good; oppressive ideas and behaviors are not." The antibias curriculum "sets up a creative tension between respecting differences and not accepting unfair beliefs and acts" (Derman-Sparks, 1989, p. x). To implement this approach requires careful planning, self-assessment, and communication with others. It takes dedication and commitment but provides many rewards for children and adults alike.

Derman-Sparks and Edwards (2010) identify four goals for antibias education:

1. Each child will demonstrate self-awareness, confidence, family pride, and positive social identities.

2. Each child will express comfort and joy with human diversity; accurate language for human differences; and deep, caring human connections.

3. Each child will increasingly recognize unfairness, have language to describe unfairness, and understand that unfairness hurts.

4. Each child will demonstrate empowerment and the skills to act, with others or alone, against prejudice and/or discriminatory actions (pp. 4–5).

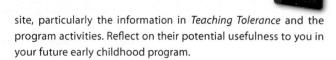

Technology Explorations and Activities . . .
SOUTHERN POVERTY LAW CENTER

Many excellent Internet resources are available to assist you in thinking about and preparing for diversity in your future early childhood program. One such option is the Southern Poverty Law Center (SPLC). It was founded in 1971 as a small, nonprofit, law civil rights organization dedicated to making the promises of the civil rights movement a reality for all (Southern Poverty Law Center, 2010). It has grown into an influential organization that has won numerous landmark legal decisions that promote civil rights for all. The SPLC publishes a magazine both in print and online titled *Teaching Tolerance* that includes activities for adults working with children. Do an Internet search for the SPLC and read some of the information on the site, particularly the information in *Teaching Tolerance* and the program activities. Reflect on their potential usefulness to you in your future early childhood program.

Research, Reflect, and Respond

1. After reading the information available on the Internet site, what are your thoughts on the SPLC? Why do you feel this way?

2. Review several articles in different issues of *Teaching Tolerance*. How could you use the information in your future early childhood program?

3. Read some of the activities listed on the website and critique their usefulness to you. Why did you like them or find the activities less useful?

Early childhood professionals interested in implementing an antibias curriculum should take a five-step approach (Derman-Sparks, 1989; Derman-Sparks & Phillips, 1997) to ensure success:

Step 1. Make a personal commitment. To make this curriculum a reality, you must spend considerable time and energy. Diversity issues must be a high priority.

Step 2. Organize a support group. The perspectives and feedback from peers are essential for rethinking the teaching of diversity.

Step 3. Do consciousness-raising (self-analysis) activities. Self-analysis was described earlier in the chapter. Become aware of your own feelings toward cultural, racial, sexual, and ableness differences.

Step 4. Make a plan for implementing the curriculum. Through an evaluation of the physical environment, a critique of current activities, and observations of children, make plans for implementing antibias activities.

Step 5. Move slowly and carefully. Integrating diversity into the curriculum is hard work and requires careful planning. Moving more slowly helps ensure success.

Using Toys That Promote Diversity

One important way to encourage an acceptance of diversity in early childhood settings is by providing toys and equipment that portray similarities and differences between people. Swiniarski (1991) suggests that toys are an excellent way to introduce young children to global education. As children play with these materials and notice their similarities and differences across cultures, multicultural learning takes place naturally:

Four-year-old Natalie is playing with a plastic replica of a giraffe in the block area. This is her first experience with the toy giraffe, so as the adult stops to observe block play, Natalie asks about this animal. Where does it live? What does it eat? How big is it? Her curiosity leads to finding some picture books and other materials that describe the habitat of giraffes. Natalie is gaining understanding of a place with people and animals that are different from herself and her surroundings.

A variety of toys are common worldwide (Swiniarski, 1991). They include

- Dolls
- Toy animals
- Musical instruments
- Puzzles
- Construction toys
- Movement toys (cars, trucks, planes)
- Puppets

The cultural uniqueness of these toys is generally in their presentation or decoration. By including toys from around the world as play materials in early childhood settings, children have many important opportunities to recognize and discuss

Puppets with disabilities help children recognize and discuss similarities and differences among people.

similarities and differences. Cultural discussions and understandings become a natural part of the day.

In addition to culture-specific toys, options are available for providing children with playthings that allow them to explore aspects of ableness. Dolls with disabilities, for example, are available through some toy vendors. Wheelchairs (both toy and real) are another possibility for use in early childhood settings. Other options are sure to present themselves if you are actively looking for them.

Toys and materials can also be purchased that encourage discussion and thinking regarding gender issues. One of the best examples of this is the variety of puzzles that are available depicting women in nontraditional work roles. Female doctors, police officers, and airline pilots are representative of this option. Some flannel board sets and dolls provide additional opportunities for discussing gender differences and roles.

Diversity through Games

Like the toys just described, many games from around the world can be used to enhance young children's understanding of different cultures. As with toys, games played by children around the world have more similarities than differences (Kirchner, 2000). Whether engaged in running and tag activities, ball games, or manipulative and guessing games, children play in very similar ways throughout the world. For example, the game Kick the Can, which has its origins in Canada, is played with slight variations in India (where it is called *Esha Desai*), Holland (*Burkuit*), Sweden (*Paven Bannlyser*), and Japan (*Kankai*) (Kirchner, 2000).

These games, in addition to being fun, provide opportunities for children to play out aspects of different cultures. For example, in the game Antelope in the Net (appropriate for 7- to 10-year-olds), which originated in the Congo, one child is chosen to be the antelope, and the rest form a circle (the net) around the antelope. Children forming the net hold hands and chant, "Kasha Mu Bukondi! Kasha Mu Bukondi!" ("Antelope in the net"). The antelope tries to break out of the net by crawling under, climbing over, or running through the tightly held hands. If the antelope is caught, the child who traps him or her becomes the new antelope (Hatcher, Pape, & Nicosia, 1988). In playing this type of game, children are naturally exposed to aspects of another culture and can begin to appreciate both the similarities and differences to their own.

Quality Children's Literature

Books for young children can be wonderful options for addressing diversity issues in early childhood settings. A good book can captivate the interests of children while introducing people and events that are new to them. Often, books can lead to in-depth discussions and activities that help children understand the complexities of diversity topics (Green & Oldendorf, 2005; Marshall, 1998; National Association for the Education of Young Children, 1993).

For example, to introduce the topic of diverse abilities, the book *Someone Special, Just Like You* (Brown, 1991) could be read and then discussed by young children. This book is a collection of photographs depicting children with special needs engaged in a variety of activities. The situations children have encountered will naturally lead to further discussions and activities, thus increasing awareness and understanding of this area of diversity.

When selecting books on diversity, consider the following:

- Try to find books that represent children in your class.
- Look for books that introduce new information and ideas to children.
- Make sure to balance your selections to ensure that children are introduced to a variety of topics (Yokota, 1993).

The Visual–Aesthetic Environment

Another excellent way to increase opportunities to discuss diversity is with the pictures and posters you use to decorate the room. These visual accessories should include people from different cultures, and individuals with special needs engaging in real-world, everyday activities. Reproductions of artwork from around the world can also be used to decorate the walls. All of these visual options can help children see that diversity is a natural part of their lives and can open up new opportunities for discussing these important topics. The *Developmentally Appropriate Practice* feature found in this section gives you some suggestions about where to find diverse pictures and posters to use in your early childhood program.

Displays of artifacts from different cultures may also be used to stimulate discussions about similarities and differences among people around the world. For example, a traditional African doll purchased by a family member during a recent trip there could be introduced at group time and used to discuss dolls in different cultures. While these items may be too fragile or special to be put in a play center,

Developmentally Appropriate Practice . . .
DIVERSITY THROUGH PICTURES

Early childhood professionals collect many different things that will be useful to them in their programs. One such collection is often a picture file. When put on the walls in centers or used as discussion starters for small- or large-group activities, pictures can help young children develop important insights about diversity. If you create a picture file, be sure to also include nonstereotypic people of color, diverse families, pictures of individuals with special needs, religious diversity, and examples of men and women in nontraditional roles. Some potential sources of good photos for a diverse picture file include the following:

- Magazines such as *National Geographic*, *Ms.*, or *Ebony* can provide many good pictures when carefully selected.

- Internet photos of different ethnic groups, religious affiliations, diverse families, and people with special needs can be downloaded and printed with a good color printer.

- Calendars made by organizations dealing with diversity may have excellent pictures that can be collected.

- Photographs of children and families in your early childhood program or community and photos from your travels may also be useful.

- Posters from organizations focusing on children and families (such as the National Association for the Education of Young Children or the Council for Exceptional Children) are useful.

using artifacts for group time experiences and then placing them on display can be a productive use of these materials.

Playing a variety of musical styles during the day is yet another way to introduce young children to cultural similarities and differences. Discussing these musical pieces at group time may stimulate further understandings of people around the world.

Meaningful Diversity Experiences

Taking advantage of the cultural, gender, religious, family, and ableness differences that exist within your early childhood setting and community is an effective way to build meaningful experiences into the curriculum. By bringing diverse people into the program and having children interact with them, awareness is heightened, and discussions of similarities and differences increase. These natural interactions can occur while adults read children a book, assist with their math problems, or build in the block corner. They can be important and meaningful steps in understanding diversity.

Informal interactions can be combined with other more focused activities to add meaningful diversity experiences to the curriculum. Having a family member whose first language is something other than English come in to tutor children in her native language is one example of this more organized approach. Another option could be to have a community member help children prepare a favorite meal that exemplifies his cultural heritage. When caregivers and teachers involve people in their programs or communities who can add these experiences to the curriculum, everyone benefits. The *Celebrating Diversity* feature found in this section discusses another important diversity experience that you can build upon: holidays. As the families you serve become increasingly diverse, you will

Celebrating Diversity ...
HOLIDAYS

The holidays we celebrate have their roots in family and culture. Some, such as Christmas and Hanukkah, are directly linked to religious beliefs. Others, like Halloween and Groundhog Day, have become traditional celebrations over time. In either case, the appropriateness of celebrating these holidays needs to be carefully determined. Kostelnik, Soderman, and Whiren (2011) identify several potential problems with these celebrations. Because children often have many opportunities to celebrate these events outside the program setting, blocks of children's lives tend to be dominated by holidays, leaving less time for other important learning options. In addition, the authors emphasize that caregivers and teachers who choose to celebrate holidays in early childhood settings run the risk of adding to cultural or religious stereotypes. The decision about whether or not to celebrate specific holidays is best made collaboratively among early childhood professionals, families, and children (National Association for the Education of Young Children, 2007).

The traditions surrounding holidays that are valued by different people can provide important opportunities for children to learn about diversity. When holidays are chosen carefully, and activities are planned that respect the cultures and religious perspectives represented by each of the children in your group, they can be a positive element of the curriculum. The National Association for the Education of Young Children (2007) provides the following suggestions for making decisions about holidays:

- Families and early childhood professionals need to ask why children should learn about this holiday and whether it is developmentally appropriate.
- Celebrations should be connected to specific children and families within the group.
- Children should be encouraged to share their feelings and information about the celebrations they have.
- Every group (but not every holiday) represented within the early childhood setting should be honored through celebration of a holiday.
- Activities should demonstrate respect for the customs of different cultures.
- Families and early childhood professionals should work together in planning these special events.

1. Do you think that holidays that come from different cultures and religious groups constitute meaningful diversity experiences as described in this chapter? Why or why not?

2. How do you feel about celebrating holidays that conflict with your religious/cultural heritage? Discuss these feelings with others.

need to consider and build upon the different religious and cultural traditions represented in your program.

English Language Learners and the Curriculum

As large numbers of immigrant families continue to enter the United States, the number of children in early childhood programs whose first language is something other than English is growing rapidly. Children living in immigrant families total 21% of U.S. children. In many states, however, these percentages are much higher (Mather, 2009). For example, the percentage of immigrant families is higher in California, Texas, and New York because these locations are the starting off points for many immigrant families. Many of these children and their families have limited English proficiency. In 18 states, the number of children with limited English proficiency grew by 200% between 1992 and 2002 (Zehr, 2005).

Because English language learning children are working hard to acquire a second language, caregivers and teachers will need to adjust their materials, activities, and teaching strategies to assist them in these efforts. The National Association for the Education of Young Children (1995), in their position statement on responding to linguistic and cultural diversity, suggest the following strategies for creating a positive learning environment for English language learners:

- **Acknowledge and support home language and culture.** Caregivers and teachers need to realize that home language and culture are very important to healthy child development. Child attitudes about self are enhanced when these aspects of home life are valued. In addition, learning English as a second language improves when home language and culture continue to be an important part of the child's life (Nieto, 2004).

- **Provide multiple ways for children to demonstrate success.** Early childhood professionals can build on the strengths of each child by allowing them to present their capabilities through such avenues as art, music, and dramatization. As young children experience success in these areas, their confidence and overall development will flourish.

- **Understand that second language learning can be difficult.** Because it is a complex process, linguistic competence takes time. Developing the English language skills needed for academic learning may take children as long as 5 to 8 years (Lake & Pappamihiel, 2003).

- **Involve families.** As families get involved, they have opportunities to assist with their child's learning and development as well as share their language and culture with others in the class. In addition, building relationships with families who speak languages other than English at home will give you the opportunity to emphasize the importance to the child of maintaining the home language and culture.

Integrating Curriculum for Individuals with Special Needs

Despite attempts over the last 30 years to include children with special needs in pre-K through grade 12 programs, individuals with special needs are often misunderstood and are only reluctantly accepted in educational settings by adults and children alike. Much has yet to be done to more adequately integrate individuals with special needs into American society. Early childhood professionals must take important first steps in their programs to help this process along.

Develop inclusive environments. While many of the techniques, methods, and materials used with children who do not have special needs are also effective for children with special needs, other strategies are often needed. The following four guidelines (Wolery & Wilbers, 1994) can help early childhood professionals more effectively design the physical space for children with special needs:

1. **When needed, help children learn to play with toys and materials.** Some young children with special needs may benefit from initial adult assistance in playing with early childhood materials. With sensitive guidance, they can greatly benefit from play experiences.

2. **Select toys and materials that appeal to children.** Through careful observation, you can learn what play materials children with special needs enjoy. These should be provided on a regular basis to encourage creative play experiences.

3. **Provide play materials that engage children in playing, interacting, and learning.** When possible, toys and materials for children with special needs should be selected to promote learning identified in their IFSP for children under age 3, or IEP for older children.

4. **Adapt toys and materials where needed.** Some toys and materials cannot be manipulated because of physical limitations. Adaptations such as battery-powered toys that can be operated with switches, and wheelchair-accessible sand play areas outdoors help ensure that all children benefit from quality play experiences.

In addition to implementing these strategies as you work with children with special needs, it is also important to be aware of and use **assistive technology** to support their learning and development. *Assistive technology* is a term used to describe devices and services that improve the functional capabilities of children with disabilities. The Individuals with Disabilities Education Act requires that children have access to assistive technology as needed. An example of assistive technology for young children with cerebral palsy would be voice recognition software that allows the child to speak to the computer and have the speech converted to written text. Not all assistive technology is of the "high tech" variety. A simpler example of assistive technology is the foam pencil grip that can be slipped over the exterior of a pencil allowing young children to have an appropriately positioned grasp as they engage in writing tasks.

Strengthen social interactions. Creating a physical space that provides quality play experiences for all children is an important step in an inclusive program. Equally valuable are the social interactions that are encouraged. Adults must first be aware of the ways in which they relate to children with special needs. Many techniques, such as observing, supporting, facilitating, and expanding children's play and interactions with others, are useful with all children. Other more specialized techniques may be needed with some children. One useful adult interaction is a **prompt**, which can be defined as help given to assist a child in engaging in specific skills (Heward, 2009). Prompts can be verbal, gestural, modeled, or used for physical assistance.

Interaction between children with special needs and their typically developing peers is another dimension that you must work to enhance. There are two important reasons to encourage these exchanges. First, social interactions help the groups understand one another better and establish effective relationships that can grow with time. Second, when children with special

Including children with special needs in early childhood settings benefits all.

needs interact with others, they have peers who model appropriate and adaptive behaviors.

These interactions between children with special needs and other children often do not occur spontaneously. You will need to support and encourage these exchanges. One effective strategy is to encourage children to engage in social interactions in small-group, rather than large-group, settings. Whenever possible, children with special needs should be placed in these small groups with peers who are especially competent in the growth areas identified in their IEP or IFSP.

Collaborate with other professionals. A variety of professionals are frequently involved in providing services for children with special needs. The following disciplines are regular collaborators in caring for young children with special needs:

- Special education
- Psychology
- Speech/language pathology
- Occupational therapy
- Social work
- Nutrition
- Nursing
- Audiology
- Medicine

The collaboration of professionals in these disciplines to provide support for young children with special needs has been mandated by legislation for many years. The IEP and IFSP both require this collaboration. Few are prepared, however, for the complexities of the interactions required. To succeed, all the professionals involved need to begin these collaborative efforts with an understanding of who should participate and what each professional's role should be, a willingness to communicate often and well, and a desire to adjust roles and responsibilities as needed in the best interests of the child.

 Joley is 4 years old and uses a wheelchair. Her mother is a single parent, so Joley spends almost 9 hours each day in the Sunshine Child Care Center. In addition to the adults she works with in the program, Joley spends time with a physical therapist twice a week. A psychologist works with her on anger control issues biweekly, and a school district special educator comes to the home once a month to assist her with oral language skills. Although Joley is benefiting from the assistance of a number of professionals, the coordination of these people and services is a challenge.

Gender and the Curriculum

What are the components of gender equity that should concern us in early childhood settings? Do these include how we communicate with both sexes? Should we focus on equitable opportunities for boys and girls to participate in activities? What about adult perceptions of gender roles and how they influence interactions with children? Each of these questions defines an important element of gender equity that must be addressed by concerned educators when planning the curriculum.

Language. The words we use to communicate with children send powerful messages that influence many aspects of development, including attitudes about gender. Take, for example, the seemingly innocuous phrase: "Hey, you guys!" If addressed to a group of boys, there is obviously no problem. But what about using that same phrase to communicate with a mixed-sex group or a gathering of girls? Is there a hidden message here that may be inappropriate? A small thing perhaps, but it is often these finer nuances that children focus on as they make assessments about the relative value of being a boy or girl.

Language has other subtle influences on children. Consistently using words that suggest dependence, weakness, or submission to describe the behavior of girls, and other descriptors that imply strength, independence, and dominance in relationship to male behaviors can lead to inappropriate gender definitions by young children. Although most of us try to avoid these categorical descriptions of boys and girls, some of the words we use to talk to young children may be sending a different message. Careful self-assessment is needed to make sure we use appropriate language as we interact with both sexes throughout the day.

Accessibility to materials and activities. Research on the play behaviors of children suggests that certain activities are dominated by boys and others by girls. Boys tend to take on more active/aggressive roles with cars and trucks, construction toys, and blocks. Girls, however, often are involved in dress-up activities, artwork, and housekeeping activities (Van Alstyne, 1932). While these gender differences are hardly surprising to most of us, it is important to plan a variety of activities that are attractive to both boys and girls. The *Developmentally Appropriate Practice* feature in this section gives ideas for making the dramatic play area more appealing to boys.

Although many of the more traditional play interests of boys and girls can lead to productive learning, children should be encouraged to move out of their comfort zones to engage in other activities. For example, it is important for boys to be involved in doll play and housekeeping activities. Eventually, most will become fathers and need to learn appropriate nurturing behaviors. Similarly, girls need experiences with blocks so that they can begin developing a foundational understanding for learning mathematics and science (Chaille & Britain, 2003).

Without conscious adult intervention, however, most children will continue doing what they find comfortable. Early childhood professionals can help break children out of their comfort zones in three major ways:

1. **Encourage children to try new activities.** Make suggestions, point out interesting options, and redirect children to play activities not normally chosen.
2. **Provide novel materials that are more likely to attract children to areas not usually chosen.** For example, marble painting or gluing and painting wood sculptures are two activities that might encourage boys to play in the art center.

Developmentally Appropriate Practice...
GENDER-NEUTRAL DRAMATIC PLAY ACTIVITIES

One important way in which early childhood professionals can encourage both boys and girls to engage in dramatic play is to plan activities that are of interest to both sexes. Selecting these more gender-neutral materials and themes to complement traditional dramatic play activities like dress-up and doll play help make this center more attractive to all children. Following are a few examples of gender-neutral themes and basic materials for creating these centers. After reading the examples presented, see if you can identify some additional options that could be included in early childhood settings.

- **Airplane.** Child-sized chairs arranged in rows to simulate airplane seating, headphones from the listening center for pilot headsets, small suitcases, simulated plane tickets, and a large photograph or poster of the cockpit of an airplane provide the basic ingredients for this theme.

- **Camping.** A small tent, sleeping bags, flashlights, lantern, camp stools, and a pretend campfire can be used to create a camping theme.

- **Post office.** Junk mail, mailboxes, postal carriers' bags, envelopes, pretend stamps, stamp pad, paper, writing utensils, and some pictures of postal carriers and post offices will get children started on this exciting play theme.

- **Boating/fishing.** A small inflatable rubber raft, sticks with string for fishing poles, magnets for the string ends, paper "fish" with paperclips attached, blue colored paper cut to represent the water, and pictures of boats and people fishing will attract many children for this dramatic play theme.

3. **Model nontraditional play as an adult.** Female caregivers and teachers can spend time building with blocks, while males can engage in housekeeping roles.

Attitudes. Adult attitudes about gender are a complex mix of formal and informal learning experiences. Family values, influential adult role models, experiences throughout the growing-up years, and the media all have a significant impact on the development of gender identity. Unless adults are particularly introspective, it is often hard to identify their true attitudes. Yet, it is important to do so for the sake of young children. Our feelings about gender issues will strongly influence those under our care. Thus, a key starting point is to raise our own consciousness about attitudes toward gender. Although some may be obvious, others are much more subtle. As emphasized earlier, it is helpful to work with a support group to discuss these issues. For example, you might read the books *What Is a Boy?* and *What Is a Girl?* (Waxman, 1976a, 1976b) and then discuss your reactions with others. These books contain photos that show the anatomic differences between boys and girls and discuss problems associated with gender stereotyping. Would you feel comfortable reading these books to young children? Why or why not? As this kind of reflection takes place, you can begin to understand your own attitudes toward gender issues at a deeper level and how they may affect the curriculum you develop for the early childhood setting.

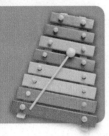

summary

Attitudes toward Diversity

Effectively addressing diversity in the early childhood setting begins with an under-standing of attitudes about race/culture, gender, sexual orientation, people with special needs, English language learners, and religious diversity.

Encouraging an Acceptance of Diversity

Adults in early childhood settings should understand their own attitudes toward diversity, spend time discussing with children the similarities and differences between people, and provide opportunities for children to interact with diverse people.

Inappropriate Responses to Diversity

Two inappropriate responses to diversity are to ignore it or to try to teach about diversity using what has been called the tourist approach.

Integrating Diversity throughout the Curriculum

Caregivers and teachers can integrate diversity throughout the curriculum by including toys and games that promote diversity, by presenting diverse children's literature, including diversity in the visual-aesthetic environment, and by providing meaningful diversity experiences. Early childhood professionals need to plan carefully for English language learners, individuals with special needs, and issues of gender equity as they prepare an antibias curriculum.

for reflection and discussion

1. Describe how your own religious beliefs may influence the ways in which you work with children and families.
2. List strategies you will consider using to bring children in contact with a diverse range of people. Discuss your ideas with others.
3. Describe the tourist approach to diversity and the problems with this strategy.
4. What will you do to make sure that both boys and girls have equal opportunities to learn and grow in your early childhood setting? Talk your ideas over with others.

MyEducationLab

Go to Topics 10: Cultural & Linguistic Diversity and 11: Special Needs/ Inclusion in the MyEducationLab (www.myeducationlab.com) for *Teaching Young Children*, where you can:

- Find learning outcomes for Cultural & Linguistic Diversity and Special Needs/Inclusion along with the national standards that connect to these outcomes.
- Complete Assignments and Activities that can help you more deeply understand the chapter content.
- Apply and practice your understanding of the core teaching skills identified in the chapter with the Building Teaching Skills and Dispositions learning units.
- Examine challenging situations and cases presented in the IRIS Center Resources.
- Access video clips of CCSSO National Teachers of the Year award winners responding to the question, "Why Do I Teach?" in the Teacher Talk section.
- Listen to experts from the field in Professional Perspectives.
- Check your comprehension on the content covered in the chapter with the Study Plan. Here you will be able to take a chapter quiz, receive feedback on your answers, and then access Review, Practice, and Enrichment activities to enhance your understanding of chapter content.

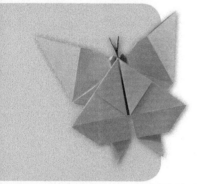

9

Planning
The Physical
Environment: Indoors

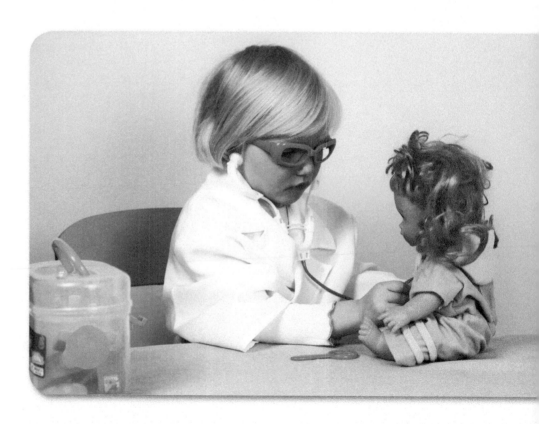

IN THIS CHAPTER YOU WILL

- Address basic issues related to planning an indoor environment for young children.
- Learn about the typical centers found in early childhood settings.
- Develop an understanding of indoor environments for infants and toddlers.
- Read about preschool settings and how they are organized.
- Study the physical organization needed for developmentally appropriate primary classrooms.

It's planning time once again, and you are thinking through the past week with your 4-year-old children in preparation for next week's activities. As usual, the children have engaged in many creative play scenarios in the different centers. The block area has been home to the toy dinosaur collection, and children have been building fences and enclosures to hold their favorite creatures. After discussing block play with the assistants, you decide to leave the dinosaurs out for another week. Interest is strong, and the toys are stimulating imaginative play.

It is early in the school year, so the dramatic play center still contains fairly basic materials, including shirts, hats, dresses, and shoes for dressing up. A mirror, stuffed chair, and chest of drawers are the major pieces of furniture in the center. For next week, you decide to add some jewelry, hair clips, and neckties for accessories.

The library center contained several books on dinosaurs during the past week. You have read several of them at group time and then made sure children could browse through them on their own. You will add two new books and a flannel board story for the coming week.

In the manipulative center, three puzzles will replace others that the children have not used recently. You will put away the Legos for a while and make Tinker Toys available. One of your assistants has agreed to make a new batch of play dough for this center as well.

The planning in the preceding scenario exemplifies the efforts of early childhood professionals to prepare their indoor environments. Each week, you will need to carefully and thoughtfully prepare the setting for developmentally appropriate play and learning. After observing young children at work and play, and consulting with other early care professionals, you should enliven the indoor environment by removing items not being used and adding new materials for creative play. Because child-initiated and child-directed activities are so important to young children, they need indoor environments that are constantly new and inviting.

 Planning Guidelines

Quality environments for young children do not just happen. They require careful planning and considerable work. To understand the complexities of creating quality environments, begin with an understanding of the fundamental of room organization. After addressing basic considerations, you will read about selecting equipment and materials, changing the physical environment, health and safety issues, and creating environmentally friendly spaces for young children.

Basic Considerations

There are a number of things to keep in mind as you prepare quality indoor spaces for young children. The space available for each child, the availability of basic materials and equipment, program goals, clues from the environment about how the space is to be used, incompatible centers, spaces for varying group sizes, personal spaces, and the importance of assessing the physical space—all need to be considered as you begin preparations for the physical space.

Physical space available. One of the most basic factors in room organization is the size and physical characteristics of the space available to you. The *NAEYC Early Childhood Program Standards and Accreditation Criteria* (National Association for the Education of Young Children, 2005) requires programs seeking accreditation to provide a minimum of 35 square feet of usable indoor space for each child in a preschool or primary classroom. In addition to the floor space requirements, such things as the window placement, heating and cooling vents, doors, and floor coverings (carpeting and vinyl) also influence planning for children's indoor play spaces. Each of these elements has significant implications for organizing early childhood settings. For example, the placement of doors in the room defines natural corridors for entrance and exit. These spaces must be left open for ease of use and safety. You must consider these fixed areas of the environment, particularly in the initial planning of play spaces.

Available basic equipment. A second basic consideration is the availability of basic equipment such as tables, chairs, room dividers, and storage cabinets. These items will have a significant impact on room design. Additional resources such as unit blocks, table toys, computers, and dramatic play equipment also influence the overall planning of the physical space.

Jamie is getting her kindergarten classroom ready for the coming school year. She has good storage units for the unit blocks, plenty of dividers for sectioning off space for centers, and enough chairs and tables for her expected enrollment. Dramatic play equipment, however, is scarce; she will need to look for a toy microwave oven and a child-sized sink. In addition, as she looks through the manipulative toys available to her, it becomes obvious that she will need to carefully plan the use of puzzles. With only 10 sets, she will need to rotate puzzles in and out regularly to maintain interest. However, Jamie has an abundance of different construction sets like Legos. Her children will have many options available for this type of play throughout the year.

Program goals. Another basic planning element for the indoor environment is the program goals (Mitchell & David, 1992). If, for example, a top program priority is the development of fine and gross motor skills, then equipment, materials, and centers need to promote these activities. In a preschool program emphasizing this goal, much indoor space would be devoted to materials and equipment such as an indoor climber, slide, balance beam, and tumbling mats. However, in a setting where social/emotional development was the program's top priority, more space and materials would be used to meet that goal.

Clues regarding use. It is important that the environment itself gives children clues about how the space should be used (Hyson, 2008). Following are some examples:

- **Seating.** An art center with a table and five chairs effectively limits the number of children who can participate there at any given time.
- **Center charts.** A chart can be posted at the entrance to each center with symbols depicting the number of children allowed in the area at a time. A kindergarten math center chart with three smiley faces tells children the expected capacity for that area.
- **Pictures and posters.** The pictures and posters on the walls in various centers also give children clues about the uses of the space. Pictures of children cooperatively building with blocks, for example, make clear the behaviors you expect in that center.

Incompatible centers. As much as possible, incompatible activities should be physically separated. Some centers promote active, noisy play, while others encourage quieter times. Typically *active/noisy centers* include these:

- Blocks
- Music
- Housekeeping/dramatic play
- Woodworking
- Sand/water play

Quiet centers that should be separated from those previously listed include the following:

- Art
- Books/library
- Computers
- Writing

Whenever possible, centers from these two categories should be separated. Having a noisy center like the block area near the library area creates unnecessary distractions for children. The banging of blocks and the creative discussion that often accompany the construction process may prevent a child who is concentrating on a book from becoming deeply involved in the story. It would be better to put the block area next to the dramatic play center, for example. These activities are more compatible in most early childhood settings.

In addition to separating noisy and quiet centers, some indoor areas are wet/messy while others should be kept dry. The dry centers should be separated from those that require water and other liquids. For example, the art center (wet/messy)—with paints, glue, marking pens, crayons, and other messy activities—needs to be separated from the library corner (dry).

Spaces for different group sizes. Indoor environments should provide spaces that accommodate gatherings of different numbers of children.

- **Large group.** Generally, early childhood professionals set aside one area for whole-class meetings. In early childhood settings, this is usually referred to as *circle time,* which requires an area large enough for children and adults to gather together in a circle formation, with everyone sitting on the floor. Often, this space is used for other activities, such as music and movement, outside of group times.

- **Small groups.** Spaces are also needed for many different small-group activities in early childhood settings. For example, many programs have a snack time in the mid-morning and again in the afternoon. Children usually gather together at tables for these food breaks, in groups of three to five, to enjoy a nutritious snack with an adult. When the early childhood program is set up in centers, adults also create several small-group spaces that accommodate two to six children for various center activities.

- **Solitary activities.** Indoor space also should make solitary activities a possibility for young children (Readdick, 1993). Caregivers and teachers sometimes overlook this necessary element when planning program space. Solitary time allows children the chance to reflect and regroup at different times during the day, before returning to the important tasks of socializing with others. Large pillows, an old bathtub, a reading loft, large cardboard boxes, beanbag chairs, and child-sized stuffed chairs can all be used to create spaces where children can get away from others for a time.

An indoor sandbox provides opportunities for individual and small-group play.

Personal spaces. Both adults and children also need to have areas that they can call their own. These personal spaces need not be large or complex but should help create a home for each person's materials. At the prekindergarten level, a cubby for coats, boots, and completed projects is a common element. At the primary level, desks can provide an area for more personal items. As children mature, the perceived importance of this private area increases. If desks are unavailable or undesirable, you should create other personal spaces for children. You also need a spot for yourself for things like lunches, coats, purses, and umbrellas. Pictures of family members, a favorite coffee mug, and other personal items help create a more inviting work environment for adults. A desk or other work space can also be put to effective use in or near the early childhood setting.

Assessing the physical space. One final consideration in planning the physical space is the need for assessment techniques to evaluate environmental quality. One option is to evaluate the complexity of the play units. Kritchevsky and Prescott (1969) have identified three different complexities in units:

- **Simple unit.** This play material or piece of equipment has only one use, and it is obvious to children. A toy truck or a stacking toy is an example of a simple unit.
- **Complex unit.** This play option has subparts, or different materials, that the child can manipulate. A sand table with digging equipment is a complex unit.
- **Superunit.** A superunit has three or more play materials juxtaposed. A block center that includes two different kinds of blocks and accessories such as toy trucks is a superunit.

Athough all three unit types are valuable in early childhood settings, the complex units and superunits are most attractive to children and hold their interest longest. Kritchevsky and Prescott (1969) suggest that by assigning a value of one to simple units, four to complex units, and eight to superunits, you can determine the total number of play spaces available in an indoor environment. Dividing that total by the number of children gives the number of options available to each child. Having two play options per child is considered highly desirable.

Harms and Clifford (1980) developed a second, more extensive, environmental assessment procedure. This well-respected rating scale was most recently revised in 2005 (Harms, Clifford, & Cryer, 2005). Called the **Early Childhood Environment Rating Scale**, this assessment tool is organized into seven separate subcategories that allow the adult to evaluate spaces for young children from inadequate (1) to excellent (7). The seven categories are:

- **Personal care routines.** All routines that relate to children's health, comfort, and safety.
- **Furnishings and display for children.** Furniture, storage shelves, and display space to facilitate child growth and development.
- **Language-reasoning experiences.** Experiences, materials, and interactions to facilitate basic reasoning discussion among children about such things as cause and effect.
- **Fine and gross motor activities.** The use of small muscles in the hands and the larger muscles in the arms and legs.
- **Creative activities.** Open-ended activities and materials available in centers such as art, block, and dramatic play.
- **Social development.** Positive self-concepts and interaction skills.
- **Adult needs.** The needs of adults for a comfortable and efficient space for teaching.

With training and practice, the Early Childhood Environment Rating Scale can be an effective tool for assessing the indoor space. It can help identify both the strengths and limitations of the physical space. The same basic rating scale has been revised to focus more specifically on other early care settings. One such modification is an environmental rating system for infants and toddlers. Called the **Infant/Toddler Environment Rating Scale (ITERS)**, this instrument is being used effectively to assess the physical spaces of very young children (Harms et al., 2003). Similarly, Harms and Clifford (2007) have published the **Family Day Care Rating Scale (FDCRS)**, and Harms, Jacobs, and White (1995) created the **School-Age Care Environment Rating Scale (SACERS)**.

Observing Development...
ASSESSING THE INDOOR PHYSICAL SPACE

Choose one of the age groups within early childhood (infants/toddlers, preschoolers, or primary-age children) and assess the indoor physical space using the guidelines provided here.

1. Sketch a floor plan of the room, including all centers, tables, chairs, entrances, and exits. The approximate sizes of spaces would be helpful, but is not essential.

2. Take careful notes listing the toys and equipment found in the indoor environment for each center and space you observe.

3. Look for evidence of health and safety considerations or attempts to create a more environmentally friendly environment for young children.

Reflect and Apply

1. Compare the floor plan you sketched with the discussion in this chapter about planning an indoor environment for young children. What are the similarities and differences?

2. Based on your notes about toys and equipment in the early learning environment, do you think children had good opportunities to engage in quality play experiences? Why or why not?

3. Did you find evidence of caregivers or teachers planning healthy, safe, and environmentally friendly spaces for young children? Describe what you found.

A third way in which indoor space can be evaluated is in terms of its **spatial density**. Johnson, Christie, and Wardle (2005) define spatial density as the amount of space per child in a play setting. It can be calculated by measuring the total area of the indoor setting, subtracting the unusable space (things like a desk for adults, spaces too small for play, or areas that are off-limits for some reason), and then dividing that area by the number of children using the space. If the spatial density is less than 25 square feet per child, the play area is too crowded. Research indicates there will be less gross-motor activity and more aggression in these settings (Smith & Connolly, 1980).

The *Observing Development* feature in this section provides a framework for informally assessing an indoor early childhood setting. Observing an indoor environment will provide you with additional insights on creating quality learning environments for young children.

Selecting Equipment and Materials

An important function of early childhood professionals is the selection of appropriate equipment and materials for center activities. Because children need many choices and adults have limited budgets for purchasing equipment and materials, it is essential to make good decisions about what to buy and use in the program.

Criteria for selection. Each center in an early childhood setting requires specialized materials that the adult can make or purchase commercially. Consider the following criteria for selecting materials for young children:

- **High initial interest.** Novelty and attractive physical characteristics make toys and equipment of high interest to young children.
- **Versatility in use.** Equipment that allows children to explore and use it in open-ended ways is best. More creativity is possible, and children tend to use the materials longer.

- **Minimal adult supervision.** Quality materials require little or no explanation or supervision by adults to use. They are of appropriate size for the ages of the children playing with them.
- **Continuing appeal.** Good toys are so inviting and interesting that children cannot resist playing with them over and over again. They continue to stimulate the use of imagination, language, cognition, and both large and small muscle movement.
- **Encourage cooperative play.** Because one of the goals of early education is to stimulate social learning, most play materials should promote interaction among small groups of children. Rather than stimulate conflict and arguments, good toys should encourage cooperation and playing together.
- **Enhance self-concept.** Play materials should reflect children's cultural, racial, gender, and physical differences. When these differences are evident in the materials selected, children have more positive self-concepts.
- **Durability.** Program materials receive frequent use and must be durable enough to withstand frequent cleaning and the banging, dropping, and general wear-and-tear of use by young children.
- **Safety.** You should not purchase toys made of toxic materials, toys that can splinter or break, equipment that can pinch or cut, and materials that easily catch fire.
- **Options for children with special needs.** Toys and equipment should be accessible (usable) by children with special needs, available in every center, and developmentally appropriate.

Commercial materials. Many different commercial companies produce toys and equipment for use in early childhood settings. Toys can come from general purpose, specialty, and multicultural companies:

General Purpose Companies. Companies that produce and sell equipment for every center are often referred to as general purpose companies. Their catalogs are extensive and provide many selections. While general purpose companies make it easy to purchase a variety of products from one source, specialty companies may provide some material and equipment options that are of higher quality. Some examples of general purpose companies are

- Lakeshore Learning Materials
- Community Playthings
- Constructive Playthings
- Kaplan Companies

Specialty Companies. Companies that produce materials that either fit a specific approach to early care and education or focus on limited aspects of the curriculum are specialty companies. While some of these specialty companies have branched out and provide equipment and materials that go beyond their specialty, they are best known for a particular product. Some examples of this type are

- **Niehuis Montessori.** Best known as a site for purchasing Montessori materials.
- **ETA Cuisenaire.** Cuisenaire rods are colored wooden manipulatives that are used in preschool and primary classrooms to teach mathematical concepts.
- **Angeles Group.** Best known for their high-quality, durable tricycles.

Multicultural Companies. Some relatively new companies focus their energies on promoting multicultural play materials for the early childhood setting. These companies are generally smaller but provide many unique options for play equipment and materials. Some examples include

- **Asia for Kids.** Books, dolls, and games representing the Asian culture.
- **Smithsonian Folkways.** The nonprofit arm of the Smithsonian Institute. Dedicated to recording and distributing music from around the world.
- **Dolls Like Me.** Sells dolls and other multicultural toys.

Adult-made equipment. To save money, many early childhood professionals make their own materials for use by children. In addition to saving money, adult-developed equipment and materials can also be more closely matched to the developmental needs and interests of a specific group of children (Leigh, 2004). Ideas for these options come from a variety of sources:

- Imitations of commercial equipment
- Ideas from other professionals
- Curriculum books for early care and education

Although early childhood professionals are generally the source of ideas for noncommercial play materials, families and other volunteers can be a big help in the actual construction of these items. Using carefully planned instructions, these adults can work on projects for early childhood programs in their spare time and greatly reduce your time commitment. The *Developmentally Appropriate Practice* feature in this section provides one example of an adult-made project.

Changing the Physical Environment

Children's play can be characterized as fluid and changing. It mirrors the interests, developmental needs, and growth of those engaging in play. Sensitive early childhood professionals continually plan for changes in the indoor environment to facilitate these important experiences for individual children. Each week, adults should critique the uses of existing play equipment and make decisions about what should be kept out or put away and about whether any new materials should be added. By carefully observing children at play, you can plan centers and activities that are stimulating and developmentally appropriate.

Observe and listen to children. To effectively plan play environments for young children, adults need to carefully observe what children are doing as they interact with toys and with one another (Van Hoorn, Nourot, Scales, & Alward, 2011). In the dramatic play center, for example, which clothes and accessories are the children using? What play themes are the children enacting? What are the children saying as they play? This information is invaluable to adults as they make decisions about toys and equipment to add or put away. If, for example, you observe children playing out travel themes in the dramatic play center, you could put out props like suitcases and travel brochures to further stimulate this play type.

Adults working with children meet regularly to discuss the play experiences observed before planning for the next week. This sharing of information can be very beneficial in selecting center materials and activities. Specifics about individual children and general patterns of behavior become more obvious and make curricular decisions easier.

Developmentally Appropriate Practice . . .
ADULT-MADE GAMES

Games provide wonderful opportunities for children to learn in playful and meaningful ways. Unfortunately, many commercially produced games have little direct connection to what is being taught in early childhood settings. In addition, if they are available commercially, they are expensive to purchase. One alternative is to use the format of some commonly played games and adapt them to fit the concepts you want taught. For example, variations of the traditional Bingo game can be constructed to teach a wide variety of academic subjects. Sugar and Sugar (2002) provide many good examples of games that can be constructed and used by teachers in the primary classroom.

One example of an adult-made game that could be used effectively in early childhood settings is a *concentration game*. You may remember this option from your own childhood. Typically, a concentration game has sets of matching cards made from cardboard that are usually about 2 or 3 inches on each side. The game generally has 16 to 20 matching pictures, shapes, words, or math problems and solutions. The game maker can use pictures from magazines, hand-drawn shapes, or printed words or math problems to personalize the game for a specific group of children and the concepts to be learned. To play the game, two children place the cards face down on the floor or table, mix up the cards, and then take turns picking two cards in an attempt to get a match. If the cards do not match, they go back in the same positions, face down. When a match is found, the player gets to keep the cards in her pile. The game continues until all matches are made.

This concentration game is relatively easy to construct and can be modified for many potential uses in early childhood settings. For example, it could be effectively used for memorizing arithmetic facts at the primary level. One card from each set would display an arithmetic fact such as 3 + 4 = and the second card would then display the correct answer. When two or more children play together, they can support one another in learning math facts in this enjoyable game format.

Provide program consistency. This planning process for young children's play environments must include careful thought about the need for both consistency and change. A consistent environment gives young children a sense of security and comfort. In their home away from home, they need to experience a familiar routine and activities that are interesting without being overwhelmingly different: the younger the child, the greater the need for consistency.

Adults create this *familiar, comfortable environment* in the following ways:

- The general arrangement of furniture in each center is consistent.
- Some materials are always available to children (e.g., basic art materials in the art center).
- Routines for use and storage of play materials are well-defined and known to children (e.g., blocks stored in clearly marked places on shelves that children can reach).
- Blocks of time for daily creative play experiences are consistent.

Juaquim is new to your second-grade classroom. Although it is nearing the end of the school year, he just arrived with his family as they prepare to work in the berry fields for the summer. Juaquim has been in three different schools this year, each of which has been very different in terms of classroom organization, adult expectations, and teaching philosophies. He will benefit significantly from being in an environment that remains relatively consistent for the rest of the school year.

Rotate materials through centers. Providing for change in early childhood settings also means adding new play materials each week and removing other items that have served their current purposes. Adults often meet weekly to discuss each center and make decisions about equipment changes. Some guidelines for determining toy needs for each center include the following:

- Make sure materials are available in centers to challenge each child to higher levels of development.
- Provide options that build on children's interests.
- Change approximately a third of the materials available in each center weekly.
- Make sure equipment and toys match the curricular goals and themes.

As new materials are added, it is important to maintain interest and enthusiasm for the play environment. Strategies to consider for accomplishing this task include the following:

- Discuss new toys and equipment at group times.
- Engage in play with children, using materials that have been overlooked or underutilized.
- Give children ideas about how to use new toys or materials in their play.
- Casually leave materials out at the beginning of an activity period to remind children of their availability.

Health and Safety Considerations

The health and safety of children are essential for optimal development, and you must consider these when planning the indoor environment. By taking responsibility for these issues, adults free children to actively interact with the people and objects around them.

Planning a healthy environment. When considering materials for early childhood programs, you must avoid any materials that would pose potential health risks. For example, many infant/toddler programs substitute cornmeal or rice for sand because of the tendency for children of this age to put everything into their mouths. Similarly, nontoxic markers and crayons should be used with all young children. Lead poisoning from old paint (prior to 1977), contaminated drinking water, and certain pieces of imported dishware are potential health hazards for young children that can be prevented by careful adult planning (Marotz, 2009).

Providing a sanitary environment for young children is also important in minimizing diseases. The more common problems such as colds and influenza can be controlled with regular cleaning of the physical environment and careful hand-washing techniques. Other communicable diseases such as hepatitis and pinworm infestation also require attention to good hygiene for successful management. Concerns over dealing with children infected with human immunodeficiency virus/acquired immune deficiency syndrome (HIV/AIDS) (Aronson & Shope, 2004) have led to the use of disposable gloves and careful hand washing when dealing with children's body fluids.

Another important aspect of a healthy environment for young children is the inclusion of materials and foods that assist in developing positive personal health habits. With the growing concerns about obesity and lack of physical activity in young children (Winter, 2009), you will need to plan indoor spaces that encourage active play and healthy eating habits:

- Plan spaces where infants and toddlers can crawl, pull themselves up in preparation for walking, and engage in early manipulative skills.
- Consider an area for climbing, tumbling, and balance activities for preschool children.
- Include books on health and nutrition in the reading corner (Renck & Jalongo, 2004).
- Establish healthy food choices for young children for lunches and snacks (Kalich, Bauer, & McPartlin, 2009).

Safety concerns. The organization of the physical environment can assist in accident prevention. Due to limited experiences and developing physical skills, children need a carefully prepared setting. Electrical outlets, stoves, air-circulating fans, and climbing equipment are some examples of equipment that should be of concern to early childhood professionals. Medicines, cleaning agents, and insecticides are other materials that adults must store out of the reach of children or outside the early childhood setting to avoid accidental poisonings.

In many circumstances, adults need to demonstrate or teach children safe use of equipment. For example, assisting children in holding and properly using a sharp knife in a cooking activity helps promote safety. Providing safety goggles for the woodworking bench and demonstrating good sawing techniques will also help prevent accidents in those areas. Although this advanced preparation will not prevent all problems from occurring, it helps create an environment where children can explore and experiment with greater freedom.

Environmentally Friendly Indoor Spaces

The world as we know it is gradually changing. The impact of fossil fuels and other pollutants is leading to global warming and the many negative side effects this brings about (Hoot & Szente, 2010). But global warming can be slowed and perhaps even reversed if we all take steps to be thoughtful stewards of our planet. As an early childhood professional, you have an important role to play in helping young children learn about, and participate in, caring for the environment.

Song (2008) suggests that environmental education for young children should begin with the development of a passionate caring, rather than an emotionally detached, perspective on the topic. Environmental educator David Sobel (1996) states it this way: "What's important is that children have an opportunity to bond with the natural world, to learn to love it, before being asked to heal its wounds" (p. 10).

So, in your future indoor space for young children you can develop a love of nature and help children learn to "heal nature's wounds" by doing such things as the following:

- Bringing in good books about the environment, such as Eric Carle's three-book set titled *All Around Us* (Crawford, 2010) to be read and discussed at group time or in the book corner.
- Growing plants, studying them to understand their complexities, and learning what it takes to keep them healthy (Hachey & Butler, 2009).
- Keeping a pet indoors, studying its history and uses by humans, and learning to care for a living creature (Meadan & Jegatheesan, 2010).

- Having a recycle area that allows children and adults to collect and prepare materials for reuse.
- Using recycled materials in the art area whenever possible for art projects.
- Planning a long-term study of the weather based on Internet sources as a way to learn more about climate change and its effects (Marrero & Schuster, 2010).

 ## Centers-Based Early Childhood Programs

Early childhood settings are organized differently depending on the ages of the children served and the educational environment. However, as described earlier in this chapter, indoor space is often arranged into centers. Using low dividers, tables, child-sized furniture, and an assortment of storage units, caregivers and teachers create small areas within the room that children can use for specific play and work-oriented tasks. At the preschool level and below, programs are often completely centers-based. Quality kindergarten through third-grade environments can be partially or fully organized around centers. Although not all of the areas described next are found in every early childhood setting, these centers are common to many indoor play spaces for young children.

As you begin to think about developing centers, remember to consider diversity as an important factor in their set-up. It is essential that the areas you create include materials and activities that are relevant to the cultures represented by your children and the community in which you are located. For example, you could include pictures on the walls of adults and children from Native American, Hispanic, Asian, or African-American heritage, depending on the composition of your program and community. Including dolls with different skin tones helps all children appreciate the centers you create. Playing music from different cultures is another strategy to make your program more inclusive for all children.

Art Center

The art center is an essential element of early childhood settings. Located near a water source for easy clean-up, this area ideally should have a vinyl floor covering or other similar surface. Furniture typically includes a child-sized table and chairs, storage shelves for art supplies, and an easel. A quality art area includes materials such as crayons, markers, and paper of various types that are available daily, and other materials that change regularly (usually each week).

Fixed materials	Materials that change
Easel(s)	Scrap paper for collages
Scissors	Watercolors
Crayons	Fingerpainting materials
Rulers	Screen painting
Staplers	Sponge painting
Scrap paper	Tissue paper for collages
Washable marking pens	Wood scraps, glue, paint

Manipulative Center

Developing fine motor skills, enhancing early mathematical understanding, and encouraging creative expression are typical goals for the manipulative center. Dodge, Colker, and Heroman (2002) identify four categories of toys found in manipulative areas:

- *Self-correcting toys* fit together in a way that lets children know when they have used the materials correctly. Puzzles are good examples of this type of toy, as are most Montessori materials. The *Celebrating Play* feature found in this section describes puzzle use in more detail.

- *Open-ended toys* are unstructured in their use. Creative exploration is stimulated. Legos, Lincoln Logs, and Bristle Blocks all fit this category.

- *Collectibles* are scrounged materials that children use in open-ended ways. Families and early childhood professionals can save plastic bottle caps, buttons, and old keys for sorting, matching, and comparing activities, for example.

- *Cooperative games* engage children in pairs or small groups in simple activities that de-emphasize winning and losing. Lotto games, concentration activities, and matching toys provide additional opportunities for quality play in this center.

Celebrating Play . . .
PUZZLES IN PRESCHOOL SETTINGS

Puzzles are a traditional and important part of learning at the preschool level. The first puzzles for children were produced in 1760 by John Spilsbury, an Englishman (Maldono, 1996), and have been part of teaching and learning since that time. What is the attraction of these manipulatives for young children? When they work with puzzles, children are often intensely focused and frequently complete the same puzzle over and over again. Maldono (1996) explains it this way:

> Children are interested in puzzle making because they can be active as observers, problem solvers, and learners, with little or no assistance from adults and others. The intrigue involved in puzzle making is that fragments come together to complete an image. Through puzzle making, young children experience satisfaction by putting things together where they belong. Contentment is achieved by the mere fact that things that look broken are fixed. (p. 4)

Good puzzles should have the following characteristics (Maldono, 1996):

1. **Puzzles should match the child's developmental abilities.** For example, most 2-year-olds need puzzles that have knobs and depict a single whole object like a car. In contrast, 4-year-olds are typically ready for knobless puzzles of 12 to 18 pieces.

2. **Puzzles should be attractive and durable.** They should be colorful and include clearly recognizable items. Because of high usage, they also must be sturdy.

3. **Puzzles should reflect items that are familiar to children.** They should represent items that children have seen or had experiences with, such as foods, vehicles, and animals.

4. **Puzzles should be solvable.** While being challenging, they should be something the child is motivated to complete and be successful with. Some children may be ready for more complex puzzles of 100–150 pieces (Barron, 1999), while others (typically) are challenged by puzzles with 20 or fewer pieces.

1. Do you enjoy doing puzzles, crosswords, or Sudoku as an adult? If so, what do you find attracts you to this activity?

2. Read one of the two articles referenced in this feature. In terms of overall development, what can children potentially learn from puzzle use?

Literacy Center

A literacy center should be a quiet oasis for children to engage in early reading and writing experiences. The main ingredients for this area include comfortable spots for children to sit and read or be read to, storage/display shelves for books, a table for writing activities, and a collection of quality children's literature. The adults can rotate a variety of book types in and out of the library area to maintain involvement among all children:

- Picture books (no words)
- New award-winning books
- Classic books
- Nursery rhymes and poetry
- Homemade children's books
- Books addressing multicultural and diversity issues (see the *Celebrating Diversity* feature in this section for examples)
- Content-oriented books that complement themes

Other materials can be added to this center to provide meaningful experiences with written language. In addition to books, an assortment of emergent literacy activities such as flannel board story figures, a listening center (with headsets), and magnetic board letters help stimulate the language arts. Notebooks with lined paper, pens and pencils, and chalkboards with chalk are other common options. When combined with quality books, this center can entice children to sit and read, be read to, or engage in early writing activities.

Celebrating Diversity . . .
CHILDREN'S BOOKS ABOUT DIVERSE CULTURES

There is a large and growing collection of books for children that provide wonderful stories about diverse children and their families. As a future early childhood professional, you will want to either start your own collection of quality books or keep an annotated bibliography so that you can use these and other children's books in your own program one day. Here are some good examples of books about diverse cultures (Braus & Geidel, 2000):

So Much by Trish Cooke (2000) is a picture book for young children that shows a series of African-American extended-family members arriving home to hug and love a young baby.

Abuela by Arthur Dorros (1991) is a story about Rosalba and her grandmother (Abuela) who take a walk in New York City. The inclusion of Spanish words adds further learning opportunities to this story.

The First Strawberries by Joseph Bruchac (1993) is a Cherokee story about the first man and woman on Earth. When the man gets angry at the woman and she runs away, he asks the sun god to put something in her way to get her to stop running. The sun god creates strawberries, which she stops to enjoy.

Hush by Mingfong Ho (1996) is a lullaby describing the author's childhood memories of falling asleep in her native Thailand to the sounds of green frogs, water buffalo, monkeys, and more.

Peek! A Thai Hide-and-Seek by Mingfong Ho (2004) depicts the Thai version of hide-and-seek played with animals of the jungle.

1. Are you aware of other good examples of children's books depicting diverse cultures? What do you like about these books?

2. In what ways do children's books about diverse cultures help young children understand and accept differences among people?

Early childhood professionals need to plan the environment to accommodate children with special needs.

Block Center

Blocks have tremendous potential for creative play and learning. This center is essential in every early childhood setting, including primary classrooms (Harris, 1994; Hirsch, 1996). The basic elements needed for this area are a set of wooden unit blocks, a collection of large hollow blocks (often constructed of wood), a carpeted floor for block building, low shelves for organized storage of blocks and ease of access, and accessories such as toy trucks or animals that the adult rotates in and out of the center regularly. The *Developmentally Appropriate Practice* feature found in this section provides information on the mathematical learning potential of blocks in early childhood settings.

Although children use unit blocks imaginatively by themselves, the accessories you provide will help stimulate further creative play in this area. Consider rotating these added props in and out of the center weekly to encourage play related to current themes. Some examples of accessories that are often used include the following:

- Toy farm animals
- Transportation toys (trucks, airplanes, etc.)
- Small wooden or plastic people/figures
- Dollhouse furniture
- Zoo animals
- Hats (construction, police, etc.)
- Play money
- Writing materials (for signs)

Housekeeping Center

As the name implies, the housekeeping center is designed for young children to engage in dramatic play focused on home themes. Typically, the housekeeping area contains materials such as a child-sized sink, stove, refrigerator, microwave, china cupboard, table and chairs, toy dishes, silverware, pots and pans, a telephone and/or cell phone, and a small broom and dustpan set. The adult can rotate accessories such as pretend foods (empty cans/boxes collected from homes or plastic food replicas), pictures of people engaged in housekeeping tasks, and additional cooking utensils in and out of this area to create new interest in playing here.

Younger children (ages 4 and below) are particularly attracted to the housekeeping center, so including it as a permanent option with little change to the basic equipment makes good sense. If space is limited or children are somewhat older, the housekeeping area may be effectively combined with the dramatic play center.

Developmentally Appropriate Practice . . .
UNIT BLOCKS AND LEARNING MATHEMATICS

Unit blocks are generally made from smooth, sanded hardwood and come in sizes that are proportional in length and width to the basic unit, which is 5½ × 2¾ × 1⅜ inches. Every other block has a mathematical relationship to this basic unit.

One of the wonderful aspects of block play is that children can engage in exciting building projects while learning key concepts that will prepare them for later learning. For example, block play provides opportunities for children to acquire an early knowledge of math. Preschool play with blocks has been shown to be a good predictor of later school achievement in mathematics (Wolfgang, Stannard, & Jones, 2001). Saunders and Bingham-Newman (1984) identify some important mathematical understandings that are being developed in block play:

- **Seriation.** Children learn to order by size (smallest to largest or the reverse) as they build steps, towers, and other block shapes. Seriation is essential in such math activities as counting, understanding greater than and less than, and measuring.

- **Classification.** As they match or sort blocks on the basis of a given characteristic (such as block length or shape), children are learning a skill that will help them understand our number system. We use classification as we group four hundreds, eight tens, and six ones together to form the number 486.

- **Estimation.** Children develop estimation skills as they determine how many blocks will be needed to build their structures and consider the amount of space required for their structures.

- **Measurement.** Because unit blocks are proportional to one another, they are excellent tools for learning about unit measurement. When we measure in inches, we are using a unit of measurement. Children who play with unit blocks use them to measure the different structures they are building.

- **Comparisons.** As they construct with blocks, children recognize differences in height, width, shape, and weight. Greater than, less than, and equal to are three essential mathematical comparisons that are used regularly in problem solving.

Dramatic Play Center

The importance of imaginative play has been clearly documented (Singer, Golinkoff, & Hirsh-Pasek, 2006; Singer & Singer, 1990), so this type of play needs to be incorporated into early childhood settings at every opportunity. Although imaginative play can occur in any center, a separate space devoted to dramatic activities is crucial. When located next to, or combined with, the housekeeping center, an imaginative play area is a popular addition to the early childhood program. Early childhood professionals often begin the school year by stocking the dramatic play center with a few basic materials such as dress-up clothes, a mirror, dolls and doll beds, a chest of drawers, and a coat rack. Gradually new accessories such as jewelry, hats, and a child-sized briefcase can be added to stimulate more interest.

A common practice for many early childhood professionals is the creation of prop boxes containing materials needed for specific dramatic play themes. Because these boxes are portable, you can organize materials for children to use either indoors or outside. Some examples of prop box themes include supermarket, shoe store, repair shop, office, camping, and airplane. The *Developmentally Appropriate Practice* feature in this section describes some typical items found in four different prop boxes.

Developmentally Appropriate Practice . . .
DRAMATIC PLAY PROP BOXES

Prop boxes are a convenient way to organize the materials needed for dramatic play themes. When sturdy boxes of consistent size are used, the props can be easily stored when not in use. Tape a list of needed materials on the inside lid of the box so that a quick check can be made for missing items before using the box. Here are some ideas for specific prop boxes (Myhre, 1993):

Office prop box	**Beach party prop box**	**Repair shop box**	**Grocery store prop box**
Telephone	Beach towels	Clipboard	Cash register
Typewriter/keyboard	Sunglasses	Wrenches and screwdrivers	Plastic foods
Pads of paper	Straw hats	Safety glasses	Play money
Desk accessories	Water bottles	Nuts and bolts	Empty food containers
Paper	Life preserver	Toolbox	Grocery bags
File folders	Air mattresses	Scrap wood	Grocery cart
Envelopes	Picnic accessories	Workbench	Baskets

The Music Center

Musical experiences provide important learning opportunities for young children and create a more pleasant environment for them (Kreeft, 2006; Shore & Strasser, 2006). Group times that include singing, movement to music, and the use of instruments are common in most early childhood settings. In addition, it is important to encourage other experiences with music. A music center can often be incorporated into the indoor space for this purpose. A CD player; an open, carpeted area; storage shelves; an assortment of music-making materials; and a piano are common items found in this area. It is best to start the year with one or two instruments on the shelf and gradually add more as the year progresses. Many adults stock the group-time area with music materials so that these are available for circle activities and free choice times.

As with every center, you should move instruments and musical options in and out of the area to maintain interest and use. Materials that can be rotated through this center include

- Rhythm sticks
- Cymbals
- Triangles
- Bells
- Drums
- Autoharp
- Scarves (for movement to music)

Music-making experiences are an important part of the early childhood curriculum.

Discovery/Science Center

A discovery/science center provides opportunities for young children to develop an understanding of science. Children can use a small table with displays of interesting materials to learn basic scientific principles and concepts. Additional storage space for other science-oriented materials is useful in this center as well. Materials to consider for the discovery/science area include these:

- Plants
- Rocks
- Shells
- Magnifying glass
- Balance scales
- Aquarium
- Animal/insect cages
- Small appliances to take apart and explore

Other Creative Centers

Although the preceding areas are considered essential in the early childhood settings, several other possibilities can be incorporated as well. These additional centers provide many play opportunities that cannot be easily duplicated in other ways. Space limitations are the most common reason for not including them. One important option that may get left out because of space limitations is a place for families when they spend time in the program. The *Family Partnerships* feature in this section provides some thoughts on creating a place for them.

Family Partnerships...
A PLACE FOR FAMILIES?

Space in most early childhood settings is at a premium. It is often difficult to find room for every desired option. Despite this major problem, if early childhood professionals want to help families and other volunteers feel welcome in their programs, having a spot they can call their own makes good sense. Consider some creative options, such as making your desk and surrounding space available as a family/volunteer corner during the day. Or create a small gathering spot just outside the door with equipment that could be moved back inside at the end of the day. Another option would be to use a space such as a snack table or circle-time area for volunteers during parts of the day when they are not needed by children. The family corner might also be used as a break area for staff, enhancing its usefulness during other times of the day and providing opportunities for volunteers and early childhood professionals to interact informally in this setting.

The items needed for a family/volunteer area vary according to the age of the children and the flexibility of your physical space. Furniture and accessories could include the following:

- Comfortable stuffed chair, desk, or a small couch with end table(s)
- Family bulletin board with information on current program activities
- Copies of program newsletters
- Articles of interest to families
- Library of parent education books
- Hot water dispenser or a coffeemaker for coffee and tea

When you combine as many of these ingredients as possible into this space, you will create a welcoming environment for visiting adults.

1. What sorts of things make you feel welcome in a new place? What similar items could you include in a family corner?

2. In addition to a family/volunteer corner, what else could you do to your indoor space to make it a more welcoming environment for family members and the community?

Woodworking center. Real, child-sized saws and hammers, wood, nails, safety goggles, a woodworking table with built-in vises, and hand drills are the basic ingredients for the woodworking center (Huber, 1999). Additional accessories could include an old stump for simple nailing practice, glue, C-clamps, and wood rasps. For younger children, or just for a change, Styrofoam can be substituted for wood.

Some adults prefer to have this activity take place outdoors; however, with enough space and proper supervision, it can be effectively managed indoors. Also, the noise, mess, and potential safety issues tend to frighten some early childhood professionals away from providing woodworking activities. With preparation and careful adult supervision, however, this center can be an exciting and safe place for children. Consider beginning with simple woodworking projects that can be expanded as your confidence and the abilities of the children increase (Bisgaier & Samaras, 2004).

Sand/water play center. The attraction of natural materials such as sand and water is strong, especially with prekindergarten children. Their sensory nature and flexible uses make these materials popular in early childhood settings. Sand and water play should be considered essential for the outdoor setting and, if space permits, are important options indoors (Chalufour & Worth, 2004; Chalufour & Worth, 2006). Although it requires considerable work on the part of caregivers and teachers, a sand/water table can be regularly changed from sand to water (or the reverse) to create added interest in this center. For infants and toddlers, consider materials like dried peas, beans, or cornmeal as alternatives to sand because of the tendency of very young children to put everything in their mouths.

Child-sized sand/water tables are available commercially that hold either sand or water. A vinyl floor (or protective covering), water-repelling smocks, and accessories for mixing and pouring sand or water complete this center. Sample accessories include the following:

- Funnels
- Measuring cups
- Waterwheel
- Spoons
- Small buckets
- Hand trowels
- Basters
- Pitchers

Writing center. Providing many opportunities for early writing experiences is essential for the literacy development of young children. You can do this by making sure writing materials are available in the art, block, dramatic play, and library centers. This will greatly increase the likelihood that children will incorporate writing into their play (Kissel, 2008; Love, Burns, & Buell, 2007). In addition, older children should have a separate center that focuses specifically on writing activities.

The materials needed for a separate writing center are relatively simple:

- Variety of writing instruments, such as pencils, pens, crayons, and markers
- Recycled paper for rough drafts
- Lined paper and paper for finished writing
- Heavier-weighted paper for book covers
- Dictionary or word file
- Staplers
- Typewriter
- Computer

Computer center. Although there is some controversy about computer use for young children, most early educators believe that when properly regulated, computer use can be an important activity for children age 3 and older (Bewick & Kostelnik, 2004; Copple & Bredekamp, 2009). With quality, play-oriented software, children can learn a great deal and have fun at the same time.

To provide maximum benefit from a computer, you should place it in the indoor environment rather than in a separate computer room shared by the entire program. It should be available to children as another choice during center time. With two or three chairs at the computer, several children can use it cooperatively.

Probably the biggest drawback to computer use is the high cost of the hardware. Many prekindergarten programs in particular have very limited budgets, and committing $1,000 or more to a quality computer system is difficult. Despite their many benefits, computers should not be a higher priority than an ample collection

Recycled paper saves money and is environmentally friendly.

of unit blocks, for example. Although a good set of blocks may cost as much as a computer, the fact that they are real-world materials that can be manipulated in a virtually limitless number of ways makes them a higher budget priority when funds are limited.

Infant/Toddler Environments

Having studied basic planning guidelines and typical centers found in indoor settings, you will now learn how these ideas can be applied to specific age groups within early childhood. The following sections describe developmentally appropriate infant/toddler, preschool, and primary spaces. While there are many similarities in indoor spaces across ages, there are also significant differences.

Developmental Considerations

As you begin thinking about indoor spaces for infants and toddlers, it is important to know and incorporate some basic information about child development into the planning process. For example, it is important to remember that much of a young child's day is spent in routines. Eating, sleeping, and toileting activities are significant parts of the curriculum. Special areas for routines are important in infant/toddler programs (Catron & Allen, 2008). A changing area with a table and access to water for clean-up is a necessity. Separating it from the eating and play centers also makes good sense. Establishing similar spaces for sleeping and eating that can be used throughout the day are also necessary.

Infants and toddlers are in what Piaget calls the *stage of sensorimotor intelligence.* They learn about their world through sight, sound, taste, smell, and touch. Sensory materials that infants and toddlers can easily manipulate are important. Because most infants and toddlers learn a great deal by putting things in their mouths, significant issues for this age are the safety and cleanliness of play materials (Lowman & Ruhmann, 1998; Post & Hohmann, 2000). Caregivers must avoid toys that might break or splinter when chewed or that are small enough to swallow. Because regular cleaning is necessary as well, equipment should be durable enough to withstand frequent washing. The following is a sampling of toys that can be valuable in an infant/toddler program:

Crib toys

Beads (large, bright, on sturdy cord)
Clutch balls (large, with finger holds, soft material)
Cradle gyms (things to push, pull, manipulate)
Mobiles
Rattles
Squeeze toys

Play equipment

Large soft blocks for stacking and climbing
Pull toys
Stacking toys
Mirrors

Musical toys

Sorting toys

Pegboard with large pegs

Interesting smells (cut flowers, spices, etc.)

Texture balls

In addition to sensory experiences, young children learn about themselves and their environment through physical movement. Infant/toddler programs need materials that stimulate motor development. Climbing, crawling, walking, and stacking activities address the developmental interests of this age. Providing simple, age-appropriate equipment and materials such as foam blocks for stacking, and padded incline planes for walking on will help make the infant/toddler space more interesting and challenging for these ages.

Spaces and Centers

Figure 9–1 provides an example of the elements found in a developmentally appropriate infant/toddler program. Take note of the following options:

- Changing table near the bathroom.
- Quiet area with cribs for rest and nap times.
- Active play area with small climber, tumbling mat, and large vinyl blocks.
- Reading area with rug and pillows.
- Social area with manipulative toys and blocks.
- Art and water play areas.
- Comfortable adult chairs and rockers for holding and cuddling young children.

 **Preschool Spaces**

Indoor environments for preschool children are somewhat different in their organization than those for infants and toddlers. For example, in preschool settings there is no need for a changing table or cribs for naps. In addition, adults generally use child-sized chairs for sitting and only one or two adult chairs are needed. These differences, and others, free up more space indoors for a greater variety of centers and activities. Read on for more information on planning developmentally appropriate indoor environments for preschool children.

Planning Considerations

As discussed earlier, play is a primary vehicle for learning during the preschool years. For this reason, programs for this age are typically organized into centers. They often include areas for art, books/quiet activities, blocks, manipulatives, housekeeping, and dramatic play (Curtis & Carter, 2003; Dodge, Colker, & Heroman, 2002). They also regularly include sand/water play, music, and discovery centers. Children have daily opportunities to spend large blocks of time in the centers they select, engaged in creative play activities.

Figure 9–1

Infant/Toddler Classroom

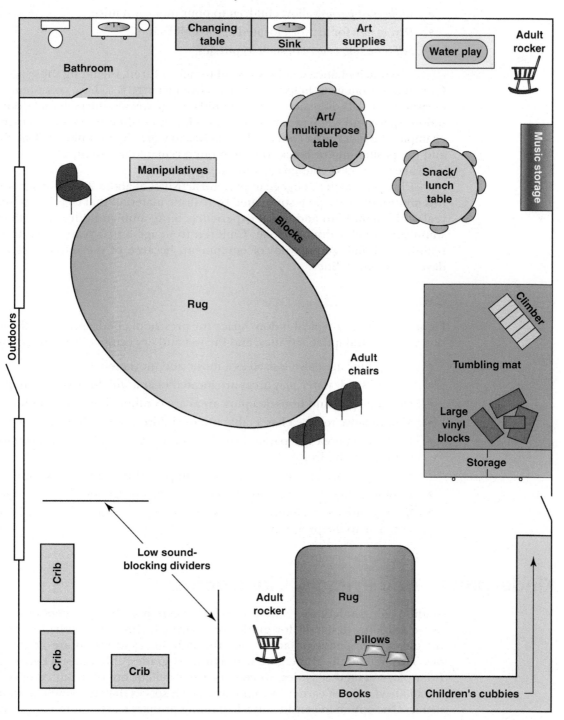

As children move toward greater and greater autonomy, experiences and materials must allow for increasing independence (Mitchell & David, 1992). Following are some examples:

- *Child-sized pitchers* allow children to pour their own juice
- *Drying rack* for artwork located at the child's level
- *Self-correcting materials*, such as puzzles

Too much change can be stressful for all children, including those age 3 to 5. One simple strategy to help reduce stress from change is to have consistency in the environment. Although accessories should change weekly, the general layout of the indoor space and the basic structure of each center often remain unchanged. For example, the block area contains low shelves to store the unit blocks. This shelving and the positioning of blocks on them often remain consistent, while the accessories (like toy trucks) change each week.

Children begin to engage in pretend activities at about 2 years of age. Initially, this important play type is stimulated by realistic materials that clearly resemble the real-world item. With additional experience, more ambiguous toys are effective in stimulating quality dramatic play. Children from age 3 to 5 years often need both realistic and ambiguous types of equipment, because of the differences in their developmental abilities.

Center Organization

Figure 9–2 shows a typical indoor space for preschool children. Notice the separation of active and quiet activities, and the wet and dry centers. Note the following:

- Group time area also is used as a music and movement space.
- Art and sand/water play areas are located near a sink for easy clean-up.
- Dramatic play and housekeeping areas are combined into one center.
- Manipulative toy area has a table where children can build with center toys.
- Book/quiet area is separated from other activities and includes comfortable seating for children.
- Science/discovery center is a permanent part of the indoor environment.
- Computer area is set up with two chairs to encourage social interactions.
- Storage area for children's coats and personal items is located near the entrance to the program.

 # Kindergarten and Primary Classrooms

Traditionally, kindergarten classrooms have been more like preschool rooms than like classrooms designed for grades one through three. Recently, however, with the growing emphasis on academics, the differences in set-up are now less obvious. Throughout the kindergarten and primary grades, children still benefit greatly from play-oriented activities, so centers are excellent options. But centers should be balanced, at least earlier in your career, with spaces that are viewed as more academic. One option to consider as a beginning primary teacher is to have temporary centers that children use a few times a week and then gradually make those temporary centers permanent.

Figure 9-2

Preschool/Kindergarten Classroom

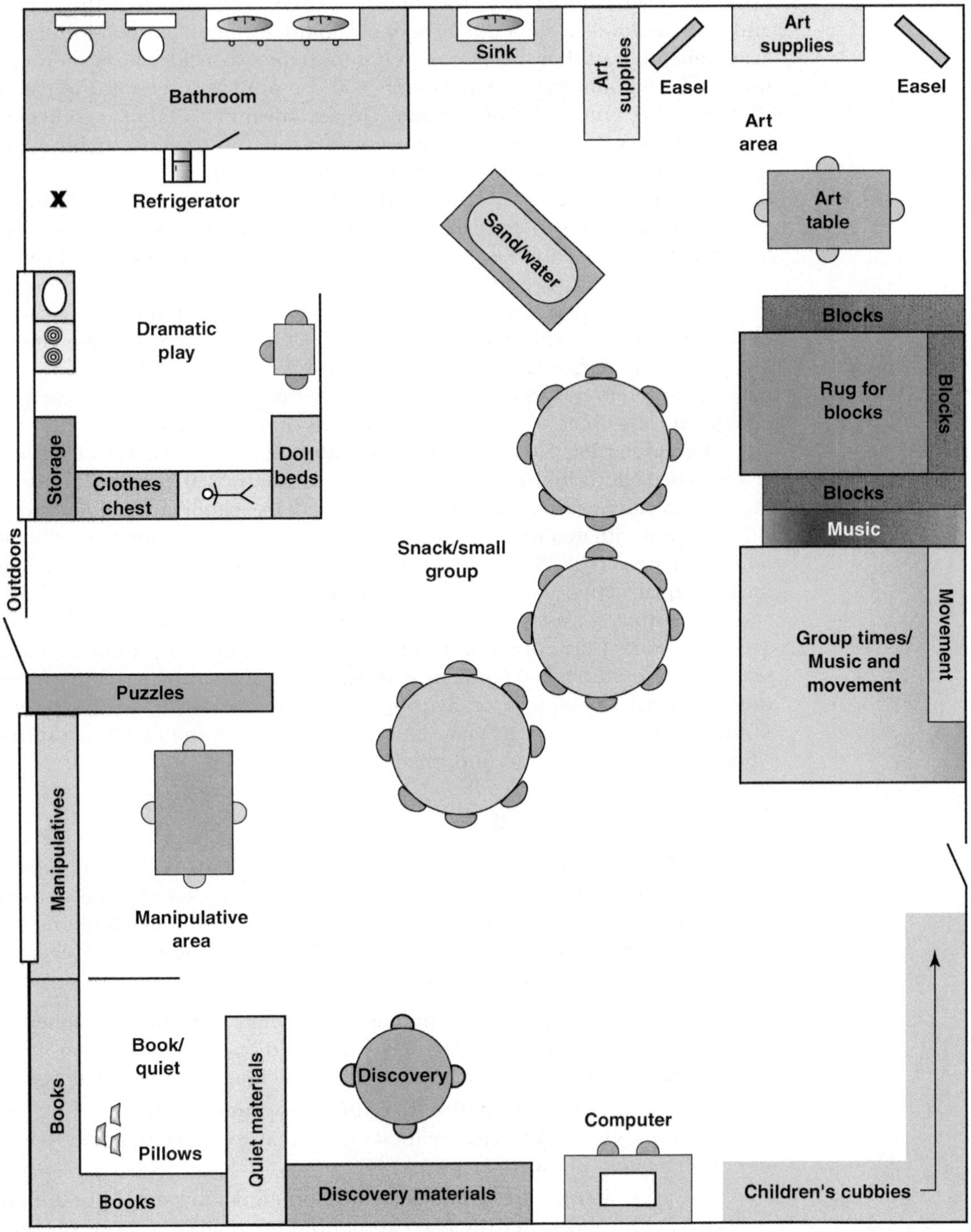

Bathroom

Sink

Art supplies

Easel

Art supplies

Easel

Art area

X

Refrigerator

Sand/water

Art table

Dramatic play

Blocks

Rug for blocks

Blocks

Storage

Clothes chest

Doll beds

Blocks

Music

Outdoors

Snack/small group

Group times/ Music and movement

Movement

Puzzles

Manipulatives

Manipulative area

Books

Book/ quiet

Quiet materials

Discovery

Computer

Pillows

Children's cubbies

Books

Discovery materials

Academic Issues

One very special consideration in planning kindergarten and primary classrooms is the importance of more traditional academic learning. Regardless of your feelings about its relative importance for young children, your success at the kindergarten and primary levels is dependent on your ability to show that children are making academic progress. For this reason, it is important to consider how you prepare and use your classroom space. The centers you use must be organized to clearly show their learning potential. You will need to demonstrate to families, other teachers, and administrators that what you are doing is not only good for children, but provides an exciting learning environment for them as well.

A quick look at most kindergarten- through third-grade classroom environments indicates that centers are not in widespread use. One or two areas at most may be available for free choice activities. Many teachers, administrators, and families with children at this level are yet to be convinced of the learning potential inherent in centers and playful experiences. Children, however, benefit significantly from these opportunities (Singer et al., 2006; Wasserman, 2000), and teachers at the kindergarten and primary levels need to slowly add centers to their classrooms. This process (which may take several years to complete) allows for careful preparation of each area and time to educate other adults about the benefits of centers and play.

A good starting point for including centers in a primary classroom is to provide activities that allow children to practice academic skills. Mathematics, library, and writing centers can be readily linked to the elementary school curriculum and will provide children with quality play experiences that extend their understanding in these important areas (Hill, Stremmel, & Fu, 2005). Center use can then be expanded to include equally important centers such as blocks, dramatic play, art, and music.

The primary classroom also needs spaces for cooperative learning and small-group activities. Clustering four to six desks together or using child-sized tables that seat four to six students is a practical arrangement for teachers who want their children to engage in frequent small-group work. With these small groups in the middle of the classroom, the centers can be on the periphery, and children can use them when not engaged in large- and small-group activities.

Areas and Centers

Figure 9–3 gives an example of a good indoor space for primary-age children. It combines some centers with more traditional work space for this age. If you choose to teach kindergarten or primary children, you might consider building the number of centers to this level after 3 to 5 years of teaching experience. Note, in particular, the following components of this indoor floor plan:

- The math/science area has a traditional academic focus and is designed for small groups to investigate/use the materials found on the shelves there. It is a good starting point for center activities in the kindergarten and primary classroom.

- The writing center is another traditional learning area that provides opportunities for children to engage in activities that you have planned for that area with student input.

- The art center has tremendous creative potential, but should be added to primary classrooms after the first two options are established and operating successfully. Kindergarten classrooms should have this option available at once.

Figure 9–3

Primary Classroom

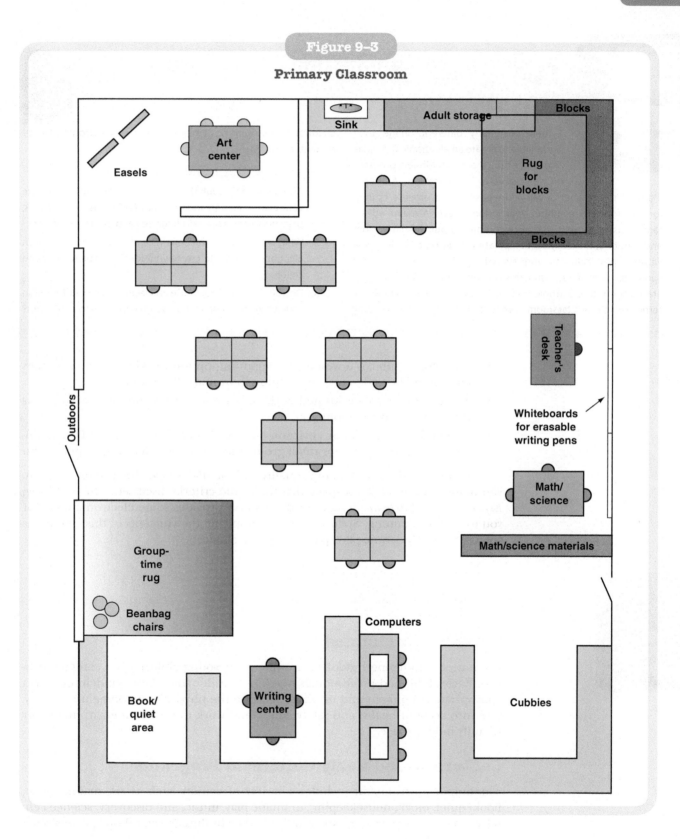

Technology Explorations and Activities . . .
PLANNING INDOOR SPACES FOR YOUNG CHILDREN

There are many different online tools available to create an electronic floor plan for your future early childhood program. One example is Classroom Architect. Many of the teacher-developed websites also provide options for electronically planning your indoor space. A major advantage of using these is that once you have input the dimensions and furniture, it is easy to manipulate the set-up of your spaces without physically moving everything. Using your desktop computer or a tablet, you can save considerable time and create a variety of electronic options for indoor spaces. Do an Internet search for Classroom Architect or simply search for early childhood classroom floor plans to find an electronic planner that interests you.

Research, Reflect, and Respond

1. After looking through the options and selecting one, create your own imaginary indoor space for infants and toddlers, preschool children, or kindergarten and primary students.

2. What do you see as the benefits and drawbacks of using an electronic planner to create your ideal floor plan for young children?

3. Do you think you would use an electronic planner to design your future indoor space for young children? Why or why not?

- The block center is a wonderful beginning option for kindergarten settings and should be added as a later option in primary classrooms.
- The computer area is located in the classroom, with a minimum of two seats for each available computer.
- The desks in this indoor environment are clustered in groups of four to encourage opportunities for small group and cooperative learning experiences.

Having read about creating quality indoor play spaces for young children, you might want to create a space that meets the criteria discussed. The *Technology Explorations and Activities* feature in this section provides some electronic tools for you to do this planning. Spend some time applying the concepts of this chapter as you create an electronic play space for young children.

Summary

Planning Guidelines

Planning a stimulating indoor environment for young children is a complex process. Early childhood professionals need to consider some basic guidelines, select appropriate equipment and materials, change the physical environment regularly, take into account health and safety issues, and work to create an environmentally friendly indoor space.

Centers-Based Early Childhood Programs

The indoor environment includes a variety of centers such as art, manipulative, book/quiet, block, housekeeping, dramatic play, music, and discovery/science center. Each of these areas must be carefully planned by the early childhood professional.

Infant/Toddler Environments

There are numerous developmental considerations when planning indoor spaces for infants and toddlers. These considerations create the need for elements such as a diaper changing area and cribs for napping that are not found in other early childhood settings.

Preschool Spaces

Preschool programs are typically organized into centers and often include areas for art, books/quiet activities, blocks, manipulatives, housekeeping, and dramatic play. They also regularly include sand/water play, music, and discovery centers.

Kindergarten and Primary Classrooms

Kindergarten and primary classrooms must be organized in ways that demonstrate the academic potential of each area. Classroom teachers should start with fewer centers as they begin their careers and slowly add academic and then more creative options for children to use.

for reflection and discussion

1. Do you believe it is important to have an environmentally friendly early childhood setting? Why or why not?

2. Choose an age of children within the early childhood range that is of interest to you. Write a few paragraphs about the centers and materials that you would consider important for this age group.

3. Plan an indoor environment for infants/toddlers, preschool age children, or the primary grades. Make the drawing to scale (such as ¼ inch equals one foot), and identify the number of children the space could accommodate and the number of square feet available per child. Identify the centers and other spaces in your plan. Share your plan with others and incorporate their feedback as appropriate.

MyEducationLab

Go to Topic 5: Program Models in the MyEducationLab (www.myeducationlab .com) for *Teaching Young Children* where you can:

- Find learning outcomes for Program Models along with the national standards that connect to these outcomes.

- Complete Assignments and Activities that can help you more deeply understand the chapter content.

- Apply and practice your understanding of the core teaching skills identified in the chapter with the Building Teaching Skills and Dispositions learning units.

- Check your comprehension on the content covered in the chapter with the Study Plan. Here you will be able to take a chapter quiz, receive feedback on your answers, and then access Review, Practice, and Enrichment activities to enhance your understanding of chapter content.

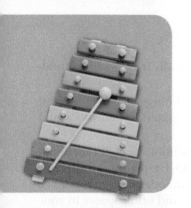

10

Planning The Physical Environment: Outdoors

IN THIS CHAPTER YOU WILL

- Gain knowledge of important planning guidelines for quality outdoor play spaces.

- Get ideas for creating a variety of outdoor play areas for young children.

- Develop an understanding of the elements needed for infant/toddler playgrounds.

- Address the components of quality preschool playgrounds.

- Study what is needed to create a developmentally appropriate playground for kindergarten and primary children.

Marika and Nikky are excited about spending some time outdoors today and are ready to get started. For several days, these eager third graders have been planning to do some gardening activities. The story about growing things and the visit from an expert gardener seem to have stimulated their interest. During project time over the past week, they have been formulating their plans. After reading portions of several books on gardening, they drew a map to scale of the portion of the garden area assigned to them and indicated the vegetables they will grow. Marika wrote a list of procedures for the planting and care of their vegetables, while Nikky gathered from her family all the seeds they will use and identified the proper planting depths for each. With shovels, trowels, row markers, and seeds in hand, they are ready to begin. It is exciting to see how children's interests can become the basis for playful learning opportunities in the outdoor setting.

Given opportunities to do so, most young children eagerly engage in creative experiences outdoors. The chance to explore the natural wonders found outside the indoor setting—combined with opportunities to run, jump, climb, and shout—makes this a valuable learning environment for children. Early childhood professionals need to be sensitive to the importance of this environment and plan for creative play experiences there.

Importance of Outdoor Play

Think about a favorite play experience you remember from your own childhood. What were you doing? Were you playing alone or with others? Were you indoors or outside? Many people find that they remember outdoor play experiences most fondly. In a study of college students' memories of their favorite play experiences, more than 75% were outdoor events (Henniger, 1993). What makes outdoor play experiences so memorable for many adults? There are a variety of possible explanations:

- **Sensory experiences.** Outdoor play provides children with many opportunities for sensory experiences. The sights, sounds, smells, and textures found outside are attractive to children and make that setting more interesting.

- **Greater sense of freedom.** The independence associated with the outdoors is another reason that many of us remember outdoor play experiences so vividly (Rivkin, 1995). Running, jumping, shouting, and getting involved in messy activities can be accomplished outdoors with little adult involvement.

- **Opportunities for risk taking.** Smith (1990) suggests that outdoor play encourages children of all ages to engage in behaviors that are more dangerous. This risk taking element is exciting and motivates many children to play. New, Mardell, and Robinson (2005) emphasize the few opportunities children have for risk taking and argue for allowing them more purposeful options.

In addition to children's interests in this setting, there are other reasons for promoting outdoor play. The National Association for the Education of Young Children emphasizes the importance of outdoor play as an integral part of developmentally appropriate practices for young children. Daily outdoor play experiences are considered essential for all children from birth through age 8. They provide opportunities to use large and small muscles, learn from materials outdoors, and experience the freedom only the outdoors can allow (Copple & Bredekamp, 2009; National Association for the Education of Young Children, 2005). The American Academy of Pediatrics, along with the American Public Health Association and the National Resource Center for Health and Safety in Child Care and Early Education (2010) also emphasize the importance of outdoor play for overall childhood health. They recommend at least two or three periods of outdoor play each day. The *Technology Explorations and Activities* feature describes a website that promotes the importance of, and activities for, outdoor play. Take some time to explore this website and reflect on the importance of outdoor activities for young children.

 Arturo and Cindy are swinging side by side on their preschool playground. As they move back and forth, Cindy talks of her new baby brother. Mandy joins them, and as they swing the children decide to pretend to be a mom, dad, and baby out for a picnic in the park.

Outdoor activities provide many opportunities for learning and development. A creative, well-planned playground can stimulate a wide variety of positive play experiences for young children (Sutterby & Thornton, 2005). Swings, slides, and wide-open spaces encourage sensorimotor play outdoors and provide opportunities for aerobic activities to strengthen young hearts and lungs. Vigorous physical activity is one important component of an early childhood program that promotes healthy living and helps children avoid obesity (Sutterby & Frost, 2002; Winter,

Technology Explorations and Activities...
LET'S MOVE OUTDOORS

In this chapter you have read about the value of outdoor play for young children. The U.S. Departments of the Interior (DOI) and Agriculture (USDA) are working together to encourage more families and children to get outside and enjoy. They, along with the National Association for Sport and Physical Education (2004) emphasize the importance of children spending at least 60 minutes each day in active and vigorous play to stay healthy. The DOI and USDA have created a website titled *Let's Move Outdoors* that contains many good ideas for where to go and what to do outdoors. Use your computer or tablet to do an Internet search for this website and review the information you find there.

Research, Reflect, and Respond

1. Search the Internet for other sites that encourage children and families to spend time outdoors in natural settings. Describe what you find, including the information on the *Let's Move Outdoors* site.

2. How will you encourage children and families to spend time outdoors? Share your thoughts with a small group.

3. Create a one-page letter to families describing some simple strategies they could use to encourage young children to spend more time outside.

2009). A sandbox with digging tools and accessories can stimulate creative construction activities, and children can use an old boat for a variety of sociodramatic play themes. In fact, every aspect of the child's development can be enhanced when adults develop quality outdoor play spaces. With careful planning and preparation of the playground, children can have rich and memorable experiences there.

Committing to the Outdoor Environment

Outdoor play areas should be an extension of the indoor environment. With proper equipment and planning, outdoor play can stimulate all aspects of children's development and provide a valuable opportunity for learning. If this perspective is to become a reality, adults working with young children must set aside much of their traditional thinking about playgrounds and begin viewing the outdoors differently. Although fixed equipment is useful, it should be considered secondary in importance to the movable options described throughout this chapter. Children learn best by physically manipulating the materials and equipment in their environment, and these options should be readily available to them outdoors.

This new way of thinking about play outdoors can be easily and inexpensively implemented. Early childhood professionals, with the help of families and community members, can either construct or purchase simple pieces of playground equipment and materials. Locating and using additional donated materials will encourage further creative play experiences. If you think creatively about what is available to children indoors and bring those materials or similar ones outdoors, they will add diversity to the outdoor play options. Finally, consider adding natural elements such as plants, gardens, and trees to the outdoor area so that young children can experience and grow in their appreciation of these important outdoor elements (Rosenow, 2008). When these steps are taken, children will have a play space outdoors that truly stimulates all aspects of their development and provides them with rich and varied playground experiences.

Family Partnerships . . .
ENCOURAGING OUTDOOR ACTIVITIES

A sad fact of life today for many young children is that they have few opportunities for outdoor play at home. One reason for this is the high level of television viewing, video game playing, and computer use by young children. Youngsters who used to run outside and play when they were bored are now plopping down in front of their favorite electronic device and spending much of their free time there. This problem is compounded by the fact that many well-meaning families are scheduling activities such as youth sports, music lessons, and dance classes to fill up the rest of a young child's waking hours. Despite the undisputed value of these and other activities, many young children simply have very little "free time" in which to get involved in outdoor play. Potential safety issues also make it difficult for many families to send their children outdoors for extended periods of unsupervised time. Finally, finding handy playmates for outdoor activities is another potential cause for the decrease in outdoor play.

Regardless of the reasons for the decline, families need to be strongly encouraged to provide their children with quality outdoor play experiences. One creative option would be to get families interested in organizing a "walking school bus" (Paquette, 2008). Basically, families volunteer to have a designated adult walk a pre-arranged route, stopping to pick up and deliver children to and from their homes each day. While this option won't work for all children, it can provide valuable exercise and outdoor time for children who live near the school. At a family meeting to discuss the walking school bus, you could talk about the benefits of outdoor activities and then work to recruit volunteers to get the project organized.

1. What are your thoughts on the importance of outdoor activities for young children? How would you convince families of its importance?

2. Is the idea of a walking school bus something you could get excited about? Why or why not? Are there other creative ideas for outdoor activities that you would suggest to families?

This rethinking of the outdoor space must also include a commitment to plan and facilitate play in this setting. Each week you must plan new and interesting play options outdoors, regularly organizing and changing this space. Already-busy caregivers and teachers must find the time to plan for creative outdoor play just as they do for indoor play. Likewise, adults must spend time outdoors with children, committing to the interactions needed to ensure that outdoor play experiences are facilitated much like indoor play.

A part of your commitment to play outdoors should include efforts to encourage families and children to spend more time outdoors. You will need to convince them of its importance and then provide practical ideas that make it easy and fun to be outside. The *Family Partnerships* feature in this section discusses this issue in more depth.

 Planning Guidelines

If outdoor play is to live up to its potential, you must commit time and energy to planning and preparing the space. Planning should occur weekly so that children experience new and exciting opportunities for play and learning outdoors. The outdoor play setting should be viewed as an extension of the indoor environment and must be an important part of the curriculum planning done by early childhood professionals (Esbensen, 1987).

Basic Considerations

Several considerations help make the outdoor play space a quality one for young children. These guidelines provide the basic ingredients children need for positive playground experiences:

- The playground should be located next to the indoor setting.
- Sand, water, and plant life are important parts of the natural world that should be included outdoors (Chalufour & Worth, 2006; Ogu & Schmidt, 2009).
- Playgrounds should provide at least 75 square feet of outdoor space for each child (National Association for the Education of Young Children, 2005).
- A balance of sunny and shady areas will help the play yard appeal to the greatest number of students.
- Large, grassy areas should be included for children's games and large muscle activities.
- A tall, sturdy fence helps children feel safe and secure in the outdoor setting.
- A covered area provides opportunities for play during very hot or rainy weather (Esbensen, 1987).
- Playgrounds should have areas that encourage group activities and private places for when children need time to themselves.

Fixed equipment. Playgrounds contain a variety of equipment and materials to stimulate children's play. The structures found most often on playgrounds today are pieces of fixed equipment such as swings, slides, and climbers (Frost, Brown, Thornton, & Sutterby, 2004). These larger pieces of equipment are designed to be permanent and immovable. They provide consistency in the outdoor environment and add important play opportunities for children. An ideal playground environment should include a variety of fixed equipment that children can use in creative ways. Swings, slides, climbers, a sandbox, dramatic play structures, and permanent storage facilities are all important pieces of fixed equipment needed for exciting outdoor play.

Swings provide children with many opportunities to practice coordinating large muscle movements as they pump vigorously with arms and legs. The exhilarating experience of moving back and forth on a swing as fresh air blows briskly over the child's face adds excitement and pleasure to this activity. When more than one swing is available, children will often gather at the swing set to talk and enjoy good friendships as they glide through the air. For other children, swinging can be an opportunity to separate themselves from the crowd and spend time thinking or regaining composure following a difficult experience elsewhere.

Slides and climbers are found on most playgrounds and provide many play opportunities for children.

Dottie has just reached the top of the largest climber on her elementary playground for the first time. She cannot wait to tell her older brother, who has been "bugging" his first-grade sister to "climb the mountain," about her accomplishment.

The challenge of moving step by step to the top of an imposing structure and then looking down at the rest of the world is an important one for the young child and can give a sense of power and accomplishment. Many modern playground structures provide children with several different ways to reach the top of the slide. This challenges children to try different approaches as they build confidence in their climbing abilities. Sliding itself provides other risk-taking opportunities and sensory experiences that are pleasurable for children.

The *sandbox* is another traditional piece of fixed equipment found on most playgrounds that adds important play options for children. In the sandbox, children spend many happy hours building, tearing down, and building again using simple child-sized tools and accessories such as spoons, scoops, and sifters (Baker, 1966). The joy of digging in the sand, mixing sand and water, and creating a child-sized world of hills and valleys or a pretend lunch of molded sand is often a richly rewarding experience for children. The sandbox tends to draw children together and encourages them to play near or with others in creative ways. It allows the shy child opportunities to engage in parallel play in preparation for more social activities in the future.

Fixed equipment for dramatic play is also valuable on the playground. Although not as commonly found on playgrounds for young children (Frost, et al., 2004), these dramatic play structures help stimulate the important types of play that can and should occur outdoors. Some options for fixed equipment include the following:

- **Playhouse.** A child-sized house structure stocked with small furniture is one example of a creative piece of equipment that is useful in stimulating dramatic play.
- **Old boat.** A smaller boat that has outlived its usefulness on the water can still be productively employed for dramatic play on the early childhood playground.
- **Small car.** The frame of a small car that has had the windows removed and all sharp edges sanded or covered can also provide children with many happy hours of dramatic play.

Another essential piece of fixed equipment is the *storage shed*, a lockable building at least 10 × 12 feet. If the outdoor environment is to reach its true potential, there must be some way of storing loose parts. Making the outdoor environment an extension of the indoor program requires storage spaces similar to those found indoors. It allows you to change the materials available to children so that the new items stimulate increased interest and involvement.

The following items can be effectively stored outdoors for children's use:

- Construction materials (large and small)
- Dramatic play props
- Sand toys and digging equipment
- Materials for children's games
- Wheeled toys
- Art materials

Movable equipment. Although the fixed playground equipment previously described provides many valuable options for children, movable materials are also needed. Remember how children learn during their early years. Hands-on manipulation of toys and equipment in their world provides young children with many opportunities for growth and development (Kamii & DeVries, 1978). When early childhood professionals plan for learning indoors, they create centers that are rich with materials children can manipulate. Similar opportunities for manipulating toys and equipment are needed outdoors so that children can learn from these experiences as well (Maxwell, Mitchell, & Evans, 2008).

> Gordy, Brianna, and Meghan are busily constructing a small fort from lightweight interlocking bricks. Having completed the walls, they are now debating what to use for a roof. They have two small pieces of plywood or some cardboard scraps available to them. All three children are excited about the play opportunities this new structure will bring to the playground. They have asked permission to keep the structure in place for several days so that they can enjoy it over an extended period of time.

Although most outdoor play areas for young children currently have limited numbers of play materials that can be manipulated, these options can and should be added. In addition to the tricycles, old tires, and sandboxes typically found on playgrounds, children can effectively use other materials such as child-sized cable spools, commercially produced outdoor blocks, and gardening tools. The *Developmentally Appropriate Practice* feature in this section describes another inexpensive and creative movable equipment option. As you read this feature, consider the possibilities of plastic rain gutters and how they might fit into your future plans as an educator.

The **Adventure Playgrounds** of Europe provide other examples of movable equipment that children can use effectively outdoors (Buck, 2009). A trained play leader guides children in their Adventure Playground experiences. They play with scrap lumber, bricks, tires, rope, hammers, nails, saws, a fire pit, and animals (for petting, feeding, and care). Through playful experiences in which they move, manipulate, and build, children gain valuable insights into the world around them. Many of the materials and equipment used on Adventure Playgrounds can be adapted for use outdoors in early childhood settings.

Developmentally Appropriate Practice...
PLAYING IN THE GUTTERS

Sue Dinwiddie (1993) suggests a simple and creative way to provide children with quality materials that they can move and manipulate outdoors. Adults introduced the children, ages 2½ to 5, in her preschool program to plastic rain gutters. After purchasing three 10-foot segments of gutter at the local lumberyard, Dinwiddie cut them into the following lengths with a hacksaw:

- Two 5-foot pieces
- Three pieces approximately 3½ feet in length
- One piece 7½ feet long, and the remaining piece 2½ feet long

Initially, the adults set the gutters up ahead of time so that they sloped down to the sandbox and the water table. They placed pitchers, pots, and buckets near the gutters for children to use. The children were then free to experiment with pouring sand and water down the gutters.

As you might expect, this activity attracted many children and held their interest for extended periods. They experimented with different slopes for the gutters and tried a creative assortment of materials such as balls and boats to send down the gutters. This inexpensive, durable option is an excellent example of movable equipment that young children can use productively.

Variety of play options. Traditional playgrounds were designed to stimulate physical/motor play (Frost & Wortham, 1988). Although this is an important goal, playgrounds can encourage a wide range of other play types. Research on children's play outdoors indicates that this environment, when properly prepared, can stimulate a wide assortment of play behaviors (Maxwell et al., 2008; Rivkin, 1990).

Play types that can be effectively promoted outdoors include the following:

- **Active physical/motor play.** With the emphasis on active lifestyles, it is important to encourage young children to engage in vigorous running, climbing, digging, and swinging activities that have been the traditional hallmark of outdoor play.

- **Solitary play.** Young children need many opportunities to get off by themselves for quiet reflection and play. This can be encouraged through the use of cardboard and wooden boxes (that children can crawl inside), barrels, and natural plantings that create a small space for individual children.

- **Construction play.** When you provide young children with a variety of building materials outdoors, they will engage in construction play (Maxwell et al., 2008).

- **Imaginative play.** Outdoor prop boxes containing dress-up materials, construction materials, and toys for dramatic play can be carried to the playground to stimulate imaginative play themes (Hanvey, 2010).

- **Games with rules.** Children who are developmentally ready for this play type can be given materials such as balls of various sizes and kinds so that they can engage in games with rules.

Including natural elements. Children today are often disconnected from much of the natural world (Rosenow, 2008). Safety concerns, more structured activities, and fewer open areas to explore mean that today's children have lost precious opportunities to see, touch, and enjoy the many wonders of nature. Louv (2005) describes this as *nature-deficit disorder* and believes it is a root cause of attention difficulties and the higher rates of physical and emotional illnesses in young children. It is, therefore, critical for early childhood professionals to take the time to add natural elements to the outdoor setting. Adding these elements can involve families and communities (Starbuck & Olthof, 2008), increase opportunities to develop a love of the natural world (Song, 2008), and help children develop an understanding of the need for environmental stewardship (Hoot & Szente, 2010). You can add natural elements in several ways:

- Grow flowers or vegetables in wooden planter boxes (Rosenow, 2008).

- Take seasonal field trips to nature centers in your local community that enhance opportunities to experience, and learn from, natural settings (Bailie, 2010).

- Put up bird feeders and then study the birds. Take a walk around the local neighborhood, looking for different bird populations (Russo, Colurciello, & Kelly, 2008).

- Plan and grow a garden with the help of families and community members (Starbuck & Olthof, 2008).

- Enlist the help of families and community members who have an interest in plants and trees to create interesting kid-friendly plantings for children to explore.

- Consider a pet, either indoors or out, for young children to care for and learn from (Meadan & Jegatheesan, 2010). You could also have families bring pets for shorter periods of time and enjoy them in the outdoor setting.

Selecting Equipment and Materials

Because outdoor play areas are often used by several different groups of children in the same school or child-care center, individuals are rarely able to make decisions on their own regarding new additions of equipment and materials. Adults need to make their preferences known to administrators so that positive changes can be made to benefit children using the playground. As opportunities arise for adding equipment and materials to the outdoor environment, early childhood professionals should consider several options. Commercial materials, donated items, and adult-made equipment all can enhance the play value of the outdoor setting.

Commercial equipment. Commercial equipment for outdoor gross motor play is readily available for early childhood settings. Many playground companies provide large permanent structures that cost from $4,000 to $20,000 or more. If you purchase all of your materials through commercial providers, the playground will be an expensive area to equip. When estimating costs for commercial structures, make sure to include the cost of the structure itself, installation costs (typically, 35% to 40% of the purchase price), and surfacing costs for the material placed under and around the equipment for safety purposes. In addition to the larger permanent play structures, commercial companies also sell some smaller movable equipment such as metal climbers, plastic interlocking panels, and tricycles.

Donated materials. Even if your budget for outdoor equipment is small, you should not let the expense of commercial options stop you from creating an exciting playground for children. Other free or inexpensive options exist. With some creative thinking, you can locate quality materials for outdoor play and have them donated to your program. Some commonly found materials that can be used effectively on the playground include old car and truck tires, boards, small cable spools (the kind that hardware stores use to hold chain and rope before sale), PVC pipe and connectors, and lumber for woodworking projects. Other larger items could include large tires from earth-moving equipment, wooden pallets used for storing materials in warehouses, an old parachute, and cargo netting from overseas shipping activities. Creative adults who get excited about the possibilities of outdoor play can undoubtedly come up with a much longer list than this. The key is to think imaginatively about the materials in your community that could be used by young children on the playground, and then get the community involved in providing them.

Adult-made equipment. Many of the materials that businesses and others donate to your early childhood program can be used to construct low-cost equipment that can serve the same purposes as the more expensive commercial playground structures. For example, a simple tire swing constructed from donated materials has just as much play potential as the more expensive options available through commercial companies (Marston, 1984). More complicated structures can be built with the assistance of knowledgeable professionals who create interesting outdoor play spaces for young children (KaBOOM, 2010). Movable equipment can also be constructed by interested family members and others with skills in metal and/or woodworking. Wooden boxes of different sizes, cleated boards to connect smaller pieces of equipment, a steering wheel mounted in a wooden box, and 55-gallon barrels with stands are a few examples of simple equipment that can be designed and built.

Planning for Change in the Outdoor Environment

 Kate Ortega is a committed, hard-working kindergarten teacher. She understands the importance of planning for creative play and takes time each week to change her centers indoors to stimulate student interest. Recently, she realized that the outdoor environment also required change. Kate now includes time to plan special materials and activities for use on the playground as well.

If we are to make the outdoor setting an integral part of the educational environment, we must plan and prepare the playground with the same care and concern that is used for the indoor setting. Adults must change outdoor material and equipment on a regular basis so that children approach playing outdoors with the same sense of excitement and joy as they do indoor explorations.

For example, when preparing for play in the manipulative center, early childhood professionals decide which new puzzles and manipulative materials to place on the shelves so that children can have new and interesting opportunities on a regular basis. Other items can then be put away until later in the year. This same planning process must occur for the outdoor setting as well. Providing outdoor prop boxes, adult-movable equipment, and child-movable materials that change regularly help create the newness and challenge that are so important to a quality playground.

Outdoor prop boxes. A prop box (also referred to as a *play crate*) is a collection of materials organized around a chosen theme to stimulate creative play. The selected props are typically put in a sturdy box that can be easily stored when not in use (Odoy & Foster, 1997). Prop box themes and materials are limited only by the imaginations and creativity of the adults doing the planning. Jelks and Dukes (1985) describe several prop boxes for the outdoor setting including options such as dress up, gardening, and science projects. Prop boxes can have important benefits when used on the playground:

- The additional props stimulate more dramatic and construction play outdoors (Maxwell et al., 2008).
- Prop boxes make it easy to add change to the outdoor setting.
- Social interactions, academic learning, and literacy skills can all be enhanced through the use of prop boxes (Hanvey, 2010).
- They are versatile and can be used effectively both indoors and outdoors.

Hatcher, Nicosia, and Pape (1994) make several suggestions for planning and constructing prop boxes that also apply to outdoor prop boxes. The box itself should be clearly labeled on the outside to help you locate the needed materials. A theme-related picture attached to the outside of the box can help stimulate children's thinking about the topic, just as pictures on the walls indoors give children ideas about play in early childhood centers. Inside the lid, an itemized list of props, and ideas for setup and use can be included. This can be particularly helpful when prop boxes are shared among several groups of children in larger programs. To aid in storage, all the props should fit in the box and all boxes should be of a uniform size and shape. Finally, making the prop boxes accessible to children and easy to move in and out of designated play areas will make it possible for children to determine their own themes and select the needed play materials. The *Developmentally*

Developmentally Appropriate Practice...
IDEAS FOR OUTDOOR PROP BOXES

As you think about prop boxes for the playground, you may want to consider several alternatives. First, many of the themes and materials you plan for indoor prop boxes can be productively used on the playground as well. In addition, the topics for prop boxes may well come from the children themselves. If they show an interest in pet grooming, for example, creating a prop box with that theme makes excellent sense. Finally, remember that the outdoor setting is particularly attractive for certain play themes. Since "real" camping experiences are outdoor activities, for example, having a camping prop box makes sense. With these thoughts in mind, here are some possible outdoor prop box themes and some basic materials that you may want to collect for each:

- **Post office.** This prop box could be used either indoors or on the playground. With paper, writing utensils, junk mail envelopes, and holiday stickers for stamps, children could write their own letters and then use a canvas bag to deliver their mail around the playground. Shoe boxes could be decorated for mailboxes, tricycles could serve as delivery vans, and the playhouse could be converted to a post office with the use of a few key signs.

- **Pet shop.** If children were to show an interest in caring for pets, you could collect several stuffed animal "pets" and then add some old hairbrushes, combs, sponges for "bathing," animal collars, leashes, a toy cash register, and paper money to create a pet shop at an outdoor table. A pet care book with photos would also help stimulate creative play with these materials.

- **Fishing.** For children who have experienced fishing trips or had stories about fishing read to them, a fishing prop box can provide hours of fun. A fishing pole can be made by attaching a string to a stick. A magnet on the end of string is then used to "catch" laminated fish with paper clips attached. A playground structure can be decorated like a boat and a pretend campfire can be set up with a frying pan to add further elements to the play.

- **Camping.** Make sure to read stories about camping experiences for those who have not been camping themselves, and then provide a piece of plastic or a small tarp to construct a tent-like structure outdoors. Some possibilities for this prop box include a canteen and compass for hikes, materials for a pretend campfire, cooking utensils, and some empty food containers.

- **Gas station.** A gas station sign attached to an outdoor table or on the side of a play structure (or building wall) near the tricycle path can be the start of a gas station area. From there you can add a cash register, paper money, sections of hose, and cleaning supplies to generate some creative play with existing tricycles that have suddenly been transformed by children into automobiles.

Appropriate Practice feature in this section provides more specific information about materials that can be collected and used in outdoor prop boxes.

Adult-movable equipment. When planning for indoor play, early childhood professionals consider the physical arrangement of the larger equipment and make periodic adjustments to ensure that children experience change and have interesting new play options on a regular basis. This same philosophy can be implemented on the playground as well; at least some of the materials and equipment should be moved on a regular basis by adults (Henniger, 1993). Rearranging these movable materials will increase the creative play potential outdoors. Some examples of this type include the following:

- **Sand table.** Moving the sand table to a new part of the outdoor play area may encourage children to use it in different ways. Emptying the sand and replacing it with water adds other elements of change to the outdoor setting.

Children need opportunities to manipulate play materials outdoors.

- **Lightweight modular climbing equipment.** Smaller climbing equipment made from aluminum or other lightweight materials can be rearranged periodically to encourage new interest or stimulate different large muscle activities.

- **Woodworking table.** Making a woodworking table and related materials available at different times during the year will stimulate more construction play activities outdoors.

- **Movable wooden or plastic boxes.** Large wooden or plastic boxes that are 2 to 4 feet on a side can be moved to new locations on the playground periodically and rearranged into interesting patterns.

Child-movable equipment. In addition to larger, adult-movable equipment, it is important to have smaller pieces that children can manipulate. Commercial options are available through various providers. Outdoor blocks, larger building sets (often plastic for durability and weather resistance), tricycles, and wheeled toys are examples of these materials. Children also can move and manipulate donated materials such as small cable spools, used tires, and cardboard boxes. For example, when tires are available on the playground, children can use them to roll, sit in, or wash. Tires can also be used as props in pretend play themes.

By moving equipment themselves, children gain important understandings of their world and see themselves as more competent and capable. Children begin to feel in charge of this environment, just as they do when they manipulate materials indoors. This sense of power and accomplishment is very important in the child's development and must be encouraged as much as possible in early childhood settings.

Health and Safety Considerations

The elementary school nurse has been working overtime to patch up children's scrapes and bruises from playing outdoors. A kindergarten girl fell and scraped the palms of both hands on the asphalt. Another child cut her head on a metal brace while running under the slide. A third-grade boy sprained his ankle when he slipped and fell off the climber and landed on a log border around the structure.

Despite the many potential health and safety hazards found on most playgrounds, the preceding scenario does not occur regularly. Yet, if the outdoor setting is to meet its potential for stimulating creative play, it not only must be rich with materials and equipment but also must be constructed and maintained to protect children from unnecessary health and safety problems. Currently, many outdoor play spaces for young children could do much better in this area. Playground injuries and health-related problems are common. As adults become more aware of the issues, many of the following problems can be avoided.

Playground injuries. The federal government first became concerned about playground injuries in the mid-1970s. The Consumer Product Safety Commission (CPSC) coordinated studies of playground safety (Frost & Henniger, 1979) and found a variety of problems that needed correction. By far the biggest problem then and now is the surfacing under and around play equipment. Large numbers of children across the nation fall from playground equipment onto hard-packed surfaces and receive injuries that range from scrapes and bruises to concussions—and worse. In addition, equipment on many playgrounds is not appropriate to the developmental abilities of children. Injuries often result when children attempt to use slides, climbers, and swings designed for older children. Equipment design problems in which exposed bolts, sharp edges, and pinch/crush points cause unnecessary injuries are common. Early studies also found that placing pieces of equipment too close together causes injuries as children move around the playground.

Unfortunately, statistics indicate that playground injuries today are similar in number to those from the 1970s. The Consumer Product Safety Commission (2008) indicates that more than 150,000 children are treated in hospital emergency rooms each year for more significant injuries associated with playgrounds. Continued efforts clearly must be made to further reduce these preventable injuries on the playground. Table 10–1 provides information on how to reduce the most serious problem—falls onto hard surfaces.

Safety guidelines. Because of the just-described injuries, the CPSC developed a set of safety guidelines for equipment on playgrounds. These guidelines, which have gone through several revisions (Consumer Product Safety Commission, 2008), are designed to assist playground equipment manufacturers and concerned adults in

Table 10–1   Protecting against Falls

Shock-absorbing materials under and around play equipment help prevent injuries from falls. Typical options include wood chips, sand, and pea gravel. But how much is needed to protect against falls of different heights? The following statistics from the Consumer Product Safety Commission provide some initial guidelines. The commission's manual (1997) provides more specifics.

Material	Uncompressed depth of material
	*9 inches
Shredded/recycled rubber	10 feet
Wood chips	10 feet
Sand	4 feet
Pea gravel	5 feet

*Minimum recommended depth. Protects for falls up to this height.

Note: From *Public Playground Safety Handbook* by the Consumer Product Safety Commission, 2008, Washington, DC: Consumer Product Safety Commission.

creating outdoor environments that are safer places for children to play. Although these guidelines are voluntary, equipment manufacturers and others are strongly encouraged to follow them. To date, compliance has been mixed (Frost, Wortham, & Reifel, 2012). Equipment that is less than ideal in terms of safety is still being produced and used outdoors for children.

Health considerations. In addition to creating playgrounds that are free from unnecessary safety hazards, planners must consider health-related issues. One such potential problem is the use of toxic materials on the playground. Chemicals sprayed on plants and coatings on wood surfaces are two examples of problem areas. Poisonous plants are also more common than might be expected and should be excluded from outdoor play areas. Consult an expert in your area for specific information on plants to avoid. Another consideration is to provide regular maintenance of the playground. Picking up trash and litter will help prevent unwanted injuries and infections from these materials. Standing water can attract insects and disease agents and should be removed from the play yard. Sandbox areas should be covered when not in use to protect them from animal droppings. Regular cleaning of the sand can also protect children from potential health hazards.

The adult's role. Caregivers and teachers have important roles in ensuring a healthy and safe place for children to play outdoors. When actively involved in facilitating outdoor play, you can substantially reduce potential injuries and increase the quality of the experiences children have in that setting. The following list outlines some important considerations in creating a climate for quality outdoor play:

- *Allow plenty of time* for outdoor play. Thirty minutes or more are needed for creative play experiences.
- *Plan with children* for creative playground use. Talk to them about how the equipment can be used.
- *Take time to prepare the outdoors* for children. This will mean that more acceptable and new options will be available to children on a regular basis.
- *Let children know the acceptable and unacceptable behaviors outdoors.*
- *Periodically inspect equipment* for needed repairs and safety hazards.
- *Spend time interacting with children* in this setting.

 Outdoor Play Areas

Many early childhood professionals view the playground as an outdoor learning environment. These adults carefully organize the environment to provide children with the best possible play experiences. Just as the indoor space is divided into centers to encourage different play types, the playground can be organized into defined areas to stimulate creative play. Esbensen (1987) suggests organizing the outdoors into seven play zones: transition zone, manipulative/creative zone, projective/fantasy zone, focal/social zone, social/dramatic zone, physical zone, and natural element zone. The playground areas identified next are modifications of the play zones defined by Esbensen.

Transition Area

Shawna has just walked out the door and is slowly scanning the playground to see what others are doing. While others are already involved in play activities, she often needs time to think through her options and warm up to the idea of playing outdoors.

As children leave the relatively quiet indoor environment to engage in more active outdoor play, a transition area helps many children adjust. This area could include quieter activities such as painting and water play. If possible, the transition area should be covered, making it more usable in hot and cold weather conditions (Johnson, Christie, & Wardle, 2005) and have child-sized tables and chairs for sit-down activities.

Manipulative/Construction Area

Another important space in outdoor play settings for young children is the manipulative/construction area. Fine motor development can be enhanced by providing puzzles, small blocks, beads, and other manipulative materials typically found indoors. The addition of a woodworking bench and other building materials also encourage construction play in this area (Burlingame, 2005). Creative materials such as play dough, clay, and art activities can stimulate other important play experiences.

Storage is a necessity for this outdoor area to keep materials safe when they are not in use. A shed can be used for many of these items, or an already existing piece of outdoor equipment may have a handy corner that could be used as a storage nook. Another possibility is to store construction materials indoors and bring them outside in boxes or crates when needed.

Dramatic Play Area

Trentin and Tessa are excitedly playing commuter on the preschool playground. After filling their trikes with gas from the toy gas pump, they both motor over to the playhouse to end their busy workdays and play with their families.

While dramatic play occurs spontaneously on the playground, providing creative props will stimulate even higher levels of this important play type. Boys, in particular, seem to engage in more pretend play in this setting when quality materials are available (Maxwell et al., 2008). A permanent structure such as a playhouse can serve as a valuable gathering spot for the dramatic play area. If possible, this structure should also have storage space to accommodate the many props needed for creative dramatic play. Other structures, such as a small stripped car body or a steering wheel mounted in a wooden box, also encourage imaginative play experiences for young children.

Physical/motor play is important for all young children.

Physical Area

Large-muscle development can be encouraged outdoors in many ways. Mounds, hills, grassy areas, asphalt or concrete surfacing, and winding, figure-eight tricycle paths challenge children to use their large muscles in new and interesting ways. Tricycle paths should be a minimum width of 4 feet to allow children to pass each other as they meet. Open spaces for running, skipping, and simple games are useful. Climbers, slides, and swings all help develop physical skills as well (Sutterby & Thornton, 2005). This area should allow risk taking by children and should challenge them with a variety of options and levels as they mature physically. This area should be separated from the quieter activities found elsewhere.

Sand/Water Play Area

The sandbox has been a traditional and important part of early childhood playgrounds. From Margaret McMillan's Open-Air Nursery (Braun & Edwards, 1972)

Developmentally Appropriate Practice . . .
SAND AND WATER PLAY

Sand and water are two natural materials that young children are attracted to and thoroughly enjoy. They should be made available for play in both the indoor and outdoor settings. Yet, in order for children to fully explore and enjoy these elements, other props and tools should be provided to stimulate creative play. As with all areas in the indoor environment, these materials should be rotated regularly to increase interest and novelty. For ease of use, you may choose to store different collections of props and tools in separate baskets or storage bins so that you can pull them out quickly and easily. The following examples are intended to give you ideas about materials to collect for use with either sand or water:

Props	Tools
Miniature toy people	Tin cans of various sizes
Toy boats, cars, airplanes	Plastic cups, bowls, measuring cups
Toy animals, water creatures	Metal spoons and forks of various sizes
Plastic dolls	Hand shovels, trowels, rakes
Toy dump trucks, tractors	Plastic milk jugs
Sticks, branches, rocks	Funnels

Sand play is an enticing activity throughout the early childhood years.

in the nineteenth century to the present time, sandbox play has been encouraged outdoors. This area should be large enough to accommodate several children at the same time. A variety of digging, mixing, and pouring utensils enrich the play experiences children can have there. Other accessories such as toy trucks, boats, plastic animals, and human figures add to the creative play potential of the sandbox. A permanent cover for the sandbox helps protect it from animal use during non-play periods. Ideally, the sandbox should also be near a water source so that children can combine sand and water for messy but thoroughly enjoyable play experiences. The *Developmentally Appropriate Practice* feature in this section provides additional information about props and tools that help facilitate these important play options.

Natural Areas

After several weeks of spring rains, today is a beautiful, sunny day. Awesta and Chrissy are skipping joyfully across the open grassy area of the playground, laughing and talking along the way. The dew on newly budding leaves sparkles in the sunlight, while the fragrant aromas of spring fill the air.

Part of the wonder and joy experienced by children outdoors comes from the natural elements found there (Rivkin, 1995). The sights, smells, and textures of this environment are unique and exciting for children (Rosenow, 2008). To enhance this aspect of outdoor play, adults should provide a variety of trees, bushes, and plantings. Choosing flowering shrubs and trees for spring blooms, other trees for shade in the warmer seasons, and yet other plantings for vivid fall colors will help make the outdoor setting interesting all year. An assortment of natural materials also allows children to experience different textures, leaf sizes, colors, and smells throughout the growing season. Rather than a single, large grouping of natural plantings in one area, several smaller groupings of trees and plants throughout the play yard can add interest and beauty to this environment. Families and interested community members may assist in planning, planting, and caring for these natural elements. A garden/digging spot that is separate from the sandbox can also be included in the natural area (Starbuck & Olthof, 2008). Child-sized shovels, rakes, and gardening tools allow children to dig, plant, and care for an assortment of interesting plantings. Young children might enjoy growing a variety of flowers, fruits, and vegetables in a garden plot. Now that you have read about outdoor play options, take some time to actually observe an outdoor play area designed for young children. The *Observing Development* feature in this section provides guidelines for this observation.

Observing Development...
OUTDOOR PLAY OPTIONS

Choose one of the groups within early childhood (infants/toddlers, preschoolers, or kindergarten/primary children) and observe outdoor play options in that early childhood setting. Sketch the playground space, labeling all the fixed and movable options, looking specifically for options that do the following:

1. Stimulate physical activity.
2. Encourage dramatic play experiences.
3. Take advantage of natural elements and/or gardening spaces.
4. Provide areas for sand and water play.
5. Lead to construction play.

Reflect and Apply

1. Review your sketch and any notes you have taken. Then discuss which materials and equipment are designed to stimulate each of the types of play described previously. What sorts of material and equipment described in this chapter did you *not* see in the outdoor setting?

2. Did you see materials and equipment that children or adults could move on the playground? What could be done to increase the amount of movable equipment and materials on the outdoor space you observed?

3. Reflect on the quality of the outdoor play space you observed when compared with the ideas presented in this chapter.

Infant/Toddler Environments

Just as indoor environments reflect the developmental abilities and interests of young children, playground planners must consider these same factors in their planning. An infant/toddler playground will look much different from a play space created with 4- and 5-year-old children in mind. Similarly, before children with special needs can engage in outdoor play, the playground planner must understand the children's physical conditions and must alter equipment and space to allow equitable access.

Developmental Considerations

You may be surprised to learn that outdoor time is important for children even at the infant/toddler stage. Recently, educators have begun to focus on outdoor play environments for infants and toddlers and have discovered that children this age find the outdoor setting richly rewarding (Lowman & Ruhmann, 1998). Because infants and toddlers learn a great deal through the use of their senses, the outdoors provides many new opportunities for extending learning and encouraging early physical play (Honig, 2004; Parish & Rudisill, 2006).

Developmentally, infants and toddlers are growing daily in their locomotor skills. They perfect sitting, crawling, standing, and walking as they interact with people and objects in their environment. Socially, these very young children are becoming aware of others and beginning to interact with them. They are developing language and intellectual skills through playful exchanges with adults, other children, and playthings. Although indoor settings certainly enhance these developing abilities, the outdoors provides another rich opportunity for growth (Williams, 2008).

Areas and Equipment

Outdoor play environments for the infant and toddler should not be simply scaled-down versions of the complex play structures found on playgrounds for older children (Lowman & Ruhmann, 1998). Many simple additions can be made to the natural elements found outdoors for this age group. Small hills, ramps, low steps, and tunnels may all be useful in facilitating physical development. A pathway with different textures to walk on and touch is another creative option. Infants and toddlers often select push toys, riding toys, dolls, and toy vehicles that help stimulate creative play (Winter, 1985). Another simple option to stimulate creative play outdoors is to have children make their own equipment with some adult assistance (Schilling & McOmber, 2006). Examples of this type include paddles for balloon bouncing and ribbon sticks for creative movement. Finally, infants and toddlers also enjoy sand and water play. Because of the tendency of very young children to put everything in their mouths, an edible substitute for sand is usually needed for infants and young toddlers.

Figure 10–1 provides a sample design for an infant/toddler playground. As you review this design, look especially at the following:

- The *covered porch*, which allows young children to use the outdoor setting in both hot and rainy weather.
- The *ramp and grassy hill* designed to take advantage of the toddler's interest in learning to walk.
- The *adult seating*, to encourage caregivers to observe and participate in outdoor activities with young children.
- The separate *sand and water play areas* to encourage young children to use these important natural elements.
- The *tunnel* for crawling and climbing experiences.
- The *trees and plants* that bring nature into the outdoor play area.

 Preschool Playgrounds

With increased physical, social, and intellectual skills, preschool children require outdoor play spaces that provide greater challenge and more variety than those created for infants and toddlers. If you are planning an outdoor play space for the preschool years, factor in the extra time it will take to plan and rearrange the various areas you create for quality play experiences in this setting.

Planning Considerations

During the preschool years, children are developing greater social awareness and increasingly want to interact with their peers. Playground equipment for this age should help facilitate social skills by bringing children together for play experiences. While group size remains fairly small, be sure to have several places where groups of three to five children can gather to play.

Physical skills during the preschool years are also developing rapidly. Children need equipment that challenges their abilities in running and climbing, and in complex tasks like throwing a ball. Because young children are not getting

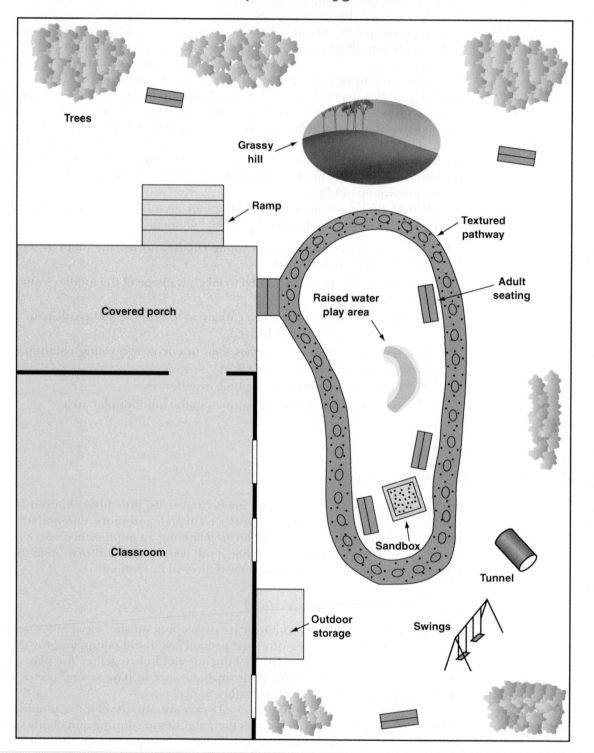

Figure 10-1

Infant/Toddler Playground

Trees

Grassy hill

Ramp

Textured pathway

Adult seating

Covered porch

Raised water play area

Classroom

Sandbox

Tunnel

Outdoor storage

Swings

Developmentally Appropriate Practice . . .
WOODWORKING OUTDOORS

While it is probably more common to have woodworking activities indoors, there are good reasons to conduct these important learning experiences on the playground. Hammering and sawing are both rather noisy and messy, so working outdoors makes good sense. In addition, playgrounds provide more space so that children are less likely to inadvertently injure themselves with a swing of a saw or hammer.

If finding storage space for a quality woodworking table is a problem, consider the following simple alternatives for outdoor woodworking activities:

- Find a large *cable spool* and use it as an outdoor woodworking bench that can be left out in the wind and rain. These durable wooden spools, available from your local telephone company, will survive several years of hard use outdoors.

- A *play crate* or *toolbox* can be used to store woodworking tools, wood, and safety goggles indoors when not in use.

- Smaller *tree stumps* create wonderful hammering experiences for young children and can be left outdoors without storage. When the stumps are filled with nails (use large-headed roofing nails approximately 1¼ inches long), use a chain saw to cut off the top portion and let the children begin again (Leithead, 1996).

- Use other materials for hammering and sawing. For example, children can easily manipulate larger *Styrofoam* chunks and use them much like wood for hammering and sawing. Another option would be heavy-duty *cardboard tubes* (one source for such tubes is your local newspaper for the center tubes that hold rolls of newsprint).

these experiences as frequently outside the preschool setting, it is essential that they be included as options in the outdoor environment (Sutterby & Thornton, 2005). In addition, 3- to 5-year-old children need a variety of equipment choices that encourage them to expand their skills to a new level. Fixed and movable equipment options that can be adjusted or that have varying levels of physical challenge built in are best suited for this age group. The *Developmentally Appropriate Practice* feature in this section describes another important consideration for the preschool playground. A woodworking table can be a very productive addition to the outdoor setting.

Preschool children engage actively in pretend play sequences. It is important to include a variety of materials outdoors that encourage dramatic play themes and stimulate this play behavior. Children this age can use fixed equipment, such as an old boat or car body, creatively. Smaller props such as dress-up clothes and theme-related toys can also promote dramatic play. Prop boxes can be stored indoors and used periodically for outdoor play.

Area Organization

Establishing a preschool playground requires effort on the part of the early childhood professional to provide a variety of creative options. Figure 10–2 shows a sample playground design for children 3 through 5 years of age. Take particular note of the following:

- The *covered patio,* used as a transition area, includes the woodworking table, a table for art activities, and manipulative materials brought from the indoor setting.
- The *storage area* for sand and water toys, wheeled toys, and gardening tools.

Figure 10–2

Preschool Playground Design

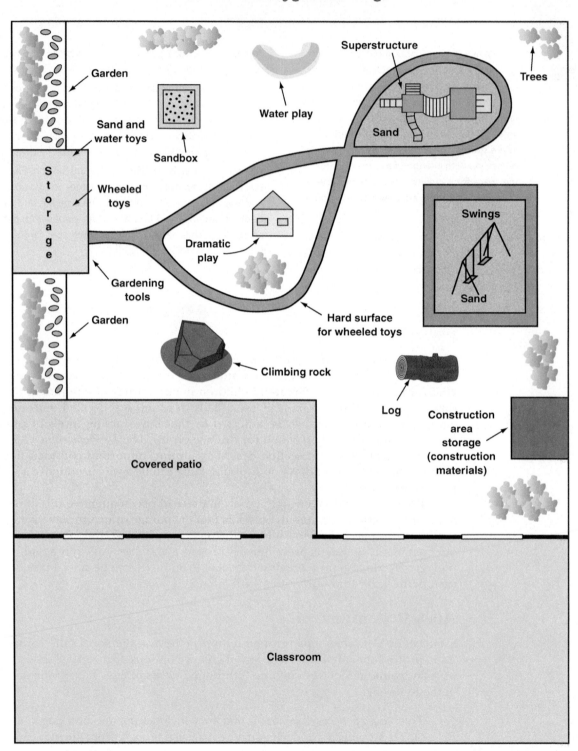

Garden

Sand and water toys

Wheeled toys

Gardening tools

Garden

S t o r a g e

Sandbox

Water play

Superstructure

Trees

Sand

Swings

Sand

Dramatic play

Hard surface for wheeled toys

Climbing rock

Log

Construction area storage (construction materials)

Covered patio

Classroom

- A *separate storage area* for larger construction materials used by children and for adult-movable equipment.
- The *gardening areas and natural elements* (climbing rock, log, trees, and plantings) added to the playground.
- A *complex, multifunctional superstructure* that includes steps, slides, suspended bridges, ramps, and climbers.
- The *sand* under and around the superstructure and swings to protect against injuries during falls.
- A *dramatic play structure* to encourage imaginative play outdoors.

Kindergarten and Primary Playgrounds

If they are to be successfully used, kindergarten and primary playgrounds need to be separate from those used by children in the upper elementary grades. The developmental abilities of children at this age, while higher than those at the preschool level, are much different from those of older children. In addition, because school playgrounds are often accessible after school hours, sturdy locking storage is a necessity if teachers plan to use any movable parts or equipment.

Primary children continue to benefit from quality outdoor experiences.

Issues Concerning Recess

If you are interested in teaching in the kindergarten or primary grades, you need to be aware of the growing trend toward fewer and fewer recess times for young children. Since the late 1980s, schools have cut back on recess so they can provide more time for academic instruction (Elkind, 2006; Jarrett & Waite-Stupiansky, 2009; Zygmunt-Fillwalk & Bilello, 2005). Statistics indicate that 20% of all schools in the United States have decreased recess time (Center on Education Policy, 2008), with 7% of first graders and 8% of third graders never having recess (Parsad, Lewis, & Greene, 2006). This comes at a time when evidence is mounting that decreased activity levels are a significant factor leading to higher obesity rates in children (Winter, 2009) and that increased physical activity levels can improve children's academic performance (Carlson, 2009; Shephard, 1997).

As indicated earlier, the outdoor setting is also an important place for children to engage in dramatic play. Although many primary-age children begin to show interest in other play activities, growing evidence indicates that children this age still need, and should be encouraged to engage in, dramatic play experiences (Singer, Golinkoff, & Hirsh-Pasek, 2006; Smilansky & Shefatya, 1990). This is particularly true for children from low-income families where dramatic play skills may develop at later ages. The materials and equipment described previously for preschool dramatic play should also be available for the primary-age child.

Carla is an active second-grade child who loves to play jump-rope games and hopscotch and to create her own challenges while twirling on the bars during outdoor time. When some props for camping were made available, she also spent long periods of time engaged in dramatic play around this theme.

Finally, recess time is virtually the only time young children can engage in games with rules. Piaget suggests that primary children are transitioning into the stage of concrete operations. As this process takes place, children become more interested in, and more able to play, games with rules (Piaget, 1962). Teachers can effectively introduce traditional team games such as soccer, baseball, and basketball, especially if competition is minimized. With an emphasis on skill building and enjoyment of the game, many children can benefit from these more structured play events during recess times. More spontaneous games that have entertained children for generations can also be introduced to young children during the primary grades. Multicultural games from around the world can open up additional playful alternatives for children (Kirchner, 2000).

Celebrating Play...
THE SOCIAL VALUE OF RECESS

Until their time in kindergarten, most children have many opportunities for socializing with their peers in the early childhood setting. As they engage in play activities in various centers, children have time to talk to and interact with others. Beginning in kindergarten and continuing through the primary grades, however, the opportunities for extended socialization are often limited. Time on the playground is one of the few opportunities that many kindergarten and primary children have to interact with their peers. The following quotations are designed to get you thinking about the potential benefits of this outdoor time:

> Recess encourages all areas of children's development. As children interact, they use language and nonverbal communications: they make decisions and solve problems, and they deal with the emotional trials and tribulations of their interactions. (Pelligrini & Holmes, 2006)

> Recess is one of the few times during the school day when children are free to exhibit a wide range of social competencies—sharing, cooperation, negative and passive language—in the context that they see as meaningful. Only at recess does the playground become one of the few places where children can actually define and enforce meaningful social interaction during the day. (Pelligrini & Glickman, 1989)

If children are going to experience the previously described social values of recess, families and school boards will need to be convinced of its value. Jambor (1994) suggests several strategies for promoting recess time:

- Educate administrators by providing them with articles about the importance of recess.

- Help families and other teachers understand the importance of recess by describing the social and cognitive benefits.

- Provide in-class recesses to give students more time for play and socialization.

- Write letters and opinion pieces for the local newspaper, school board members, legislators, and others. Don't be afraid to speak out often for the importance of recess.

1. Read an article about the importance of recess, and list the benefits cited.

2. Watch children at play on an elementary playground. Describe the kinds of social interactions you observed. Do you think recess provides valuable opportunities for developing social skills?

The *Celebrating Play* feature in this section provides yet another reason for continuing to provide recess for kindergarten and primary children. Take some time now to read about the social value of recess.

Children with Special Needs

It is also important to include quality outdoor play experiences for children with special needs. Kindergarten and primary teachers need to prepare the outdoor environment to accommodate all children. Two basic considerations should be kept in mind. First, early childhood professionals must be aware that their involvement and assistance are essential when working with children with special needs. Although they can playfully engage in activities outdoors that stimulate their physical, intellectual, and social/emotional development, children with special needs often need more modeling, encouragement, and reinforcement. The adult should provide this helping hand to ensure that these children get the most out of their play situations.

Second, the child with special needs must be able to use the available equipment. For example, many playground surfaces create obstacles. Sand is a great shock-absorbing material under and around swings, but sand makes it very difficult for a child using a wheelchair to get close enough to use the swings. Similarly, fixed playground equipment without ramps are not accessible to students using wheelchairs and to others with physical disabilities. Depending on the nature of the child's special needs, other playground modifications may be necessary if we are to make the outdoor environment truly accessible to all children. The *Celebrating Diversity* feature in this section provides additional information to help you facilitate outdoor play for children with special needs.

Equipment and Its Organization

The outdoor space at this level may look a bit different from the outdoor space for preschool children. This is due to the addition of games with rules as an important play type for kindergarten and primary children and the more public nature of playgrounds in most settings. More open spaces and greater numbers of fixed pieces of equipment are typically found in these settings. While the need for movable equipment remains very high, most schools will need to be convinced of its importance. Figure 10–3 provides a sketch of a quality outdoor play space for kindergarten and primary children. Take particular note of the following:

- The *space for games with rules* (a hard surface of either concrete or asphalt).
- The *quiet area* created from natural plantings to make a space where children can get off by themselves (yet is easy to supervise).
- The *storage areas* for construction toys, balls, games, jump ropes, and quiet activities near the classroom.
- The *dramatic play structure* for children who want this opportunity on the playground.
- The *wheelchair accessible protective surfacing* under and around the superstructure.
- The *gardening and water options* available near the classroom.
- The *covered patio* for hot and rainy day activities.

Figure 10–3

Primary Playground

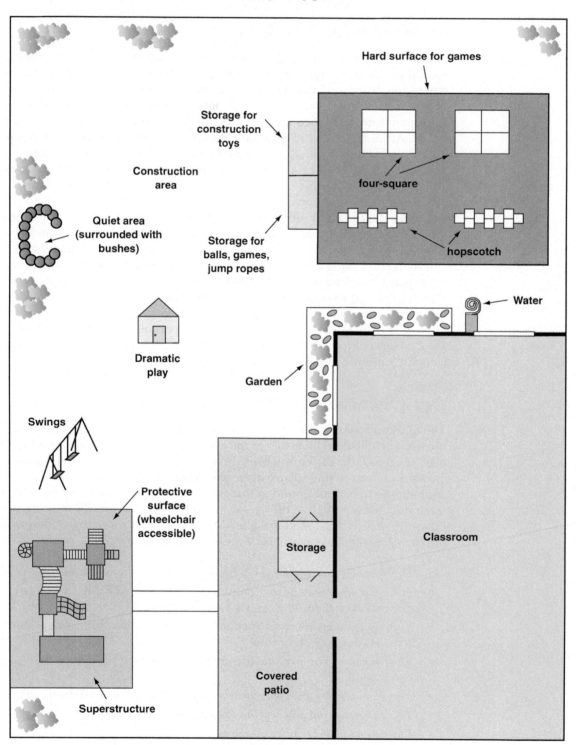

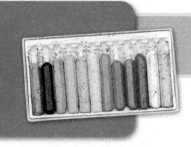

Celebrating Diversity . . .
ACCESSIBLE OUTDOOR PLAY FOR CHILDREN WITH SPECIAL NEEDS

All children, including those with special needs, benefit from playing outdoors (Schappet, Malkusak, & Bruya, 2003). An essential first step in facilitating their natural interests in this setting is to provide quality playground equipment and materials that are accessible to them (National Association for the Education of Young Children, 2005). The largest group of children typically excluded from using playground equipment are those using wheelchairs. Connecting all playground equipment with hard-surfaced pathways that are at least 5 feet wide allows movement between pieces of equipment. In addition, using absorbent materials that can hold wheelchairs under all equipment will ensure accessibility for children with special needs (Consumer Product Safety Commission, 2008). Wood mulch is the most common material used under and around equipment that meets federal guidelines for wheelchair accessibility.

Remember, however, that while it is essential that playground equipment be made accessible, it should not be done at the expense of other children who use the playground. For example, surfacing an entire playground with wood mulch meets the Americans with Disabilities Act guidelines for accessibility by wheelchair, but it takes away options for grass and other hard surfaces that are important for children as well.

The U.S. Access Board (2005) identifies more specific guidelines for playgrounds that are in compliance with the Americans with Disabilities Act. They include the following:

- **Ground-level play equipment.** One of each type (swings, slides, etc.) must be accessible.
- **Elevated structures.** Half of all elevated options (platforms, elevated forts, etc.) must be accessible.
- **Dramatic play equipment.** Structures such as playhouses can be made accessible by simply placing them on the edge of accessible pathways.
- **Water play, sandboxes, and garden areas.** These play options should be placed on the edge of playground pathways and raised so that wheelchairs can be moved under or next to them.

1. Take a look at a playground for young children. What did you see that would indicate accommodations for children with special needs? Share your findings with classmates.

2. What special safety issues might children with special needs face on the playground? How would you handle these safety concerns?

summary

Planning Guidelines

In addition to understanding general guidelines for planning quality playgrounds for young children, it is important to know about the value of fixed equipment, movable equipment, and the importance of having a variety of play options outdoors. Planning for change outdoors and thinking through health and safety issues are other important considerations when planning playgrounds for kindergarten and primary children.

Outdoor Play Areas

When planning the outdoor environment, it is important to include a transition area that helps children move from the indoor area outside, a manipulative/construction area, a dramatic play area, a place for physical activities, a sand and water play spot, and natural areas.

Infant/Toddler Environments

When planning outdoor areas for infants and toddlers, it is important to consider their developmental needs first. Outdoor spaces should include areas for adult seating, practice areas for walking and crawling, natural areas, sand and water play, and outdoor storage.

Preschool Playgrounds

Playgrounds for preschool children should be safe, yet challenging spaces where children can practice their growing physical skills, engage in dramatic play, spend time constructing, participate in gardening and enjoy the natural world, and provide areas for sand and water play.

Kindergarten and Primary Playgrounds

Teachers of kindergarten and primary children need to be aware of the growing trend to decrease the amount of time spent outdoors during recess, despite the many identified values of this activity. Planning should include areas for games with rules, dramatic play, quiet areas, a transition zone, and opportunities for children with special needs.

for reflection and discussion

1. How important is the idea of movable outdoor play equipment and what could you do to include these options in the early childhood setting of your choice?

2. Choose an age within the early childhood range. Write a few paragraphs about the gardening activities that you think would be appropriate for these children. Share your ideas with others.

3. Plan an outdoor environment for infants/toddlers, preschool children, or the primary grades. Make your drawing to scale (for example, ¼ inch equals one foot). Identify the square footage of the play space and the number of children the space could accommodate. Share your plan with others and incorporate their feedback as appropriate.

MyEducationLab

Go to Topic 5: Program Models in the MyEducationLab
(www.myeducationlab.com) for *Teaching Young Children*, where you can:

- Find learning outcomes for Program Models along with the national standards that connect to these outcomes.
- Complete Assignments and Activities that can help you more deeply understand the chapter content.
- Apply and practice your understanding of the core teaching skills identified in the chapter using the Building Teaching Skills and Dispositions learning units.
- Check your comprehension on the content covered in the chapter with the Study Plan. Here you will be able to take a chapter quiz, receive feedback on your answers, and then access Review, Practice, and Enrichment activities to enhance your understanding of chapter content.

11
Developmentally Appropriate Curriculum

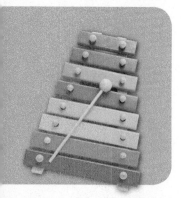

IN THIS CHAPTER YOU WILL

- Study the elements of developmentally appropriate curriculum.
- Learn about integrated curriculum.
- Identify observation strategies to use in early childhood settings.
- Understand the steps in developing activities and lessons for young children.
- Clarify the importance and types of assessment used in early childhood programs.

Mary Beth's mother just finished talking to you following the Open House. She is concerned about allowing children time for project learning in your second-grade classroom. The curriculum has so many required components that taking major blocks of time for child-selected, playful learning just doesn't seem right to her. This conversation is no surprise to you as the classroom teacher. Having recently modified your activities to provide a more developmentally appropriate curriculum, you expected this response from some of your families. The letter you sent home before the school year began emphasized this shift and encouraged families to come in to see the learning that was taking place. Although several did drop in, others still need to be convinced. Tonight's discussion on developmentally appropriate practice seemed to help others understand as well. However, time and more positive communications appear to be needed before this issue can be fully resolved.

When combined, all of the activities, experiences, and interactions available to children in early childhood settings makes up what is called the **curriculum**. In quality programs for young children, this curriculum is child-centered, adult-supported, and playful (Copple & Bredekamp, 2009). Often, this approach to teaching and learning will generate the kind of response just described. Families, other early childhood professionals, and administrators need to be convinced that a curriculum that includes freedom of choice, manipulation of real-world materials, and child-directed learning is appropriate for young children. This is particularly true at the primary level. When the more traditional curriculum is replaced with one that actively engages children in learning through hands-on manipulation of materials in their environment, adults who are unfamiliar with this approach need more information before they can accept it as valuable for young children.

Creating a Developmentally Appropriate Curriculum

The curriculum in early childhood settings is grounded in what the National Association for the Education of Young Children calls **developmentally appropriate practice (DAP)**. In DAP, "All teaching practices should be appropriate to children's age and developmental status, attuned to them as unique individuals, and responsive to the social and cultural contexts in which they live" (Copple & Bredekamp, 2009, p. xii). It is based on three important kinds of knowledge:

1. Knowledge of child development and learning
2. Understanding the unique developmental abilities and interests of individual children
3. Knowledge of the social and cultural settings of children and families

DAP has five interrelated dimensions (Copple & Bredekamp, 2009). They include the following:

1. **Creating a caring community of learners.** Developmentally appropriate practice views the creation of positive relationships among adults, children, and families as fundamental.
2. **Enhancing child development and learning.** A major responsibility of caregivers and teachers is to provide for healthy development and learning opportunities for all children.
3. **Planning curriculum to achieve important goals.** Taking into consideration the age and experience of the learners, social and cultural values, and family input, early childhood professionals are responsible for developing the content of the early childhood curriculum based on important learning goals.
4. **Assessing learning and development.** In developmentally appropriate programs, assessment is integrated into daily activities and provides valuable information for planning and implementing the curriculum.
5. **Establishing and maintaining strong family–school relationships.** DAP recognizes the importance of families and strives to develop and strengthen home–school relationships.

Due to the unique makeup of each child and the diverse mix of children found in every early childhood setting, it is not possible to simply pick up a teacher's guide and begin interacting in developmentally appropriate ways. The developmentally appropriate curriculum must be tailored to the needs and interests of the children involved. Although this is a more difficult approach, the end result is an early childhood setting in which active, excited learners grow to their full potential. Virtually any topic can be addressed in a developmentally appropriate curriculum. For example, the *Developmentally Appropriate Practice* feature in this section provides information on how tragedy can be effectively addressed with young children.

Bredekamp and Copple (1997) identify nine guidelines for a developmentally appropriate curriculum:

1. The curriculum provides for all aspects of the child's development (physical, social, emotional, and cognitive).
2. The curriculum for young children is intellectually interesting and meaningful to them.

Developmentally Appropriate Practice . . .
COPING WITH TRAGEDY THROUGH ART

Young children encounter tragedy in many different ways. World events like the September 11, 2001, World Trade Center disaster; wars; and famine are regularly viewed by young children on television programs. A death in the local community, a serious illness of a schoolmate, and the loss of a family member are other tragedies faced by young children. Early childhood professionals need to provide ways for children to process this difficult information. Gross and Clemens (2002) describe how 2- to 5-year-olds used their artwork to respond to the tragedy of September 11:

> On September 12, 2001, when five-year-old Joshua drew a picture of a hurricane, I asked him, "Tell me about your drawing." Joshua replied, "It's a hurricane." I wondered if his violent image arose from seeing frightening images on television, and I used a neutral question to let him say what was on his mind: Toni (adult): "What's happening in your hurricane?" Joshua: "It hurts people. It knocks down towers." (p. 44)
>
> A few minutes after my discussion with Joshua, four-year-olds Emma and Emily began a quarrel in the dramatic play area. I saw Emily crying. Toni (adult): "What's happening with you?" Emily: "I don't *want* to be the girl who is burning!" Toni: (turning to Emma) "Do *you* want to be the girl who is burning?" Emma: (drawing back) "No!" Toni: (noticing that both children look frightened) "Maybe this play is too scary. Maybe you'd like to paint this story?" (Emma went directly to the art center and painted what she was feeling; Emily took nearly two weeks before she could do so.) (p. 45)

In both instances, young children who were faced with a difficult tragedy expressed their feelings through artwork. For many children, this can be a useful tool in working through the conflicting feelings and difficult emotions surrounding a tragedy. Gross and Clemens (2002) suggest several steps you can take to help yourself and the children under your care deal with tragic events:

- Find people who can discuss with you (the adult) practical ideas for dealing with tragedy.
- Have children who have expressed an idea in one art medium share it again in other art forms. Taken together, these different pieces provide even greater validation of what the child is feeling.
- Make sure children have access to open-ended art materials daily, so they are accustomed to expressing themselves through art.
- Let children know that freely expressing themselves through their artwork is fully accepted by you as the adult. Foster relationships in the early childhood setting that encourage this same attitude among children.
- Use neutral language and open-ended questions that help children talk more deeply about the works they have created.

3. New knowledge is built upon already existing understandings and abilities.

4. Much of the time, traditional subject matter areas are integrated, rather than taught separately, to help children make more meaningful connections and develop richer concepts.

5. Although learning concepts and skills is important, the early childhood curriculum should also emphasize the development of problem-solving skills and an interest in lifelong learning.

6. An age-appropriate curriculum for early care and education has intellectual integrity. It challenges children to use the concepts and tools of the different disciplines.

7. While supporting the child's home culture and language, a quality curriculum also strengthens the ability to participate in the shared culture.

8. Goals for the curriculum are reasonable and attainable for most children.

9. Technology used in early childhood settings is physically and philosophically integrated into the curriculum. To see an example of how technology might be used in early childhood settings, read the *Technology Explorations and Activities* feature found in this section.

Developmentally appropriate curriculum for young children is created through a cyclical process consisting of three main elements:

- **Identify children's needs and interests.** Early childhood professionals use an understanding of child development and observations of children in their programs to determine their needs and interests. These are then used as the basis for curricular planning.
- **Plan the curriculum.** After organizing the indoor and outdoor physical spaces, early childhood professionals identify goals and objectives, plan activities and lessons, and develop a daily schedule of events.
- **Engage in assessment.** Standardized tests, developmental screening, observations, documentation, and portfolios are used by early childhood professionals to determine the effectiveness of planned activities and to identify future needs and interests of young children.

This curriculum implementation cycle is summarized in Figure 11–1 and discussed in more detail in the following sections.

Identify Children's Needs and Interests

Creating a developmentally appropriate curriculum begins with an understanding of children's needs and interests. Rather than planning activities based on what well-meaning adults think that children should know and be able to do, in a developmentally appropriate program the child's needs and interests come first. Early childhood professionals use two primary tools to identify these needs and interests: an understanding of child development, and observations of children in early childhood settings.

Technology Explorations and Activities . . .
READING IS FUNDAMENTAL (RIF) READING PLANET

The Internet is a wonderful place to find materials that can be used by children for quality learning experiences. As you plan for a developmentally appropriate curriculum, review the options available online.

For example, there are many good sites for electronic books that can either be read by the computer, or that children can read for themselves. Be sure to explore the Reading Is Fundamental (RIF) Reading Planet website. RIF is the oldest and largest nonprofit literacy organization in the United States. Their highest priority is meeting the literacy needs of young children from birth through age 8. Part of that effort is to provide electronic books and games that help children develop their literacy skills.

Research, Reflect, and Respond

1. Do an Internet search for Reading Is Fundamental and spend some time reviewing the materials available on this site. Pay particular attention to the Reading Planet portion of the website.

2. What are the strengths and limitations of the activities available there for use by young children?

3. As an early childhood professional, would you recommend this site to families? Why or why not? Would you use this site in your early childhood program?

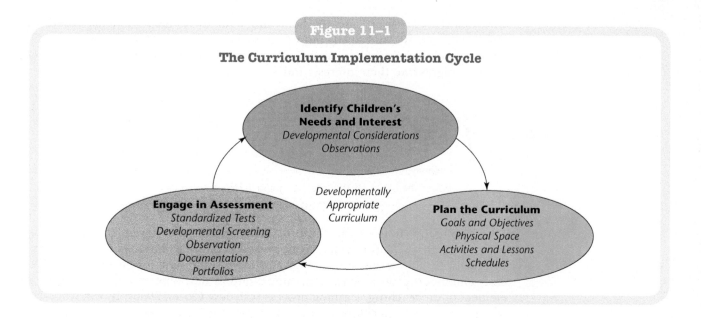

Figure 11–1

The Curriculum Implementation Cycle

Identify Children's Needs and Interest
Developmental Considerations
Observations

Developmentally Appropriate Curriculum

Plan the Curriculum
Goals and Objectives
Physical Space
Activities and Lessons
Schedules

Engage in Assessment
Standardized Tests
Developmental Screening
Observation
Documentation
Portfolios

Developmental considerations. Quality planning in early childhood settings requires an in-depth knowledge of all aspects of child development. These understandings are used to plan activities that build upon the young child's social, emotional, physical, linguistic, and intellectual abilities. Because of the developmental differences that exist across age groups, activities and lessons will vary markedly among infant/toddler, preschool, and primary settings.

Caregivers at the infant/toddler level need to know, for example, that children are learning a great deal through the use of their senses. The environment should be richly furnished with materials that engage the child's sight, touch, hearing, taste, and smell. Colorful crib hangings, pictures of human faces, mirrors, and cheerful room furnishings all help create an exciting visual environment. Similarly, toys that infants and toddlers can shake, drop, squeeze, and push are effective tactile stimulants. By actively exploring these and other sensory materials, children are learning a great deal about their ever-expanding world.

Although developmental considerations are different during the preschool years, they are equally important in curriculum planning. For example, an understanding of emotional development at this age should influence the selection of books read to children. Reading and discussing books like *William's Doll* (Zolotow, 1985) and *Girls Can Be Anything* (Klein, 1973), for example, should be helpful to children as they struggle with stereotypic expectations.

During the early elementary years, curriculum planning is strongly influenced by local school district and state guidelines. At the same time, however, teachers at this level must develop lessons and use materials that match the developmental abilities and interests of primary children. For example, children at this age are developing the basic physical skills needed for games like baseball and basketball. While many children show an interest in these activities, they often become frustrated with the competitive element. The creative adult can teach the physical skills needed while encouraging children to play noncompetitive versions of these sports. Through an understanding of both the physical and the emotional aspects of typical primary-age children, the teacher can successfully introduce modifications of traditional sports activities.

Observation. Caregivers and teachers who want to develop curricula based on childhood interests and needs must find effective strategies for identifying them. Observing children as they work and play provides adults with many opportunities to gain insights into their interests and needs.

 As Juanita and Sharena play in the dress-up area in their preschool program, they are talking about Sharena's mom, who is pregnant and expecting a new baby in a few months. After listening to their conversation for a few minutes, you realize that this issue is important to both these girls and several other children in the class. Raul has a new baby sister, and Maggie's mom just mentioned the other day that she was going in for a pregnancy test. Perhaps this topic could be part of the focus for the upcoming discussion on families.

Taking time to make these informal observations of children in your program is not easy. Preparing for each activity, assisting children who need your help, and working with both large and small groups leaves little time for anything else. Yet, early childhood professionals frequently mention that observation is an essential element of the teaching/learning process (Curtis & Carter, 2006). By carrying writing materials and checklists around throughout the day, you can also engage in more formal observation strategies and develop a much clearer understanding of children's needs and interests as they make future curriculum plans. It may also be useful to tape record or videotape children's activities to document more completely what is being observed.

Plan the Curriculum

Once children's needs and interests have been identified, the actual process of planning the curriculum can begin. This typically starts with identifying program goals and objectives and is followed by organizing the indoor and outdoor physical spaces, creating activities and lessons, and planning the daily schedule.

Goals and objectives. Creating a strong curriculum for young children requires a clear sense of what you are trying to accomplish. **Curriculum goals** are broad learning outcomes that identify the key results anticipated from the educational process. Goals are often created as part of a program-wide mission statement identifying its philosophy and values. **Objectives** are more specific and describe in detail what children are expected to know or do.

When identifying key goals for an early childhood curriculum, it is important to make sure they align (are consistent) with state and national standards (Gronlund, 2006). For example, before an early childhood program identifies its curriculum goals for mathematics, it should first understand the state standards for early mathematical learning and those of the National Council of Teachers of Mathematics (2000).

In a developmentally appropriate program for young children, the curriculum goals should include all aspects of child development. Following are examples of common expectations in programs for young children:

- Physical goals (2-year-olds)
  1. Scribble using large crayons or other similar art materials.
  2. Develop the ability to engage in running activities for short distances.

- Social goals (4-year-olds)
  1. Learn to control nonproductive impulses such as hitting and taking things without asking.
  2. Listen when others are speaking, take turns talking, and use other conventions of communication.
- Emotional goals (5-year-olds)
  1. Use words to describe and deal with feelings experienced.
  2. Develop a sense of competence at school-related tasks.
- Cognitive goals (8-year-olds)
  1. Use the scientific method to explore materials presented.
  2. Know and use the arithmetic operations of addition, subtraction, multiplication, and division.

Curriculum objectives identify specifically what you expect children to know and be able to do. Objectives are used when specific activities or lessons are planned. Like goals, objectives should be identified for all aspects of child development. An example of curriculum objectives for 5-year-olds on emotions could have the following objectives:

1. Children will correctly use the terms angry, sad, and happy in identifying emotions expressed in pictures.
2. Children will be able to verbalize a situation in which they were angry, sad, or happy.
3. Children will correctly describe a behavior that would make others angry, sad, or happy.

Physical space. An important element in curriculum planning for early educators is the preparation of the physical setting itself. Since young children learn best through the manipulation of real world materials, the toys and equipment provided in early learning settings need to change regularly to excite and interest them. Both the indoor and outdoor environments require careful initial preparation and continued planning and change if developmentally appropriate curriculum is to be developed.

Most indoor early learning settings are arranged into centers that require thoughtful planning on a regular basis. For example, a literacy center in a kindergarten program often contains a collection of books, tapes, and writing materials that children can use during center time. You will need to rotate books in and out of this center to maintain interest and to provide materials to supplement learning that has taken place in small and large group activities. Similarly, tapes and writing materials will need to be changed on a regular basis. Early childhood professionals typically change at least a portion of each center's materials weekly.

Outdoor environments also need careful planning and preparation so that the needs and interests of children

Preparing a visually appealing and texture-rich crib area is an important part of developmentally appropriate practice for infants.

are met. For example, the sandbox toys, water play materials, construction toys, and dramatic play prop boxes on a preschool playground are often changed weekly to promote continued interest and to stimulate quality play in that setting.

Activities and lessons. Once the physical environments are prepared, much remains to be done to develop specific events for each day. The early childhood professional begins by creating **long-term plans** to provide a sense of direction for several weeks or months, or even the entire school year. Because they are general plans, they provide a flexible framework for building a more specific curriculum as the year progresses. Weekly and daily **short-term plans**, based on children's interests and needs, identify the specific activities in which children will be engaging.

Adam, a 4-year-old child in your preschool program, has just shared his rock collection during show and tell. Children were attentive and asked him many good questions about his specimens. You have decided to add some books about rocks to the library next week and will ask Adam if he would be willing to have his rock collection available for observation at the science table.

After identifying children's interests, the adult must make decisions about procedures to be followed and the materials that will be needed. One strategy is to brainstorm possible pathways to investigate the topics selected. For example, an interest in the postal service by 7-year-olds could be studied in many different ways, including the following:

- Read written information about mail carriers and the postal service.
- Invite a postal employee into the program to talk about her work.
- Set up a post office center where children can create and send mail to one another.
- Visit a local post office to tour the facilities and see how mail is sorted and moved.
- Take a neighborhood walk to notice the different mailboxes that families use for their mail.

Once activities have been selected, you must plan times during the week when they can be implemented, organize the materials, schedule guests and field trips, and identify specific procedures for each activity. Experienced early childhood professionals do this by making relatively brief notes to themselves. When you begin your own planning, however, you may find that more detailed written plans for activities and lessons are necessary for their success.

As you plan activities and lessons for young children, also plan for the guidance strategies you will use to prevent problems. The *Developmentally Appropriate Practice* feature in this section describes some ideas you should consider.

Schedules. In addition to carefully planning lessons and activities for young children, it is important to think about how all these events fit together to form a daily schedule, like the one shown in Figure 11–2. You will need to consider several important issues as a schedule is created:

- **Length of the program day.** As the day lengthens, early childhood professionals must plan rest/nap times, snacks/meals, outdoor options, and playtimes to accommodate the longer time span.

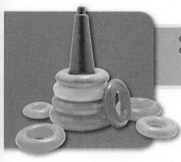

Developmentally Appropriate Practice . . .
PLANNING GUIDANCE STRATEGIES

Much of the guidance in the early childhood settings consists of preventing problems from occurring in the first place. This can be accomplished by planning ahead and defining potential problems. For example, a cooking activity can get out of hand quickly if you leave part way through the process to gather some forgotten ingredients or needed utensils. Sharp knives or tempting taste treats may be too much for children while you are away. So, as you plan for activities, take time to think about what you can do to prevent problems from occurring as children proceed through them. Consider the following:

- **Gather all needed materials.** As in the previous cooking example, having all the materials needed for planned activities together and ready to go can prevent many problems from occurring in the first place.
- **Consider space needs.** Some activities have specific space needs for safety and freedom of expression. For example, woodworking activities often involve hammers and saws, and cramped spaces can lead to inadvertent accidents when children move with these relatively dangerous tools. Another enjoyable activity for young children is movement to music with colorful scarves. To move freely and creatively, however, requires considerable space for each child.
- **Provide several popular toys.** When setting up a creative play center, include more than one of the same popular toy so there are fewer problems with sharing. For example, having two or three popular trucks in the block center makes it possible for several children to engage in similar play themes.
- **Think about potential conflicts.** Part of your planning should include thoughts about potential conflicts that might occur between children and ways in which these conflicts can be resolved. In the computer area, for example, several children might want to use a new software program at the same time. You could set a time limit and have a buzzer go off when time is up or set up two or three chairs at the computer so that several children can work together using the same software.
- **Plan for clean-up time.** Although many activities are exciting for young children, cleaning up the messes made can be less attractive. Cleaning up a creative fingerpaint activity, for example, could be facilitated by assigning different roles to children. Some could be responsible for hanging up wet paintings, others could put away paints, and a third group could be responsible for wiping the table clean.
- **Schedule time for transitions.** It takes time for children at all levels within the early childhood range to transition from one scheduled activity to the next. Children may need directions on where to go or what they need to take with them, or information about the things they will see or do. It will also take time to physically move from one activity to the next. Planning for these transition times helps make them smoother and less traumatic for children and adults.

- **Large blocks of time.** When implementing a play-oriented, theme-based curriculum, children need large blocks of time to engage in creative learning activities. Typically, 30- to 60-minute periods both indoors and outdoors make these quality experiences possible.
- **A balance of active/quiet times.** Schedule planning must also take into consideration the need to have periods of both high physical activity and calmer, quieter times. These should be mixed throughout the program day.
- **Meeting children's needs.** The physical needs of young children require scheduled times as well. You will need to include time for snacks and meals, toileting, and rest/nap/quiet times.
- **Smooth transitions.** Younger children often struggle with transitions. Planning consistent times during the day for transitions helps make these times less stressful. The schedule should include times for arrival, departure, and clean-up after play.

Figure 11–2

Figure 11–2

Daily Schedules

The sequence of events for an early childhood classroom varies from one room to the next, but a sample schedule for full day programs at both the prekindergarten primary level follow.

4-Year-Old Program		Second-Grade Classroom	
7:00 a.m	Arrival, breakfast, limited centers	8:45 a.m	Arrival, greetings
8:30 a.m	Opening group	9:00 a.m	Opening group time
8:45 a.m	Indoor centers	9:15 a.m	Center planning time
10:00 a.m	Toileting, snack	9:30 a.m	Learning centers
10:30 a.m	Outdoor time	10:30 a.m	Outdoor play
11:30 a.m	Lunch	11:00 a.m	Reading
Noon	Group time, story	11:45 a.m	Lunch/outdoors
12:30 p.m	Quiet time	12:30 p.m	Story time
2:00 p.m	Center time	1:00 p.m	Mathematics
3:00 p.m	Snack	1:45 p.m	Library/music/physical education
3:30 p.m	Physical education/ outdoors	2:30 p.m	Silent, sustaining reading
4:15 p.m	Limited centers	2:50 p.m	Closing group
5:00 p.m	Departure	3:15 p.m	Departure

- **Consistent sequence of events.** During the early childhood years, children are just beginning to understand time; therefore, beginning center activities each day at 9:15 is less important for this age than the fact that this experience follows group time. When activities follow a consistent sequence, children are more secure and content with the day. This de-emphasis on rigid starting and ending points for activities provides additional flexibility to the day and enhances learning.

Engage in Assessment

After you have planned the curriculum for young children, you will need to take one more important step to complete the developmentally appropriate curriculum cycle. You will need to use one or more of the many informal or formal assessment strategies available. When you use **assessment**, you are working to understand the impact of your activities and lessons on young children and making decisions about future directions for the curriculum.

There are two broad categories of assessment: formative and summative. **Formative assessment** is used throughout the curriculum implementation cycle to check the effectiveness of the lessons and activities, and to determine whether children are understanding. Generally more informal in nature, formative assessment gives early childhood professionals the feedback they need to modify activities as they go through a unit of study to meet the needs and interests of children. For example, a third-grade teacher listens carefully to children's conversations as they work with manipulatives in the math center during center time. In doing so, she is using formative assessment to determine whether the vocabulary terms that were introduced are being used correctly. If children are struggling with these terms, a class review may need to be added before continuing with other parts of the unit. **Summative assessment** is used at the end of a unit of study to provide evidence of what children know and are able to do. These assessment strategies may be more formal and are organized to promote record keeping. A preschool child's drawing and labeling of the parts of a plant, for example, could be a formative assessment used to document the learning that has taken place in studying plant growth.

Assessment is used to understand and improve the learning of all children. Therefore, assessments must take into consideration cultural, linguistic, and ability-level differences among children while addressing the needs of diverse families (National Association for the Education of Young Children & National Association of Early Childhood Specialists in State Departments of Education, 2003). Some examples of strategies used to assess young children include these:

1. Informal and formal observations
2. Taking time to talk to young children about what they are learning and what they want to know
3. Collecting and analyzing the products of childhood play and work
4. Recording through photographs, audio recordings, or video recordings of children's activities
5. Administering oral or written tests

The Integrated Curriculum

 Mariah and Jasmine are working intently at the kitchen table in Mariah's home. These second-grade children recently returned from the local community's Independence Day ceremonies. Intrigued by the concept of Independence Day, they researched the topic via the Internet and became fascinated with the clothing from the colonial period of American history. After making a list of interesting tidbits gleaned from websites, they are now busy sketching out some articles of clothing they hope to make for their dolls. With some adult assistance, this interest could become a long-term project with considerable learning potential. Language, mathematics, and social studies are just a few of the naturally occurring curriculum elements built into this experience. Mariah and Jasmine are engaging in an integrated learning experience at home.

An **integrated curriculum**, as described in the previous example, consists of learning experiences that include multiple subject matter areas as a natural part of the curriculum. Good integrated learning often includes mathematics, social studies, literacy learning, and more in a format that is of interest to young children.

The integrated curriculum is an essential component of developmentally appropriate practice (Copple & Bredekamp, 2009). As young children interact with

Hands-on manipulation of materials is an important part of an integrated curriculum.

the things and people in their world, they use a holistic approach to gain knowledge and understanding. When children play with blocks, for example, they don't focus on mathematical understandings or science principles or the social learning that is taking place. They are learning all these things and more as they build with the blocks and interact with other children and adults. Caregivers and teachers need to recognize that this is the child's natural way of knowing and plan an integrated curriculum.

Why Implement an Integrated Curriculum?

One important reason for using an integrated curriculum is evident from the preceding example: It is a natural way of learning that matches what children and adults do outside the early childhood setting. Krogh (1995) describes buying a car as an example of integrated adult learning in the real world. Reading ads and brochures, computing payments, investigating fuel efficiency and engine power, considering the car's aesthetic appeal, and negotiating with the salesperson require language, mathematics, science, art, and social studies learning. This is definitely an integrated (and complicated) real-world educational experience. Clearly, the lives of both children and adults are full of these naturally occurring integrated learning times.

Integrated learning makes the curriculum more relevant. Mathematics, for example, can be taught as a series of procedures and rote memorization tasks. Unfortunately, this approach fails to make mathematics meaningful and interesting to children. However, when adults demonstrate the usefulness of mathematics in real-life situations, such as computing the time it will take to save allowances to buy a pair of roller blades, children can see the relevance of their learning and get excited about mathematics. The *Celebrating Play* feature in this section provides additional strategies for developing an integrated mathematics curriculum. Similarly, reading has little value until these skills can be applied to written topics that are of interest to children.

The integrated curriculum also takes advantage of the child's natural way of learning (Isenberg & Quisenberry, 2010). That is, hands-on manipulation of materials is more likely in an integrated approach. Typically, this curriculum is organized around themes of interest to children. For example, a theme or unit on birds for a second-grade classroom could emphasize activities that include reading, mathematics, science, and social studies learning, all of which involve children in reading, talking about, and manipulating materials.

A quality program based on integrated learning also allows for more in-depth study of the themes chosen. Because all content areas are considered in the planning of thematic units, longer blocks of time can be spent engaging in these learning activities. Rather than breaking the afternoon into half-hour segments for the study of mathematics, reading, social studies, and science, a first-grade teacher could plan

Celebrating Play . . .
REINVENTING MATHEMATICS

Constance Kamii and Georgia DeClark (1985), a researcher and primary teacher, respectively, wrote *Young Children Reinvent Arithmetic*, a book describing the benefits of young children reinventing their mathematical understandings through real-world experiences. Based on the theories of Jean Piaget, this book presents a detailed account of children constructing arithmetic understanding through play. The authors developed a complete first-grade mathematics curriculum based entirely on group games and activities that focus on everyday events in the lives of children. Some examples of activities and games of this type include the following:

Voting

In DeClark's first-grade classroom, she strongly encouraged voting on many issues throughout the day. This allowed children to use arithmetic skills in meaningful ways. For example, children had a chance to vote on the number of times they needed to practice writing letters in their journals. One child suggested six times on each line, and a second child thought nine times was more appropriate. Children then voted on which option they preferred, with 20 preferring six times, and 5 wanting the nine repetitions.

On this occasion, after the votes were recorded, one child wanted to change his vote from nine repetitions to six. This allowed the class to discuss the results of adding one vote to the first column and removing one from the second. Meaningful mathematics was being practiced.

Group Games

Kamii and DeClark used some common card games to promote additional arithmetic practice in more fun ways for first-grade children. The card game War is one example. Children use a deck of cards and split them into equal piles (one for each child playing). Each child turns the top card up in her stack, and the child with the card having the highest value wins that set of cards. Tic-tac-toe is an example of a board game that DeClark encouraged as well. Although this activity does not build arithmetic skills, it helps children decenter (see things from another's perspective), which is important to growth in intellectual functioning.

1. What do you see as the strengths and limitations of reinventing mathematics or any other curriculum area through play?
2. Why is play critical to this approach to learning? What is the role of play in the reinvention process?

---

and present an exciting thematic unit on community helpers using a larger block of time. Children can use graphing skills, for example, to chart the number of fires in the community within the last year. Children read and discuss books on community helpers. A trip to the police station helps children learn more about their community. Letters of thanks to visiting community helpers provide writing experiences. This type of integrated learning experience gives children more time to develop deeper and more relevant understandings of the concepts being learned.

Planning and Preparation

At first glance, the planning needed for integrated learning may seem less complicated than what is needed for a more traditional approach. After all, it is a natural way of learning outside the early childhood setting, and little preparation is needed for those experiences. Why can't we just gather some good materials and then turn children loose with them and see what they come up with?

Unfortunately, planning an integrated curriculum is not that simple. This approach is definitely more complicated and demanding for the early childhood professional than a more traditional curriculum. More planning and preparation are required rather than less. For one thing, no how-to manuals clearly and specifically lay out a strong integrated curriculum for young children. Although good

This primary student demonstrates learning from a long-term thematic study of undersea life.

books that provide effective guidance for the planning process are available (see, e.g., Kostelnik, Soderman, & Whiren, 2011; Mitchell & David, 1992), they are, of necessity, general in their focus. Because integrated learning should be based on interests and abilities, themes selected and activities used will vary from one program to the next.

The starting point for planning an integrated curriculum is to select appropriate *themes*. The adult should base the choice of topics primarily on the needs and interests of children, which will vary from one group of children to the next. Children in coastal Alaska, for example, would probably be interested in the life cycle of salmon, whereas those in Arizona would be more likely to find a study of cacti relevant. Although childhood needs and interests are the most important factors in selecting themes, it is also important to consider your own interests. You will be spending large blocks of time and energy preparing the materials and activities needed for the themes chosen. If the topic is something you can get excited about as an adult, the children are much more likely to do the same. After selecting an appropriate theme, follow these planning steps:

- **Learn about the topic selected.** To do this, the adult becomes a learner and reads books and related written materials, explores field trip possibilities, talks to others who are more expert on the subject, and engages in some of the same activities that children may later explore. This process should be an exciting one—an opportunity to learn and grow as an adult while preparing for children's learning.

- **Find and organize materials related to the theme.** This is time-consuming but important in thematic planning. Because understanding during the early childhood years is best gained through hands-on manipulation of materials, finding objects that enhance learning about the chosen topics is essential. Books, puzzles, props for play, and pictures are all examples of materials that you can collect and use for specific themes. Resource books such as those by Mayesky (2002) are useful at this point in the planning process to help locate appropriate materials.

- **Reflect on what you want the children to learn.** This will bring focus to the thematic planning. What is it, specifically, that you want children to gain from the activities you are planning? Once this question has been answered, the activities themselves are more easily identified. At this point, spend some time identifying the relationships between this specific theme and the overarching goals and objectives for the school year. The objectives should clearly fit with your overall plan.

- **Identify open-ended questions to encourage inquiry.** Good questions can help children focus their energies on the most important aspects of the activities presented and encourage them to dig for deeper understandings of key concepts. The process of identifying appropriate questions can begin with the children themselves. Ask children what they already know about the upcoming theme. What do they need clarified? Are there questions they want answered? Obviously, younger children will need more assistance with this discussion, but beginning in the preschool years this planning step can provide much helpful information in developing the theme.

- **Plan activities and lessons related to the theme.** This usually starts with a process called *webbing*. Basically, webbing is a brainstorming technique that provides a visual overview of the content to be emphasized in a unit. The adult begins by writing the theme title in the middle of a page and drawing curriculum spokes for each area to be addressed. Typically, language, mathematics, science, art, music and movement, and social studies are each represented as a spoke. For each of these areas, then, the early childhood professional identifies as many activities as possible that address the separate curricular domains. Other early childhood professionals, resource books, and the Internet are all useful in adding items in this brainstorming effort. A major advantage of the webbing process is that it quickly identifies areas of the curriculum that are either overrepresented or underrepresented. At this point, it is easy to add or delete items to better balance the curriculum. After developing a written overview of the thematic unit, you will need to create lessons and activities using the planning strategies discussed earlier in this chapter.

- **Invite family participation.** Get families involved in the planning, preparation, and teaching of thematic activities. Collecting materials at home, helping organize a field trip, assisting in the early childhood setting, and making suggestions for activities and events are all tasks that families can do. Not only will their participation make your job easier, it will increase the likelihood that what is learned in the early childhood program will be reinforced at home. When families are involved in curriculum planning and teaching, children benefit.

- **Determine a closing event or activity.** Plan an event or activity that brings a positive ending to the unit of study. For the theme of pets, for example, you might hold a pet show as a closing event. Children and families could bring pictures, videos, and pet accessories to share with the rest of the class. In addition to being an enjoyable event, the closing activity allows children to summarize what they have learned and get ready to move on to the next theme. It brings closure to the unit activities.

- **Evaluate the theme and what children have learned.** This is the final step in planning for thematic learning and should actually be ongoing throughout the teaching and learning activities. You can collect children's written observations and samples of their work, and use them to assess the successes and areas for improvement in the unit. These materials can then be shared with families and others to document the child's growth through thematic teaching.

The Project Approach

As children learn about, and become interested in, the integrated curriculum themes, they engage in more in-depth investigations of components of the theme that are of particular interest to them. At some point, a theme may actually evolve into a project. A **project** is an in-depth investigation about a topic that incorporates children's questions, interests, and theories about that topic. It is a type of integrated learning in which children take on much of the responsibility for the directions for, and elements of, the work to be accomplished.

Over the last several years, many early childhood professionals have become interested in involving children in group projects. This trend has been strongly influenced by the impressive results of project work done by young children in prekindergarten programs in Reggio Emilia, Italy (Hendrick, 2004). Although this approach to teaching is not new, it is currently receiving considerable attention by many adults in early learning settings.

Typically, a small group of children in an early childhood setting embark on project learning when they discover they have a number of questions about a

Computers with Internet access provide a wealth of information for project work.

particular topic. The following situation is an example of how children become interested in a subject, which can then lead to an in-depth investigation:

> One day after a rainstorm, 5-year-old children noticed a large puddle in the schoolyard and asked to go outside to play. As they explored the puddle, stamping their boots, floating leaves, and making circles by casting pebbles, they noticed that their reflections were upside down. This discovery surprised them and led them to pose many questions and hypotheses. (Edwards & Springate, 1993, p. 9)

Edwards and Springate (1993) describe how adults took advantage of the interests of these children to create a project that led in many different directions. Children wondered what would happen if everything in the world was upside down. This concept was then discussed and explored. The rainy day also got children thinking about where water goes after the storm. They began a study of the underground areas of city streets. Each new insight led to further questions and new areas for investigation as the project continued to expand, grow, and change. At all times, the children's interests and questions provided direction for the project, while adults helped focus their efforts and suggested materials and activities to explore the issues raised.

Katz and Chard (1989) describe three phases of a project. Phase one is called *getting started* and is the time when children and the adult spend several discussion periods selecting and refining the topic to be investigated. Phase two, *field work*, is the direct study of the project selected and may include field trips, activities, careful observations, drawings, models of the concept being studied, and discussions of findings. The final phase, *culminating and debriefing events*, consists of concluding activities that help children summarize their new learning.

It should be clear from this discussion that project learning parallels the thematic approach described earlier. The major difference is that in project learning, the activities chosen and the new directions taken are not clearly defined before beginning the study but rather are based on questions children pose along the way. When caregivers and teachers implement integrated curricular themes, children often take those initial understandings and build on them as they engage in project learning. Adults continue to carefully guide projects through the materials and equipment they make available and the interactions they have with children (Edwards & Springate, 1993).

Observation in Early Childhood Settings

Observations are a time-honored component of early childhood education. Pestalozzi, Montessori, Piaget, and Gesell are just a few of the key historical figures in the field who have used informal and formal observations of children to better understand child development and behavior (Braun & Edwards, 1972). Model early childhood programs today, including High/Scope (Epstein, 2007), Montessori (Lillard, 1972), Bank Street (Mitchell & David, 1992), Waldorf (Edwards, 2002), and Reggio Emilia (Hendrick, 2004) all emphasize the importance of informal and formal observations. They are essential tools used by early childhood professionals in both planning and assessing the curriculum. The following paragraphs explain informal and formal observations, give reasons why early educators use observations, provide strategies for becoming an objective observer, and describe several useful observation strategies.

Informal and Formal Observations

There are two primary categories of observations. One is spontaneous, while the other tends to be more structured. **Informal observations** are when you take a moment or two between other activities to simply stop and listen, and to observe what children are saying or doing. **Formal observations**, on the other hand, are written and have more specific purposes. Both types have important roles in early childhood settings. An informal observation, which can occur at any time during the program day, is an opportunity to carefully and thoughtfully watch young children at play or work. While the observation itself may be spontaneous and appear casual, it is an important opportunity to see if the activities planned are meeting children's needs and helping them in their understanding of the world.

After reviewing the state science standards and being reminded that observation and scientific inquiry are important goals for her children, Kiana has created a science center in her second grade classroom and put several different plants there for children to observe and investigate. She has taken time to discuss observations and scientific inquiry in small groups and now wants to see if the children are using that knowledge effectively as they spend time in the center. Kiana takes a few minutes before her next literacy circle time to informally observe the group excitedly engaged in the science center.

Formal observations come in many different forms and are used for a variety of purposes. Many formal observations use a preprinted form that early childhood professionals carry with them through much of the program day. Although they require more time to prepare, formal observations give you helpful data on the effectiveness of your curriculum and its impact on child learning and development.

Awesta is concerned about Elvio, a new 4-year-old child in her preschool program. He has been very sullen and withdrawn through much of the first week. Awesta knows that Elvio has been enrolled in several programs in the past and that no detailed records exist about his behavior and development. She decides to spend 30 minutes observing during free play time this afternoon. Awesta has developed a simple form for making running record observations and plans to sit quietly and observe Elvio during this time. She will be recording as much of the words, interactions, and behaviors as she can so that she can develop a more complete understanding of this new student.

Uses for Observations

Early childhood professionals use observations throughout the program day to do the following:

1. **Build relationships.** During observations, early childhood professionals listen carefully and reflect on what individual children are doing. They develop better understandings of each child, which can then lead to stronger relationships (Jablon, Dombro, & Dichtelmiller, 2007).

2. **Document behaviors.** There are many times throughout the program day when you will want to make an accurate record of the behaviors engaged in by young children. How many times did 10-month-old Frieda need her diaper changed today? When did 3-year-old Jimarcus engage in appropriate social play this week? How well is 5-year-old Beth doing in pronouncing the "th" blend in her oral communications? You will want this data and much more to share with families and other professionals in your program.

3. **Identify progress and potential problems.** Observations provide opportunities to collect information on individual children and record the progress they are making in all aspects of their development. Social relationships, cognitive understandings, physical and emotional health, and linguistic abilities can all be observed as you go through the program day.

4. **Assess the curriculum.** Early childhood professionals need relatively quick and effective strategies to determine if the activities, lessons, and materials being used in the early childhood setting are meeting the needs and interests of young children. Observations, while not your only option, will be an important component of your curriculum assessment (Copple & Bredekamp, 2009).

Taking time to observe children as they work and play can pay big dividends.

Becoming an Objective Observer

While it may seem that observations are a simple matter of looking, listening, and recording what you see in the early childhood setting, making quality observations actually requires careful thought and practice. You will need practice in order to record all the important details that are needed for a useful observation. Equally challenging is making sure that your observations are objective and free from bias.

We all bring our own unique perspectives to the times when we observe children. One person, for example, might believe that a loud and boisterous first grader is simply being an active, busy, and fun-loving child while the next would see this as rude and inappropriate behavior for the school setting. All of our personal experiences shape who we are and give us a distinctive approach to observing young children. In some instances, our perspectives create a bias against individual children (Jablon et al., 2007).

To avoid this potential for bias, make sure that you record the behaviors and words used by children, rather than your interpretation of what those words and actions mean. If it is important to include your interpretations, make sure there is a clear distinction between what was actually observed and your interpretation of those observations. It might be something as simple as putting your interpretive comments in parentheses, rather than including them in the actual observation. Keeping complete and accurate records of what you observe also reduces the potential for bias.

Observation Strategies

In addition to the informal observations, there are several other observation strategies that you should learn to use now as you spend time in early childhood settings. They include the following:

1. **Anecdotal records.** These observations consist of brief written descriptions that capture the essential actions and activities of children in early childhood settings. They should include when the observation was made (date and time), who was observed, what the children were doing, and what was said. Despite the limited time available for making good observations, you should make every effort to provide as much detail as possible to clarify what was occurring. It is also important to separate what is actually seen and heard from your interpretation of events. One simple way to do this is to include insights in parentheses that go beyond the actual behaviors. Brief, specific notes should be made throughout the day to identify what children are learning. The *Observing Development* feature in this section uses an anecdotal record observation with

Observing Development...
ANECDOTAL RECORDS

Choose one of the age groups within early childhood (infants/toddlers, preschoolers, or primary-age children) and observe a young child, using an **anecdotal record**, for a minimum of 10 minutes. Use the sample observation below as a guide for your own observation.

Janeen, age 4, Lynwood Montessori Preschool, 1–1:30 p.m., May 23

1:00 J. is sitting on the floor with a small rug sample in front of her. She has taken a tray from the shelf of the daily living center. Removing the bowl with dried peas and placing it in front of her, she then places a second bowl and a spoon beside the first. J. slowly spoons the dried peas from one bowl to the next. When done, she begins the process again, spooning back and forth four times before giving a short sigh (appears contented) and placing. . . .

1. Before beginning your observation, head your paper with the date and time of the observation, approximate age of the child, and a pseudonym for the child.
2. Record as much of the behaviors and language of the child as you can.
3. Separate what you actually observe from your interpretations of the child's behaviors by putting interpretations in parentheses.

Reflect and Apply

1. After you have cleaned up your notes and rewritten the observation you have made, go back and reflect on your work. What difficulties did you have in doing an anecdotal record observation? Were you able to easily separate what you actually observed from your interpretation of the behaviors?

2. What do you see as the strengths of anecdotal record observations in early childhood settings? Will you plan to use them in your future program?

young children. Make an effort to use this important observation tool in an early childhood setting. Anecdotal records require considerable practice and thought to do well. A sample follows:

8/29/12, 9:30 a.m., Pat and Marcie (both age 3), Block Area. On the rug in the block area, Pat says: "Let's make a barn and pasture for our horses! Then we can play farm." (The class went on a field trip to a farm last week.) Marcie replies, "What about all the other animals? Where will the pigs and cows and chickens go?"

2. **Checklists.** A checklist consists of characteristics or behaviors that the adult marks off each time they are observed. For example, you might want to develop a checklist to record how many times certain children visit the art center and use specific materials provided there. This could help you determine when to change the materials available so that the environment will continue to stimulate creative expression for the targeted children. Figure 11–3 provides an example of a checklist for an infant/toddler program. Checklists can also be used to assess childhood behaviors. You could create a checklist to determine the number of times an individual child has an angry exchange with other children or with adults prior to planning intervention strategies for her.

3. **Rating scales.** Rating scales are similar to a checklist, but provide for adult interpretation of the targeted behavior. The adult observes a behavior of interest and uses her professional judgment to rate the quality of the behavior. The rating scale itself identifies different ratings of a particular behavior that the

---

Figure 11–3

Infant/Toddler Observation

Teachers and earegivers can develop checklist to record occurrences of nearly any type of child behavior. The following checklist could be used by infant/toddler care givers to assess **Oral Language Development**.

Child's Name *Meghan*   **Parent(s)** *Anita Smith*
Observer *Adrienne*   **Birth Date** *9/10/10*

Directions: Mark the appropriate category each time you observe one of the following verbalizations from the targeted child.

Oral Language Development

Vocalization	✓	✓	✓	✓	✓	✓			
Single-word utterance	✓	✓							
Two-word sentence	✓								
Three or more words									

Figure 11–4

Primary Rating Scale

Teachers and caregivers can develop simple rating scales to assess nearly any type of child behavior. The following rating scale could be used by primary teachers to assess performance during independent reading.

Independent Reading Assessment

Child's Name Ari_____   Date October 15____

Circle the number of the phrase that best describes the child's behavior during independent reading:

1. Refuses to read, disrupts others nearby.
2. Opens book and appears to read when teacher is near.
3. Reads with limited success when prompted by teacher.
4. Reads independently but needs assistance with difficult words.
5. Independently reads without teacher assistance.

adult can quickly circle. Figure 11–4 provides an example of a rating scale for primary independent reading.

4. **Running records.** A longer narrative story that describes a child, a group of children, or an activity over an extended period of time is called a running record. This observation method requires more time, energy, and skill to complete. The observer must accurately make notes that describe the child's actions, speech, and apparent feelings. When done well, however, the running record provides a more detailed and descriptive look at the behaviors of a particular child.

Planning Activities and Lessons

When you take the time to understand children's needs and interests, prepare the indoor and outdoor environments, and create a schedule for your program day, the process of planning activities and lessons then becomes an interesting and creative part of the curriculum planning process. The starting point for this step is to brainstorm possible ways to investigate the topics you and the children have selected. Once activities have been selected, you must then make written plans for these events. The next two sections of this chapter describe the creation of effective activity and lesson plans.

Activity Planning

 Ryan and Amy are building together in the block area of their kindergarten classroom. Following a recent field trip to a local dairy farm, the play during center time has focused on this theme. Amy and Ryan are no exception. They are busily constructing a fenced pasture and barn for their dairy herd. It is clear from the conversation that much has been learned from the field trip, and the play theme is allowing them both to consolidate their understandings of this topic.

Because play opportunities like those of Amy and Ryan are such an important part of the early childhood curriculum, planning for these experiences is a high priority. It should be clear, however, that because play is open-ended and child-directed, the activity plans themselves must take into consideration this important element. Flexibility is a key component of activity plans.

Early childhood professionals use many different formats for written activity plans, each of which has its own strengths and limitations. The essential elements include these:

- Purposes for the activity
- Materials and preparation needed
- Procedures to follow
- Variations that may be introduced
- An evaluation component

Figure 11–5 provides an example of a mathematics activity plan for a second-grade classroom. Initially, as you are learning about curriculum planning, developing

Figure 11–5

Mathematics Activity Second Grade

Purposes

1. Identify the geometric shapes of a square, triangle, and parallelogram.
2. Use the tangram shapes to build a pattern matching those on accompanying cards.

Materials and Preparation

1. Tangram puzzle pieces (three sets). Each set consists of seven geometric shapes that fit together to form a square.
2. Pattern cards.
3. Select pattern cards of varying difficulties to challenge ability levels of different children.

Procedures

1. Discuss tangrams at group time, describing how they can be used to create patterns illustrated on accompanying cards.
2. Place tangram sets and pattern cards in the mathematics center for children to use during choice time.
3. Observe the mathematics center for tangram use, assisting children as needed.

Possible Variations

1. Encourage interested students to create their own pattern cards that others can use with the tangram sets.
2. Consider having some children work in pairs to solve puzzle patterns. Joint problem solving may be an important confidence booster for some students.

Assessment Strategies

1. Observe students working with the tangram sets to see if they are enjoying the task and using effective problem-solving strategies as they work.
2. Discuss tangrams at group time to see if students use appropriate terminology for shapes and to determine if pattern cards are at an appropriate level of difficulty.

such detailed activity plans is necessary to ensure successful learning experiences for all children. Every piece of play material found in the early childhood setting should have a specific purpose, and the adult should clearly understand procedures for their use. However, with several centers and perhaps hundreds of options available to children, writing detailed plans for each experience is overwhelming for a full-time worker. Therefore, it is important to engage in these detailed planning steps now so you will be successful with the abbreviated written plans you will use in your future career.

Lesson Planning

 Group time is the next scheduled event for your 4-year-olds. Today, after singing two or three songs, a story is planned followed by a movement activity, a brief discussion of family similarities and differences, and more singing. This is a busy, but typical agenda.

To make group times like this one positive experiences, you must carefully plan what you will do and say and organize the events into an effective sequence. Lesson planning can help ensure the success of group times. Although similar to the previously described activity plans, lesson plans tend to be more structured in identifying procedures, questions, and comments. Although still flexible, lesson plans often focus more on specific learning and predetermined procedures. A typical lesson plan includes objectives, introduction, content, methods and procedure, closure, resources and materials, and evaluation. A sample plan for a preschool group time appears in Figure 11–6.

Assessment

As stated earlier, assessment is an essential dimension of developmentally appropriate practice. The National Association for the Education of Young Children and the National Association of Early Childhood Specialists in State Departments of Education (2003), in their joint position statement on curriculum, assessment, and program evaluation, state: "To assess young children's strengths, progress, and needs, [early childhood professionals must] use assessment methods that are developmentally appropriate, culturally and linguistically responsive, tied to children's daily activities, supported by professional development, inclusive of families and connected to specific, beneficial purposes" (p. 10).

To be effective, developmentally appropriate curriculum as described in this chapter needs to be assessed using techniques that are consistent with this joint position statement. Five assessment strategies used in developmentally appropriate early childhood settings are (a) standardized tests, (b) developmental screening, (c) observation, (d) documentation of children's work, and (e) portfolios. Each of these assessment strategies will be described in more detail later.

Standardized Assessments

Standardized assessments are carefully developed tests created by professional designers in an attempt to accurately measure a child's performance compared with other children or in relation to some standard or objective. When used properly,

Figure 11–6

Group-Time Lesson Plan for 4-Year-Olds

Objectives

1. Students will participate in songs, listen to the story and be involved in the movement activity.

2. Children will be able to identify the root system, stems and leaves in three drawings of plants.

Introduction

1. "I brought a special living thing from my home today to share with the class. It if hidden in this brown grocery bag. It sits on my window sill at home. I water it once a week. Can anyone guess what it is?"

2. After giving children an opportunity to guess the bag's contents, remove the plant, and discuss it roots, stems, and leaves.

3. "Today at group time, we are going to spend time talking about plants and how they grow. Let's begin by singing a new songs."

Content

1. Introduce a new song about flower gardens. Sing two familiar songs.

2. Read a story about plants.

3. Perform a movement activity to music.

4. Discuss plants.

5. Sing concluding songs.

Methods and Procedure

1. Sing "Flower Garden" from *Piggyback Songs* and one or two other student choices for songs.

2. Read *In the Garden* by Eugene Booth.

3. Play "Over in the Meadow" by Raffi (*Baby Beluga* tape), and have children move to the music.

4. Sing concluding songs chosen by children.

Closure

1. Put a plant and drawings of plants out in the science area for children to use during free play time.

2. Have been seeds, pots, and soil available outdoors for students interested in growing their own plants.

Resources and Materials

1. Plant from home, book audiotape, and plant drawings

2. Bean seeds, pots, and soil for planting activity.

Assessment Strategies

1. As children discuss plant components during group time, can they accurately identify them?

2. Do children spend time observing the plant and drawings placed in the science center? Do they use appropriate terminology in describing what they observe?

standardized assessments are an important component of early childhood assessment. Developmental screening instruments, discussed in the next section of this chapter, are examples of standardized assessments that can be used effectively with young children.

Many say, however, that standardized assessments are problematic for children of all ages. When used to measure academic progress, standardized assessments have been criticized for testing the wrong content and being biased against children from minority cultures (Kohn, 2000). The No Child Left Behind Act of 2001 has led to significant increases in the use of standardized tests in public schools and in early childhood settings to determine academic progress. For example, despite significant concerns on the part of many adults, standardized achievement tests have been used biannually in Head Start programs since 2003 (Meisels & Atkins-Burnett, 2005).

Standardized assessments have been criticized by many for discriminating against non-White children (see the *Celebrating Diversity* feature in this section) and for how the results of standardized tests are used. For example, the No Child Left Behind Act of 2001 mandates that all states test performance in reading and mathematics annually in third through eighth grade. Many states are using these test results to make critical "high-stakes" decisions about students, teachers, and schools:

> "High-stakes" tests are those directly linked to decisions regarding children's entry into a program or promotion or retention, that are used for evaluating or rewarding teachers or administrators, that affect the allocation of resources to programs, and that result in changes in the curriculum. (Meisels & Atkins-Burnett, 2005, p. 3)

But because child development is so variable, the results of standardized assessments often are an inaccurate measure of the true abilities of young children. Rather than relying solely on standardized measures, caregivers and teachers should use multiple assessment strategies to help them develop more accurate pictures of the abilities of the children they teach (Copple & Bredekamp, 2009).

Developmental Screening in Early Childhood

Developmental screening can be defined as a short standardized assessment administered by a trained adult to identify children who may have a disability or learning problem (Meisels & Atkins-Burnett, 2005). If a potential concern is identified, then further, more in-depth assessments by specialists are encouraged. For example, a developmental screening for vision problems could lead to a referral to an optometrist or ophthalmologist for a more comprehensive exam.

A commonly used developmental screening instrument is the Denver II (Frankenburg, Dodds, Archer, Shapiro, & Bresnick, 1992). Designed to be used with children from 2 weeks to 6 years of age, this assessment screens in four categories: personal/social, fine motor/adaptive, language, and gross motor development. The Denver II takes approximately 20 minutes to complete and can be administered by early childhood professionals, specialists, or trained volunteers.

The Role of Observation in Assessment

As mentioned earlier, observation is an important tool in determining children's needs and interests for curriculum planning. It is an equally valuable technique for assessment purposes. Because the physical space plays such an important role in early care and education, observing how children use their environment is an important part of evaluation. Do children avoid some areas or use other areas too often? Can children move easily from one center to the next? Which materials are children using? These questions need to be answered through careful observations of the environment. An observation instrument that assesses physical space is the

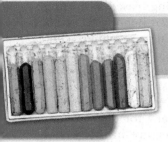

Celebrating Diversity . . .
CLOSING THE ACHIEVEMENT GAP

Throughout the history of American schooling, a troubling phenomenon has been the disparity in performance between many African-American and Hispanic children and their more privileged White peers. While the former score at the lower end of the performance scale, their White counterparts typically do considerably better. One indicator of this achievement gap comes from statistics published by the National Black Caucus of State Legislators (2001). They state that while 30 of every 100 White kindergartners continue their schooling through college, only 16 of every 100 Black children earn a college degree. While some progress has been made since the publication of this major report (Kober et al., 2010a, 2010b), much is yet to be done. There are many factors cited for this continuing gap. Following are three of the most significant factors:

- **Standardized tests.** Standardized tests have been criticized for many things, including the very real possibility that they discriminate against children from non-White cultures. Kohn (2000) states it this way: "For decades, critics have complained that many standardized tests are unfair because the questions require a set of knowledge and skills more likely to be possessed by children from a privileged background" (p. 46).
- **Low household income.** Children who are raised in a low-income family typically have fewer educational resources at home and poorer health care and nutrition. These children tend to have lower academic performance in schools (National Center for Education Statistics, 2010).
- **Underfunded inner-city schools.** Because a large proportion of minority students live in inner-city environments, they attend schools in their local community. These schools are typically underfunded and, consequently, children generally receive a poorer quality of education (Carey, 2003).

Regardless of the causes, professionals at all levels must commit time and energy to ensuring that all children have equitable opportunities to learn and grow. If we truly want "no child left behind," early childhood professionals, families, and communities must work together to meet the needs and interests of children from all cultures and socioeconomic backgrounds.

1. Have you had direct experience with children who have achieved at lower rates because of their ethnicity or socioeconomic status? What could have been done to assist them in being more successful?

2. Read one or more of the articles referenced in this feature. Based on this reading, are you willing to commit to meeting the educational needs of all children, regardless of ethnicity and socioeconomic status? What do you see as the challenges you will face with this commitment?

Early Childhood Environment Rating Scale (Harms, Clifford, & Cryer, 2005). It is designed to evaluate indoor preschool spaces. Similar instruments are available to assess infant/toddler (Harms, Cryer, & Clifford, 2003), family day care (Harms & Clifford, 2007), and school-age environments (Harms, Jacobs, & White, 1995).

An additional rationale for using observations of children in assessment is the emphasis on developing the whole child. Identifying physical skill development, listening to the oral language children use as they play, and studying social interactions are all examples of important evaluation strategies that you can implement. Observations are often the best way to assess these aspects of the child's development.

 Raylynn is a cheerful first grader who is having difficulty learning to read. She tries hard, seems interested in books, and comes from a home that emphasizes the importance of school. Yet, her progress is agonizingly slow and difficult. Some careful observation may be needed to help determine the problems she faces. After several observations in the book corner, the teacher has decided to refer Raylynn for a vision test. She seems to have difficulty seeing the printed letters and words clearly.

Early childhood settings have many children like Raylynn. They struggle with some aspect of learning or development, but the specific cause is not easily determined. Observations can again be useful in identifying the root problems and in helping you to choose effective strategies for intervention.

Documentation of Children's Learning

When caregivers and teachers collect artifacts such as children's artwork and writing, photographs, observations, and video/audiotapes of children engaged in work and play, they are providing **documentation** of childhood learning (Helm & Katz, 2010). This is an important form of assessment in early learning settings. Although documentation has been a part of early learning for many years, it has become more widely used due to the popularity of the Reggio Emilia program. Documentation of learning is central to their approach.

Documentation strategies should be based on the goals and objectives you have identified for the theme or project being addressed. The artifacts selected are typically displayed in some way in the program. For example, children's work can be collected and hung on a bulletin board or placed in a notebook that is then available in one of the centers. Documentation typically includes samples of the work done by *all of the children* engaged in the theme or project.

Some examples of documenting childhood learning include the following:

- **Recording children's discussions.** Videotapes or audiotapes of children's questions and comments on a theme or project provide clear evidence of their understandings. Consider recording these conversations at the beginning, middle, and end of the project so that you can document the growth children make.
- **Photographs of children's work.** Photographs can be used as a vivid portrait of the work children do throughout the course of a theme or project. The ease and minimal costs of digital photography make this option for documenting children's work even more attractive in the early childhood setting.
- **Samples of children's work.** Sketches, drawings, three-dimensional representations, and writings collected at the beginning, middle, and end of a theme or project provide further evidence of childhood learning. Displaying them prominently in the indoor setting provides opportunities for children, early childhood professionals, and families to discuss and reflect on the themes and projects addressed.

The Portfolio and Its Use

While documentation of childhood learning consists of a collection of artifacts from all the children engaged in thematic or project learning, **portfolios** are important assessment tools used to compile and organize information about *individual children* (Harris, 2009). The artifacts collected for portfolios are much like those previously mentioned for documenting learning, only now they provide evidence of individual childhood learnings. Although the use of portfolios in education is a relatively new assessment technique, the concept has been around for a long time. Artists and photographers, for example, have long used collections of their best work to demonstrate their abilities to others. DeFina (1992) presents seven assumptions about portfolios:

1. **They represent a systematic effort to collect meaningful works.** Selecting and updating the best materials for a portfolio require considerable planning and preparation by both the child and the adult.

2. **Children should be actively involved in selecting pieces to include in the portfolio.** Because children create many of the materials found in their portfolios, they need to be major participants in choosing items to include.

3. **Portfolios can contain materials from early childhood professionals, families, peers, and school administrators.** Including items from a variety of sources adds important dimensions to this assessment tool.

4. **Portfolios should reflect the actual daily learning activities of children.** Portfolios should measure what children have accomplished in day-to-day experiences.

5. **Portfolios demonstrate the child's progress over time.** Growth is best documented over a longer period. Ideally, portfolios should follow children from one year to the next. They are excellent tools for communicating with families, as discussed in the *Family Partnerships* feature found in this section.

6. **Portfolios may have subcomponents.** Some children may want to separate finished projects from works that are still in progress. Having sections for notes about items in the portfolio, activities in progress, and best works may help the organization of the portfolio.

7. **A variety of media can be used.** Written work, art projects, audiotapes, and videotapes are examples of the different media that may be found in portfolios.

Shores and Grace (1998) suggest a 10-step approach for developing portfolios:

1. **Establish a portfolio policy.** Before actually beginning to use portfolios, adults need to create a brief set of guidelines defining what will be saved and how these materials will be used.

2. **Collect work samples.** After deciding what materials will be saved, both you and the child should participate in collecting samples of work to place in the portfolio either temporarily or for the longer term.

3. **Take photographs.** An effective portfolio should include photographs of children's activities in the program. Photos document efforts that cannot easily be placed in the portfolio (a block construction or an outdoor play activity would be examples of this type).

4. **Conduct learning log conferences.** A learning log is written by you and the individual children and includes records of their plans and accomplishments. You will need to meet regularly with each child to talk over recent activities.

5. **Conduct interviews.** Interviews are extensions of learning log conferences that allow you to gain deeper insights into what individual children know and can do.

Family Partnerships...
SHARING PORTFOLIOS WITH FAMILIES

Harris (2009) makes a strong case for using portfolios as a communication tool with families. As a kindergarten teacher who uses portfolios for a number of purposes, she indicates that the top benefit of portfolio assessment is that it allows you to share actual evidence of child performances, rather than having to simply talk or write about them. At an open house for families at the beginning of the year, Harris explains portfolio assessment and how it is used to document each child's progress. She also offers to make them available for family review at any time during the school year. Harris then uses portfolios as evidence of childhood progress at each midyear and end-of-year conference. She typically includes the following in children's portfolios:

Work samples. Drawings, writing samples, photos of play activities, etc.

Observations. Written observations of children's activities throughout the day.

Checklists. Lists of behaviors observed over a period of time.

Rating scales. A regular assessment by the caregiver or teacher of specific traits.

Interviews. A short summary of answers children and families give to basic questions posed by the early childhood professional.

1. Imagine yourself as an early childhood professional in an infant/toddler program. Could you see yourself using portfolios with this age group? Why or why not?

2. What would be your biggest challenge in implementing a portfolio assessment system for your preferred early childhood setting?

6. **Make systematic records.** In this step, early childhood professionals use observations to collect data on specific issues concerning growth and development. For example, you may wish to know if a 4-year-old child can skip. You can observe the child on the playground for evidence of this ability.

7. **Make anecdotal records.** As part of the portfolio process, adults must also recognize important spontaneous events that occur in the early childhood setting and make brief, clear written records of these activities to include in the portfolio.

8. **Prepare narrative reports.** These reports can be viewed as being similar to a report card, summarizing an individual child's progress during a specified period of time.

9. **Conduct three-way portfolio conferences.** Children participate in these family–teacher conferences where the entire portfolio is reviewed to demonstrate progress in all aspects of development since the last reporting period. Many educators consider this process of reflection on past performance and future directions essential (Smith, 2000).

10. **Use portfolios in transitions.** As the child moves from one early childhood program to the next, a smaller representative sample of materials from the full portfolio should be passed along to the next early childhood professional. This pass-along portfolio can then be used for making initial curriculum and activity planning decisions for this child.

summary

Creating a Developmentally Appropriate Curriculum

Several general guidelines can help early childhood professionals begin the process of creating a developmentally appropriate curriculum. The implementation cycle for developmentally appropriate curriculum consists of three important steps. After identifying children's needs and interests, early childhood professionals plan the curriculum, and then engage in assessment.

The Integrated Curriculum

The integrated curriculum is a natural way of learning that makes the curriculum more relevant for children and allows for more in-depth study. Projects are a type of integrated curriculum in which topics of interest to children are studied in-depth.

Observation in Early Childhood Settings

Informal and formal observations are useful in building relationships, documenting behaviors, identifying progress and potential problems, and assessing the curriculum. It is important to be an objective observer as you use anecdotal records, checklists, rating scales, and running records in your work with young children.

Planning Activities and Lessons

Early childhood professionals plan for both activities and more formal lessons with young children. Activity plans are designed to be more open-ended and are particularly useful in getting ready for play-oriented events. Lesson plans are used in group settings that have more specific outcomes for children.

Assessment

Standardized assessments, developmental screening, observations of children, documenting childhood learning, and portfolio development for individual children are important assessment alternatives in early childhood settings.

for reflection and discussion

1. Discuss with an early childhood professional the concepts presented here on developmentally appropriate practice. What are the strengths and challenges of this approach? Share what you learn with others.
2. Assume a group of children you are working with gets very interested in butterflies. Outline a program project that builds on this interest and engages young children in an integrated curriculum. Share your project with others and incorporate their feedback as appropriate.

3. Discuss with others what you see as the challenges of making good observations in early childhood settings.

4. Using the format for activity planning described in this chapter, plan an art activity for young children and share your plan with others.

5. What do you see as the strengths and weaknesses of using standardized tests in early childhood settings?

MyEducationLab

Go to Topics 4: Observation/Assessment, 6: Curriculum Planning, and 8: DAP/Teaching Strategies in the MyEducationLab (www.myeducationlab .com) for *Teaching Young Children,* where you can:

- Find learning outcomes for Observation/Assessment, Curriculum Planning, and DAP/Teaching Strategies along with the national standards that connect to these outcomes.

- Complete Assignments and Activities that can help you more deeply understand the chapter content.

- Apply and practice your understanding of the core teaching skills identified in the chapter with the Building Teaching Skills and Dispositions learning units.

- Listen to experts from the field in Professional Perspectives.

- Check your comprehension on the content covered in the chapter with the Study Plan. Here you will be able to take a chapter quiz, receive feedback on your answers, and then access Review, Practice, and Enrichment activities to enhance your understanding of chapter content.

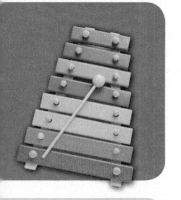

12

Health
and Wellness

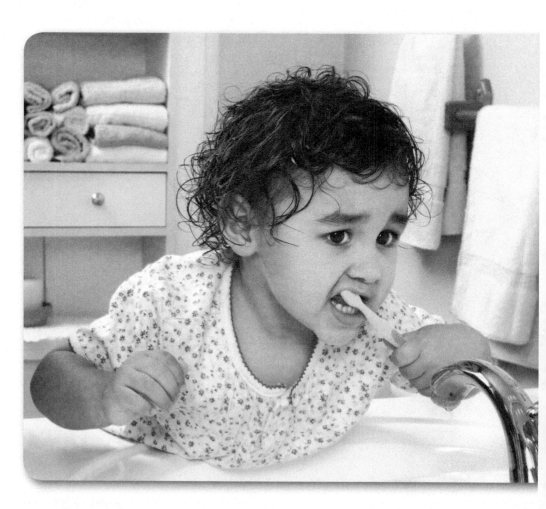

IN THIS CHAPTER YOU WILL

- Learn about the importance of health and wellness in early childhood settings.
- Study the role of physical education for young children.
- Investigate health education and its importance in early childhood programs.
- Gain insights into safety education for young children.

Friday afternoon, at last! It has been a busy, exciting week in your first-grade classroom. The cool, crisp weather of fall seems to be reflected in the children's active behaviors. As you sit down to plan for the coming week, you are reminded of the difficulties children had in staying on task this past week—too much sitting and listening for many of your students. To make the classroom day more manageable and enjoyable for children, you decide to add tasks that will lead to more active student involvement. This will include new physical development activities during the school day. Several ideas come to mind. Perhaps it is time to bring out the math manipulatives during center times. In addition to their usefulness in teaching mathematical concepts, the Cuisenaire Rods and Unifix cubes give children opportunities to develop fine motor skills. Another option is to provide art materials for times when children have finished other projects. The easel and art activity table will give students additional play options that also enhance small muscle development. Songs like "Head, Shoulders, Knees and Toes" can add some spice to your group-time activities. An obstacle course in the gym for bad weather days can supplement the outdoor play that is so important to the development of large muscle skills. It certainly makes a difference when plans for the next week are fun and include active participation on the part of children. Combining learning and physical activity makes good sense.

The health and wellness curriculum for young children has several important parts. As indicated in the previous scenario, one element should focus on children spending much of their day moving and doing so that they can learn about the world in their natural and preferred way. Integrated learning experiences that blend physical activity with academic and social experiences promote a developmentally appropriate curriculum for young children. In addition to promoting physical development, they also stimulate social, emotional, and cognitive learning.

But health and wellness experiences for young children should also include learning about healthy living and steps they can take to be safe. Children need to know that nutrition, physical activity, positive body image, medical and dental health, and preventing illness are all parts of healthy living. To make sure that young children are safe, early childhood professionals need to talk about such things as firearms, poisons, fire hazards, abuse and neglect, and what to do in case of an emergency.

This chapter begins by addressing the critical importance of health and wellness for young children. Additional sections will address the physical, health, and safety education curricula. As an early childhood professional, you will need to engage young children in developmentally appropriate experiences in each of these areas.

Importance of Health and Wellness

MyEducationLab

Visit the MyEducationLab for *Teaching Young Children* to enhance your understanding of chapter concepts with a personalized Study Plan. You'll also have the opportunity to hone your teaching skills through video- and case-based Assignments and Activities, IRIS Center Resources, and Building Teaching Skills and Disposition lessons.

As with virtually every aspect of development, the early years are a formative time for developing habits and knowledge that can become the basis for life-long health and wellness. For this reason, it is important for you to know all you can about the importance of health and wellness as you consider working in an early childhood setting. The following paragraphs will discuss the importance of physical health and safety education in early childhood settings. Internet resources can provide you with additional information and ideas for health and wellness. The *Technology Explorations and Activities* feature in this section provides some initial sites for your review.

Physical Education and Its Importance

During the first days of life, children begin using their bodies to learn about the world around them. Piaget (1950) suggests that sensory and motor experiences are the basis for all intellectual functioning for approximately the first 2 years of life.

Technology Explorations and Activities . . .
HEALTH AND WELLNESS SITES ON THE INTERNET

Several Internet sites have good information that can help you create a health and wellness curriculum for young children. KidsHealth and Healthy Habits for Life Sesame Workshop are two good examples. Do an Internet search for one or both of these sites and spend some time reviewing the contents that you find there. As you review the website, think about the ages of the young children you plan to work with and reflect on the value of this content for that group.

Research, Reflect, and Respond

1. What did you like about the content you found on the website you reviewed? Was there anything you saw that might not fit with what has been described in this book as developmentally appropriate practice?

2. How would you use the information you found on the website in your work either with children or with their families?

3. Was there anything that might be useful to you personally in your own health and wellness efforts?

Physical activity is a natural way for children throughout the early childhood years to enhance all aspects of their learning about the world:

- **Physical development and social skills.** Movement activities are especially well-suited to helping children develop social skills. Coordinating the movements of the group in parachute play, for example, allows children to create a dome overhead and to sit inside at the same time. Simple games like this for young children also require cooperation and positive social skills.

- **Motor skills and emotions.** Physical activity has long been viewed as a positive way to release the pent-up energy generated from strong emotions. For example, vigorous physical activity such as running outdoors is generally considered an acceptable way to get rid of angry feelings. More subtle, perhaps, is the use of art materials for emotional release. Children painting at the easel or molding with play dough or clay may well be playing out their feelings in a socially acceptable way.

- **Connections to cognitive development.** Physical competence is fundamental to cognitive development during early childhood. Montessori (1967) stated that, for learning to reach its full potential, it must be directly connected to physical movement for the young child. This *unity of mental and physical activity* is at the heart of the Montessori method of education. When the motor skill is directly related to the task being learned, children can understand concepts more completely and quickly.

- **Creating an integrated curriculum.** Physical activities provide wonderful opportunities for children to engage in an integrated curriculum. The *Developmentally Appropriate Practice* feature in this section gives an example of this type. Using play dough, young children are provided exciting opportunities to learn a variety of important concepts.

Developmentally Appropriate Practice . . .
INTEGRATING CURRICULUM WITH PLAY DOUGH

Play dough can be found in almost every early learning environment. It is highly attractive to young children and leads to many hours of creative play. But as Swartz (2005) emphasizes, there is much that children learn as they use play dough. In addition to enhancing social and emotional development, and learning in the arts, Swartz outlines how this seemingly simple material can provide integrated learning experiences in the following cognitive areas:

- **Language development.** Because of the interactive nature of play dough use, children need to listen, understand the communications of others, speak, and practice their oral communication skills as they mold and manipulate their play dough constructions.

- **Science understandings.** The tactile experience of manipulating play dough helps children develop a deeper understanding of how matter changes (physics) and encourages them to use scientific thinking as they observe changes, make predictions, and talk through differences in the materials they are using.

- **Mathematics concepts.** Mixing up a new batch of play dough with adults engages children in mathematical learning as they measure and count recipe ingredients. Discussions about shape, relative size (greater than, equal to, or less than), height, length, and weight provide additional opportunities for children to develop mathematical understandings.

- **Literacy learning.** When paper and writing utensils are added to the play dough area, children can make signs and labels, and can create stories related to their play efforts.

- **Physical development.** The fine motor skills needed for writing and drawing are refined as children roll, poke, and shape their play dough creations.

Although early childhood professionals working with young children traditionally have not considered physical fitness a major element of the curriculum, mounting evidence indicates that they should encourage young children to be more active. While obesity levels for children of all ages continue to rise (Crosnoe, 2010), physical activity levels are declining (Pate et al., 2008) with more than 80% of a preschool child's day spent in sedentary activity. An increased emphasis on physical fitness can be of significant help in the following areas:

- Reducing health risks due to high blood pressure and heart disease. The first signs of arteriosclerosis (hardening of the arteries) are appearing as early as age 5 (Poest, Williams, Witt, & Atwood, 1990).

- Reducing the likelihood of Type 2 diabetes, which is occurring more frequently in young children (Sorte & Daeschel, 2006).

- Increasing the activity levels of young children. Many are spending 3 to 5 hours each day sitting in front of a television screen or playing on the computer (Sorte & Daeschel, 2006). This inactivity needs to be counter-balanced with more focused attention on physical fitness.

The National Association for Sport and Physical Education has developed two sets of curriculum standards that provide physical activity guidelines for young children. In *Active Start: A Statement of Physical Activity Guidelines for Children Birth to Five Years* (National Association for Sport and Physical Education, 2002), the organization provides guidelines for infants, toddlers, and preschoolers. Figure 12–1 shows an overview of these guidelines for toddlers. In 2004, the National Association for Sport and Physical Education published the second edition of *Moving into the Future: National Standards for Physical Education*. This document includes benchmarks for children in grades K–2. Figure 12–2 summarizes standard 4 for this age group.

Figure 12–1

Toddler Physical Activity Standards

Guideline 1:	During the day, toddlers should have at least 30 minutes of structured physical activity.
Guideline 2:	A minimum of one hour of unstructured physical activity is needed, with blocks of no more than an hour of sedentary time (other than sleeping).
Guideline 3:	Toddlers need to develop basic movement skills required for more complex physical activities.
Guideline 4:	Indoor and outdoor areas for toddlers must meet or exceed safety standards for large muscle activities.
Guideline 5:	Caregivers should understand the importance of, and support, toddlers' movement skill development.

Source: Based on information from *Active Start: A Statement of Physical Activity Guidelines for Children Birth to Five Years,* by the National Association for Sport and Physical Education, 2002, Reston, VA: Author.

Figure 12–2

Physical Education Standard 4: K–2

Students are expected to reach and sustain physical fitness as an important part of healthy development.

Based on this standard, K–2 children should be able to do such things as:

Bear their body weight for climbing and hanging by the hands.

Hop, jump, gallop, and run for timed segments without tiring.

Travel hand-over-hand along a horizontal ladder (monkey bars).

Recognize that fitness consists of several important components.

Source: Based on information from *Moving into the Future: National Standards for Physical Education* (2nd ed.), by the National Association for Sport and Physical Education, 2004, Reston, VA: Author.

Gardening is a wonderful way to learn about health and nutrition.

The Values of Health Education

One reason for the increased national interest in physical activity levels of young children is the rapid rise in childhood obesity. Research tells us that the percentage of obese children ages 2 to 5 has doubled since 1976 and obesity levels for children 6 through 11 have increased from 6.5% to 19.6% (Ogden & Carroll, 2010). When combined with the growing numbers of children who are overweight, these statistics are truly alarming (Ogden, Carroll, & Flegal, 2008). This very large rate of increase can be attributed to two main factors: "eating too much and moving too little" (Sorte & Daeschel, 2006, p. 40). Children, starting at a very early age, need to understand the importance of good health and the steps that need to be taken to maintain a lifetime of good health (Winter, 2009).

Health education has a number of key components that must be included as part of the curriculum in early childhood settings:

- **Nutrition.** Young children are surrounded by messages on television, in stores, and over the Internet in which poor nutrition is prominent (Henry J. Kaiser Family Foundation, 2004; Powell et al., 2007). High-sugar cereals, processed foods with numerous additives and salt, and drinks with caffeine and sugar are portrayed as enticing alternatives for children. As an early childhood professional, you will need to educate young children and their families about good food choices and model those choices by providing nutritious snacks and meals.

- **Medical and dental health.** Not all children have ready access to quality medical and dental care through family health plans. In 2009, more than 8.1 million young children were without coverage (Children's Defense Fund, 2010). Nor do they all receive the guidance at home that they need to be physically and emotionally healthy. You may need to help children and their families find care options in your community and help children learn about what can be done to develop and maintain healthy bodies.

- **Healthy body image.** Another important component of a health education program for young children is to help them develop a healthy body image (Huber, 2009). Media images promote the notion that being thin is the essence of beauty and elegance, particularly for young women. This can lead to significant eating disorders that begin in the early years (Natenshon, 1999). It is important for young children to learn that bodies come in all shapes and sizes and to respect the healthy differences they see.

- **Illness prevention.** Children and families need to know how to prevent childhood illnesses that range from common colds and flu to more serious concerns such as diphtheria, tetanus, whooping cough, measles, and mumps. These latter concerns can all be readily prevented through simple vaccinations (National Institutes of Health, 2008). Educating children and families about illnesses and their prevention is another important part of the curriculum.

Safety Education and Young Children

Part of the responsibility of every early childhood professional is to ensure the safety of all the children in their care. Maslow (1968) indicates that safety and security are two of the most basic human needs. It is only when children feel safe and secure in their environments that they can learn and grow to their full potential. It is essential that this need be met in both early childhood and home environments. You will need to educate both children and families about the following safety issues as part of your developmentally appropriate curriculum:

- **Environmental risks.** While it is never possible to remove all environmental risks, it is important to remove unnecessary ones from both indoor and outdoor early childhood environments. For example, you will want to keep cleaners and poisons out of the reach of children, preferably in locked cabinets. Small items that can be swallowed by very young children and toys with lead-based paint also should be excluded. Outdoors, protecting children from sharp edges and protruding bolts are other ways that you can eliminate unnecessary risks.

- **Accidents.** It is important to educate young children about the risks of injury from such things as electric shock, traffic, poisons, and fire. These topics, and more, should be included in the discussions you have with both children and families. In addition, despite your best efforts to prevent accidents from occurring, you must be prepared to deal with the cuts, bruises, bites, and more serious injuries that can occur in early childhood settings. In addition to knowing basic first aid, you should be aware of initial procedures for such things as blocked airways, poisoning, and complications associated with asthma and diabetes.

- **Child abuse and neglect.** One of the most unpleasant issues that early childhood professionals face is that of child abuse and neglect. It is heart wrenching to think that innocent and defenseless young children can be subjected to abuse and/or neglect by adults. Yet statistics indicate that there were nearly 450,000 confirmed cases of abuse/neglect in the United States in 2008 (U.S. Department of Health and Human Services, 2008). You will need to be aware of the signs of child abuse and neglect so that you can report any concerns to the proper authorities.

Working with Families

Families can be major contributors in every area of their child's growth and development, including issues of health and wellness. During their early years, children not only spend more time at home than they do in early childhood settings, they also absorb the values and attitudes of those around them. For example, if children consume processed foods and drinks at home that are high in sugar, salt, and preservatives, they are likely to think that this is normal and might resist efforts on your part to help them learn about and enjoy more healthy alternatives. To effect long-term change in eating habits, families will need to learn about, and get excited about using, easy-to-prepare and nutritious alternatives. Similar support is needed from families if greater levels of physical activity are to become a reality. Safety issues, accidents, abuse and neglect, and emergency preparedness are also closely linked to attitudes and understandings of family members.

In some instances, families unwittingly engage their children in activities that are less than ideal for health and fitness. The *Family Partnerships* feature in this section gives an example of this type. Organized sports for children less than 7 or 8 years of age are generally considered inappropriate because of the children's level of intellectual development (Piaget, 1962). Read the feature now for more information on this topic.

Family Partnerships . . .
ORGANIZED SPORTS FOR YOUNG CHILDREN

If you have spent any time around youth sports activities, you know that families are enrolling children as young as 3 or 4 years of age in a variety of organized sports. Baseball, soccer, basketball, and football are all being played by young children, with eager family members providing encouragement to their young charges. With proper leadership and adult support, these activities can provide positive social outlets and enjoyable fitness experiences for young children beginning at age 7 or 8.

David Elkind (2001), however, reminds us that most children during the early childhood years are not ready for highly competitive sports and games. He suggests that families who push their children into early competitive activities are hurrying them to grow up too quickly and adding extra stress to their lives. Underwood (1981) puts it this way:

> To visit on small heads the pressure to win . . . is indecent. To dress children up like pros in costly outfits is ridiculous. In so doing, we take away many of the qualities that competitive sports are designed to give to the growing process. (p. 73)

Many well-meaning families create unnecessary structure in their children's lives by introducing them to early competitive sports. Although these activities for young children are improving, with more appropriate coaching and fewer fanatical family members shouting from the sidelines, most young children benefit at least as much from more unstructured, vigorous play activities as they do from organized sports. Families and children need to hear this message repeatedly from a variety of experts so they can stand up to the pressure from others to get involved in too many organized sports activities at an early age.

1. Do you think David Elkind is right in saying that early organized sports place unnecessary stress on the lives of young children? Why or why not?

2. What can or should you do in your work with families to share your ideas about the value and/or problems with organized sports for young children?

You can help families become more health and fitness conscious by providing them with information and activities that are developmentally appropriate. This family education effort should build upon the positive things that are already occurring and should take minimal time and effort for families to implement. Regular communications through newsletters, e-mail correspondence, books and articles that can be checked out to read at home, and group meetings can help families understand their roles in facilitating health and fitness.

Physical Education

Although children rather naturally engage in physical activity, it is necessary for early childhood professionals to incorporate activities and periodically teach the skills needed for healthy motor development (Tucker, 2008). By planning for and encouraging physical activity during play and by teaching developmentally appropriate motor skills, early childhood professionals can assist children in an important aspect of their development and help children be more physically fit.

Basic Considerations

Regardless of the skill being learned or the ability levels of individual children, early childhood professionals can use several general guidelines to promote physical development (American Academy of Pediatrics, American Public Health Association, & National Resource Center for Health and Safety in Child Care and Early Education, 2010; Benelli & Yongue, 1995; King & Gartrell, 2003; National Association for Sport and Physical Education, 2002):

- Create time in the daily schedule for children to engage in both play-oriented and adult-directed movement activities.
- Plan for physical pursuits both indoors and outdoors.
- Make sure all children get involved in a variety of motor activities. The *Celebrating Diversity* feature in this section provides some thoughts on physical activities for children with special needs.
- Evaluate your responses to both boys and girls to ensure equitable opportunities for physical movement.
- Identify your expectations for children's motor development. Consider these goals as you plan your curriculum.
- Establish clear rules for children as they engage in movement activities. Two basics: Respect one another's personal space, and keep noise to a minimum.
- Identify for children the boundaries for physical activities. Where are they allowed to play the game, toss the ball, or move to music? What are the boundaries in terms of appropriateness? The *Developmentally Appropriate Practice* feature in this section discusses strategies to address boundaries for violent play themes in early childhood settings.
- Integrate physical development activities into all areas of the curriculum. Mathematics, science, art, and music are just some of the possibilities for integration.
- Observe children carefully as they engage in physical activity to determine strengths and areas for improvement. It should also form the basis for future planning.

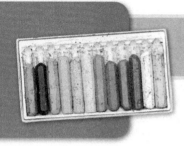

Celebrating Diversity . . .
MOVEMENT ACTIVITIES FOR CHILDREN WITH SPECIAL NEEDS

Although physical skills may present many challenges to children with special needs, the benefits of involvement include these:

- Better coordination
- Improved listening skills
- Enhanced expressive abilities

Although these are important reasons for including children with special needs, perhaps the most significant reason is improved self-concept (Gallahue & Ozman, 2005). Many disabilities make it harder for children to participate in physical tasks, or when they do get involved, the outcome is different from that of other children. This can lead to a distorted body image. Involving children with special needs in successful movement activities can help them feel good about themselves.

Here are some planning considerations for including children with special needs (Flynn & Kieff, 2002; Watson & McCathren, 2009):

- Make sure that all children can succeed with the tasks you include.
- Consider modifying movement activities or materials to make them positive experiences.
- Include music as an important component that can help improve response, motivation, and enjoyment.
- Consult with families and special educators for other insights in planning for physical activities.

1. Take a look at playground equipment for young children. What adaptations would be needed (or were made) to make them accessible to children with special needs?

2. Talk to a physical education teacher who works with primary children to find out the benefits and problems of involving children with special needs in movement activities. What did you learn?

- Use materials and equipment for physical development that are developmentally appropriate and meet the diverse needs and abilities of children.
- Remember that children need repeated opportunities for practice as they learn new skills.

Instructional Strategies for Physical Education

Pica (2004) describes three teaching methods for early childhood physical education. The direct approach, guided discovery, and exploration are all effective in different situations for teaching motor skills. Some physical activities are best taught through the *direct approach*. The Hokey Pokey is a traditional dance activity that young children thoroughly enjoy. By describing, modeling, and imitating the necessary steps, caregivers and teachers can help children quickly learn this dance. This approach has the advantage of allowing the adult to discover if any children are having trouble following the directions or producing the desired movement. *Guided discovery* is a child-centered approach that allows for inventiveness and experimentation as the early childhood professional guides children toward an appropriate solution to a problem. For example, you could use a series of questions to lead children to discover what skills are needed for a forward roll. Guided discovery gives children an important role in learning the physical skill being taught. Finally, the *exploration approach*, also referred to as divergent problem solving, should be used as much as possible. When children explore, they produce a variety of responses to each challenge. For

Developmentally Appropriate Practice . . .
GUIDING VIOLENT PLAY

One thing you have undoubtedly discovered by now is that young children love to imitate significant others. Unfortunately, many of the role models for young children come from the television programs and movies they watch. Many of these programs include violent characters such as those in the classic cartoon about Wile E. Coyote, the movie *The Secret of NIMH,* and adult action heroes like Jet Li. It should come as no surprise, then, that we sometimes find even very young children engaged in play of a violent nature. Although children typically do not intend to hurt one another, the end result of violent play is often just that. In addition, it is important for young children to learn better strategies than violence for dealing with disagreements. Consider the following strategies for guiding children away from violence in their play:

- **Avoid pretend weapons.** Make sure no toys resembling weapons are brought from home. Suggest nonviolent uses for sticks and other neutral objects that children pretend are weapons.

- **Redirect play themes.** If children are playing out a cartoon theme such as "Dragon Ball Z" and becoming violent, try to redirect the play without entirely changing the theme. Having some knowledge of the characters being imitated helps with this task.

- **Rehearse verbal responses.** Be prepared with simple, direct responses to violent play. "I won't let you play in that way. Someone might get hurt." "You need to find another way to play Teen Titans so that no one gets hurt."

- **Remain calm, but firm.** Your responses to violent play will impact how children accept your intervention. Make sure to use a calm but firm voice.

- **Model appropriate behavior.** In some situations, it may be effective to actually join in the play and through your actions show children more appropriate ways to interact.

- **Seek family support.** Make sure to share with family members both the importance of intervening in violent play and the strategies you are using in school, so that they can support you at home.

---

example, asking children to balance on two body parts should result in many different responses from a group. Extending and refining children's initial responses to a specific challenge gives them many opportunities for practicing movement skills.

Physical Development and Play

As has been emphasized throughout this text, play is critical to a child's overall development. Childhood play enhances every aspect of growth, including physical development. As adults plan for motor development, it is essential to consider how play can be used to develop movement skills. Careful planning of the indoor and outdoor environments and the adult's comments and questions are both important.

Early childhood professionals should select play equipment to stimulate gross and fine motor development and perceptual-motor skills. Toys and equipment that could be used include the following:

Gross Motor	Fine Motor	Perceptual-Motor
Climber	Water play	Rhythm instruments
Digging area	Small blocks	Dance scarves
Large balls	Crayons	Pattern blocks
Wheeled toys	Legos	Body part puzzles
Tumbling mats	Sand play	Sound cylinders

Fine motor skills are developed as children manipulate toys.

When quality toys and equipment are available to young children, they will use them in play to develop motor abilities naturally.

During free-play time, your primary role is to serve as facilitator. By asking the right questions, making appropriate comments, and redirecting children to more positive options, early educators assist in overall development. When the focus becomes physical development, adult verbalizations help facilitate these skills in children:

- "Suzanna, where should you put your hands so that you can reach the next level on the climber?"
- "Adrianne, your handwriting has improved so much lately! You have learned how to make *b*s and *d*s correctly and are printing so much clearer now. Congratulations!"
- "Eddie, let me show you how I use a saw to cut a board. Watch how I push and pull the saw blade across the wood."

By actively facilitating physical skills during play, you can help emphasize these important abilities throughout the school day. The *Observing Development* feature in this section is designed to help organize your observation of play in an early childhood setting and reflect on its importance.

Observing Development...
ACTIVE PLAY

Choose one of the age groups within early childhood (infants/toddlers, preschoolers, or primary-age children) and observe the activity levels of three young children playing indoors using the rating scale below. Observe for a minimum of 10 minutes.

Activity level	Child one	Child two	Child three
Rate each child once each minute: 1 = low; 2 = medium; 3 = high			
Minute 1			
Minute 2			
Minute . . .			

Reflect and Apply

1. Based on your ratings of three children, what can you say about their activity levels in an indoor early childhood setting?

2. How might the adults increase activity levels of children?

3. What do you think the results for activity levels would have been if you had observed children outdoors?

Organized Physical Activities

Although infants and toddlers benefit most from using play-oriented activities to develop motor skills, you can introduce more adult-directed tasks during the preschool and primary years. These activities should be fun for children, include specific guidance on how to perform various skills, and allow for many opportunities to practice newly learned movements (Benelli & Yongue, 1995; National Association for Sport and Physical Education, 2002).

- **Throwing activities.** Children can learn to step forward with the opposite foot when throwing. Use of a target, such as a decorated sheet, helps ensure success. Beanbags and smaller soft balls are better for throwing tasks. Verbal cues help the child learn appropriate motions.

- **Catching activities.** A bright, colorful ball helps the younger child follow it visually. Yarn balls, balloons, and beach balls are good beginning items for catching. If the person throwing can toss at a consistent speed and height, children will have more success in catching.

- **Striking activities.** As in throwing, children will be more successful in striking an object when they step forward with the leg closest to the target. A soft ball, placed on a batting tee at waist level, creates an easier target for preschool and early primary children. A bat made from a plastic 2-liter bottle and a dowel rod is helpful for many young children.

- **Kicking skills.** Targets help children improve their kicking skills. A large sheet or plastic 2-liter bottles set up like bowling pins make good targets. Children should be told to step beside the ball as they kick it with their dominant leg. Watching the ball also helps improve success rates with kicking.

- **Balancing tasks.** These activities can initially be practiced on the floor. Walking forward and backward on a line drawn on the floor, and then using an uneven surface such as a rope or hoop, will help children develop the skills needed to walk on a balance beam.

Organized physical activities can help children develop more complex movement skills.

- **Jumping activities.** Jumping off low platforms is an enjoyable event for most young children. Providing safe, stable alternatives for jumping is a good beginning here. This can be followed by having children practice jumping vertically and horizontally.
- **Spatial awareness.** Children need to practice moving, dodging, balancing, and stopping without invading the personal space of others. Music and movement activities provide many opportunities for spatial awareness.
- **Fitness activities.** Although young children tire easily from vigorous activity, it is important to encourage walking, running, and jumping for fitness. Make sure to have fun, and downplay the competitive element. The important thing is to get children engaged in aerobic movement.

Games and Activities: Indoors

As caregivers and teachers plan for organized physical activities indoors, they should integrate them with other activities whenever possible to take advantage of the young child's natural ways of learning. The *Developmentally Appropriate Practice* feature in this section describes some options for integrating movement and music in early childhood settings. In addition, by using key curriculum resources such as Pica (2004), and building ideas for involvement around children's needs and interests, adults can implement a strong motor skills program.

Following are some movement activities that may be adapted for use in early childhood settings.

- **Magical marching.** Having children march to music, swinging their arms and raising their knees, can be a fun fitness activity. A variety of musical recordings are available that encourage a range of marching speeds. Accompanying the music with a drumbeat can be helpful for younger children. Either pretending

Developmentally Appropriate Practice . . .
INTEGRATING CURRICULUM THROUGH MOVEMENT AND MUSIC

One popular and effective strategy for developing an important part of an integrated curriculum is combining movement and music. Each complements the other in supporting learning and development. In addition, children find this combination of activities particularly enjoyable. The following examples highlight the benefits of this approach:

- **Signing and singing the ABC Song.** The small muscle skills needed to sign the alphabet challenge young children and also motivate them to learn the ABCs while doing an enjoyable task. It is also a good way to introduce children to an important aspect of life for deaf and hard-of-hearing children.

- **Head, Shoulders, Knees, and Toes.** Children learn body parts, practice coordinated movements, and have fun singing this traditional song.
- **Silk scarves and movement to music.** Many children love the combination of free flowing movements to music and holding colorful billowing silk scarves. Creative movement, balance, and timing are all being practiced when this activity is encouraged (Dow, 2010).
- **The Eensy Weensy Spider.** In addition to practicing fine motor skills, very young children experience a simple story sequence that fascinates them over and over again. They are developing a deeper understanding of an important early literacy skill.

to play a musical instrument as children march or actually including simple rhythm instruments can add variety and interest to this task. Allowing children to assume special pretend roles such as drum major, baton twirler, and flag bearer add further opportunities for playfulness.

- **The bunny hop.** Children love to pretend, and animals are a favorite theme. Why not combine these interests with physical movement? Children can pretend to be rabbits and hop across the rug. Remind children to avoid leaping into another child's path. Then consider other hopping creatures. Frogs and kangaroos are two other possibilities. Keep children actively involved yet under control for some exciting hopping experiences. Other animals may be the starting point for additional movement possibilities (horses? crabs? elephants?).

- **Quick, freeze!** Movement and music go together very well in early childhood. Play an instrumental piece of music, and ask children to move any way they like until the music stops. They must then "quick, freeze" in the position they were in when the music stopped. Use a variety of musical styles and rhythms to encourage different movements and to add interest to the activity. Make sure to stop the music at unexpected times so that children must be careful listeners as well as creative movers. Props such as scarves and streamers help self-conscious children focus more on the prop and move more productively to the music.

- **Hit the bull's-eye.** Beanbags make great initial throwing instruments for young children. They are easy to grasp, weighted for good distance, and soft enough to be safe when the toss is off target. Paint a large bull's-eye on an old donated sheet and cut a hole in the center for the beanbags to be tossed through, attach it securely by one edge to the ceiling, and have children practice tossing the beanbags at the target. Tape on the floor at varying distances from the target can add further challenges for children as they become more accurate in their tosses.

- **Finger frolics.** Young children love to engage in activities that involve their fingers and hands. A variety of finger plays and action songs are available that allow children to practice fine and gross motor skills. "Five Little Speckled Frogs," "The Eensy Weensy Spider," and "Head, Shoulders, Knees and Toes" are well-known examples of fine and gross motor activities combined with games and singing. These activities promote early mathematical understandings as well (Geist & Geist, 2008). Repeat them often, because children enjoy them even more with practice.

- **Catch me if you can.** The eye–hand coordination needed for a young child to catch a ball or other objects is greater than might first be expected. Begin by having children catch their own bounced ball. Next, have an adult who can toss accurately throw a beach ball or other large, soft object for catching. Learning to toss an object into the air and then catch it is yet another step in the process. Catching tends to be more difficult than tossing activities for many children. They may be afraid of being hit by whatever is being tossed. Be sensitive to this as you introduce the activity.

- **Balancing circus.** Balance activities can follow a sequence from fairly simple to more complex. A good beginning for young children is to have them pretend to be circus high-wire performers and walk on a line taped to the floor. Next, they can walk on a small rope secured to the floor. Have children walk forward, placing one foot in front of the other. Later, they can practice moving sideways along the rope and then backward. Older children can use the same procedures with a low balance beam as they gain skill and confidence in moving and balancing.

Games and Activities: Outdoors

The outdoor environment provides children with many opportunities for motor skill development. The wide-open spaces and fewer restrictions beckon children to move. Integrated learning opportunities can be planned to entice a wide range of children to engage in active play. The American Academy of Pediatrics, the American Public Health Association, and the National Resource Center for Health and Safety in Child Care and Early Education, in a joint publication in 2010, recommend at least two or three opportunities each day for outdoor play activities. The *Developmentally Appropriate Practice* feature in this section describes the integrated learning potential associated with a mud center set up on the playground. Outdoor free-play activities like this are full of opportunities for large and small muscle movement that may be particularly enticing to young boys (King & Gartrell, 2003). Early childhood professionals organize many similar events to encourage further practice in movement outdoors.

Rough-and-tumble play. Before looking at more adult-organized activities outdoors, you should be aware of an important component of outdoor play, particularly for boys. Bobbie and D. J. are two very active first-grade students. On the

Developmentally Appropriate Practice . . .
INTEGRATING CURRICULUM IN A MUD CENTER?

Do you have any fond memories of playing outside with mud; making mud pies, mud sandwiches, or other interesting concoctions? It is a sensory experience that many people fondly remember. For many children today, however, playing in mud is a rare opportunity at best (Jensen & Bullard, 2002). Apartment life, city existence, and even growing up in rural areas today just do not seem to be as compatible with the messy joys of mud play. Early childhood professionals should consider setting up a mud center either indoors or on the playground. With careful planning, children can again experience this valuable play experience.

Jensen and Bullard (2002) list the materials they used to set up a mud center on their school playground:

- **An old stove.** Some sort of discarded stove or oven that can be left outdoors as the focal point for mud play is essential. A box made to look like a stove could also be used.

- **Dirt and water.** Some containers are needed for the supply of dirt that is needed to make mud, along with a water source. If a hose or faucet is not close by, be sure to have several buckets of water for mixing and clean-up.

- **Cooking utensils.** One of the key dramatic play themes generated by this center will be cooking activities, so having pots and pans, items for stirring and mixing, empty containers of spices and condiments, and dishes available helps stimulate this theme.

- **Smocks.** Because of the mess, it is best to have several smocks for children to put over their clothes to avoid getting dirty.

- **Writing materials.** A recipe box, recipe cards, and writing utensils help stimulate literacy-related activities in this center as well.

- **Table and chairs.** Providing a spot where "meals" can be served adds another fun element to the dramatic play in this center.

playground, they love to wrestle and chase each other across the grass. This type of vigorous activity is referred to as *rough-and-tumble play* (Pelligrini & Perlmutter, 1988). Wrestling, play fighting, chasing, and fleeing behaviors are common when children engage in this play. Although at first glance this activity may seem to lead to more aggressive behavior, research indicates that rough-and-tumble play has positive educational and developmental value, especially for boys, and should be encouraged (Pelligrini, 1987).

This play type is clearly valuable in getting children to engage in high-energy activity that stimulates cardiovascular fitness and large-muscle use (Sutterby & Frost, 2002). As such, it is an important element of physical development activities in early childhood settings. You will need to carefully observe as children engage in rough-and-tumble play to make sure the activity remains positive. Intervention may be needed to redirect the play in new ways.

Organized activities. The outdoors is an ideal place for adults to lead children in organized physical development activities. The larger spaces and reduced noise restrictions make the outdoors valuable for developing motor skills. There are many good resources for children's games and activities that can be used effectively with young children outdoors (see, e.g., Kamii & DeVries, 1980; Kirchner, 2000; Orlick, 1978). With careful selection and planning, these games and activities will be popular with children and provide many opportunities for growth. Good games for young children should have simple rules, include all children who want to participate, and be noncompetitive.

 The children in your second-grade classroom have been struggling at recess to implement a game of kickball. They are arguing over how to choose teams, and they have hurt feelings regarding winning and losing. Rather than discourage their obvious interest in this active game, you decide to plan for this activity later in the week. After discussing the problems with competition at group time, you take children out to recess, arbitrarily assign students to teams, and then show them how they can play the game and de-emphasize the competitive element. The next week, you notice that several children have spontaneously chosen your modified game and are actively and happily involved during recess.

This example highlights one of the biggest problems with organized games for young children: competition. Piaget (1962) suggests that until about 7 or 8 years of age, children are often not cognitively or emotionally ready for games with rules, many of which contain significant amounts of competition. Losing is difficult for young children and should be downplayed in games (Rivkin, 1995). With creativity and thought, adults can modify most games so that competition is reduced or eliminated. Orlick (1978) identifies many new noncompetitive game options and describes ways in which traditional competitive games can be made more cooperative. Examples of each type follow:

- **Fish gobbler.** In a large grassy area with enough space for all the children to spread out, the caller (known as the Fish Gobbler) says, "Ship," and children run to a designated spot on the playground. When the caller announces, "Shore," children run to a second location. When the caller says, "Fish Gobbler," children drop quickly to the grass. While lying on their stomachs, they link arms, legs, or bodies together so that the Fish Gobbler cannot come by and gobble them up. Later, the adult can add other directions such as "Sardines" or "Crabs," and children can respond with appropriate motions.

- **Nonelimination musical chairs.** Even though chairs are removed when the music is stopped, as in the traditional version, the object of this game is to keep everyone involved. Children simply come up with creative ways to share the remaining chairs. They must work together to make sure the game can continue.

- **Tug of peace.** Rather than playing the traditional game of tug of war, where children compete in teams and pull against each other, introduce children to the tug of peace. In this game, children work together with a rope to meet a specific objective. For example, in small groups, children can cooperate to create a geometric pattern such as a triangle or rectangle, or letters of the alphabet. Small groups can then be combined to form larger groups for more complex tasks.

Although many of the ideas suggested earlier for indoor use can be effective on the playground, these additional options provide a larger sample of outdoor physical activities for children during the early childhood years.

- **The roadrunner.** After discussing the Roadrunner cartoon and how fast he runs, encourage children to practice being roadrunners on the playground. A poster mounted indoors with the designated trail and decorated with individual roadrunners who have made the trip may encourage others to try it as well. Praise individuals (avoid comparing children to downplay competition) and have children challenge themselves to run longer distances as the year progresses.

- **The bumblebee.** Children enjoy pretending and can move creatively to music or a drumbeat. Combine these interests into a playground movement activity. Talk about how a bumblebee travels through the air and what body parts children could move to imitate the bee. Question them about which body parts they can move slowly or quickly. Give children plenty of room, and have them pretend to be bumblebees. This activity can be expanded by asking children to suggest other things they could imitate. They will probably come up with a long list. Discuss the movements required, and then have children practice different rates of speed by pretending to be the creatures they have suggested.

- **Mountain climbing.** Using an obstacle course is a fun way for children to develop their physical skills outdoors. A combination of movable climbers, ladders, boards, wooden boxes, tires, cable spools, and barrels can challenge children to climb over, crawl under, and step through the skills course. Encourage pretending by discussing mountain climbing/hiking at group time and suggesting that the obstacle course is actually a mountain trail that the children can explore. After several days of exploring the trail, change it and give it a new name, such as the jungle or the forest.

- **La piñata.** A favorite multicultural celebration can also be a good introductory striking experience for young children. A piñata attached to a rope and hung from a stationary piece of outdoor equipment makes a large target for this age group. Depending on children's abilities, the piñata can remain at a fixed height for younger children, or it can be raised and lowered to increase the challenge for older ones. The bat should be light enough for children to swing easily and wide at the striking end to ensure success in hitting the target.

Choose a piñata that can be broken by children, fill it with healthy treats, and give each child a chance to strike away.

- **Traffic jam.** Wheeled toys like tricycles and wagons help young children develop leg muscle coordination. Pretend city streets laid out by adults on the playground can be a fun way to encourage children to pedal and steer in and around various obstacles. Stop signs, turn indicators, a simple ramp to drive over, traffic cones, and a pretend gas pump can stimulate good exercise that children will enjoy for many days. Changing the traffic patterns every few days will help maintain interest in this activity.

- **Parachute play.** Group activities with a parachute can help promote cooperation and allow for both large and small muscle use. Begin by demonstrating how to grip the parachute: either palms down, palms up, or alternating. Children can use the parachute to create waves by using different large arm movements to make it go up and down. Experiment with different positions (sitting, kneeling, standing) and a variety of motions as children gain confidence in manipulating the parachute. For a more advanced activity, place a lightweight ball on the parachute and have children keep it bouncing.

Health Education

As a society, we are continuing to grow in our understanding of what it takes to become and remain healthy individuals. Take, for instance, the relatively new emphasis on the importance of vitamin D and the problems that can occur if we are deficient in this important vitamin (Holick, 2007). Deficiencies of vitamin D have been found to lead to slowed growth in childhood and osteoporosis (bone weakness) in later life. This is but one example of societal changes in understanding. However, it highlights the fact that you will need to remain current regarding the latest information on health and wellness so that you can assist the young children in your care in this important aspect of their development.

Nutrition

Nutrition clearly influences the young child's behavior. A good diet helps children be more alert, attentive, and active in early childhood settings. Poor nutrition will generally have the opposite effects and may lower the child's resistance to illnesses. Overeating and malnutrition also contribute to many problems in childhood, and early childhood professionals need to address these issues. An alarming number of young children are overweight or obese due to both poor nutrition and their increasingly sedentary lifestyles. Convenience/fast foods high in fat and sugar, combined with aggressive advertising by the companies producing them, have been major factors leading to the rapid increase in overweight and obese young children (Sorte & Daeschel, 2006).

One way to counterbalance the poor nutrition choices that bombard children and families is to provide nutritious alternatives in your early childhood setting. The American Academy of Pediatrics, along with the American Public Health Association and the National Resource Center for Health and Safety in Child Care and Early Education (2010) published a set of nutrition standards for early childhood programs. Following are some of the options you should consider including in your program:

- **Fruits and vegetables.** The American diet tends to be low in fruits and vegetables. A recent report indicates that less than a third of all Americans meet the dietary guidelines for these important foods (Centers for Disease Control, 2010). Yet fruit and vegetable consumption has been positively linked to long-term good health and weight management. Fruits and vegetables are relatively low-cost and easy to prepare. Including them as snacks and as part of meals makes excellent sense in early childhood settings.

- **Low salt and sugar foods.** High levels of both salt (Institute of Medicine, 2010) and sugar (Welsh et al., 2010) have been shown to increase the risk of heart disease. By choosing foods that are low in salt and sugar, you can help young children develop healthier eating habits.

- **Real foods.** Michael Pollan has written several popular books that emphasize the importance of eating healthy foods, including one titled *In Defense of Food* (Pollan, 2008). Part of his message is that most of us are eating things we call food that wouldn't be recognized as real food by our grandparents. Much of what we eat is highly processed and includes many preservatives and color enhancers. Although the effects of these additives is unclear, we continue to eat them in large quantities. Pollan encourages us to abandon these habits in favor of food choices that have limited additives.

- **Smaller portion sizes.** In our super-sized society, we tend to think that more is better. But when it comes to food, less is generally the best choice (Fisher et al., 2007). One way to encourage smaller portion sizes is to eat from smaller plates and bowls. Children can always come back for more, if needed.

- **Water and milk for drinks.** While it should be clear that carbonated beverages are not a good drink for young children, it may surprise you to know that large amounts of fruit juice can be a problem as well (Dennison, Rockwell, & Baker, 1997). Because of the high sugar levels in fruit juice, a better option for most young children is water or milk.

Cooking is another common and fun way to help teach young children about good nutrition. By providing examples of inexpensive and healthy foods that can be simply prepared, children learn about important alternatives to the fast food that they see so frequently. For example, a fruit salad is easy and fun for young children to prepare and provides a healthy alternative to high-sugar or fatty cooking projects. Something as simple as peeling and cutting carrots for snacks is another good example of a cooking experience that many young children would enjoy. While cooking, you can talk informally with children about the many benefits of healthy food choices.

Modeling good nutrition in your early childhood setting also means taking the time to communicate often and well with families about the importance of good food choices. By communicating clearly with them about healthy snacks and treats brought from home for consumption in the program, families can be reminded about good nutrition. You can also have articles on good food choices available to share with interested families and include summaries of important nutrition information in newsletters that you send home to them.

With very few exceptions, families want the best for their children. In many instances, however, they need guidance in knowing what can be done to encourage healthy development. Without putting families on the defensive or making them feel like they are failures, you will need to help them learn about providing good nutrition and a healthy diet for their young children. While many families do well in this area, others eat foods high in fat, sugar, salt, and preservatives.

Providing resources (see, e.g., Marcon, 2003; Wanamaker, Hearn, & Richarz, 1979) for simple, nutritious alternatives to fast foods and communicating with families about the importance of healthy diets will make a difference in the overall physical development of young children. The *Developmentally Appropriate Practice* feature in this section provides examples of some nutritious snacks and meals that you can model in your early childhood setting and share with families.

Healthy Body Image

Take a look around you the next time you are in a large group of people. Notice the differences that exist in body types. People literally do come in all shapes and sizes. But, then notice what is presented on television, in movies, and through most popular print media. While there are exceptions, for the most part slim body types are portrayed as the ideal. As a society, we can and should work to educate people to the dangers of being overweight and obese. At the same time, however, we need to help young people, beginning in the early years, to accept and like the body type they have. Being too thin can be a serious problem, with anorexia and bulimia being common concerns. Eating disorders are considered a mental health issue and carry the highest death rate of any such issue (Birmingham et al., 2005).

Young children develop patterns of behavior during these years that often last a lifetime. Teaching respect and care for one's body is an essential element of the

Developmentally Appropriate Practice . . .
NUTRITIOUS SNACKS AND MEALS

It is important that snacks and meals for young children be healthy and nutritious. In addition to the obvious physical benefits to children, these healthy food options model for families some positive alternatives to the high salt and sugar foods that are found in many homes. By selecting easy-to-prepare foods that children like to eat, families can be shown that good nutrition is easy, inexpensive, and enjoyable for all involved. In the early childhood setting, simple options also mean that children can benefit from being involved in the actual food preparation for additional learning experiences.

The following ideas should get you started thinking about healthy options for young children:

Banana smoothie. Combine two peeled bananas, two cups of strawberries or other fruit, one cup of milk, and one cup of plain yogurt in a blender. Blend until smooth.

Ants on a log. On 2- to 3-inch pieces of cleaned celery, spread a layer of peanut butter and then top with a row of raisins.

Fruit salad. Wash, clean, and peel the fruits of your choice. Be sure to have a good variety of seasonal alternatives. Chop fruit into small pieces and mix them together in a large bowl.

Yummy bagel sandwich. Cut bagels of your choice in half lengthwise (an adult task unless you have a special bagel cutter), add a slice of cheddar cheese, a round slice of apple (green is best), and a dash of cinnamon. Bake 5 to 10 minutes at 350 degrees.

At the prekindergarten level, serving nutritious snacks and meals can be an effective way to show families the positive benefits of good nutrition. If you teach at the primary level, you can ask families to provide nutritious mid-day snacks from a list that you develop. Also be sure to share the importance of good nutrition as you communicate with families in newsletters and via e-mail.

early childhood curriculum. This role should be the responsibility of caregivers and teachers with support from the early childhood program and community. WebMD (2010) suggests that you can help by doing the following:

- Reminding children that young bodies continue to change and grow as they mature. They need to understand that if they are eating healthy foods and getting good exercise, those body changes are just a part of growing up.
- Reinforcing the idea that there is no one ideal body type.
- Being careful about the language you use to talk about your body and the bodies of others. Avoid using fat and ugly, for example, as descriptors of body types.
- Emphasizing each child's abilities and positive personality traits rather than focusing on their appearance.

Medical and Dental Health

Although good medical and dental care is commonplace in many households, other children and families do not have adequate coverage. Low-income families and those without medical and dental insurance may be unable to afford these services. Many programs for young children include curricular information on the importance of good medical and dental care and provide referrals to low-cost alternatives for families.

Early childhood professionals must also be alert to health problems that could lead to later difficulties for children. Providing for vision, hearing, and speech screening is a common first step that programs can take to help identify potential health problems. Careful observation by adults can also be helpful in discovering other concerns.

 You have overheard Rachel complaining of headaches for the last several days in your third-grade classroom. With the school's annual standardized tests scheduled for tomorrow, Rachel's headaches may be related to stress. You decide to call her family to discuss the problem further.

Illnesses

A final component of health education is an emphasis on identifying and, where possible, preventing the spread of childhood illnesses. As an early childhood professional, you will need to make initial assessments of potential childhood illnesses so you can get the sick child the care she needs as soon as possible. Early identification will also help control the spread of illnesses to others. Even if your program has a nurse to help in these matters, the program staff will always be the first line of contact for sick children, so you should be prepared to help identify these and other common childhood illnesses (Downs, 2010):

- **Colds, ear infections, the flu.** These illnesses are experienced in many homes and early childhood settings. The runny noses, painful ear canals, fevers, and other symptoms associated with these illnesses are observable and, when treated early, can help save children from considerable pain and can prevent the spread of these illnesses.
- **Fifth disease.** This strangely named disease is caused by a virus and may affect as high as 20% of all children by age five. It produces a red rash on the cheeks

that looks like someone has slapped the child's face. While it is generally not a serious illness, it can be spread through contact with the saliva or nasal discharge from an infected child.

- **Hand, foot, and mouth disease.** With this disease, an initial fever is followed by blisters in the mouth and then a rash on the palms of the hands and soles of the feet. It is caused by a virus and usually goes away after a week to ten days.
- **Croup.** Caused by another group of viruses, croup is best distinguished by the "barking" cough that comes with it. Croup may become serious enough to cause hospitalization because children have trouble breathing deeply.
- **Strep throat.** This is a bacterial infection that leads to a very sore throat and high fever. In some instances, the strep throat will lead to *scarlet fever,* which is seen as a bright red rash that starts on the chest and stomach.
- **Impetigo.** This is a bacterial skin infection. It is the third most common skin infection in children, and is especially common in ages 2 to 6. Impetigo creates itchy bumps that weep liquid and are very contagious to other children and adults.
- **Whooping cough.** This contagious bacterial infection can be a problem for children and adults, but is most serious for infants. It gets its name from the child's hard and rapid cough that causes him to run out of breath and "whoop" when attempting to inhale. More than half of all children under 12 months who catch whooping cough need to be treated in a hospital.

The above list of illnesses is only a portion of the childhood diseases that you will need to be aware of in your future work with young children. While the list of illnesses is long, the good news is that there are some very good Internet resources that you can go to for help in identification and prevention. One such site is Medline Plus, a service of the U.S. National Library of Medicine (2010). This site contains a long list of links to important information about childhood illnesses. A second important Internet site is WebMD (2010). It provides a wealth of information, in layman's terms, that would be helpful in your work with young children.

In addition to identifying illnesses in children, you will need to lead efforts to prevent them in your early childhood setting as well. By *emphasizing good nutrition and physical activity* with young children, you can help improve overall childhood health. Healthy children are more able to fight off the bacteria and viruses they will encounter. Another important prevention strategy is to *promote personal hygiene* in the early childhood setting. When you integrate good health habits into program activities, like hand washing before eating and after toileting, young children learn and practice these important routines. Hair grooming, brushing teeth, and caring for a runny nose are other aspects of good personal hygiene. Head Start programs are especially effective in emphasizing this component of the health education curriculum.

Healthy Adults

You don't have to look very far in American culture to see that many adults are not living healthy lifestyles. Overweight and obesity issues, for example, are affecting growing numbers of adults (Hedley et al., 2004). And exercise is a distant memory for many others. Time constraints and misinformation often lead adults to unhealthy lifestyles. But, if we are going to expect children to live healthy lives and become fully functioning adults, early childhood professionals need to reflect on their own levels of health to see if they are modeling what they are asking children to do. As a significant role model for young children, you should be doing these things:

- **Eating healthy foods and talking about it with children.** It is clearly important to do this in the early childhood setting. But to be truly meaningful to children, they need to hear that you eat healthy foods at home and are willing to talk to them about your food choices and the rationale you used in making those choices. Will you be able to practice what you preach?

- **Exercising regularly.** Do you have some favorite exercise routines that work for you? Can you spend some time talking about those routines with children? If you like to hike, for example, you could show them photos of some of your favorite places and talk about why you like this activity so much. As much as you can, share with children the excitement and satisfactions that come from exercise. If you don't currently have an exercise plan, can you find a way to add even a small amount to your busy schedule?

- **Discussing your own body type.** Are you comfortable enough with your personal body type to talk with children about it? They certainly notice what you look like physically, even if they don't talk about it. By talking about your physical attributes and those of other adults, focusing on the positive, children can begin to accept the differences in body types they see in people all around them.

- **Talking about strategies you use to stay healthy.** In addition to healthy eating and exercise, are there things you do to maintain good physical and emotional health? Are you making sure to get enough sleep? What do you like to do for fun? What friendships or family members do you call upon when you have a difficult issue to work through? Can you share these strategies with the children you work with?

 ## Safety Education

The final component of health and wellness is safety education, which requires a two-pronged approach. You should first work to create safe indoor and outdoor environments for young children. At the same time, your safety education curriculum needs to include time spent educating young children about safety issues in early childhood settings and in the home. This portion of the health and wellness curriculum should include an understanding of, and the ability to deal with, environmental risks, accidents, and child abuse and neglect.

Before looking at these safety issues, however, there is another important safety consideration that you must be prepared to address as an early childhood professional. With the high rate of divorce and the emotional custody battles that come from some of them, it is critical that you release children from your care only to court-designated family member(s). You should ask families for copies of relevant court documents and understand the implications of them for your work with children (Bergen County Bar Association, 2006). Keep careful records and document who picks up children at any point in your program day. A simple sign-in and sign-out form for all families may be the best and easiest alternative. You may need to discuss this issue with individual children as well. When family members are fighting over custody, it is critical that children hear from you in clear and unemotional terms the conditions that you have for releasing them from the early childhood setting.

Environmental Risks

Both the indoor and outdoor environments have numerous risk factors that can and should be avoided:

- **Falls.** Children of all ages need to be protected from risks and injuries associated with falls from furniture and equipment. An infant, for example, should never be left unattended on a changing table. Similarly, indoor and outdoor climbing equipment for preschool and primary children should have shock-absorbing materials such as foam mats under and around it to prevent injuries from falls (Consumer Product Safety Commission, 2008). When appropriate, children should be taught correct foot placement and hand grips on the climbing equipment to decrease the likelihood of falls.

- **Burns.** Take a careful look at your indoor environment to see what might cause burns among young children. Do you have a radiator that gets very hot to the touch? What about hot liquids for coffee and tea for adults? Are there cooking activities for which you use a hot plate or stove? Do matches get left unattended in the early childhood setting? You will need to take steps to avoid each of these environmental risks by carefully preparing the indoor setting so that children will not be injured by them.

- **Poisons.** Indoors, it is important to lock up all medicines so that children can never access them. Even relatively low doses of things such as aspirin can cause significant injury to young children. Household cleaners are another example of poisonous substances that should be kept under lock and key. Outdoors, it is important to avoid having poisonous plants such as foxglove accessible to young children (National Resource Center for Health and Safety in Child Care, 2002).

Amelia, a 4-year-old, knows she can explore the materials on the shelves in her preschool program. She is encouraged to take the blocks and build with them or create art projects from the many options available in that center. But what about under the sink near the snack area? As she opens the cupboards to investigate, she finds two different cleaning agents among the sponges and rags. Luckily, Mrs. Abbot, her teacher, notices Amelia's inquisitiveness and redirects her to more appropriate areas. Furthermore, Mrs. Abbot decides to bring up the issue of storing cleaners in a more secure area at the next staff meeting.

- **Small and sharp objects.** Very young children (under age 3) tend to put small objects in the mouth as a way to explore some of their characteristics. This can be dangerous, so small objects should be avoided both indoors and on the playground. Similarly, sharp objects such as knives and pointed scissors should be kept out of the reach of young children.

- **Suffocation.** Plastic bags and plastic wrap can quickly and effectively cut off a young child's air supply, causing suffocation. You will need to keep these materials stored safely away and also take the time to talk with children about the hazards of placing plastic over the nose and mouth. Outdoors, be sure to check play equipment for sharp angles that might catch a young child's hood and cause the air supply to be cut off through the child's throat.

- **Traffic hazards.** Is your early childhood setting located on or near a busy street? If so, is there a high-quality fence to keep children from wandering off during outdoor play? It is also important to teach children simple strategies to improve safety when moving along a street where cars are present. For example, when taking a walking field trip through the local community, have several adult volunteers participate. Each adult can be responsible for a small group of 3 or 4 children, all of whom are holding hands and "connected" to an adult.

While avoiding unnecessary risks in early childhood settings, remember that reasonable risks are considered a healthy part of growing up. Bunker (1991) reminds us that children acquire self-confidence and self-esteem in part through successful physical activities. As children master and refine basic motor skills, they see themselves as more competent and capable. The preschool child who has mastered the monkey bars and exclaims for all the world to hear, "Hey, look at me!" is feeling good about himself and his accomplishment. The *Celebrating Play* feature in this section describes this connection between risk taking and emotional development. Part of the excitement of many physical tasks is the element of risk that accompanies them. Read the feature to learn more about the importance of physical play and risk taking.

Celebrating Play . . .
PLAY AND RISK TAKING

Smith (1990) suggests that a major attraction of playing outdoors is the opportunity to take risks. It is exciting to engage in play that might lead to accident or injury. Children do not want to be injured, but the possibility makes play more fun. This attitude is certainly contrary to what most adults want children to experience. That may be one reason why adults are frequently absent when children engage in their favorite play experiences outdoors. Kids want to take risks; adults prize safety in play.

Sutterby (2009) describes how today's children have very limited opportunities at home to engage in risk-taking behaviors. Families are worried about injuries and concerned about strangers in the neighborhood who may be child predators. They are hesitant to allow children to play unsupervised outdoors. These fears, combined with increasing levels of more structured activities, such as music lessons, after-school programs, and organized sports leads to fewer opportunities for young children to have experiences that their parents and grandparents found highly beneficial.

When early childhood professionals allow risk taking to take place, children are challenged to extend themselves both physically and emotionally in their motor play. When children have a safe play environment where they are free to explore and stretch their skills, they gain confidence in their abilities and want to spend more time in building them further. Because of the decline in active play and the resulting lack of physical fitness in many children, you should seriously consider this issue of risk taking and work to balance healthy risk taking with safety needs. In this way, children can explore more freely and spend the amount of time they need in physically active play.

1. Think back to your favorite play experiences and try to remember any that had elements of risk taking. Describe the play and its risk-taking elements. Do you think that the risks you took were an important reason why you enjoyed this play so much? Why or why not?

2. Do you think playgrounds and indoor-play environments for young children should include risk-taking opportunities? Describe the rationale for your response. What could you provide or do to allow at least some risk taking?

Accident Prevention

Although one of your primary responsibilities as an early childhood professional should be to address the environmental risks in your early childhood program, there are important ways to help young children avoid accidents outside your setting, too. You will need to discuss with children the risks of several significant problem behaviors. Passing this information on to families is another important component of accident prevention.

- **Water safety.** You should carefully check water temperature before placing an infant or toddler in bath water. To avoid potential drowning, never leave a child unattended in even the shallowest of baths. Discuss with preschool and primary children the risks of drowning in rivers, lakes, and swimming pools. This can reinforce what families are hopefully sharing with young children at home.

- **Fire safety.** Adult smoking is the leading cause of death from fires (Hall et al., 2006). Children playing with matches is another significant concern both in early care settings and at home. You will need to spend time talking with children and sharing with their families information about fire safety and what to do in case of a fire.

- **Firearm safety.** According to a recent study, approximately 24% of all households had one or more firearms in the home (Forbis et al., 2007). Many of the children you will be working with will be in environments where guns are common and safety issues need to be addressed. While many of us would rather not have to address this issue, children would be at risk if they did not have basic information about gun safety. Four thousand children in the United States were killed from gunshot wounds in 1998 (Forbis et al., 2007). It is also critical to share this information with families, unemotionally but clearly, in an effort to decrease the possibilities of injury or death from gunshot wounds.

Abuse and Neglect

Child abuse and neglect is a highly emotional topic that frequently is covered up and not discussed by either young children or adults, making it very difficult to diagnose and treat. Awareness of the problems of abuse and neglect led to the passage of the *Child Abuse and Treatment Act* in 1974. This law was most recently reauthorized in 2003. To receive federal assistance based on this act, all 50 states passed legislation that requires you as an early childhood professional (among many others) to report suspected cases of child abuse and neglect (Hmurovich, 2009). You may be one of the first to notice the signs and symptoms of abuse and neglect, and you must be prepared to report it using your state-mandated guidelines. Nearly 32% of all victims of child abuse and neglect were children under 4 years of age (U.S. Department of Health and Human Services, 2008). An additional 24% were 4 to 7 years of age. For these reasons, it is critical that you have a good working knowledge of this complex issue.

There are four main categories of abuse and neglect (Child Welfare Information Gateway, 2008):

1. **Neglect.** Neglect is defined as the failure of family members and others to meet the basic needs of the child. Not providing adequate food, shelter, or medical care are examples of neglect. Approximately 59% of the total child

abuse and neglect reports were for neglect (U.S. Department of Health and Human Services, 2008).

2. **Physical abuse.** Any purposeful physical injury by an adult or family member is considered physical abuse. Bruises, broken bones, and burning are examples of physical abuse. A little more than 10% of abuse and neglect cases were physical abuse (U.S. Department of Health and Human Services, 2008).

3. **Sexual abuse.** Sexual abuse occurs when an adult uses a child for sexual pleasure of any type, or exposes the child to others through physical contact or photos in a sexually explicit way. Nearly 8% of cases were for sexual abuse (U.S. Department of Health and Human Services, 2008).

4. **Emotional abuse.** Also referred to as psychological abuse, emotional abuse occurs when the child's emotional development or self-worth is impaired by the behavior of adults or family members. Emotional abuse accounts for approximately 4% of the total (U.S. Department of Health and Human Services, 2008).

To effectively report suspected cases of child abuse and neglect, you will need to have a basic understanding of key signs and symptoms. While the signs and symptoms presented here don't automatically mean that abuse or neglect is taking place, they provide indicators that may help you decide when to seek more professional help in diagnosis.

- **Physical abuse** (Pressel, 2000)
  A pattern of physical injuries that are not a typical part of the child's history.
  Bruises and fractures in areas that are unlikely to be from accidents.
  Patterned bruises from objects.
  Bruises and burns in very young children who are not yet mobile.
- **Neglect** (Morton & Salovitz, 2001)
  Inadequate supervision at home (child-reported).
  Poor personal hygiene.
  Malnutrition.
  Failure to obtain emergency medical, mental health, or dental care.
- **Sexual abuse** (American Humane Association, 2010)
  Sudden and dramatic change in general behavioral patterns.
  Bowel problems.
  Excessive fears of an individual.
  Complaints or symptoms of soreness of vagina or anus.
- **Emotional abuse** (Kimball, 2003)
  Evidence of adult substance abuse.
  Belligerant or verbally abusive communications from family members to early childhood professionals.
  Temper tantrums.
  Bullying.

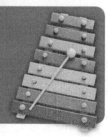

summary

The Importance of Health and Wellness

The early childhood years are critical for the development of lifelong habits of health and wellness. Physical, health, and safety education are all important elements of the developmentally appropriate curriculum.

Physical Education

With growing numbers of overweight and obese children and the corresponding decline in physical activity levels, it is becoming increasingly important for early childhood professionals to promote organized physical activities, both indoors and on the playground, to improve the overall health and well-being of young children.

Health Education

The health education program in early childhood settings should include nutrition, medical and dental health, and illness as topics for discussion. You should be prepared to model and discuss healthy living with young children.

Safety Education

Safety education for young children includes environmental risks and accident prevention. In addition to preparing the early childhood environments to be safe places for children, you will need to discuss these topics with children. As a mandated reporter of child abuse and neglect, you should be able to recognize signs and symptoms and be prepared to follow your state guidelines in reporting suspected cases.

for reflection and discussion

1. What personal health and wellness goals do you need to set in order to be a good role model for young children?
2. For the age of children you are most interested in, plan three or four physical education activities that you think would be appropriate. Discuss these with others and incorporate their feedback as appropriate.
3. What roles should the early childhood professional play in promoting good nutrition education with young children?
4. Write a few paragraphs about what you see as the biggest challenges of working with abused children and their families.

MyEducationLab

Go to Topic 7: Curriculum/Content Areas in the MyEducationLab (www.myeducationlab.com) for *Teaching Young Children*, where you can:

- Find learning outcomes for Curriculum/Content Areas along with the national standards that connect to these outcomes.
- Complete Assignments and Activities that can help you more deeply understand the chapter content.
- Apply and practice your understanding of the core teaching skills identified in the chapter with the Building Teaching Skills and Dispositions learning units.
- Examine challenging situations and cases presented in the IRIS Center Resources.
- Check your comprehension on the content covered in the chapter with the Study Plan. Here you will be able to take a chapter quiz, receive feedback on your answers, and then access Review, Practice, and Enrichment activities to enhance your understanding of chapter content.

13

Supporting Emotional and Social Development

IN THIS CHAPTER YOU WILL

- Learn about how you can support emotional development.
- Study the social development curriculum.
- Recognize the impact of stress on emotional and social development in children and its influence on adults.

Andrea has changed over the past few weeks from an excited, busy 5-year-old in your kindergarten classroom to a withdrawn and anxious child. Her life was turned upside down recently with the sudden death of her father. It is affecting her ability to relate to other children and has led to a short attention span as well as lackluster play experiences.

Some other children in the group, although not experiencing the same dramatic loss, live in single-parent homes and have limited contact with their fathers. They are wrestling with their own related problems.

You have decided to provide materials and activities in your classroom that can assist children in working through these stressors. Many excellent children's books are available that deal with living in single-parent homes, and you can add some to the library corner. A puppet family is another good possibility for the dramatic play area. In addition, now may be the time for that unit on families that you have been planning to introduce.

The problems of separation and loss are only two of many issues that young children and their families face today. Combine these stressors with the more normal challenges of emotional and social development, and it becomes clear that the curriculum in early childhood settings must address these important topics. A quality program for young children recognizes the value of guiding the growth of emotional development, social skills, and the coping strategies necessary to deal with the stresses of modern life.

Supporting Emotional Development

Emotional development in young children consists of a gradual growth in the ability to recognize, label, and appropriately respond to their feelings. Each step is important to emotional health and must be learned through repeated interactions with others. Your role as an early childhood professional will be to observe children expressing emotions, reflect on how these emotions impact the early childhood program, and apply strategies to identify and accommodate the emotions. Nissen and Hawkins (2010) outline three components of emotional competence that you will want to promote in your early childhood setting:

1. **Emotional expressiveness.** Children will need to work on their ability to positively express the emotions they experience.
2. **Emotional knowledge.** Young children will need help in identifying emotional expressions in others and responding in positive ways.
3. **Emotional regulation.** Young children will need to learn to manage the feelings they experience during social interactions.

Figueroa-Sanchez (2008) emphasizes the importance of positive emotional development and indicates that it is as fundamental as literacy skills in the healthy development of children. She states that early childhood professionals must build what she calls emotional literacy as an important foundation for early learning. It is important to build the vocabulary, concepts, and social skills needed for effectively managing emotions. Goleman (1995) presents the same case when stating:

> Emotional life is a domain that, as surely as math or reading, can be handled with greater or lesser skill, and requires its unique set of competencies. And how adept a person is at those is crucial to understanding why one person thrives in life, whereas another, of equal intellect, dead ends: Emotional aptitude is a meta-ability, determining how well we can use whatever other skills we have, including raw intellect. (p. 83)

What Are Emotions?

Emotions are feelings that come in response to other people, experiences, or circumstances. Stimuli from the environment cause physiological responses in the body that lead to feelings such as anger, fear, sadness, or surprise (Arnold, 2010).

 Seven-year-old Kimberly was severely bitten by a pit bull at age 3 and has since been fearful around dogs of all sorts. When she sees a dog, her heart rate goes up, and she literally begins to shake as she runs to her father for protection. Although not all emotional responses are as clearly defined as Kimberly's, we each have our own physical reactions to stimuli. These feelings are real and must be recognized and dealt with in positive ways.

Researchers who have studied emotional development suggest that young children are genetically programmed with **core emotions** that include joy, anger, sadness, and fear (Plutchik, 1980). These intense, relatively pure emotions serve as the foundation for the later emergence of more **complex emotions** such as frustration, annoyance, jealousy, and boredom.

MyEducationLab

Visit the MyEducationLab for *Teaching Young Children* to enhance your understanding of chapter concepts with a personalized Study Plan. You'll also have the opportunity to hone your teaching skills through video- and case-based Assignments and Activities as well as Building Teaching Skills and Disposition lessons.

Dealing with Feelings

Young children have much to learn about their feelings. Because it is very difficult to change their emotional responses to situations and people, it makes more sense to help them respond appropriately. You will need to help children recognize, label, and accept the feelings they have, and engage in appropriate responses to them.

Recognizing and labeling feelings. Before responding appropriately to emotions, children need to recognize that they are having an emotional reaction and then give it a name. Through most of the early childhood years, early childhood professionals will need to help children with this task. When the adult sensitively recognizes the emotional signs and gives them a label, children gradually develop the ability to do the same.

Six-year-old Ara is playing with a car in the block corner, and he briefly leaves the area to get a drink of water. Upon his return, Ara sees that Adrienne has taken the car he was using. With a loud scream, Ara rushes into the center, grabs his vehicle, and violently kicks down the block structure Adrienne has constructed. The teacher enters the area, takes Ara by the hand, and leads him away to a quiet corner of the room. She gets down to the child's level and says, "I can tell by your scream and kicking that Adrienne made you very angry when she took the car you were using." The teacher needs to continue her discussion with both Ara and Adrienne, but these initial comments make it clear that she has provided a label for Ara's feelings.

Accepting feelings. The emotions children experience can often be powerful and seem almost overwhelming to them. Children need to know that it is normal to have strong feelings and that it is important to accept them as a natural part of life. Unfortunately, many adults have not learned this lesson and try to deny their own feelings or those of children. Often, they make comments to children such as: "You're okay. There is nothing to be afraid of!"

The words adults use in communicating with children about emotions help them accept their feelings. The teacher dealing with Ara in the preceding example could add the following to her initial comment: "It's okay to be angry. Everybody gets angry sometimes." This will help Ara accept the strong emotion he experienced. Also remember that you are a role model for children in terms of how you express your own feelings. Be sure to use words and actions for your own feelings that are consistent with what you are expecting from children.

Appropriate responses to emotions. As children learn to recognize, label, and accept their feelings, they also need assistance in developing suitable responses. Although hitting, kicking, crying, or withdrawal may be the natural reaction for many children, they must learn to use words or other positive actions to more effectively deal with emotions.

Children's emotions are often clearly observable in their facial expressions and body language.

The teacher dealing with Ara in the preceding example could finish her discussion with him by saying:

"Ara, even though you are angry, I can't let you scream or kick playthings in the classroom. Can you think of a better way to let Adrienne know that you are angry?" If the child is unable to come up with another option, the teacher can then suggest acceptable alternatives.

Bullying

Bullying is a growing concern among early childhood professionals. While many would assume that bullying behaviors start in late elementary school and beyond, you may find early forms of bullying occurring in the preschool setting. Coy (2001) suggests that racial bullying may be seen as early as 3 or 4 years of age. Preschool bullying is typically in the form of name-calling and is intentionally passed from a family member on to the young child.

Bullying is generally viewed as having three main forms (Piotrowski & Hoot, 2008):

- **Physical bullying.** Physical contact that causes discomfort to another child is physical bullying.
- **Emotional bullying.** Excluding and ignoring other children are examples of emotional bullying.
- **Verbal bullying.** Language that is intended to belittle other children is considered verbal bullying. Some have called this relational aggression or psychological bullying (Espelage & Swearer, 2003).

While there may be a variety of causes for bullying, research indicates that it often stems from emotional immaturity (Crick & Grotpeter, 1995). Children who feel inferior, inadequate, or insecure, for example, may find that the power and control that comes from bullying is hard to resist. You will need to be alert to signs of emotional immaturity in young children and help them become more positive in their emotional responses.

Following are some strategies you can teach children to use when they have been bullied:

- **Tell an adult.** Children need to know that they have a right to be safe and that telling an adult is not "tattling" (Esch, 2008). Children's books, like *Jody and the Bully* (Anders, 1996) can help children see that telling a trusted adult is the first step in bringing resolution to bullying activities.
- **Use defined strategies to counter verbal bullying.** Children will need to learn key phrases or simple behaviors that they can use when another child bullies them verbally. When name-calling occurs, for example, children could respond with "Stop talking to me like that" or "Can't you think of something else to say?" (McNamee & Mercurio, 2008). An effective behavioral response may be to simply walk away from the bully.
- **Spend time in groups.** Bullies try to isolate a person that they perceive to have less power and engage in behaviors that belittle that one person. Children who spend their time in groups are less likely to be the object of bullying.
- **Fighting back doesn't work.** The old strategy of standing up to the bully and fighting back doesn't work (Piotrowski & Hoot, 2008). It tends to escalate the conflict, which increases the chance that someone will be more seriously hurt.

You may also be able to purchase and use a bullying/violence prevention curriculum in the early childhood setting. One example is the Second Step program developed by the Committee for Children (2010). Two options are available: a curriculum designed for preschool through kindergarten children and one designed for elementary children. The preschool/kindergarten program uses puppets, songs, and photo-lesson cards to present ideas for preventing bullying and violent childhood behaviors. Lesson cards and DVDs are used in the elementary curriculum to generate role-play situations and discussions on eliminating bullying and violence. Research on the effectiveness of the elementary program is encouraging, with studies showing significant gains in more pro-social behaviors following the implementation of this curriculum (Cooke et al., 2007; Frey et al., 2005).

Materials and Activities for Emotional Development

Many teachable moments for emotional development are spontaneous and come from the lives of children themselves. In addition, early childhood professionals can use a variety of materials and activities in the early childhood setting to help children learn about dealing with feelings. The following materials are effective in helping children to express their feelings in positive ways:

- **Art materials.** Clay, play dough, and paints (including finger paints) are all examples of materials that many children use regularly to express their feelings. Playing with a lump of play dough or painting a picture can be a healthy release for many children.

- **Dramatic play props.** Dolls, puppets, dress-up clothes, and housekeeping materials can encourage children to act out the experiences that lead to strong emotions. By playing them out, they can understand their feelings better and gradually work to set them aside. The *Celebrating Play* feature in this section describes a classic study of how children used play as a therapeutic tool to work through traumatic experiences they faced.

- **Books.** Many excellent children's books are available that address children's emotional issues. The story lines of these books bring up difficult issues (e.g., divorce or death) or the more normal emotions we all experience, thereby helping children begin to deal with the feelings involved. For example, *Dinosaurs Divorce* (Brown & Brown, 1988) is a book that helps young children understand and begin to talk about the complex set of emotions that exist when parents divorce.

- **Sand and water activities.** Playing with sand and water has a definite therapeutic value. When this play is combined with small figurines and dramatic play props, children can once again play out their emotional concerns. Some professional therapy techniques use sand to encourage disturbed youngsters to play out their severe emotional traumas (Yawkey & Pellegrini, 1984).

- **Music.** Tapes and CDs are available that either provide a calming background for program activities or address specific emotional issues. An example of the latter is Rosey Greer's "It's All Right to Cry" (in Marlo Thomas's *Free to Be You and Me*).

- **Internet resources.** The *Technology Explorations and Activities* feature in this section gives some examples of Internet resources that are available to support emotional development in young children. Take some time now to read the information and explore the Internet options that are available for use with young children.

Technology Explorations and Activities . . .
EMOTIONS AND FEELINGS GAMES

Games, when used appropriately in the early childhood setting, can be very effective teaching tools. Because emotions and feelings are often difficult concepts for young children to understand, games may prove helpful in teaching children to recognize and respond appropriately to the emotions they experience. Do an Internet search for the Do2Learn company. They have a variety of games that can be purchased for use with young children. In particular, the Feelings Game and a game called Faceland are offered as good ways to help children understand and respond to feelings and emotions. Review the online materials available and reflect on their usefulness.

Research, Reflect, and Respond

1. What do you see as the strengths and limitations of the two games? Do they seem appropriate for use by young children? Would you use either game in your work with young children?

2. Search the Internet for other emotions and feelings games. What did you find? Were there other options that you thought were better than the ones reviewed earlier?

Celebrating Play . . .
PLAY AS THERAPY

In a classic study on children and play, Brown, Curry, and Tittnich (1971) describe the reactions of several kindergarten children to the following situation:

On September 26, 1968, the children at the Arsenal Family and Children's Center witnessed a tragic accident outside the play yard. In this accident a man, who had been working on lights 20 feet above the ground, was catapulted from the bucket of his crane-like machine onto the concrete below. Because he did not have his safety helmet on, his head was severely injured. All this occurred only a few feet from the kindergarten playground which was occupied by 12 observant children. (p. 27)

You can imagine the scene: children standing around excitedly watching the man working high up in the air changing lights, followed by hushed silence as the man falls and strikes his head on the concrete. At that point, the early childhood professional decides to let the children stay outdoors because she wants them to see that people who get hurt receive aid quickly. In all likelihood, all 12 children remain glued to the fence until the ambulance comes to take the injured man away to the hospital. Still dazed and confused, the children are then taken indoors where they are encouraged to talk about what they have seen.

The authors go on to describe the longer-term reactions of these children to the accident they observed. With encouragement from concerned adults, these children began to incorporate both indoor and outdoor play themes that included falling, injuries, and others coming to provide assistance. These play sequences were repeated over and over again for a period of several months with small modifications as children explored new aspects of the situation. For example, at one point they pretended they were wearing safety helmets and, thus, avoided serious injury. After this extended period of play, children were eventually able to work through their anxieties about the difficult situation they had observed and move on to other play themes. For these children, play was a therapeutic tool.

1. Can you remember any therapeutic play sequences that you, your friends, or other children you have known engaged in? If so, describe them.

2. Do you think play can serve as an important therapeutic tool to help children work through many, if not most, of the stressors they face? Why or why not?

Facilitating Social Competence

The process of **socialization** begins at birth and continues throughout childhood. It involves learning to relate to a variety of people in many different circumstances (Oden, 1987). For example, relating to families is different from interacting with caregivers and teachers, grocery clerks, strangers on the street, and peers. Children also must learn that different environments call for varying social skills. It is generally okay to shout, run, and get dirty outdoors; the indoor setting tends to be a somewhat quieter environment. Similarly, churches, drugstores, and swimming pools each have their own environmental requirements for social interactions.

Historically, early educators have placed a heavy emphasis on encouraging positive social development (Braun & Edwards, 1972). More recent research helps substantiate the value of this emphasis (Joseph & Strain, 2003). Hartup (1992) puts it this way:

> Indeed, the single best childhood predictor of adult adaptation is *not* IQ, *not* school grades, and *not* classroom behavior, but, rather the adequacy with which the child gets along with other children. Children who are generally disliked, who are aggressive and disruptive, who are unable to sustain close relationships with other children, and who cannot establish a place for themselves in the peer culture are seriously "at risk." (p. 2)

Ellen Galinsky (2010), in an important new book titled *Mind in the Making,* describes seven essential life skills that every child must have in order to be successful. Two of those seven have strong implications for children who are working to develop social competence:

- **Perspective taking.** To be successful in a variety of situations, including social interactions, children must learn to take the perspectives of others into consideration. By seeing things as others see them, children gradually learn that people come to any interaction with differing thoughts, experiences, likes, and dislikes. While this is difficult for young children because of their natural tendency toward egocentrism (Flavell, 1963), perspective taking is a key step in becoming a social being.
- **Communicating.** Being a good communicator is essential to virtually every interaction we have with others. Think about your relationships with other adults and the problems that occur when communications are not what they should be. Anger, frustration, and misunderstandings are often the result. On the other hand, when the message sent is understood by the one receiving it, effective communication takes place and social relationships are strengthened. Good communication is essential for young children to learn as they work to build social relationships with families, other adults, and peers. The *Developmentally Appropriate Practice* feature in this section provides suggestions for creating an environment in which positive communications are more likely to occur.

Given the importance of quality social skills, it is helpful to have a list of positive attributes to encourage in early childhood settings. McClellan and Katz (1997) provide a checklist of social skills as a guide for early childhood professionals:

- Approaches others positively
- Expresses wishes and preferences clearly

Developmentally Appropriate Practice...
CREATING A POSITIVE VERBAL ENVIRONMENT

Good communications are more likely to occur when you create a positive verbal environment. Meece and Soderman (2010) provide a number of good tips that will assist you in this effort:

- **Know and respect each child as an individual.** By warmly greeting each child every day, calling them by name, and using supportive touch, you send each child the message that you care about them.

- **Show children that you are interested in them and what they do.** Get close to the child and down on their level to communicate. Engage in childhood play from time to time as a way to show interest.

- **Speak courteously.** Be patient and polite in your communications so that you model for children how you want them to communicate. Avoid interrupting children as they work to communicate with you or others.

- **Ask different kinds of questions.** Modeling what you hope young children will do in their communication with you and others, ask children questions that make them think, that show your own curiosity, and that are open-ended and require more lengthy responses.

- **Make sure your expectations are clear.** Children need to know what to do, rather than what they are to avoid. "Walk indoors, please" would be an example of this.

- **Give children choices.** When children have true choices in the early childhood setting, they learn to make better decisions about their social interactions.

- Asserts personal rights and needs appropriately
- Is not easily intimidated by bullies
- Expresses frustration and anger in positive ways
- Easily joins others in work or play
- Participates in discussions and makes contributions to activities
- Is able to take turns
- Shows an interest in others
- Can negotiate and compromise in interactions with others
- Accepts and enjoys people of diverse ethnic groups
- Uses appropriate nonverbal communication such as smiling and waving

The Center on the Social and Emotional Foundations for Early Learning, funded by Head Start and the Child Care Bureau (Center on the Social and Emotional Foundations for Early Learning, 2010), is a national consortium that provides practical information for families, early childhood professionals, and others on topics of social and emotional development. The Center produces a series of briefs titled *What Works?* that are available online and include practical tips in both English and Spanish for adults interacting with children. Currently, 22 briefs can be downloaded by early childhood programs and families. For example, Brief 8 is titled *Promoting Positive Peer Social Interactions*. It gives examples of evidence-based practices that adults can use to support children's social interactions with their peers. Because all of the briefs are available online, they provide quick and useful information to early childhood professionals working to support emotional and social development in early childhood settings.

Building a Sense of Self

Social and emotional development strongly influence one another in childhood (Denham et al., 2003) as can be seen in the relationship between a child's self-concept and social development. **Self-concept** can be defined as how people feel about themselves and is generally considered to be a component of emotional development. It has three dimensions (Kostelnik et al., 2009):

- **Competence.** A person's belief that he/she can accomplish tasks and achieve goals
- **Worth.** A person's sense of being valued by others
- **Control.** The degree to which people feel they can influence events around them

Self-concept is seen as a significant factor in emotional development, but it also plays a role in the socialization process. Children with strong self-concepts think of themselves as competent and likable. They look forward to the challenges of social interactions, and expect to do well. Individuals with low self-concepts, however, often feel inadequate in social situations and fear rejection.

Obviously, we want to promote positive self-concepts in early childhood settings and need to engage children in activities and interactions that enhance perceptions of themselves. Canfield and Wells (1994) suggest the following principles for building a positive self-concept:

- Early childhood professionals can either positively or negatively influence self-concept. Learn and use the positive strategies.
- Building a strong self-concept is not easy. It takes time and considerable energy.
- Although they are harder to change, try to influence central beliefs, such as feelings about academic ability, social skills, or attractiveness.
- Relate the successes and strengths you observe in children to one another. This enhances those central beliefs.
- All the little things you do—such as calling children by their names and complimenting them for positive interactions—help build strong self-concepts. When these interactions are sincere, specific, and occur regularly, children see themselves as more competent.

The *Developmentally Appropriate Practice* feature in this section provides additional ideas for enhancing self-concepts of young children.

Adult–Child Relationships

Caregivers and teachers in early childhood settings are an important factor in the development of children's social skills. Their efforts to relate effectively with children, create a positive climate, and develop strategies to deal with problems are all significant in this process.

Without question, adults are models of behavior that young children imitate (Bandura, 1989). Children listen to the words that you use to communicate with others and then try them out in their own speech. They use polite comments like "please" and "thank you" far more often in settings where early childhood professionals regularly use them. Children imitate smiles, eye contact, and physical touch when they see adults using these important nonverbal skills. Children also observe and imitate the techniques adults use to resolve problems with children and other adults.

The climate that early childhood professionals create influences children's developing social skills, too. Glasser (1990) calls this *building a friendly workplace* and identifies several strategies that are helpful to consider:

- Avoid becoming adversarial in relationships with children.
- Create an atmosphere where courtesy prevails.
- Show an interest in children's lives, and share some information about yourself as a person.
- Ask children for advice and help whenever you can.
- Develop close, caring work relationships with children.

Developmentally Appropriate Practice . . .
ENHANCING SELF-CONCEPT

Early childhood professionals can strengthen children's self-concepts in two major ways. The first is through their daily interactions with them. Dreikurs, Grunwald, and Pepper (1982) call this *encouragement*; it is the adults' efforts to let children know they trust and believe in them. The second method of building self-concept is through *planned activities*. Examples of each type follow. The Center on the Social and Emotional Foundations for Early Learning (2010) provides additional examples of both encouragement and planned activities for you to consider.

Encouragement

Although every child reacts differently to adult interactions, children often view these behaviors as encouraging:

- Smiling, a pat on the shoulder, a hug
- Spending time finding out about a child's weekend
- Praise for work well done
- Pointing out a child's strengths
- Displaying a child's work
- Attending an after-school sports event

Planned Activities

Planned events, while contrived, are still very productive in helping children feel good about themselves. The titles for these activities are playful descriptors of their intent.

- **I Like. . . .** Choose one member of the group each day, and have children share things they like about that person. With younger children, come prepared with several things you like about the targeted child so that many examples can be presented. Make sure that every child eventually has a chance to be the center of attention for this activity.

- **Person of the Week.** While it is important to recognize and value every child every day, creating a Person of the Week allows you to get to know each child in a special way. For example, you might display a bulletin board created by family members and the child that includes pictures and other highlights of family life. Another option would be to invite family members into the early childhood setting to share more about their lives and to get to know the other children.

The way early childhood professionals organize and enhance the physical environment also influences the overall climate. For example, a comfortable child-sized couch or several throw pillows create an inviting space for reading or other quiet activities. Decorating the walls with children's artwork and creative writing delivers an important message that this work is valued by those who work and play there. Careful attention to these details in the beginning of the program year can pay big dividends later.

The intervention strategies that early childhood professionals use to address the socialization problems that come up throughout the day also have a great influence on the skills children develop.

Margaret is an active, busy 4-year-old in your child-care program. She is a natural leader, and others in the group often follow her direction. Margaret is playing in the block center and decides that she wants to use the dump truck Deforrest is filling with blocks. She says, "Deforrest, if you let me use the truck, I'll play with you later." New to the group and naturally shy, he reluctantly agrees rather than cause conflict.

How should the adult intervene in this situation to help both children learn better strategies for interacting? Deforrest needs to develop positive ways to stand up for himself while becoming a part of the group. Margaret has to learn she cannot always have her own way and needs to channel her leadership abilities in more positive directions. One possible response is, "Margaret, Deforrest is using the truck right now. When he is finished, I hope you will ask him again to play with you." The intervention strategies you use to deal with this situation and others will help determine how effectively both children learn to relate in social settings.

Family–child relationships are another important factor in the young child's developing social abilities. In addition to being role models for appropriate (or inappropriate) interactions, families provide the foundations for effective social and emotional development. During the infant/toddler years, a key role of families is to help young children develop a basic sense of trust that others will meet their social/emotional needs (Erikson, 1963). When this occurs, infants and toddlers are more likely to be ready for other social interactions outside the home. Similarly, families provide infants and toddlers with the opportunity to form strong attachments with at least one primary caregiver (Bowlby, 1969). These attachment bonds give children the confidence they need to feel good about themselves and be secure enough to interact with others in social situations.

Peer Interactions

Relationships with early childhood professionals help children develop social skills. Interactions with peers are the proving ground for these unfolding abilities. Developing peer relationships is an important step for children and one that is difficult to accomplish. Infants and toddlers spend most of their time interacting with adults and only gradually move toward the more challenging task of socializing with peers. Preschool children are becoming more aware of their peers and beginning to build relationships with

Young children spend considerable energy building and maintaining friendships.

them. Primary children find that budding friendships consume increasingly larger proportions of their time and energy.

One of the reasons young children struggle with peer relationships is their level of cognitive development. Piaget suggests that young children are egocentric (Flavell, 1963). They have difficulty seeing issues from the perspective of others. Other research (see, e.g., Newcombe & Huttenlocher, 1992) suggests that children may be less rigid in their perspective-taking than Piaget originally believed; however, it is only gradually and through repeated interactions with peers in play and work situations that children consistently recognize that others may have opinions, attitudes, and needs that are separate from their own.

Play, both indoors and on the playground, is one of the best settings for the development of social skills (Van Hoorn, Nourot, Scales, & Alward, 2011). Most play sequences include several children and require effective communication, compromise, leaders, and followers to be successful. Children have many opportunities to practice all aspects of their developing social skills as they engage in play themes. Jambor (1994) suggests that for school-age children, recess time on the playground is one of the few opportunities they have to engage in meaningful social experiences. Unfortunately, because of the current heavy emphasis on cognitive learning brought about by the No Child Left Behind Act of 2002, as many as 40% of the school districts in the United States have reduced or eliminated recess for young children (Zygmunt-Fillwalk & Bilello, 2005).

As children engage in play activities and other interactions with peers, they develop important social skills:

- **Making friends.** The essentials of friendship are commitment and reciprocity between two people who are fairly equal in power. Early friendships often set the stage for making and keeping friends later in life (Hartup & Moore, 1990).
- **Sharing and helping.** Taking turns with toys, helping with a puzzle, and sharing food at snack time are examples of behaviors that children engage in regularly when encouraged to do so. When adults practice these skills, it helps them develop into caring adults who support and encourage one another.
- **Cooperation.** When children willingly and without coercion by an authority figure support and assist one another, they are engaging in cooperative activity. Play provides many opportunities for cooperation.
- **Respecting rules.** Rules or conventions for appropriate conduct are an important part of all social interactions. Listening when another is speaking is just one of the rules that children must learn to follow if they want to participate effectively in social interactions.
- **Problem solving.** Social interactions often lead to disagreements that must be resolved. Children learn problem-solving strategies to deal with these conflicts.
- **Expressing feelings.** Although children often express their feelings toward others in inappropriate ways (hitting, kicking, biting, name-calling), they also quickly learn that these approaches get in the way of friendships and being part of a group. More appropriate ways of communicating feelings are needed.

The *Observing Development* feature in this section provides an opportunity to observe the social interactions of young children in an early childhood setting. Take some time to complete this observation and reflect on what you saw.

Observing Development . . .
SOCIAL RELATIONSHIPS

Choose one of the age groups within early childhood (infants/toddlers, preschoolers, or primary-age children), *observe* social relationships using the sample observation form that follows as a guide for your own observation, and make an x or check every time you see one of the listed behaviors.

Central Elementary School playground, 11:00–11:30 a.m.

Physical Proximity (attempts to be close)	X X
Physical Distance (walks, runs away from others)	
Verbal Communication	X X X X
Sharing and Helping (taking turns, sharing toy)	X
Cooperating (working together for common goal)	
Expressing Feelings (verbal or physical)	X

Reflect and Apply

1. Compare and contrast the social skills of the children you observed. What observed strengths and limitations did you find?

2. Reflect on the reasons for the differences you saw. Were there behaviors that led to either problems or positive interactions? What would you consider to be the reasons for the social skill differences observed?

Guiding Social Interactions

When children have conflicts or problems in their interactions with peers and others, you will need to step in and provide assistance. Because young children are just beginning to develop their social skills, this guidance should be provided calmly and in easily understood language so that children can learn to make better choices as they interact with others. Two approaches may be useful to you in guiding social interchanges:

Guided participation. Based on the theory of Lev Vygotsky (1962) and the concept of the zone of proximal development, guided participation takes place when the adult provides just the right amount of support to help the young child learn new skills and knowledge that will assist him in social development (Petty, 2009). Guided participation helps young children solve problems and build social skills that they need for social play activities (Rogoff et al., 1993). Guided participation is a three-step process (Petty, 2009):

- **Assess the circumstances.** The adult must first determine that a problem has come up in the play situation and communicate the issue to the children involved. For example, Mioki and Saul are playing in the block area and Saul has tried to take a block from Mioki's stack. She is currently holding it to her chest and refusing to let go. The caregiver could assess the situation and say, "It appears that Mioki doesn't want you to use that block right now."

- **Inquire about the child's understanding of the problem.** As you continue to guide the responses in a potential conflict, it is important to find out if the child has an accurate understanding of the situation. In the previous example, the adult could ask, "Why do you think she won't let you have it?"

- **Respond to the problem behavior.** Responses should give children the opportunity to think about possible alternatives. In addition, the adult should continue to monitor the play activities until no further assistance is needed. "Saul, when you want a block for your play, you can ask Mioki if you can use it, or look for another block like it on the shelf."

Conflict resolution. Another effective approach in guiding young children's social interactions is called conflict resolution. First applied in adult situations, these problem-solving approaches have now been adapted to early childhood settings. One popular example of this type is being promoted by the HighScope program in Ypsilanti, Michigan. Best known over the last several decades for their highly regarded early childhood curriculum model, HighScope has more recently created a conflict resolution approach for young children from 18 months to 6 years of age. As with most conflict resolution programs, the HighScope option promotes a six-step method for helping adults work through emotional and social conflicts (Evans, 2009):

- **Approach calmly.** Your behavior helps set the tone for the interactions. Using a calm manner will help diffuse emotions. Calmly stopping any hurtful activities is the first step in conflict resolution.
- **Acknowledge children's feelings.** Verbalize the emotions you see children expressing. "Mary Lynne, I can see that you're sad because Rashard hit you."
- **Gather information.** Even if you saw what happened, getting children to verbalize their perspectives on what occurred and why can be important. "Rashard, why did you hit Mary Lynne?" "Mary Lynne, were you doing anything that might have made Rashard mad?"
- **Restate the problem.** Using brief, clear statements, summarize the problem as you see it. Make sure that the children agree with your statement. "So, Mary Lynne, you called Rashard a twit. That made him mad and he hit you."
- **Ask for solutions.** Hopefully, children will volunteer possible solutions on their own. "Mary Lynne, what could you do differently next time? Rashard, what about you?" With very young children, you may need to assist by providing at least one alternative. After all the solutions are presented, make sure to discuss them and choose the best solution together.
- **Follow up as needed.** Always check back with children who have been through a problem-solving session to make sure they are following the agreed-upon solution.

The Environment and Materials

In many instances, the curriculum for developing social skills occurs spontaneously as children interact with peers or other adults. For example, as early childhood professionals quietly assist children in finding alternatives to hitting as an expression of anger, they are engaging in an informal social development curriculum. As important as these informal teaching/learning opportunities are, however, adults need to make a conscious effort to plan for social skill development. This curriculum is described in the following paragraphs.

The physical setting in which young children interact is an important element of the socialization process. Careful planning of space helps make positive interactions more likely. The following suggestions should be considered in organizing space:

- **Space to be social.** The physical space should invite children to interact with one another. Clusters of desks or child-sized tables and chairs, centers

Early childhood professionals use puppets to model appropriate social interactions.

designed for small groups of children, large throw pillows, and open spaces for gathering are examples of this type. The *Developmentally Appropriate Practice* feature in this section provides additional information on social spaces for infants and toddlers.

- **Access to work and play spaces.** If you want children to interact spontaneously with their peers and others on a regular basis, you will need to provide ready access to the spaces available to them. Children who are free to explore their environment for major parts of the school day will naturally have more social interactions with others.

- **Pictures that depict social activities.** When selecting pictures for the walls in different centers, try to find ones that show adults and children engaging in pro-social behaviors.

- **Materials that foster cooperation.** A mural for an art project, computer software that takes two or more to play, and noncompetitive board games are examples of materials that children can use to strengthen social skills.

- **Fewer options to encourage sharing.** Having just one piece of popular equipment (e.g., a special dump truck) for children may lead to major conflicts. Having too many pieces, however, eliminates the opportunity to practice sharing. The best option is to have fewer pieces than children would like so that some sharing is needed.

- **Books dealing with social skills.** A variety of children's books deal with socialization issues. One such example is *A Friend Is Someone Who Likes You* (Anglund, 1983). You should rotate books in and out of the library/book center that provide children with examples of positive social interactions.

The daily schedule of events is another way the environment influences the development of social skills. When early childhood professionals provide adequate time for children to work and play in small groups or as a class, more productive interactions take place. It is critical to remember that short time blocks are seldom effective for socialization and may in fact be counterproductive.

Children need time to warm up to the idea of working or playing with others, time to plan what they are going to do, opportunity to engage in the activity, and a cooling-off period. Even for primary-age children, these blocks of time are seldom productive if they are shorter than 20 or 30 minutes.

Activities and Themes

The social curriculum plan should also include activities that promote the developmental skills emphasized in the early childhood program. You can choose from a rich assortment of options. A sampling of ideas for activities follows:

- **Songs.** Singing and music are wonderful learning tools for all areas of the curriculum. Social development is no exception. Some songs are appropriate for every

Developmentally Appropriate Practice . . .
SOCIAL SPACES FOR INFANTS AND TODDLERS

Curtis and Carter (2006) remind us that infants and toddlers in early care settings engage primarily in social interactions with adults. They go on to state that the true curriculum at this level is centered specifically on relationships: "For infants and toddlers, responsive interactions are what curriculum is about" (p. 109). Caregivers working with very young children must then create spaces that enhance these social interactions. They should facilitate adult–child and child–child interactions and help young children feel a sense of belonging (Curtis & Carter, 2003). Here are some ideas for creating these social spaces:

- **Create engaging spaces for routines.** Many of the interactions that caregivers have with infants and toddlers center around the routines of the day. Diaper changing, toileting, washing up, and eating are important social opportunities. Make each of these spaces engaging for both adults and children through your choice of color, pictures, and comfortable equipment.

- **Give your environment a cozy, home-like feel.** Providing a home-like environment helps infants and toddlers feel safe, secure, and connected. Comfortable stuffed chairs, rugs, and indirect lighting are some examples of materials that can add this home-like feel to the early childhood setting.

- **Add a sense of softness to the room.** When furniture, lighting, pictures, and colors are selected that create a sense of softness, both children and adults will be more likely to engage in quality social interactions.

- **Remember to plan for the outdoor setting.** The outdoor setting provides many more opportunities for social interactions. Include comfortable seating for both children and adults that encourages social interactions. Use colorful plantings, a variety of natural textures, and purchased materials that add a sense of softness and coziness to the outdoor setting as well.

---

age within the early childhood range. Examples that fit this category from a songbook by Warren (1991) titled *Piggyback Songs for School* include "Helping," "Friends," "Be My Friend," and "Here We Are Together."

- **Play materials.** The equipment available to children in centers also influences the potential for social learning. Dolls, dramatic play props, and puppets are all examples of materials that encourage social learning opportunities. The *Celebrating Diversity* feature in this section provides additional information on the value of dolls in discussing and understanding diversity topics in the early childhood setting.

- **Games.** Games for young children should be noncompetitive. Many excellent books on childhood games are available to promote positive social interactions. Four examples are *Group Games in Early Education* (Kamii & DeVries, 1980); *The Cooperative Sports and Games Book: Challenge Without Competition* (Orlick, 1978); *The Second Cooperative Sports and Games Book* (Orlick, 1982); and *Everybody Wins: 393 Non-Competitive Games for Young Children* (Sobel, 1984).

- **Community workers.** An important aspect of social development is learning about and effectively relating to people in the community. Having construction workers, firefighters, doctors, and others as guests in your program provides children with opportunities to better understand and interact with these people.

- **Discussions.** Reading a good book about social relationships or using a similar discussion starter can help generate a productive dialogue with children about social skills. For example, reading *Alexander and the Terrible, Horrible, No Good,*

Celebrating Diversity . . .
THROUGH THE USE OF DOLLS

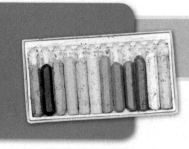

The toys we have available for young children tell a great deal about what we value as early childhood professionals. If we provide colorful, inviting options that encourage children to explore and experiment, we are telling them that we value these attributes. Similarly, if we value diversity in our early childhood programs, it is important to provide toys that demonstrate this commitment. One important option to consider is to have dolls of all types available for children to play with. For example, there are several manufacturers currently producing high-quality dolls with skin tone differences and clothing options that are representative of African-American, Native-American, and Asian cultures. When these dolls are placed in the early childhood setting, Caucasian children can play out events in which multicultural children participate in natural ways. Children of color unconsciously see their ethnicity respected and valued through the provision of quality dolls. All children are more likely to engage in productive dialogue about diversity when these multicultural dolls are available.

In addition to the multicultural dolls just described, several companies are producing dolls with special needs that are being used in early childhood settings. A doll without a leg and equipped with crutches, or a doll in a wheelchair, can be a useful toy in any program. These toys may be particularly valuable in settings where there are no children present with these special needs. With these dolls, children can play out their understandings of disabilities and be reinforced by the adult or other children when they are correct and learn from others when they have misunderstandings. Again, all children benefit as conversations and play themes focus more directly on issues related to children with special needs.

A more controversial option is the anatomically correct doll. Several companies are producing boy dolls complete with penis and testicles and girl dolls with vaginas. The intent is to let young children naturally explore these sexual differences in their play. By asking direct questions, young children receive matter-of-fact responses from caring adults about sexual differences and the reasons for them. As you might expect, this early introduction of sexual topics is not always well-received by families and others. Despite the good intentions of this approach, many families see this as an infringement upon their responsibility for addressing this issue.

1. Do you think a diverse collection of dolls can help young children develop deeper understandings of both the similarities and differences among people? Why or why not?

2. How do you feel about including anatomically correct dolls in early childhood settings? Give a rationale for your response.

Very Bad Day (Viorst, 1972) can lead to a lively discussion of what can be done to support someone who has a bad day. When discussions like this include topics being experienced by children, meaningful communications can take place.

- **Group learning projects.** For primary children, the teacher can assign group projects that require children to work together to complete tasks. More formally referred to as **cooperative learning**, these projects can be effective in developing social competence (Magnesio & Davis, 2010). They help build social skills and provide quality integrated learning opportunities. The *Developmentally Appropriate Practice* feature in this section describes a group project that encourages social development as part of an integrated learning experience.

Thematic teaching can also be used to stimulate social learning. Cooperation is a theme that early childhood professionals can use to build social skills. Following are examples of center materials and activities that might be used in a unit on cooperation:

- *Pictures* in centers showing adults and children cooperating will help create the right atmosphere for the theme.
- *Cooperative block building* can be encouraged both verbally and by providing a large map of a city that children can use as the foundation for creating their own city.

Developmentally Appropriate Practice . . .
INTEGRATING PRIMARY CURRICULUM THROUGH GROUP PROJECTS

As children at the primary level grow in their ability to interact with their peers, group learning experiences become meaningful opportunities for social development and cognitive learning. Early childhood professionals need to assist young children in becoming more environmentally aware. They need to understand the interrelationships that exist between all living things and their surroundings. As primary children study the environment, they learn science, study the broad goals of the society, use math skills, and engage in social interactions with peers and adults. Following are some ideas for helping primary children become more environmentally aware through group projects:

- **Pick up trash on the school playground.** Have children collect trash from the school playground and bring it into the classroom for study. Small groups can work to identify health and safety hazards related to the specific materials found.

As a class, discuss ways in which the school community can become more aware of the problems associated with playground litter and strategies for eliminating the problem. Communicate these findings to others in the school.

- **Plant trees to create more green space.** Have small groups of children study the impact of different fossil fuels on the environment. Research the positive benefits of planting trees to help overcome this problem. Purchase small trees that children can plant somewhere in your local community. Notify the local newspaper or television station for possible coverage of this community project.

- **Recycle common household materials.** Have children bring bags of newspaper, plastic containers, and recyclable metals to class. Have small groups investigate the processes used in recycling these different materials. Take the items collected to a local recycle center. Write letters to family members sharing the results of this recycling effort.

- *Difficult puzzles* in the manipulative center can be completed by two or more children.
- *Cooperative sand structures* can be part of the outdoor activities. Adults can give pairs or small groups of children their own tools for building.
- *Mural art projects* allow children to work on a common art activity.
- *Group fingerpainting* is an art project that encourages children to work together.
- *Post office* props in the dramatic play area help children cooperate as they take different roles related to writing, sending, and receiving mail.
- *Books* on cooperation such as *Sharing* by Newman (1990) support the theme.
- *Commercial music recordings* such as Fred Rogers' *Let's Be Together Today* or Marlo Thomas's *Free to Be You and Me* can be available for use in the music center.

 ## Stress as a Factor in Emotional and Social Development

When we think about stress, we generally associate it with adult life rather than childhood. Over the last few decades, however, more and more people have been concerned about the levels of stress that even young children experience. David Elkind (2001) has been one of the most visible and well-known spokespersons for this issue.

Stress has always been a part of childhood. Making friends, going to grandma's house, learning about the world around them, and living in a family are all examples of the normal stresses of growing up. But what Elkind and others are concerned about are the additional stressors children face today. While not every stressor is problematic, each has an additive effect that can eventually make life more difficult for children. Divorce, remarriage, violence and sexual themes on television, unsafe home environments, natural disasters, and the increased pressures of schooling are examples of potential stressors.

This combination of both normal and extra stress is making it difficult for many children to deal successfully with areas of their social/emotional development. If stress is allowed to build, most children eventually reach a point of feeling overwhelmed, and developmental progress suffers. For example, a common response from children of divorce is that they feel responsible for their parents' breakup (Elkind, 2001). If these feelings are not worked through with the assistance of caring adults, they can cause children to devalue themselves as individuals and may negatively affect not only their overall self-esteem but their social development as well.

It is difficult for young children to appropriately process televised violence.

Stress Factors

What are the major factors causing children stress? In addition to the ones already mentioned, the following list helps clarify the most significant issues.

Family circumstances. The most common stressor faced by today's children is divorce. However, remarriage, two-career families, and gay parents are other examples of family situations that can cause children stress. For example, a young child in a two-career family may experience what Elkind (2001) calls *change overload* from being shuttled between early morning care, school, and late afternoon supervision. Families who are homeless, or who live in high crime areas add other stressors to the lives of young children.

Early pressure to excel. Many well-meaning families inadvertently put stress on their children by involving them in too many extracurricular activities. While some young children benefit from early musical experiences, competitive sports programs, and computer camps, more often these experiences add stress to their lives. A more specific example of early pressure to excel comes from the writings of Glenn Doman (1961). In his book, *Teach Your Baby to Read*, and through the Institutes for the Achievement of Human Potential (2010), Doman has been encouraging families for more than 40 years to teach their infants and toddlers to read. Although it is possible to teach some children to read at very early ages, there is no research to indicate that this approach has any long-term value for these early readers. For most children, this activity only adds to their stress level.

Media stress. For a variety of reasons, television is a stressful media experience for children (Center for Communication Policy, 1997). One reason is that young children have difficulty separating fact from fantasy and therefore struggle to understand and cope with the violence and sexual themes they regularly encounter. Television advertising has also been criticized because of the unhealthy foods and low-quality toys promoted and the conflicts that arise in interactions with families (Notar, 1989). Movies, popular music, and even some children's books (Carlsson-Paige & Levin, 1986) have also been cited for their stressful impact on children.

Child abuse and neglect. Families under stress may react in very inappropriate ways to children. Physical abuse in the form of beatings, sexual relations between family members, and blatant neglect may result. As an adult working with young children, you need to be aware of these symptoms and be ready to report possible child abuse and neglect to the proper authorities. The *Child Abuse Prevention and Treatment Act*, originally enacted by the federal government in 1974 and reauthorized most recently in 2003, requires mandatory reporting of suspected cases of child abuse. All 50 states have passed similar legislation requiring teachers and other selected

Family Partnerships . . .
REDUCING STRESS AT HOME

Stress is an all-pervasive force within our society. We all face it in many different forms. In some instances, the stressors are deeply rooted and difficult to address. The loss of a loved one, for example, causes deeply felt stress that may take years and professional assistance to resolve. Other stressors are more a matter of lifestyle choices and can be resolved with careful thought and effort. For example, lack of sleep causes most people to be irritable and have poor work performance. With careful planning, however, this stressor can be eliminated. As a future early childhood professional, you can help families address this latter category of stressors. When you do, happier and healthier children are the result.

As you work to assist families in reducing the stress in their lives, it is important to keep the following in mind:

- **Remind without belittling.** "Lecturing" families about the importance of good nutrition, for example, will have little chance of changing behaviors. You will need to be nonjudgmental as you share useful information with them.

- **Share information from other experts.** Avoid setting yourself up as the expert. First of all, you probably are not, and second, families will resent your attitude. Find others in the community, state, or nation that can share their knowledge and insight with families.

- **Use a variety of reminders.** There are a number of different ways to send the same message. Meetings with families, a class newsletter, a video or book that families can check out, or a notice regarding a community event are all useful tools to share your ideas. By using a variety of approaches, you are more likely to reach a greater number of families.

- **Avoid a critical attitude.** You will probably never fully know all the problems and stresses faced by each of the families you work with. Avoid being critical of them or your helpful advice will go unheeded. Time and repeated discussions may be needed before changes can take place.

- **Be a good role model.** With families, just as with children, you will need to model the message you are sharing. If you want families to be aware of the importance of active outdoor experiences as a stress reliever, make sure you engage in these activities yourself so that they can see that you are "practicing what you preach."

1. How effective are you right now in reducing the unnecessary stresses in your own life? Is this something you will need to work on before helping families to do the same? Describe your current efforts to reduce stress in your life. What else could you be doing?

2. Is it important to help families reduce the stress in their lives? Why or why not?

professionals to report cases of child abuse to the proper authorities. Make sure you know the specific legal regulations for the state in which you plan to teach.

Growing up too quickly. Elkind (2001) suggests that many children today are being pressured by society to grow into adulthood too quickly. He calls these children "hurried" and sees this push to grow up as a pervasive element in American society. Consider, for example, the clothing we now buy for our children. There is virtually no distinction between adults and children in the clothes we wear. When youngsters are dressed like adults, we expect them to engage in adult-like behavior. A related example is the proliferation of beauty contests for young girls. With adult hair styles, makeup, and clothes, very young children are placed in high-stress situations where they are expected to act like miniature adults. In many other ways, children are being hurried into adulthood too quickly. Can you identify other examples of this type?

Helping Children Cope

Clearly, children need adult assistance in working through both the normal stresses of development and the added complications of living in modern American society. Several good strategies are available to help children deal with stress (Elkind, 2001; McCracken, 1986):

- **Be aware of the times we hurry children.** This recognition is the first step in helping children deal with their stress.
- **Analyze the distinctive effects of stress on each child.** The temperament, age, developmental level, and individual child's perception of the stress all influence the impact of stress. Some children have an incredible ability to manage seemingly overwhelming circumstances; others struggle unsuccessfully to deal with much lower levels of stress.
- **Eliminate stressors whenever possible.** This is easy to say and much harder to do. However, early childhood professionals and families can work together to reduce stress by doing such things as making sure children eat right, get plenty of rest, slow down, have time to talk about issues and concerns, and avoid inappropriate television programming. The *Family Partnerships* feature in this section discusses positive ways that you can help families reduce the stress in their lives.
- **Take time to have fun with kids.** When you get to know children better by occasionally eating lunch with them or playing a game for fun, relationships are strengthened and children are fortified to better deal with the next stress to come their way.
- **Be respectful of children.** Elkind (2001) suggests that showing respect is a simple, direct way to let children know that we value them. Just knowing that adults care is a support to children under stress.
- **Encourage childhood play.** Elkind states, "Basically, play is nature's way of dealing with stress for children as well as adults" (Elkind, 2001, p. 197). When children can repeatedly play out the issues they are struggling to understand, they can make sense of them and gradually be able to set them aside. From the serious problems of a disturbed child (Axline, 1964) to the more mundane struggles of young children everywhere, childhood play is one of the best techniques available to work through stress.

Adult Stress

Just as the stresses of life are often high for children, the same can be said for adults. Your personal life mirrors those of society in general, with family, financial, and job stressors creating tensions and pressures that can get in the way of quality interactions with children. If left unchecked, these stresses can reach a breaking point and you may find that you are no longer able to cope.

To maintain the balance needed for effective work with young children, adults need to make sure to preserve their own social/emotional well-being. It is critical for you to do the following:

- **Eat healthy foods, exercise regularly, and get adequate rest.** You may readily encourage children to live a healthy lifestyle but sometimes forget that these same strategies also apply to the stresses you face. Choosing a healthy lifestyle will help you better assist young children on a daily basis. You will be more likely to have both the physical energy and the emotional stamina to positively engage children throughout the day. In addition, by modeling healthy living you will be much more likely to influence families and children in their lifestyle choices.

- **Maintain social relationships with other adults.** The social and emotional demands of working with young children are draining on adults, making it easy for some to spend less energy on their own social needs. But when this happens, you lose valuable opportunities for personal growth and end up shortchanging the children that you are trying to serve. Just as you encourage young children to begin a lifelong journey of social and emotional growth, you need to remember to take time for continued personal growth.

- **Take time for self.** Hobbies, interests, and time to simply reflect and "be" are necessary for healthy emotional development. Early childhood professionals who neglect this aspect of life may gradually become overwhelmed by the stresses of life and work.

- **Know your limits.** As the role of the early childhood professional continues to expand (Allison, 1999), they must frequently reassess what they can reasonably expect to accomplish in their work with children and what should be referred to other professionals. Although we sometimes like to think that we can meet all of our children's needs all of the time, the reality is that this is just not possible. Knowing your limits is another important component of personal well-being.

Supporting Emotional Development

Children experience a wide range of emotions; adults can help them deal with their emotions by helping them to identify, accept, and respond appropriately to their feelings. Bullying is becoming an increasingly significant issue in early childhood settings. Art materials, dramatic play props, books, sand and water play activities, and music provide important opportunities for emotional development.

Facilitating Social Development

You can enhance children's social competence by helping them develop a positive sense of self, by promoting strong adult–child relationships, and by enabling effective peer interactions. Guided participation and conflict resolution can both be used in early childhood settings to assist in the development of social skills. You will need to be aware of the environment, materials, activities, and themes that are part of a quality social development curriculum.

Stress as a Factor in Emotional and Social Development

Children need help in coping with both the normal stresses of development and the added complications of life in the twenty-first century. This will positively influence the child's social and emotional development. The stress of everyday life can also influence the adult's interactions with children. Reducing adult stress leads to more positive interactions with children.

for reflection and discussion

1. What should adults be doing in early childhood settings to reduce/eliminate bullying?
2. List three or four strategies that you will use to build adult-child relationships. Share your thoughts with others.
3. How does stress influence teaching and learning? What will you do to reduce your own stress and that of children in your care?

MyEducationLab

Go to Topic 2: Child Development/Theories in the MyEducationLab (www.myeducationlab.com) for *Teaching Young Children*, where you can:

- Find learning outcomes for Child Development/Theories along with the national standards that connect to these outcomes.
- Complete Assignments and Activities that can help you more deeply understand the chapter content.
- Apply and practice your understanding of the core teaching skills identified in the chapter with the Building Teaching Skills and Dispositions learning units.
- Check your comprehension on the content covered in the chapter with the Study Plan. Here you will be able to take a chapter quiz, receive feedback on your answers, and then access Review, Practice, and Enrichment activities to enhance your understanding of chapter content.

14

Mathematics, Science, and Social Studies Learning

IN THIS CHAPTER YOU WILL

- Study the elements of the cognitive curriculum.
- Address issues relating to mathematics instruction.
- Identify the science curriculum for young children.
- Understand the importance of social studies in early childhood settings.
- Learn about integrating cognitive learning throughout the curriculum.

Michael and Eric are fascinated by their discoveries from morning recess. Using the bug catchers from the science center, they have managed to capture a ladybug, two spiders, and several ants. After creating separate homes for each of their bugs with leaves, sticks, and dirt, the boys are off to the computer to see if they can find out what their new friends like to eat. These second graders are learning to navigate the Internet and soon find some sites to explore.

During the afternoon recess, Michael and Eric scour the playground for food for their bug collection and additional materials for the habitats (a term they learned from the web search). Following recess, they record what they have learned in the science center journal. The boys also make plans to describe their bug collection at tomorrow's sharing time. They talk with the teacher about what they want to do and how long it will take.

Eric decides to take home one of the books in the science center to help him prepare for tomorrow's presentation. Michael has agreed to spend some more time browsing the Internet on his family's home computer to gather additional information for sharing time. Both boys leave school flushed with excitement and ready to continue learning about bugs.

In the situation just described, Michael and Eric are engaged in constructivist learning as they actively explore their personal interest in bugs. As they study the living creatures found on the playground, both boys are developing mathematics and science understandings. They are engaged in the process of cognitive development.

The word *cognition* has its roots in the Latin word *cognoscere*, which means "to know." **Cognitive development** is the continuing process of learning about the world and all of its many components. As young children actively explore topics of interest to them, they come to deeper understandings of their world. By manipulating real objects and interacting with others, children acquire facts, concepts, and relationships. While all aspects of the early childhood curriculum include elements of cognition, mathematics, science, and social studies are essential. The experiences you prepare for young children in these three key subjects should engage them in the kinds of active learning described next.

The Cognitive Curriculum

A major role of early childhood education is to facilitate children's intellectual understandings of their world. Preparing for mathematics, science, and social studies learning is a central component of education at all levels, including the early years. Therefore, early childhood professionals must clearly understand how this part of the curriculum should be presented in early childhood settings. In the traditional approach, commonly used in public education, students learn through direct exchanges with their teachers; however, in early learning, leaders promote playful interactions with people and things as an important avenue for cognitive development (Copple & Bredekamp, 2009). While adult-directed learning has its place, most of the emphasis is on active, child-centered learning.

Learning Facts

Think back to your elementary school years and how you were taught mathematics, science, and social studies. Unless your experience was unusual, much of your time was spent on learning facts. Mathematics emphasized number facts such as the multiplication tables. Science probably included tasks like studying the parts of a flower. Social studies provided additional opportunities to memorize names and dates associated with important events or people.

How much of this information do you remember today? Most people find that they retain only a small portion of the facts they have learned. Although the instruction may have been both fun and intellectually stimulating at the time, the facts themselves are often forgotten. Does this tell you anything about the value of a cognitive curriculum that places heavy emphasis on learning facts?

Make no mistake: *The learning of facts is often an important task.* Could you successfully balance your checkbook without ready recall of addition and subtraction facts? Likewise, a basic knowledge of motor vehicle laws is necessary every time you drive a car. Every adult needs to know many essential facts to function as a productive member of society. However, when rote memorization of information becomes the primary focus of the learning process, a child's development suffers.

In many instances, the factual information learned in early childhood settings is secondary to other more important goals. Take, for example, Michael and Eric's science experiences described at the beginning of this chapter. As they explore the Internet, read books on bugs, and talk to others, they are learning facts. But it is the *process of scientific learning* that is most important and will lead to the greatest long-term benefits.

If learning facts should not be the primary focus of the cognitive curriculum in early childhood, what should? Educators have consistently emphasized three goals: (a) fostering critical thinking, (b) encouraging problem solving, and (c) promoting lifelong learning (Copple & Bredekamp, 2009; Galinsky, 2010; National Council of Teachers of Mathematics, 2000; Olson & Loucks-Horsley, 2000).

Critical Thinking

Caregivers and teachers in early childhood settings need to recognize the importance of promoting critical thinking in children. Today's citizens are bombarded with information from so many different sources that it is difficult even for adults to make sense of it all. You will need to help children learn to examine data critically to determine what is useful in making specific decisions and what is not.

Piaget effectively describes the importance of critical thinking:

> [An essential] goal of education is to form minds which can be critical, can verify, and not accept everything they are offered. The great danger today is of slogans, collective opinions, ready-made trends of thought. We have to be able to resist individually, to criticize, to distinguish between what is proven and what is not. So we need pupils who are active, who learn early to find out by themselves, partly by their own spontaneous activity and partly through materials we set up for them. (Ripple & Rockcastle, 1964, p. 5)

Galinsky (2010) says this about critical thinking:

> At its core, critical thinking is the ongoing search for valid and reliable knowledge to guide beliefs, decisions, and actions. Like the other essential life skills, critical thinking develops on a set course throughout childhood and into adulthood, but its use must be promoted. . . . It parallels the reasoning used in the scientific method because it involves developing, testing, and refining theories about "what causes what" to happen (p. 9)

Problem Solving

Another important goal for the cognitive curriculum is to help children become successful problem solvers. On a daily basis, each of us encounters situations that we must evaluate and deal with. Children need to develop skills in first recognizing and then solving the problems that come their way. The ability to approach issues confidently, identify possible strategies for dealing with them, and then resolve them successfully requires considerable cognitive skill.

A major tool for encouraging problem solving in early childhood settings is the creative play experience. As children engage in play, they naturally encounter many problems that require resolution.

Shauntel and Blythe are playing in the sandbox outdoors. They are trying to create a tunnel connecting their two holes in the sand. Shauntel suggests trying to use sticks from the playground to strengthen the walls of their tunnel. Although the sticks help, both girls are disappointed in the results. Blythe adds a second option when she proposes they try digging their holes deeper and connecting farther down in the sandbox. This option, however, makes it difficult to make the bend needed to join the holes. After talking through their dilemma yet again, they decide to try moistening the sand with water so that it will remain firmer through the digging process. They have found a workable solution.

Because there are no right or wrong answers in play, children can feel free to experiment, explore, and problem solve as Shauntel and Blythe have done. Tegano, Sawyers, and Moran (1989) put it this way:

> When playing, young children openly and spontaneously express themselves because they are in a nonthreatening environment. The creative process—defining the problem, generating ideas and solutions, evaluating solutions, converting solutions into outcomes—is enhanced in an open, "psychologically safe" environment. (p. 93)

The *Observing Development* feature in this section is designed to get you into an early childhood setting to observe materials that encourage playful interactions that lead to cognitive development. Spend some time observing in a program for young children and reflect on the role of these materials on cognitive development.

Lifelong Learning

A final goal for the cognitive curriculum is to instill in children a love of learning that will help them continue to grow intellectually throughout their lives. While young children tend to be naturally curious about the world around them, the schooling

Observing Development . . .
MATERIALS FOR COGNITIVE LEARNING

Choose one of the age groups within early childhood (infants/toddlers, preschoolers, or primary-age children), and spend time observing the early childhood environment for evidence of materials available for playful cognitive learning. Review chapter content for examples of materials you might see; then create a table like the one here to record how many different examples you observe in each of the categories listed:

Materials for Cognitive Learning, Manchester Elementary Kindergarten, November 10

	Books	Manipulatives	Dramatic play	Music	Natural materials
Mathematics	X X	X X X			X
Science					X
Social Studies	X X		X X X		X

Reflect and Apply

1. Which category of materials (books, manipulatives, etc.) were the most prevalent in the program you observed? Do you think they were effective in stimulating cognitive learning? Why or why not?

2. Were any of the materials you expected to see not available for children to use? Reflect on why that may have been the case.

3. Of the three subject matter areas (mathematics, science, social studies), which had the most materials for cognitive learning? Reflect on the reasons for this. Which area had the least materials and why?

process has often been accused of dampening enthusiasm. Albert Einstein (1949) said this about education:

> It is in fact nothing short of a miracle that the modern methods of instruction have not yet entirely strangled the *holy curiosity of inquiry* [emphasis added].... It is a very grave mistake to think that the enjoyment of seeing and searching can be promoted by means of coercion and a sense of duty. (p. 17)

Einstein is implying that when instruction consists of hands-on discovery learning, children are much more curious and motivated to understand their world. Project learning is one important way in which young children engage in discovery learning. The *Developmentally Appropriate Practice* feature in this section describes preschool children who are involved in project learning through the study of pizza. Play in the early childhood classroom is another important option for discovery learning. As children engage in center activities, they are spontaneously and naturally involved in cognitive development and are motivated to learn more. This playful way of knowing is essential in stimulating a positive attitude toward lifelong learning.

The Constructivist Approach

It should be clear from the preceding discussion that traditional educational methods in which the early childhood professional dispenses knowledge to children who are passive recipients are not compatible with the goals described for the cognitive curriculum. A much more effective and developmentally appropriate approach is referred

Developmentally Appropriate Practice . . .
INTEGRATING CURRICULUM: THE PIZZA PROJECT

Helm and Beneke (2003) describe a project conducted in a licensed child-care center for children from 3 to 5 years of age in which mathematics, science, art, social studies, and early literacy experiences were integrated through the study of pizza. The project began after children identified several topics of interest to them, voted on their priorities, and selected pizza as their first option. Both counting and graphing skills were used in this initial step as sticky notes were used to record children's votes on a large graph on the wall. After having children share what they already knew about pizza, children were given the opportunity to draw and talk about this topic. A staff member then brought in pizza pans, chef hats, and pizza tools from her part-time job in a pizza parlor and discussed their use prior to putting them in the dramatic play center. Children were encouraged to touch, draw, and label these tools. Additional science and math learning opportunities were integrated when pizza toppings were counted, smelled, cooked, and observed when left without refrigeration.

After this initial phase of exploration, children began a more in-depth investigation of how pizza was made, and then delivered, by arranging two field trips to a local pizza parlor. One of the adults created a book of photos to give children ideas about what they could expect to see on their trips. The first visit was used to familiarize children with the general operations of a pizza parlor. Children took clipboards and had some initial questions they wanted answered. Of special interest on this first visit were the oven and the machine used to grind meat and cheese. During the second field trip, many children sketched and labeled items of special interest and then made their own pizzas using the tools they had been playing with in the classroom. After returning to the program center, children modified the dramatic play area to make it more like the real pizza parlor, including the construction of a grinder and pizza warmer. Further math, social studies, and early literacy learning experiences were incorporated into these activities. The culminating activity for the project was a pizza party that included a sharing time to show families what children had learned from their pizza explorations.

to as **constructivist education**. Grounded in the developmental theories of Jean Piaget (1950) and Lev Vygotsky (1978), this approach to early education promotes the idea that children build their own understanding of the world through activities based on personal interests. As they manipulate real-world objects and interact with the people around them, children create for themselves an understanding of the world.

Chaille and Britain (2003) have identified four characteristics of children that make the constructivist approach the best match for early learning:

1. **Young children are theory builders.** The constructivist position suggests that knowledge is built by children themselves as they make educated guesses about why things work the way they do and then test out their theories in the real world. Children do this naturally and without prompting by adults.

2. **Cognition requires a foundation of physical knowledge.** Children are naturally motivated to understand the physical world around them (Helm & Katz, 2010). This knowledge of how objects and materials such as balls and cubes work lays the foundation for the more abstract understandings that come later.

3. **Children acquire increasing autonomy and independence.** As young children mature, they gradually move from dependence on adults for meeting their needs to more independent functioning. Healthy youngsters have a strong need to experiment, explore, and discover on their own.

4. **Young children are social beings.** Children are naturally social and spend considerable effort planning and interacting with others. These interchanges are an important part of the learning process. Children construct many understandings through their social exchanges with adults and peers.

DeVries and Zan (1995) identify the following strategies for creating a constructivist early childhood setting:

- **Cultivate an atmosphere of respect.** Children need to work and play in an environment in which they are respected as individuals and encouraged to experiment and explore without fear of poor treatment by adults or peers. This atmosphere allows children to engage in the construction of knowledge as they interact with people and things.

- **Allow children to be active learners.** The best learning occurs when children are allowed to pursue their own interests and physically manipulate the things in their environment. A child's mental functioning is enhanced when physical activity also takes place.

- **Foster social interactions.** When cognitive tasks allow for social interchange, childhood learning is enhanced. Sharing ideas with others helps clarify misunderstandings and provides additional perspectives that enrich the learning experiences.

- **Emphasize self-regulation and reflection.** As adults help children take responsibility for their learning experiences, children become more independent and self-confident in seeking new knowledge. Encouraging reflection leads to an attitude of questioning that is at the heart of critical thinking.

Family Roles

Families are children's first and best teachers. They play crucial roles in cognitive development. Families need to support early learning in three important ways: (a) encourage the importance of intellectual growth, (b) assist in classroom learning, and (c) engage children at home in cognitive tasks.

Families of children with special needs can show support by helping to create an Individualized Family Service Plan (IFSP) or an Individualized Education Program (IEP) for their children. The *Family Partnerships* feature found in this section provides more information on this important support opportunity.

Supporting the importance of cognitive development. Families, early childhood professionals, and community members generally agree about the importance of learning mathematics, science, and social studies concepts and readily concede the values of cognitive development. Achievement in these areas is necessary for success in work and life.

The content and process of this learning, however, are not always agreed upon. Many of these differences of opinion come from the family members' own schooling experiences as children. If social studies learning, for example, focused on the memorization of names, dates, and significant historical events, these families typically feel that this approach to learning is appropriate for their own children. "It worked for me," they think, "so why shouldn't it work for my kids?"

Approaches focusing on rote learning, however, have proven to be ineffective for many children. The constructivist approach described earlier in this chapter is a much more positive technique for encouraging cognitive development (DeVries & Kohlberg, 1987; Kamii & DeVries, 1978). Because it is new to many families,

Family Partnerships . . .
IFSP AND IEP MEETINGS

As a future early childhood professional, you will need to participate in creating either an Individualized Family Service Plan (IFSP) or an Individualized Education Program (IEP) for each of the children with special needs in your classroom. By federal law, every child identified as having special needs must have a detailed learning plan developed and revised annually through group meetings that include the early childhood professional, the special educator, other educational specialists (such as a speech therapist, occupational therapist, psychologist, physical therapist), and family members. Because of the critical role of families in early development, children under age 3 and their families receive an IFSP (Bruder, 2000). After age 3, planning for children with special needs is usually in the form of an IEP.

Families are strongly encouraged to participate in the finalization of either the IFSP or IEP. While many of these meetings are friendly and collegial, some are marked by considerable tension that can stem from a variety of sources. For example, program personnel may fail to understand the heavy physical and emotional burdens families bear as they provide 24-hour care for their child with special needs. When these tensions are present, a relatively simple request from educational personnel for assistance from home can be met with anger or helplessness on the part of the family.

Another source of tension comes when early childhood professionals and programs are unable to provide services that are either expected by families or mandated by federal law. Due to limited funding and a lack of qualified personnel, many programs find it difficult to fully meet the needs of children with special needs. When this happens, educational personnel tend to get defensive, while families may become frustrated as they see their children's need go unmet. Careful planning and an understanding attitude can help reduce the tensions in these stressful meetings.

1. Choose a special need of interest to you and take some time to learn more about family stresses associated with that special need. What did you learn that could be shared with others?

2. You are more likely to resolve problems when they are addressed in a strong relationship. What could you do to strengthen your relationships with families that have children with special needs?

caregivers and teachers must help them understand this approach. As families see constructivist learning in action, discuss the approach with others, read about its benefits, and observe the results of these efforts, they can become strong advocates of this alternative to memorization and rote learning.

Assisting with classroom learning. Families who help out in early childhood settings are assisting with cognitive development. Reading to children, helping individual children with integrated learning projects, and going on class field trips are examples of this support. More mundane tasks like preparing materials for an art project or constructing a game help free up the professional's time for more direct assistance in cognitive learning. The family members' presence in the classroom also sends children the message that their own work is important, which motivates them to do their best.

Families who are unavailable during the school day can help out at home by gathering the ingredients for the upcoming science project, saving materials for mathematics manipulatives, or making telephone calls for the field trip next week. Tasks like these give families important roles to play when they cannot come into the classroom.

Home learning tasks. Families have many unique opportunities to promote cognitive understanding outside the school environment. Often, however, they do not take advantage of them because family members fail to recognize the value of the many informal learning experiences that exist around them. Setting the table for dinner, for example, gives young children the chance to count and to practice one-to-one correspondence (one fork, spoon, and knife for each person) as they assist with a household chore. Likewise, a trip to the grocery store can be a great opportunity to practice money concepts and to discuss the rationale for buying some foods but not others.

Many early childhood professionals send home lists of simple activities that can be built into daily life to promote cognitive development. These home-learning tasks should be easy to prepare and fun to do. Following are some good ideas for home learning activities:

- **Cooking activities.** Have children help with cooking. It can teach number concepts, fractions, measurement, and much more.
- **Backyard science.** Encourage exploration outdoors for insects, leaves, and rocks. Plant seeds and bulbs in the garden. Children engaged in these kinds of activities are classifying, observing, and experimenting with variables as they play with the materials outdoors.
- **Play games with children.** Children, for example, can learn to discriminate among size, shape, and color as they play simple card-matching games. Families often need suggestions for making competitive games more cooperative.
- **Visit museums.** Explore the resources within the community, including museums of interest to children. When these experiences include things children can touch and manipulate, the interest will be greater. Museums provide wonderful opportunities for learning, especially about the subject of history.

 ## Mathematics and Young Children

When many of us recall our own early mathematical experiences, memories of rote learning with little connection to real life often predominate. However, mathematics can be an exciting, interesting, relevant topic for investigation. With the constructivist approach, young children can learn a broad assortment of topics through manipulation and discovery and make mathematical connections to real issues in the world around them.

In 2000, The National Council of Teachers of Mathematics (NCTM) published a set of national standards for prekindergarten through grade 12 mathematics. In it they identify five content strands and their applications in early childhood settings:

1. **Number and operations.** During the early childhood years, young children should be learning basic concepts about numbers. Primary children are also ready to develop understandings of mathematical operations such as addition, subtraction, and multiplication.

2. **Algebra.** Although most people assume that algebra should be taught in middle school and high school, the NCTM suggests that young children benefit from engaging in algebraic reasoning. The *Developmentally Appropriate Practice* feature in this section describes some examples of this type.

3. **Geometry.** Young children can be introduced to basic geometric shapes and analyze them using mathematical reasoning skills.

4. **Measurement.** Because of its practical applications in real life, there are many opportunities to engage young children in meaningful measurement activities. Options abound to measure height, width, weight, and volume of the natural and man-made equipment and materials around them.

5. **Data analysis and probability.** Statistical reasoning gives children opportunities to formulate questions and collect data to answer their inquiries. For example, primary children could estimate the number of marbles it would take to fill a jar and then check on the accuracy of their estimates.

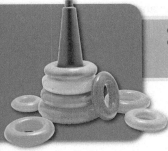

Developmentally Appropriate Practice . . .
ENGAGING PRIMARY CHILDREN IN ALGEBRAIC REASONING

In algebra, unknown elements of arithmetic operations are designated by letters or symbols. For example, $3 + x = 5$ would be a simple algebraic expression. While more complex problems challenge even the best of mathematicians, even very young children can engage in meaningful algebraic reasoning (Bamberger, Oberdorf, & Schultz-Ferrell, 2010). Transforming typical arithmetic problems into algebraic expressions allows children to develop deeper understandings of the structure and properties of mathematics. Barton (2005) provides examples from elementary school classrooms in rural Oregon where teachers are successfully engaging young children in just this type of algebraic reasoning:

- One teacher challenges her second- and third-grade students by saying: "I'm thinking of a two-digit number that's less than 50. It's an odd number and the difference between the digits is two" (p. 6). With the assistance of "placeholder" pockets and numbered cards, children were able to identify three possible solutions.

- Another group of students plays a game to refine their understanding of place value. If they randomly draw three cards from a selection of nine in which each card has a different numeral written on it, what would be the largest three-digit number they could create? What would be the smallest? If there were 18 cards, two each with the numerals 1 through 9 printed on them, what would be the largest and smallest three-digit numbers that could be created?

- Returning from recess, each student in a first- and second-grade classroom is handed a piece of blank paper and asked to create a mathematical equation and then discuss it with the class. One student's problem is $(¼ \times 4) + 3 = 12 \div 3$. When asked to talk about how you would solve this problem, a student replies, "You have a circle and you divide it in four, and then color in one part and another and another and another, because there's four one-fourths and that equals one whole" (Barton, 2005, p. 8).

Copley (2010) suggests a framework for teaching mathematics in early childhood settings that has three essential components:

- **Curriculum.** What is taught should form the foundation for long-term mathematical understandings. It should be integrated with other content areas and be based in the real world of children. With books, mathematics materials, and visual models, you can create a math-rich environment that allows children to learn from the objects and people around them.

- **Instruction.** Plan experiences that allow children to engage in problem solving and mathematical reasoning as they learn more about their world. Expect that *all* children can and should learn mathematics.

- **Assessment.** To know which mathematical understandings need to be presented in the early childhood setting, you will want to assess the specific content knowledge of each child. By observing and interacting with young children, you can collect multiple sources of evidence to make sure you are accurately assessing child understandings.

Classification

During the early childhood years, children develop cognitive understandings that are foundational to learning the mathematical content described in the NCTM standards. One such understanding is the ability to classify. Putting objects or ideas that have similar characteristics into groups demonstrates **classification** competence. Figure 14–1 provides a visual example of classification by color.

Although this cognitive ability seems simple for us as adults, children require considerable practice and time to understand classification. For example, a 3-year-old child given a set of colored blocks and asked to "put blocks together that are the same" may playfully organize and reorganize the blocks, not really using any logical thinking in creating his groupings.

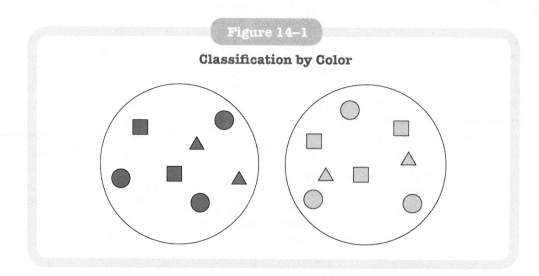

Figure 14–1

Classification by Color

Classification skills are fundamental to many mathematical concepts. For example, writing the numeral 43 requires an understanding of the "tens place" and "ones place" as different groupings. In addition, the study of algebraic functions places a heavy emphasis on the ability to classify; for example, "Consider n to be the set of all integers greater than zero."

Caregivers and teachers can provide many opportunities to practice classification. Mary Baratta-Lorton (1976), in her classic book *Mathematics Their Way*, provides many good ideas for simple materials that can be used in sorting and classifying tasks:

- People in the classroom
- Buttons for grouping
- Old bottle caps
- Natural materials for sorting such as acorns, leaves, rocks, and shells
- Nuts and bolts
- Teacher-directed activities using geoboards (square board with 25 regularly spaced pegs over which rubber bands can be stretched)

Seriation

Ordering objects from smallest to largest is referred to as **seriation**. This sequencing can be based on height, weight, shades of color, or any other characteristic. This is another important cognitive task for young children to master. It is essential to understanding the number system.

Children must be given many opportunities to practice seriation to truly make sense of it. Although some cognitive understanding of seriation is seen in many children at age 3 or 4, often the concept is not fully developed until age 8 or 9. Piaget spent considerable time studying the growth of this developmental task (Flavell, 1963).

Many excellent commercial materials are available to give children practice with seriation. One well-known example is Montessori's cylinder block. Each rectangular block has several wooden cylinders that fit into holes ordered from smallest to largest in the block. Children practice their sequencing skills by finding the right cylinder for each hole. Cuisenaire Rods can also be used for seriation activities. These multicolored rods begin with a small cube as the basic unit and grow step by step to the longest rod, which is 10 units in length.

Patterning

Being able to recognize and create visual, auditory, spatial, and numerical **patterns** is another important mathematical understanding. The discipline of mathematics is logical and based on patterns of all sorts. The number system, for example, with groupings of 10 has a clear pattern that children must recognize to truly understand its complexities.

Students must also master patterns in arithmetic, algebra, and geometry. You can provide young children with many meaningful opportunities to engage in patterning activities (Eisenhauer & Feikes, 2009). Following are some examples of appropriate materials and activities:

- Stringing beads in patterns
- Constructing designs with pattern blocks
- Repeating clapping patterns

- Listening to musical patterns
- Building with Unifix cubes (plastic cubes that can be snapped together to form patterns)
- Playing with Cuisenaire Rods

Number Concepts

Children's understandings of number concepts develop rapidly during the early childhood years. While a 3-year-old often is just beginning to understand that "1" is a small number and others are larger, 5-year-olds have typically mastered basic number concepts through "9" (Murray & Mayer, 1988). During the primary years, children develop the ability to count forward and backward, skip count (counting by twos, fives, tens, etc.), and understand numbers into the hundreds (Charlesworth, 2005; Ginsberg, Boyd, & Sun Lee, 2008).

Counting. Much of the preschool child's understanding of numbers comes from repeated counting experiences. Many songs and finger plays (e.g., "Five Little Speckled Frogs" and "Ten Little Monkeys") give children enjoyable opportunities for rote counting experiences. The day-to-day life of the classroom and home provide many other meaningful opportunities to count and understand numbers. Discussing the calendar at group time, counting crackers in the snack bowl, and finding out how many ladybugs were caught on the playground are examples of these natural opportunities for counting.

It is important to remember that primary-age children often use counting as an aid in solving addition and subtraction problems. Although this strategy eventually becomes cumbersome and slow, it helps many children make the transition to more mature arithmetic skills. Using concrete materials as an aid in counting is still a necessity for many primary-age children and should be made available for those who need them.

Arithmetic skills. During the primary years, children learn about addition, subtraction, and multiplication. However, part of the problem with the traditional approach to teaching these skills is that not all children are cognitively ready to begin when the teacher starts the instruction. Some may need more counting experience first, while others should spend additional time developing basic number concepts. When the teacher uses a constructivist approach and allows children to manipulate materials and discover arithmetic understandings as they work on real-world problems, children are much more able to set their own pace and conquer the task.

Many primary children benefit from using concrete materials in counting activities.

Measurement

The ability to quantify materials in the world should also be emphasized during the early years. Finding the height, weight, volume, and dimensions of objects are examples of **measurement**. Piaget's work tells us that until children have reached the stage of concrete operations (about age 7 or 8) they have difficulty measuring using standardized units such as inches, pounds, and liters (Flavell, 1963). Younger children, however, can learn much when given the opportunity to measure with nonstandard units.

The preschool and kindergarten child can engage in the following types of informal measurement activities:

- Use blocks to measure tables, floor space, and other elements of the classroom environment (Anderson, 2010).
- Find out how many plastic cups of sand or water it takes to fill containers in the sand or water play area.
- Use a balance to compare weights of different objects.
- Trace full-body silhouettes of children and have them compare heights.

Children in the primary grades can engage in many of these same activities but with the use of standardized units of measurement. Children this age can use and understand rulers, weight scales, and one-cup containers. Measurement activities should remain meaningful and relevant to the children's lives. To achieve this goal, consider weighing the class guinea pig, measuring the dimensions of playground equipment, and discovering how many liters of water are needed to fill the classroom sink.

Geometry

The study of two- and three-dimensional shapes and how they are related to one another is called **geometry**. Although this topic is often thought of as part of the high school mathematics curriculum, it is highly applicable in early childhood settings as well. Young children develop these geometric understandings from playing with materials such as unit blocks, pattern blocks, and paper for origami.

Another effective manipulative that is becoming more popular in early childhood settings is the tangram (Lee, Lee, & Collins, 2010). A tangram has seven puzzle-like pieces: two small triangles, one medium triangle, two large triangles, one square, and one parallelogram. Children use these pieces to make their own shapes or to copy the shapes shown on accompanying cards. As they create these shapes, they develop a deeper understanding of spatial relationships and geometric shapes. This type of active learning with a creative mathematical manipulative is an excellent example of developmentally appropriate mathematics.

In addition, you can help children develop geometric understandings by identifing the many shapes that exist in the early childhood setting and outdoors on the playground. By casually pointing them out and naming them, children grow to understand basic geometric concepts in the world around them. There are also a number of good children's books on geometry, such as *My Very First Book of Shapes* (Carle, 1985), which can be read to children to encourage further discussions of geometric concepts.

The Language of Mathematics

Preschool provider: (*holding up a ball*)	"We're going to talk about shapes today. This ball is a circle."
Kindergarten teacher: (*writing on the chalkboard*)	"This is how we write the number '5'."
Second-grade teacher: (*demonstrating with manipulatives*)	"I have five popsicle sticks in my right hand. and seven in my left. Which hand is holding less?"

In each of these situations, caregivers and teachers have used inaccurate terms to describe mathematical concepts. In the first, the preschool provider has used a two-dimensional term to describe a three-dimensional object (sphere). The kindergarten teacher in the second situation should have used the word *numeral* rather than *number* to describe the representation on the chalkboard. In the last situation, the correct term is *fewer*, rather than *less*. These common errors that many adults make daily seem like fairly minor issues. Is it really worth the effort it would take to use accurate terms?

Tracy (1994) makes a strong case for refining the language we use to teach mathematics. Language directly influences the concepts children develop. Because mathematics is such a precise field of study, early childhood professionals need to use accurate language with children. Not only do they understand concepts more easily when precise language is used, but children also enjoy using the more interesting terms. *Rhombus, ellipse, cube, rectangle*, and *numeral* are all words that children can learn and enjoy. Adults should refine the language they use by first recognizing the terms that may cause misunderstandings and then working to identify and consistently use more appropriate words to describe the mathematical concepts being presented. Although this is not an easy task, the benefits to children are worth the effort.

In addition to using accurate mathematical language, early childhood professionals also need to provide young children with more exposure to meaningful math vocabulary. Rudd et al. (2008), in their research on mathematical language used in prekindergarten classrooms, found that adults regularly used effective language to describe spatial relationships, but provided limited verbal descriptions of other key math concepts. There was, for example, a very low incidence of language around key concepts such as seriation and patterning. By using accurate mathematical language more regularly, you can help children develop deeper understandings of the related concepts.

Science Learning

Just as mathematical concepts are an important part of the early years, science surrounds young children in their daily lives. What makes some things float and others sink at the water table? How does a flower grow? What does an ant eat? What makes a person grow? How do fish breathe? Why does a magnet pick up some things but not others? When you prepare an environment that allows children to manipulate and discover the answers to these and other important questions, the science curriculum will be a major success.

Science consists of two main components: content and process. Content is the actual body of knowledge developed over time by the scientific community. The study of plants (botany) is an example of science content that can be presented to young children in developmentally appropriate ways. The **scientific process**, often referred to as **scientific inquiry**, consists of the methods and attitudes used by scientists to gather information and solve problems. As young children measure the growth of a plant over time and record their findings in a table, they are collecting data and engaging in an important step in the scientific process.

Scientific Content

The National Academy of Sciences (1996) published a set of national standards for science education. In these standards, they grouped the sciences into three broad

Cooking is an example of a valuable science activity in early childhood settings.

categories: **physical science** (physics and chemistry), **life science** (botany and zoology), and **earth and space science** (geology and astronomy). For each grouping, the National Academy of Sciences identified broad categories of content to be learned by students in the primary grades. Content for the life sciences, for example, should focus on these:

- Helping students understand the characteristics of different living organisms
- Developing understandings of life cycles for living things
- Identifying relationships between organisms and the environments in which they live

Early childhood professionals can find many opportunities to build developmentally appropriate science content into their work with young children. By focusing on real world explorations, you can make science learning meaningful and fun for them. For example, Ogu and Schmidt (2009) describe an inquiry-based approach to the study of rocks and sand that is an excellent example of science content that can be addressed in developmentally appropriate ways. After teachers noticed children were making collections of rocks and pebbles from the playground and elsewhere, they began an in-depth study to help them develop deeper understandings of this aspect of their natural world. The following paragraphs provide several additional examples of developmentally appropriate science activities.

Early physics experiences. **Physics** can be defined as "the science of matter and energy and of interactions between the two" (Chaille & Britain, 2003, p. 76). When we provide children with opportunities to discover the physical properties of objects, they learn physics concepts. Sprung (1996) provides three examples of appropriate physics activities:

- *Ramp experiments* provide children with opportunities to roll objects down ramps that they construct (DeVries & Sales, 2011). Through this, children learn about such things as the properties of inclined planes. Zan and Geiken (2010) provide additional examples of using ramps in fun and intellectually rigorous ways to teach early physics. By simply adding wooden cove molding and marbles to the block center, they began engaging young children in exciting learning experiences.
- *Water experiments* allow children to explore the properties of water. For example, funnels of different sizes let children experiment with the rate at which water moves through varying diameters.
- *Tinkering experiments* permit children to tinker with objects to see how they work. For example, children can take apart and put back together old appliances that adults have made safe.

The *Celebrating Play* feature in this section gives another example of how physics principles can be learned within the larger context of an integrated learning experience.

Celebrating Play...
INTEGRATING SCIENCE CURRICULUM THROUGH BLOCK PLAY

Although many materials in the early childhood classroom can be used for hands-on science learning, unit blocks are among the best alternatives for all ages. Mary Moffitt (1996), in a classic book on block play, says it this way:

> [S]cience content is better learned through the development of processes of inquiry, such as observing, comparing, classifying, predicting, and interpreting. Block building is a medium that is particularly well adapted for children to use these processes. Children's scientific thinking is stimulated as they discover and invent new forms, compare and classify different sizes and shapes, test ideas of "What will happen if . . .?," or learn to use clues to predict outcomes because they have become familiar with the properties of the blocks with which they build. (p. 27)

She describes how children who play with blocks learn about their properties, such as size, shape, and weight, and then use this knowledge as they construct during their play. As they build, children learn about their block structure as a system and the importance of the various elements to that system, which are both important scientific concepts. They also learn about the interaction of forces within a system. Gravity, for example, influences such things as equilibrium, balance, and stability. In block play, children are also learning about space as they build up or create a pattern on the floor. Beginning measurement skills are practiced as they compare the length, height, and depth of block structures. Children develop basic understandings of architectural forms as they create tunnels, build bridges, and add ramps to their block structures. Because block building is an open-ended activity, children have many opportunities for language learning, developing mathematical understandings, and engaging in creative thinking and scientific reasoning.

1. Finish reading this section of the chapter on science learning in the early childhood classroom. Then think about the possibilities for teaching important science concepts through the use of unit blocks. Do you think blocks are a useful tool in science learning? Give a rationale for your thinking.

2. Although not commonly found in the primary classroom, do you think blocks could be effectively used for science learning at that level? Why or why not?

Early chemistry experiences. **Chemistry** is defined as the study of substances and what happens when they are combined or come in contact with one another. Here are a few examples of chemistry activities for young children:

- **Cooking activities.** When mixing ingredients and cooking foods, teachers and children can observe and discuss the changes that are taking place in the materials used.
- **Mixing liquids of different viscosities.** Mix liquid corn oil and water, for example, and observe the results. To add an element of ecology, mix motor oil and water, and then try to figure out ways to separate the two liquids.
- **Engage in bubble-making activities.** The process of making bubble solutions can be a fun chemistry project. It often takes some effort to get the best solution. Using different items to blow bubbles adds an element of physics to the project.

Early life science experiences. **Botany** is the scientific investigation of plants. Young children are motivated to learn about plants when they can do so through hands-on experiences. Gardening is an excellent example of an activity that brings botany to life in early childhood settings. Planting and growing vegetables, herbs, flowers, and other plants in a garden bed gives young children many wonderful opportunities for science learning. Clemens (1996) describes four different types of gardens that adults can effectively use with young children:

- **Container gardens.** By using small containers such as milk cartons or purchased pots, you can convert nearly any spot into a small garden area for children. Each container can hold a different type of plant, or each child can have his own container garden.

- **Square-foot gardens.** Another option is to mark off a small area that can be a garden spot for a specific class. Because each garden is small, more classrooms can participate in the fun of gardening. It does not take much space to enjoy creative gardening activities.

- **Conventional gardens.** Having a somewhat larger space where vegetables and flowers can be planted in traditional rows can be another good option. It requires more upkeep but is workable if the space is available.

- **Raised gardens.** A raised garden bed is created by using some sort of wood or rock border to build the garden bed up several inches above the ground. This arrangement makes the bed easier to plant and weed and can allow for the addition of soil amendments to aid in growing. Additionally, the soil warms earlier in the spring for planting.

You may also want to consider indoor gardening activities. Hachey and Butler (2009) provide additional options for gardening indoors. Whether you engage in indoor or outdoor gardening activities, these experiences have great potential for helping children learn science concepts and strategies. Children can predict, experiment, draw conclusions, observe patterns, and understand interactions among plants, insects, and birds. They can learn about the growth process of plants and how it varies among species. Children can study and understand the effects of rain, drought, wind, and sun.

Zoology is the study of animals. Children love the opportunity to feed, hold, and learn more about all sorts of living creatures. Guinea pigs, rabbits, mice, hamsters, turtles, frogs, lizards, and gerbils are examples of animals that you can bring into the early childhood setting for children to study as part of the zoology curriculum (Meadan & Jegatheesan, 2010). Field trips to the zoo or a local farm can provide additional opportunities for learning about animals.

The examples presented here illustrate that scientific content does not have to be mysterious or foreign to young children. Early childhood professionals can develop similar methods for introducing geology and astronomy concepts to young children. Strong early childhood programs have been presenting children with opportunities such as these to study scientific content since the beginning of this century (Sprung, 1996).

For both mathematics and science learning, adults working with young children need to be sure that *all* children are learning this important content. A solid foundation in mathematics and the sciences is critical for later success in many occupations. As the *Celebrating Diversity* feature in this section emphasizes, however, we are currently failing to help all children learn in these areas. Read the feature now for more insights into this important issue.

The Scientific Process

The *processes* used to study science are even more important than the content. Early childhood professionals need to promote the same techniques that scientists themselves use in their inquiries. This process consists of the following steps:

1. **Identify a problem for investigation.** Scientists must first recognize that a situation needs to be studied. You can help young children identify problems using simple questions or statements like, "Abby, do you know what a spider eats?" (Ogu & Schmidt, 2009).

2. **Collect data.** Once a problem is identified, a scientist works to collect information that may be useful in solving the problem. For young children, practicing good observation techniques and documenting what they find is a primary way to collect data (Blake, 2009).

3. **Generate possible solutions to problems.** Following the collection of data, scientists formulate several hypotheses or solutions for the problems they face. Likewise, play situations provide many opportunities for children to generate answers to the problems they encounter.

4. **Test solutions.** Some potential solutions simply will not work, while others are only partially successful. The only way to work through a problem is to keep trying until success is achieved. Adults can help children know that it is normal to fail many times before finding an option that works.

5. **Draw conclusions and share with others.** Once the testing has taken place, the scientist summarizes his findings and shares the results of his investigations with others.

Celebrating Diversity...
HELPING ALL CHILDREN LEARN MATH AND SCIENCE

Because of the importance of mathematics and science in today's world, all children must have the opportunity to succeed in these fields. Unfortunately, however, statistics indicate that this currently is not the case. For example, although women represent 45% of the total workforce, only 27% are scientists and engineers (Peet, 2010). In mathematics performance, White students have consistently achieved higher scores than their Black or Hispanic peers, and Asian-American students perform better than White students (Viadero, 2000; Wenglinsky, 2004). What can be done to improve this situation? Although attitudes change slowly, and it will be difficult to improve conditions quickly, the following two ideas can be important first steps.

Equal Opportunities to Participate

Most early childhood professionals believe that they encourage boys, girls, all cultures, and all socioeconomic groups to participate at the same level in science and math activities. However, research suggests this is not the case (American Association for the Advancement of Science, 1999). For example, consider the way early childhood professionals typically set up a block center. The accessories provided most often are those that interest boys: trucks, airplanes, zoo animals, and so on. When the block center includes materials more attractive to girls, both genders will use it to learn important

math and science concepts. You should also become aware of how you are verbally encouraging children to engage in science and math activities. Either videotaping or audiotaping a portion of the day can help uncover times when you need to increase the positive feedback you give to young girls.

Get the Support of Families

Families play a significant role in all of child development, including how children perceive the importance of science and mathematics. If family members support the value of these subjects, assist with simple learning experiences around the home, and encourage play and reading activities to replace typically high levels of television viewing, children will be much more successful in math and science. Unfortunately, this role is often hard for many family members who were themselves low achievers in these subjects. Thoughtful family education and involvement are needed to correct this difficult situation.

1. Do you think that helping all children learn math and science will be a significant issue for you as a future caregiver or teacher? Why or why not?

2. What is your own personal skill level in science and math? Do you think that your understandings will either positively or negatively influence your work with young children in these areas? Why or why not?

Scientists also approach problems with *attitudes* or ways of thinking that help them succeed. These approaches do not come easily to young children, and they will need assistance in using them. You can model these attitudes while providing the guidance necessary to ensure that children use these approaches themselves. Wolfinger (1994) identifies five qualities that are essential to scientific investigations:

- **Objectivity.** This is perhaps the most difficult attitude to model and encourage in children. Basically, objectivity is the ability to look at all sides of an issue before making a decision. Many adults struggle with being objective. Children, because of their egocentrism during the early childhood years, also find this difficult. Adults must work hard to model appropriate objectivity as they work with children.

- **Willingness to suspend judgment.** A scientist waits until all of the evidence is in before making a decision. The early childhood professional must again be a good model by demonstrating a willingness to suspend judgment in problems encountered with children.

- **Skepticism.** Although this word often carries a negative connotation, the skeptic is one who questions all things. Rather than simply accepting the first idea that comes to mind, the scientist questions, searches for additional information, and critically evaluates the available data. Guide children through this process as they approach science activities.

- **Respect for the environment.** Scientific inquiry should never be damaging to any part of the natural environment. Taking fallen leaves on a nature walk rather than stripping live ones from a tree, keeping insects alive for observation and study rather than killing them, and using organic methods for controlling insects in a garden bed are all examples of environmentally friendly approaches to science activities.

- **Positive approach to failure.** When children make predictions for solutions to a problem, many will prove to be wrong. However, much is learned from failure. It helps refine an understanding of the problem and may lead to future solutions. Adults need to work hard to let children know that it is perfectly acceptable to make predictions that end up being wrong. Children can then learn from their misperceptions.

 # Young Children and Social Studies

Social studies help children understand relationships between people and environmental factors that influence their lives. In the adult world, this broad topic includes the disciplines of history, psychology, economics, sociology, anthropology, geography, and political science. Young children are keenly interested in these topics when they are presented to them in developmentally appropriate contexts.

The National Council for the Social Studies (2010) has identified 10 thematic strands for social studies content in the schools:

1. **Culture.** Studying the similarities and differences among cultural groups.
2. **Time, continuity, and change.** Understanding history and its influences on life today.
3. **People, places, and environments.** Developing an awareness of people and places around the world.
4. **Individual development and identity.** Studying how individuals learn and grow.

5. **Individuals, groups, and institutions.** Understanding the influences of groups and institutions on individuals.

6. **Power, authority, and governance.** Developing knowledge of how governments operate at all levels.

7. **Production, distribution, and consumption.** Gaining insights into how goods and services are developed and distributed.

8. **Science, technology, and society.** Studying the relationships among science, technology, and society.

9. **Global connections.** Understanding the interdependence of people around the world.

10. **Civic ideals and practices.** Developing insights into being a citizen in a democratic society.

Each of these 10 strands has relevance in early childhood settings. For example, the study of Culture (strand 1) can begin early as children begin to recognize and discuss similarities and differences among children in the program. The *Developmentally Appropriate Practice* feature in this section describes a project of this type. A second example of meaningful social studies learning for young children would be to organize an investigation of food production and distribution through field trips to a local produce garden and farmer's market (Production, Distribution, and Consumption, strand 7). Mindes (2005) provides additional examples of developmentally appropriate social studies activities for children in early childhood settings.

The social studies curriculum for infants and toddlers centers around learning to relate to their primary caregivers (strand 3). Crying, smiling, touching, staring, and vocalizing are early attempts to understand and communicate with family members and significant others. Gradually, as children enter the preschool years, they begin to expand their sphere of learning about people, relationships, and the environment. Developing an understanding of self and family, relating to friends and relatives, and developing relationships in early childhood settings are all examples of this growing interest in broader social studies learnings. Primary children are expanding these same understandings as their relationships in the school and community continue to grow. The following sections describe, in more detail, opportunities for young children to learn more about themselves and others.

Understanding Self

The young child's social studies interests begin with an understanding of self (Mindes, 2005). Although this is a lifelong process for each of us, it is during the early childhood years that children become aware of their physical, emotional, and intellectual selves and begin to understand how they are similar to and different from others. Much of this learning about self is informal and comes from interactions with parents, teachers, peers, and others. At the same time, more structured experiences help children learn about themselves. Even the complex and difficult topics of race and social class become meaningful to children when materials and activities are made available in the early childhood setting (Lee et al., 2008).

A more structured study of children's physical selves, for example, might include the following activities:

- **Create body art.** In the art center, children can create their own handprints and footprints and can have an adult trace their bodies on large sheets of paper for decoration.

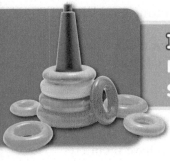

Developmentally Appropriate Practice . . .
INTEGRATING CURRICULUM THROUGH CONSTRUCTIVIST SOCIAL STUDIES

One interesting way to involve children in valuable social studies experiences is to provide them with handmade cloth dolls with no facial features. Wien, Stacey, Keating, Rowlings, and Cameron (2002) describe the 6-month constructivist curriculum they developed with children from 27 months to 3½ years of age. After the adults noticed that many of the children were frequently taking dolls and washing, feeding, combing hair, and carrying them around the early childhood setting, each child in the program was offered a handmade cloth doll without any distinguishing facial features. "Art consultant Rhonda Wakely-Fortin designed and constructed the dolls in a resplendent variety of skin tones and body shapes, from skinny mahogany to plump peach. She also devised simple shapes for facial features and hairpieces, which she enclosed in plastic zipper bags" (p. 33). The intent behind these dolls was to create a sense of surprise and mystery in very young children and give them opportunities to think about and discuss what they saw.

This project, based on the Reggio Emilia approach, began with the early childhood professionals audiotaping the conversations of children as they were presented with the dolls. Without exception, the first thing children noticed and discussed was the lack of eyes, making comments like, "My doll cannot see you" (p. 34). Children began a rather lengthy study of their own eyes. They then made decisions about the color of eyes their own dolls should have and glued on appropriate colors of felt pieces. A field trip to a local optometrist provided additional opportunities to discuss eyes and eyeglasses. After several weeks, the discussion and resulting activities moved on to the topic of hair. Children were invited to come along when one of the adults got a haircut at a local hair salon. A book was later created from photographs, drawings, and children's comments about the visit. With permission, a lock of hair from each child was cut and placed on laminated index cards and added into the book. Hairpieces from the art consultant were also placed on a table for children to glue onto their dolls. As the project continued, further investigations included a study of noses and mouths and the construction of doll beds. Throughout this experience, these very young children constructed new knowledge about themselves and others through their handmade dolls.

- **Take photos.** Take photographs of children in the class, discuss similarities and differences at group time, and then mount the pictures on a bulletin board so that children can study them in more detail. Or use a digital camera to create a computerized bulletin board for study and sharing with others.

- **Read stories.** Collect several books that talk about children's physical selves, and read them at group time. Two examples are *Teach Me About Series: My Body* (Berry, 1986) and *Bodies* (Brenner, 1970). Make the books available during center time for children to browse.

- **Sing songs.** Many songs help children understand their physical selves. Some examples include "Head, Shoulders, Knees and Toes," "You Are Special" (Mr. Rogers), and "Getting to Know Myself" (Hap Palmer).

Understanding Others

Throughout the early years, children are expanding their knowledge of human relationships as they interact with family members, early childhood professionals, peers, and others. Understanding relationships within the family is

An understanding of self begins during the first year of life.

an important starting point for this growing knowledge base. Families influence almost every facet of the young child's early development and generate much interest as a topic of discussion in the classroom. Here are some ideas for the study of families:

- **Family of the week.** Make sure each family in your classroom has a special week when they can share with others some elements of their lives at home. Invite families into the classroom; have them create a bulletin board, family scrapbook, or videotape that helps others know about them; encourage families to share occupations, hobbies, and family traditions.

- **Holiday celebrations.** Every family is shaped by their cultural roots. This can be celebrated through the sharing of special holiday traditions. Take advantage of the diversity of families within the classroom to learn about similarities and differences among cultures.

- **Family volunteers.** Encouraging family members, relatives, and older siblings to spend time helping out in the classroom can be an effective way for children to learn about family differences through casual interactions and projects (Cohen, 2009).

- **Family foods.** Have families sign up to provide special snack foods that are popular in the home. Food is a great socializer and can be another way to initiate conversations about similarities and differences among families.

- **Family jobs.** Family members can share their work responsibilities with the class. A photo essay, videotape, field trip, or personal sharing time (with appropriate work props) can be a way to learn more about families.

A second important component of understanding others is the study of community relationships. A frequent starting point for this discussion is learning about community helpers. What does a police officer do? How does a firefighter control a burning building? Why does the doctor listen to my chest with her stethoscope? Children are fascinated by these issues and many more. Taking a field trip to these community work sites or inviting the workers into the classroom makes for exciting social studies learning. An electronic field trip might be a good supplement to real-world field trips for some children. The *Technology Explorations and Activities* feature in this section provides some examples of this option.

Many areas of community relationships remain hidden to children unless we take the time to point them out. Where does the garbage go once the truck picks it up? How do grocery stores work? Who fixes the city street when it needs repair? Children are curious about these issues and more. Adults should make sure that the early childhood program has many opportunities to address the complexities of community relationships.

Technology Explorations and Activities . . .
ELECTRONIC FIELD TRIPS

Through the Internet, young children can gain cognitive understandings by taking "electronic field trips" to popular places that are difficult for most children and families to visit in real life. For example, the Smithsonian Institute has a page for children that encourages them to take virtual tours of Smithsonian exhibits and provides activities designed to enhance understandings on a wide variety of topics. Do an Internet search for the Smithsonian Institute, locate the links that relate specifically to children, and review the options you find there. There is a wealth of information, so allow yourself enough time to carefully study what you find.

Research, Reflect, and Respond

1. Was the material you found at the Smithsonian site developmentally appropriate for children within the early childhood range? Why or why not?

2. How would you use some of this information in your own early childhood setting?

3. Search the Internet for other virtual field trip possibilities and compare what you find to the materials on the Smithsonian website.

Integrating Cognitive Learning throughout the Curriculum

It should be obvious at this point that cognitive development occurs throughout the day as children interact with adults, peers, and materials in their environment. Intellectual understanding is not limited to specific topics taught at set times. Rather, all that the child does, hears, and sees provides the raw material for cognitive growth.

Every center within the early childhood classroom and in the outdoor environment encourages intellectual development. These activities can include playing with blocks, painting in the art center, digging in the garden, and reading books in the library center. As you prepare each of these centers, plan for developmentally appropriate materials and activities that enhance learning opportunities for young children. These preparations will vary with the ages and developmental abilities of the children in the program.

Infant/Toddler Materials and Activities

Piaget (Ginsburg & Opper, 1969) describes the infant/toddler's cognitive functioning as sensorimotor intelligence. By this he means that children at this age are learning about their world through sensory and motor exploration. Sights, sounds, tastes, and physical manipulation provide many opportunities for intellectual growth.

To integrate cognitive learning throughout the infant/toddler environment, caregivers need to provide materials and activities that children can experience through sensory/motor activity (Geist, 2009). Some examples follow:

- Mobiles in cribs, pictures of human faces around the room, and picture books to stimulate visual exploration
- Blocks, stacking toys, and push–pull toys for physical manipulation

- Balls made of different materials, texture sheets, water play activities; corn-meal, rice, or dried peas in a dishpan; food experiences that include a variety of textures for tactile stimulation
- Talking to and holding children to develop relationships and communicate caring
- Music-making materials, sound discrimination toys for auditory stimulation, and recorded music

Children Ages 3 through 5

Most preschool and kindergarten classrooms are organized into centers with schedules that allow children to spend large blocks of time playfully exploring the indoor environment and playground. Early childhood professionals should provide materials for each center that enhance children's cognitive understandings (Eisenhauer & Feikes, 2009). Examples for each center follow.

Block center. Unit blocks are among the best materials in the early childhood classroom for cognitive learning. Counting, shape recognition, understanding stability and balance, and developing beginning mapping skills are just a few of the many learning opportunities they provide (Chalufour & Worth, 2004; Hirsch, 1996). The accessories that are added can help facilitate other learning. For example, multicultural family figures placed in the center help children realize that families are diverse (Lee et al., 2008). With the assistance of thoughtful adults, children can begin to discuss and understand these diversity issues.

Art center. Providing paints of different textures and colors, and a variety of brushes and applicators allows children to explore the properties of the art materials and how they can be used to create different paintings. Conceptually, children learn to recognize patterns, identify colors and shapes, and develop an understanding of symmetry as they playfully explore these materials (Schirrmacher, 2006).

Manipulative center. Legos, Bristle Blocks, Tinker Toys, puzzles, simple matching games, and most of the typical materials found in the manipulative area help children develop concepts of color, size, and shape. Children practice patterning, one-to-one correspondence, and counting skills as they work with manipulatives as well (Singer, Golnikoff, & Hirsch-Pasek, 2006).

Book center. The pictures and text in any good children's book have great potential for stimulating conceptual growth. Books about understanding relationships, those with specific information on science and math topics (e.g., different types of birds), and books addressing feelings are just a few of the possibilities for learning (Griffiths & Clyne, 1991; Jacobs & Crowley, 2010). Providing a variety of books that focus on specific themes and changing them regularly will stimulate many learning opportunities in math, science, and social studies (Sackes, Trundle, & Flevares, 2009).

Dramatic play/housekeeping center. As children play out themes in these centers, they learn properties of real-world materials by using toys (e.g., a toy stethoscope), grow in their understanding of roles (doctors, nurses, and other health workers), and gain information from other players ("Hey, doctors don't do it that way, they . . .") (Miles, 2009).

Music center. Play with musical instruments can be useful in building conceptual knowledge. Striking a xylophone, for example, and then discussing what causes the sound can be an excellent learning opportunity. Many songs (e.g., "Five Little

Speckled Frogs") also contain conceptual information that children learn as they sing (Parlakian & Lerner, 2010).

Discovery center. The science materials in this center have clear potential for stimulating cognitive development. Examining, classifying, and reading about different rocks is one example. Measuring a plant's growth and charting it on a graph is another possible learning activity for this center.

The Primary Grades

Although interest in other options is growing, the traditional elementary school curriculum tends to teach cognitive subjects in isolation from one another. That is, math, science, and social studies are each taught at a distinct time during the school day. This segmented approach is in direct conflict with constructivist learning. Children in constructivist classrooms learn through manipulation and discovery, which are much more open-ended in terms of outcomes. Any given task generally provides opportunities for cognitive growth in many different areas.

One highly appropriate technique that engages children in constructivist learning is called the *project approach*. Children who have decided to pursue a particular subject in more depth form a small group to take on a project. Katz (1994) describes a project involving an investigation of balls. For this project, a kindergarten teacher asked the children to collect from home, friends, relatives, and others as many old balls as they could. She developed a study web by asking what the children might like to know about the balls. The children collected 31 different kinds of balls, including a gumball, a cotton ball, a globe of the earth, and an American football (which led to a discussion of the concepts of sphere, hemisphere, and cone).

The children then formed subgroups to examine specific questions. One group studied the surface texture of each ball and made rubbings to represent their findings; another measured the circumference of each ball with pieces of string; and a third tried to determine what each ball was made of.

As children engaged in their study of balls, new questions arose, groups shared information, and the children learned concepts of science, math, and social studies. Excited children learned rapidly from this project.

Although not all experiences in the primary classroom can be organized around projects, this option clearly works well and leads to important conceptual growth. By beginning with student interests and assisting children as they construct their projects, exciting learning opportunities can take place. The *Developmentally Appropriate Practice* feature in this section provides additional examples of integrated learning through projects.

Project learning allows children to study topics in depth and learn from their peers.

Developmentally Appropriate Practice...
INTEGRATING COGNITIVE CURRICULUM WITH PROJECT LEARNING

Project learning is an excellent vehicle for facilitating cognitive development. Projects provide numerous opportunities for young children to engage in math, science, and social studies learning as activities unfold. Following are examples from different writers of projects that could be effectively implemented in the early childhood classroom:

- **Conversations about leaves.** Preschool children are often fascinated by the process of leaves turning color and finally dropping from the tree. After collecting leaves, examining and categorizing them, and then drawing and painting pictures of leaves (science, math, and art experiences), children and adults can hold a group meeting to discuss their observations and theories related to the subject. This conversation would then lead to other science experiments, data collection, and art experiences to address their questions about how, when, and where leaves fall (Hendrick, 2004, p. 144).

- **Housing costs.** Primary children who experience a classmate who moves, a parent remarrying, or classmates moving into new housing may be interested in a project about housing costs that includes mathematics, social studies, and literacy activities. After discussing the sorts of furnishings children would like in their "ideal house," a webbing of categories of materials needed to furnish a house (appliances, furniture, kitchen supplies, etc.) could be created. Children could then work in small groups to first estimate and then find actual costs for the various categories investigated and share their results with others (Kostelnik, Soderman, & Whiren, 2011).

- **Climate and people.** What are the effects of climate on how people live? Young children may be curious about why people in Florida or California wear winter clothing that is different from that worn in Minnesota or New York. Students could " collect data—look at weather maps; make weather charts; read stories about weather and clothes; consult the weather channel on TV or the Internet; and draw, cut, and paste pictures—to explore climatic differences" (Mindes, 2005, p. 13).

summary

The Cognitive Curriculum

The goals of the early childhood mathematics, science, and social studies curricula include an emphasis on critical thinking, problem solving, and lifelong learning rather than an overemphasis on the learning of facts. The Constructivist Approach is valued and emphasized in early childhood settings to engage children in the cognitive curriculum. Families have important roles in supporting cognitive learning.

Mathematics and Young Children

Mathematics learning for young children includes classification, seriation, patterning, number concepts, measurement, geometry, and problem-solving experiences. Early childhood professionals should provide developmentally appropriate activities for each of these categories. The math language used by adults should be accurate and descriptive of the concepts being presented.

Science Learning

An understanding of scientific content, process, and attitudes is essential to the science curriculum. When addressed in developmentally appropriate ways, the physical and biological sciences are all important topics for learning in the early childhood classroom.

Young Children and Social Studies

The social studies curriculum helps young children understand relationships between people and environmental factors that influence their lives. Knowledge of self and others are two key elements of the early childhood social studies curriculum.

Integrating Cognitive Learning throughout the Curriculum

It is important to integrate cognitive learning with other components of the early childhood curriculum at the infant/toddler, preschool, and primary-age levels. As children engage in playful interactions with peers and materials provided in the early childhood setting, they are growing in their understanding of math, science, and social studies.

for reflection and discussion

1. How will you encourage problem solving in your future early childhood program? Share your ideas with others.
2. List two or three math activities that you would consider using with young children. Note which aspects of math learning they promote.
3. What is the scientific attitude and how can you promote it in early childhood settings?
4. Describe ideas you might use to help children understand similarities and differences in families.
5. Develop a plan for integrating cognitive learning throughout the curriculum. Share your idea with others and incorporate their feedback as appropriate.

─ MyEducationLab ─

Go to Topic 7: Curriculum/Content Areas in the MyEducationLab (www.myeducationlab.com) for *Teaching Young Children*, where you can:

- Find learning outcomes for Curriculum/Content Areas along with the national standards that connect to these outcomes.
- Complete Assignments and Activities that can help you more deeply understand the chapter content.
- Apply and practice your understanding of the core teaching skills identified in the chapter with the Building Teaching Skills and Dispositions learning units.
- Examine challenging situations and cases presented in the IRIS Center Resources.
- Check your comprehension on the content covered in the chapter with the Study Plan. Here you will be able to take a chapter quiz, receive feedback on your answers, and then access Review, Practice, and Enrichment activities to enhance your understanding of chapter content.
- Use the Online Lesson Plan Builder to practice lesson planning and integrating national and state standards into your planning.

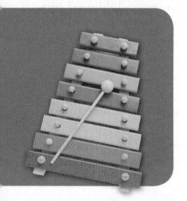

15

Language and Literacy Learning

IN THIS CHAPTER YOU WILL

- Investigate the development of language and literacy in young children.

- Study techniques for facilitating language and literacy learning.

- Develop strategies to encourage family involvement in language and literacy development.

Your class of 4-year-olds is playing during their free choice time indoors. For the moment, children are productively interacting with peers and play materials, so you have time to step back and observe what is taking place. With a notepad in hand, you focus your attention on the play themes unfolding around you.

Blake and Abby are in the art center, involved in the fingerpainting activity there. "Ooo, ooo, ooo. Goo, goo, goo!" chimes Blake as he smears the shaving cream mix in large circular motions on his tray. "Boo, hoo, hoo. You're full of moo!" responds Abby as she looks up from her painting. Both children giggle and then return to their art project.

Terrance and Stuart pretend to be shopper and grocery clerk in the store set up in the dramatic play area. As Terrance brings his groceries up to Stuart for bagging, he says, "Say, you got any peanut butter? Ah love my peanut butter!" Sorry," replies Stuart, "We're out. How about some beans?" "Nah, beans and me don't get along too well," responds Terrance. "I'll buy what I've got." They continue to dramatize their play theme while chatting.

Tina is in the book corner with a parent volunteer, and the two of them are absorbed in reading the book *Mike Mulligan and His Steam Shovel* (Burton, 1939). They have read the story once and are just beginning a second reading at Tina's request. This time, she stops the parent periodically to ask questions about the steam shovel and Mike Mulligan. Tina is fascinated by the story.

The children in this early childhood setting are engaged in language and literacy learning. No direct instruction is taking place, but as they play and communicate, they are intuitively learning how language works, practicing its many nuances, and gaining insights into the meanings of written language.

Language and literacy competence are at the heart of the human experience. The ability to communicate with others enables us to learn and grow, while enriching our lives. Adults working with children during the early childhood years need considerable knowledge about language and literacy learning so that they can facilitate these important experiences.

Language and literacy learning, though clearly related, are generally thought of as complementary processes. **Language** can be defined as either oral or hand-signed communication between humans. Every culture arbitrarily assigns meaning to sounds. Then people within the culture use combinations of these basic units to create words and sentences that communicate messages to others. Rules govern the ways in which sounds are used to form words and how words are combined to form sentences. Speakers of the language intuitively (but usually not consciously) understand these rules.

Literacy is the ability to make meaning from language in written form. Literate people can read and write the language of their culture. Cultures arbitrarily assign meaning to written symbols and construct systems to organize these symbols on the written page. Literacy is the ability to interpret the intended message of these symbols (reading) and to use them to communicate information to others (writing).

Language and Literacy Development

The process of learning language may appear effortless, but in reality it is a major undertaking for young children. Those who study language acquisition have considerable difficulty even explaining it. The next several sections should help you understand how children complete the complex process of learning to speak the language of their culture. Following that is a discussion of literacy skills and how they develop in young children.

Theoretical Perspectives

Theorists have proposed three different views of how children learn language. Those who believe in **behaviorism** argue that children acquire language through the same stimulus–response connections that influence learning in all areas (Skinner, 1957). Children hear language spoken by family members and others, imitate that speech, and are rewarded for their efforts. This positive reinforcement encourages them to communicate more.

While behaviorist theory helps explain some aspects of language learning, other perspectives add further insight into how children develop linguistic competence. The **maturationist** theory suggests that every child, regardless of culture, intellectual ability, or socioeconomic status, inherits the genetic capability for language. When children are exposed to language, this innate ability, or **language acquisition device (LAD)**, allows them to gradually make sense of the rules for oral communication (Chomsky, 1965).

A third view of language learning is the **interactionist theory of language acquisition**. Proponents of this theory suggest that language acquisition combines an innate ability with environmental influences. These two factors interact in complex ways as children learn language. The writings of both Piaget (1959) and Vygotsky (1962) support the interactionist view.

Language Development

Children vary in the rate at which they learn language, but eventually almost every child masters the complex linguistic system in which she or he is immersed. This process begins in infancy and continues throughout the early childhood years (Birckmayer, Kennedy, & Stonehouse, 2010).

Infancy. Even newborn infants work to communicate with others and are beginning to learn about their linguistic system (Kuhl, 1993). Crying is the earliest form of infant communication, and family members quickly learn the many different messages children send in this way: "I'm wet." "Feed me!" "I'm sleepy."

At the same time, infants are attending to the oral language of caregivers and others. They notice changes in sounds, rhythm, and intonation. At about 3 or 4 months of age, children start to coo and babble. Gradually, infants begin to recognize and babble the sounds of the specific language they must eventually master (Birckmayer et al., 2010).

Near the end of the first year of life, children begin to speak words. To the great thrill of their families, "mama" or "dadda" are often the earliest words spoken. Many infants have expanded their initial vocabulary to about a dozen words by their first birthday.

Toddlerhood. Toddlers proceed rapidly in their acquisition of language. By the end of the second year of life, children's vocabularies may include as many as 50 words. Many of these words carry much more meaning than the adult equivalent. This is referred to as **holophrastic speech**. For example, "More!" may well mean, "Give me more milk right now! I'm still hungry!"

As toddlers mature, they begin the process of stringing two words together to form simple sentences. A toddler who wants to go in the car with Daddy, for example, may say, "Me go!" Often referred to as **telegraphic speech** because of limited word usage, these two-word sentences are a major step forward in the young child's use of language.

The preschool years. The language understanding of children during the preschool years continues to expand rapidly. Vocabulary increases at an amazing rate, with new words added almost daily. Sentences move quickly beyond the two-word stage to more complex combinations. During the preschool years, young children refine their understanding of the rules of communication and become more proficient at carrying on a conversation with others.

The primary grades. Growth in vocabulary and sentence complexity continues throughout the primary grades. By this time, children have mastered most of the grammar needed for oral language communication. They are adding the finer nuances of linguistics: learning about humor, multiple meanings of words and phrases, and the importance of intonation in communications.

Linguistic Systems

When adults study language, it is generally divided into five main elements or systems. Children, also, must master each of these systems to become competent in communicating with others. Without any direct instruction, youngsters learn about phonology, morphology, semantics, syntax, and pragmatics (McNeil, 1970).

Phonology is the system of sounds used to make up words in a specific language. Cultures assign arbitrary meaning to these sounds, and speakers use consistent rules to combine the sounds into words. Phonology also includes an understanding of the intonations used to add meanings to combinations of sounds.

A second linguistic system is **morphology**. Language learners must understand the rules for combining sounds to form words within a specific language. The rules for creating plurals (*apples*) and tense (*went* for past tense; *will go* for future tense) are examples of morphology. This system is complex and varies within individual languages as well as from one language to the next.

The **semantics** of language is a third system children must master. This involves the meanings given to words. For some words, like *hat*, this is a relatively simple task; other words vary in meaning depending on the context. How many different meanings, for example, exist for the word *nurse*? Because young children are literal, many words or phrases are difficult to comprehend. "I've got a frog in my throat" may actually be a frightening concept to a 3-year-old struggling to understand the semantics of this statement.

A fourth linguistic system, **syntax**, refers to the procedures for combining words into phrases and sentences. Even nonsense words acquire some meaning when placed in phrases and sentences. "The crog slagged zuppily across the waggor" contains many nonsense words, but even young children can find meaning in this sentence because of the syntax, or placement of the words.

The final linguistic system is **pragmatics**; it consists of adapting language to different social situations. A 5-year-old learns that talking to a baby is different from interacting with peers, for example. Recognizing that "please" and "thank you" are expected in many social interactions is another aspect of pragmatics. Children gradually learn that certain words, phrases, and styles of communication are appropriate in some situations and not in others.

Literacy Development

Like the development of speech, literacy awareness and learning begin in infancy. The 8-month-old child who cuddles up on her father's lap to look at a picture book is developing early reading skills. The 18-month-old scribbling on a piece of paper is preparing for writing in later childhood. Through these and other early experiences, very young children slowly learn reading concepts such as beginning in the front of the book and moving sequentially to the back, reading each line of print from left to right, and being aware that print has meaning (Bennett-Armistead, Duke, & Moses, 2005; Bobys, 2000; National Institute for Literacy, 2008).

Traditional view. The idea that even infants engage in meaningful literacy learning is relatively new. The more traditional view has been that language and literacy development are different (Genishi & Dyson, 2009). While language learning occurs naturally, the traditional view held that formal reading and writing instruction should begin around age 6, when children have developed the mental and physical maturity needed for these tasks. Furthermore, this traditional view promoted the idea that children should be taught reading and writing through the use of basal readers, worksheets, and handwriting practice.

Emergent literacy. The idea that learning to read and write has much in common with oral language development is called **emergent literacy** (Sulzby & Teale, 1991). This approach promotes the idea that children begin learning about reading and writing in infancy. With appropriate materials and supportive adults, young children construct knowledge about print and gradually become more literate (Yaden, Rowe, & MacGillivray, 2000). By immersing the child in a print-rich environment and providing guidance during the discovery process, adults help children grow into readers and writers. Emergent literacy includes a process in which children develop **phonemic awareness**, which is defined as the "understanding and conscious awareness that speech is composed of identifiable units, such as spoken words, syllables, and sounds" (International Reading Association, 1998, p. 197). Phonemic awareness has been closely linked to success in reading and writing (Manning & Kato, 2006) and can be integrated into playful adult/child interactions in early childhood settings. Yopp and Yopp, 2009, for example, suggest that you could read *The Hungry Thing* (Slepian & Seidler, 1967) so that children can hear the silly requests the hungry thing wants to eat, such as featloaf instead of meatloaf. Young children learn phonemic awareness when they are exposed to this type of word play.

 # Language and Literacy Learning

Young children often learn language and literacy skills together as they interact with peers, family, and others. For example, when an adult reads a story to a child, there is the potential for learning new words and their pronunciation while developing a deeper understanding of print and its meaning. However, in many situations, language and literacy learning occur separate from one another. When you play a rhyming game with a young child, for example, considerable language learning takes place but there are few direct links to greater understanding of the reading and writing processes. For these reasons, the content that follows begins with a discussion of language learning experiences and is followed by information on facilitating literacy in early childhood settings.

Facilitating Language Learning

Maria Montessori (Lillard, 1972) promoted the idea of **sensitive periods** in the child's life. During these blocks of time, children have a keen interest in certain aspects of their development. The early childhood years are generally considered by Montessori to be the sensitive period for language; therefore, adults should do all they can during this time to assist children in the development of linguistic competence.

The International Reading Association (IRA) and the National Association for the Education of Young Children (International Reading Association, 1998) have published a joint position statement on developmentally appropriate language and literacy practices. They identify the following strategies as critical for oral language development:

- **Infants and toddlers.** Taking time to talk to very young children through the course of the day and responding to their language attempts. Playing with, singing to, and using finger plays are also very important strategies.
- **Preschool children.** Children need strong, nurturing relationships, opportunities to play, and real-world experiences to expand vocabulary.
- **Primary children.** You should continue strategies identified previously for preschool children, while providing individualized attention to children experiencing language learning difficulties, and supporting ELL students by providing opportunities to strengthen first language learning.

Informal conversations. When early childhood professionals engage in informal conversations, children can learn a great deal about language and the world around them. These casual interactions do not need to be long or carefully planned ahead of time. Some suggestions for making these conversations more productive follow:

- **Show interest by listening carefully to what the child has to say.** Give the child your full attention as he speaks. This will encourage further discussion by the child (Birckmayer et al., 2010).

- **Use open-ended questions to get the child to elaborate on what has already been said.** In response to "Grammy's in Vermont," you could say, "That sounds like fun. What is she doing there?"

- **Build language into routines.** Toileting, eating, and sleeping activities are significant components of the day for very young children. Adults should take advantage of these times to talk positively with the child as they assist in meeting the child's needs.

- **Model good communication by speaking courteously and using good grammar and proper word choice.** Make sure that the verbal and nonverbal messages you send do not contradict one another and that you are being a positive role model for children.

- **Build on the child's interests as you communicate.** This will help make conversation attractive to the child. For example, a simple response to a child interested in insects might be, "Janet, I found a new book on insects yesterday in the school library. Would you like to look at it during silent reading?"

There are many opportunities for informal conversations throughout the day.

- **Expand vocabulary by using words that children may not know but that are relevant to their lives.** Labeling the emotions children express, using precise terms for science and math concepts, and identifying occupations within the community are examples. Wasik (2006) provides many other examples of building vocabulary for young children.
- **Be sensitive to children.** Listen when the child is speaking, lead the conversation when it is appropriate to do so, and try to avoid interrupting productive play time or interactions with peers to engage in conversation.

Play. Childhood play provides numerous opportunities for language learning. Garvey (1990) describes how children engage in playing with language. As they vocalize, children explore how to combine sounds, learn about syntax, and experiment with fantasy and nonsense. Garvey shares the following example of two 5-year-olds playing with language:

> **Girl 1.** Mommy, Mommy, I got new friends called Dool, Sol, Ta.
> **Girl 2.** Dool, Sue, and Ta? (both girls laugh)
> **Girl 1.** Those are funny names, aren't they?
> **Girl 2.** No, its Poopi, Daigi, and Dia . . . Diarrhea. (both laugh again)
> (Garvey, 1990, p. 71)

Language is also an important part of the play experience itself. Children use **metacommunication statements** to structure and organize the play. Designating the make-believe properties of an object ("Let's pretend this stick is a fishing pole"), assigning roles ("You be the daddy, I'll be the baby"), and planning the story line

Celebrating Play . . .
DEVELOPING LANGUAGE SKILLS THROUGH PHYSICAL ACTIVITY

When playful physical activities are combined with language training, young children benefit. Connor-Kuntz and Dummer (1996) studied children 4 to 6 years of age in special education, Head Start, and typical preschool classes. They provided some of these students with guided physical activities only, but gave the rest both guided physical activities and additional language skills training.

Children in the latter group were given natural opportunities to learn language concepts related to their physical activities such as these:

- Around
- Over and under
- Front and behind
- Above and below
- Distance
- Height
- Shape

Children who received these additional language experiences, including those with impaired cognitive and language abilities, showed improvements in their language skills. Furthermore, these children showed gains in their motor skills equivalent to those receiving the physical training alone.

1. Do the results of this study make sense to you? Why should playful physical activities combined with adult-led language enrichment lead to improved language skills? Discuss this with others.

2. Describe some ways to combine physical activity with language learning in an early childhood setting.

("First, we'll cook dinner, and then we'll sit down and eat") are all examples of meta-communication statements for enacting play sequences.

The language used in play provides additional opportunities for developing linguistic competence. The conversation necessary to engage in pretend play is one good example of this language usage: "Hush, baby! Mommy is on the telephone." Children must communicate in other types of play as well. Two girls constructing a block tower, for example, use language to discuss their intent and rationale for placement of blocks, ask each other for feedback as they proceed, and discuss alternatives while they build.

The physical activity associated with play also has a positive influence on language development. The *Celebrating Play* feature in this section describes a study in which this relationship is explored in more detail. Read the feature now to learn more about play and development.

Language-rich experiences. The motivation to expand vocabulary and communicate with others is greatly enhanced when children have adventures that excite them in some way. You can provide children with diverse experiences to assist in language development. Good books can be that kind of opportunity for many children. By touching on issues that are meaningful or interesting to children, books become a starting point for further investigation and communication.

Another language-rich experience, particularly for infants and toddlers, is the lullaby. These age-old melodies are used traditionally to calm children in preparation for naps or evening sleep times. Honig (2005) makes it clear, however, that these soothing songs are an important language learning experience as well. As early childhood professionals combine music and movement in enchanting

Developmentally Appropriate Practice . . .
INTEGRATING CURRICULUM THROUGH A TRIP TO THE POST OFFICE

Mrs. Riley's first-grade class is off for a field trip to the community post office. With the help of several family volunteers, the children arrive safely at mid-morning and are greeted by postal workers who have prepared a tour of the facilities. Children see where the mail arrives in big trucks and how it is unloaded, sorted, and prepared for delivery. They also see how mail on its way to other cities is prepared for shipping. Students watch postal workers assist customers who need stamps and those who need their packages mailed. It is a busy morning.

Upon returning to the classroom, children spend time as a large group talking with Mrs. Riley about what they saw. She records their comments on the overhead projector. Later, she will combine this written record with student illustrations to construct the monthly newsletter for families. In addition, Mrs. Riley has set up the dramatic play center as a post office with pretend stamps, envelopes, paper, writing instruments, and mailboxes for each member of the class. Children can spend free time writing, sending, and reading their mail. The center is buzzing with activity throughout the day.

In addition, two other centers have been modified for this study of mail services. The library corner has three new books with mail-related themes: *What's It Like to Be a Postal Worker?* (Matthews, 1990), *The Postman's Palace* (Henri, 1990), and *Here Comes the Mail* (Skurzynski, 1992). Mrs. Riley introduced these books at group time, and children are eagerly browsing through them with the adult volunteer. In the process, they recognize many of the procedures that they saw earlier at the post office. Bookmaking is the theme of the writing center, and several children spend time there working on tales about the trip to the post office. They draw pictures of remembered events and then dictate stories to the parent volunteer. Children add their finished books to the library corner and read them to other interested children.

lullabies, young children are learning language in meaningful and enjoyable ways. Lullabies also have stress-reducing properties for both children and adults.

Field trips, too, can spark children's interests in a topic that can lead to important language learning. Traveling to a nearby pond to collect tadpoles, insects, and underwater plant life could be an excellent starting point for a science unit and a great way to generate individual and group discussion on these topics. Every community has many potentially beneficial sites for field trips. The *Developmentally Appropriate Practice* feature in this section describes a field trip to the post office and how it can provide a rich integrated learning experience for young children.

Taking advantage of people and events in the community may be yet another language-rich experience for young children. For example, a retired volunteer who is good at communicating with young children could come into the early childhood setting and talk about his experiences as a child. Participating in a community-sponsored musical concert or going to see a play or puppet show for young children can provide other experiences that children can talk about at home or in the classroom.

The power of storytelling. Storytelling is another important tool for language and literacy learning that should be an integral part of the teaching/learning process for young children (Curenton, 2006). Isbell (2002) states:

> The experience of hearing a story told is more personal and connected to the listener. The *storyteller* can maintain eye contact and adapt the telling of the story to specific listeners. . . . Listeners, regardless of their language skills or reading abilities, can understand the story because it is communicated through words, vocal intonation, gestures, facial expressions, and body movement. . . . Storytelling promotes expressive language development—in oral and written forms—and presents new vocabulary and complex language in a powerful form that inspires children to emulate the model they have experienced. (p. 26)

Almost any book can be told as a story, but the best options typically include repetitive phrases, unusual words, and actions that you can incorporate into the story. Early childhood professionals can also make up their own stories or tell children about some of their own or others' interesting life experiences. With practice, storytelling can be an easy and enjoyable part of the day for early educators (Birckmayer et al., 2010). Raines and Isbell (1999) and Isbell and Raines (2000) offer tips for storytelling and provide more than 30 stories for caregivers and teachers who are interested in using storytelling with young children.

After children have experienced quality storytelling by the early childhood professional, Whaley (2002) suggests that group storytelling can help motivate young children to engage in this experience themselves. She provides several ideas for group storytelling:

1. **Round-robin or sentence stories.** Select story topics that are familiar to young children (animal stories and fables are good choices), begin a story, and then ask children to determine what will come next. Depending on developmental abilities, it may be best to first have children decide the next steps as a group and later have individual children add a sentence at a time to the story.

2. **Theme stories.** Have children choose the theme for the story (e.g., a story about monkeys) and then create your own story, focusing on the identified theme.

3. **Descriptive stories.** Once children have gained confidence in round-robin storytelling, help them expand their language by using more descriptive words to tell their stories. For older children, instead of "The cow walked across the street," you could encourage them to say, "The brown and white cow walked slowly across the busy street as cars honked their horns in anger."

4. **Picture stories.** Children can choose photographs, or pictures from magazines, as the starting point for their stories. As they describe what they see and think is happening, their story unfolds.

5. **Grab bag stories.** Prepare a bag full of familiar objects. Have children take one from the bag to tell their own story or to add to a group story already in progress.

Second language learning. An option that is growing in popularity, both at the prekindergarten and primary levels of education, is second language learning for all children. For much of the world, learning a second language is an expected part of the schooling process. In addition to the native language, children are also learning English from an early age. Two examples from the United States highlight the growing interest in having all children learn a second language here:

- **Bennington College Early Childhood Center.** This early learning center for children ages 2 to 6, located in rural Vermont, operates a dual language immersion program for predominantly English-speaking children, with one adult who speaks only English and another who speaks only Spanish (DeBey & Bombard, 2007).

- **Nellie Muir Elementary.** Beginning in kindergarten, children here are instructed for 80% of the day in Spanish and 20% in English. This mix changes gradually until fifth grade when it reaches 50% in each language (Barton, 2006). Children in the program are a mix of Spanish native language speakers and English native language speakers.

Language Learning Materials

Virtually every toy and piece of equipment in the early childhood classroom can lead to language learning. Some options, however, are particularly important in stimulating linguistic exploration. These include the following:

- **Flannelboard stories.** For younger children, having a board covered with flannel material and figures that relate to popular books helps them to retell familiar story lines. Older children can also benefit from a collection of flannel pieces to tell their own stories. You can either make or purchase commercial flannel pieces to use in the classroom.

- **Magnetic boards.** As the name implies, pieces stick to a metal board rather than flannel. Adults can attach magnetic strips to the backs of figures, that children can then manipulate to tell familiar or invented stories. Commercial materials are also available for magnetic boards.

- **Puppets.** Puppets are another versatile way to provide extensive language experiences. Handmade and commercial puppets stimulate increased verbal interactions in the classroom. Many quiet children become much more verbal with puppets on their hands. They may also be a powerful tool for second language learning. Akcan (2005) describes a first-grade classroom in which children use a daily puppet theater as a tool for practicing French as a second language.

- **Dramatic play props.** As children use props and play out themes, they engage in many linguistic interactions. Some examples of useful props include restaurant supplies, camping materials, doctor's office props, grocery store goods, and barber/beauty shop supplies.

Assisting with Emergent Literacy

Language and literacy learning are related but not identical processes. Although almost all children learn oral language, many find reading and writing more difficult. Traditionally, reading and writing have been more formally taught, and many children have struggled with the pressures placed on them to understand a process they may not be ready to master. To improve chances for success, early childhood professionals use an emergent literacy approach (Sulzby & Teale, 1991) whereby children begin learning about reading and writing in infancy and continue throughout the early childhood years. With appropriate materials and supportive adults, young children engage in meaningful reading and writing experiences and gradually become more literate (Yaden et al., 2000).

The National Association for the Education of Young Children and the International Reading Association, in their joint position statement on reading and writing (International Reading Association, 1998), identify the following strategies for promoting reading and writing in young children:

- **Infants and toddlers.** Reading books one-on-one, beginning in infancy, is the single most important strategy. Casually demonstrating characteristics of books as they are read (words proceed from left to right and the reader moves from the top of the page to the bottom, etc.) can also be meaningful with very young children.
- **Preschool children.** Like those working with infants and toddlers, early childhood professionals also read books to individuals and groups, model effective reading and writing behaviors, create print-rich environments so that young children see and use written language throughout their day, and encourage play experiences that include literacy tools.
- **Primary children.** In addition to continuing the previous strategies, primary children need opportunities for daily independent reading, meaningful daily writing experiences, small group work focused on literacy instruction, and individualized instruction for those who are either struggling or demonstrating advanced skills.

This emergent literacy perspective means that early childhood professionals working with prekindergarten children need to provide experiences that lead to discoveries about reading and writing. For example, traditional rhyming, skipping, and word games are an enjoyable way for young children to begin developing phonemic awareness (Bryant, MacLean, Bradley, & Crossland, 1990). When combined with songs, finger plays, and books in which rhyming and alliteration are prominent, children are able to develop phonemic awareness in preparation for reading and writing (Yopp & Yopp, 2009). This emergent literacy perspective also changes the approaches that primary teachers should use with their children. Teachers at this level are finding meaningful literacy alternatives to the traditional basal readers, worksheets, and handwriting exercises so often found in the primary grades (Gaffney, Ostrosky, & Hemmeter, 2008; Tunks & Giles, 2009).

Observing Development . . .
EMERGENT LITERACY EXPERIENCES

Choose one of the age groups within early childhood (infants/toddlers, preschool children, or primary children) and observe (for a minimum of 30 minutes) the emergent literacy materials and experiences in that setting. Track whether the material or activity is adult-led or child-initiated. For example, a child selecting a book (include title, if possible) and sitting down to read it would be a child-initiated activity. Provide as many details as you can about the materials and activities observed. Use the following chart to summarize your findings.

Emergent Literacy Materials and Activities, Kickerville Preschool, 4-Year-Old Class

Adult-led (materials and activities)	Child-initiated (materials and activities)
• Book on frogs (adult reads to two children) • Stories about winter break (adult writes down what children dictate and then children illustrate)	• Computer game (Reader Rabbit) that engages children in literacy activities • Children choose from 15 books in the reading center, sit on the rug, and look through the text

Reflect and Apply

1. Compare and contrast what you read in this chapter with the adult-led emergent literacy activities you observed in the early childhood setting.

2. Do you think the adult-led or the child-initiated emergent literacy activities observed were the most helpful in facilitating language and/or literacy learning? Why do you feel this way?

3. If you were the early childhood professional in this setting, what else would you have done to promote language or literacy learning there?

Children's artwork can be used to stimulate both oral and written language.

Seeing emergent literacy activities in practice can help you understand the types of materials and activities that work best for young children. The *Observing Development* feature in this section provides a format for making this observation. Spend some time in an early childhood setting observing emergent literacy activities and then consider the implications of what you saw.

Print-rich environments. Caregivers and teachers at all levels within the early childhood range need to provide children with meaningful written materials that can lead to literacy learning. The most obvious of these are books. Beginning in infant/toddler programs (Kupetz & Green, 1997), adults should provide children with access to a wide variety of books and should read to individual children or small groups (Gaffney et al., 2008).

There are several key elements of a print-rich environment:

• **A variety of materials for reading.** In addition to books, early childhood settings should display many types of print that serve real-life functions (labels on food items, restaurant menus, road signs, etc.). Where possible, provide print in the children's home languages as well (Love, Burns, & Buell, 2007). If, for example, you have Spanish-speaking children in your classroom, provide signs and labels in Spanish as well as English.

- **Diverse writing materials.** A well-equipped writing center should be the focus of these activities, with materials available throughout the room that encourage children (or adults) to record important written communications (title of artwork, description of block structure, story to accompany flannelboard figures, etc.).

- **Displays of children's written products.** You can help children see the importance of writing by displaying their stories, books, and letters to friends and families.

- **Integrated printed materials.** Written materials should be connected with ongoing activities in the classroom. Gardening activities outdoors could be connected to teacher-recorded stories of children's gardening experiences, labeling of plant rows, recordings of plant growth, and books in the library center about aspects of gardening (Hachey & Butler, 2009).

- **Literacy as part of routines.** Literacy activities can be highlighted during the routines of the school day. The attendance charts, hot and cold lunch counts, daily schedule, Pledge of Allegiance, and weather chart can be used for meaningful reading and writing experiences (Perlmutter, Folger, & Holt, 2009).

Developmentally Appropriate Practice . . .
INTEGRATING CURRICULUM THROUGH STORY SONGS

Shelly Ringgenberg (2003) provides good evidence that music can be an important tool for language learning. She experimented with both conventional storytelling and what she calls story songs where well-known stories are matched with a simple tune and sung with children. Ringgenberg found that children not only remembered more words from the story songs, but also that they were very popular with all ages of children in her preschool class.

Ringgenberg (2003) suggests three graduated steps in the creation of story songs:

1. **One musical phrase.** Take a story familiar to children and create a musical phrase to use with a repeating portion of the story. For example, in the story *Brown Bear, Brown Bear, What do you See?* (Martin, 1967) the phrase "Brown Bear, Brown Bear, what do you see?" is repeated several times. By creating a simple melody (or using a melody from a well-known song such as "Mary Had a Little Lamb"), you can tell the story and then sing the repeating phrase with children.

2. **Melody for an entire story.** The next step is to try creating a song for an entire story. Again, choose a story that you and the children both know well, one that includes repetition and rhythm, and set it to a tune you create or to a familiar tune. For example, you could use the tune of "Frére Jacques" to sing the story *I Went Walking* (Williams, 1989). To make the story and song match, repeat each line: "I went walking, I went walking. What did you see? What did you see? I saw a black cat. I saw a black cat. Looking at me. Looking at me."

3. **Create your own story songs.** A third type of story song is one you create totally on your own. Write your own story about people and events that are meaningful to you and the children, create a tune (or use a well-known favorite), and put them together for a creative experience with young children. The nice thing about children is that they accept your efforts without criticism and simply enjoy your creation along with you. You do not have to be an accomplished musician to have fun with this option.

Making the oral and written language connection. Young children need meaning-ful opportunities to grasp the connections between oral and written language. Un-derstanding that what is said can be written down and that printed information can be spoken are important steps during the early childhood years. The *Developmentally Appropriate Practice* feature in this section discusses the use of songs to help children make these oral and written language connections.

An important technique that many early childhood professionals use to help children make these connections is the **language experience approach**. Children dictate information about personal experiences while an adult writes them down. The adult can then read the story back to them and encourage them to practice reading their dictated work. Christie, Vukelich, and Enz (2011) describe three lan-guage experience options:

- **Group experience stories.** Following a shared group experience such as a field trip to the bakery, the class can discuss the highlights of the event and together create a story about the activity. As the group dictates the story, the adult writes it down and then reads the completed story, asking children to join in choral reading. Group experience stories can be copied and sent home to give families further informa-tion about school activities and provide opportunities for reading at home.

- **Individual experience stories.** These stories come from individual children, who dictate them to you. An example of this type is a child creating a picture book of his family's trip to the zoo with space at the bottom of each page for the dictated story. The *Technology Explorations and Activities* feature in this sec-tion describes the use of photographs as another interesting option for creat-ing individual or group experience stories. Read the information now and reflect on the implications for early learning.

- **Classroom newspaper.** First, children share interesting things that have happened to them. The adult then records these experiences and compiles

Technology Explorations and Activities...
LITERACY EXPERIENCES AND PHOTOGRAPHS

Photographs are a wonderful way for young children to have meaningful writing and storytelling experiences. With digital photography, it is an easy, low-cost option that you can incorporate into your early childhood setting (Neumann-Hinds, 2007). For example, you could take digi-tal photos of the field trip to the bakery and have children orga-nize the pictures into an electronic slide show. The children could also narrate a story to accompany the pictures, and the whole show could be presented at an open house for families. In some instances, children can also take their own photographs to summa-rize a work/play project and then write or tell the story of what they have accomplished as a way to document their learning.

Research, Reflect, and Respond

1. One free photography program that can be used to advantage in early childhood settings is Photo Story. Do an Internet search for this Microsoft product and review the possibilities for young children. Can you see yourself using this product in an early childhood setting? Why or why not?

2. Do an Internet search for "photography for kids." Review the options you find and summarize some of the best ideas for use in early childhood settings.

3. What do you see as the strengths and limitations of using digital photography in early childhood settings?

them into a newspaper to share with families. Older children can often do much of this work themselves (Sahn & Reichel, 2008). If you have an overabundance of news items, it may be necessary to limit the number of children sharing their stories, making sure that all the children eventually have a chance to have their stories recorded.

Literacy learning through play. Many different play types can effectively stimulate literacy understandings. Dramatic play, for example, can lead to early reading and writing experiences.

Liam, Jerome, and Erika are playing in their preschool classroom's restaurant. Liam is the cook, Jerome is the waiter, and Erika is the customer. Erika pretends to read the menu and gives her order to Jerome, who pretends to write it down by making scribbles on his notepad, and then takes it to the cook. As these children engage in dramatic play, they are dealing with many beginning literacy concepts.

Construction play in the block area can also lead to reading and writing opportunities.

Chad and Marshall, two third graders, have just finished building a castle based loosely on a book they recently read in the library center. Now they are interested in writing their own story about medieval times and life in a castle. They plan to spend time on the Internet collecting more information about castles before engaging in their literary efforts.

Each center in the early childhood classroom should be equipped with literacy-related materials that children can use in their play (Love et al., 2007). Pencils and paper for writing, signs created by adults and children, magazines, newspapers, and an old typewriter are examples of options to include. Bartel (2005) and Wellhousen and Giles (2005) provide two different examples of centers (art and blocks, respectively) that have been enriched with literacy materials.

Reading to children. Many experts consider reading books and other printed materials to young children the most important way to develop their early literacy skills. The Commission on Reading (Anderson, Hiebert, Scott, & Wilkinson, 1985) states, "The single most important activity for building the knowledge required for eventual success in reading is reading aloud to children" (p. 23). This process should begin in infancy and continue throughout the early childhood years, both at home and in school. In addition to developing literacy skills, reading to children has social and emotional benefits as well (Knopf & Brown, 2009).

Kupetz and Green (1997) provide the following guidelines for reading to children:

- Read to children when they are in the mood for it.
- Choose books appropriate to the age of the children.
- Read stories that are of interest to you as well.
- Have special reading times as part of the routine of the day.
- Allow the children to assist you in the reading process.
- Use your voice to show interest and help tell the story.

A comfortable center where children can go to read with others is an essential component of every early childhood setting. In addition to displaying plenty of reading options, this area should invite children to participate in the wonder of books. You should provide children with cozy pillows to lie on and good lighting. Other options might include a child-sized chair or couch, a loft area, or even a bathtub stuffed with pillows to create an inviting space that will attract children to engage in reading activities. Take extra care in preparing this corner of the classroom.

Formal literacy instruction. Although children continue to construct their own understanding of reading and writing during the primary grades, classroom teachers also implement formal literacy instruction. For the last several decades, literacy experts have debated the relative merits of **phonics instruction** (teaching the relationships between sounds and sound combinations to their written counterparts) and **whole language learning** (helping children construct reading and writing understandings from meaningful literacy activities). While early educators tended to lean toward the whole language approach, many current researchers and writers are suggesting that reading instruction in the primary grades must integrate both phonics instruction and the whole language approach to be successful (International Reading Association, 1998; Snow, Burns, & Griffin, 1998).

Children's Books

Every early childhood setting should have an excellent collection of books to entice children into the library corner. The International Reading Association (1998) suggests that a classroom library for elementary children should have a minimum of five books for every child. Some of these books can remain in the center throughout the year, but most books should be rotated in and out of the room on a regular basis.

Over the course of the year, early childhood professionals may literally need hundreds of children's books for their library centers. Although you can check out books from school and public libraries, developing your own collection also makes good sense. Consider the following resources for building your own library of quality children's literature:

- Commercial publishers (expensive but important resources)
- Used bookstores
- Internet purchases through eBay, Amazon, or other booksellers
- Garage sales
- Public library sales
- Family donations

Selecting books. With literally thousands of children's books available, you will need guidelines for making good selections of children's literature. Machado (2007) provides several criteria that should be helpful in this process:

- **Attention span, maturity, and interests.** Books should match the attention span, maturity, and interests of the children using them. These characteristics vary widely across the early childhood range. For example, even within a homogeneous age group, attention spans vary greatly. Books chosen should reflect this diversity.
- **Broad literary and artistic tastes.** Texts should include a variety of types such as fiction, nonfiction, picture books, and predictable books. Provide books by a

variety of authors, including ethnically and culturally diverse writers and illustrators to encourage breadth in children's literature (Harper & Brand, 2010).

- **Writing style.** The book should be interesting to young children, and the vocabulary and story sequence should be appropriate for the targeted children. Repetition of words, actions, or rhymes makes the book more enjoyable to young children. Humor and silliness that children can understand can add to the attractiveness of an author's writing.

- **Educational value.** The content of the book should add to the child's knowledge of the world. Books that add new vocabulary in the areas of childhood interest should be considered. The issues faced by characters in the books should be similar to those encountered by children and their families, and the solutions should be workable for real-world problems.

Each year approximately 500 new children's books are published. Many of these would be excellent choices for families, early childhood professionals, and librarians to use with young children. To help make the selection of new books easier, the Children's Book Council and the International Reading Association, in 1975, began publishing a list of books that children enjoy reading. Every fall, the most popular choices of children are published in *The Reading Teacher*, a journal of the International Reading Association, with a brief summary of each book's content. Called the **Children's Choice Awards**, this annual list of books is appropriate for children throughout the early childhood and elementary/middle school years. Approximately 10,000 children participate in the selection process each year, helping ensure that the books chosen will have wide appeal. These awards, although not the only source of information, help make it easier for adults to select good literature for children to read. Two other ways to recognize quality children's literature are through the **Newbery** and **Caldecott awards**. The Newbery is awarded for the year's most distinguished new book for children. The Caldecott is awarded for the best illustrated book of the year.

Books for infants and toddlers. It is never too early to integrate literacy experiences into young children's lives. Adults can begin by sharing books with infants and toddlers so that the wonder and excitement of print communications can be a part of their lives. Kupetz and Green (1997) describe five types of books that are appropriate for this age:

- **Rhythmical language books.** Books with rhymes and lullabies (e.g., *Mother Goose*) are some of the first to interest very young children.

- **Point-and-say books.** Containing pictures or photographs of familiar animals, toys, family members, and the like, these books allow the adult to point to pictures and say their names. Eventually, children can do the pointing and become more involved in the reading.

- **Touch-and-smell books.** Children are presented with different textures to touch and/or a variety of smells to get them actively involved in exploring these books.

- **Board books.** These durable books are made of board-like materials that withstand the banging and chewing of young children. Children can thus spend more time independently exploring these books.

- **Early picture storybooks.** Many toddlers are ready for books with simple story lines and clear illustrations that help tell the story.

Books for preschool and primary children. There are a number of different types of books for preschool and primary children. Be sure to include samples of each type in your book corner so that you can meet the interests and needs of all your children:

- **Action books.** These books contain mostly pictures and have pop-ups, pull tabs, and other movable parts to encourage active child participation. While these are of strong interest to many young children, these books are easily damaged, making them more difficult to maintain in group settings.
- **Informational books.** Books that share specific content on topics of interest to young children through words and pictures fit this category. A story about how milk is produced (Carrick, 1985) or the life of a squirrel (Lane, 1981) are examples.
- **Picture books.** Books of this type contain mostly pictures and have limited print. Young children can learn many of the conventions of reading books (e.g., reading each page from left to right and top to bottom) while enjoying the pictures.
- **Predictable books.** These books have repetitive patterns that make it easy for children to predict what comes next. Many of the Dr. Seuss books, such as *Green Eggs and Ham* (Seuss, 1960), fit this category.
- **Storybooks.** Although they contain pictures on most pages, these books also provide children with an interesting story line to follow. *Leo the Late Bloomer* (Kraus, 1971) is an example of this type.
- **Wordless books.** Children can use the pictures in these books to tell their own stories. An example is *Frog Goes to Dinner* (Mayer, 1974).
- **Beginning chapter books.** These books are more adult-like. They have limited pictures, complex plots, and are organized into chapters. Parents or teachers often read these books to primary-age children. Judy Blume's book, *Freckle Juice* (1970), is a popular example of this type.

Writing Tools

Just as children's books are important tools for emerging readers, certain materials are particularly helpful in fostering early writing experiences. The following items provide playful ways for children to experiment with producing written language:

- **Magnetic boards.** When used with a set of magnetic letters, the board provides children with unlimited ways to combine letters into words. Without actually needing to draw letters with their own hand, children can experiment with writing.
- **Paper and writing instruments.** Stock each center with paper and writing materials of all types for children to manipulate. Children can effectively use lined paper, unlined paper, recycled paper, notepads, notebooks, pencils, pens, marking pens, crayons, and so on for writing activities.
- **Child-sized chalkboards.** The unique feel, shape, and smell of chalk make it an inviting writing instrument for young children. Child-sized chalkboards let

Language and literacy skills can be enhanced with software programs and quality Internet sites.

children sit comfortably and work on their own writing tasks. In addition, chalk is easy to erase, allowing children to change what they have written.

- **Tracing materials.** Montessori (Lillard, 1972) developed a set of shapes that children can trace around with a writing instrument. These and similar materials help develop the fine motor skills necessary for writing.

- **Typewriters.** Young children are fascinated with how things work. An old manual or electric typewriter not only gives them a chance to see a machine at work but also encourages children to write something—or pretend to do so. Preschool children, in particular, can benefit from this option.

- **Computers.** Computers have made word processing easy and enjoyable for everyone, including young children. Several software designers have created excellent programs that help primary children engage in quality writing experiences. In addition, younger children can benefit from having a computer in the classroom to simply type letters and words on the screen.

Writing Instruction

Do you remember how you were taught to write? For many people, teachers in the primary grades assigned topics that were used to practice writing skills. At the beginning of the school year, a popular tactic was to ask children to write about events that occurred over summer vacation. Or perhaps you remember story starters like, "The sun was going down over the dusty plains. Exhausted from the day's travels, the riders dismounted from their horses and. . . ." While children can learn from these experiences, it is much better to teach writing and then allow children to choose their own topics (Brown, 2010; Kissel, 2008).

Labeling drawings is an important step forward in literacy learning.

One way to teach writing is to teach children how good writers do their work. Good writers think about what they want to write (prewrite); read and reread what they draft; revise their drafts through adding, deleting, and reorganizing; and edit for spelling, grammar, and punctuation problems. This process is often referred to as teaching the **writing workshop** way (Brown, 2010). This relatively new approach includes the following:

- Children choose their own topics for writing (Perlmutter et al., 2009).

- Writing should be done for real audiences (peers, family members, and others) rather than imaginary audiences.
- Initially, writing should focus on what the writer wants to tell others. Once that is achieved, the writer should polish the grammar, spelling, and punctuation.
- Children should have the opportunity to do many drafts so they can create a quality piece of writing.
- In addition to needing plenty of time, children need the chance to talk to the teacher and peers about their writing.
- Children should be allowed to write in a variety of categories (narrative, persuasive, informative).

The *Developmentally Appropriate Practice* feature in this section addresses another option for teaching writing. It discusses the value of combining drawing and writing in the early childhood classroom. This approach builds on the child's natural progression in the use of writing instruments.

Formal Reading Instruction

As with many issues in education, there has been a tendency in reading instruction to emphasize *either* phonics *or* whole language learning rather than including both as important elements of the reading curriculum. In a joint position statement of the International Reading Association and the National Association for the Education of Young Children (International Reading Association, 1998), leading educators in both fields strongly advocate for reading instruction that includes both phonics and whole language learning. Since there is great diversity in student abilities and experiences, this integrated approach is likely to be the most effective for all children.

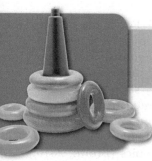

Developmentally Appropriate Practice . . .
INTEGRATING CURRICULUM THROUGH DRAWING AND WRITING

Baghban (2007) describes the importance of encouraging young children to draw as a way to build writing skills by demonstrating the connection between their drawings and their early writing experiences. She suggests that children in early childhood settings use their drawing as a bridge to early writing: "Children draw pictures and write to organize ideas and construct meaning from their experiences" (p. 21). Baghban outlines children's movements from scribbles to labels and stories as they develop writing skills:

- **Scribbles.** Very young children produce scribbles for their drawings and writing. There is a strong desire on the part of young children to make marks that are a product of their actions. This cognitive awareness is an important step in the young child's developing sense of self.

- **Labels.** As children mature, they begin to realize that drawing and writing are separate processes, and they start to draw and write on the same page. At approximately 4 to 6 years of age, they draw and then provide labels for their drawings. This is often the child's first meaningful writing and leads to beginning attempts to read what they have written to others.

- **Stories.** After children gain experience and confidence in drawing and labeling, they gradually want to express more in their writing and do so by creating simple stories. At approximately 6 to 7 years of age, children use their drawings as inspirations for these longer stories.

The reading curriculum should include the following elements (International Reading Association, 1998):

- **Daily reading experiences.** Children should be read to and should engage in independent reading activities.
- **Systematic code instruction.** Phonics instruction should be included as a part of meaningful reading experiences.
- **Daily writing experiences.** Because it is an integral part of the literacy experience, students gain additional insights into reading as they engage in teacher-supported writing experiences.
- **Small group work.** Both instruction and interaction in small groups allow children to become better readers.
- **Challenging curriculum.** By providing an overall curriculum that is exciting and challenging, children expand their knowledge of the world and increase their vocabularies.
- **Individualized instruction.** For children who are advanced and those needing additional assistance in learning to read, teachers must work to individualize the reading instruction so that motivation and progress remain strong.

Addressing the Needs of Diverse Language and Literacy Learners

A growing number of children are learning not one, but two, languages during the preschool and primary years. Immigrant children whose parents speak Spanish, for example, are continuing to refine understandings of their native language and learning English at the same time. These English language learners (ELLs) face unique challenges in early childhood settings. Because the number of ELL students in U.S. schools has more than doubled during the last 15 years (Waters, 2007; National Center for Education Statistics, 2010), early childhood professionals must be prepared to provide extra assistance to these learners.

Genishi and Dyson (2009), however, suggest that even though diverse early childhood settings are the norm, practices in support of ELL students have not kept pace. The *Celebrating Diversity* feature in this section provides insights and additional information on this important topic.

 ## Encouraging Family Involvement

While families play significant roles in all aspects of the young child's development, none are more critical to academic success than the promotion of language and literacy learning. Families who create an environment in the home that stimulates positive communications and demonstrates the importance of written language provide their children with an invaluable asset that is difficult to duplicate.

For many families, one of the most difficult hurdles to overcome is the belief that what they do in the home really does not make a difference in language and literacy development. They may need to be educated about the importance of their role. Articles from professional journals, workshops for families on language

Celebrating Diversity . . .
SUPPORTING ENGLISH LANGUAGE LEARNERS

Growing numbers of young children come to the early childhood classroom speaking languages other than English at home. Data from the U.S. Census Bureau (2000) indicate that nearly one in five American families speaks a language other than English at home, with Spanish, Chinese, Tagalog (Filipino), Korean, Vietnamese, Arabic, Hindi, and Russian being the most common. Early childhood professionals working with young children must be prepared to support these English language learners (ELLs) as they work to master a new language.

Lake and Pappamihiel (2003) identify four main components of a developmentally appropriate language environment for young ELL students:

1. **Conversation.** Teachers must make time to engage ELL students in direct conversation to stimulate their understanding and use of oral language. While avoiding overcorrecting and judging these children, regular and natural conversations help children practice and build confidence in their English-speaking abilities.

2. **Understanding and acceptance.** Much has been written about the process of second language acquisition. You will need to understand and accept the additional steps children must take. Lake and Pappamihiel (2003) emphasize that even though young children take only 1 to 2 years to develop basic interpersonal communication skills, it often requires 5 to 8 years to acquire the language competence needed for academic success.

3. **Experience.** ELL children need meaningful experiences to use as the basis for productive oral language communications. Early childhood professionals should plan a variety of meaningful experiences with ELL students in mind.

4. **Children's literature.** Quality children's literature that values the differences among children can help young ELL students feel good about themselves and stimulate oral language learning (Harper & Brand, 2010). A collection of books like *Someone Special, Just Like You* (Brown, 1991) will add important insights for the whole class.

1. Think about the positive aspects of having English language learners in early childhood settings. How will these children enrich your life and the lives of other children?

2. Read an article about ELL students and then think about the implications for your future teaching. What changes will you need to make in your teaching when you have ELL students in your room?

and literacy learning, and informal discussions with individuals can provide ideas to help promote this concept.

Families who speak languages other than English in the home may need extra assistance from you in feeling like they can make a difference in language learning at home. In many immigrant families, for example, adults typically speak languages other than English and have limited English-speaking ability themselves. Before these families can support English-language learning at home, they need to feel that you respect and value their heritage and native language (Potter, 2008). Translating written materials to the language used at home, creating labels in the home language to use in the early childhood setting, and inviting family members to come into the program to share their language and culture with the group will help families feel valued. As these relationships grow, families will be more willing to support language and literacy activities at home.

One of the most important tasks that all families can participate in is to read to their young children. The more opportunities that children have to experience the pleasures of reading with family members, the easier it becomes for them to learn

Family Partnerships...
INVOLVING FAMILIES IN READING

One of the most important things you can do as an early childhood professional is to develop ways to successfully involve families in reading aloud to their children at home. The research indicates that this is the single most important activity needed for success in reading (International Reading Association, 1998). While this may seem to be a simple task, it actually requires careful planning and constant effort. Families lead busy lives and often forget (or do not realize) that this effort is critical to success in reading.

While the following list of suggestions is not complete, it should get you thinking about what you can do to increase the likelihood of families and children sitting down together to read.

- **Provide a rationale for reading.** Because of their busy lives, families need to be highly motivated to spend some of their precious time reading to children. Collect research and writing that supports this position and send home regular reminders in newsletters or other written communications summarizing the views expressed.

- **Suggest good children's literature.** There are literally thousands of books available to children of all ages and reading abilities. Families need guidance about what books might be appropriate for their children and where they might be found. Send home lists periodically (you may wish to tie them to the concepts you are emphasizing in class) so that families will consistently know about quality literature they can read.

- **Prepare reading backpacks.** Prepare one or more backpacks, each equipped with a good children's book, a note to the family explaining what they should do and why, and some suggestions for extending the reading task into other activities. At the end of each day, send a backpack home with one of the children to use overnight. Make sure every child regularly has the opportunity to take home the backpack.

- **Conduct family meetings.** It may be useful to have families come together for an evening meeting in which you explain the importance of reading aloud to children and provide some examples of quality children's literature and where it can be found. Discussing this topic with others may also encourage "reluctant family readers" to get involved in this important task.

1. Talk to an early childhood caregiver or teacher about the challenges of involving families in reading to their children. From your discussion, do you think most families believe that reading to their own children as infants, toddlers, and preschoolers is an important task? Why or why not?

2. Do you enjoy reading for pleasure? How will you work to instill this attitude in the children you teach?

---

to read. The *Family Partnerships* feature in this section provides several suggestions to help you get families involved in this valuable experience.

Taking Advantage of Daily Living

As families are being convinced of their important role in language and literacy development, many need specific ideas about how they can assist in this process. Many of the activities that families and children engage in daily are excellent opportunities for encouraging oral and written language understandings. Following are examples of these natural learning opportunities that are a part of family life:

- Spend some time each day giving individual attention to each child in the family. Talk about your life or what is happening in the child's day; make it a pleasant time of sharing.

- Try to extend the child's vocabulary by adding new and interesting words to your communications.

Families need to take advantage of the many opportunities for meaningful print experiences that exist in the home.

- Take time to point out meaningful print in the child's world such as names on food containers and road signs.
- Make trips to the grocery store (and similar chores) learning opportunities by talking about the things being purchased and pointing out and discussing labels and brand names.
- Become a skilled questioner to promote thinking and effective communication.
- Be a good conversationalist. Listen carefully to what the child has to say, and try to build on his comments in your responses.

Simple Home Learning Tasks

The natural opportunities for language and literacy learning just described make a big difference, but other more specific tasks are also valuable. These should be easy to prepare for and require a limited time commitment by family members. The following examples show how diverse these home learning tasks can be:

- Read, read, and read some more to your child. These times should be enjoyable for both the adult and child. Reading one or more books before bed each night is an excellent habit to develop.
- Create a writing center in the home with paper and writing instruments that the child can use to create her own stories and books.
- Make books with young children. If needed, a family member can write down the child's story and the child can then illustrate it.
- Do things together as a family: visit the zoo, browse through museums, spend time at the public library, and attend musical concerts. Spend time talking and writing about these special events after returning.
- Encourage children to write thank-you cards, birthday messages, and letters to friends and relatives. Make sure children see you doing the same.
- In homes with computers and Internet access, family members can help children send e-mail messages to friends and other family members.

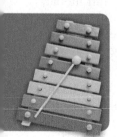

summary

Language and Literacy Development

To assist with language and literacy development, early childhood professionals need to understand different theoretical perspectives, the developmental patterns associated with growth in verbal communications, linguistic systems, and literacy development.

Language and Literacy Learning

Language learning is enhanced when adults communicate often and well with young children, provide interesting activities that promote discussion, and create an environment that encourages peer and adult-child interactions. Supporting literacy learning requires an understanding of the importance of print-rich environments in learning to read and write, recognition of the role of play in literacy learning, and the critical importance of reading to children.

Encouraging Family Involvement

Families need to be educated about their critical roles in language and literacy learning. They can take advantage of daily living experiences and be involved in simple home learning tasks to assist in language and literacy learning.

for reflection and discussion

1. In 3 to 4 paragraphs, briefly describe literacy development in young children.
2. Identify and discuss with others three or four ideas for stimulating language learning through peer interactions.
3. How will you promote family involvement in language and literacy learning for an age group within the early childhood range? Write 2 to 3 paragraphs describing your strategy.

MyEducationLab

Go to Topic 7: Curriculum/Content Areas in the MyEducationLab (www.myeducationlab.com) for *Teaching Young Children*, where you can:

- Find learning outcomes for Curriculum/Content Areas along with the national standards that connect to these outcomes.
- Complete Assignments and Activities that can help you more deeply understand the chapter content.
- Apply and practice your understanding of the core teaching skills identified in the chapter with the Building Teaching Skills and Dispositions learning units.
- Examine challenging situations and cases presented in the IRIS Center Resources.
- Check your comprehension on the content covered in the chapter with the Study Plan. Here you will be able to take a chapter quiz, receive feedback on your answers, and then access Review, Practice, and Enrichment activities to enhance your understanding of chapter content.
- Use the Online Lesson Plan Builder to practice lesson planning and integrating national and state standards into your planning.

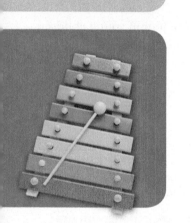

16

The Creative Arts

IN THIS CHAPTER YOU WILL

- Define creativity as it applies to young children.
- Clarify the roles of art in early childhood settings.
- Understand music and its importance in the creative arts curriculum.
- Reflect on early drama, theater, and dance experiences for young children.

Your kindergarten classroom has just begun its morning schedule. Children gather at circle time for opening activities, two or three familiar songs, a movement activity using silk scarves and selected music, and a discussion of the activities available in the classroom centers. You explain that a finger painting activity will be available in the art center in addition to the regular art supplies. As children wander off after group time, you watch as Jaylani and Amanda head straight to the art corner to get involved in finger painting. They are tentative at first as they get their hands covered with the gooey paint and shaving cream mix. Soon, however, they are happily weaving intricate patterns on the tabletop. They spend nearly 20 minutes exploring this activity before moving on to another center. Matt and Karen have discovered some new materials in the music center and are busily exploring the music-making potential of these new instruments. The shallow drum and homemade stringed instrument are the main attractions. As they pluck and tap, they sing their newly created song about the "Eensy Weensy Tadpole." Three new puppets have been added to the dramatic play center. Kayla and Pieter are using them as props for a story they plan to share with others. Both children are enthusiastically acting out their roles as the story unfolds. This is just a small sampling of the musical, artistic, and dramatic activities that your students regularly experience. Each day many new options are available for children to explore.

Quality early childhood programs are full of opportunities for creative expression and learning through music, art, and dramatic expression. Like the children in the example, young people want and need a wide variety of outlets for their creativity. When they are given the right materials and allowed the freedom to explore in their own special ways, children delight in art, music, drama, and dance experiences.

In addition to the many specific benefits of artistic expression, the arts also provide excellent opportunities for integrated learning experiences (Bartel, 2005).

The Association for Childhood Education International (ACEI) recommends that all children be allowed to express themselves through the arts. The association developed a position paper that states the following:

> The creative process, contrary to popular opinion, is socially supported, culturally influenced, and collaboratively achieved. In taking this position, ACEI acknowledges that several challenges must be addressed by educators throughout the world. First, we need to redefine creative teaching and confront misconceptions about creative thinking. Second, we need to provide students with role models of motivation and persistence in creative thought, and arrive at more capacious ways of assessing creative processes and products. Finally, educational institutions and the larger societies in which they exist need to reflect deeply on what they hope children will become. We need to do more than prepare them to become cogs in the machinery of commerce. The international community needs resourceful, imaginative, inventive, and ethical problem solvers who will make a significant contribution, not only to the Information Age in which we currently live, but beyond to ages that we can barely envision. (Association for Childhood Education International, 2003, p. 2)

 What Is Creativity?

Before looking specifically at art, music, and dramatic expression, a discussion of the concept of creativity itself is necessary. Creative activity takes place throughout the day in the early childhood settings. E. Paul Torrance (1992), a leading researcher and writer in this area, suggests the following as a rather whimsical description of creative activity:

Creativity is digging deeper.
Creativity is looking twice.
Creativity is crossing out mistakes.
Creativity is talking/listening to a cat.
Creativity is getting in deep water.
Creativity is getting out from behind locked doors.
Creativity is plugging in the sun.
Creativity is wanting to know.
Creativity is having a ball.
Creativity is building sand castles.
Creativity is singing in your own way.
Creativity is shaking hands with the future.

Defining Creativity

Clearly, the activities that Torrance includes under the broad umbrella of creativity are many and varied. Defining the term, therefore, is difficult. In general, however, definitions of creative activity have two common criteria: novelty and appropriateness (Starko, 1995).

To be creative, an idea or product must be *new*, or *novel*. The key question that must be asked, however, is novel to whom? Does the idea or product need to be new to humankind? If so, very, very few of us are creative. Creative acts would be limited to the Mozarts and Einsteins of the world. However, if ideas or products are new to the person who produced them, then most people engage in creative activity. This latter description makes the most sense when working with young children.

The second criterion for judging an act as creative is *appropriateness*. For adults, this means that activities are creative when they are acceptable and useful by some set of criteria. These criteria vary from one culture to the next and between groups of adults. Whereas some might view an adult's photo essay of migrant farm workers as creative, others could see it as meaningless and therefore not appropriate.

Once again, the lines blur as we apply the criterion of appropriateness to children. Using adult standards of appropriateness to evaluate children's artwork, musical productions, or dramatic presentations, for example, makes little sense. We cannot expect beginning artists and musicians to produce creative materials rivaling those of adults. Rather, when children's efforts are meaningful to them, they are appropriate.

Take, for example, 7-year-old Shawnna, who spent the past 30 minutes in the art center painting at the easel. Shawnna has been intently creating a picture of her home and front yard, carefully choosing colors and creating a good representation of that environment. Are her efforts novel and appropriate as defined earlier? From Shawnna's perspective, it is a new activity that she finds meaningful and useful. Adults should view her efforts as a creative activity.

Characteristics of Creative Individuals

The list of characteristics associated with creative individuals is lengthy and varies from one researcher to the next. Torrance (1962) identifies the following seven characteristics of highly creative young children:

- **Curiosity.** Creative children have a healthy curiosity; they consistently ask meaningful questions and manipulate materials in the environment.
- **Flexibility.** Creative children are flexible. When one approach to a problem does not work, they simply try something else.
- **Sensitivity to problems.** Creative children can sense missing elements and quickly identify problem situations.
- **Originality.** Creative children commonly have unusual ideas and create original products.
- **Independence.** Creative children are comfortable working alone as they play with ideas or materials. Creative individuals often work with others, but they can accomplish much on their own.
- **Redefinition.** Creative children combine ideas or materials in new and unusual ways.
- **Penetration.** Creative children gain much insight from spending time thinking deeply about ideas and problems.

Assisting with the Creative Process

It is counterproductive to think about formally teaching children to be creative; however, early childhood professionals and families have important roles to play in facilitating creativity. Several key ingredients are needed for children to be creative individuals:

- **Adults who value creativity.** Children need to know that the creative process is important in the adult world and that it enriches each of our lives. The ideas and products of highly creative adults, including their new solutions to the everyday problems faced by adults, help make life more enjoyable and pleasant. By valuing originality with our words and actions, we can help children grow into more creative adults.

- **Low-risk early childhood settings.** As children solve problems, explore, and experiment, they need to know that failure is acceptable and normal. Wasserman (1992) puts it this way: "Inventions of the new do not come from duplicating what is already there. They come from minds that are unafraid to take risks to try" (p. 135). Creativity is possible only when you encourage children to experiment with ideas that may not work. They learn from these failures and come back with even better, more creative solutions.

- **Freedom to explore.** Children need large blocks of time for exploration and experimentation if creativity is to take place. They must also be free to choose the activities that interest them and to mess around with materials in their own unique ways. Although these activities are often noisy and messy, this freedom to explore will pay big dividends in terms of creative activity.

- **Open-ended materials.** Interesting art materials, such as colorful paints and a variety of paper textures, help children produce imaginative works that express their unique personalities and developmental abilities. A variety of musical instruments provides additional options for creative expression. Props for dramatic play, storytelling, and dance encourage further creative expression.

Creativity and Play

During group time today, your 4-year-olds requested "The Eensy Weensy Spider" once again for music. Then Adam suggested a variation he called "The Eensy Weensy Caterpillar." It was a big hit. Following group time, Adam and Marika stayed on the rug and spent another 10 minutes creating their own playful modifications to "The Eensy Weensy Spider." They developed words and hand movements for "The Eensy Weensy Frog" and "The Eensy Weensy Bird."

Perhaps you have noticed already that many of the characteristics associated with creative individuals also apply to children at play. In fact, play and creativity are closely linked. Take another look at the list of characteristics of creative individuals presented earlier in this chapter. Most, if not all, of the characteristics of creative individuals are also found when children engage in play. Although it is possible to play and not be creative, or for creativity to occur outside of the play experience, the two often take place together.

Children can be very creative in their play.

It is sometimes difficult to assess the creative potential of the playful experiences children have. An option that fits this category, but many find difficult to assess, is the use of electronic games. The *Technology Explorations and Activities* feature in this section looks at the creative potential of the Nintendo Wii. Read the feature now and reflect on the value of electronic games for young children.

Technology Explorations and Activities . . .
NINTENDO WII: CREATIVE TECHNOLOGY?

A popular piece of technology in many homes today is the Nintendo Wii. Like the Microsoft Xbox and the Sony PlayStation, the Wii is a video game system that can be used by children and adults to play a wide variety of games. What makes the Wii unique is its wireless controller that allows the user to pretend to engage in activities such as bowling and to compete with other participants. Find someone who owns a Nintendo Wii and spend some time playing with one or more of its many games. Before you do, reread the section on creativity in this chapter and use this information to do an evaluation of the system for use by young children.

Research, Reflect, and Respond

1. Do an Internet search for information about the Wii, Microsoft Xbox, and Sony PlayStation. Are there significant differences among these systems that would affect how they are used by young children?

2. Based on your personal use of the Wii and the content in this chapter on creativity, do you think that young children who use the Wii are engaging in creative activity? Why or why not?

3. For the age range you are interested in working with, would you recommend the Wii to families who asked your opinion of this technology? Give a rationale for the response you make.

Highly creative adults often describe their creative acts as playing around with ideas or materials. Goertzel and Goertzel (1962) describe the lives of famous people such as the Wright brothers, Frank Lloyd Wright, Thomas Edison, and others as filled with playful explorations and discoveries. Wasserman (1992) quotes Richard Feynman, a Nobel Prize winner in physics, as saying this about his playfulness:

> Why did I enjoy doing it [physics]? I used to play with it. I used to do whatever I felt like doing. It didn't have to do with whether it was important for the development of nuclear physics, but instead whether it was interesting and amusing for me to play with. (p. 139)

This ability to simply play around with physics concepts eventually led to a discovery that won Feynman the Nobel Prize.

While play will not allow most of us to reach this high level of creativity, our lives are clearly enriched when children and adults alike engage in quality play experiences. Albert Einstein (1954), considered one of the greatest thinkers of the twentieth century, clearly felt that play was necessary for creative thinking when he stated, "Play seems to be the essential feature in productive thought" (p. 26). Bringing a playful mindset to everyday situations and problems can benefit us all.

The *Celebrating Play* feature in this section suggests another reason for encouraging play in childhood and adulthood. David Elkind (2003) asserts that besides its great potential for learning, play should be a part of our lives for the sheer pleasure of the activity. Read the feature now for important insights on this aspect of play.

Celebrating Play . . .
FOR THE FUN OF IT

Throughout this text there has been an emphasis on the learning potential associated with childhood play. Children enhance physical, social, emotional, linguistic, and intellectual knowledge as they engage in creative play experiences. Early childhood professionals need to understand these many benefits and be prepared to share them with families, administrators, and concerned others.

While strongly supporting the many benefits of play, David Elkind (2003) makes a case for simply allowing children to play for the sheer fun of the activity. He believes that while childhood is an important time for developing skills for the future, it should also be enjoyed in the present through play. He justifies this position in the following way:

> I first recalled Freud's response when asked what was necessary to lead a happy and productive life. He replied, *"Lieben und Arbeiten"* (loving and working). With all due respect to Freud, I believe he should have added a third activity, namely, *Speilen* (playing). I believe that play is as

fundamental a human disposition as loving and working. We play because we are programmed to play; it is part of human nature, and of animal nature as well. (p. 46)

Take a moment to consider the importance of play in adult lives. Although the play of adults may be different from that of children, is it not equally true that adults need to engage in playful activities to have balanced and meaningful lives? Doesn't "all work and no play" make for a dull adult existence? Healthy adults, just like healthy children, consistently take time for play "just for the fun of it."

1. What do you think of this perspective on childhood play? Should we allow children time to play for the sheer fun of the activity? Why or why not? What are the potential dangers in this approach?

2. Do you believe that adults need play for a healthy lifestyle? Cite the reasons for your response. Describe how you engage in play or how you could increase play in your adult life.

The Young Artist

Art, music, and drama are not the only ways for young children to express their creative talents; however, they are important options in early childhood settings. The foundation laid in these early years often determines whether or not individuals enjoy the creative arts throughout their lives. In this section, you will read about the importance of the arts in early childhood programs and then address more specifically the essential elements of the art curriculum.

Why Include the Arts?

Historically, all of the creative arts have received less emphasis in schools than the more academic subjects such as mathematics, reading, social studies, and science. Consequently, at all levels of public education, when faced with budget cuts or time constraints, the arts, music, and drama programs are often the first to be cut or de-emphasized. This attitude has influenced many families and early childhood professionals at the prekindergarten level as well. To counter this attitude and make sure that art is being encouraged, some primary classrooms are using volunteer art docents. The *Family Partnerships* feature in this section provides more information on this option.

Recently, the creative arts have been recognized by many as central to the curriculum for the twenty-first century. For example, the Arts Education

Family Partnerships . . .
THE ART DOCENT IN PRIMARY CLASSROOMS

Because of budget cutbacks and the higher priority of academic subjects such as mathematics and reading, many schools and school districts have chosen to do without trained art educators. While understandable from a fiscal standpoint, this approach leaves regular classroom teachers with the responsibility of carrying on this important component of the curriculum with very little background or training in the arts. The result is that many young children get little or no exposure to art on a regular basis.

One way that some primary classrooms are attempting to keep the art education curriculum alive and well in difficult financial times is to seek and train volunteers to serve as art docents. The word *docent* comes from the Latin word *docere*, which means "to teach" or "to lead." After receiving training from an art professional, docents travel from classroom to classroom to share an art education curriculum that would otherwise not be taught.

Families and community members with a passion for art are accepting the challenge and assisting with art education activities in the classroom (Hansen, 2008). They may lead a field trip to a local museum to view important works on display, prepare activities that help students understand the different styles of famous artists, or share techniques for using different art media (such as watercolors and chalk). By sharing their excitement and expertise in art, art docents help young children begin to develop an interest in art that can be strengthened through later school and life experiences.

1. What do you see as the strengths and limitations of having art docents deliver the art curriculum to young children?

2. How high a priority should art education be in the primary classroom? Is it of equal or lesser importance than the more academic subjects? Give reasons for the position you take.

Partnership (2004), which was founded in 1995, includes more than 100 national organizations that have joined forces to promote the arts as essential components of the subject matter that students must master in public school if they are to succeed in later life. Christensen and Kirkland (2010) emphasize the importance of the arts in children's developing a sense of self, in understanding others who are different from themselves, and in gaining new historical perspectives. Soundy and Drucker (2009) describe the benefits of drawing in developing problem-solving skills in young children. The Task Force on Children's Learning and the Arts (Bruce, 1998) says this about early education and the arts:

> The arts motivate and engage children in learning, stimulate memory and facilitate understanding, enhance symbolic communication, promote relationships, and provide an avenue for building competence. The arts are natural for young children. Child development specialists note that play is the business of young children; play is the way children promote and enhance their development. The arts are a most natural vehicle for play. (p. v)

Ernest Boyer (1987) has identified three main reasons for including the creative arts as significant parts of the curriculum:

- The arts help children express feelings and ideas that are difficult to share using words.
- Caregivers and teachers can integrate the generally splintered academic world of children through the arts. Seeing connections and finding patterns across disciplines can be accomplished through the arts (see also Soundy & Qui, 2007).
- The arts provide the child with a universal language that is useful in communicating with others.

Misconceptions about Art

Looking more specifically at art education in early childhood settings, Jalongo (1995) suggests that many people have misconceptions about art, and we need to take actions to counteract them. She identifies five misconceptions that we should actively work to overcome:

- **Art is a nonessential element of the curriculum.** This misconception is widespread and needs to be carefully addressed by early childhood professionals. First of all, communicating to others through the medium of art is an essential element of our humanity and cannot be taken lightly. Second, children practice considerable higher-level thinking skills as they engage in art activities. Art needs to be considered an essential component of learning and development rather than an unnecessary frill.
- **Discovering talent is the goal.** Our job as early childhood professionals is *not* to discover the next Picasso or Monet. Every child should be encouraged to participate in art. When you work with young children, you should emphasize the process of art rather than the products produced.
- **You must have performance skills in art to teach it.** It is most important to share with children an enthusiasm for art and its production. This does not

require strong performance skills. When early childhood professionals communicate excitement, provide materials for creative art experiences, and facilitate children's efforts, a rich curriculum in art is ensured.

- **Creative art experiences are adult-centered.** Although it is possible to assist children in their creative efforts (see the information on Reggio Emilia later in this chapter), the process of creative thinking and expression must come from within the child. Making an art pattern for children to cut out and decorate is not helpful in stimulating creativity. Shidler-Lattz and Ratcliff (1998) make it clear that when we force children to "color within the lines," we end up with frustrated students who are likely to avoid art altogether.

- **The early childhood professional is uninvolved.** While you cannot directly teach creative art, much can be done to ensure that quality art experiences take place. In addition to providing quality materials, early childhood professionals need to ask appropriate questions, make helpful comments, and guide the creative efforts of young children.

Developmental Trends in Art

 Rhonda, at 18 months, is a very busy young girl. At her child-care center, she is particularly interested in playing with paper and pencils. Rhonda has been fascinated with her older sister's pictures and stories and spends several minutes each day creating her own artful scribbles. To the untrained eye, they appear to be simply scratch marks on paper. But to Rhonda, they are important first steps in communicating with others.

As children mature both physically and mentally, their progress in art moves from rather random scribbles during the infant/toddler years to more recognizable art during the primary grades. Many researchers, including Rhoda Kellogg (1969), have carefully studied these developmental trends. Kellogg's collection of children's paintings and drawings from the United States and other countries around the world totals over a million samples.

Fox and Schirrmacher (2012) summarize the research of Kellogg and others and identify the following stages in children's art:

- **Scribbling and mark-making stage (birth to about age 2).** Kellogg identified 20 basic scribbles that young children use as the foundation for future art activities. These change from simple dots and lines to the more complex motions needed to create an imperfect circle. Children begin by making random marks and gradually move to more controlled and purposeful scribbling.

- **Personal symbol and design stage (approximately 2 to 4 years of age).** During this period, children make scribbles and marks in specific areas on their paper to create personal symbols and designs. For example, a large imperfect circle with four lines protruding at odd angles might become an early symbol for the human figure. The young child includes whatever features he views as important and omits those elements that he considers insignificant. Preschool children begin to create artwork that more closely represents objects and people in the real world.

An example of a young child's early scribbling.

- **Attempts at public representation (approximately 4 to 7 years of age).** At this point, children modify their personal symbols and gradually produce art that is more recognizable to others. They include more details, as accurate representation becomes increasingly important to children. For example, if a child is drawing his mother, who has brown hair and blue eyes, the drawing will contain these details.
- **Realism stage (late primary years and up).** Children at this point strive hard to include even the smallest of realistic details as they create their artwork. This attempted photographic realism emphasizes size, placement, proportion, and other elements as children try to produce replicas of people, places, and things they have experienced.

The Early Childhood Art Curriculum

The content of the art program for young children may appear straightforward; however, many experts suggest that it involves more than just the production of art using a variety of media. Opportunities for making art are only one part of the larger curriculum that young children need to explore.

Fox and Schirrmacher (2012) identify four central elements in a strong art program:

- **Sensing and experiencing.** When children use their senses and engage in meaningful experiences, these experiences form the foundation for creative expression. Art is an expression of these events to others.
- **Making art.** Children need to express themselves by making art with diverse art media.
- **Learning about art, artists, and artists' styles.** The natural interest of young children in learning about community helpers can be extended to include artists. Local artists using a variety of styles and media can tell their stories and share works with children.
- **Aesthetics.** Aesthetics is the study of beauty in color, form, and design. With assistance, children can come to appreciate beauty in different artworks and in the natural world around them.

One approach to the art curriculum being used in early childhood settings is **discipline-based art education**. The Getty Center for Education in the Arts (Alexander & Day, 1999) has been a major proponent of this approach. Designed for children in the primary grades and beyond, it promotes developing the technical skills needed in art production and teaching four disciplines that help children create, understand, and appreciate art:

- Art production
- Art history
- Art criticism
- Aesthetics

The Adult's Role in Art Experiences

You can facilitate creative art experiences in early childhood settings in many ways. An important first step is *providing a variety of appropriate materials* for children to explore. Tempera paints, watercolors, chalk, and clay are all examples of diverse art materials that children can use productively during the prekindergarten and primary years. By rotating exciting materials in and out of the art center, early childhood professionals provide children with experiences using different materials. It also helps maintain a high level of interest in making art. The *Developmentally Appropriate Practice* feature in this section describes some of the typical materials and equipment that are found in a high-quality art area for young children.

Another way early childhood professionals support quality art experiences is by *valuing creativity*. Unfortunately, many well-meaning adults can permanently damage the creative abilities of young children with their comments and interactions. Rather than shutting down the creative expressiveness of young children, we need to let children know, through both words and actions, that we value their unique uses of art materials. That kind of emotional climate will keep children motivated to engage in art activities.

During center time, Mrs. Duncan's first-grade students are engaged in a variety of activities, including art. Aletha is using the colorful cloth scraps to create an intricate design on her paper. Mrs. Duncan takes a moment to carefully observe Aletha at work and then says, "Aletha, I'm impressed with the variety of colors you are using and the wonderful designs being created. Very interesting!" Mrs. Duncan is showing Aletha that she values her creative efforts in art.

Developmentally Appropriate Practice . . .
PERMANENT ART MATERIALS AND EQUIPMENT

Caregivers and teachers should give careful consideration to the materials and equipment provided for art activities in early childhood settings. A well-stocked art center will attract considerable interest from young children. Many art centers contain two distinct categories of materials and equipment: those that remain in the area on a permanent basis and those that are changed regularly (generally every week). Following are examples of typical materials and equipment that are a permanent part of the early childhood art center.

Materials

Paper (scrap, recycled, colored, etc.)

Crayons, marking pens, pens, and pencils

Scissors, hole punches, and staplers

Rulers, protractors, and compasses (for older children)

Glue, glue sticks, and rubber cement

Equipment

Easel (having two is preferable)

Child-sized table and chairs

Shelves for storing materials

Trays for holding paper

Drying space/spots for completed projects

Children also benefit when adults *describe and/or demonstrate appropriate uses for art tools and materials.* When you casually describe to a child using a paintbrush how the position of the brush allows the artist to make different strokes, you are providing the child with valuable "just-in-time" art instruction. Because children learn in different ways, some will find it more helpful to watch the adult demonstrate how to use materials rather than listening to a verbal description. In both instances, children can benefit from this one-on-one assistance in using art tools and materials.

It is critical, however, that these demonstration efforts *avoid the use of models.* Models that the adult constructs have no place in early childhood settings. They send children the message that their art is of poor quality because it can never look as good as your example. Models also say to children that there is a right way to use these materials. This can lead children to believe that their art work is of low quality. When adult words or actions give children this impression, they quickly come to the conclusion that they are not "good in art," and they lose their motivation to engage in art experiences.

Caregivers and teachers in early childhood settings also need to *emphasize the process of art rather than the product.* Creative acts occur when children have plenty of opportunities to explore and experiment. This means that many of the products will be the result of "messing around" with materials. Although it is important to teach children specific art techniques, an emphasis on the product makes it less likely that the much-needed experimentation will take place. You should:

- Put away patterns, ditto masters, and pre-marked papers.
- Throw out coloring books.
- Avoid "cookbook" art activities.
- Enjoy the freedom that basic materials provide (Syzba, 1999).

Talking about art with children is another important way to guide the developing artists' work. The wrong questions and comments can be damaging to children.

Children benefit when adults talk about art with them.

Although well-meaning, questions such as "What is it?" may be difficult to answer and emphasize the product rather than the process of art. Making appropriate comments and asking the right questions require thoughtfulness and insight (Swann, 2009). Engel (1996) suggests that adults must learn to look more carefully at children's art so that they can respond in positive ways. She identifies six questions that teachers can ask themselves as they prepare to talk with children about art:

- What is it made of (size, tools, medium)?
- What does the adult see (lines, angles, shapes, symmetry, colors, overlaps)?
- What does it represent (design, story, scene, symbol)?
- How is it organized (perspective, composition, action, view, completion)?
- What is it about, what is the nature of involvement (violence, peace, love, sadness, persuasion, information)?
- Where does the idea come from (imagination, observation, literature, imitation, TV, messing around)?

Finally, early childhood professionals need to *display children's art in the early childhood setting*. The message adults must convey is that art is a means of expression for all, not just something for a select few who demonstrate special talent. Displaying artwork from each child helps both family members and children value the creative activities of each classmate. Adults should place art at the child's eye level and rotate it regularly to make sure children fully appreciate the artwork of their peers. Bakerlis (2007) describes how displaying children's artwork can also be a wonderful tool to educate families about the importance of art in the lives of young children.

Take some time to observe art activities in an early childhood setting. The *Observing Development* feature in this section will help you make that observation and reflect on the importance of art for young children.

Observing Development . . .
CHILDHOOD ART

Choose one of the age groups within early childhood (infants/toddlers, preschoolers, or primary-age children) and *observe* for childhood art.

Focus on a specific child and observe at least 20 minutes of an art experience. Create an anecdotal record form like the sample that follows to record what you observe:

Townsend Elementary, Mrs. L.'s Kindergarten Class, 2:00–2:30 p.m., December 8

2:00 Mrs. L. dismisses children from group time and they seek out activities in the individual centers. Three girls and one boy enter the art center for a finger painting project (the three girls appear to be close friends). After putting on their smocks, . . .

Reflect and Apply

1. Compare the art activity you observed with those described in this chapter. Was the activity developmentally appropriate? Did the child you observed engage in creative activity?

2. Would you change the activity you observed in any way to make it a better experience for young children?

3. What other art activities might you consider using in this early childhood setting if you were working there?

The Art of Reggio Emilia

The model preschool program known as Reggio Emilia is well known for its artwork. Seefeldt (1995) describes it as having rather amazing results:

> Stunning displays of art surround you. Brightly colored drawings and paintings, surrealistic in appearance and depicting all kinds of animals—giraffes, zebras, horses, lions, and tigers—decorate the walls. A mural of children playing in a field of red poppies hangs from the ceiling. Shelves and pedestals hold sculptures. (p. 39)

This is not a description of what most early childhood professionals in the United States regularly experience. What makes the artwork of children in the Reggio Emilia approach so astonishing? The maturity and complexity of the productions are truly amazing. Certainly, the children are no different from those in preschool programs in the United States. So, where do the differences come from?

Seefeldt (1995) argues that in Reggio Emilia, adults consider art *serious work*. They organize the art program around three principles:

- **Understanding cognitive theories of art.** A basic premise of cognitive theories is that art is an important form of communicating ideas and feelings to others. Art becomes a language of expressing cognitive understandings to others.
- **Motivating children to produce art.** Children who are provided with quality experiences can be motivated to express their learning to others through art. Deeply meaningful experiences can lead to amazing art.
- **Selecting teaching strategies.** Adults in the Reggio Emilia program are actively involved in teaching young children the skills they need to succeed in art. This is done individually as the child demonstrates a need for instruction. Modeling appropriate techniques, physically assisting the young child from time to time, and providing specific verbal feedback are all used to teach art to young children.

Art Activities

Many idea books are available to assist teachers of young children in planning creative art and music activities. *Creative Resources for the Early Childhood Classroom* by Herr and Libby-Larson (2004) and *The Complete Book of Activities, Games, Stories, Props, Recipes, and Dances for Young Children* by Silberg and Schiller (2003) are two examples of resource guides that are useful in planning for art and music. Teachers and caregivers should take care to adapt the suggestions in these or other idea books to meet the needs and interests of specific children. Similarly, the ideas that follow may need modifications to succeed with the children you know.

Infant and toddler art activities. A major consideration for infant and toddler art is that nearly everything at this age ends up in the mouth. Whatever materials you provide should be safe to ingest and be objects that cannot cause choking.

- *Pudding* can be used as an enjoyable finger painting activity with infants and toddlers. While using food for non-eating activities should be generally discouraged because it models waste, this might be one exception that you would want to make if you are working with infants and toddlers and they will eat most of the pudding at another time during the day.

- *Play dough* is another activity that very young children can enjoy with adult supervision. Make sure it is non-toxic and keep it in larger pieces to discourage children from putting it in their mouth.

- *Place artwork within the view of infants and toddlers* as they participate in various routines. By including a variety of types of art, you will provide young children with early art appreciation experiences.

Preschool art ideas. The following are selected examples of creative art experiences for preschool children:

- *Mural painting* can be a fun outdoor activity for young children. Tape a large sheet of butcher paper to any exterior wall, and let children collectively paint to their hearts' content. Alternatively, provide children with buckets of water and paintbrushes of different sizes and encourage them to paint the walls and other structures with water.

- *Straw painting* with glossy paper and straws. Children put small amounts of fairly runny paint on the paper and then blow through the straws to create interesting images and mixing of paints. Be sure to instruct younger preschoolers to blow out rather than suck up through their straws.

- *Crayon rubbings* with a definite texture, such as leaves, coins, or sandpaper are good options for crayon rubbings. Place a piece of newsprint on top of one of the objects and have children rub the flat side of the crayon over the paper. Let children experiment with objects of their own choosing to make rubbings.

- *Working with clay* is more difficult for young children than working with the more traditional play dough. However, with careful preparation, it can be a very positive experience (Rogers & Steffan, 2009). It may be possible to create finished fired pottery, but these products are not nearly as important as giving children the opportunity to mold and manipulate the clay.

- *Attending an art show* put on by older students can be a positive experience for preschool children. These older artists can talk to preschool children about the art they have created.

Primary art suggestions. Fox and Schirrmacher (2012) have many good suggestions for primary-age children. They remind us that, at this age, the young artist is still eager to mess around with materials, exploring their properties and enjoying the process of art. Possible ideas for art include the following:

- *Paper, glue, scissors, crayons, and paint* should be readily available as basic art supplies. Consider making them permanent supplies in the primary classroom so that students can count on their availability.

- *Chalk and pastels* are new options that delight primary children. Although messy, they allow children to blend colors in beautiful combinations. Light chalk on dark paper, wet chalk, and pastels on heavy paper are options to consider.

- *Crayon shavings* can be used to make interesting art projects for primary children. The teacher can scrape old broken crayons with a dull knife to create the shavings needed for the project. To create attractive designs, the children place the shavings on a piece of waxed paper and put another sheet of waxed paper on top. The teacher presses these with a warm iron, through a protective sheet of plain paper. Before adding the second piece of waxed paper, children can include other items—such as glitter, bits of ribbon, or tissue paper—to individualize their creations.

- *Drawing or sketching* is of interest to some children at the primary level. Simple sketches of each other, objects in the room, or things at home may be attractive options for many primary-age children. Brookes (1986) provides excellent ideas for helping children develop their creative drawing abilities.

- *Stars and snowflakes* can be created as a fun winter-time activity. Coffee filters (flat-bottomed rather than conical) are just the right shape, size, and thickness for creating individually designed stars or snowflakes. By folding the filters into quarters, snipping off small pieces, and carefully unfolding the paper, children can easily create and then display their efforts on classroom windows.

Music and the Young Child

Just as art provides many opportunities for young children to express themselves, music draws others into creative activities in early childhood settings. When adults carefully prepare the environment with appropriate materials and encourage musical experiences, children become willing participants in a variety of musical activities. For many children, there is something captivating about music that draws them into experiences that are enjoyable and that enhance many areas of their growth and development.

The Importance of Music in Early Childhood

The technical quality of musical productions at this age shows that children are just beginning to develop their skills. However, most children are genuinely interested in and enjoy musical experiences. Just as with the child's developing art abilities, the foundations for later musical production and enjoyment are built during the early childhood years. Ball (1995) cites longitudinal research that reveals that musical aptitude (the potential to learn music) becomes stabilized by age 9. The clear implication is that if we want to help children develop the basic skills necessary for musical expression later in life, they need many opportunities to experience music during the early childhood years. The *Celebrating Diversity* feature in this section describes a formal music instruction program that many families are choosing for their young children as a strategy for developing early musical talent.

There are many reasons for including music in the curriculum. The following benefits of music for young children are listed frequently (Campbell, 1998; Zur & Johnson-Green, 2008):

- **Psychomotor skills.** As children strike the xylophone, tap their rhythm sticks, beat a drum, or move to music, they are refining their control over large and small muscle movements.

- **Perceptual skills.** Recognizing a familiar tune and imitating it or tapping out a rhythmic pattern are examples of how music allows children to develop perceptual abilities.

Celebrating Diversity . . .
EARLY MUSICAL TALENT

Many families with very young children are enrolling them in formal musical instruction in either violin or piano as early as age 2. The Suzuki method (International Suzuki Association, 2010), begun in Japan in 1928, is now a popular approach for early musical training in the United States. While not specifically designed for gifted and talented children, the program often attracts families who believe their children are highly capable.

The Suzuki method assumes that just as young children learn language early and well by being immersed in a language-rich environment, they can learn music by listening, repeating, and practicing until they have mastered simple tunes such as "Twinkle, Twinkle, Little Star." Family members are an essential part of the Suzuki approach, encouraging their children to spend time each day listening to the music being learned and practicing their musical skills. In a relatively short time, many of these young children can play very complex music. By emphasizing perfection in form and production, the Suzuki method has helped a great many very young children develop the skills they need to perform complex musical pieces that often astound adult listeners. While not all children continue to develop their musical skills after their early successes, some do become truly gifted musicians.

1. Do you have any personal experience with the Suzuki method? Has a family member or friend been involved in this approach? What was the experience like?

2. Some would suggest that these more formal music experiences are pushing children at too early an age. Do you think programs such as the Suzuki method are creating stress for young children? Why or why not?

- **Affective development.** Music naturally leads to emotional responses and provides many children with important and appropriate ways to express their feelings.
- **Cognitive growth.** Musical experiences have been found to enhance the reasoning abilities of young children. Children develop higher-level thinking skills and memory through musical activities (see also Edelson & Johnson, 2004; Krull, 2003; Shore & Strasser, 2006).
- **Social skills.** Many musical experiences encourage participation, sharing, and cooperation. These important social skills need constant reinforcement in the early childhood classroom in natural and meaningful ways.
- **Cultural understandings.** Multicultural musical experiences help familiarize children with an important aspect of different cultures. This can lead to meaningful discussions of the similarities and differences between cultures. Children also identify with music from their own culture and react positively when you include this music in the early childhood setting.

Musical Development

John and Astra are sitting on the circle time rug and singing along with their favorite music CD by Raffi. These busy 3-year-olds then decide to add some music-making of their own to the activity. John takes a drum off the shelf, while Astra locates a triangle to use for her rhythm instrument. They restart the tape and sing along while keeping a reasonably accurate beat with their instruments. John and Astra are progressing normally in their musical development.

Figure 16–1

Milestones in Musical Development

Infants	Toddlers	Three-year-olds	Four-year-olds	Five-year-olds	Six-, Seven-, Eight-year-olds
React to loudness, softness, human voice	Listen to music, repeat some phrases, enjoy making music	Better voice control, master simple songs	Can learn basic musical concepts, sing complete songs from memory	Maturing sense of pitch, rhythm, and melody	Singing voices approaching maturity, enjoy silliness and word-play

Researchers who have studied the development of musical abilities in young children generally describe their results in terms of typical performance at different ages rather than identifying stages of development (Campbell & Scott-Kassner, 2006). The following abilities are milestones in musical development (see also Figure 16–1).

- *Infants* respond to the loudness and softness of sounds; react to the human voice, particularly the primary caregiver's; and express lively reactions to action songs and more subdued responses to lullabies.

- *Toddlers* discriminate among sounds and may try to approximate them; listen to music, enthusiastically responding to certain songs while repeating repetitive phrases; enjoy making sounds with musical instruments or common household items; and may sing or hum casually as they play.

- *Three-year-olds* develop better voice control and can master simple songs; many have favorite tunes they recognize; they can play rhythm instruments with a basic understanding of beat.

- *Four-year-olds* can learn basic musical concepts such as pitch, duration, tempo, and loudness; are able to classify musical instruments by sound, shape, size, and pitch; sing complete songs from memory with improving rhythm and pitch; and have an average singing range of five notes.

- *Five-year-olds* have a maturing sense of pitch, rhythm, and melody; like longer songs with predictable elements; reproduce a melody in an echo song; and extend their singing range to six notes.

- *Six-, Seven-, and Eight-year-olds* have singing voices that approach maturity; can sing in tune with up to 10 notes; are beginning to develop a sense of harmony; enjoy silliness and wordplay in songs; have a greater awareness of printed music and its role; often have well-established musical preferences; and may show an interest in playing a musical instrument.

Movement and Music

For many adults, the urge to respond to music through some sort of movement is nearly overpowering. Swaying, toe tapping, and dancing are common responses to a familiar and enjoyable piece of music. It should come as no surprise, then, that young children also have a natural desire to move in some way as they listen to, and produce, music of all types. There is also good evidence to indicate that movement plus music equals learning in early childhood settings (Foley, 2006; Palmer, 2001). Adults should provide numerous opportunities for children to combine these elements throughout their time in early childhood settings. Here are some ways to encourage movement and music:

- **Include finger plays.** Many of the songs that young children enjoy are combined with finger, hand, and body movements. For example, "Where Is Thumbkin?" is a popular preschool finger play/song combination that young children love.
- **March to music.** Stepping in time to music as you move around the classroom can be an enjoyable way to help children begin to understand musical rhythms.
- **Use rhythm instruments.** Children of all ages enjoy using rhythm instruments to strike the beat of the music they are listening to or singing. Including a variety of rhythm instruments in the music center allows children to learn more about rhythm as they move to music in meaningful ways.
- **Provide space for movement and music.** Opportunities for movement and music in your program are facilitated when a larger open space is available. Children can then move freely and without coming in contact with others as they listen to, or make, their own music. The group time area is one possible space for movement and music activities in many classrooms.

The Music Curriculum for Young Children

The early childhood music curriculum has four main elements that should be present in all settings. *Listening to music* is the first of these components. For example, you could lead a group activity in which you play recordings of different musical styles, instruments, or old favorites and help children listen more carefully to the elements of the music. Another option would be for individual children to put on headphones and listen to recorded music during free time. Finally, you could play music at different times during the day to create a pleasant atmosphere in your program. In all these instances, children are refining their musical listening skills in an enjoyable setting.

A second component of the music curriculum is *responding to music through movement.* Young children have an almost irresistible urge to move to the music they hear. Adults can encourage this through modeling, group movement and music activities, and providing materials and space for movement. Many songs for young children also include hand motions; adults can teach these, and children can use them when singing. You could also create a marching band with musical instruments and a lively CD recording. Another option would be for children to use scarves and streamers in the music corner as they move to music during free play.

A third important component of the music curriculum is that children must have many *opportunities to make music.* Singing enjoyable songs is one way to have fun making music. Many excellent songbooks and recordings (see Flohr, 2004, for example) can provide children with a variety of singing experiences. Playing different musical and rhythmic instruments gives great pleasure to young children as well. Rotating these options in and out of the early childhood setting adds further interest to this facet of music-making. Making music is an important way for children to engage in creative expression; encourage them to create new verses for familiar

Developmentally Appropriate Practice . . .
SINGING SONGS WITH YOUNG CHILDREN

Singing should be an integral part of the curriculum in early childhood settings. Songs can strengthen conceptual understandings, make more routine activities such as clean-up time more pleasant, and add an enjoyable interlude to the day. If you enjoy singing, so will young children. You can even make up songs that can be sung to familiar music and create your own music curriculum.

Singing to Strengthen Conceptual Understanding

Many songs allow children to learn while they sing. The following is an example for mathematics:

Four Little Horses

> Four little horses, galloping through town
>
> Two are white and two are brown
>
> Two gallop up and two gallop down
>
> Four little horses galloping through town.

You can create your own tune for this song and, using fingers for horses, merrily sing about four, six, eight, or even five little horses.

Singing During Routines

Songs are a good way to alert children to the start of routines like snack, clean-up, and outdoor time. Here is an example:

Brushing Teeth

> (Sing to the tune of "Mulberry Bush")
>
> This is the way we brush our teeth,
>
> brush our teeth, brush our teeth.
>
> This is the way we brush our teeth
>
> so early in the morning.
>
> (Herr & Libby-Larson, 2004, p. 189)

Singing for Fun

Songs with hand motions or full-body involvement are often popular with young children and are frequently requested. "The Eensy Weensy Spider" and "Head, Shoulders, Knees and Toes" are two traditional favorites.

---

songs and develop their own musical and rhythmic expressions. The above *Developmentally Appropriate Practice* feature provides additional ideas on using singing not only as an important music-making opportunity, but also as a key learning experience in early childhood settings.

The final component of the early childhood music curriculum is to help children begin to *understand music and music-making*. For example, children need to acquire a vocabulary that helps them describe musical experiences. Children can learn and then use musical terms such as *pitch, duration, tempo,* and *loudness* to help them describe both their own and others' musical experiences. You can also present the appropriate names for musical instruments and simple explanations of how each makes music. Learning that music communicates feelings and identifying the emotions generated by specific pieces is yet another way for children to begin developing a cognitive understanding of music.

For some people, the thought of developing and teaching a music curriculum for the early childhood classroom is a worrisome one. They are concerned that their own perceived lack of musical abilities will be a hindrance to their children. The *Developmentally Appropriate Practice* feature on page 453 makes it clear that for those who consider themselves nonmusicians, there are still plenty of opportunities to include meaningful music activities throughout the day.

Developmentally Appropriate Practice...
MUSIC FOR THE NONMUSICIAN

Does all this discussion about music make you nervous? Would you consider yourself below average in musical abilities? If you have not had any musical training, the thought of encouraging young children to engage in these activities may seem daunting. The good news is that you really do not need to be highly proficient musically to have a strong program for young children. Jalongo (1996) suggests five ways the nonmusician can use recorded music to create quality experiences for young children:

- **Choose music that is at a comfortable pitch.** Young children's voices are still maturing, and music that has a high pitch is harder to sing. Singers such as Raffi and Ella Jenkins have many recordings that are easy for children (and adults) to sing along with because of the lower pitch.
- **Expand your musical repertoire.** Try to avoid sticking to only familiar music. Borrow some recorded music from the library or other adults, and work on expanding your musical horizons. This helps ensure that students are getting richer musical experiences.

- **Become familiar with the best music available for young children.** Several musical awards are presented regularly for children's music, such as the Parent's Choice Seal of Approval. Professional journals also review recordings, and these can be helpful in selecting quality options. Talking to other adults and music specialists can provide additional insight.

- **Provide a wide range of musical styles, including ethnic music.** Recordings of songs sung in different languages and others that use culturally specific instruments can be excellent additions to the early childhood classroom.

- **Arrange many opportunities for quiet listening.** Set up a CD player with headphones and a basket of CDs for listening times. Background music at different times during the day can provide another productive listening experience.

Facilitating Musical Experiences

Adults play important roles in facilitating quality musical experiences. Having positive attitudes about music and taking time for adequate planning and preparation can help ensure exciting musical adventures. The following guidelines identify specific strategies that you can use.

- **Prepare the classroom environment.** Careful planning and preparation are the essential starting points for good musical experiences (Kemple, Batey, & Hartle, 2004). Thoughtful selections of songs to sing, music to play, and instruments for children to use will strengthen the music curriculum (Achilles, 1999). While children love to repeat favorite songs and enjoy the opportunity to thoroughly explore musical instruments, it is also important to have new materials and songs to maintain interest.

- **Encourage creative expression.** You will need to allow young children the freedom to experiment and explore with music. At the same time, take time to let them know that what they are doing is valued. When you value creative musical expression, children will be more likely to engage in this activity. As they make up songs or new verses to familiar tunes and create their own rhythmic expressions, children are truly making music in meaningful ways.

- **Emphasize enjoyment.** The quality of musical expression should *not* be the focus of the early childhood music curriculum. Children have yet to develop the skills needed for quality performance. Rather, the emphasis should be on enjoying a variety of musical experiences. Developing a love of music during the early years can help maintain interest and involvement in later life.

- **Make music fun.** You have a major role to play in making musical experiences fun for young children. It is important, for example, to demonstrate your own excitement. If you are animated and involved, children will be, too. Active participation in musical experiences increases the likelihood that children will find them fun. Adding props to songs, selecting motivating music, and providing quality musical instruments also help make these activities more fun for children.

- **Observe carefully.** Observations serve several purposes in the early childhood music curriculum. They help you determine which music materials are being used and when change is needed. Observations will also help you recognize who is participating and what can be done to get others involved. Through observations, you will be able to assess children's musical understandings and then plan activities to meet any deficits.

Music Activities

As you begin work in your new early childhood setting, you will need a variety of effective activities to use with young children as part of the music curriculum. Following are examples of typical options for infants and toddlers, preschool children, and children in the primary grades.

Infant and toddler music activities. Programs for infants and toddlers spend much time and effort dealing with the routines of young children's lives (Watson & Swim, 2008). Toileting, bathing, eating, and sleeping activities consume much of the day. For this age, a music curriculum should be integrated with these activities whenever possible. These might include the following:

- *Playfully singing* to young children while diapering, feeding, or preparing them for naps is enjoyable (Honig, 2005).
- *Playing background music* during the routines of the day introduces infants and toddlers to pleasant musical experiences.
- *Placing rattles and other noisemakers within reach* of young children can lead to playful exploration during diaper-changing times.

Preschool music ideas. Many different types of musical experiences, including those that are combined with movement, can be valuable for preschool children. The following suggestions provide a beginning list of ideas for this level:

- *Scarves* can be combined with a music CD to provide hours of fun for young children. Collect silky scarves from families, and use these to help children move to music. Have the scarves available in the group time area with music to fit the mood you want to encourage. Help children realize that they need to avoid collisions with others, and simply turn them loose. This is a favorite activity for many children.
- *"I Know an Old Lady"* is a classic song about an old lady who swallows a fly (and much more). It is often sung with primary-age children. However, with props for the flannel board, this song has considerable appeal for younger students. The catchy tune, combined with much repetition, makes it a hit.
- *Marching band* is an exciting option for many preschool children. With a good collection of rhythm instruments—such as cymbals, bells, and drums—children

Music and movement provide wonderful opportunities for creative experiences.

can practice making music by marching around the classroom (or outdoors) in time to a good piece of music with a clear beat. The addition of hats and a band leader (the adult initially) makes the activity even more attractive to young children.

- *Music appreciation* can begin during the preschool years. Choose several pieces of music that create different moods for you as an adult. Have children close their eyes and listen to each piece, imagining that they are doing something as they listen. Talk about what children imagined and how the music created that mood. Add your own insights.

Primary music activities. The continued development of motor skills and cognitive understanding makes it possible for teachers to plan and implement increasingly complex music activities for primary-age children. The following examples are designed to get you thinking about the possibilities for this level.

- *Making music* is a highly motivating activity for primary children and should include many different ways to make music. The *Developmentally Appropriate Practice* feature in this section describes some multicultural musical instruments that can be effectively used with primary children. More complex musical instruments can also be introduced at this time. The autoharp, for example, is an excellent instrument that both teachers and children can use. When the autoharp has clear markings for chords, children who have learned songs that the teacher has played can recreate the appropriate chords by reading a song card. Orff instruments, designed by the German composer Carl Orff, are other examples of more complex instruments that produce beautiful musical tones. The metallophone, for example, is like the traditional xylophone, but produces rich alto and bass tones on bars of thick metal.

- *Continue singing* with primary children. Singing songs remains a high priority for children at this age. With increasing musical abilities, children can enjoy singing songs in rounds. A classic example is "Row, Row, Row Your Boat." Silly songs with child-oriented humor are also very popular, especially when sung in unusual voices, such as an underwater voice, or the voice of a robot or baby. It is great fun and provides many opportunities for creative expression.

- *Increasing the variety of music for listening* is productive with primary children. They can enjoy listening to and discussing classical music. Edwards (2010) suggests the following for young children: Mozart, Symphony no. 39 in E Flat and Symphony no. 41 in C; Chopin, Sonata no. 3, op. 58; Beethoven, String Quartet no. 3 in D Major and String Quartet no. 4 in C; Bach, Brandenburg Concerto no. 106.

- *Attending live concerts* is another good activity at this age. Primary-age students, with their longer attention spans can benefit from live musical experiences. Having a middle school or high school band come to play would be one option. Taking a field trip to listen to a live performance is another possibility.

Developmentally Appropriate Practice . . .
MULTICULTURAL MUSICAL INSTRUMENTS

Early childhood professionals can use a diverse collection of multicultural musical instruments in early childhood settings. Although it is important to avoid being stereotypic, presenting traditional instruments can open up a productive dialogue about the similarities and differences between cultures. In addition, the musical experiences can be very rewarding for children. Here are a few examples of instruments that you may want to consider as part of the music curriculum:

- **Rain stick.** This instrument comes from Chile and is made from a long, cylindrical, dried cactus, with the spines pounded inward and sealed with small pebbles inside. Tipping the stick allows the stones to bounce off the cactus spines and create a pleasant tinkling sound.

- **Ocarina.** This instrument, also called a vessel flute, originated in South America. Made from clay, it has a small built-in mouthpiece and several holes for making different musical notes. More appropriate for primary-age children,

this instrument requires careful handling and cleaning between players.

- **Drums.** No one culture holds a monopoly on drums. They come from many different places and make a wide range of sounds. African, Chinese, Brazilian, and Native American cultures all have diverse drums that can be used in the early childhood classroom. Children enjoy trying out the many different varieties and talking about similarities and differences.

- **Guiro.** This traditional rhythm instrument originated in Mexico and is a favorite for all ages. Shaped somewhat like a shortened, hollow baseball bat with grooves running horizontally around the instrument, the player taps or rubs a short stick over the grooves on the exterior of the guiro to keep time with the music.

- **Shakeree.** This rhythm instrument comes from Africa and consists of a large gourd with seeds strung over its exterior in an intricate pattern. Shaking the gourd causes the seeds to make a rattling sound similar to maracas.

Creative Dramatics, Theater, and Dance

During most of the early childhood years, young children engage in creative dramatics, theater-like activities, and dance as they play. However, other options can be considered to integrate these important activities into the early childhood curriculum. Following a discussion of the role of dramatic play in facilitating theater and dance skills, other ideas for implementing theater and dance will be described.

Dramatic Play

Throughout this textbook, play has been emphasized as an important experience that facilitates learning in all areas of development. Dramatic play occurs when children pretend an object is something other than what it is (a stick becomes a fishing pole) or they pretend to be someone other than themselves (a young girl pretends to be a mother). Children typically begin to engage in dramatic play at about age 3 (Piaget, 1962). When they pretend to be their favorite superhero or take on the roles of adults who are important in their lives, they are engaging in early forms of creative dramatics and theater. Young children spontaneously act out unrehearsed stories and themes that are of interest to them. These early experiences are the basis for later, more formal, dramatic activities.

Most of this dramatic play should involve informal opportunities to act out themes of the children's own choosing. The primary role of the early childhood professional is to provide quality dramatic play props, observe what young children do with them, and facilitate this important play type as needed. The dress-up clothes in the dramatic play center, props for housekeeping activities, and materials that can be used to act out a theme such as a shoe store are all examples of quality dramatic play props for young children.

Theater

In addition to the informal creative dramatics activities described previously, children at the primary level are also ready for more structured activities in this area. Akcan (2005) describes how a puppet theater can be used for both creative dramatics activities and as a powerful second language learning tool. Each afternoon, different groups of three children in a French-immersion class present a short story using child-made puppets and a story that they created over several days of school work. By sharing the story in French and later responding to comments from the rest of the class who serve as an audience for the daily performances from rotating groups, children are engaging in drama activities that also strengthen their language learning skills.

In preparation for the puppet theater, student groups work with the classroom teacher to develop a story that includes the following:

- Location or setting
- Characters
- Goal of the characters
- Obstacles faced by characters in reaching goal
- Story resolution

Children then create their stories, prepare their puppets, practice, and present their puppet play to the class. This is both an effective model for meaningful second language learning and a productive strategy for helping primary children learn story elements and present them in a logical sequence. Dramatic presentation activities are wonderful opportunities for academic learning in the primary classroom and are another early form of theater that young children enjoy greatly.

Another effective strategy for introducing theater to young children is to take them to live performances (Friedman, 2010). Because young children can readily engage in pretend activities through their play, it is easy for them to get absorbed in a live theater performance. At the same time, because they have difficulty distinguishing fantasy from reality, performances must be selected carefully so that frightening costumes and troubling events are minimized (Friedman, 2010). For these reasons, taking groups of young children to theater designed specifically for young children is the best option. Even those designed for children should be previewed, if possible, and discussed with the children beforehand.

Dance

Most early childhood professionals have had fewer experiences with dance than with some of the other creative arts. If this is true for you, it may make you less comfortable in planning creative dance experiences for young children. But by adding some simple props to your early childhood setting, some beginning dance activities can be implemented. Just as dramatic play is the basis for much of the early theater experiences of young children, so, too, can movement activities be seen as the foundation for a more formal dance curriculum. The earlier example of using scarves, music, and an open space to allow children to engage in creative movement and dance is a typical and productive way to help young children become comfortable in expressing themselves through body movement. In addition, there are other, somewhat more structured ways that dance can be added to the early childhood curriculum.

By making some simple adaptations to free choice movement activities, you can help children develop their early dance skills. For example, Dow (2010) describes a movement/dance activity in which children march to a specific piece of music. After they become comfortable with marching, they can be asked to vary their movements and march backwards, or march very slowly, or march like they are barefoot on a hot pavement. By varying the music, adding new props, and guiding young children's movements through creative questions, children can have great fun as they engage in movement/dance activities.

Planning for these activities does not need to be extensive or costly. For example, most of the equipment you will need is already available to you in the early childhood setting. Musical CDs, instruments, scarves (from the dress up area), streamers, and small flashlights are all examples of easily found items that can be used in dance activities (Dow, 2010). An open space such as a gymnasium or empty room will allow children to move without being hindered by tables, chairs, and other furniture. Then, with some thoughtful consideration of the prompts you could use to encourage creative movement, your dance curriculum is off and running.

summary

What Is Creativity?

An understanding of the creative process is central to the teaching of art, music, creative dramatics, and dance. Studying definitions of creativity, the characteristics of creative individuals, how adults can assist with the creative process, and the relationships between play and creativity provides the foundation needed to understand this complex process.

The Young Artist

Although some consider art education less important than other parts of the curriculum, there is a strong rationale for including art in early childhood settings. Understanding developmental trends in art, the content of the early childhood art curriculum, and the adult's role in art experiences allows early childhood professionals to create appropriate and interesting art experiences for young children.

Music and the Young Child

Music is another important element of the early childhood curriculum. When caregivers and teachers understand the developmental patterns children follow in their musical growth, create appropriate content for the music curriculum, find ways to facilitate musical experiences, and include appropriate materials and activities for young children, they can implement exciting musical experiences in early childhood settings.

Creative Dramatics, Theater, and Dance

Dramatic play provides a wonderful opportunity to engage young children in early drama and theater experiences. As they take on roles and pretend to be someone else, they expand their ability to engage in creative dramatics. Puppet theater can be used for more structured drama activities with children. Movement and dance activities can be readily added to the early childhood curriculum and are popular with young children.

for reflection and discussion

1. What do you see as the key characteristics of creativity in young children?
2. In 3 to 4 paragraphs, explain what important roles adults play in developing and implementing creative art activities for young children.
3. List and describe two or three music activities that you will want to use in your future early childhood setting. Share your ideas with others and incorporate their feedback as appropriate.
4. What is the role of more structured theater activities for children in preschool or the primary grades?

MyEducationLab

Go to Topic 7: Curriculum/Content Areas in the MyEducationLab (www.myeducationlab.com) for *Teaching Young Children*, where you can:

- Find learning outcomes for Curriculum/Content Areas along with the national standards that connect to these outcomes.
- Complete Assignments and Activities that can help you more deeply understand the chapter content.
- Apply and practice your understanding of the core teaching skills identified in the chapter with the Building Teaching Skills and Dispositions learning units.
- Examine challenging situations and cases presented in the IRIS Center Resources.
- Check your comprehension on the content covered in the chapter with the Study Plan. Here you will be able to take a chapter quiz, receive feedback on your answers, and then access Review, Practice, and Enrichment activities to enhance your understanding of chapter content.
- Use the Online Lesson Plan Builder to practice lesson planning and integrating national and state standards into your planning.

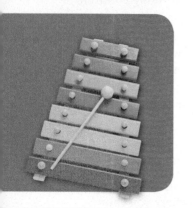

17

Technology and Young Children

Kesara and Mark are playing at the computer in their preschool classroom. Like the rest of their classmates, these 4-year-old children fearlessly experiment with the computer as they navigate through the art program they are using. As they draw and paint on the computer screen, Mark and Kesara talk about their creation. "Let's try the stamps" insists Kesara as they change the background color from white to green. "Okay, I want butterflies in our picture, and they have some in the stamp part," Mark says. The two children work to negotiate additional elements of their project as play continues over the next 15 minutes. Once the picture is complete, they print it out, show it to two interested classmates, and then take off for the block corner to engage in additional play.

The scene just described is becoming commonplace in many early childhood settings. Early childhood professionals and families are coming to recognize the value of computers and other technologies for young children and are providing opportunities to use them on a regular basis. Children are enthusiastically using a variety of technologies as effective tools for exploration, learning, and play.

Until fairly recently, however, many adults questioned the value of technology in early childhood settings. During the 1980s, for example, as computers became more accessible to children in prekindergarten–12 education, some early educators voiced concerns associated with computer use by young children, such as developmental readiness (Barnes & Hill, 1983), lack of social interactions (Heller & Martin, 1982), and the move away from concrete, real-world materials (Cuffaro, 1984).

Writing and research from the 1990s to the present have generally been supportive of computer and technology use by young children. Socialization issues (Baron, 1991), concerns over software options (Shade, 1992), and developmental appropriateness (Clements & Sarama, 2003) have been addressed to the satisfaction of many early educators. While it is clear that the hands-on manipulation of real world materials is extremely valuable for young children, there is also a place for the many technology options that are so commonly used by society at large (Copple & Bredekamp, 2009).

This chapter discusses the appropriateness of computers and other forms of technology as learning tools in early childhood settings beginning at age 3. Although a growing number of technology options for infants and toddlers are being produced and marketed to families (see, for example, Matte, 2010), most early childhood specialists consider these alternatives developmentally inappropriate (American Academy of Pediatrics, 2010; Galley, 2000; Jacobson, 2006; National Association for the Education of Young Children, 1996). However, with careful selection and planning, activities involving technology for children 3 and older can successfully complement the other more traditional activities of young children (Technology and Young Children Interest Forum, 2008).

Television and Video Games

Television and video games are examples of technologies that are very common in most homes. Many children spend several hours each day watching television and/or playing video games at home. In addition, some early childhood settings include television as an option for early literacy skills (Moses, 2009). While some suggest that young children should have nothing to do with either of these options, others say that limited use of these technologies can be positive for young children. In the sections that follow, the positive and negative attributes of television and video games will be discussed.

Television and Young Children

Television is one form of technology that has been available to families and early childhood programs for many years. Much has been written about the problems young children encounter as they interact with this technology. The amount of time spent viewing, the content of programming, and issues with advertising are all concerns that have been voiced about television viewing. An additional concern is the recent effort to promote television and video options for infants and toddlers. For example, a recent DVD series published by Sesame Beginnings uses popular *Sesame Street* characters such as Big Bird and Elmo to entice very young children to watch television programming at a very early age (Jacobson, 2006). The National Association for the Education of Young Children (2005) and the American Academy of Pediatrics (2010) clearly identify this as developmentally inappropriate practice for infants and toddlers. Despite these valid criticisms and concerns, limited television viewing in early childhood settings may be useful as children move beyond toddlerhood. In this section, we will look at both the limitations and potential for effective television viewing.

Time spent viewing. One major concern voiced about television use is the large amount of time children spend viewing. Statistics vary regarding the amount of time spent watching television because many of the studies have been based on self-reported data or "best guesses" done by family members (Roberts & Foehr, 2008). In one study, children in the United States were found to watch an average of 23 to 28 hours of television weekly (Hurst, 2004). Another found children spending an average of 14 hours a week interacting with some form of screen media (television, DVDs, computers, video games), with television viewing averaging about one and a quarter hours each day (Rideout & Hamel, 2006). A third study also indicated that 30% of children from birth to age 3 and 43% of 4- to 6-year-olds have a television in their bedroom (Rideout, Vandewater, & Wartella, 2003). Children often spend more time watching television than they spend in school, playing, or interacting with adults (Persson & Musher-Eizenman, 2003). Even if all the programming being watched were excellent, spending this much time in front of the television significantly decreases the child's opportunities for other valuable experiences. During the early childhood years, the activity that television most likely replaces is play.

Let's create a typical day in the life of a 5-year-old child to see the potential impact of an average level of television viewing:

7:00 a.m.	Wake up, dress, breakfast, television
8:30 a.m.	Leave for kindergarten
2:30 p.m.	After-school care (with 1 hour of TV viewing)
5:00 p.m.	Home, computer or video game (½ hour), dinner
6:30 p.m.	Television (1½ hours)
8:00 p.m.	Prepare for bed

It does not take much imagination to see that this child has little time for anything other than regular routines and about 3 hours of television viewing. The TV has crowded out most of the opportunities for socializing with others, being read to, or playing.

Because of the large amount of time many young children spend watching television, there are fewer opportunities for active physical play. This is seen by many as a major contributing factor in childhood obesity and health problems (American Academy of Pediatrics et al., 2010; Sorte & Daeschel, 2006). The lack of vigorous physical activity in the early years may well lead to a more sedentary lifestyle as an adult, compounding health and fitness problems in later life.

Sex, violence, and advertising. A careful analysis of television programming during prime time also shows considerable content that is inappropriate for young children. Sexual themes and acts of violence are often cited as problem areas (Cortes, 2000; Hurst, 2004; Thornton, 2002). Children view a variety of adult-oriented sexual situations and many different acts of violence on a daily basis. It is estimated that the average child sees more than 200,000 acts of violence on television, including 40,000 murders by the age of 18 (Hurst, 2004). The ability of children to make sense of these situations is limited, at best, and leads to considerable confusion and misunderstanding. If something is on television, does that mean it is acceptable in the real world? Young children are struggling to define the borders between reality and fantasy. Unfortunately, television often blurs this already unclear distinction. The results are painfully evident in the inappropriate behaviors of young children.

Another problem area associated with television viewing is the advertising to which children are exposed. It is estimated that the average child sees approximately 40,000 commercials a year, many of them specifically targeting children as consumers (Kunkel, Wilcox, Cantor, Palmer, Linn, & Dowrick, 2004). The following concerns regarding children and TV advertising have been identified (Kunkel et al., 2004):

- Commercial recall and product preference
- Parent–child conflict over products purchased

- Materialistic attitudes
- Unhealthy eating habits
- Positive attitudes toward alcohol consumption

Redeeming aspects. The preceding discussion suggests that television viewing has a strong negative impact on the lives of young children. Although research supports this perspective, other evidence indicates that children can benefit when they spend time watching quality programming. Educational programs like *Sesame Street* and *Between the Lions* are receiving good reports in terms of their impact on preparing children for school (Moses, 2009). Regular viewing of these programs has helped improve early literacy and mathematics skills (Rath, 2002; St. Clair, 2002; Wright & Huston, 1995). Although many television programs have limited value, educational programming may be a positive experience for many young children.

Guidelines for family television use. Families play critical roles in technology use. Most homes have an abundance of technology options and need to plan carefully how young children will use them. For example, one study showed that 26% of all 2- to 4-year-old children and 39% of all 5- to 7-year-olds have television sets in their bedrooms (Kunkel et al., 2004). You will need to assist families in developing good strategies for managing the many technology options available to them and their children.

Perhaps the most universal piece of technology found in American homes is the television. Very few are without at least one, and most have two or more. Many families provide little guidance and supervision for young children's viewing. The following ideas may help families deal more effectively with the television:

- *Collect articles* from professional literature that provide information about the problems and benefits of television viewing. The ones discussed in this section are all good examples for your collection.

- *Encourage families to limit television viewing* by suggesting alternatives that are healthier for the child's overall development. When provided with specific suggestions for simple play experiences, families can take the difficult step of turning off the television for at least part of the child's free time. The *Family Partnerships* feature in this section provides some beginning thoughts on options families can consider to replace at least a portion of television viewing.

- *Suggest that families discuss* what children are watching. Whenever possible, parents should watch television with their children and talk about the negative ideas that are being presented. This can help children be better consumers of the programs they watch.

- *Move the television* to a room not at the center of family life. This will help encourage other more valuable activities when family members gather.

- *Avoid isolating family members* by placing television sets in shared living spaces, rather than in a more private setting. When a TV is placed in a child's bedroom (a more private space), the child is more likely to view inappropriate programming, spend more time viewing, and have fewer conversations with other family members about content.

Family Partnerships . . .
ALTERNATIVES TO TELEVISION

While many families understand at some level that they and their children probably watch too much television, they may need to understand the rationale for cutting back on their viewing and find good alternatives that are easy to organize and pleasurable for all concerned. As an adult working with young children, you will need to remind families regularly of creative and fun alternatives to television. Perhaps including a column in each edition of your newsletter or holding a group meeting to discuss this topic would work for you. Whatever method you choose, be ready with a long list of good alternatives to TV viewing. Here are a few ideas to get you started:

- **Family reading time.** Encourage families to set aside time each evening for reading. Even 15 or 20 minutes can be valuable in motivating interest in reading. Children need to see other family members engaged in reading, and children can benefit greatly from being read to. Be sure to provide lists of quality children's literature and possible locations so that it will be easy for families to find good selections.

- **Game night.** Reserving one evening a week for a short game can be an enjoyable alternative to television viewing. Once again, families can benefit from some information about good game options. You might send home a description of a simple game played in the early childhood setting that families would enjoy at home.

- **Family play time.** Many families have gotten out of the habit of playing together. With regular reminders and simple suggestions, this can be another important addition to family routines. Things like singing and acting out "Row, Row, Row Your Boat" with infants and toddlers, building block structures with preschoolers, and helping a primary-age child construct a "fort" using an old blanket are examples of things you could share. When they are relatively short and simple to prepare, families will be more likely to commit to this activity.

- **Getting outside.** Going for a walk around the neighborhood, visiting a local park, or planting a small garden are all options that get everyone out of the house and engaged in fun activities together. Families often need reminders to get involved in these enjoyable tasks as well.

1. Are you a good role model for reasonable television viewing? If so, describe your alternatives to TV viewing. If not, identify strategies you could use to bring better balance to this part of your life.

2. How do you feel about this role in working with families? Will you be comfortable in suggesting alternatives to television? Why or why not?

The Video Game Dilemma

Matt and Alan rush home from their second-grade classroom and head straight to the video game shelf. They select a favorite game, plug it in, and spend the next 45 minutes deeply engrossed in manipulating their joysticks. Their animated conversation and intense focus show that both boys are definitely excited about the game.

Many children like Matt and Alan find video games highly motivating, and the number of homes with these games continues to grow. In a study of low-income families, approximately 75% of the homes had video games for young children (Wright & Huston, 1995). In one study of 4- to 6-year-olds who have video games, girls spent an average of 53 minutes a day playing them while boys averaged an hour and 8 minutes (Rideout et al., 2003).

The debate over value. Although children typically spend slightly less time playing video games than watching television, many adults are concerned about video game use. Fantasy, violence, and autonomous action rather than cooperation are frequently

Video games are used extensively by young children.

cited as problem areas (Funk, 1993; Rideout et al., 2003). For some children, another issue is the large amount of time spent playing these games. Again, this leaves little time to engage in other more important activities such as vigorous physical activity and creative play.

However, some adults believe that video games offer benefits over television viewing. While TV is a passive activity, video games may increase a child's eye–hand coordination and improve attention to detail. Others suggest that these games can be a nonthreatening way to introduce children to computers (Henry J. Kaiser Family Foundation, 2002). Finally, many children also gain a sense of accomplishment from playing (Cesarone, 1994).

One influential writer, Seymour Papert (1993), suggests that video games give insight into the potential power of computers to transform the way children learn. He states that families and early childhood professionals should try to understand why video games captivate children. "Any adult who thinks one of these games is easy need only sit down and try to master one. Most are hard, with complex information—as well as technique—to be mastered" (p. 4). Video games, according to Papert, allow children to explore and experiment in situations with predetermined rules and to learn a great deal from these experiences. Papert wants computers to provide similar types of playful interactions for children.

Video games in the home. Many of the issues families face regarding video games are similar to those discussed earlier for television viewing. One major concern is the amount of time some children spend playing video games. Families should be encouraged to help their children find other activities when they spend too much time with video games. Another significant issue is the level of violence portrayed in some games. Many children are negatively influenced by the violence they see (Funk, 1993). The following problems are associated with violence (Levin, 1998; National Association for the Education of Young Children, 1998):

- Children who view violence tend to see it as an acceptable way of resolving conflict.
- Children become less sensitive to the suffering of others.
- Anxieties may increase in some children. They may be more fearful of the world around them.

Selection of video games should be carefully made after a thorough review of the content of the games.

 ## Computers and Young Children

When the National Association for the Education of Young Children first published its description of developmentally appropriate practice in 1987, it did not mention computers (Bredekamp, 1987). At that time, fewer computers were being used by young children, and there was considerable disagreement among leaders in the field (Mageau, 1993) regarding their appropriateness. After much discussion, however, NAEYC approved and published a position statement describing effective technology use in the early childhood classroom (National Association for the Education of Young Children, 1996). This document, which is currently being updated, emphasizes the following points:

1. The caregiver or teacher must exercise professional judgment to ensure that each opportunity for computer use is age appropriate, individually appropriate, and sensitive to cultural diversity.

2. When implemented properly, technology can stimulate children's cognitive and social skills.

3. Computers should be integrated into the classroom environment and used by children as simply another learning option.

4. All children should have equitable access to computers in the schools.

5. Software selected for use should avoid stereotyping any group of people and avoid the use of violence as a problem-solving strategy.

6. Early childhood professionals and families should work cooperatively to advocate for quality hardware and software options for young children.

7. Early childhood educators need training in appropriate computer use, including its implementation as a tool for working with other professionals.

Computers and Play

A key element of developmentally appropriate practice is encouraging children to interact playfully with the materials and people in their environment. Play is a primary means for learning in early childhood settings, and they must be carefully planned to promote childhood play. If the computer is to become an important option for young children, it must also encourage playful behaviors.

The software available to children is the key ingredient to playful computer use. When it is designed to be used creatively by children, the potential for playful interactions is greatly enhanced. Many companies produce software for the early childhood age range. Some, however, have been more actively involved in creating playful products for young children. As a future early childhood professional, you will need to review potential software carefully to be sure that it is developmentally appropriate and playful.

When characteristics of play are discussed in relation to computer use, we can see that while much of the software available for young children age 3 and above is of lower quality, other options facilitate playful interactions in early childhood settings (Henniger, 1994):

*   **Play is active.** Rather than being a passive event, play is generally associated with physical activity. Yet, the level of physicalness varies from one play event to the next. Puzzles, for example, require small muscle movements similar to those needed for manipulating a computer mouse and keyboard.

*   **Play is child selected.** Good play experiences are chosen by the child from a variety of available options. When caregivers and teachers place computers in program space like any other early childhood center and make them available to children during choice time, playfulness is enhanced.

*   **Play is child directed.** Children can engage in quality play events with limited adult intervention. Independent use of the computer requires careful software selection, because much of what is currently available requires considerable adult assistance.

- **Play is process oriented.** In play, the process is more important than any product the child may create. Computers should allow children to enjoy the process of exploring and experimenting without emphasizing an end product.
- **Play stimulates imagination and creativity.** Many play experiences allow children to use their imaginations and be creative in their interactions with people and things. Drill-and-practice software (discussed later in this chapter) discourages these important characteristics. There is only limited availability of more creative software options.
- **Play is a low-risk activity.** Play provides an opportunity for children to experiment and explore with little risk of failure. Software that is difficult for children to use independently or that requires specific responses makes it more likely that children will fail. Drill-and-practice software again receives low marks in this category.

As the preceding discussion indicates, the key ingredient in developmentally appropriate computer use is the software selected. Out of the hundreds of options being marketed, excellent software is available. However, much of what is offered has limited play value. You will need to examine each piece of software carefully to ensure that young children have quality computer experiences. Having read about software and play, take time now to review the *Celebrating Play* feature in this section and respond to the questions presented as a way to summarize your thoughts and feelings about the impact of computers on play in early childhood settings.

Social Interactions

An early concern about computers was that they would isolate children, thereby discouraging the social experiences that are essential to development. When we think about how adults use computers, this concern seems justified. To accomplish tasks on the computer, most adults need to shut out other distractions and focus their energies on manipulating the keyboard and mouse. It becomes a solitary activity.

Yet, with children, this problem can be easily overcome. By simply putting more than one chair out at each available computer and encouraging children to help each other as they work their way through various software programs, you can significantly enhance social exchanges. Laptop computers and their mobility may also increase the opportunities for social interactions. Research indicates that in at least some instances, computer use can be more social than other more traditional activities for young children (Clements & Sarama, 2003).

Developmental Abilities

Another frequently cited concern is the issue of developmental readiness. Do children have the cognitive skills needed to understand and manipulate the computer? Early detractors suggested they do not. Barnes and Hill (1983) argued that, developmentally, children need to be in Piaget's stage of concrete operations (approximately age 8) before they are ready to use the computer. At that point, they suggest, children can more effectively manage the symbol world of the computer. Similarly, Cuffaro (1984) was concerned that preschool children should use concrete, real-world materials rather than the more abstract, symbol-oriented computer.

Celebrating Play . . .
THE COMPUTER'S IMPACT ON PLAY

While there are those who believe that technologies such as computers have no place in early childhood settings, there is a growing body of evidence that suggests young children can benefit from appropriate computer use (Clements & Sarama, 2003). With quality technology products and appropriate preparations by the early childhood professional, benefits include social and emotional growth as well as language and cognitive learning. Still, there are those who harbor lingering doubts about the impact of computer use on childhood play. Some worry that technology will replace other play activities in the classroom. Others are concerned about the potential for social isolation. A third concern is that technology will take away opportunities for creative expression that are so prevalent in play.

Fischer and Gillespie (2003) addressed these concerns and others after carefully observing a typical Head Start classroom in rural Iowa. First, they found that when a variety of creative learning centers (such as blocks, art, dramatic play, and technology) are made available to children, they spend time in each of the options rather than focusing only on computer use. The technology center simply becomes one of several good choices among the many available, and children continue to take part in the more traditional play experiences. Second, they discovered that children engage in considerable social interaction as they use technology in the early childhood setting. They felt that the portability of laptop computers helped facilitate these social exchanges. Finally, observations led them to conclude that creativity can prosper when open-ended developmentally appropriate software is made available to young children. Fischer and Gillespie concluded that technology can have a positive impact on play and the young child's development.

1. Based on what you have read in this chapter, what do you see as the positive and negative influences of computers on childhood play?

2. Should preschool programs include a technology center as one option for children during playtime? Why or why not?

Although young children need many opportunities to manipulate objects in the real world, they can use symbols in their play from a very early age. Consider the following situation:

Aletha and Selena (both age 4) are playing in the dress-up area of their preschool classroom. Following their recent trip to the fire station, they have decided to dress up as firefighters and pretend to put out a fire. Aletha describes the scene: "Let's say the wall is the apartment building on fire. It has three stories, and there are people hollering for us to quick, put out the fire! You hold the hose, and I'll get the water started!"

Clearly, these two girls are using a wealth of symbols in their pretend play. They are envisioning complex situations that are not physically present, and they are manipulating these symbols successfully in play.

Young children can manage the symbol world of the computer, although it is one step removed from real objects and interactions (Clements & Sarama, 2003). When computers are one of many choices, they can provide quality experiences that expand, rather than detract from, the young child's learning opportunities.

Assistive Technology

Computers and technology are potentially powerful tools for assisting children with special needs. For example, computers help some children with attention deficits focus more effectively on their learning tasks; children with autistic tendencies may improve their interactions with peers as they use the computer together; and children with visual impairments have increased opportunities for learning and communicating with others via computers (Keramidas & Collins, 2009; Poel, 2007).

In many instances, computers require special adaptations to be successfully used by children with special needs. Assistive technology is the general descriptor for all the hardware and software modifications needed and also includes other devices children with special needs require to enhance their learning opportunities and ability to communicate with others (Keramidas & Collins, 2009). For example, voice recognition software is an assistive technology that can enable a visually impaired child to tell the computer what to do. Touch screens, trackballs, and simplified keyboards are just a few options that make the computer more accessible to children with special needs. Early childhood professionals can consult experts in the field to locate assistive technology options for children with special needs. When these options are made available, children can move from dependent to more independent learning (Mulligan, 2003; Poel, 2007; Snider & Badgett, 1995). The *Celebrating Diversity* feature in this section provides additional information on assistive technology.

Computers in Early Childhood Settings

If children are to use computers in developmentally appropriate ways, you will need to incorporate computers physically into the classroom space. When technology is readily accessible on a daily basis, it becomes just another tool that children can use to further their knowledge about the world. Computers become integrated into the learning experiences that take place. This natural connection helps make technology developmentally appropriate for young children (National Association for the Education of Young Children, 1996).

To integrate computers effectively into early childhood settings, consider the following:

Early childhood professionals play an important role in effective computer use.

- Set up a computer center with open access during designated times during the program day.
- Place the screen and keyboard at appropriate heights for the children using them.
- Organize each computer with at least two chairs to encourage more than one child to use the computer at a time.
- Make sure that the adult can easily observe children working at the computer so that she can help as needed.
- Develop activities that make it more likely that children will use the computer as a regular part of their school day.

Interacting with children using computers. Davis and Shade (1994) suggest three key roles for caregivers and teachers as they interact with children using computers:

1. **Educator as instructor.** When the computer is brought into the early childhood setting, adults will need to help children learn how to use the technology.

Celebrating Diversity . . .
ASSISTIVE TECHNOLOGY

Public Law 100–407, The Technology-Related Assistance for Individuals with Disabilities Act, was passed in 1988 to ensure that children with special needs and their families have access to technology resources. Children benefit significantly from having this technology in their early childhood classrooms (Keramidas & Collins, 2009; Mulligan, 2003). Roblyer, Edwards, and Havriluk (1997) identify two major benefits:

- **Improved motivation and self-concept.** Children with special needs spend more time on instructional tasks and have improved self-confidence when provided with assistive technology.
- **Enhanced communication and interaction with others.** Assistive technology also helps children with special needs express themselves more effectively in their communications with others.

Recently, many tools have been designed to make technology more useful to children with special needs. Some examples follow:

- **Alternate input devices.** Some students with physical disabilities find it difficult to use the keyboard and mouse to enter information into the computer. Touch screens, alternative keyboards, and voice-controlled devices are examples of hardware that help these students.
- **Substitute output devices.** Children with visual impairments need mechanisms such as enlarged computer images, speech devices that tell what the program is doing, or printers that produce Braille.
- **Equipment to assist deaf learners.** Captioned video that provides subtitles for television and other video presentations is one example.

1. Visit an early childhood program that includes children with special needs. Review their assistive technology and describe how children used it.
2. Observe a child with special needs using assistive technology. What benefits can you see? Discuss this with others.

---

2. **Educator as coach.** As children become more comfortable with the computer, the early childhood professional becomes more of a facilitator by providing assistance as needed and guiding children into appropriate uses of the technology.
3. **Educator as model.** Children should see adults using the computer as well. Recording children's oral stories, creating charts and signs for the early childhood setting, and incorporating computers into small-group activities are some examples of this modeling.

Internet safety. In addition to making good decisions about the software available to children, planning the environment for computer use, and interacting with children in positive ways, caregivers and teachers must also be prepared to restrict access to inappropriate Internet sites. The growth of content on the Internet each year has been phenomenal. In addition to websites designed specifically for adults, more people of all ages are using Facebook, YouTube, and Twitter. While much of the content on many of these Internet sites is inappropriate and even harmful to children, there is also valuable content that you may want to use with young children. The *Technology Explorations and Activities* feature in this section provides an opportunity to explore some possible Internet options for young children.

Technology Explorations and Activities . . .
VIDEO-SHARING WEBSITES

There are a number of video-sharing websites available for children and early childhood professionals. They include youtube.com, teachertube.com, ehow.com, vimeo.com, hulu.com, and viddler.com (An & Seplocha, 2010). Although most people first think of these sites as providing entertainment for children and adults, they may also offer some useful content. Spend some time reviewing videos on youtube.com. After doing your own search of the site, search for "At the Dentist—Role Play" and watch that short video. Search also for "preschool songs" and watch two or three song videos. You may also want to review one or more of the other video-sharing sites mentioned above and then respond to the following questions.

Research, Reflect, and Respond

1. Did you find any videos that you would consider using in an early childhood setting? Describe what you saw as the negative and positive aspects of the videos you observed.

2. If you found a video that you would use with young children, describe how you would use it in an early childhood setting. If no such video was found, describe what you would want in a video you would use with young children.

3. Were there resources available on any of the video-sharing websites that would be useful to you as an early childhood professional? Describe what you found.

If you choose to provide access to these or other sites, be sure to carefully monitor usage to make sure children are making appropriate content choices. Software options such as Net Nanny and Cyber Patrol Parent Controls can also help by blocking unwanted content from reaching young children and should be considered in early childhood settings that provide Internet access to children.

Selecting Software Programs

One of the major challenges facing early educators who want to use computer technology in their classrooms is to choose appropriate software. Numerous options are available, and new products are regularly being developed; therefore, it is difficult for even the experts to keep up with all the choices. Thousands of software options make selections mind-boggling for many. Although each of these decisions is personal, some guidelines may help make the process more manageable. In general, there are two ways to purchase and/or use software for young children. The first is the more traditional purchase of a compact disk (CD) that contains the actual software program. This disk can either be loaded onto the computer hard drive or uploaded from the CD each time you want to use the product. More frequently, you can purchase or use software that is automatically downloaded from an Internet site. Several general guidelines are described below that can help you in selecting appropriate software in either format.

Guidelines for Software Selection

Before purchasing or using software options with young children, it is important to try them out. Although many provide children with positive experiences, numerous

The best way to evaluate computer software is to spend time using it.

others are inappropriate and should be avoided. Your most important task, therefore, is to select the best software from the thousands of options available.

The following characteristics should provide guidelines as you conduct a review of the software under consideration. When all of these characteristics are evident, the software is a good option to use in early childhood settings (Henniger, 1994):

- **Minimal adult instruction and interaction.** Materials in a good early childhood program have a significant characteristic in common: they can all be used with little or no adult instruction or assistance. Good software should have this same quality. You should be able to install the software on the hard drive or download it from the Internet and then turn children loose to explore its possibilities.

- **Easy to enter and exit.** Quality programs should also allow children to enter the software and later exit without assistance. This seemingly small characteristic can make a big difference in the child's confidence level in approaching and using the computer. When software is user-friendly, children will be more likely to try it out and have greater success along the way.

- **Verbal/pictorial instructions.** Because most children in the early childhood years are either nonreaders or beginning readers, the instructions for software use should be verbal or pictorial rather than written.

- **Child manipulated.** Good software allows children to experiment, explore, and manipulate the program as they see fit. They then take control and use the software in ways that are interesting and developmentally appropriate. Children will spend more time with these options and learn more along the way.

- **Stimulates imagination and creativity.** When children play, they frequently use their imaginations as they creatively work through roles and situations. Quality software should encourage these important qualities.

- **Simple in design, complex in use.** The best play materials for children are simple in design, yet can be used in virtually unlimited ways. Blocks are a good example of this concept. Without overwhelming the young child with too many choices, a good software program should allow the child to manipulate and explore for long periods of time. Imaginative, creative experiences are often the result.

Much of the software available for young children does not meet these criteria. Haugland and Shade (1994) estimate that approximately 70% of the software developed for young children has limited value. One type of program that should be used less often, drill-and-practice software, requires children to respond with one right answer to closed-ended questions and leaves little opportunity for independent, creative manipulation. Although some drill-and-practice software has value in teaching early math and reading skills, this option should comprise only a small portion of the programs in the early childhood classroom. The *Developmentally*

Appropriate Practice feature in this section provides some ideas for effective use of drill-and-practice software.

Good software can be organized into several categories. Although not all programs in these areas are developmentally appropriate, they tend to be better options for young children. These categories include the following:

- **Storyboard software.** Shade (1995) states that these programs allow children to build a story by first picking a background and then adding their own choices of objects and people, much like the more traditional flannelboard stories children create.

- **Draw/paint programs.** Some software programs allow children to use the computer much like an electronic easel. Children can draw pictures, paint, use electronic stamps, and use a variety of other options to create an art project on the computer screen.

- **Electronic books.** With the growth of CD-ROM software, many stories have been computerized with excellent graphics and sound capabilities that allow the computer to read to the child.

- **Writing/publishing software.** Several good programs let children write and publish their own stories. They are designed for children in the primary grades and above and often let children illustrate their creations as well.

With the hundreds of titles available, it is difficult for most teachers and caregivers to find the time to adequately review software before purchasing. Fortunately, good resources can help narrow the list of options down to a manageable size:

- **Children's Technology Review.** Formerly called Children's Software Review, this company produces a monthly electronic newsletter that can be purchased

Developmentally Appropriate Practice . . .
DRILL-AND-PRACTICE SOFTWARE

Estimates indicate that nearly three-fourths of all software being produced for young children is drill-and-practice. In this software, the computer prompts the user to respond in a specific, predesigned way to problems it poses.

Despite the fact that these programs can be used less creatively by children (much like *self-correcting toys* such as the Montessori graduated cylinders), some drill-and-practice software does make rote learning experiences more interesting. As long as it is not the primary type of software available, you can use some drill-and-practice software programs in early childhood settings. The following examples highlight some effective uses of this type of software:

- **Learning arithmetic/number facts.** Most of us can remember the traditional flash cards used to teach basic arithmetic facts. This approach, although effective in many ways, is not exciting. Several software companies have produced much more motivating ways to learn these basic facts. "Math Rabbit" by The Learning Company and the "Math Blaster" series by Knowledge Adventure are good examples.

- **Spelling.** Another routine task faced by children in the primary grades is learning appropriate spellings of words. The "Spelling Blaster" by Knowledge Adventure presents more interesting activities for children.

- **Prereading and reading activities.** Letter recognition and phonics activities can be effective supplements to the whole language approach to reading. Knowledge Adventure, Disney Interactive, and The Learning Company all produce software programs that help with these tasks.

for an annual fee. It contains reviews of children's software and other new media (Children's Technology Review, 2010). Edited by Warren Buckleitner, this publication provides professional evaluations of more than 100 software titles and new media in each issue.

- **Association for Library Service to Children (ALSC).** Each year on its website, the ALSC publishes top picks for interactive software for young children (Association for Library Service to Young Children, 2010). They provide a description of the product, the cost, and a website where you can go for further information.

- **Parenting websites.** Numerous websites provide reviews of children's software by educators, families, and children. While many lack specific expertise in software design and review, their input is valuable in making initial assessments of software possibilities. An example of this type is *SuperKids Educational Software Review* (SuperKids Educational Software Review, 2010).

Helping Families Select Computer Software and Video Games

Families play critical roles in technology use. While many homes have computers, Internet service, and video game options for children, there is limited information regarding the best programs and games for young children. With the thousands of software titles and games available, it is difficult for families to choose the ones that will best meet their children's needs and interests. You can help in several ways:

- **Software and video game review options.** Perhaps the most useful assistance that you can provide is to share with families resources for rating software and games. The resources presented earlier can help families select appropriate software and games for home use.

- **Share software selections from the early childood setting.** Consider having the software options you are using in your early childhood program available for families to review. For example, you may want to take time during an open house to let families examine available software.

- **Characteristics of quality software.** In the program newsletter or in a group meeting, you could provide families with information on the limitations of drill-and-practice software and the characteristics of playful software.

Other Technologies and Their Uses

While television and computers are important technologies that affect the lives of young children, other technologies can also provide positive learning opportunities in early childhood settings. Digital cameras, video recorders, DVD players, and an assortment of Internet tools can all be used in a variety of interesting ways by young children. These options will be described in the sections below.

Digital Cameras

Digital cameras are an inexpensive and common option for young children to use. One important benefit of using a digital camera is that you don't have to worry about taking a bad photo or taking too many pictures of an event or person.

Digital cameras provide many opportunities for learning.

Just push the delete button and you can continue to take more photographs. This allows children to experiment with the camera and develop their photographic skills without risk of failure. Besides being a highly motivating activity for young children, there is evidence to suggest that photography enhances learning as well (Einarsdottir, 2005; Neumann-Hinds, 2007). Following are some ways to use digital photography in an early childhood setting:

- **Picture walks.** Have children take pictures while taking a walk through the local neighborhood or as part of a field trip (Byrnes & Wasik, 2009). Later, have them talk about their pictures to help build vocabulary.

- **Collect data.** Children can use the digital camera to collect data for a science activity (Neumann-Hinds, 2007). For example, taking photographs each week of a plant and its growth provides a record of what is observed and measured.

- **Document learning.** Photographing a completed block structure or an early writing experience can document for families and others the progress that the child is making in his or her development.

- **Photo-narration.** A child can take photographs of objects or events and then describe the photographs to an adult who writes down the narrative (Marinak, Strickland, & Keat, 2010). This early literacy experience helps children make connections between their oral language and the written word.

- **Create picture books.** Photography can form the basis for exciting writing activities for young children. Creating a story narrative with pictures and then assisting the child in writing about what is happening in the photographs can be highly motivating for young children (Baskwill & Harkins, 2009).

Video/Audio Recorders and Players

It is clear that children are exposed to video/audio recorders and players from an early age and are comfortable with their use. A recent study by the Kaiser Family Foundation (2010) indicates that young people from 8 to 18 use a music/audio player an average of 2 hours and 31 minutes each day. Cell phones are also being used regularly by younger children, most of which have cameras and video recorders built into the phone itself. While studies indicate that heavy media use can lead to lower academic performance (Kaiser Family Foundation, 2010), there are times when video/audio recorders and players can be used effectively in early childhood settings:

- **Music for fun and learning.** Music is an enjoyable and educational addition to any early childhood setting. Having a music player available for listening pleasure throughout the day is a time-honored element of developmentally appropriate practice. In addition, many songs can be used to teach concepts to young children. Another option would be to audio record young children's musical expressions for assessment purposes or simply as a fun way to share the child's music making with others.

- **Video recordings of activities and events.** A good cell phone with a video recording option can be an enjoyable and easy way for either children or adults to record some of the activities and events that occur in early childhood settings. For example, a short video of a child playing in the block center would be a good record of the materials used and peer interactions. For families who can't come into the early childhood setting, longer video recordings could be made to provide information about events taking place there.

Internet Tools

Information available over the Internet continues to grow rapidly. Much of this content is directed at young children, while other options may be valuable in your work with families. In many ways this wealth of information is a positive development and should encourage you to search for helpful sites. But you will also need to carefully review the content on each site before encouraging children and families to go there. Not all website content is of equal value. You may want to do an Internet search for "educational search engines" and find an option that helps you do an initial sorting of potentially valuable sites (Technology and Young Children Interest Forum, 2008).

Web pages for children. While you will probably find many good curriculum ideas and resources for your early childhood program on the Internet, be aware that several websites can be used to extend and enrich other activities you plan for young children. To avoid overwhelming them, provide them with a small number of select sites and help them become comfortable in using them. Lisenbee (2009) suggests the following website options for prekindergarten children:

- **Storyline Online.** The Screen Actors Guild Foundation sponsors this website, which provides streamed video of several high-quality children's books being read by well-known actors. Additional ideas for activities to accompany these stories are also presented.
- **Starfall.** This website is provided as a free public service and is designed to help children learn to read using phonics. The site is well designed and allows children to navigate through the games and activities independently.
- **WeatherBug.** This site may need more adult guidance to use. It provides live local weather reports that include current temperature, wind speed, and future weather forecasts. Since this site provides live weather "snapshots," wind speeds in particular can change rapidly and are of high interest to young children.

Now that you have read about technology options for young children, spend some time observing in an early childhood setting to see which of these options are available and the effectiveness of their use. The *Observing Development* feature in this section provides a framework for making this observation.

Observing Development...
TECHNOLOGY USE IN EARLY CHILDHOOD SETTINGS

Choose either prekindergarten or primary children and observe the technology they use. Create a rating scale like the sample below to make your observation. Circle the number that best matches your assessment for each technology available:

Technology	Adult supervision			Social interaction			Supports program learning		
Computer	5	3	1	5	3	1	5	3	1
	High		Low	High		Low	High		Low
Digital Camera	5	3	1	5	3	1	5	3	1
	High		Low	High		Low	High		Low
Visual/Audio Recorders/ Players	5	3	1	5	3	1	5	3	1
	High		Low	High		Low	High		Low
Other Technnologies	5	3	1	5	3	1	5	3	1
	High		Low	High		Low	High		Low

Reflect and Apply

1. Based on what you observed in the early childhood setting, do you think technology was effective in stimulating learning and development for young children? Why or why not?

2. Of the technologies you observed, what was the most interesting to young children? Was the technology being used in developmentally appropriate ways?

3. If you had been the early childhood professional in the setting you observed, could you have done anything to enhance developmentally appropriate technology use?

Tools for communicating with families. Because of the increasing numbers of families using a variety of technologies, you should consider communication strategies that incorporate technology (Mitchell, Foulger, & Wetzel, 2009). There are two main strategies that could strengthen your ability to better communicate with families. The first is through e-mail messages. This quick and inexpensive option can be used successfully to share a positive experience from the classroom day, seek assistance with a field trip, or remind families of upcoming events. Make sure to use your best writing skills in preparing these messages. The other technology option that you may want to consider is creating a classroom homepage. The *Developmentally Appropriate Practice* feature in this section provides more information on this option.

Developmentally Appropriate Practice...
CREATING A PROGRAM WEBPAGE

Creating a website for your early childhood program can typically be done with a minimum of computer expertise. If you are part of a larger program that already has a website, it is relatively simple to add a link on that site for your own use. But even starting from the very beginning, there are many good resources that can assist you in creating a website (Mitchell et al., 2009). If you choose to create a website, be sure to share the same information in other ways so that families without Internet access can still be informed. The uses of a website as a communication tool are many, and include (Charland, 1998; Mitchell et al., 2009):

- Sharing discipline procedures
- Identifying homework and grading policies
- Discussing home learning tasks
- Asking for assistance in the early childhood setting or at home
- Getting feedback from families via a comments form
- Sharing the calendar of program events for the week or month
- Opening a dialogue with parents on a variety of topics relevant to the classroom, such as issues surrounding television viewing

summary

Television and Video Games

Television has a significant impact on young children's lives. They spend a large amount of time viewing TV, often watching programs with sexual themes, violence, and misleading advertising. Both strengths and weaknesses are associated with children's use of video games. Children who use these games extensively are limited in the time they have for other play options.

Computers and Young Children

Although computers are viewed as inappropriate for infants and toddlers, with appropriate software and assistive technology (when needed), children age 3 and above can use computers in developmentally appropriate ways when playful software is used.

Selecting Software Programs

Selecting quality software is the teacher's or caregiver's most important task if computers are to be effectively used. There are literally thousands of software options, but only a limited number that are appropriate for use in the early childhood classroom.

Other Technologies and their Uses

Digital cameras are an easy and fun way for children to engage in quality learning experiences and to document their learning. Audio and video recorders and players can be a positive experience when used in developmentally appropriate ways by young children. Internet websites, when selected carefully, can be positive learning opportunities for young children. Having a program website to communicate with families is an effective strategy.

for reflection and discussion

1. Would you encourage the use of video games at home or in the early childhood setting? Why or why not?

2. How important are computers in early childhood programs? Would you place a higher value on computers than some of the more traditional items (such as blocks) found in many programs? Discuss your thinking with others.

3. Search for a software program that you think is a quality option for young children and share it with others.

4. Write 2 to 3 paragraphs explaining the strengths and limitations of using digital cameras in early childhood settings. Discuss your conclusions with others.

MyEducationLab

Go to Topic 7: Curriculum/Content Areas in the MyEducationLab (www.myeducationlab.com) for *Teaching Young Children*, where you can:

- Find learning outcomes for Curriculum/Content Areas along with the national standards that connect to these outcomes.

- Complete Assignments and Activities that can help you more deeply understand the chapter content.

- Apply and practice your understanding of the core teaching skills identified in the chapter with the Building Teaching Skills and Dispositions learning units.

- Examine challenging situations and cases presented in the IRIS Center Resources.

- Check your comprehension on the content covered in the chapter with the Study Plan. Here you will be able to take a chapter quiz, receive feedback on your answers, and then access Review, Practice, and Enrichment activities to enhance your understanding of chapter content.

- Use the Online Lesson Plan Builder to practice lesson planning and integrating national and state standards into your planning.

glossary

Absorbent mind Montessori believed that during the first 3 years of life children learn in ways that are different from adults. She felt that they unconsciously absorb information from the environment around them and, like a sponge, simply soak up information into their developing minds.

Active listening A guidance technique where the teacher listens carefully to what the child is saying and doing, then repeats back in her own words what she has heard the child say.

Adventure Playgrounds Seen mostly in Europe, these playgrounds provide a trained play leader and a variety of materials for children to move, manipulate, and enjoy. Examples of materials include scrap lumber, bricks, tires, rope, hammers, nails, saws, a fire pit, and animals.

Advocacy Early childhood professionals promoting the causes of children and families.

Anecdotal record A written summary of teacher observations of young children as they work and play in the classroom or on the playground.

Antibias curriculum An approach to integrating diversity throughout the curriculum that was developed by Louise Derman-Sparks. The program provides general principles that allow teachers and caregivers to create an appropriate curriculum for their classrooms.

Assessment Techniques used to understand the impact of classroom activities and interactions on the growth and development of young children.

Assistive technology A term used to describe devices and services that improve the functional capabilities of students with disabilities.

Associate of Arts in Teaching A community college degree option that is intended to better prepare students who are planning to complete a 2-year degree and then transfer to a 4-year college or university to pursue state teacher certification.

Association for Childhood Education International (ACEI) This professional organization for teachers focuses on children from birth through adolescence. The early years have been a major interest of many members. Members receive the journal *Childhood Education* and have the opportunity to participate in national and regional conferences.

Associative play Beginning at about 3½ years of age, children start to engage in true social play. They borrow and loan play materials, and group members are engaged in similar activities.

Atelier A special workshop area in the Reggio Emilia classroom designed for recording in visual form what students learn as they engage in projects of their own choosing.

Atelierista A person hired to work in a Reggio Emilia school who assists the other teachers and helps children develop documentation to summarize learning experiences.

At-risk Children who are at risk may experience developmental delays due to negative genetic or environmental factors such as poverty, low birth weight, or maternal diabetes. These children have not been identified as having disabilities, but, without adequate intervention, they may develop problems.

Attachment An emotional bond that occurs between two people and is essential to healthy relationship building. The work of John Bowlby suggests that this bonding begins at birth and is well under way by about 6 months of age. Establishing at least one significant attachment bond during the first 2 years of life is considered critical to healthy social and emotional development.

Attention-deficit/hyperactivity disorder (ADHD) ADHD is characterized by a short attention span and a tendency to be restless and impulsive.

Bank Street approach An early childhood program model developed at the Bank Street College in New York in the 1930s. This model continues to have a strong influence on theory and practice in the field.

Before- and after-school care A child-care option for parents who work either before or after regular school hours. These programs may be provided at the school, or children may travel to other sites to receive care.

Behavior modification Based on the theoretical perspectives of behaviorism, the three basic techniques of positive reinforcement, punishment, and ignoring are used as guidance and discipline strategies with children.

Behaviorism A psychological approach to teaching and learning in which actions by the teacher and others in the learning environment reinforce desired behavior of students. This approach has limited appropriate applications in the early childhood classroom.

Body awareness The child's ability to locate, name, and correctly describe body part functions.

Botany The scientific investigation of plants.

Caldecott award Award given to the best illustrated children's book of the year.

Casa dei Bambini (Children's House) Located in the slums of Rome, Casa dei Bambini was where Maria Montessori further developed her theories about children and refined her teaching techniques.

Checklist An observation instrument, often created by teachers and caregivers, to record the numbers and types of behaviors young children display in early childhood settings.

Chemistry The study of substances and what happens when they are combined or come in contact with one another.

Child-care centers Programs located in buildings either designed for young children or remodeled to be used with them. Large numbers of children are typically enrolled in these programs, with several teachers hired to work with different groups of children.

Children with disabilities The federal government has defined categories of disabilities for children and provides assistance to schools based on these categories. Specific mental, emotional, and physical disabilities, as well as combinations of disabilities, are all defined by the federal government.

Children with special needs Children who need specialized assistance, support, and/or materials in the early childhood setting to maximize their growth and development.

Children's Choice Awards An annual list of books that are appropriate for children throughout the early childhood and elementary/middle school years.

Classification Putting objects or ideas with similar characteristics into groups.

Classroom centers Spaces in early childhood classrooms where children can independently explore materials and activities of their own choosing in playful ways. Typical centers in the preschool classroom include such things as blocks, dramatic play, and art.

Cognitive development The continuing process of learning about the world and all of its many components.

Cognitive play A framework for categorizing childhood play that identifies the types of intellectual functioning occurring in play. As they mature, children engage in higher levels of intellectual functioning in play.

Cognitive structures theory of play Piaget suggests that one of the two major ways that children learn about the world is by taking in information from the environment and fitting it into already existing concepts. He calls this process assimilation. When children play they are engaging primarily in the process of assimilation.

Competence A part of self-esteem that suggests you can accomplish tasks and achieve goals.

Complex emotions Emotions are feelings that come in response to other people, experiences, or circumstances. Complex emotions include frustration, annoyance, jealousy, and boredom.

Construction play Children from about 2 to 3 years of age engage in construction play where they make something out of the materials available to them.

Constructivist approach The belief held by most early childhood educators that children create knowledge of the world for themselves as they interact with the people and things in their environment.

Constructivist education The belief that individuals actively construct knowledge on an ongoing basis as they constantly receive new information and engage in experiences that lead us to revise our understanding of the world.

Constructivist learning Learning that emphasizes children creating knowledge about the world through interactions with the people and things in their environment.

Control The part of self-esteem that describes the degree to which people feel they can influence the events around them.

Cooperative play Beginning at about 4½ years of age, children's social play demonstrates division of labor, working on a group project, or cooperating to attain a common goal.

Cooperative-competitive play Social play type for older children beginning at about age 7 or 8 that involves activities formally patterned toward team victory. Organized team sports such as soccer and baseball are examples of this play type.

Co-playing A type of adult involvement in play where the teacher actually enters the children's play but allows them to control the activities.

Core emotions Emotions are feelings that come in response to other people, experiences, or circumstances. Core emotions are intense, relatively pure emotions that include joy, anger, sadness, and fear.

Corporate child care Child care that is provided on-site at business locations as a convenience and service to employees. Some corporations manage the child-care program themselves, while others contract with child-care providers to offer the service on-site.

Curriculum All of the activities, experiences, and interactions available to children in early childhood settings.

Curriculum goals Broad learning outcomes that identify the key results anticipated from the educational process. Goals are often created as part of a school-wide mission statement identifying the philosophy and values of the program.

Deficiency needs The two most basic levels of needs in Maslow's hierarchy of needs. These physiological and safety and security needs are considered deficiency needs because their absence causes physical illness.

Developmental interactionalist model A concept of the Bank Street model for early learning. The curriculum in this model addresses all aspects of child development in a setting that encourages both interpersonal interactions and learning experiences that integrate intellectual, social, and emotional understandings.

Developmental screening A short assessment administered by a trained adult to identify children who may have a disability or learning problem.

Developmentally appropriate practice (DAP) Basing the curriculum on an in-depth understanding of child development and learning. Rather than focusing first on what is to be learned, the teacher in a developmentally appropriate classroom begins by working hard to understand the developmental abilities of the class and then makes decisions about what should be taught.

Disabled/disability A child who is disabled or has a disability is unable to do something or has difficulty with a specific task.

Discipline That part of the guidance process in which the adult is responding to children who misbehave.

Discipline-based art education An approach to art education that promotes developing the technical skills needed in art production, plus the teaching of four disciplines that help children create, understand, and appreciate art: art production, art history, art criticism, and aesthetics.

Discovery learning Jerome Bruner's emphasis on the importance of learning through active physical and/or mental manipulations of materials or problems to discover answers to issues presented.

Documentation/documenting learning experiences A concept associated with the Reggio Emilia program where young children create a record (picture, story, photograph, etc.) summarizing for others the work they have accomplished and the processes they have used in discovering new knowledge.

Dramatic play From about age 3 to 7, in their cognitive play, children pretend that one object is something else or take on a role other than being children.

Early Childhood Environment Rating Scale An extensive and well-respected environmental rating scale.

Early Head Start A federally funded program focusing on children younger than age 3. A part of the Head Start program, this more recent option is a result of the growing awareness that working with very young low-income children pays big dividends to society.

Early intervention programs Programs designed to help identify young children's special needs and assist them in growth and development. Options for infants and toddlers are most common and often combine limited small-group experiences with home visits where the parent and home visitor work together to support the young child's development.

Earth and space science That portion of the sciences consisting of geology and astronomy.

Ecological model Urie Bronfenbrenner created an influential theory of human development that has been called an ecological model to describe the many different systems that contribute to the overall development of the child.

Educational Resources Information Center (ERIC) An important reference system that can provide quick and detailed assistance in locating information on children and families. This computer-based information retrieval system is free of charge to users.

Egocentric/egocentrism Piaget's belief that children during the early childhood years have a difficult time seeing things from any perspective other than their own. Taking things literally is another characteristic of egocentrism.

Emergent literacy The idea that learning to read and write has much in common with oral language development.

English language learners Children whose first language is other than English and who are learning a second language, typically in the school setting.

Family Day Care Rating Scale (FDCRS) An environmental rating tool used to assess the physical space in family child-care settings.

Family home child care Early childhood programs that operate out of the caretaker's home and enroll only a small number of children.

Fine motor development The smaller muscles in the hands and feet, which gradually mature during the early childhood years so that children can engage in such activities as cutting, lacing, buttoning, painting, balancing, and writing.

Formative assessment Generally more informal in nature, this form of assessment is used throughout the curriculum implementation cycle to determine the effectiveness of lessons and activities and to check on child understandings.

Formal observations Those times when the early childhood professional records the actions and/or words of children to better understand the impact of the curriculum on growth and development.

Functional play From birth to about age 2, children play by engaging in simple, repetitive muscle movements. This is the lowest level of cognitive functioning in play.

Games with rules At approximately 7 years of age, children engage in cognitive play activities requiring them to agree to a set of rules before beginning play and accept the defined penalties for breaking the rules.

General developmental abilities The average/normal cognitive, social, and emotional abilities that can be expected of children at specific ages.

Geometry The study of two- and three-dimensional shapes and how they are related to one another.

Gifted Children who are gifted demonstrate excellence in an aspect of development that is well beyond most children of the same age.

Gross motor development The large muscles of the arms and legs, which gradually develop in young children so that they can do such things as walk, run, throw, and catch.

Growth needs The higher levels of needs in Maslow's hierarchy of needs. They are the individual's attempts at becoming a more satisfied and healthy person.

Guidance All the adult does or says to influence the behavior of the child.

Guidance techniques Since guidance is listed in the glossary, I don't think this term needs a definition.

Head Start A federally funded program begun in 1964 that provides quality comprehensive care to low-income children who are 3 to 5 years of age. In addition to the more traditional curriculum, Head Start provides resources and assistance with medical, dental, nutritional, and mental health needs.

Hierarchy of human needs Abraham Maslow's theory that a person's most basic needs must be met before higher level needs can be successfully addressed.

Hierarchy of needs Abraham Maslow's concept that basic needs such as food, shelter, and clothing must be satisfied before higher-level needs such as belongingness and affection can be met.

Holophrastic speech At around 2 years of age, children use one word utterances like "more" to communicate complete thoughts such as "I want more milk."

I-Message This guidance strategy helps children understand the impact of their actions on others. It is a statement that includes the personal pronoun I, the feelings experienced by the adult, and the actions of the child that caused those feelings.

Ignoring A behavior modification technique where the teacher refrains from giving any verbal or nonverbal feedback for inappropriate behaviors that are attention-seeking.

Individual Education Program (IEP) Individualized learning and development plans for children with special needs beginning at age 3. These plans are designed collaboratively by teachers and caregivers, educational specialists, and families.

Individualized Family Service Plan (IFSP) Individualized learning and development plans designed by caregivers, educational specialists, and families for infants and toddlers with special needs.

Individuals with Disabilities Education Act In 1990, after several revisions, Public Law (PL) 94–142 was renamed the Individuals with Disabilities Act (IDEA). IDEA was last amended in 2004. The intent of this law has been to educate all children with special needs in classrooms with their normally developing peers to the greatest extent possible.

Infant/Toddler Environment Rating Scale (ITERS) A rating tool that is being effectively used to assess the physical spaces of very young children.

Informal observations Times when the early childhood professional takes a moment or two between other activities to simply stop and listen and observe what children are saying or doing.

Integrated curriculum Learning experiences that include multiple subject matter areas as a natural part of the curriculum. Good integrated learning often included mathematics, social studies, literacy learning, and more in activities that are of interest to young children.

Interactionist theory of language acquisition This theory suggests that language acquisition combines an innate ability with environmental influence. The two factors interact in complex ways as children learn language.

Key experiences Teachers in the High/Scope program emphasize eight important areas of study as they plan for their time with children.

Language Either oral or hand-signed communication between humans.

Language acquisition device (LAD) A theory of language acquisition suggesting that children have an innate ability when exposed to language to gradually make sense of the rules for oral communication.

Language experience approach A strategy used to help children make connections between oral and written language. Children dictate information about personal experiences while an adult writes them down.

Learning disabilities Children with learning disabilities are found in almost every classroom. Although they have no outward signs of problems, these children struggle with one or more basic learning tasks.

Life science That portion of the sciences consisting of botany and zoology.

Literacy The ability to make meaning from language in written form.

Logicomathematical relationships Understanding that objects can be organized into groups according to common characteristics and ordered from smallest to largest.

Long-term plans Curriculum plans that give a sense of direction for several weeks, months, or even the entire school year. Because they are general plans, they provide a flexible framework for building a more specific curriculum as the year progresses.

Looping A situation where a teacher remains with the same students for 2 or more years. For example, a first-grade teacher could work with the same students from first through third grades before "looping" back to a new group of first-grade students at the end of the 3-year period.

Maturationist Those who believe that physical and mental growth are determined primarily by heredity. Arnold Gesell is considered a maturationist.

Measurement Finding the height, weight, volume, and dimensions of objects. These are important mathematical abilities.

Metacommunication statements Verbalizations used to structure and organize play. "Let's pretend this rope is a snake." "First we'll go to the market, then the toy store."

Military child care An early childhood program funded by the federal government as a benefit to those engaged in military service around the world.

Morphology The rules for combining sounds to form words within a specific language.

Movement skills Those physical skills needed for basic locomotion, stability, and manipulation.

Multiage classroom Classroom organization in which two or more grades are grouped together for instruction. For example, rather than having separate groups of 5-, 6-, and 7-year-old children, students are mixed together and provided instruction in the same room.

National Association for the Education of Young Children (NAEYC) The largest professional association specifically organized to meet the needs of early childhood teachers and caregivers. Members receive the journal *Young Children* and are invited to participate in local, state, and national professional meetings to enhance their knowledge and skills as educators.

Natural and logical consequences Discipline strategies that help children make a clear link between their inappropriate behavior and the consequence for that activity. Natural consequences occur without adult intervention, while logical consequences are established by the early childhood professional.

Newbery award A prestigious award for the year's most distinguished new book for children.

No Child Left Behind Act of 2001 Federal legislation that provides financial incentives to schools that make good academic progress as measured on standardized tests, and penalizes those that demonstrate poor performance.

Objectives Specific learning outcomes in early childhood settings that describe in detail what children are expected to know or do.

Open-Air Nursery Margaret and Rachel McMillan opened this nursery school program in the late 1800s in London to help combat health problems of low-income children. The Open-Air Nursery was designed for children from 1 to 6 years of age and emphasized outdoor play.

Parallel play From about 2½ to 3½ years, children's social play consists of playing beside, but not with, others. There is an awareness of the children nearby but little interaction with them.

Parent cooperative An early childhood program in which each family unit is expected to spend a specified number of hours each month helping out in the classroom to keep the costs of schooling low.

Patterns The ability to recognize and create visual, auditory, spatial, and numerical patterns is an important mathematical understanding.

Phonemic awareness A developing awareness in children that oral language consists of sounds, syllables, and words.

Phonics instruction Teaching the relationships of sounds and sound combinations to their written counterparts.

Phonology The system of sounds used to make up words in a specific language.

Physical science That portion of the sciences consisting of physics and chemistry.

Physics The scientific study of the properties of matter and energy.

Plan-do-review sequence In the High/Scope model of early childhood education, the teacher encourages children to plan the tasks they want to accomplish during free-choice time, engage in those activities, and then spend time later in the day reflecting on what they learned.

Play as arousal seeking A theory of play based on the drive for optimal arousal. In an attempt to avoid boredom on the one hand and overstimulation on the other, people strive to reach just the right level of excitement. Play is a major opportunity for most of us to be stimulated.

Play experience Open-ended learning opportunities where children select interesting materials and use them in their own unique ways. Play materials usually do not require demonstration by the teacher.

Play tutoring A form of adult involvement in play where the adult takes at least partial control of the play situation to give directions or suggestions.

Portfolio An important assessment tool used by teachers and caregivers to compile and organize information about individual children. It includes materials such as examples of children's work, assessments, and observations made by teachers and caregivers.

Positive reinforcement Anything that immediately follows a behavior and increases the likelihood that the behavior will occur more often in the future.

Practitioner A person, who, in addition to presenting new and interesting ideas about child development and learning, has actually worked in the classroom teaching young children.

Pragmatics The understandings necessary for adapting language to different social situations.

Pre-exercise theory A theory of why children play that sees this activity as an opportunity to practice the skills necessary for adult life.

Pretend communication statements Verbalizations used during play that are appropriate to the roles children have adopted. "Hush, baby! Mom is on the telephone!"

Problem-solving strategies A form of guidance that is a co-operative effort in which both the student and teacher work through the issues of concern together.

Progressive movement An education effort often attributed to John Dewey that began in the 1920s and questioned the traditional methods and content of American schooling. Progressive education emphasized active learning and the importance of social interactions in teaching and learning.

Project An in-depth investigation about a topic that incorporates children's questions, interests, and theories about that topic.

Project approach Early childhood programs that place heavy emphasis on in-depth investigations of topics of interest to children and teachers. The Reggio Emilia program uses the project approach.

Project Follow Through A federally funded program begun in 1969 as a way to continue providing assistance to primary-age children from low-income families who had completed programs like Head Start.

Prompt Help given to assist a child in engaging in specific skills. Prompts can be verbal, gestural, modeled, or physical.

Psychoanalytic theory of play Based primarily on the work of Sigmund Freud, play is seen as being motivated by the pleasure principle. Pleasure is achieved, according to Freud, through wish fulfillment in play.

Public Law (PL) 94–142 Federal legislation enacted in the mid-1970s that requires public schools to provide all children age 3 and older who have special needs with a free and appropriate public education. Later revisions of this act extended the availability of these programs downward to include birth to age 3.

Punishment Any event or action that follows a behavior and decreases the likelihood that the behavior will occur again.

Redirection A form of guidance in which the teacher verbally redirects the child from his current activity to a more desirable one.

Relaxation theory A theory of why people play suggesting that we engage in play because of a deficit of energy. When we engage in tasks that are relatively new to us or that are demanding in some way, fatigue sets in and relaxation through play is needed to replenish our energy.

Restitution A form of punishment in which the teacher insists that the child engage in activities that correct or "make up for" the problem the child created.

School-Age Care Environment Rating Scale (SACERS) An environmental rating tool used to assess the physical space in primary school classrooms.

School-based child care Child care provided in public and private school settings. These programs are housed primarily in elementary schools, but some high schools have a child-care option for teen parents.

Scientific process/scientific inquiry The methods and attitudes used by scientists to gather information and solve problems.

Self-esteem/self-concept This is a psychological concept that refers to a person's subjective assessment of her abilities and skills.

Semantics The meanings given to words in a language.

Sensitive periods Montessori believed that children pass though numerous genetically programmed blocks of time during which they are especially eager and able to master certain tasks.

Seriation Ordering objects from smallest to largest.

Short-term plans Curriculum plans made weekly and daily to identify the activities in which children will be engaging. Whenever possible, teachers and caregivers should base these activities on children's interests.

Social play A description of categories of childhood play that is based on the social interactions occurring in play. As they mature, children gradually become more able to relate effectively with others in their play.

Social studies The study of relationships between people and environmental factors that influence their lives.

Socialization A process that begins at birth and continues throughout childhood. It involves learning to relate to a variety of people in many different circumstances.

Solitary play Until about 2½ years of age, children do not engage in social play. They play with toys that are different from those of children playing nearby and make no attempt to get close to or interact with others.

Spatial awareness In physical development, a child's ability to control his body as it moves through space.

Spatial density The amount of space per child in a play setting. It can be calculated by measuring the total area of the indoor setting, subtracting the unusable space, and then dividing that area by the number of children using the space.

Spatiotemporal relationships Relational concepts such as up/down, over/under, and inside/outside. Event sequences and cause-and-effect relationships are also included.

Stages of intellectual development The best-known and most influential aspect of Piaget's work is his definition of stages of intellectual development that children pass through on their way to mature thinking. During the early childhood years, children spend most of their time in the sensorimotor and preoperational stages of intellectual development.

Standardized tests Carefully developed exams created by professional designers in an attempt to accurately measure a child's performance in relation to other children or to some standard or objective.

Summative assessment A form of evaluation used at the end of a unit of study to provide evidence of what children know and are able to do.

Surplus energy theory A classical theory of why we play suggesting that each of us generates a finite level of energy that must be expended. Our first priority is to use that energy for survival. What is left over accumulates until it reaches a point where it must be used up through play.

Syntax The procedures for combining words into phrases and sentences in a specific language.

Telegraphic speech Abbreviated two-word sentences used by young 2-year-old children to communicate their complex thoughts.

Theorist A person who has identified and discussed important issues related to children and teaching, but has not actually put these ideas into practice working with children.

Theory of multiple intelligences Howard Gardner's belief that intelligence, rather than being a single, general capacity that each of us possesses, is of at least eight distinct types. The intelligences include linguistic, logicomathematical, spatial, musical, bodily kinesthetic, interpersonal, intrapersonal, and naturalistic.

Three-way conference A parent–teacher conference that includes the child. In some instances, the child leads all or part of the conference discussion.

Unity of the mental and physical Montessori's belief that full development of the intellect is not possible without physical activity.

Verbal thought Vygotsky's study of language and thought suggests that the two are separate very early in life. During the preschool years, however, language and thought begin to partially overlap to form what he called verbal thought.

Whole language learning Helping children construct reading and writing understandings from meaningful literacy activities.

Work task An activity in a Montessori classroom where children choose the materials they want to spend time with during work times. But, unlike free play, these items are used in very specific ways. Before the child is allowed to spend time independently on a work task, the teacher demonstrates how the materials are to be used.

Worth The component of self-esteem that represents the extent to which you like and value yourself.

Writing workshop A process for teaching writing in which the student first thinks about what she wants to write (prewrite), then drafts, revises her drafts, and finally edits for spelling, grammar, and punctuation problems.

Zone of proximal development A concept developed by Lev Vygotsky. It can be defined as the gap between the child's independent performance of a task and that which he can perform with the help of a more skilled peer or adult. Children who are functioning in their zone are being challenged and are growing with the assistance of others at a maximum rate.

Zoology The scientific study of animals.

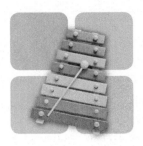

references

Aboud, F. (1988). *Children and prejudice.* London: Basil Blackwell.

Achilles, E. (1999). Creating music environments in early childhood programs. *Young Children, 54*(1), 21–26.

Administration for Children and Families. (2010a). *About Head Start.* Retrieved June 30, 2010 from http://eclkc.ohs.acf.hhs.gov/hslc/About%20Head%20Start.

Administration for Children and Families. (2010b). *Head Start stories.* Retrieved August 2, 2010 from http://eclkc.ohs.acf.hhs.gov/hslc/Family%20and%20Community%20Partnerships/New%20Parental%20Involvement/Engaging%20Parents/famcom_bul_00111_081505.html.

Ainsworth, M. (1973). The development of infant and mother attachment. In B. Caldwell & H. Ricciuti (Eds.), *Review of child development research* (Vol. 3, pp. 121–143). Chicago: University of Chicago Press.

Akcan, S. (2005). Puppet theater time in a French-immersion class. *Young Children, 60*(2), 38–41.

Alexander, K., & Day, M. (Eds.). (1999). *Discipline-based art education: A curriculum sampler.* Los Angeles: J. Paul Getty Trust.

Allison, J. (1999). On the expanded role of the teacher. *Childhood Education, 75*(5), 258–259.

American Academy of Pediatrics. (2006). *The importance of play in promoting healthy child development and maintaining strong parent–child bonds.* Retrieved November 2, 2006 from www.aap.org/pressroom/playFINAL.pdf.

American Academy of Pediatrics. (2010). Policy statement: Media education. *Pediatrics.* Retrieved December 22, 2010 from http://pediatrics.aappublications.org/cgi/reprint/peds.2010-1636v1.

American Academy of Pediatrics, American Public Health Association, & National Resource Center for Health and Safety in Child Care and Early Education. (2010). *Preventing childhood obesity in early care and education programs.* Elk Grove Village, IL: Authors.

American Association for the Advancement of Science. (1999). *Dialogue on early childhood science, mathematics, and technology education.* Washington, DC: Author.

American Humane Association. (2010). *Child sexual abuse.* Retrieved October 21, 2010 from www.americanhumane.org/about-us/newsroom/fact-sheets/child-sexual-abuse.html.

American Montessori Society. (2010). *American Montessori Society.* Retrieved July 5, 2010 from www.amshq.org/.

American Psychological Association. (2010). *Lesbian and gay parenting.* Retrieved July 30, 2010 from www.apa.org/pi/lgbt/resources/parenting-full.pdf.

An, H., & Seplocha, H. (2010). Video-sharing websites. Tools for developing pattern languages in children. *Young Children, 65*(5), 20–25.

Anders, E. (1996). *Jody and the bully.* New York: Grosset & Dunlap.

Anderson, C. (2010). Blocks: A versatile learning tool for yesterday, today, and tomorrow. *Young Children, 65*(2), 54–56.

Anderson, R., Hiebert, E., Scott, J., & Wilkinson, I. (1985). *Becoming a nation of readers: The report of the Commission on Reading.* Washington, DC: National Academy of Education.

Anglund, J. (1983). *A friend is someone who likes you.* San Diego, CA: Harcourt Brace Jovanovich.

Annie E. Casey Foundation. (2010). *2010 Kids count data book.* Retrieved July 30, 2010 from http://datacenter.kidscount.org/databook/2010/?cmpid=18.

Aries, P. (1962). *Centuries of childhood.* New York: Vintage Books.

Arnold, C. (2010). *Understanding schemas and emotions in early childhood.* Thousand Oaks, CA: Sage Publications.

Aronson, S., & Shope, T. (Eds.). (2004). *Managing infectious diseases in child care and schools: A quick reference guide.* Elk Grove Village, IL: American Academy of Pediatrics.

Arts Education Partnership. (2004). *Strategic plan 2004–2006.* Retrieved January 8, 2004 from aeparts.org/PDF%20Files/AEPStratPlan.pdf.

Association for Childhood Education International. (2003). *The child's right to creative thought and expression. A position paper of the Association for Childhood Education International.* Retrieved April 18, 2007 from www.acei.org/creativepp.htm.

Association for Library Services to Children. (2010). Great interactive software for kids. Spring 2010. Retrieved December 23, 2010 from www.ala.org/ala/mgrps/divs/alsc/awardsgrants/notalists/gisk/index.cfm.

Association Montessori Internationale. (2010). *Association Montessori Internationale.* Retrieved July 5, 2010 from www.montessori-ami.org/.

Association of Waldorf Schools of North America. (2010). *Waldorf education: An introduction.* Retrieved July 6, 2010 from www.whywaldorfworks.org/02_W_Education/index.asp.

Atlas, J., & Lapidus, L. (1987). Patterns of symbolic expression in subgroups of the childhood psychoses. *Journal of Clinical Psychology, 43*, 177–188.

Axline, V. (1947). *Play therapy.* Boston: Houghton Mifflin.

Axline, V. (1964). *DIBS: In search of self.* Boston: Houghton Mifflin.

Baghban, M. (2007). Scribbles, labels, and stories. *Young Children, 62*(1), 20–26.

Bailie, P. (2010). From the one-hour field trip to a nature preschool: Partnering with environmental organizations. *Young Children, 65*(4), 76–82.

Baker, K. (1966). *Let's play outdoors.* Washington, DC: National Association for the Education of Young Children.

Bakerlis, J. (2007). Children's art show: An educational family experience. *Young Children, 62*(1), 88–91.

Ball, W. (1995). Nurturing musical aptitude in children. *Dimensions of Early Childhood, 23*(4), 19–24.

Bamberger, H., Oberdorf, C., & Schultz-Ferrell, K. (2010). *Math misconceptions. PreK–grade 5.* Portsmouth, NH: Heinemann.

Bandura, A. (1989). Social cognitive theory. *Annals of Child Development, 6,* 1–60.

Bang, Y. (2009). Helping all families participate in family life. *Young Children, 64*(6), 97–99.

Bank Street College. (2010). *About Bank Street College.* Retrieved July 6, 2010 from www.bankstreet.edu/aboutbsc.

Baratta-Lorton, M. (1976). *Mathematics their way.* Menlo Park, CA: Addison-Wesley.

Barbour, C., Barbour, N., & Scully, C. (2011). *Families, schools, and communities: Building partnerships for educating children* (5th ed.). Upper Saddle River, NJ: Merrill/Prentice Hall.

Barnes, B., & Hill, S. (1983). Should young children work with microcomputers—Logo before Lego? *The Computing Teacher, 10*(9), 11–14.

Baron, L. (1991). Peer tutoring, microcomputer learning and young children. *Journal of Computing in Childhood Education, 2*(4), 27–40.

Barron, M. (1999). Three- and four-year-olds completing 150-piece puzzles? Impossible! *Young Children, 54*(5), 10–11.

Bartel, V. (2005). Merging literacies: A case study. *Childhood Education, 81*(4), 196–200.

Barton, R. (2005). When 1 + x = 2. *Northwest Education, 11*(2), 6–9.

Barton, R. (2006). Creating believers: Weaving together English, Spanish, and Russian, an Oregon school district aims at biliteracy for all students. *Northwest Education, 11*(3), 6–11.

Baskwill, J., & Harkins, M. (2009). Children, parents, and writing. Using photography in a family literacy workshop. *Young Children, 64*(5), 28–33.

Baumgartner, J., & Buchanan, T. (2010). Supporting each child's spirit. *Young Children, 65*(2), 90–95.

Bee, H., & Boyd, D. (2010). *The developing child* (12th ed.). Boston, MA: Allyn & Bacon.

Benelli, C., & Yongue, B. (1995). Supporting young children's motor skill development. *Childhood Education, 71*(4), 217–220.

Bennett-Armistead, S., Duke, N., & Moses, A. (2005). *Literacy and the youngest learner.* New York: Scholastic.

Bergen County Bar Association. (2006). *Child custody for educators and school mental health professionals.* Retrieved October 25, 2010 from www.njsbf.org/images/content/1/1/11094/childcustody.pdf.

Berk, L. (1994). Vygotsky's theory: The importance of make-believe play. *Young Children, 50*(1), 30–39.

Berry, J. (1986). *Teach me about series: My body.* Danbury, CT: Grolier.

Berson, I., & Baggerly, J. (2009). Building resilience to trauma: Creating a safe and supportive early childhood classroom. *Childhood Education, 85*(6), 375–379.

Bewick, C., & Kostelnik, M. (2004). Educating early childhood teachers about computers. *Young Children, 59*(3), 26–29.

Birckmayer, J., Kennedy, A., & Stonehouse, A. (2010). Sharing spoken language. Sounds, conversations, and told stories. *Young Children, 65*(1), 34–39.

Birmingham, C., Su, J., Hlinsky, J., Goldner, E., & Gao, M. (2005). The mortality rate of anorexia nervosa. *International Journal of Eating Disorders, 38*(2), 143–146.

Bisgaier, C., & Samaras, T. (2004). Young children try, try again using wood, glue, and words to enhance learning. *Young Children, 59*(4), 22–29.

Blake, S. (2009). Engage, investigate, and report: Enhancing the curriculum with scientific inquiry. *Young Children, 64*(6), 49–53.

Bloom, B. (1964). *Stability and change in human characteristics.* New York: John Wiley & Sons.

Blume, J. (1970). *Freckle juice.* Scarsdale, NY: Bradbury.

Bobys, A. (2000). What does emerging literacy look like? *Young Children, 55*(4), 16–22.

Boutte, G., & McCormick, C. (1992). Authentic multicultural activities. *Childhood Education, 68*(3), 140–144.

Bowlby, J. (1969). *Attachment and loss: Vol. I. Attachment.* New York: Basic Books.

Bowman, B., & Moore, E. (2006). *School readiness and social-emotional development: Perspectives on cultural diversity.* Washington, DC: National Black Child Development Institute.

Boyer, E. (1987, January). Keynote address to the National Invitational Conference sponsored by the Getty Center for Education in the Arts, Los Angeles.

Bramble, L. (2010). *About corporate day care facilities.* Retrieved June 30, 2010 from www.ehow.com/about_6324524_corporate-daycare-facilities.html.

Bramlett, M., & Mosher, W. (2002). *Cohabitation, marriage, divorce, and remarriage in the United States.* Washington, DC: National Center for Health Statistics.

Braun, S., & Edwards, E. (1972). *History and theory of early childhood education.* Belmont, CA: Wadsworth Publishing.

Braus, N., & Geidel, M. (2000). *Everyone's kids' books.* Brattleboro, VT: Everyone's Books.

Bredekamp, S. (Ed.). (1987). *Developmentally appropriate practice in early childhood programs serving children from birth through age 8.* Washington, DC: National Association for the Education of Young Children.

Bredekamp, S. (1993). Reflections on Reggio Emilia. *Young Children, 49*(1), 13–17.

Bredekamp, S. (1996). 25 years of educating young children: The High/Scope approach to preschool education. *Young Children, 51*(4), 57–61.

Bredekamp, S., & Copple, C. (Eds.). (1997). *Developmentally appropriate practice in early childhood programs* (rev. ed.). Washington, DC: National Association for the Education of Young Children.

Brenner, B. (1970). *Bodies.* New York: Dutton.

Bright Horizons Family Solutions. (2010). *Enhanced employee health, well-being, and engagement through dependent care supports.* Retrieved June 28, 2010 from www.brighthorizons.com/healthystudy/health_and_wellness_report_updates.pdf.

Bronfenbrenner, U. (1974). *Is early intervention effective?* (Vols. 1 & 2). Washington, DC: U.S. Government Printing Office.

Bronfenbrenner, U. (1979). *The ecology of human development.* Cambridge, MA: Harvard University Press.

Brookes, M. (1986). *Drawing with children: A creative teaching and learning method that works for adults, too.* New York: G.P. Putnam's Sons.

Brown, K. (2010). Young authors. Writing workshop in kindergarten. *Young Children, 65*(1), 24–28.

Brown, L., & Brown, M. (1988). *Dinosaurs divorce.* New York: Little Brown and Company.

Brown, N., Curry, N., & Tittnich, E. (1971). How groups of children deal with common stress through play. In N. Curry & S. Arnaud (Eds.), *Play: The child strives toward self-realization* (pp. 26–38). Washington, DC: National Association for the Education of Young Children.

Brown, T. (1991). *Someone special, just like you.* New York: Holt, Rinehart & Winston.

Bruce, C. (1998). *Young children and the arts: Making creative connections.* Washington, DC: Arts Education Partnership.

Bruchac, J. (1993). *The first strawberries.* New York: Dial Books.

Bruder, M. (2000). *The Individual Family Service Plan (IFSP).* ERIC Digest #E605. Retrieved February 23, 2004 from http://ericec.org/digests/e605.html.

Bruner, J. (1960). *The process of education.* New York: Vintage Books.

Bruner, J. (1966). *Toward a theory of instruction.* Cambridge, MA: Harvard University Press.

Bruner, J. (1972). The nature and uses of immaturity. *American Psychologist, 27,* 687–708.

Bryant, P., MacLean, M., Bradley, L., & Crossland, J. (1990). Rhyme and alliteration, phoneme detection, and learning to read. *Developmental Psychology, 26*(3), 451–455.

Buck, D. (2009). A good adventure playground is never finished. *London Play News,* Summer 2009, pp. 1–7. Retrieved February 3, 2011 from www.londonplay.org.uk/file/1446.pdf.

Bunker, L. (1991). The role of play and motor skill development in building children's self-confidence and self-esteem. *The Elementary School Journal, 91*(5), 467–471.

Bureau of Labor Statistics. (2009). *Occupational outlook handbook, 2010–2011 edition.* Retrieved June 30, 2010 from www.bls.gov/oco/ocos069.htm.

Burlingame, H. (2005). The four seasons kindergarten. *Play, Policy, & Practice, 9*(2), 1–6.

Burton, V. (1939). *Mike Mulligan and his steam shovel.* Boston: Houghton Mifflin.

Byrnes, J., & Wasik, B. (2009). Picture this: Using photography as a learning tool in early childhood classrooms. *Childhood Education, 85*(4), 243–248.

Campbell, B. (1992). Multiple intelligences in action. *Childhood Education, 68*(4), 197–201.

Campbell, P. (1998). *Songs in their heads: Music and its meaning in children's lives.* New York: Oxford University Press.

Campbell, P., & Scott-Kassner, C. (2006). *Music in childhood: From preschool through the elementary grades.* Belmont, CA: Thomson Schirmer Press.

Canfield, J., & Wells, H. (1994). *100 ways to enhance self-concept in the classroom* (2nd ed.). Boston: Allyn & Bacon.

Capizzano, J., & Main, R. (2005). *Many young children spend long hours in child care.* Washington, DC: Urban Institute. Retrieved January 20, 2011 from www.urban.org/url.cfm?ID=311154.

Carey, K. (2003). *The funding gap: Low-income and minority students still receive fewer dollars in many states.* Retrieved October 5, 2003 from www2.edtrust.org/NR/rdonlyres/EE004C0AD7B8-40A6-8A03-1F26B8228502/0/funding2003.pdf.

Carle, E. (1985). *My very first book of shapes.* New York: Harper & Row.

Carlson, F. (2006). *Essential touch: Meeting the needs of young children.* Washington, DC: National Association for the Education of Young Children.

Carlson, F. (2009). Rough & tumble play 101. *Child Care Information Exchange, 31*(4), 70–73.

Carlsson-Paige, N., & Levin, D. (1986). The butter battle book: Uses and abuses with young children. *Young Children, 41*(3), 37–42.

Carrick, D. (1985). *Milk.* New York: Greenwillow.

Carter, P. (2005). The modern multi-age classroom. *Educational Leadership, 63*(1), 54–58.

Cascio, E. (2010). What happened when kindergarten went universal? *Education Next, Spring 2010.* Retrieved June 28, 2010 from http://educationnext.org/files/ednext_20102_62.pdf.

Casey, L. (2008). The role of play in assessing, evaluating, and intervening with children with developmental delays. *Play, Policy, and Practice Connections, 11*(2), 2–4.

Casey Family Foundation. (2008). *Fact sheet: Educational outcomes for children and youth in foster and out-of-home care.* Retrieved July 30, 2010 from www.casey.org/Resources/Publications/pdf/EducationalOutcomesFactSheet.pdf.

Castle, K. (1990). Children's invented games. *Childhood Education, 67,* 82–85.

Castro, D., Bryant, D., Peisner-Feinberg, E., & Skinner, M. (2004). Parent involvement in Head Start programs: The role of parent, teacher, and classroom characteristics. *Early Childhood Research Quarterly, 19*(3), 413–430.

Catron, C., & Allen, J. (2008). *Early childhood curriculum: A creative play option* (4th ed.). Upper Saddle River, NJ: Merrill/Prentice Hall.

Center for Communication Policy. (1997). *The UCLA television violence monitoring report.* Retrieved December 22, 2003 from The University of California at Los Angeles website: www.ccp.ucla.edu/pages/VReports.asp.

Center on Education Policy. (2008). *Instructional time in elementary schools: A closer look at changes for specific subjects.* Retrieved August 30, 2010 from www.cep-dc.org/_data/n_0001/resources/live/InstructionalTimeFeb2008.pdf.

Center on the Social and Emotional Foundations of Early Learning. (2010). *About us.* Retrieved November 2, 2010 from http://csefel.vanderbilt.edu/about.html.

Centers for Disease Control and Prevention. (2010). *Attention-deficit/hyperactivity disorder.* Retrieved July 14, 2010 from www.cdc.gov/ncbddd/adhd/data.html.

Centers for Disease Control and Prevention. (September 10, 2010). State specific trends in fruit and vegetable consumption among adults: United States 2000–2009. *Morbidity and Mortality Weekly Report, 59*(35), 1–6.

Cesarone, B. (1994). Video games and children. *ERIC Digest,* EDO-PS-94-3. Urbana, IL: ERIC Clearinghouse on Elementary and Early Childhood Education.

Chaille, C., & Britain, L. (2003). *The young child as scientist: A constructivist approach to early childhood science education* (3rd ed.). New York: Longman.

Chalufour, I., & Worth, K. (2004). *Building structures with young children.* St. Paul, MN: Redleaf Press.

Chalufour, I., & Worth, K. (2006). *Exploring water with young children.* St. Paul, MN: Redleaf Press.

Charland, T. (1998). Classroom homepage connections. *T. H. E. Journal, 25*(9), 62–64.

Charlesworth, R. (2005). *Experiences in math for young children* (5th ed.). Albany, NY: Delmar.

Charlesworth, R. (2011). *Understanding child development* (8th ed.). Albany, NY: Delmar.

Child Welfare Information Gateway. (2008). *What is child abuse and neglect?* Retrieved October 21, 2010 from www.childwelfare.gov/pubs/factsheets/whatiscan.pdf.

Children's Defense Fund. (1999). *The state of America's children: Yearbook 1999.* Washington, DC: Author.

Children's Defense Fund. (2010). *The state of America's children 2010.* Washington, DC: Author.

Children's Technology Review. (2010). *Children's Technology Review,* December 2010. Retrieved December 23, 2010 from http://childrenstech.com/about.

Chomsky, N. (1965). *Aspects of a theory of syntax.* Cambridge, MA: MIT Press.

Christensen, L., & Kirkland, L. (2010). Early childhood visual arts curriculum. *Childhood Education, 86*(2), 87–91.

Christie, J., Vukelich, C., & Enz, B. (2011). *Teaching language and literacy—Preschool through the elementary grades* (4th ed.). New York: Longman.

Clemens, J. (1996). Gardening with children. *Young Children, 51*(4), 22–27.

Clements, D., & Sarama, J. (2003). Young children and technology. What *does* the research say? *Young Children, 58*(6), 34–40.

Clothier, S., & Poppe, J. (2010). *New research: Early education as economic investment.* Retrieved June 30, 2010 from www.ncsl.org/IssuesResearch/HumanServices/NewResearchEarlyEducationasEconomicInvestme/tabid/16436/Default.aspx.

Cohen, L. (2009). Exploring cultural heritage in a kindergarten classroom. *Young Children, 64*(3), 72–77.

Coleman, J. (1966). *Equality of educational opportunity.* Washington, DC: U.S. Government Printing Office.

Comenius, J. (1896). *School of infancy.* Boston: Heath.

Committee for Children. (2010). *Second Step: A violence prevention curriculum.* Retrieved November 3, 2010 from www.cfchildren.org/programs/ssp/overview/.

Connor-Kuntz, F., & Dummer, G. (1996). Teaching across the curriculum: Language-enriched physical education for preschool children. *Adapted Physical Activity Quarterly, 13*(3), 302–315.

Consumer Product Safety Commission. (2008). *Public playground safety handbook.* Retrieved August 27, 2010 from www.cpsc.gov/cpscpub/pubs/325.pdf.

Cooke, M., Ford, J., Levine, J., Bourke, C., Newell, L., & Lapidus, G. (2007). The effects of city-wide implementation of Second Step on elementary students' prosocial and aggressive behaviors. *The Journal of Primary Prevention, 28*(2), 93–115.

Cooke, T. (2000). *So much.* Cambridge, MA: Candlewick Press.

Copley, J. (2010). *The young child and mathematics* (2nd ed.). Washington, DC: National Association for the Education of Young Children.

Copple, C., & Bredekamp, S. (Eds.). (2009). *Developmentally appropriate practice in early childhood programs serving children from birth through age 8* (3rd ed.). Washington, DC: National Association for the Education of Young Children.

Corbett, C., Hill, C., & Rose, A. (2008). *Where the girls are: The facts about gender equity in education.* Washington, DC: American Association of University Women.

Cortes, C. (2000). *The children are watching: How the media teach about diversity.* New York: Teachers College Press.

Costello-Dougherty, M. (2009). Waldorf methods to use in your classroom. *Edutopia,* October, 2009, Retrieved September 19, 2011 from http://www.edutopia.org/waldorf-public-school-morse-tips.

Coulton, C., Theodos, B., & Turner, M. (2009). *Family mobility and neighborhood change.* Washington, DC: The Urban Institute.

Council for Professional Recognition. (2010). *CDA credential.* Retrieved June 30, 2010 from www.cdacouncil.org/.

Coy, D. (2001). *Bullying.* ERIC Clearinghouse on Counseling and Student Services. ERIC Document Number ED 459405. Retrieved November 2, 2010 from www.ericdigests.org/2002-3/bullying.htm.

Crawford, P. (2010). It's not easy being green. . . But great books can help: Literature and resources for helping children to care for the earth. In J. Hoot & J. Szente (Eds.), *The earth is our home. Children caring for the environment.* Olney, MD: Association for Childhood Education International.

Crick, N., & Grotpeter, J. (1995). Relational aggression, gender and social-psychology adjustment. *Child Development, 66,* 710–722.

Crosnoe, R. (2010). Obesity as an educational issue. *Teachers College Record.* Retrieved April 26, 2010 from www.tcrecord.org.

Cuffaro, H. (1984). Microcomputers in education: Why is earlier better? *Teacher's College Record, 85,* 559–567.

Curenton, S. (2006). Oral storytelling: A cultural art that promotes school readiness. *Young Children, 61*(5), 78–89.

Curtis, D., & Carter, M. (2003). *Designs for living and learning: Transforming early childhood environments.* St. Paul, MN: Red Leaf Press.

Curtis, D., & Carter, M. (2006). *The art of awareness: How observation can transform your teaching.* Upper Saddle River, NJ: Merrill/Prentice Hall.

Dallas County Community College District. (2010). *2010–2011 catalog. Associate of Arts in Teaching degree.* Retrieved June 30, 2010 from https://www1.dcccd.edu/cat1011/academicdegrees/aat.cfm?use_nav=acad_info.

Damon, W. (1983). *Social and personality development: Infancy through adolescence.* New York: W.W. Norton.

Daniel, J. (2009). Intentionally thoughtful family engagement in early childhood education. *Young Children, 64*(5), 10–14.

Daniel, J., & Koralek, D. (2005). Embracing diversity in early childhood settings. *Young Children, 60*(6), 10–11, 66.

Darling-Hammond, L., & Bransford, J. (Eds.). (2005). *Preparing teachers for a changing world.* San Francisco: John Wiley & Sons.

Davis, B., & Shade, D. (1994, December). Integrate, don't isolate! Computers in the early childhood curriculum. *ERIC Digest,* EDO-PS-94-17. Urbana, IL: ERIC Clearinghouse on Elementary and Early Childhood Education.

Davis, G., Rimm, S., & Siegle, D. (2011). *Education of the gifted and talented* (6th ed.). Columbus, OH: Merrill.

Dearden, R. (1968). Play as an educational process. In *The philosophy of primary education: An introduction.* London: Routledge and Kegan Paul.

DeBey, M., & Bombard, D. (2007). Expanding children's boundaries: An approach to second-language learning and cultural understanding. *Young Children, 62*(2), 88–93.

DeFina, A. (1992). *Portfolio assessment.* New York: Scholastic Professional Books.

Deiner, P., & Qui, W. (2007). Embedding physical activity and nutrition in early care and education programs. *Zero to Three,* September 2007, pp. 13–18.

Denham, S., Blair, K., DeMulder, E., Levitas, J., Sawyer, K., Auerbach-Major, S., & Queenan, P. (2003). Preschool emotional competence: Pathway to social competence? *Child Development, 74,* 238–256.

Dennison, B., Rockwell, H., & Baker, S. (1997). Excess fruit juice consumption by preschool-aged children is associated with short stature and obesity. *Pediatrics, 99*(1), 15–22.

Derman-Sparks, L. (1989). *Anti-bias curriculum: Tools for empowering young children.* Washington, DC: National Association for the Education of Young Children.

Derman-Sparks, L. (1994). Empowering children to create a caring culture in a world of differences. *Childhood Education, 70*(2), 66–71.

Derman-Sparks, L. (1999). Markers of multicultural/antibias education. *Young Children, 54*(5), 43.

Derman-Sparks, L., & Edwards, J. (2010). *Anti-bias education for young children and ourselves.* Washington, DC: National Association for the Education of Young Children.

Derman-Sparks, L., & Phillips, C. (1997). *Teaching/learning anti-racism.* New York: Teachers College Press.

Derman-Sparks, L., & Ramsey, P. (2006). *What if all the kids are white?* New York: Teachers College Press.

DeVries, R., & Kohlberg, L. (1987). *Constructivist early education: Overview and comparison with other programs.* Washington, DC: National Association for the Education of Young Children.

DeVries, R., & Sales, C. (2011). *Ramps and pathways: A constructivist approach to physics with young children.* Washington, DC: National Association for the Education of Young Children.

DeVries, R., & Zan, B. (1995). Creating a constructivist classroom atmosphere. *Young Children, 51*(1), 4–13.

Dewey, J. (1929). *Democracy and education.* New York: Macmillan.

Dinwiddie, S. (1993). Playing in the gutters: Enhancing children's cognitive and social play. *Young Children, 48*(6), 70–73.

Dodge, D., Colker, L., & Heroman, C. (2002). *The creative curriculum for early childhood* (4th ed.). Beltsville, MD: Gryphon House.

Doman, G. (1961). *Teach your baby to read.* London: Jonathan Cape.

Dorros, A. (1991). *Abuela.* Boston, MA: E.P. Dutton.

Dow, C. (2010). Young children and movement. The power of creative dance. *Young Children, 65*(2), 30–35.

Downs, M. (2010). *Nine childhood illnesses: Get the facts.* Retrieved October 18, 2010 from http://children.webmd.com/features/childhood-illnesses-get-the-facts.

Dreikurs, R., Grunwald, B., & Pepper, F. (1982). *Maintaining sanity in the classroom* (2nd ed.). New York: Harper & Row.

Eck, D. (2001). *A new religious America: How a "Christian country" has become the world's most religiously diverse nation.* San Francisco: Harper.

Edelson, J., & Johnson, G. (2004). Music makes math meaningful. *Childhood Education, 80*(2), 65–73.

Edwards, C. (2002). Three approaches from Europe: Waldorf, Montessori, and Reggio Emilia. *Early Childhood Research and Practice, 4*(1). Retrieved July 5, 2010 from http://ecrp.uiuc.edu/.

Edwards, C., Gandini, L., & Forman, G. (Eds.). (1998). *The hundred languages of children: The Reggio Emilia approach to early childhood education* (2nd ed.). Norwood, NJ: Ablex.

Edwards, C., & Springate, K. (1993). Inviting children into project work. *Dimensions of Early Childhood, 22*(1), 9–12, 40.

Edwards, L. (2010). *The creative arts: A process approach for teachers and children* (5th ed.). Upper Saddle River, NJ: Prentice Hall.

Einarsdottir, J. (2005). Playschool in pictures: Children's photography as a research method. *Early Child Development and Care, 175*(4), 523–541.

Einstein, A. (1949). Autobiographical notes. In P. A. Schilpp (Ed.), *Albert Einstein: Philosopher and scientist.* Evanston, IL: The Library of Living Philosophers.

Einstein, A. (1954). *Ideas and opinions.* New York: Crown Publishers.

Eisenhauer, M., & Feikes, D. (2009). Dolls, blocks, and puzzles: Playing with mathematical understandings. *Young Children, 64*(3), 18–24.

Eli Lilly and Company. (2010). *One decision, many benefits.* Retrieved June 30, 2010 from www.lilly.com/careers/docs/FTE.pdf.

Elkind, D. (2001). *The hurried child: Growing up too fast too soon* (3rd ed.). Boulder, CO: Perseus Books.

Elkind, D. (2003). Thanks for the memory. The lasting value of true play. *Young Children, 58*(3), 46–50.

Elkind, D. (2006). *The power of play: How spontaneous, imaginative activities lead to happier, healthier children.* Cambridge, MA: Da Capo Press.

Ellis, M. (1973). *Why people play.* Upper Saddle River, NJ: Prentice Hall.

Engel, B. (1996). Learning to look: Appreciating child art. *Young Children, 51*(3), 74–79.

Epstein, A. (2007a). *Essentials of active learning in preschool.* Ypsilanti, MI: High/Scope Press.

Epstein, A. (2007b). *The intentional teacher.* Washington, DC: National Association for the Education of Young Children.

Epstein, A. (2009). *Me, you, us: Social-emotional learning in preschool.* Washington, DC: National Association for the Education of Young Children.

Epstein, J. (1995). School/family/community partnerships: Caring for the children we share. *Phi Delta Kappan, 76*(9), 701–712.

Epstein, J. (2006). Families, schools, and community partnerships. *Young Children, 61*(1), 40.

Erikson, E. (1963). *Childhood and society* (2nd ed.). New York: W. W. Norton.

Erikson, E. (1968). *Identity: Youth and crisis.* New York: W. W. Norton.

Esbensen, S. (1987). *An outdoor classroom.* Ypsilanti, MI: High Scope Press.

Esch, G. (2008). Children's literature: Perceptions of bullying. *Childhood Education, 84*(6), 379–382.

Espelage, D., & Swearer, S. (2003). Research on school bullying and victimization: What have we learned and where do we go from here? *School Psychology Review, 32*(3), 365–383.

Evans, B. (2007). *I know what's next: Preschool transitions without tears or turmoil.* Ypsilanti, MI: High Scope Press.

Evans, B. (2009). *You're not my friend anymore.* Ypsilanti, MI: High Scope Press.

Fields-Smith, C., & Neuharth-Prichett, S. (2009). Families as decision-makers. *Childhood Education, 85*(4), 237–242.

Figueroa-Sanchez, M. (2008). Building emotional literacy: Groundwork to early learning. *Childhood Education, 84*(5), 301–304.

Fischer, M., & Gillespie, C. (2003). One Head Start classroom's experience. Computers and young children's development. *Young Children, 58*(4), 85–91.

Fisher, J., Arreola, A., Birch, L., & Rolls, B. (2007). Portion size effects on daily energy intake in low-income Hispanic and African American children and their mothers. *American Journal of Clinical Nutrition, 86*, 1709–1716.

Flavell, J. (1963). *The developmental psychology of Jean Piaget.* New York: D. Van Nostrand.

Flohr, J. (2004). *The musical lives of young children.* Upper Saddle River, NJ: Prentice Hall.

Flynn, L., & Kieff, J. (2002). Including everyone in outdoor play. *Young Children, 57*(3), 20–26.

Foley, M. (2006). The music, movement, and learning connection: A review. *Childhood Education, 82*(3), 175–176.

Forbis, S., McAllister, T., Monk, S., Schlorman, C., Stolphi, A., & Pascoe, J. (2007). Children and firearms in the home: A southwestern Ohio ambulatory research network study. *Journal of the American Board of Family Medicine, 20*, 385–391.

Forum on Child and Family Statistics. (2010). *America's children in brief: Key national indicators of well-being 2010.* Retrieved July 30, 2010 from www.childstats.gov/americaschildren/index.asp.

Foster, S. M. (1994). Successful parent meetings. *Young Children, 50*(1), 78–81.

Fox, J., & Schirrmacher, R. (2012). *Art and creative development for young children* (7th ed.). Albany, NY: Delmar.

Frankenburg, W., Dodds, J., Archer, P., Shapiro, H., & Bresnick, B. (1992). The Denver II: A major revision and restandardization of the Denver Developmental Screening Test. *Pediatrics, 89*(1), 91–97.

Frawley, T. (2005). Gender bias in the classroom. *Childhood Education, 81*(4), 221–227.

Freud, S. (1938). *An outline of psychoanalysis.* London: Hogarth.

Frey, K., Nolen, S., Edstrom, L., & Hirschstein, M. (2005). Effects of a school-based social-emotional competence program: Linking children's goals, attributions, and behavior. *Journal of Applied Developmental Psychology, 26,* 171–200.

Friedman, S. (2010). Theater, live music, and dance. *Young Children, 65*(2), 36–41.

Froebel, F. (1886). *Education of man.* (J. Jarvis, Trans.). New York: Appleton-Century-Crofts.

Froebel, F. (1906). *Mother-play and nursery songs.* New York: Lothrop, Lee, & Shepard.

Fromberg, D. (2002). *Play and meaning in early childhood education.* Boston: Allyn & Bacon.

Fromberg, D., & Bergen, D. (Eds.). (2006). *Play from birth to twelve: Contexts, perspectives, and meanings.* New York: Routledge.

Froschl, M., & Sprung, B. (1999). On purpose: Addressing teasing and bullying in early childhood. *Young Children, 54*(2), 70–72.

Frost, J. (1968). *Early childhood education rediscovered.* New York: Holt McDougal.

Frost, J., Brown, P., Thornton, C., & Sutterby, J. (2004). *The developmental benefits of playground equipment.* Olney, MD: Association for Childhood Education International.

Frost, J., & Hawkes, G. (1970). *The disadvantaged child* (2nd ed.). Boston: Houghton Mifflin.

Frost, J., & Henniger, M. (1979). Making playgrounds safe for children and children safe for playgrounds. *Young Children, 34*(5), 23–30.

Frost, J., & Sweeney, T. (1996). *Cause and prevention of playground injuries and litigation.* Washington, DC: Association for Childhood Education International.

Frost, J., & Wortham, S. (1988). The evolution of American playgrounds. *Young Children, 43*(5), 19–28.

Frost, J., Wortham, S., & Reifel, S. (2012). *Play and child development* (4th ed.). Upper Saddle River, NJ: Merrill/Prentice Hall.

Funk, J. (1993). Reevaluating the impact of video games. *Clinical Pediatrics, 32,* 86–90.

Furman, R. (1995). Helping children cope with stress and deal with feelings. *Young Children, 50*(2), 33–41.

Gaffney, J., Ostrosky, M., & Hemmeter, M. (2008). Books as natural support for young children's literacy learning. *Young Children, 63*(4), 87–93.

Galinsky, E. (2010). *Mind in the making.* New York: HarperCollins.

Gallahue, D., & Ozman, J. (2005). *Understanding motor development: Infants, children, adolescents, adults* (6th ed.). New York: McGraw-Hill.

Galley, M. (2000). Computer companies give birth to "lapware" for babies. *Education Week,* May 10, 2000, p. 5.

Gandini, L. (1993). Fundamentals of the Reggio Emilia approach to early childhood education. *Young Children, 49*(1), 4–8.

Gardner, H. (1983). *Frames of mind: The theory of multiple intelligences.* New York: Basic Books.

Gardner, H. (1993). *Multiple intelligences: The theory in practice.* New York: Basic Books.

Gardner, H. (1999). *Intelligence reframed.* New York: Basic Books.

Gartrell, D. (2006). Guidance matters: The beauty of classroom meetings. *Young Children, 61*(6), 54–55.

Gartrell, D., & Gartrell, J. (2008). Understand bullying. *Young Children, 63*(3), 54–57.

Garvey, C. (1990). *Play* (enlarged ed.). Cambridge, MA: Harvard University Press.

Gates, G. (2003). *Gay and lesbian families in the census: Couples with children.* Washington, DC: The Urban Institute.

Geist, E. (2009). Infants and toddlers exploring mathematics. *Young Children, 64*(3), 39–41.

Geist, K., & Geist, E. (2008). Do re mi, 1-2-3: That's how easy math can be. *Young Children, 63*(2), 20–25.

Genishi, C., & Dyson, A. (2009). *Children, language and literacy: Diverse learners in diverse times.* New York: Teachers College Press.

Gennarelli, C. (2004). Family ties. Communicating with families: Children lead the way. *Young Children, 59*(1), 98.

Gesell, A., & Ilg, F. (1949). *Child development: An introduction to the study of human growth.* New York: Harper & Brothers.

Gestwicki, C. (2010). *Home, school and community relations* (7th ed.). Albany, NY: Delmar.

Ginott, H. (1972). *Teacher and child.* New York: Macmillan.

Ginsburg, H., Boyd, J., & Sun Lee, J. (2008). Mathematics education for young children: What it is and how to promote it. *Social Policy Report, 22*(1), 12–13.

Ginsburg, H., & Opper, S. (1969). *Piaget's theory of intellectual development.* Upper Saddle River, NJ: Prentice Hall.

Ginsburg, K. (2007). The importance of play in promoting healthy child development and maintaining strong parent-child bonds. *Pediatrics, 119*(1), 182–191.

Glasser, W. (1969). *Schools without failure.* New York: Harper & Row.

Glasser, W. (1990). *The quality school.* New York: Harper & Row.

Goertzel, M., & Goertzel, R. (1962). *Cradles of eminence.* Boston: Little, Brown.

Goleman, D. (1995). *Emotional intelligence.* New York: Bantam.

Gonzalez-Mena, J. (2010). *50 strategies for communicating and working with diverse families.* (2nd ed.). Upper Saddle River, NJ: Pearson Education.

Gordon, T. (1974). *Teacher effectiveness training.* New York: Wyden.

Gorter-Reu, M., & Anderson, J. (1998). Home kits, home visits, and more! *Young Children, 53*(3), 71–74.

Green, C., & Oldendorf, S. (2005). Teaching religious diversity through children's literature. *Childhood Education, 81*(4), 209–218.

Griffiths, R., & Clyne, M. (1991). *Books you can count on: Linking mathematics and literature.* Portsmouth, NH: Heinemann.

Gronlund, G. (2006). *Make early learning standards come alive: Connecting your practice and curriculum to state guidelines.* St. Paul, MN: Redleaf Press.

Gropper, N., & Froschl, M. (1999, April). *The role of gender in young children's teasing and bullying behavior.* Paper presented at the American Educational Research Association Annual Meeting, Montreal, Quebec.

Gross, T., & Clemens, S. (2002). Painting a tragedy. Young children process the events of September 11. *Young Children, 57*(3), 44–51.

Guimps, R. (1890). *Pestalozzi: His life and work* (J. Russell, Trans.). New York: Appleton.

Hachey, A., & Butler, D. (2009). Seeds in the window, soil in the sensory table. Science education through gardening and nature-based play. *Young Children, 64*(6), 42–48.

Halgunseth, L. (2009). Family engagement, diverse families, and early childhood education programs. *Young Children, 64*(5), 56–58.

Hall, J., Ahrens, M., Rohr, K., Gamache, S., & Comoleti, J. (2006). *Behavioral mitigation of smoking fires through strategies based on statistical analysis.* Washington, DC: U.S. Fire Administration.

Hallahan, D., Kauffman, J., & Pullen, P. (2009). *Exceptional learners: Introduction to special education* (11th ed.). Columbus, OH: Merrill.

Hanford, E. (2009). *Early lessons.* Retrieved May 24, 2010 from www.americanradioworks.org/features/preschool/.

Hansen, L. (2008). Parents as partners in art education. *Young Children, 63*(5), 90–95.

Hanvey, C. (2010). Experiences with an outdoor prop box. Addressing standards during recess. *Young Children, 65*(1), 30–33.

Harms, T., & Clifford, R. (1980). *Early childhood environment rating scale.* New York: Teachers College Press.

Harms, T., & Clifford, R. (2007). *Family day care rating scale* (rev. ed.). New York: Teachers College Press.

Harms, T., Clifford, R., & Cryer, D. (2005). *Early childhood environment rating scale (ECRS)* (rev. ed.). New York: Teachers College Press.

Harms, T., Cryer, D., & Clifford, R. (2003). *Infant/toddler environment rating scale* (rev. ed.). New York: Teachers College Press.

Harms, T., Jacobs, E., & White, D. (1995). *School-age care environment rating scale.* New York: Teachers College Press.

Harper, L., & Brand, S. (2010). More alike than different. Promoting respect through multicultural books and literacy strategies. *Childhood Education, 86*(4), 224–233.

Harris, M. (2009). Implementing portfolio assessment. *Young Children, 64*(3), 82–85.

Harris, T. (1994). The snack shop: Block play in a primary classroom. *Dimensions of Early Childhood, 22*(4), 22–23.

Hartup, W. (1992). Having friends, making friends, and keeping friends: Relationships as educational contexts. *ERIC Digest,* EDO-PS-92-4. Urbana, IL: ERIC Clearinghouse on Elementary and Early Childhood Education. ERIC Document Reproduction Service No. ED 345 854.

Hartup, W., & Moore, S. (1990). Early peer relations: Developmental significance and prognostic implications. *Early Childhood Research Quarterly, 5*(1), 1–18.

Haskins, R. (2010). *The impact of early experience on childhood brain development.* Washington, DC: The Brookings Institution.

Hatcher, B., Nicosia, T., & Pape, D. (1994). *Interested in inviting and sustaining play behaviors? Prop boxes offer promise!* Paper presented at the Annual Conference of the Association for Childhood Education International, New Orleans, LA.

Hatcher, B., Pape, D., & Nicosia, T. (1988). Group games for global awareness. *Childhood Education, 65*(1), 8–13.

Haugland, S., & Shade, D. (1994). Software evaluation for young children. In J. Wright & D. Shade (Eds.), *Young children: Active learners in a technological age* (pp. 17–24). Washington, DC: National Association for the Education of Young Children.

Hearron, P., & Hildebrand, V. (2009). *Guiding young children* (8th ed.). Upper Saddle River, NJ: Merrill/Prentice Hall.

Hedley, A., Ogden, C., Johnson, C., Carroll, M., Curtin, L., & Flegal, K. (2004). Prevalence of overweight and obesity among U.S. children, adolescents, and adults 1999–2002. *Journal of the American Medical Association, 291*(23), 2847–2850.

Heidemann, S., & Hewitt, D. (1992). *Pathways to play: Developing play skills in young children.* St. Paul, MN: Redleaf Press.

Heimes, M. (2009). Building positive relationships. *Young Children, 64*(1), 94–95.

Heller, R., & Martin, C. (1982). *Bits 'n bytes about computing.* Rockville, MD: Computer Science Press.

Helm, J., & Beneke, S. (2003). *The power of projects: Meeting contemporary challenges in early childhood classrooms.* New York: Teachers College Press.

Helm, J., & Katz, L. (2010). *Young investigators: The project approach in the early years* (2nd ed.). New York: Teachers College Press.

Hemmeter, M., Ostrosky, M., Artman, K., & Kinder, K. (2008). Moving right along. . . Planning transitions to prevent challenging behavior. *Young Children, 63*(3), 18–25.

Hendrick, J. (Ed.). (1997). *First steps toward teaching the Reggio way*. Upper Saddle River, NJ: Merrill/Prentice Hall.

Hendrick, J. (Ed.). (2004). *Next steps toward teaching the Reggio way: Accepting the challenge to change* (2nd ed.). Upper Saddle River, NJ: Merrill/Prentice Hall.

Henniger, M. (1993). Enriching the outdoor play experience. *Childhood Education, 70*(2), 87–90.

Henniger, M. (1994). Software for the early childhood classroom: What should it look like? *Journal of Computing in Childhood Education, 5*(2), 167–175.

Henri, A. (1990). *The postman's palace*. New York: Macmillan Children's Book Group.

Henry J. Kaiser Family Foundation. (2002). *Key facts: Children and video games*. Menlo Park, CA: Author.

Henry J. Kaiser Family Foundation. (2004). *The role of media in childhood obesity: Issue brief*. Menlo Park, CA: Author.

Herr, J., & Libby-Larson, Y. (2004). *Creative resources for the early childhood classroom* (4th ed.). Albany, NY: Delmar.

Heward, W. (2009). *Exceptional children: An introduction to special education* (9th ed.). Upper Saddle River, NJ: Prentice Hall.

High/Scope Educational Research Foundation. (2010). *The High/Scope difference*. Retrieved July 5, 2010 from www.highscope.org/.

Hill, L., Stremmel, A., & Fu, V. (2005). *Teaching as inquiry: Rethinking curriculum in early childhood education*. Boston: Allyn & Bacon.

Hirsch, E. (Ed.). (1996). *The block book* (3rd ed.). Washington, DC: National Association for the Education of Young Children.

Hmurovich, J. (2009). Child abuse and neglect prevention. *Policy and Practice*, June, 2009, pp. 11–13.

Ho, M. (1996). *Hush*. New York: Orchard Books.

Ho, M. (2004). *Peek! A Thai hide-and-seek*. Cambridge, MA: Candlewick.

Hoagie's Gifted Education. (2010). *How can I choose a school for my gifted child?* Retrieved July 5, 2010 from www.hoagiesgifted.org/choose_school.htm.

Hoefer, M., Rytina, N., & Baker, B. (2010). Estimates of unauthorized immigrant population residing in the United States: January 2009. *Population Estimates 2010*. Washington, DC: Office of Immigration Statistics.

Hohmann, C. (1996). *Foundations in elementary education: Overview*. Ypsilanti, MI: High/Scope Press.

Hohmann, M., & Weikart, D. (1995). *Educating young children: Active learning practices for preschool and child care programs*. Ypsilanti, MI: High/Scope Press.

Holick, M. (2007). Vitamin D deficiency. *New England Journal of Medicine, 357*, 266–281.

Holzman, M. (2005). Preschool's effects at 40: The news from Ypsilanti. *Education Week*, January 19, 35.

Honig, A. (2004). Exploring nature with babies. *Early Childhood Today, 18*(6), 22.

Honig, A. (2005). The language of lullabies. *Young Children, 60*(5), 30–36.

Honig, A., & Wittmer, D. (1996). Helping children become more prosocial: Ideas for classrooms, families, schools, and communities. *Young Children, 51*(2), 62–70.

Hoot, J., & Szente, J. (Eds.). (2010). *The earth is our home. Children caring for the environment*. Olney, MD: Association for Childhood Education International.

Howard, G. (2006). *We can't teach what we don't know: White teachers, multiracial schools* (2nd ed.). New York: Teachers College Press.

Huber, D. (2009). Making a difference in early childhood obesity. *Exchange*, September/October 2009, 16–18.

Huber, L. (1999). Woodworking with young children: You can do it! *Young Children, 54*(6), 32–34.

Hughes, F. (1999). *Children, play, and development* (3rd ed.). Boston: Allyn & Bacon.

Huizinga, J. (1955). *Homo ludens: A study of the play element in culture*. Boston: Beacon Press.

Hurst, M. (2004). Researchers target impact of television violence. *Education Week*, November 17, 2004, 8.

Hymes, J. (1978). *Living history interviews*. Carmel, CA: Hacienda Press.

Hyson, M. (2008). *Enthusiastic and engaged learners. Approaches to learning in the early childhood classroom*. New York: Teachers College Press.

Institute for Medicine. (2010). *Strategies to reduce sodium intake in the United States*. Washington, DC: Author.

Institutes for the Achievement of Human Potential. (2010). *About us*. Retrieved November 4, 2010 from www.iahp.org/.

International Reading Association. (1998). Learning to read and write: Developmentally appropriate practices for young children. A joint statement of the International Reading Association (IRA) and the National Association for the Education of Young Children (NAEYC). *Reading Teacher, 52*(2), 193–217.

International Suzuki Association. (2010). *The Suzuki Method*. Retrieved December 16, 2010 from http://internationalsuzuki.org/method.htm.

IPA. (2010). *The International Play Association declaration of a child's right to play*. Retrieved July 16, 2010 from www.ipausa.org/ipadeclaration.html.

Irvine, J. (2003). *Educating teachers for diversity*. New York: Teachers College Press.

Isbell, R. (2002). Telling and retelling stories. Learning language and literacy. *Young Children, 57*(2), 26–30.

Isbell, R., & Raines, S. (2000). *Tell it again 2*. Beltsville, MD: Gryphon House.

Isenberg, J., & Quisenberry, N. (2010). *Play: Essential for all children. A position paper of the Association for Childhood Education International*. Retrieved July 16, 2010 from http://acei.org/wp-content/uploads/PlayEssential.pdf.

Itard, J. (1962). *The wild boy of Aveyron* (G. Humphrey & M. Humphrey, Trans.). New York: Appleton-Century-Crofts. (Original work published 1801 and 1806.)

Jablon, J., Dombro, A., & Dichtelmiller, M. (2007). *The power of observation for birth through eight* (2nd ed.). Washington, DC: Teaching Strategies Inc. and the National Association for the Education of Young Children.

Jacobs, G., & Crowley, K. (2010). *Reaching standards and beyond in kindergarten*. Thousand Oaks, CA: Corwin.

Jacobson, L. (2006). "Sesame" videos sparking debate. *Education Week*, April 5, 2006, p. 8.

Jalongo, M. (1995). Awaken to the artistry within young children! *Dimensions of Early Childhood, 23*(4), 8–14.

Jalongo, M. (1996). Using recorded music with young children: A guide for nonmusicians. *Young Children, 51*(5), 6–14.

Jambor, T. (1994). School recess and social development. *Dimensions of Early Childhood, 23*(1), 17–20.

Jarrett, O., & Waite-Stupiansky, S. (2009). Recess—It's indispensible! *Young Children, 64*(5), 66–69.

Jelks, P., & Dukes, L. (1985). Promising props for outdoor play. *Day Care and Early Education, 13*(1), 18–20.

Jensen, B., & Bullard, J. (2002). The mud center. Recapturing childhood. *Young Children, 57*(3), 16–19.

Johnson, J., Christie, J., & Wardle, S. (2005). *Play, development, and early education*. Boston: Allyn and Bacon.

Johnson, J., Christie, J., & Yawkey, T. (1987). *Play and early childhood development*. Glenview, IL: Scott, Foresman.

Jones, N. (2008). 2, 4, or 6? Grouping children to promote social and emotional development. *Young Children, 63*(3), 34–39.

Joseph, G., & Strain, P. (2003). Comprehensive evidence-based social-emotional curricula for young children: An analysis of efficacious adoption potential. *Topics in Early Childhood Special Education, 23*(2), 65–76.

KaBOOM. (2010). *About KaBOOM*. Retrieved August 27, 2010 from http://kaboom.org/about_kaboom.

Kadish, R. (2006). *Beyond backpacks—Back-to-school issues for GLBT parents*. Washington, DC: Human Rights Campaign Foundation. Retrieved November 27, 2006 from www.hrc.org/Template.cfm?Section=Evaluating_schools1&CONTENTID=33732&TEMPLATE=/ContentManagement/ContentDisplay.cfm.

Kaiser Family Foundation. (2010). *Generation M2: Media in the lives of 8 to 18 year olds*. Retrieved January 3, 2011 from www.kff.org/entmedia/upload/8010.pdf.

Kalich, K., Bauer, D., & McPartlin, D. (2009). "Early Sprouts." Establishing healthy food choices for young children. *Young Children, 64*(4), 49–55.

Kamii, C., & DeClark, G. (1985). *Young children reinvent arithmetic: Implications of Piaget's theory*. New York: Teachers College Press.

Kamii, C., & DeVries, R. (1978). *Physical knowledge in preschool education*. Upper Saddle River, NJ: Merrill/Prentice Hall.

Kamii, C., & DeVries, R. (1980). *Group games in early education*. Washington, DC: National Association for the Education of Young Children.

Kamii, C., & Ewing, J. (1996). Basing teaching on Piaget's constructivism. *Childhood Education, 72*(5), 260–264.

Katz, L. (1984). The professional early childhood teacher. *Young Children, 39*(2), 3–10.

Katz, L. (1994). The project approach. *ERIC Digest*. EDO-PS-94-6. Urbana, IL: ERIC Clearinghouse on Elementary and Early Childhood Education.

Katz, L., & Chard, S. (2000). *Engaging children's minds: The project approach* (2nd ed.). New York: Ablex.

Kellogg, R. (1969). *Analyzing children's art*. Palo Alto, CA: Mayfield Publishing.

Kemple, K., Batey, J., & Hartle, L. (2004). Music play: Creating centers for musical play and exploration. *Young Children, 59*(4), 30–37.

Keramidas, C., & Collins, B. (2009). Assistive technology use with the birth to three population: A rural perspective. *Rural Special Education Quarterly, 28*(1), 38–48.

Kersey, K., & Masterson, M. (2009). Teachers connecting with families—In the best interest of children. *Young Children, 64*(5), 34–38.

Keyser, J. (2006). *From parents to partners: Building a family-centered early childhood program*. St. Paul, MN: Redleaf Press.

Kimball, C. (Ed.). (2003). *Child and youth security sourcebook*. Detroit, MI: Omnigraphics, Inc.

KinderCare. (2010). *About KinderCare*. Retrieved June 28, 2010 from www.kindercare.com/about/.

King, M., & Gartrell, D. (2003). Building an encouraging classroom with boys in mind. *Young Children, 58*(4), 33–36.

Kinsey, S. (2001). Multiage grouping and academic achievement. *ERIC Digest* ED448935. Champaign, IL: ERIC Clearinghouse on Elementary and Early Childhood Education.

Kirchner, G. (2000). *Children's games from around the world* (2nd ed.). Boston: Allyn & Bacon.

Kissel, B. (2008). Apples on train tracks. Observing young children reenvision their writing. *Young Children, 63*(2), 26–32.

Klein, N. (1973). *Girls can be anything*. New York: Dutton.

Knopf, H., & Brown, H. (2009). Lap reading with kindergarteners. Nurturing literacy skills and so much more. *Young Children, 64*(5), 80–87.

Kober, N., Chudowsky, N., Chudowsky, V., & Dietz, S. (2010a). *A call to action to raise the achievement for African American students*. Washington, DC: Center on Education Policy.

Kober, N., Chudowsky, N., Chudowsky, V., & Dietz, S. (2010b). *Improving achievement for the growing Latino population is critical to the nation's future*. Washington, DC: Center on Education Policy.

Koch, P., & McDonough, M. (1999). Improving parent–teacher conferences through collaborative conversations. *Young Children, 54*(2), 11–15.

Kohn, A. (2000). Standardized testing and its victims. *Education Week*, September 27, 46–47, 60.

Koralek, D. (2005). Kindergarten and beyond. *Young Children, 60*(2), 10–11.

Koralek, D. (2008). Teaching and learning through routines and transitions. *Young Children, 63*(3), 10–11.

Kostelnik, M., Soderman, A., & Whiren, A. (2011). *Developmentally appropriate curriculum: Best practices in early childhood education* (5th ed.). Upper Saddle River, NJ: Merrill/Prentice Hall.

Kostelnik, M., Whiren, A., Soderman, A., & Gregory, K. (2009). *Guiding children's social development* (6th ed.). Albany, NY: Delmar.

Kraus, R. (1971). *Leo the late bloomer.* New York: Windmill.

Kreeft, A. (2006). A well-tempered mind: Using music to help children listen and learn. *Childhood Education, 82*(3), 182.

Kritchevsky, S., & Prescott, E. (1969). *Planning environments for young children: Physical space.* Washington, DC: National Association for the Education of Young Children.

Krogh, S. (1995). *The integrated early childhood curriculum* (2nd ed.). New York: McGraw-Hill.

Krull, K. (2003). *M is for music.* New York: Harcourt.

Kuhl, P. (1993). *Life language.* Seattle, WA: University of Washington.

Kunkel, D., Wilcox, B., Cantor, J., Palmer, E., Linn, S., & Dowrick, P. (2004). *Report of the APA Task Force on Advertising and Children.* Retrieved May 5, 2007 from www.apa.org/releases/childrenads.pdf.

Kupetz, B., & Green, E. (1997). Sharing books with infants and toddlers: Facing the challenges. *Young Children, 52*(2), 22–27.

Lake, V., & Pappamihiel, N. (2003). Effective practices and principles to support English language learners in the early childhood classroom. *Childhood Education, 79*(4), 200–203.

Landau, S., & McAninch, C. (1993). Young children with attention deficits. *Young Children, 48*(4), 49–58.

Lane, M. (1981). *The squirrel.* New York: Dial.

Lee, J., Lee, J., & Collins, D. (2010). Enhancing children's spatial sense using tangrams. *Childhood Education, 86*(2), 92–94.

Lee, R., Ramsey, P., & Sweeney, B. (2008). Engaging young children in activities and conversations about race and social class. *Young Children, 63*(6), 68–76.

Leigh, C. (2004). It's all in the game. *Childhood Education, 80*(2), 59–67.

Leithead, M. (1996). Happy hammering . . . a hammering activity with built-in success. *Young Children, 51*(3), 12.

Levin, D. (1998). *Remote control childhood: Combating the hazards of media culture.* Washington, DC: National Association for the Education of Young Children.

Lillard, P. (1972). *Montessori—A modern approach.* New York: Schocken Books.

Lillard, P. (1996). *Montessori today: A comprehensive approach to education from birth to adulthood.* New York: Schocken Books.

Lisenbee, P. (2009). Whiteboards and web sites. Digital tools for the early childhood curriculum. *Young Children, 64*(6), 92–95.

Louv, R. (2005). *Last child in the woods: Saving our children from nature-deficit disorder.* Chapel Hill, NC: Algonquin Books.

Love, A., Burns, S., & Buell, M. (2007). Writing: Empowering literacy. *Young Children, 62*(1), 12–19.

Lowman, L., & Ruhmann, L. (1998). Simply sensational spaces: A multi-"s" approach to toddler environments. *Young Children, 53*(3), 11–17.

Machado, J. (2007). *Early childhood experiences in language arts* (8th ed.). Albany, NY: Delmar.

Mageau, T. (Ed.). (1993). Early childhood and school success. *Electronic Learning, 12*(5), 23.

Magnesio, S., & Davis, B. (2010). A novice teacher fosters social competence with cooperative learning. *Childhood Education, 86*(4), 216–223.

Maldono, N. (1996). Puzzles: A pathetically neglected, commonly available resource. *Young Children, 51*(4), 4–10.

Manning, M., & Kato, T. (2006). Phonemic awareness: A natural step toward reading and writing. *Childhood Education, 82*(4), 241–243.

Marcon, R. (2003). Growing children. The physical side of development. *Young Children, 58*(1), 80–87.

Mardell, B., & Abo-Zena, M. (2010). Kindergartners explore spirituality. *Young Children, 65*(4), 12–17.

Marinak, B., Strickland, M., & Keat, J. (2010). A mosaic of words. Using photo-narration to support all learners. *Young Children, 65*(5), 32–38.

Marotz, L. (2009). *Health, safety and nutrition for the young child* (7th ed.). Albany, NY: Delmar.

Marrero, M., & Schuster, G. (2010). Students making meaningful environmental connections to achieve science literacy: From local school yards to half a world away. In J. Hoot & J. Szente (Eds.), *The earth is our home. Children caring for the environment.* Olney, MD: Association for Childhood Education International.

Marshall, C. (1998). Using children's storybooks to encourage discussions among diverse populations. *Childhood Education, 74*(4), 194–199.

Marston, L. (1984). *Playground equipment.* Jefferson, NC: McFarland.

Martin, B. (1967). *Brown bear, brown bear, what do you see?* New York: Henry Holt and Company.

Martin, J., Kochanek, K., Strobino, D., Guyer, B., & MacDorman, M. (2005). Annual summary of vital statistics 2003. *Pediatrics, 115*(3), 619–634.

Maschinot, B. (2008). *The changing face of the United States: The influence of culture on child development.* Washinton, DC: Zero to Three.

Mashburn, A. (2008). Quality of social and physical environments in preschools and children's development of academic, language, and literacy skills. *Applied Developmental Science, 12*(3), 113–127.

Maslow, A. (1968). *Toward a psychology of being.* Princeton, NJ: Van Nostrand Reinhold.

Mather, M. (2009). *Children in immigrant families chart new paths.* Washington, DC: Population Reference Bureau.

Matte, C. (2010). *Giggles computer funtime for baby.* Retrieved December 22, 2010 from http://familyinternet.about.com/od/software/fr/giggles_baby.htm.

Matthews, H. (2009). *Charting progress for babies in child care project.* Retrieved June 28, 2010 from www.clasp.org/admin/site/babies/make_the_case/files/cp_rationale15.pdf.

Matthews, M. (1990). *What's it like to be a postal worker?* Mahweh, NJ: Troll Associates.

Maxwell, L., Mitchell, M., & Evans, G. (2008). Effects of play equipment and loose parts on preschool children's outdoor play behavior: An observational study and design intervention. *Children, Youth and Environments 18*(2), 36–63.

Mayer, M. (1974). *Frog goes to dinner.* New York: Dial.

Mayesky, M. (2002). *Creative activities for young children.* Albany, NY: Delmar.

McClellan, D., & Katz, L. (1997). *Fostering children's social competence: The teacher's role.* Washington, DC: National Association for the Education of Young Children.

McCracken, J. (Ed.). (1986). *Reducing stress in young children's lives.* Washington, DC: National Association for the Education of Young Children.

McMillan, M. (1919). *The nursery school.* New York: E.P. Dutton & Co.

McNamee, A., & Mercurio, M. (2008). School-wide intervention in the childhood bullying triangle. *Childhood Education, 84*(6), 370–378.

McNeil, D. (1970). *The acquisition of language: The study of developmental psycholinguistics.* New York: Harper & Row.

Meadan, H., & Jegatheesan, B. (2010). Classroom pets and young children. Supporting early learning. *Young Children, 65*(3), 70–77.

Meece, D., & Soderman, A. (2010). Positive verbal environments: Setting the stage for young children's social development. *Young Children, 65*(5), 81–86.

Meisels, S., & Atkins-Burnett, S. (2005). *Developmental screening in early childhood: A guide* (5th ed.). Washington, DC: National Association for the Education of Young Children.

Miles, L. (2009). The general store: Reflections on children at play. *Young Children, 64*(4), 36–41.

Miller, E., & Almon, J. (2009). *Crisis in the kindergarten. Why children need to play in school.* College Park, MD: Alliance for Childhood Play.

Mindes, G. (2005). Social studies in today's early childhood classroom. *Young Children, 60*(5), 12–18.

Mitchell, A., & David, J. (Eds.). (1992). *Explorations with young children.* Mt. Rainier, MD: Gryphon House.

Mitchell, E., & Mason, B. (1948). *The theory of play.* New York: Barnes.

Mitchell, S., Foulger, T., & Wetzel, K. (2009). Ten tips for involving families through Internet-based communication. *Young Children, 64*(5), 46–49.

Moffitt, M. (1996). Children learn about science through block building. In E. Hirsch (Ed.), *The block book* (3rd ed.). Washington, DC: National Association for the Education of Young Children.

Montessori, M. (1965). *Dr. Montessori's own handbook.* New York: Schocken Books.

Montessori, M. (1967). *The absorbent mind.* New York: Dell Publishing. (Original work published 1949.)

Moore, M., & Campos, D. (2010). Inspiration to teach—Reflections on Friedrich Froebel and why he counts in early childhood education. *Young Children, 65*(6), 74–76.

Morton, T., & Salovitz, B. (2001). *The CPS response to child neglect.* Duluth, GA: National Resource Center on Child Maltreatment.

Moses, A. (2009). What television can (and can't) do to promote early literacy development. *Young Children, 64*(2), 80–89.

Mulligan, S. (2003). Assistive technology. Supporting the participation of children with disabilities. *Young Children, 58*(6), 50–51.

Murray, P., & Mayer, R. (1988). Preschool children's judgments of number magnitude. *Journal of Educational Psychology, 80,* 206–209.

Myhre, S. (1993). Enhancing your dramatic-play area through the use of prop boxes. *Young Children, 48*(5), 6–11.

Nash, A., & Fraleigh, K. (1993, March). *The influence of older siblings on the sex-typed toy play of young children.* Paper presented at the Biennial Conference of the Society for Research in Child Development, New Orleans.

Natenshon, A. (1999). *When your child has an eating disorder: A step-by-step workbook for parents and other caregivers.* Hoboken, NJ: Jossey-Bass.

National Academy of Sciences. (1996). *National Science Education Standards.* Retrieved March 27, 2007 from www.nap.edu/catalog/4962.html.

National Association for the Education of Young Children. (1993). Enriching classroom diversity with books for children, in-depth discussion of them, and story-extension activities. *Young Children, 48*(3), 10–12.

National Association for the Education of Young Children. (1995). *Responding to linguistic and cultural diversity: Recommendations for effective early childhood education.* Washington, DC: Author.

National Association for the Education of Young Children. (1996). NAEYC position statement: Technology and young children—Ages three through eight. *Young Children, 51*(6), 11–16.

National Association for the Education of Young Children. (1998). *Media violence and young children: A guide for parents.* Washington, DC: Author.

National Association for the Education of Young Children. (2005). *NAEYC early childhood program standards and accreditation criteria.* Washington, DC: Author.

National Association for the Education of Young Children. (2007). *Celebrating holidays in early childhood programs.* Retrieved January 3, 2007 from www.naeyc.org/ece/1996/18.asp.

National Association for the Education of Young Children. (2009). *NAEYC standards for early childhood professional preparation programs.* Retrieved July 29, 2010 from www.naeyc.org/files/naeyc/file/positions/ProfPrepStandards09.pdf.

National Association for the Education of Young Children. (2011). *Code of ethical conduct and statement of commitment.* Revised April 2005. Reaffirmed and Updated May 2011. Retrieved October 27, 2011 from www.naeyc.org/files/naeyc/file/positions/Ethics%20Position%20Statement2011.pdf.

National Association for the Education of Young Children & National Association of Early Childhood Specialists in State Departments of Education. (2003). *Early childhood curriculum, assessment, and program evaluation: Building an effective, accountable system in programs for children birth through age 8.* Washington, DC: Authors.

National Association for Sport and Physical Education. (2002). *Active start: A statement of physical activity guidelines for children birth to five years.* Reston, VA: Author.

National Association for Sport and Physical Education. (2004). *Moving into the future: National standards for physical education* (2nd ed.). Reston, VA: Author.

National Black Caucus of State Legislators. (2001). *Closing the achievement gap: Improving educational outcomes for African American children.* Retrieved November 1, 2001 from www.nbcsl.com/news/pdf/cag.pdf.

National Center for Education Statistics. (2010). *The condition of education 2010.* Washington, DC: U.S. Government Printing Office.

National Center on Family Homelessness. (2010). *What is family homelessness?* Retrieved July 30, 2010 from www.familyhomelessness.org/Facts.

National Collegiate Athletic Association. (2003). *2003–04 Gender-equity report.* Washington, DC: Author.

National Council for the Social Studies. (2010). *National curriculum standards for social studies: A framework for teaching, learning, and assessment.* Silver Spring, MD: Author.

National Council of Teachers of Mathematics. (2000). *Principles and standards for school mathematics.* Reston, VA: Author.

National Institute for Literacy. (2008). *Developing early literacy: Report of the National Early Literacy Panel.* Jessup, MD: Author.

National Institutes of Health. (2008). Childhood diseases: What parents need to know. *MedlinePlus, 3*(2). Retrieved October 6, 2010 from www.nlm.nih.gov/medlineplus/magazine/issues/spring08/toc.html.

National Institutes of Health. (2009). *Stimulant ADHD medications: Methylphenadate and amphetamines.* Retrieved July 14, 2010 from www.drugabuse.gov/pdf/infofacts/ADHD09.pdf.

National Resource Center for Health and Safety in Child Care. (2002). *Caring for our children* (2nd ed.). Aurora, CO: Author.

National Society for the Gifted and Talented. (2010). Giftedness defined—What is gifted & talented? Retrieved July 14, 2010 from www.nsgt.org/articles/index.asp.

Neugebauer, R. (2006). For profit child care: Four decades of growth. *Exchange,* January/February 2006, pp. 22–25.

Neuman, S., & Roskos, K. (1993). *Language and literacy learning in the early years.* Ft. Worth, TX: Harcourt Brace Jovanovich.

Neumann-Hinds, C. (2007). *Picture science.* St. Paul, MN: Redleaf Press.

New, R., Mardell, B., & Robinson, D. (2005). Early childhood education as risky business: Going beyond what's "safe" to discovering what's possible? *Early Childhood Research and Practice, 7*(2), 1–18.

Newcombe, N., & Huttenlocher, J. (1992). Children's early ability to solve perspective-taking problems. *Developmental Psychology, 28*(4), 635–643.

Newman, N. (1990). *Sharing.* New York: Doubleday.

Nieto, S. (2004). *Affirming diversity: The sociopolitical context of multicultural education* (4th ed.). Boston: Allyn & Bacon.

Nissen, H., & Hawkins, C. (2010). Promoting emotional competence in the preschool classroom. *Childhood Education, 86*(4), 255–259.

North American Montessori Teachers Association. (2010). Frequently asked questions about Montessori Education. Retrieved July 5, 2010 from www.montessori-namta.org/NAMTA/geninfo/faqmontessori.html.

Notar, E. (1989). Children and TV commercials: Wave after wave of exploitation. *Childhood Education, 66,* 66–67.

Nourot, P., & Van Hoorn, J. (1991). Symbolic play in preschool and primary settings. *Young Children, 46*(6), 40–50.

Nucci, L., & Killen, M. (1991). Social interactions in the preschool and the development of moral and social concepts. In B. Scales, M. Almy, A. Nicolopoulou, & S. Ervin-Tripp (Eds.), *Play and the social context of development in early care and education.* New York: Teachers College Press.

Oden, S. (1987). *The development of social competence in children.* Champaign, IL: ERIC Clearinghouse on Elementary and Early Childhood Education. ERIC Document Number ED 281610.

Odoy, H., & Foster, S. (1997). Creating play crates for the outdoor classroom. *Young Children, 52*(6), 12–16.

Ogden, C., & Carroll, M. (2010). *Prevalence of obesity among children and adolescents: United States, Trends 1963–1965 through 2007–2008.* National Center for Health Statistics. Retrieved October 4, 2010 from www.cdc.gov/nchs/data/hestat/obesity_child_07_08/obesity_child_07_08.pdf.

Odgen, C., Carroll, M., & Flegal, K. (2008). High body mass index for age among US children and adolescents, 2003–2006. *Journal of the American Medical Association, 299*(20), 2401–2405.

Ogu, U., & Schmidt, S. (2009). Investigating rocks and sand: Addressing multiple learning styles through an inquiry-based approach. *Young Children, 64*(2), 12–18.

Olsen, G., & Fuller, M. (2008). *Home-school relations: Working successfully with parents and families* (3rd ed.). Boston: Allyn & Bacon.

Olson, S., & Loucks-Horsley, S. (Eds.). (2000). *Inquiry and the National Science Education Standards: A guide for teaching and learning.* Washington, DC: National Academies Press.

Orlick, T. (1978). *The cooperative sports and games book: Challenge without competition.* New York: Pantheon.

Orlick, T. (1982). *The second cooperative sports and games book.* New York: Pantheon.

Owocki, G. (1999). *Literacy through play.* Portsmouth, NH: Heinemann.

Paintal, S. (1999). Banning corporal punishment of children. *Childhood Education, 76*(1), 36–39.

Palmer, H. (2001). The music, movement, and learning connection. *Young Children, 56*(5), 13–17.

Papert, S. (1993). *The children's machine. Rethinking school in the age of the computer.* New York: Basic Books.

Paquette, K. (2008). Through rain, sleet, ice, and snow, the walking school bus still must go! *Childhood Education, 84*(2), 75–78.

Parish, L., & Rudisill, M. (2006). HAPPE: Toddlers in physical play. *Young Children, 61*(3), 32–35.

Parlakian, R., & Lerner, C. (2010). Beyond Twinkle, Twinkle: Using music with infants and toddlers. *Young Children, 65*(2), 14–19.

Parsad, B., Lewis, L., & Greene, B. (2006). *Calories in, calories out: Food and exercise in public elementary schools, 2005.* Retrieved August 30, 2010 from http://nces.ed.gov/pubs2006/2006057.pdf.

Parten, M. (1933). Social play among preschool children. *Journal of Abnormal and Social Psychology, 28,* 136–147.

Pate, R., McIver, K., Dowda, M., Brown, W., & Addy, C. (2008). Directly observed physical activity levels in preschool children. *Journal of School Health, 78*(8), 438–444.

Peet, J. (2010). Women engineers and scientists still making inroads. *New Jersey News.* Retrieved November 18, 2010 from www.nj.com/news/index.ssf/2010/03/women_engineers_and_scientists.html.

Pelligrini, A. (1987). Elementary school children's rough-and-tumble play. *Monographs of the Institute for Behavioral Research.* Athens: University of Georgia.

Pelligrini, A., & Glickman, C. (1989). The educational benefits of recess. *Principal, 62*(5), 23–24.

Pelligrini, A., & Holmes, R. (2006). The role of recess in primary school. In D. Singer, R. Golinkoff, & R. Hirsh-Pasek (Eds.), *Play-learning.* New York: Oxford University Press.

Pelligrini, A., & Perlmutter, J. (1988). Rough-and-tumble play on the elementary school playground. *Young Children, 43*(2), 14–17.

Pepler, D., & Ross, H. (1981). The effects of play on convergent and divergent problem solving. *Child Development, 52,* 1202–1210.

Perlmutter, J., Folger, T., & Holt, K. Pre-kindergarteners learn to write. *Childhood Education, 86*(1), 14–19.

Persson, A., & Musher-Eizenman, D. (2003). The impact of a prejudice-prevention television program on young children's ideas about race. *Early Childhood Research Quarterly, 18,* 530–546.

Petersen, S., and Wittmer, D. (2008). Relationship-based infant care. *Young Children, 63*(3), 40–42.

Petty, K. (2009). Using guided participation to support young children's social development. *Young Children, 64*(4), 80–85.

Pew Forum on Religion and Public Life. (2008). *U.S. Religious Landscape Survey.* Retrieved June 24, 2010 from http://religions.pewforum.org/reports.

Piaget, J. (1950). *The psychology of intelligence.* (M. Piercy & D. Berlyne, Trans.). New York: Harcourt, Brace.

Piaget, J. (1959). *The language and thought of the child* (3rd ed.). (M. Gabain, Trans.). London: Routledge & Kegan Paul.

Piaget, J. (1962). *Play, dreams, and imitation in childhood.* (C. Gattegno & F. Hodgson, Trans.). New York: W. W. Norton.

Piaget, J. (1965). *The moral judgment of the child.* (M. Gabain, Trans.). New York: Free Press.

Piaget, J., & Inhelder, B. (1969). *The psychology of the child.* (H. Weaver, Trans.). New York: Basic Books.

Pica, R. (2004). *Experiences in movement, birth to age eight* (3rd ed.). Albany, NY: Delmar.

Piotrowski, D., & Hoot, J. (2008). Bullying and violence in schools: What teachers should know and do. *Childhood Education, 84*(6), 357–363.

Plutchik, R. (1980). *Emotion: A psychoevolutionary synthesis.* New York: Harper & Row.

Poel, E. (2007). Enhancing what students can do. *Educational Leadership, 64*(5), 64–66.

Poest, C., Williams, J., Witt, D., & Atwood, M. (1990). Challenge me to move: Large muscle development in young children. *Young Children, 45*(5), 4–10.

Pollan, M. (2008). *In defense of food: An eater's manifesto.* New York: Penguin Press.

Post, J., & Hohmann, M. (2000). *Tender care and early learning: Supporting infants and toddlers in child care.* Ypsilanti, MI: High/Scope Press.

Potter, G. (2008). Sociocultural diversity and literacy teaching in complex times. *Childhood Education, 84*(2), 64–69.

Powell, D. (1998). Reweaving parents into the fabric of early childhood programs. *Young Children, 53*(5), 60–67.

Powell, L., Szczypka, G., Chaloupka, F., & Braunschweig, C. (2007). Nutritional content of television food advertisements seen by children and adolescents in the United States. *Pediatrics, 120*(3), 576–583.

Pressel, D. (2000). Evaluation of physical abuse in children. *American Family Physician, 61,* 3057–3064.

Quintero, E. (2005). Multicultural literature: A source of meaningful content for kindergartners. *Young Children, 60*(6), 28–32.

Raikes, H. (1993). Relationship duration in infant care: Time with a high ability teacher and infant-teacher attachment. *Early Childhood Research Quarterly, 8*, 309–325.

Raines, S., & Isbell, R. (1999). *Tell it again.* Beltsville, MD: Gryphon House.

Ramsey, P. (2004). *Teaching and learning in a diverse world: Multicultural education for young children* (3rd ed.). New York: Teachers College Press.

Rankin, B. (1993). Curriculum development in Reggio Emilia: A long-term curriculum project about dinosaurs. In C. Edwards, L. Gandini, & G. Forman (Eds.), *The hundred languages of children.* Norwood, NJ: Ablex.

Rath, L. (2002). Using *Between the Lions* to support early literacy. *Young Children, 57*(2), 80–86.

Readdick, C. (1993). Solitary pursuits: Supporting children's privacy needs in early childhood settings. *Young Children, 49*(1), 60–64.

Reggio Children. (2010). *The wonder of learning: The exhibition.* Retrieved July 7, 2010 from www.thewonderoflearning.com/exhibition/?lang=en_GB.

Reichel, S. (2006). *The parent newsletter: A complete guide for early childhood professionals.* St. Paul, MN: Redleaf Press.

Renck, M., & Jalongo, M. (2004). Children's literature about health, safety, and nutrition. *Beyond the Journal. Young Children on the Web.* Retrieved August 18, 2010 from www.naeyc.org/files/yc/file/200403/ChildrensBooks.pdf.

Rettig, M. (1998). Guidelines for beginning and maintaining a toy lending library. *Early Childhood Education Journal, 25*(4), 229–232.

Reusable Resources Association. (2010). About us. Retrieved August 2, 2010 from www.reusableresources.org/about.html.

Rideout, V., & Hamel, E. (2006). *The media family: Electronic media in the lives of infants, toddlers, preschoolers, and their parents.* Menlo Park, CA: The Henry J. Kaiser Foundation.

Rideout, V., Vandewater, E., & Wartella, E. (2003). *Zero to six: Electronic media in the lives of infants, toddlers and preschoolers.* Menlo Park, CA: The Henry Kaiser Family Foundation. Retrieved May 1, 2003 from www.kff.org.

Riley, J., & Jones, R. (2010). Acknowledging learning through play in the primary grades. *Childhood Education, 86*(3), 146–149.

Ringgenberg, S. (2003). Music as a teaching tool: Creating story songs. *Young Children, 58*(5), 76–79.

Ripple, R., & Rockcastle, V. (Eds.). (1964). *Piaget rediscovered: A report of the conference on cognitive studies and curriculum development.* Washington, DC: National Science Foundation and United States Office of Education.

Rivkin, M. (1990). Outdoor play—What happens here? In S. Wortham & J. Frost (Eds.), *Playgrounds for young children: National survey and perspectives* (pp. 191–214). Reston, VA: American Alliance for Health, Physical Education, Recreation and Dance.

Rivkin, M. (1995). *The great outdoors: Restoring children's right to play outside.* Washington, DC: National Association for the Education of Young Children.

Roberts, D., & Foehr, U. (2008). Trends in media use. *The Future of Children, 18*(1), 11–38.

Roblyer, M., Edwards, J., & Havriluk, M. (1997). *Integrating educational technology into teaching.* Upper Saddle River, NJ: Merrill/Prentice Hall.

Rogers, L., & Steffan, D. (2009). Clay play. *Young Children, 64*(3), 78–81.

Rogoff, B., Mistry, J., Goncu, J., & Mosier, C. (1993). Guided participation in cultural activity by toddlers and caregivers. *Monographs of the Society for Research in Child Development.* Serial no. 236, vol. 58.

Roopnarine, J., & Johnson, J. (Eds.). (2009). *Approaches to early childhood education* (5th ed.). Upper Saddle River, NJ: Merrill/Prentice Hall.

Rosenow, N. (2008). Teaching and learning about the natural world. Learning to love the earth . . . and each other. *Young Children, 63*(1), 10–13.

Rousseau, J. (1979). *Emile* (A. Bloom, Trans.). New York: Basic Books. (Original work published 1762.)

Rudd, L., Lambert, M., Satterwhite, M., & Zaier, A. (2008). Mathematical language in early childhood settings: What really counts? *Early Childhood Education Journal, 36*, 75–80.

Rudolf Steiner College. (2010). *Rudolf Steiner College.* Retrieved July 6, 2010 from www.steinercollege.edu/.

Russell, S. (2009). From our president. Ten strategies for effective advocacy. *Young Children, 64*(1), 6.

Russo, M., Colurciello, S., & Kelly, R. (2008). For the birds! Seeing, being, and creating the bird world. *Young Children, 63*(1), 26–30.

Sackes, M., Trundle, K., & Flevares, L. (2009). Using children's books to teach inquiry skills. *Young Children, 64*(6), 24–26.

Sahn, L., & Reichel, A. (2008). Read all about it! A classroom newspaper integrates the curriculum. *Young Children, 63*(2), 12–18.

Sanchez, X. (2007). The hospital project. *Early Childhood Research Project, 9*(1). Retrieved July 2, 2010 from http://ecrp.uiuc.edu/v9n1/index.html.

Saunders, R., & Bingham-Newman, A. (1984). *Piagetian perspectives for preschools: A thinking book for teachers.* Englewood Cliffs, NJ: Prentice Hall.

Schappet, J., Malkusak, A., & Bruya, L. (2003). *High expectations: Playgrounds for children of all abilities.* Bloomfield, CT: The National Center for Boundless Playgrounds.

Schilling, T., & McOmber, K. (2006). Tots on and beyond the playground. *Young Children, 61*(3), 34–36.

Schunk, D. (2008). *Learning theories: An educational perspective* (5th ed.). Upper Saddle River, NJ: Merrill/Prentice Hall.

Schwartz, E. (2008). From playing to thinking: How the kindergarten provides a foundation for scientific understanding. *European Journal of Psychotherapy and Counseling, 10*(2), 137–145.

Schweinhart, L. (1993). Observing young children in action: The key to early childhood assessment. *Young Children, 48*(5), 29–33.

Schweinhart, L. (2003, April). *Benefits, costs, and explanation of the High/Scope Perry Preschool Program.* Paper presented at the Meeting of the Society for Research in Child Development, Tampa, FL.

Schweinhart, L. (2004). In memorium: David P. Weikart: 1931–2003. *Early Childhood Research and Practice, 6*(1). Retrieved July 5, 2010 from http://ecrp.uiuc.edu/v6n1/weikart.html.

Schweinhart, L.J., Montie, J., Xiang, Z., Barnett, W.S., Belfield, C. R., & Nores, M. (2005). *Lifetime effects: The High/Scope Perry Preschool study through age 40.* (Monographs of the High/Scope Educational Research Foundation, 14.) Ypsilanti, MI: High/Scope Press.

Seagoe, M. (1970). An instrument for the analysis of children's play as an index of socialization. *Journal of School Psychology, 8,* 139–144.

Seefeldt, C. (1995). Art-A serious work. *Young Children, 50*(3), 39–45.

Seguin, E. (1907). *Idiocy and its treatment.* Albany, NY: Press of Brandow Printing Co.

Seuss, Dr. (1960). *Green eggs and ham.* New York: Random House.

Shade, D. (1992). Computers and young children: Software with the appeal of blocks. *Day Care and Early Education, 19*(3), 41–43.

Shade, D. (1995). Storyboard software: Flannel boards in the computer age. *Day Care and Early Education, 22*(3), 45–46.

Shepard, R. (1997). Curricular physical activity and academic performance. *Pediatric Exercise Science, 9,* 113–125.

Shepherd, T. R., & Shepherd, W. L. (1984). Living with a child with autistic tendencies. In M. Henniger & L. Nesselrod (Eds.), *Working with parents of handicapped children* (pp. 85–106). Lanham, MD: University Press of America.

Shidler-Lattz, L., & Ratcliff, N. (1998). Coloring in the lines: A tale of two children. *Young Children, 53*(1), 68–69.

Shiller, V., & O'Flynn, J. (2008). Using rewards in the early childhood classroom: A reexamination of the issues. *Young Children, 63*(6), 88, 90.

Shonkoff, J., & Phillips, D. (Eds.). (2000). *From neurons to neighborhoods.* Washington, DC: National Academy of Sciences.

Shore, R. (2003). *Kids Count indicator brief: Preventing teen births.* Retrieved August 5, 2010 from www.aecf.org/upload/publicationfiles/brief%20teen%20births.pdf.

Shore, R., & Strasser, J. (2006). Music for their minds. *Young Children, 61*(2), 62–67.

Shores, E., & Grace, C. (1998). *The portfolio book. A step-by-step guide for teachers.* Beltsville, MD: Gryphon House.

Silberg, J., & Schiller, P. (2003). *The complete book of activities, games, stories, props, recipes, and dances for young children.* Beltsville, MD: Gryphon House.

Singer, D., Golinkoff, R., & Hirsh-Pasek, K. (Eds.). (2006). *Play-learning.* New York: Oxford University Press.

Singer, D., & Singer, J. (1990). *The house of make-believe.* Cambridge, MA: Harvard University Press.

Skeels, H. (1966). Adult status of children with contrasting early life experience. *Monographs of the Society for Research in Child Development, 31*(3, Serial No. 105).

Skinner, B. (1957). *Verbal behavior.* New York: Appleton-Century-Crofts.

Skinner, B. (1974). *About behaviorism.* New York: Knopf.

Skurzynski, G. (1992). *Here comes the mail.* New York: Macmillan Children's Book Group.

Slepian, J., & Seidler, A. (1967). *The hungry thing.* New York: Scholastic.

Smilansky, S. (1968). *The effects of sociodramatic play on disadvantaged preschool children.* New York: Wiley.

Smilansky, S., & Shefatya, L. (1990). *Facilitating play: A medium for promoting cognitive, socio-emotional and academic development in young children.* Gaithersburg, MD: Psychosocial and Educational Publications.

Smith, A. (2000). Reflective portfolios: Preschool possibilities. *Childhood Education, 76*(4), 204–208.

Smith, P., & Connolly, K. (1980). *The ecology of preschool behavior.* Cambridge, England: Cambridge University Press.

Smith, S. (1990). The riskiness of the playground. *The Journal of Educational Thought, 24*(2), 71–87.

Snider, S., & Badgett, T. (1995). I have this computer, what do I do now? Using technology to enhance every child's learning. *Early Childhood Education Journal, 23*(2), 101–105.

Snow, C., Burns, S., & Griffin, P. (1998). *Preventing reading difficulties in young children.* Washington, DC: National Academy Press.

Sobel, D. (1996). *Beyond ecophobia: Reclaiming the heart in nature education.* Great Barrington, MA: The Orion Society and the Myrin Institute.

Sobel, J. (1984). *Everybody wins: 393 non-competitive games for young children.* New York: Walker and Company.

Song, Y. (2008). Exploring connections between environmental education and ecological public art. *Childhood Education, 85*(1), 13–19.

Sorte, J., & Daeschel, I. (2006). Health in action: A program approach to fighting obesity in young children. *Young Children, 61*(3), 40–48.

Soundy, C., & Drucker, M. (2009). Drawing opens pathways to problem solving for young children. *Childhood Education, 86*(1), 7–13.

Soundy, C., & Qui, Y. (2007). Portraits of picture power: American and Chinese children explore literacy through the visual arts. *Childhood Education, 83*(2), 68–74.

Southern Poverty Law Center. (2010). *Who we are.* Retrieved August 10, 2010 from www.splcenter.org/who-we-are.

Souto-Manning, M. (2010). Family involvement: Challenges to consider, strengths to build on. *Young Children, 65*(2), 82–88.

Sprung, B. (1996). Physics is fun, physics is important, and physics belongs in the early childhood curriculum. *Young Children, 51*(5), 29–33.

St. Clair, J. (2002). Using *Between the Lions* in a kindergarten classroom. *Young Children, 57*(2), 87–88.

Standing, E. (1962). *Maria Montessori: Her life and work.* Fresno, CA: Academy Guild Press.

Starbuck, S., & Olthof, M. (2008). Involving families and community through gardening. *Young Children, 63*(5), 74–79.

Starko, A. (1995). *Creativity in the classroom: Schools of curious delight.* White Plains, NY: Longman.

Steiner, G. (1976). *The children's cause.* Washington, DC: Brookings Institution.

Stone, S. (1995). Wanted: Advocates for play in the primary grades. *Young Children, 50*(6), 45–54.

Sugar, S., & Sugar, K. (2002). *Primary games: Experiential learning activities for teaching children K–8.* San Francisco: Jossey-Bass.

Sulzby, E., & Teale, W. (1991). Emergent literacy. In R. Barr, M. Kamil, P. Mosenthal, & P. Pearson (Eds.), *Handbook of reading research* (Vol. 2, pp. 82–97). New York: Longman.

SuperKids Educational Software Review. (2010). *Educational software reviews.* Retrieved December 23, 2010 from www.superkids.com/.

Sutterby, J. (2009). What kids don't get to do anymore and why. *Childhood Education, 85*(5), 289–292.

Sutterby, J., & Frost, J. (2002). Making playgrounds fit for children and children fit for playgrounds. *Young Children, 57*(3), 36–41.

Sutterby, J., & Thornton, C. (2005). It doesn't just happen: Essential contributions from playgrounds. *Young Children, 60*(3), 26–32.

Sutton-Smith, B., & Roberts, J. (1981). Play, games, and sports. In H.C. Triandis & A. Heron (Eds.), *Handbook of cross-cultural psychology: Vol. 4. Developmental psychology* (pp. 223–241). Boston: Allyn & Bacon.

Swann, A. (2009). An intriguing link between drawing and play with toys. *Childhood Education, 85*(4), 230–236.

Swartz, M. (2005). Playdough: What's standard about it? *Young Children, 60*(2), 100–109.

Swick, K., Boutte, G., & van Scoy, I. (1995, March). Family involvement in early multicultural learning. *ERIC Digest,* EDO-PS-95-2. Urbana, IL: ERIC Clearinghouse on Elementary and Early Childhood Education.

Swiniarski, L. (1991). Toys: Universals for teaching global education. *Childhood Education, 67*(3), 161–163.

Szyba, C. (1999). Why do some teachers resist offering appropriate, open-ended art activities for young children? *Young Children, 54*(1), 16–20.

Taylor, J. (1999). Child-led parent/school conferences—in second grade? *Young Children, 54*(1), 78–82.

Technology and Young Children Interest Forum. (2008). Meaningful technology integration in early learning environments. *Young Children, 63*(5), 48–50.

Tegano, D., Sawyers, J., & Moran, J. (1989). Problem-finding and solving in play: The teacher's role. *Childhood Education, 66*(2), 92–97.

Thomas, R. (1985). *Comparing theories of child development* (2nd ed.). Belmont, CA: Wadsworth.

Thornton, K. (2002). From our president. Exporting TV violence—What do we owe the world's children? *Young Children, 57*(2), 6, 74.

Torrance, E. (1962). *Guiding creative talent.* Upper Saddle River, NJ: Prentice Hall.

Tracy, D. (1994). Using mathematical language to enhance mathematical conceptualization. *Childhood Education, 70*(4), 221–224.

Trawick-Smith, J. (2010). *Early childhood development: A multicultural perspective* (5th ed.). Upper Saddle River, NJ: Merrill/Prentice Hall.

Tucker, P. (2008). The physical activity levels of preschool-aged children: A systematic review. *Early Childhood Research Quarterly, 23,* 547–558.

Tunks, K., & Giles, R. (2009). Writing their words: Strategies for supporting young authors. *Young Children, 64*(1), 22–25.

Ullrich, H. (1994). Rudolf Steiner. *Prospects, 24*(3–4), 555–572.

Underwood, J. (1981, February 23). A game plan for America. *Sports Illustrated,* 64–80.

United States Access Board. (2005). *A guide to the ADA accessibility guidelines for play areas.* Retrieved January 10, 2007 from www.access-board.gov/play/guide/intro.htm.

University of Texas. (2010). *Human development and family sciences: Applied practicum.* Retrieved June 30, 2010 from www.he.utexas.edu/hdfs/appliedprac.php?pagecat=hdfs.

University of the Incarnate Word. (2010). *Frost play research collection.* Retrieved July 5, 2010 from www.uiw.edu/frost/frostbiography.html.

U.S. Census Bureau. (2000). *Census 2000.* Washington, DC: Government Printing Office.

U.S. Department of Education. (2009). *2007 annual report to congress on the implementation of the Individuals with Disabilities Education Act, Part D.* Washington, DC: Author.

U.S. Department of Education. (2010a). *The condition of education 2010.* Washington, DC: Author.

U.S. Department of Education. (2010b). *No child left behind.* Retrieved June 30, 2010 from www2.ed.gov/nclb/landing.jhtml.

U.S. Department of Health and Human Services. (2008). *Child maltreatment 2008.* Retrieved October 7, 2010 from www.acf.hhs.gov/programs/cb/pubs/cm08/cm08.pdf.

U.S. Department of Health and Human Services. (2010). *Program performance standards for the operation of Head Start programs by grantee and delegate agencies.* Retrieved August 4, 2010 from www.access.gpo.gov/nara/cfr/waisidx_06/45cfrv4_06.html#1301.

U.S. National Library of Medicine. (2010). *Medline Plus.* Retrieved October 18, 2010 from www.nlm.nih.gov/medlineplus/.

Van Alstyne, D. (1932). *Play behavior and choice of play materials of preschool children.* Chicago: University of Chicago Press.

Van der Pool, L. (2009). Corporate day care centers feel the wrath of economy. *Boston Business Journal.* Retrieved June 30, 2010 from http://boston.bizjournals.com/boston/stories/2009/06/29/story2.html.

Van Hoorn, J., Nourot, P., Scales, B., & Alward, K. (2011). *Play at the center of the curriculum* (5th ed.). Upper Saddle River, NJ: Merrill/Prentice Hall.

Vandenberg, B. (1980). Play, problem-solving and creativity. *New Directions for Child Development, 9,* 49–68.

Viadero, D. (2000, March 22). Lags in minority achievement defy traditional explanations. *Education Week, 1,* 18–22.

Viorst, J. (1972). *Alexander and the terrible, horrible, no good, very bad day.* New York: Simon & Schuster.

Vygotsky, L. (1962). *Thought and language.* Cambridge, MA: M.I.T. Press.

Vygotsky, L. (1978). *Mind in society: The development of higher psychological processes.* M. Cole, V. John-Steiner, S. Scribner, E. Superman (Eds.). Cambridge, MA: Harvard University Press.

Wacona Elementary School. (2010). *Using digital cameras in the classroom.* Retrieved July 7, 2010 from www.wacona.com/digicam/digicam.html.

Waelder, R. (1933). The psychoanalytic theory of play. *Psychoanalytic Quarterly, 2,* 208–224.

Waldorf Early Childhood Association of North America. (2010). *The Waldorf kindergarten: The world of the young child.* Retrieved July 6, 2010 from www.waldorfearlychildhood.org/articles.asp?id=3.

Waldorf Schools. (2010). *World list of Rudolf Steiner (Waldorf) schools.* Retrieved July 6, 2010 from http://waldorfschule.info/upload/pdf/schulliste.pdf.

Wanamaker, N., Hearn, K., & Richarz, S. (1979). *More than graham crackers: Nutrition education and food preparation with young children.* Washington, DC: National Association for the Education of Young Children.

Ward, C. (1996). Adult intervention: Appropriate strategies for enriching the quality of children's play. *Young Children, 51*(3), 20–25.

Warren, J. (1991). *Piggyback songs for school.* Torrance, CA: Totline Publications.

Washington State Department of Early Learning. (2010). *Kid's potential, our purpose.* Retrieved June 30, 2010 from www.del.wa.gov/.

Wasik, B. (2006). Building vocabulary one word at a time. *Young Children, 61*(6), 70–78.

Wassermann, S. (1992). Serious play in the classroom—How messing around can win you the Nobel Prize. *Childhood Education, 68*(3), 133–139.

Wassermann, S. (2000). *Serious players in the primary classroom. Empowering children through active learning experiences* (2nd ed.). New York: Teachers College Press.

Waters, J. (2007). The universal language. *T.H.E. Journal, 34*(1), 34–40.

Watson, A., & McCathren, R. (2009). Including children with special needs: Are you and your early childhood program ready? *Young Children, 64*(2), 20–26.

Watson, L., & Swim, T. (2008). *Infants and toddlers curriculum and teaching* (6th ed.). Albany, NY: Delmar.

Waxman, S. (1976a). *What is a boy?* Los Angeles: Peace Press.

Waxman, S. (1976b). *What is a girl?* Los Angeles: Peace Press.

Weber, E. (1984). *Ideas influencing early childhood education.* New York: Teachers College Press.

WebMD. (2010). *Children's health: Body image and children.* Retrieved October 18, 2010 from http://children.webmd.com/building-healthy-body-image-for-children.

Weikart, D., Rogers, L., Adcock, C., & McClelland, D. (1971). *The cognitively oriented curriculum.* Washington, DC: National Association for the Education of Young Children.

Wellhousen, K., & Giles, R. (2005). Building literacy opportunities into children's block play: What every teacher should know. *Childhood Education, 82*(2), 74–78.

Welsh, J., Sharma, A., Abramson, J., Vaccarino, V., Gillespie, C., & Vos, M. (2010). Caloric sweetener consumption and dyslipidemia among US adults. *Journal of the American Medical Association, 303*(15), 1490–1497.

Wenglinsky, H. (2004). Closing the racial achievement gap: The role of reforming instructional practices. *Education Policy Analysis Archives, 12*(64). Retrieved March 27, 2007 from http://epaa.asu.edu/epaa/v12n64.

Whaley, C. (2002). Meeting the diverse needs of children through storytelling. *Young Children, 57*(2), 31–34.

Wickens, E. (1994). *Anna Day and the O-ring.* Boston: Alyson Publications.

Wien, C., Stacey, S., Keating, B., Rowlings, J., & Cameron, H. (2002). The doll project. Handmade dolls as a framework for emergent curriculum. *Young Children, 57*(1), 33–38.

Williams, A. (2008). Exploring the natural world with infants and toddlers in an urban setting. *Young Children, 63*(1), 22–25.

Williams, S. (1989). *I went walking.* New York: Harcourt.

Willis, C. (2009). Young children with autism spectrum disorder. Strategies that work. *Young Children, 64*(1), 81–89.

Winter, S. (1985). Toddler play behaviors and equipment choices in an outdoor playground. In J. Frost & S. Sunderlin (Eds.), *When children play* (pp. 129–138). Wheaton, MD: Association for Childhood Education International.

Winter, S. (2009). Childhood obesity in the testing era: What teachers and schools can do. *Childhood Education, 85*(5), 283–288.

Wittmer, D., & Honig, A. (1994). Encouraging positive social development in young children. *Young Children, 49*(2), 4–12.

Wolery, M., & Wilbers, J. (Eds.). (1994). *Including children with special needs in early childhood programs.* Washington, DC: National Association for the Education of Young Children.

Wolfgang, C., Stannard, L., & Jones, I. (2001). Block play performance among preschoolers as a predictor of later school achievements in mathematics. *Journal of Research in Childhood Education, 15*(2), 173–180.

Wolfinger, D. (1994). *Science and mathematics in early childhood education.* New York: HarperCollins.

Wright, J., & Huston, A. (1995). *Effects of educational TV viewing of lower income preschoolers on academic skills, school readiness, and school adjustment one to three years later.* Lawrence, KS: Center for Research on the Influences of Television on Children.

Wright, T., & Neuman, S. (2009). Purposeful, playful pre-K: Building on children's natural proclivity to learn language, literacy, mathematics, and science. *American Educator,* Spring 2009, pp. 1–40.

Yaden, D., Rowe, D., & MacGillivray, L. (2000). Emergent literacy: A polyphony of perspectives. In M. Kamil, P. Mosenthal, P. Pearson, & R. Barr (Eds.), *Handbook of reading research* (Vol. III). Mahwah, NJ: Erlbaum.

Yawkey, T., & Pellegrini, A. (Eds.). (1984). *Child's play and play therapy.* Lancaster, PA: Technomic Publishing.

Yokota, J. (1993). Issues in selecting multicultural children's literature. *Language Arts, 70,* 43–50.

Yopp, H., & Yopp, R. (2009). Phonological awareness is child's play. *Young Children, 64*(1), 12–18, 21.

Young, D., & Behounek, L. (2006). Kindergartners use PowerPoint to lead their own parent–teacher conferences. *Young Children, 61*(2), 24–26.

Zan, B., & Geiken, R. (2010). Ramps and pathways: Developmentally appropriate, intellectually rigorous, and fun physical science. *Young Children, 65*(1), 12–17.

Zehr, M. (2005). Newcomers bring change, challenge to region. *Education Week, 24*(34), 1, 17, 19.

Zellman, G., & Gates, S. (2010). *Examining the costs of military child care.* Retrieved June 30, 2010 from www.rand.org/pubs/monograph_reports/MR1415/index.html.

Zolotow, C. (1985). *William's doll.* New York: Harper & Row.

Zur, S., & Johnson-Green, E. (2008). Time to transition: The connection between musical free play and school readiness. *Childhood Education, 84*(5), 295–300.

Zygmunt-Fillwalk, E., & Bilello, T. (2005). Parents' victory in reclaiming recess for their children. *Childhood Education, 82*(1), 19–24.

name index

Abo-Zena, M., 210
Aboud, F., 215
Achilles, E., 453
Adcock, C., 68
Administration for Children and Families, 17, 185
Ainsworth, M., 92
Akcan, S., 416, 457
Alexander, K., 442
Allen, J., 253
Alliance for Play, 133
Allison, J., 376
Almon, J., 133, 140
Alward, K., 240, 366
American Academy of Pediatrics, 133, 264, 332, 462, 463
American Association for the Advancement of Science, 396
American Humane Association, 351
American Montessori Society, 67
American Psychological Association, 180, 210
American Public Health Association, 264, 332
An, H., 472
Anders, E., 358
Anderson, C., 391
Anderson, J., 193
Anderson, R., 421
Anglund, J., 369
Annie E. Casey Foundation, 177, 209
Anti-Bias Curriculum Task Force, 52
Aries, P., 53
Arnold, C., 356
Aronson, S., 242
Association for Childhood Education International (ACEI), 434
Association for Library Service to Children, 475
Association Montessori Internationale, 63
Association of Waldorf Schools of North America, 73
Atkins-Burnett, S., 317
Atlas, J., 208
Atwood, M., 328
Axline, V., 127, 375

Badgett, T., 470
Baggerly, J., 164
Baghban, M., 426
Bailie P., 270
Baker, B., 10

Baker, K., 268
Baker, S., 343
Bakerlis, J., 445
Ball, W., 448
Bamberger, H., 387
Bandura, A., 364
Bang, Y., 183
Bank Street College, 77
Baratta-Lorton, M., 389
Barbour, C., 190
Barbour, N., 190
Barnes, B., 461, 468
Baron, L., 461
Barron, M., 245
Bartel, V., 421, 434
Barton, R., 387, 416
Baryshnikov, M., 73
Baskwill, J., 476
Batey, J., 453
Bauer, D., 243
Baumgartner, J., 210
Bee, H., 208
Behounek, L., 196
Beneke, S., 383
Benelli, C., 332, 336
Bennett-Armistead, S., 410
Bergen County Bar Association, 347
Bergen, D., 122
Berk, L., 125
Berry, J., 399
Berson, I., 164
Bewick, C., 252
Bilello, T., 285, 366
Bingham-Newman, A., 248
Birckmayer, J., 409, 412, 415
Birmingham, C., 344
Bisgaier, C., 251
Blake, S., 396
Bloom, B., 47–48
Blume, J., 424
Bobys, A., 410
Bombard, D., 416
Bouttee, G., 218
Bowlby, J., 91–93, 365
Bowman, B., 167
Boyd, D., 208
Boyer, E., 440
Bradley, L., 417
Bramble, L., 19
Brand, S., 423, 428
Braun, S., 36, 37, 39, 46, 53, 55, 278, 309, 361
Braus, N., 246

Bredekamp, S., 11, 15, 67, 79, 88, 89, 90, 123, 133, 142, 252, 264, 293, 299, 303, 310, 380, 466
Brenner, B., 399
Bright Horizons Family Solutions, 12
Britain, L., 228
Bronfenbrenner, U., 56, 99–100, 193
Brookes, M., 448
Brown, H., 421
Brown, K., 425, 428
Brown, L., 359
Brown, M., 359
Brown, N., 128, 360
Brown, P., 267
Brown, T., 222
Bruce, C., 440
Bruchac, J., 246
Bruder, M., 385
Bruner, J., 15, 48, 123, 125, 134
Bryant, D., 194
Bryant, P., 417
Buchanan, T., 210
Buck, D., 269
Buckleitner, W., 475
Buell, M., 252, 419, 421
Bullard, J., 339
Bunker, L., 349
Bureau of Labor Statistics, 26
Burlingame, H., 277
Burns, S., 252, 419, 421, 422
Burton, V., 407
Burya, L., 289
Bush, G. W., 57
Butler, D., 243, 395, 419
Byrnes, J., 476

Cameron, H., 399
Campbell, P., 448, 450
Campos, D., 41
Canfield, J., 363
Cantor, J., 463
Capizzano, J., 10
Carey, K., 318
Carle, E., 243, 391
Carlson, F., 156, 285
Carrick, D., 424
Carroll, M., 329
Carter, M., 142
Carter, P., 15
Cascio, E., 14
Casey Family Foundation, 182
Casey, L., 143
Castle, K., 133

subject index